AF576506

Words of Torah

Words of Torah

A COLLECTION OF DIVREI TORAH
BY YOUNG ISRAEL RABBIS

edited and compiled by

PESACH LERNER

NATIONAL COUNCIL OF YOUNG ISRAEL

JASON ARONSON INC.
Northvale, New Jersey
Jerusalem

This book was set in 11 pt. Berling Roman by Alpha Graphics of Pittsfield, New Hampshire, and printed and bound by Book-mart Press, Inc. of North Bergen, NJ.

10 9 8 7 6 5 4 3 2 1

Library of Congress Cataloging-in-Publication Data

Words of Torah : a collection of divrei Torah by Young Israel rabbis / by National Council of Young Israel.
p. cm.
Includes index.
ISBN 0–7657–6004–5 (alk. paper)
1. Bible. O.T. Pentateuch—Sermons. 2. Festival-day sermons, Jewish. 3. Jewish sermons, American. I. National Council of Young Israel (U.S.)
BS1225.4.W67 1999 98–10687
296.4'7—dc21 CIP

Printed in the United States of America on acid-free paper. For information and catalog write to Jason Aronson Inc., 230 Livingston Street, Northvale, NJ 07647-1726, or visit our website: www.aronson.com

❖ Contents ❖

❖ Acknowledgments ❖

With praise to the Almighty, we present, in book form, a collection of weekly Divrei Torah Bulletins. These thoughts on the *parsha*, written by the rabbinate of the national Young Israel movement, are distributed each Shabbat and Yom Tov at Young Israel and many non-Young Israel synagogues throughout North America and Israel—and are currently available on the National Council of Young Israel web page (www.youngisrael.org). This volume includes Divrei Torah Bulletins from 1992–1995.

These weekly bulletins represent the various backgrounds of our rabbis and reflect the many philosophies and experiences of the writers. We hope these various outlooks will provide you with the "Many Faces of Torah."

We express a special thank you to all the rabbis of the Young Israel movement who are participating in this project.

We thank the Henry, Bertha, and Edward Rothman Foundation of Rochester, New York, Circleville, Ohio, and Cleveland, Ohio for their sponsorship of the weekly bulletin.

We thank Mr. and Mrs. Chaim S. Kaminetzky for their dedication of the softcover edition of the first year collection of the Divrei Torah Bulletins in memory of Yeshaya ben Ben Zion Isur Kaminetzky, and Moshe Shimon ben Yitzchok Aron Marcus, patriarchs of the Kaminetzky-Marcus families.

We thank Mr. Arthur Kurzweil, Ms. Dana Salzman, and all the professionals at Jason Aronson, Inc. for their encouragement, assistance, and overall patience. We are forever indebted.

And thank you to the national and international Young Israel community for your continued encouragement to all of us at the National Council of Young Israel. It is with this encouragement that we continue our *Avodat HaKodesh* on your behalf and on behalf of *Klal Yisrael*.

Rabbi Pesach Lerner
Executive Vice President
National Council of Young Israel

❖ Dedication ❖

National Council of Young Israel dedicates this book of Divrei Torah to:

The rabbi, officers, and membership of Congregation Beth Jacob, Bronx, New York.

For close to seven decades Congregation Beth Jacob on Leland Avenue in the Parkchester area of the Bronx was a center of traditional Jewish life. The synagogue was a focal point for the young and elderly of the community.

In its infancy, under the guidance of Rabbi Abraham Gris, of blessed memory, the synagogue became a place where families found a home, not only for religious activity but for the entire spectrum of Jewish life. During his lifetime, Rabbi Gris stressed a constant mix of Torah learning and good deeds bringing all families together under the canopy of Torah Judaism. Rabbi Shimon Schwartz assumed the rabbinic position in 1968, after the sudden passing of his revered father-in-law and re-energized the community.

A diminishing Jewish population forced the synagogue to close its doors in the spring of 1995 with the satisfaction of knowing that its goal of bringing Jews closer to Torah and *mitzvot* was achieved during the synagogue's tenure as a center of Jewish life.

In memory of Joe, Flora, and Lea Hyman, generous supporters of the Young Israel movement for over 50 years, both with their time and financial resources. May their memory be a blessing for us all.

In loving memory of Jacob Wertheim, devoted member and officer of Young Israel for many years. Mr. Wertheim was a quiet philanthropist to many causes. May his deeds be a blessing for us all.

In loving memory of Dorothy "Dotty" Goldberg; President, National Council of Young Israel Women's League; President, Ladies Auxiliary, Young Israel of Brighton Beach, NY and with her husband, Larry, a"h, Shofar Award recipients. Dotty and Larry were devoted to the ideals of Young Israel. Together they built a life of Torah and *Gemilas Chesed,* and gave of themselves to the Jewish community. Sponsored by National Council of Young Israel Women's League; Ruth Saperstein, President, Rozanne Polansky, Secretary, Rebbetzin Judi Steinig, Director.

With special thanks to the membership of The Inwood Jewish Center, formerly at 12 Ellwood Street, New York, NY.

In loving memory of Rochelle Lipschik.

In loving memory of Solomon J. Polansky, Dinah Polansky, Yehudah Schaum, Moish Polansky, Nathan Flaum, and Goldie Flaum of blessed memory.

In honor of our children Sari and Shlomo Drazin, Ari Naftali and Deena Tova; Ninette Polansky, Motty Polansky, and Dovey Polansky.

Dedicated by Rozanne and Joe Polansky of the Young Israel of North Bellmore, NY.

In memory of Estelle Chwat, Louis Rabinowitz, Nettie and Michael Mayer Chwat, and Shirky and Yitzchak Rabinowitz.

Dedicated by Lee Rabinowitz.

With special thanks to: Young Israel of Boca Raton, FL, Rabbi Eliyahu Rabovsky, Mr. Irving Perles, President• Young Israel of Brooklyn, NY, Rabbi Bernard Weinberger• Young Israel of Canarsie, NY, Rabbi Boruch M. Leibowitz, Mr. Abe Schwartz, President• Young Israel of Century City, CA, Rabbi Elazar Muskin, Dr. Emanuel Gottlieb, President• Young Israel of East Northport, NY, Rabbi Chaim Bausk• Young Israel of Eltingville, NY, Rabbi Daniel Yormark, Mr. Sid Stadler, President• Young Israel of Greater Buffalo, NY, Rabbi Dovid Plaut, Dr. Michael Cowen, President• Young Israel of Lawrence-Cedarhurst, NY, Rabbi Moshe Teitelbaum, Mr. Michael Kollander, President• Young Israel of Monsey-Wesley Hills, NY, Rabbi Ari Jacobson, Dr. David Schwalb, President• Young Israel of Southfield, MI, Rabbi Elimelech Goldberg, Mr. Mark Eisenberg, President• Young Israel of Windsor Park, NY, Rabbi Yehoshua Weber, Mr. Mark Fogel, President• Young Israel Shomrai Emunah of Greater Washington, MD, Rabbi Gedaliah Anemer, Dr. David Maslow, President• Congregation Sons of Israel, Allentown, PA, Rabbi Daniel Korobkin• Congregation Migdal David, Tamarac, FL, Rabbi Berel Simpser, Dr. Russel Swift, President.

❖ When You Are Honored ❖ with an *Aliyah*

Rabbi Chaim Wasserman

Young Israel of Passaic–Clifton, New Jersey

1. When called to the Torah one ought to proceed without delay, taking the shortest route possible.
2. Do not leave the *bimah* until the second person after you is called to the Torah.
3. There are no special or privileged sections of the Torah, not even those for which certain congregations remain standing. The entire Torah abounds with uniform holiness. To be insulted if one does not get called for a certain *aliyah* is nothing short of ignorance compounded by arrogance. Similarly, not to be called to the Torah by the *gabbai* should never become a source of contention within a congregation. (See *Aruch haShulchan Orach Chayim* 136:2)
4. Except for very unusual circumstances, a *kohen* should never be asked to leave the *minyan* so that he does not receive *aliyot* time after time. This is a matter which always should be referred for rabbinic determination. A *kohen* who wishes to leave the *minyan* so that other non-*kohanim* may receive an *aliyah* in his stead should also refer the matter for rabbinic guidance.

5. Before starting the first *brachah*, the Torah is opened and the *baal korei* points to the place where the reading for your *aliyah* will begin. Once you see the beginning word it is not necessary to do anything else before beginning the first *brachah*.
6. "During the *brachot*, should the Torah be opened or rolled closed?" is an often-asked question. During the *brachah* after the reading, all agree that the Torah should be rolled closed even before the *brachah* is recited. As for the *brachah before* the reading of the Torah, customs vary: Some close the Torah, while others keep it open. My preference is that the Torah remain open during the *brachah* before the reading so that, immediately following, the *baal korei* will not have to delay in spotting the beginning words of the *aliyah*. When the Torah is open, look away from the open script or close your eyes, thereby indicating that the words of the *brachah* are not actually written in the Torah.
7. Say the *brachah* out loud so that everyone may respond to it. When you complete *Borchu* be certain to repeat *Baruch HaShem ham'vorach l'olam va'ed* after the congregation has said it.
8. During the reading of the Torah follow every word inside the Torah. If one reads along with the *baal korei*, extreme care must be exercised that the *baal korei* is not confused by your audible sounds, even a whisper.
9. At all times, it is proper to wear a *tallit* when being called to the Torah. This applies also to the three others who stand near the Torah when serving as *baal korei* or *gabbaim*. Likewise, those who are called for *hagbaha* and *g'lilah* should always have a *tallit* on. It is difficult these days to maintain the practice, when the Torah is read in the afternoons, not to have a *tallit* on, especially when in most congregations there are many *talitot*, property of the congregation, that can be used even when most people do not have their own personal *tallit* with them, as is the case during *minchah* Torah reading.

   When one borrows a *tallit* belonging to someone else, a *brachah* over that *tallit* is not necessary. When using your own *tallit* a *brachah* should quickly be said so as not to detain the congregation unnecessarily.

   When one uses someone else's *tallit*, it goes without saying that it ought to be returned in a proper manner. This is especially important when using the *tallit* of a person who is not present at that time. While the *halachah* states that the owner of the *tallit* should be gratified that his property is being used for a *mitzvah* purpose, at the same time, he has an absolute right to expect that the property will be returned and replaced in a proper manner.
10. It is not uncommon for people to forget or become confused with the order of the two *brachot*. Accordingly, use a *siddur* or the chart at

the side of the Torah provided in most congregations. If you come to the Torah with a *siddur,* do not lean the *siddur* on the Torah itself.

In the event that a person began the first *brachah* incorrectly (using the words of the second *brachah*) then he should return to the words *asher bachar banu* and correct the mistake provided that he has not already concluded with the final five words "*Baruch ata HaShem noteyn haTorah.*"

If the last five words above were already recited, then the reading proceeds even though the *brachah* was incorrect. Then, at the conclusion of the *aliyah,* the *brachah* that was not recited at the beginning is then said. (See *Mishna B'rurah* 139:15, where he quotes the *Derech haChayim.*)

11. It is a widespread custom to gently lift the Torah during certain short phrases. During the *brachah* before the reading some lift the rollers slightly when saying the words *v'natan lanu et torato,* and repeat this procedure during the *brachah* at the conclusion of the *aliyah* when saying *asher natan lanu torat emet.*
12. During the reading of the Torah, the one who has been honored with the *aliyah* should hold on to the right wooden roller and be ready to help roll the Torah when the *baal korei* goes on to the next column.
13. Reaching across the Torah to extend a handshake to the *gabbai* at the far left is improper, not in keeping with respect for the Torah's holiness.
14. *Baalaei kriah* and *gabbaim* who remind a congregant about any of the proprieties associated with the receiving an *aliyah* should be thanked for their appreciation of *kavod haTorah.*
15. The honors at the end of the Torah reading of *hagbaha* and *g'lila* (lifting), rolling closed, and dressing the Torah are, according to the Talmud (*Megillah* 32a) the highest of the honors. In talmudic times, this function was given to the most prestigious person in the assembled *minyan.* How strange it is, then, why many individuals feel that the honors that do not involve the recitation of *brachot* are of lesser prestige.

    The Talmud's position is based on the premise that taking out the Torah and restoring it properly to its *aron hakodesh* constitutes the *mitzvah* of *kavod haTorah,* respect for the Torah. One who properly cares for the Torah is entitled to be properly recompensed for that effort. The Talmud indicates straightforwardly that the ones who put the Torah away are as meritorious as all the others combined who were called for *aliyot* to the Torah.

    Accordingly, consider once asking the *gabbai* for *hagbahah* or *g'lilah* (even if you are a *chiyuv*) when you deserve having an *aliyah.* In any event, when you are honored with *hagbahah* or *g'lilah*, be aware of the Talmud's position concerning its worthiness.

16. Be certain you are able to properly lift the Torah for *hagbahah*, especially when most of the parchment is on the side of your weaker hand. It is not unknown for a Torah to fall from the hands of a person not able to balance it properly.

    The task of *hagbahah* is to lift the Torah and show its writing to all present. This is why the person turns around to all sides.

    The seam between two attached parchment sheets should be rolled into the center before the *hagbahah* is performed.

17. The one doing *g'lilah* should make certain that the Torah is secure in the hands of his *hagbahah* partner and not tug at the Torah, thereby making it difficult to be held.

    Start by rolling the Torah so that the sewn seam remains in the center.

    The *gartel* (belt) is wrapped around the Torah tightly, starting on the outer side, that side of the Torah which faces the person doing *g'lilah*.

    On *Shabbat* and *yom tov*, a double knot at the end of the *gartel* should be avoided. Buckles or velcro on the end of the *gartel* obviate any problems with tying double knots.

18. *Hosafot* (additional *aliyot*) can be made within reason only on *Shabbat*, save for a few exceptional *Shabbatot* when certain halachic requirements must be maintained for specific reasons.

    Hosafot cannot be added indiscriminately. This is crucial for families celebrating a *Shabbat simchah* to understand. *Hosafot* should be anticipated as best possible in advance of *Shabbat*, and cleared with the *gabbai* and/or rabbi so that no problems occur or interfere with the Torah reading. It is entirely incorrect to assume that every three *pesukim* may constitute another *aliyah*.

PART ONE

Genesis

❖ CHAPTER 1 ❖

Bereishit

Rabbi Elias Schwartz

Young Israel of Bensonhurst
Bathbeach, New York

The Torah starts with a most important statement: "God created the heaven and the earth." This first statement lays the foundation for our lives in this world and the next:

We must know that the world belongs to God.
Perhaps, we belong to God.
God created the world for a purpose.
We are the Purpose!

We are to bring godliness down to the world in which we live. We are to endow everything we do with a spirit of godliness. We are to bring a *ruchanius* element into this material world that surrounds us on all sides. But why must the Torah give us a detailed account of *each day* of creation? Let us examine The Story of Creation carefully and learn as much as we can.

Two expressions are constantly repeated throughout the first chapter of *Bereishit*. They are:

"And God saw that it was good."
"And thus it became," usually translated, "And it was so."

Sometimes, both expressions are used when describing the day; at other times, one expression is omitted. Keep these two expressions firmly in mind as we go through the entire six days of creation.

FIRST DAY

On the first day God created the light. "God saw that it was good" is stated; "and it was so" is omitted.

SECOND DAY

On the second day, God made the firmament (*rakia*), which was a division between the waters above the firmament and the waters below it. Nothing could be seen because the waters filled the entire universe. This seems to be an *unfinished* process. We find the expression, "And it was so," but "God saw that it was good" is omitted.

THIRD DAY

On the third day, God finished the work of the second day. All the waters below the division receded and formed oceans, rivers, seas, and lakes. Dry land was seen for the first time. This, in reality, was the purpose of the division on the second day. *Both* expressions—"And it was so" and "it was good"—are found in sentences (*pesukim*) 9 and 10.

As soon as dry land was seen, God created grass, trees, flowers, and so on. Once again, we find both expressions repeated in sentences 11 and 12. In this third day, we find two elements of creation, and both parts are blessed with the words, "And God saw that it was good" and "it was so."

I remember my mother's saying, "It is *mazeldik* to move on a Tuesday because God blessed that day with *two* expressions of good."

FOURTH DAY

On the fourth day, God created the sun, moon, and stars. Both expressions are used.

FIFTH DAY

On the fifth day, God created fish and fowl. The expression, "And it was so," is omitted.

SIXTH DAY

On the sixth day, God created the animal kingdom and man. In sentences 25 and 26, referring to the animals, both expressions are stated. When God created man, the words, "And God saw that it was good" are omitted.

Man is the most important part of creation. Man is the very purpose of creation. Man is to be imbued with a Godly spirit. Yet, on man there is no stamp of approval by *HaShem*. Why?

The following chart summarizes the various occurrences of the two expressions:

Six Days of Creation

	"And God saw that it was good"	"And it was so"
First Day	✓	
Second Day		✓
Third Day	✓✓	✓✓
Fourth Day	✓	✓
Fifth Day	✓	
Sixth Day		
animals	✓	✓
man		✓

The second expression, "And it was so," is missing only in the accounts of the first and fifth days.

The second expression, "And it was so," means that something must be so forever. Once God has imprinted His words, "And it was so," this part of creation can never change.

These words were omitted on the first day because the special, beautiful light of the first day was put away for the future world. The light of the first day was "too good," and it could not stay with us forever. We must strive to be worthy of the light created on the first day. That light was taken away from our world. The lights for *our* world are the sun and the moon, which were created on the fourth day.

On the fifth day, God created the *taninim*—huge, whalelike sea giants. These sea giants could destroy our world, and so God took away one of them so that they could not multiply. Thus, this part of creation could not exist forever and could not be stamped with the words, "And it was so."

Now, let us understand why "And God saw that it was good" is omitted on the second and sixth days. On the second day, the act of creation was not yet complete; therefore, it could not be stamped with the words, "And God saw that it was good." We can learn two important lessons from this. The first is that division is not always good; unity and togetherness are generally better. Particularly is this so when a single element—in this case, water—is divided.

Chazal—the Sages—tell us there is no water—no sustenance for man other than Torah. If there is a division in the Torah world between different Torah groups, this can never be good. Let Torah views, ideals, and goals speak with one strong powerful voice and, I am sure, God will stamp this with His words "and God saw it and it is good."

The second lesson we can learn is starting something without finishing it *cannot* be good. In his commentary on *Parshat Ekev* (Deut. 8:1), Rashi tells us that we are considered to have done a *mitzvah*—and that it is counted and credit for it given—only when the *mitzvah* is fully completed (learn this Rashi inside Deut. 8:1). There are many "starter-uppers" in the world, but they leave the completion for others to accomplish.

Man: Man is different from all other creations; trees are the same today as when they first appeared on this world. Animals, fish, fowl, and birds are the same today as when they were first created. "God saw that it was good" stamped all of them with their characteristics, forever, and this indicates God's approval of them as well. Why was man *not* blessed with, "And God saw that it was good"?

Rabbi Meir Simcha Hakohen of Divinsk Russia (1843–1926) says in his Commentary on the Torah, *Meshech Chochmah* that God did not give man His approval of "goodness." Had God said, "And it was good," then man could never do anything wrong; man would not have *bechirah*, would lose his power of choice. Man could never transgress or violate a *mitzvah* of the Torah. We would not be worthy of *Gan Eden* and reward. *We* must strive to be good, to do *mitzvot*, to serve *HaShem* properly and spiritually, because *we decided to do so*. *We*, man, must weather the storms of problems that beset us as we grow. *We*, man, must elevate ourselves to be what God wants us to be. This is why God gave us the Torah.

We must put a stamp of approval upon ourselves. We are starting Torah all over again. We are at Bereishit. We are at the beginning. Start *now!* Not only will our beginning of the year be good; our end of the year will also be good.

When we fulfill all the mitzvot of the Torah, when we learn Torah regularly—daily and intensely—then, subconsciously, we will hear God's voice whispering to us, "And God saw that it was good."

Rabbi Shmuel Landesman

Young Israel of Massapequa, New York

IF ONLY WE REALIZED

Almost all of us reading this article probably believe in God. Though our belief inevitably wanes at times, we still generally believe in God—that He created the world, gave us the Torah, and so on. However, many of us tend to wonder if God really believes in *us*—if He feels a connection, if He cares. We're not always sure, but we try to repress such doubts. We will often even believe we are not supposed to have such thoughts. Therefore, this week's *Parsha* is reassuring—very reassuring. I would like to share, with regard to this issue, the approach of Rabbi Nosson Tzvi Finkel, the *Alter* of Slabodka (1849–1927), one of the major *mussar* personalities in the earlier part of this century. The Alter's legacy still affects us because his disciples founded the Yeshivot that we, our children and grandchildren have studied and do study at today.

The *Torah* recounts, in four separate places, man's being of God's image:

1. "And God created the man in His own image, in the image of God He created him." (Gen. 1:27)
2. "This is the book of the generations of Adam on the day God created man, in the likeness of God He made him." (Gen. 5:1)
3. "Whoever sheds the blood of man, by man shall his blood be shed; for in the image of God He made man." (Gen. 9:6)
4. [With regard to a sinner who received capital punishment] "his body shall not remain all night upon the tree . . . For it is an insult unto God that he is hanged" (Deut. 21:23). Rashi explains, "It is a slight to the King because man is made in the exact likeness to His image."

Chazal continue with this theme. "Beloved is man, for he was created in God's image; it is indicative of a greater love that it was made known to him that he was created in God's image" (*Avot* 3: 18). *Chazal* even incorporated this concept into the *Sheva Brachot* (Blessings recited at a wedding meal): "Who fashioned man in His image, in the image of His likeness." *Chazal* also mention that God and His *Bet Din* (court) (so to speak) deliberated and carefully planned each limb of Adam's body (*Bereishit Rabbah* 12). In fact, when the *pasuk* tells us, "And [He] breathed into his nostrils the breath of life" (Gen. 2:7), *Chazal* comment, "From who [where] did [He] breathe? From Himself He breathed [life into man]." The *Midrash Rabbah* records the *Ribbono Shel Olam* (God) as saying, "The [man] is unique among the lower beings, just as I am unique among the higher beings."

Psalm 8 says, "And You made him only a little less than God" (or "angels," depending on the commentary). The *midrash* relates that the angels made a mistake and wanted to pray to man. The source of man's uniqueness is his ability to choose between good and bad (unlike the other creatures of the world).

All too often we act less than fully in accordance with how we should act (or we may even actually sin) because we are not really in touch with ourselves as holy and spiritual beings. The Talmud *Gemarah Berakhot* 6A relates that *Hakadosh baruch Hu* puts on *tefillin* (so to speak) that contain the verse, "And who is like Your nation of Israel, a unique nation in the land." (*Divrei Hayomim*/Chronicles I: 17.21). This metaphorical anecdote reveals the extent of *HaShem*'s respect for the Jewish people. The Prophet brings forth the verse, "I love you [the Jewish people], says God." This speaks for itself and needs no elaboration. (Malachi 1:2; Haftarah of *Parshat Toldot*)

Many of us, though, when confronted with these very clear sources will respond that there may have been real spiritual connectedness and closeness back then, but we don't see it nowadays. There is actually a basis for this approach in *Chazal*. Talmud *Gemarah Shabbat* 112 says, "If the earlier ones [generations] were [like] angels we are [like] people, and if the earlier ones were people we are like donkeys."

However, the Alter of Slabodka counters this concern by pointing out that even in our "lowly" day and age we are still commanded to perform the *Torah mitzvah* "And you shall go in His ways" (Deut. 28:9). In other words, *HaShem* still feels we are capable of totally following His example. There is an additional *mitzvah*, "This is my God and I will glorify Him" (Exod. 15:2), upon which *Chazal* expound, "You should make yourself similar to Him" (*Shabbat* 133).

The Alter also emphasizes the *Gemara* (*Sanhedrin* 37)—"A person is obligated to say, 'The world was created for me.'" This is not intended to reinforce narcissistic tendencies. Rather, a person should use every opportunity in life (and in the world) as a catalyst to grow in one's service to God. As stated before, the uniqueness of man (and the feature that makes him most similar to God) is his free will. As the world continues to grow in terms of population, technology, intellectual development, and so on, there are many more opportunities for us to make proper use of our free will to grow in our service to God, to become more similar to Him. Thus, these are really exciting and special times in which we have a very unique opportunity to become our true selves—the image of God. If only we realized.

Rabbi Yitzchok M. Goodman

Young Israel of Far Rockaway, New York

THE "TRUTH" ABOUT *Shabbat*

A well-known expression in *midrashim* is that "the seal (*chosamo*) of God is truth (*emet*)." Since the Hebrew term *chosam* also means "conclusion," this statement seems to hint at the idea that *emet* might be found at the conclusion of significant statements. We find in the *Midrash Rabbah* (chapter 1) that "the opening of Your word is *emet*," followed by the first phrase in the Torah. Indeed, at the beginning and the end of the creation account, this seal is to be found. The first three words in Torah [*bereishiT barA E-lohiM*] and the last three words in the creation account [*barA E-lohiM la'asoT*] end with the three consonants of *emet* [*A/M/T*]. Examining the entire text of the creation in between these two *emet* indicators, we find several other phrases that contain this seal of *emet* in perfect order. In Gen. 1:4, [*vayar* (*A*) *E-lohiM eT*] (*haor*)—and God saw the light that it was good; Gen. 1: 21, [*vayivrA E-lohiM eT*] (*hataninim*)—and God created the sea-serpents; Gen. 1:27, [*vayivrA E-lohiM eT*] (*haadam*)—and God created man; Gen. 1:31, [*vayar* (*A*) *E-lohiM eT*] (*kol asher asah*)—and God saw all that He had made. . . .

It appears that the seal of *emet* was placed at very strategic places for good reasons. Whenever an exceptionally creative act took place that we would consider *yeish mei-ayin—ex nihilo* (something from nothing)—the additional stamp of *emet* is utilized. The very first *emet* is for the creation of matter itself; the second, for the creation of energy (light); the third, for the beginning of biological life; the fourth, for the creation of man, who, owing to the presence of a soul, is a new creation again; and the fifth, for the summary of the entire process of creation!

Why, however, did a sixth *emet* appear in the final verse, dealing with the sanctity of the Sabbath (Gen. 2:3)?

I would like to suggest a sermonic type of response. If the previous seals of *emet* came to strengthen our faith in the creative *ex nihilo* process, perhaps the final *emet* came to tell us that we, too, might seek to participate in such creation, in the way we treat the sanctity of the Sabbath. Rather than think of the Sabbath as a do-nothing day for sleeping and lounging, we should actively create a great day of Torah and sanctity to make something out of a day of seemingly no activity. How nearly this interpretation fits into the very words that spell out *emet* at this juncture—"which God created to do"! This unusually awkward phrase, which has led to numerous interpretations, now gains still another meaning with this approach: God created the Sabbath for us *to do*, or *to make* something beautiful and holy of it. Unfortunate are those who think of *Shabbat* as a day to catch their breath for the following six days of strenuous activity. Fortunate are those who find *Shabbat* to be the greatest day of activity for them, in terms of their spiritual growth and progress—as we indeed find in Exodus (31:16): "And the children of Israel shall observe the Sabbath to *make* the Sabbath [*V'shomru Yisrael et haShabbat la'asot et haShabbat*]."

WRITING ON THE HORN OF AN OX?

"And the earth was desolate and chaos [*tohu vavohu*] and darkness (was) upon the firmament" (Gen. 1:2). The *Midrash Rabbah* comments in the name of Rabbi Shimon ben Lakish that "desolate" [*tohu*] represents Babylon (*Bavel*); "chaos" [*bohu*] represents Modei and "darkness" is Greece (in the Antiochus era), because the Greeks darkened our eyes with their evil decrees, saying, "Write on the horn of the ox [*Kitvu lachem al keren shel shor*] that you have no part of the God of Israel." The "horn of the ox" reference is quite obscure, and several interpretations have been given. Here are Rav Yitzchok Yaakov Reines' and Rav Leib Gurevitz's marvelous explanations:

In Psalm 94, King David laments over the persecution that the wicked inflict upon Israel, and upon widows and orphans (. . . they murder orphans: and say, "God does not see nor . . . understand . . .). In these verses David foresaw with his holy spirit our long bitter exile and the two types of suffering we would endure.

1. The Babylonians would overrun our land and possessions, but their goal would be to increase their assets and power. With such enemies there is at least a boundary to their pillage: when they gain no further advantage they cease the killing.

2. Others will persecute and murder purely for hatred of God, Israel, and the Torah, even when no benefit is derived from the conquest and destruction. Such enemies know no bounds for their violence, since it serves their "purpose" of degrading Israel and God (as Hitler did even to the detriment of his own war effort and troop movements). Of this type, King David writes, "They say God does not see . . ."—that is, their entire intent is to prove that God does not see; this is their real goal. Such hatred characterized the Greeks when they forbade our observance of *milah*, and *Shabbat*, and so on, for they gained nothing for themselves here, but just sought to uproot Judaism.

Now, our *Chazal Baba Kama* (2:b) divided the damage done by an ox into three categories: "horn," "tooth," and "foot" (*keren, shein, regel*). Under "horn," they included all activity in which the ox has malicious intent with no gain or pleasure for itself. Thus, in our *midrash*, when *Chazal* wanted to describe the terrible *galut* in which enemies like the Greeks seek to destroy our faith, and attack out of pure hatred, they picture the enemy as saying, "Write on the horn of an ox . . . ," symbolizing that their intent is on this level of destruction of its own sake. What worse darkness is there? Thus "darkness is Greece"!

Rav Leib Gurevitz, *z"l* of the Gateshead England Yeshiva, told of his experience when he visited a museum showing ancient Greek artifacts in the hope of learning something of value in connection with the many talmudic references to the Greeks. He came upon a description of an ancient Greek invention: They sometimes had a problem providing milk for newborn babies whose mothers could not nurse them for medical reasons, or who had died in childbirth, and they searched for a kind of baby bottle with a narrow mouth. They devised one by hollowing out the horn of a large animal, such as an ox, and puncturing the narrow end. When he saw this, Rav Gurevitz suddenly understood the intent of this *midrash*: The Greeks were obsessed with wiping out the very concept of our Jewish God from the land of Israel. Knowing some human psychology, they decided that the time to begin to accomplish this goal is with small infants, since the Jewish adult is quite obstinate. Thus they decreed that every "ox-horn" (that is, every baby bottle) must proclaim the denial of God; therefore *Chazal* call the Greeks "darkness."

This "Greek psychology" should teach us a powerful lesson in the *chinuch* of our children, and how important are the early formative years for developing *Ahavat HaShem*, *Ahavat Torah*, and *Ahavat Yisrael* in their impressionable hearts.

THE AWESOME POWER OF MAN (GEN. 1:31)

"And God saw all that He had made and, behold, it was very good (*tov m'od*). . . ." This is the first time the adjective "very" was added; previously, only the word "good" was used—many times—regarding aspects of creation. A mysterious series of comments in the *Midrash Rabbah* interprets the term "very" in a strange way: it represents death, the Angel of Death, the evil inclination. This lifting of "very" from "very good" to mean evil things has intrigued many commentators.

The following represents a variation based on insights from Rabbi Yaakov Kranz, the Maggid of Dubna (1741–1804): the term *m'od* is used only after man is created. All other creatures on earth are endowed by their nature with specific limits to their abilities. No lion will ever fly, and no fish will ever live on dry land. But man has the unique ability of planning, scheming, and inventing to overcome his natural limits. Without wings, he flies into space and, without gills, lives under water. This spectacular ability has also allowed him to produce mass weapons of potential world destruction. Positively seen, the great potential of man is expressed in the Torah as very good. But *Chazal* wanted to warn us that this very uniqueness of going beyond our limits contains the potential for death, evil, and destruction; hence, they indicated that *m'od* is indeed the "angel of death."

Pursuing this concept, I would suggest that the verse in the *Shema*—"You shall love *HaShem* with all your heart . . . soul . . . and . . . might (*m'odehcha*)" may mean that our goal in life should be to dedicate our *m'od*—power of going beyond ourselves and reaching great heights—to the service of God and His Torah.

WHY WOMAN WAS FASHIONED FROM ADAM'S RIB (2:23–24)

> "And Adam said, this time [it is] bone of my bones and flesh of my flesh; let this one be called *ishah* [woman] for she was taken from *ish* [man]. Therefore, man forsakes his father and mother and clings to his wife, and they become as one flesh."

In explaining these two verses and their interconnection, Rabbeinu Avraham ben Dovid, the Ravad, develops the following very meaningful explanation:

It was one of God's marvelous deeds that only with humans did the female derive from the man (Adam's rib), contrary to natural law. This was done to teach humanity that man and woman are truly to harmonize their lives in mutual help and support as if they were one being. Adam comprehended this perfectly but understood that, in the future, all births would follow the usual rules of nature. In order to teach this idea of love and harmony to future generations, he formed the word *ishah* as a reminder that she came from *ish*.

Thus, these verses form a unity of thought: Man said, "this time [only] bone of my bones and flesh of my flesh," that is, God has fashioned this woman with my body—but how will future generations remember the lesson to be learned from this, of harmony and mutual respect? Therefore, "let her be called *ishah* [to remember] that from man she was fashioned [and thus they are one]." Therefore, man forsakes his father and mother and clings to his wife, and they become [indeed] one flesh (Ravad, introduction to *Baalei Hanefesh*).

SLAMMING THE DOOR ON EVIL (GEN. 4:7)

". . . sin crouches at the door, and his desire is to [conquer] you. . . ." This image can best be appreciated with the following comparison:

A man may have various types of visitors at his door:

1. A poor man knocks and asks for some charity. He waits humbly for a gift and will not dare to step inside, unless invited.
2. A friend comes by for an emergency loan. He sits down in the reception room and tells his tale of woe. The host leaves the room; his guest hopes that it is to bring some funds. Although he is already in the house, it would be poor manners to follow him further into the house; so he remains in his seat, waiting.
3. A creditor comes in to collect his debt. Not only does he feel free to enter the house but may follow and pursue the owner from room to room, demanding his overdue money!
4. A thief enters the house, moves freely from room to room taking all he wishes, and, if armed as well, may drive the owner from his own house.

Now let us consider: How does our evil inclination gain entrance into our minds and souls? This verse tells us to beware: sin crouches at the door [that is, like a humble beggar; it acts meekly at first, making the simplest requests: it waits patiently, but remember] its desire is you; [like the thief/robber, it ultimately seeks total mastery] and will destroy you, beware! (Rav Tzvi Hirsch Kahane, *Likutai RTZB'A*, Warsaw 5627)

Consider the powerful impact of the final phrase of this verse as well: "You shall [must] rule over it." Here, shortly after one of the first sins of history, man is informed that he has the power to rule over his evil inclination.

Rabbi Aaron S. Tirschwell

Director of Synagogue Services
National Council of Young Israel

From the presentation of the creation of the world in *Parshat Bereishit,* one would expect to learn significant insights into human nature from the very first humans whom God created. Clearly, we get a picture into man's ability to make choices, as Adam and Chava taught us about the concept of choosing sin and its consequences through the incident of the Tree of Knowledge. We also learn that man was not destined to be alone in this world; therefore, God created woman. Yet, given the traumatic situation of their son's untimely death, the Torah does not record how our first ancestors expressed their feelings toward their children.

When the Torah, in its fourth chapter describes Chava's giving birth to two sons, we are presented with the famous Cain and Hevel story, complete with Cain's slaying of Hevel. At that point, Cain is punished by *HaShem,* after which he "leaves the presence of *HaShem*" (Gen. 4:16). Immediately following this incident, the Torah goes on to list the various generations that lead us into *Parshat Noach*—without further mention of Hevel's death and his parents' subsequent mourning over the loss of his life.

We know that that the Torah usually goes out of its way to show us the actions, opinions, reactions, and emotions of major Biblical figures, especially when it comes to their dealings with their children: Avraham during the *Akeidat Yitzchak,* the reaction Yitzchak had to Yaakov's performance as Esav (*Hakol kol Yaakov—V'HaYadaim Y'dei Esav*), Yaakov's lamenting over Yosef's pseudo-death at the hands of his brothers, and so on. Why, then, weren't Adam and Chava's reactions to their son's death recorded in the Torah? As they are the first parents in the history of the world, one would think that such a monumental event in *their* lives would be recorded. Certainly, it is hard to believe that they didn't know about Hevel's death or they were uninterested in his demise.

I believe that two ideas will give us further insights into our first ancestors and a basic answer to our question. First, Adam and Chava understood Hevel's death to be another part of their punishment for eating from the *Etz HaDa'at*—just as the *pri* (fruit) of *HaShem* was taken away from Him, so did *HaShem* take the *pri* of Adam and Chava (this incident could be the first historical case of *middah k'negged middah*, that one action affects another in a similar fashion). Therefore, Adam and Chava were not at all surprised when Hevel was killed, and they accepted it as part of their punishment. Thus, the Torah did not find it necessary to record their responses to their loss.

Second, as the first parents on the face of the earth, Adam and Chava had the opportunity to be the first role-model parents—to teach all generations how to raise children, appreciate their accomplishments, and reinforce Torah values. Once they had committed the sin of the *Etz HaDaat* and their subsequent banishment from *Gan Eden*, they could no longer be considered for these role models. The Torah makes this point when it says, *Va'yehi miketez yamim* (Gen. 4:3), which, translated literally, means, "it was the end of days." Rabbi Aryeh Kaplan translated this phrase as "an era ended"; the era of *Gan Eden*, of immortality and of being Torah role models, had been lost. Only later on, through Avraham's complete sacrifice of *HaShem*, do we see a biblical figure worthy of being a Torah role model as an adult and a parent. (This point is reinforced by the Midrash that states that Adam was created before Avraham so that, if Adam sinned, Avraham's status of being our first forefather would be protected.) Because of Adam's loss of role-model status, the Torah felt it inappropriate to record the reactions of Adam and Chava to Hevel's death, from which all subsequent generations could have benefited. Given these two ideas, we can gain a deeper understanding of the ramifications of one's actions. The Torah made no mention of Adam and Chava's mourning over Hevel's death because they had committed a sin against God. This has not only removed from them the privilege of living in *Gan Eden*; it also stripped them of their potentially larger role as model Torah parents.

As we just finished the *Yamim Noraim* season, free of sin and ready to start the new year off with a clean slate, it behooves all of us to recognize our newly regained status as God's chosen children and to protect our privilege of serving as *Ovdei HaShem*.

❖ CHAPTER 2 ❖

Noach

Rabbi Sholom Steinig

Young Israel of Bayside, New York

"Noach was a righteous man; he was perfect in his generations."

This verse, which seems to praise Noach as a great man, is the source of one of the most complex rabbinic discussions about the personality of a figure in the *Chumash*. The *Gemara* in *Sanhedrin* (108a) tells us that Rabbi Yochanan explains "in his generations" to mean "in *his* generation [he was considered righteous], but not in any other," whereas Resh Lakish understands it to mean "how much more so [had he lived] in other generations." The negative opinion that Rabbi Yochanan has of Noach is consistent with his discussions elsewhere. In *Bereishis Rabbah* (32:6), Rabbi Yochanan declares Noach to be lacking in his faith, as he did not enter the ark until the water was "lapping at his ankles." And in *Sanhedrin* (ibid.), in discussing the construction of the ark itself, Rabbi Yochanan explains that the word *tzohar* should not be understood as a window in the ark, which would be the normal translation, but, rather, as a precious gem that gave off light. What do we learn from this change? The *Torah Teminah* explains that Rabbi Yochanan's view here is that just as Lot was not righteous enough to be permitted to watch the destruction of S'dom and Amorrah, so was Noach not considered on a sufficiently high level to witness the flood destroying the world. Hence, no window was permitted in the ark; only the glowing gem was allowed. With regard to "in his generation," we may be more familiar with the wording that Rashi uses in his commentary:

> There are those of our rabbis who interpret this as praise: "All the more so had he been in a generation of righteous people; he would have been even more righteous," and there are those who interpret this as discourteous: "According to his generation he was a righteous man, but had he lived in the generation of Avraham, he would not have been considered at all."

Immediately, we notice several changes in Rashi's presentation. The first is that, whereas the *Gemara* mentions the damning opinion of Noach first,

Rashi opens with the more positive view. In addition, whereas Rashi contrasts Noach specifically with Avraham, the Talmud merely mentions "other generations." Why the differences?

First, the Talmudic discussion is said in the names of the authors of the statements, Rabbi Yochanan and Resh Lakish. Since Rabbi Yochanan was Resh Lakish's teacher, it is proper to mention him first. As Rashi does not mention these Rabbis by name, he apparently felt it was more respectful to mention the praise of Noach before "insulting" him. Second, as to the mention of Avraham specifically, there are several possible responses. It can be said that Avraham, as the first *tzaddik* to live after the time of Noach, should naturally be the one to whom Noach would be compared. It could also be said, however, that since Avraham stands out as the epitome of *chesed*—acts of kindness—the failure of Noach in this area stands out even more. Whereas Avraham was known for bringing in guests and even debating with *HaShem* in trying to save the wicked people of S'dom and Amorrah, Noach didn't even question the impending flood. He just built his boat and, seemingly, ignored the threat to his neighbors. The comparison with Avraham seems almost to shame Noach. In fact, in the same verse, Rashi comments that while Noach walked *with HaShem*, implying a weakness and the need for a crutch, Avraham walked before God, indicating an inner strength and greater righteousness that allowed him to stand alone.

In defending Noach, it is possible to say that his inability to turn around the people of his time was not his fault, but theirs. The *Mizrachi* explains that Noach was not able to achieve his full potential as a *tzaddik* because of his surroundings. Had he been transported, just as he was, to the time of Avraham, he truly would not have been considered at all. The level of righteousness that he had attained was the most that could have been expected for any individual at that time, but in Avraham's generation this would have seemed insignificant indeed. However, we must keep in mind that in Avraham's presence, and in the absence of the wicked people in his generation who surrounded him, Noach would have flourished and achieved his full potential as an outstanding and unquestionable *tzaddik*. In his own time, his job was not to convert others but merely to keep his head above the surrounding wickedness. Avraham's mission in his time was to affect others; Noach's in his own was to survive. As such, he did, indeed, accomplish that for which *HaShem* intended him.

A *tzaddik hador*—the great righteous individual of any generation—is provided with what is necessary for his era, but this would not necessarily be adequate or appropriate for another. Noach was righteous for his time, and *this* is the crucial point. Comparisons do not matter. They do not even apply. Noach supporters can rest at ease: he was the right man at the right time—a *tzaddik*.

Rabbi Yaakov Feitman

Young Israel of Beachwood, Ohio

Chazal and the Torah commentaries often teach us the important lesson that the Torah is not a history book. The rule that the Torah is not necessarily chronological (*Pesachim* 6b) is a regular reminder of this dictum. The fact that many wonderful and edifying stories are not told in the Torah itself, but were left to the *midrash*, is another reflection of the reality that the Torah is far more than a compendium of anecdotes and aphorisms.

The saga of Avraham Avinu's rescue at *Ur Kasdim*, Moshe Rabbeinu as the king of the land of Kush, and many other such *midrashim* reveal to us important elements of the lives of some of our greatest progenitors.

And yet these stories did not "make it" into *Torah Shebichtav*—the Written Torah. This is in part because the narratives that are a part of the Torah present us, beyond the content of the "stories" themselves, with an eternal and infinite set of lessons and teachings, sources for *halachah* and homiletics. Even details of our history and concepts that are crucial to the people of Israel have often been left to the Sages to reveal and explicate. Although the criteria for what is included in *Torah Shebichtav* are beyond our comprehension, it is manifest that each event recorded in the Torah bears profound significance until the end of time.

Thus, it is all the more difficult to understand the place of the *Dor Hahaflagah*—the generation that built the Tower of Babel—in the Torah. The precious words of the Torah were not needed just to tell the genealogy of mankind's linguistic development. In the case of the Generation of the Flood, the Torah delineated very clearly the sin for which mankind suffered near-annihilation. *Chazal* (*Bereishit Rabbah* 38:6) note that, though it is evident that the Generation of the Flood perished because of larceny, the sin of the Generation of the Tower is undefined. The question, therefore, inevitably arises: If the Torah was not going to reveal to us the cause of its fall, why tell us the story of that era at all?

To be sure, *Chazal* themselves illuminate the apparent darkness and shine an unblinking beam upon those builders. Our Sages and the commentators through the ages have revealed and discovered devastating iniquity embedded in the Torah's description of the *Dor Hahaflagah*: "Twenty-four different forms of blasphemy issued forth from that generation," says the *Midrash Tanchumah*, although only a few of their sinful statements have come down to us. These people worshiped idols (*Avodah Zarah* 53b) and arrogantly thought that they could conquer the heavens themselves (*Rabbeinu Bechaya* in name of *Midrash Aseret Hadibrot*). They were heretics (*Ramban*) and wanted to sabotage the mission of Avraham *Avinu* at its very nascency (*Rabbi Yosef Tzvi Dushinsky*). And yet, one wonders why the Torah withheld these revelations in the world of *peshat* and left it to *Torah shebal peh*—the Oral Torah—to expose that strange generation. Surely, the Torah did not spare the Generation of the Flood. It tells us of the "great evil" and "corruption" that permeated the earth. Why the use of euphemism and innuendo concerning these rebels and renegades?

One novel approach, granted to us by the *Be'er Sheva* (commentary to *Sanhedrin* 109a), a contemporary of the *Shulchan Aruch* in the sixteenth century, suggests that, in fact, there is no practical lesson to be derived from the Tower of Babel. Rabbi Yissachar Ber Eilenberg declares that the danger caused by that generation was unique because of the once-in-history unity that existed among the nations. Since it can never happen again, there was no purpose in revealing the genesis of its iniquity. The Generation of the Flood destroyed itself because of greed and mendacity, sins that are replicated throughout history, and so its downfall needs to be studied, analyzed, and avoided. Only when *Mashiach* comes, teaches the *Be'er Sheva*, will mankind be as unified again; and then it will be a boon, not a danger to the world.

This surprising interpretation certainly explains why the Torah didn't enter into details about the *Dor Hahaflagah* but doesn't address the imperative follow-up question: Why, then, tell the tale at all?

Rabbi Reuven Margolios, in his compendium *Margoliyot Hayum* to Sanhedrin (ibid.) cites a fascinating explication by the early midrashic/ kabbalistic work *Sefer Hapliah*. There were three groups whose intent was to honor God, teaches the *Sefer Hapliah*, but who were punished, nevertheless, because their methods were terribly wrong: Adam and Eve, the Generation of the Tower, and Nadav and Avihu, the sons of Aharon.

The *Dor Hahaflagah* saw the tremendous apparent power of the stars, the constellations, and the hosts of heaven, and sought to avoid them and be under the dominion of God alone. This yearning, in and of itself, was certainly laudable. Their sense of unity and caring for each other were certainly exemplary. And yet, they went terribly astray.

What happened?

Since the *Sefer Hapliah* provided us with the context for the error of the *Dor Hahaflagah,* we must explore what that generation had in common with the downfall of both Adam and the sons of Aharon. Although these matters are esoteric and far from our understanding, *Chazal* (*Sanhedrin* 29a) did reveal to us a simple common denominator. Concerning *Adam Harishon*—the first man—the *Gemara* teaches: "From where do we derive that he who adds [to the word of God] is considered as if he diminished [His word]? The Torah teaches [that Adam and Eve] added to God's prohibition [God only commanded not to eat, and they added the prohibition against touching as well]," and therein lay the downfall of mankind.

The Torah's language about Nadav and Avihu is even more unmistakable. They offered a sacrifice "which God had not commanded them" (Lev. 10.1). *Chazal* in the *Safra—Torat Kohanim* define what they did as—they added an additional expression of their love of God upon that which had been commanded.

It is instructive to note that both in the case of *Adam Harishon* and in that of Nadav and Avihu, in addition, as we have seen, to the *Dor Hahaflagah, Chazal* enumerate many sins apparently omitted by the Torah. Of Adam, the *Gemara* (*Sanhedrin* 38b) records opinions that he was a *min* (heretic) *Moshech Beorloto* (reversed his Sign of the Covenant), and even a *Kofeir Biekor* (one who, God forbid, denied the existence of the Creator).

About Nadav and Avihu, the Sages list a litany of offenses including entering the *Mishkan* without their priestly clothing, remaining unmarried and refraining from the commandment to procreate, issuing rulings in the presence of their teachers, and other misdeeds as well.

On perhaps the most simplistic of levels, the pattern is obvious. The great, benevolent, omniscient God knows the best of intentions, we inevitably begin our slide down that slippery slope toward His denial as well.

The great benevolent omniscient God knows exactly what is best for us. When we attempt to supersede His will, even with the best of intentions, we inevitably begin our slide down the slippery slope toward his denial as well.

The Sefer Tzafnas Paneach by the Gaon of Rogatcibv explains the appellations ascribed to Adam Harishon as: *B'gufo shel Adam Harishon hayah kol minei Metziut sh'yeshnom b'olom.*

Within the body of Adam was all possible realities that exist in the world.

Adam was the repository of all future modes, approaches, sins, virtues, characters, and personalities. Thus, one major danger inherent in mankind is trying to improve or even supplement the works of the Creator.

Adam and Eve tried, to improve the world, and the world entered its instant cosmic deterioration. Nadav and Avihu attempted to rise higher or faster than God intended, and one iniquity apparently led to another.

And so it was with the Generation of the Tower. They began as decent people who had learned some of the lessons of the Flood. They not only were honest with each other but had achieved a remarkable unity and harmony amongst people. They could have created a utopian society in which paradise on earth would have been available to all.

And then they fell into the trap. God had said to "fill the earth and subdue it," and they were afraid to proliferate across the face of the earth. They thought that one can become close to God only on the high places—a thought that leads directly to idolatry (see *Avodah Zarah* 45a). All of their fine manners and excellent personality traits and characteristics became worthless because they were trying to second-guess the Creator.

That is more than a sin. It is a fatal flaw. It leads to sin, but it is more than sin. So the lesson of the *Dor Hahaflagah* had to be presented to us as a seemingly innocuous exercise in freedom of religion—good people searching for God in their own way, making up the rules as they go along. But a common language led to a babel of incoherence, and good intentions led to ultimate tragedy.

For, in the final analysis, man must know that he has been given rules to live by. These laws, being divinely ordained, cannot be subject to change or improvement, whims or fads. On the surface all can seem well, while beneath are sown the winds of anarchy and destruction. Total unity will indeed come one day (*Pesachim* 50b), but on God's own terms, when we will truly be able to say: *HaShem Echud V'shmo Echad,* God is one and His name is one.

Rabbi Fabian Schonfeld

Young Israel of Kew Gardens Hills, New York

In most cases in which we are told in the Torah of the birth of the biblical personalities, we are also told of the reasons for the names given to them by their parents. One of the exceptions to this practice is in the case of Noach. Though the portion of the week is called *Noach*, his name has already been mentioned at the end of *Bereishit*. In chapter 5, verse 29, we read, "And he called his name Noach, saying 'This one will bring us rest from our work and from the toil of our hands, from the ground which *HaShem* has cursed.'"

Rashi comments as follows: This was said in reference to the invention of the plowshare, which was attributed to Noach. Until his time, in consequence of the curse decreed upon Adam, the earth produced thorns and thistles when one planted wheat. In Noach's day this ceased (ArtScroll translation). In other words, the word Noach, which means "to rest," was meant to indicate that farmers would now be able to rest more easily from their hard work because of the plow that Noach invented.

What does a plow really accomplish? Before the soil is plowed, the seeds may be completely dispersed by the wind, or the soil may produce weeds and thorns. Seeds are not able to penetrate beyond the top soil and the surface of the land. For the wheat to grow the seeds must penetrate the hard crust of the land and begin to gestate and, eventually, find their way through the hard core of earth and grow towards heaven.

Symbolically, what is suggested here is that Noach removed superficiality from the life of the farmers; a concept that applies not only to the farming community but, in the view of the Torah, to all moments in the area of life. What Judaism rejects is superficiality in our thoughts and in our actions. If, for example, we are engaged in prayer and merely recite the words then we are said to be *mitpallel min hasafan vehachutz*—which really means to be involved only in lip service. When we study a text of Torah, we are not supposed to read it simply and to glance at the words; we are not supposed to study it superficially but rather to go beyond the surface. When we perform a *mitzvah* of *chesed*, we should not simply convey our feelings toward our fellow human beings in a superficial manner and perform this *mitzvah pro forma*. It was this concept of going beyond the surface that the plowshare invented by Noach was to accomplish.

This is why he was named Noach, as Rashi explains in the passage quoted above. Noach conveyed to the Jewish people the need not to do things purely mechanically but to probe beneath the surface. This is the meaning of Noach's name, and this is why he was given this name by the Torah.

In our commitment in the study of Torah, we must not perform the *mitzvot* toward our fellow man with a superficial and indifferent attitude. Like Noach, we must use the plowshare to reach the inner depth of our soul and of our life.

❖ CHAPTER 3 ❖

Lech Lecha

Rabbi Chaim Wasserman

Young Israel of Passaic–Clifton, New Jersey

WHY NOT START WITH *LECH LECHA*?

Echoing Rashi's comments to the Torah, the Maggid of Kosinitz, in an attempt to define the essence of Torah, also wondered why *Chumash* began with *Bereishis* and *Noach* and not with *Parshat Lech Lecha*. For, only in *Lech Lecha* do we begin learning about the activities of Avraham *Avinu*, the first Jew; everything else in the two preceding *parshiyot* are of universal significance, without any content that is specifically Jewish.

The Maggid, much like Rashi, realized that these seemingly unnecessary sections do indeed contain vital lessons by which one must understand the Torah that follows. He offered the following explanation:

Three highlights of the two *parshiyot* preceding *Lech Lecha* are (1) the murder perpetrated by Cain, (2) the generation of the great flood in the days of Noach, and (3) the plans for the Tower of Bavel. Each person, said the Maggid, possesses the very human qualities that were at the root of each of these three occurrences, and these traits must be faced and dealt with even before the rest of Torah, the specific lessons for Jews.

In the case of Cain it was jealousy (*kin'ah*) of his brother's grace in the eyes of God that led him to commit such a dastardly act. The generation of the flood was destroyed because of the unbridled lust for possessions (*ta'avah*) that characterized every social transaction (*vatimalei ha'aretz chamas*). And it was only an insatiable hunger for honor (*kavod*) that motivated the building of the tower in Bavel (*na'aseh lanu shem*).

Every person is touched by each of these three attitudes: jealousy, a lust for possession, and a drive for honor. And until one comes to proper grips with these three human dispositions, one cannot effectively approach the study of Torah or the Torah way of life, explained the Maggid.

The Gerrer Rebbe (in *S'fas Emes* to *Pirke Avot* 4:21) expanded upon the Maggid's approach by citing here the dictum of Rabbi Eleazar haKappar: Jealousy (*kin'ah*), unbridled lust (*ta'avah*), and an uncontrollable desire for honor (*kavod*) obliterate nearly all traces of a Divine image (*tzelem Elohim*) in which all humanity was fashioned. The Jew, therefore, must first learn to be a *mensch* before being able to grapple with the imperatives of Torah living. This, claims the *S'fas Emes*, is what *Chazal* meant when they taught that *Derech eretz kodmah laTorah*.

This, then, is the Divine purpose of starting the Torah with *Bereishis* and *Noach*; so that a Jew may understand first which human virtues are needed as a prerequisite for Torah study and Torah living. Without this introduction, the rest of Torah, starting with *Lech Lecha* and Avraham *Avinu*, would be seriously flawed.

WHAT IS A "YASHAR"?

The *Netziv* (Rav Naftali Tzvi Yehudah Berlin, immortal *Rosh Yeshivah* of *Volozhin*) notes in his introduction to *Bereishis* (*Ha'amek Davar, P'sichah* leSefer Bereishis) that Avraham, as well as Yitzchak and Ya'akov, were referred to as *yesharim* (morally correct) aside from being just *tzaddikim*, *chasidim*, and lovers of God. This designation of *Yesharim* (first used Bamidbar, *Parshat Balak* 23:10 by none other than Bilaam) attested to the fact that the *avos*, starting with Avraham, because of their moral perfection, were able to plead before God for the well-being of all humans no matter how removed they were from the universal demands of the Torah. What better example is there of what a *yashar* is than Avraham standing before God demanding that the entire corrupt society of S'dom be spared just in case there were *tzadikkim*, however few and however hidden, in the city.

S'dom epitomized everything that Avraham deemed evil and morally detestable. Nonetheless, he is able to call God to a *din Torah*, a Judicial court of law as it were, on behalf of these human beings. Despite one's corrupt and evil actions, the mark of a *yashar* is that he can still plead for the well-being of that person or society. The greatest among *tzaddikim* would be hard pressed to act in such a manner; not so *yesharim*. It is for this reason that the first book of the Torah, which tells of the lives and accomplishments of Avraham, Yitzchak, and Yaakov, is also called *Sefer Yesharim*.

GOING TO *THE* LAND

Eretz Yisrael is not an external entity for the Jewish people, serving merely as a means of uniting the nation and giving the people a way of existing in a physical sense or even a cultural or spiritual sense. For the Jew, *Eretz Yisrael* represents a unique entity—the very life bond of the nation. This bond is not the common and natural attachment nations have for their historical territory, which develops over the span of many years. Our bond with the land derives directly from the recognition of God that began with Avraham *Avinu*. It was then that God's covenant with the descendants of Avraham focused upon that small land, which has the watchful eye of Divine providence every moment of the year (based on Rav Avraham Yitzchon Hakohen Kook).

Avraham *Avinu* merited this land as a result of his tribulations and narrow brush with death while still in *Ur Kasdim*. For his resolute faith in the idea of One God, he was awarded, at the *Bris Bein Hab'sarim*, God's favorite land, for himself and his children, unto eternity (*Mabit* in *Beit Elokim*).

The Jewish spirit is inseparable from the Jewish people. It is impossible for either of these entities, spirit or nationhood, to reach its state of perfection away from the environment and boundaries of Torah. *Eretz Yisrael* and the Jewish nation, fused together, become the unique possession (*kinyan*) of God in this world.

To which this writer would add: Fortunate are those in the Young Israel movement who have worked relentlessly to unite the Jewish spirit with its people in the land which was so treasured (*eretz chemda*) by Avraham, Yitzchak, and Yaakov. At no time in the last two thousand years could one read the opening words of the *parsha* with such determination, certainty, and spirituality: *Lech Lecha*—Go to the land which I will show you. It will be for your benefit and ultimate enjoyment (*l'tovascha u'l'hana'ascha*).

Rabbi Elias Lauer, Z'l
Executive Director

American Friends of Yisrael Hatzair Young Israel in Israel

One would expect the Torah to have taught us that Avraham *Avinu*'s faith in *HaShem* was immediately rewarded with the fulfillment of the promises that were made to him by God. Instead we are surprised to learn that Avraham, following God's directive to leave his land, his birthplace, and his father's house, arrives in Canaan to find a famine and is forced to leave and travel to Egypt. Only later does Avraham return to Canaan *kaveid meod*—very laden—after having amassed a great fortune in cattle, silver, and gold. But why, one wonders, was there the initial delay in the fulfillment of *HaShem*'s promise of blessing?

Moreover, Rashi, in commenting on the Torah's description of the route traveled by Avraham on his return to Canaan (Gen. 13:3), quotes the *midrash* and tells us that Avraham retraced his original steps so that he could "repay his debts." What kind of debts did Avraham incur? Are we to believe that, in return for following God's commandments, Avraham not only finds famine in Canaan but incurred debt as well? Is this how we are to understand *avorechacha v'yehey brachah*? (Genesis 12:2) "And I will bless you . . . and you shall be a blessing."

There are several answers that one can give, but, of these, there is one in particular that I would like to share with you as being especially meaningful in the light of today's unfolding world events. It is the view that explains Avraham's debt, not as a monetary debt of gold or silver or anything of material value, but rather a debt of "words." Avraham had to retrace his steps because he owed an answer to so many people—an answer that he did not have when he left Canaan but which he was now prepared to give based upon his new insight of *HaShem*, learned from his experiences in Egypt.

For, when Avraham first arrived in Canaan and found famine rather than the blessing that God had promised, he became vulnerable to those who heckled him and mocked his teachings of the existence of God. "Is this how God is true to His word?" they asked. "Is this the *brachah* that you were promised?" Avraham remained steadfast in his *emunah,* he had his faith and his belief, from which no scorn or ridicule could sway him. But, though he believed that God would fulfill His promise, he had no answer for those who ridiculed him.

It is only now, when he leaves Mitzrayim laden with the great fortune that he has amassed, that Avraham realizes that the fulfillment of God's promises do not necessarily come on the very same day that the promise is made. That man must retain his faith and his *emunah* but, as the Psalmist teaches, *elef shanim k'yom echad*—in the eyes of *HaShem* a thousand years is as one day—that the fulfillment of *HaShem*'s promises may take years, centuries, or millennia but that His promises will see fulfillment according to a timetable that He alone comprehends.

It is with this new understanding that Avraham is most anxious to retrace his original steps as he returns to Canaan. He "owes" an answer to all those who mocked him. He retraces his original route to make sure that he answers all whom he could not answer before.

This explanation is particularly meaningful to us in our day, as we see events taking place in the world about us—in Israel, in particular—what obviously show the *yad HaShem*—the hand of God—but that we, with our limited capacity, do not comprehend and do not fully understand. The lesson that can be learned from Avraham is that, although we may have no answer at the moment, we must remain steadfast in our *emunah* and continue to give strength and support to those who uphold the ideals of Torah and *yahadut.* We may not have the answers now, but, with faith in *HaShem,* we, too, will ultimately have the answer.

One final thought. Following Avraham's return to Canaan, the Torah tells us of the dispute between the shepherds of Avraham and the shepherds of Lot and then adds, *v'hacannani v'haprizi oz yoshev ba'aretz*—"Canaani and Prizi then dwelled [singular] in the land." The obvious question is, why *yoshev* in the singular? We are speaking of two nations, and the plural form should have been used? The answer is as obvious as the question, and teaches us a lesson for all times. When there is division in our midst, among brethren who should be united, then our enemies become united as one.

At this crucial juncture in the history of our people, as we witness the *yad HaShem* in events that are beyond our understanding, may we be united as one with our brethren in Israel and, more particularly, with the more than sixty branches of Young Israel in Israel (known as *Yisrael Hatzair*), half of which are located in Yehuda and Shomron. They need our help and our *chizuk* and support to endure these most difficult times. May we be responsive to the needs of the hour and, in that *z'chut*, may we merit the witnessing of *U'va LeZion Goel*—speedily in our day. Amen.

Rabbi Yaakov Bienenfeld

Young Israel of Harrison, New York

In *Parshat Lech Lecha* we learn of Avraham *Avinu*'s wealth. The terminology the Torah uses for wealth is quite strange: *V'Avraham kaved meod bamikneh bakesef uvezahav* (Gen. 13:2)—"And Avraham was burdened with flock[s], silver, and gold." Why is the word "burden" used to denote wealth? A few *pesukim* earlier, the very same word—*kaved*—is used to describe the hardship of famine: *Ki kaved haraav baaretz* (Gen. 12:10). There, however, the use of the word burden seems appropriate, since a scarcity of food is certainly a hardship and a burden. In describing Avraham's possessions of gold, silver, and livestock, the word "burden" seems ill chosen. Shouldn't these material blessings make life easier and more enjoyable for Avraham instead of more burdensome?

To the great *tzaddik* Avraham, wealth was as much a burden as a blessing. Avraham knew the Talmudic dictum, *schar mitzvah behai alma lekah*—in this world we do not receive reward for our observance of *mitzvot*. Yet, in the *Kriyat Shema*, which we recite daily, we say: *Vehaya im shomoa tishmiu el mitzvotai . . . vinatati mitar artzichem bieto yoreh umalkosh viasafta deganecha vitiroschcha viyitzharecha.*—"And it will come to pass that if you continually hearken to My commandments . . . then I will provide rain for your land in its proper time, the early and the late rains, that you may gather in your grain, your wine, and your oil." The famous question then arises: If we do not receive reward in this world for our observance of *mitzvot*, why does the Torah explicitly state that if we observe the commandments we will be the beneficiaries of rain, crops, and other material goods?

The answer is that these material goods are not the end reward; they are mere instruments that enable us to continue the observance of *mitzvot*. The grain, wine, and oil are not intended to reward us but, rather, to give those who do *mitzvot*, the strength and the means to continue. When a lawyer is hired by a firm and is given an office, desk, and legal pads, or an accountant, a calculator, or a teacher, chalk and erasers, these are not considered their salary or reward but the tools and instruments necessary for them to carry out their respective jobs. So, too, *HaShem* offers us material goods as a means to continue our job of performing *mitzvot* as committed Jews. Our true reward remains intact for the World to Come.

When Avraham saw that he was blessed with an excessive amount of material goods, he understood that this could not be attributable to a heavenly reward for good deeds. That, he knew, would not be forthcoming in this world. If so, why was he the recipient of this wealth? What was its purpose?

Avraham could only conclude that these riches were not given to him as a means for self-indulgence but, rather, to facilitate an even greater level of *mitzvah* performance. He saw himself merely as a funnel through which *HaShem*'s blessings must be disbursed and distributed to others—the needy, the infirm, the abandoned. He viewed his wealth as a burden because with it came the responsibility of equitable distribution and allocation. And, though Avraham did appreciate the blessings of material things and the good that could be achieved through wealth, he also understood the burden of the responsibility that accompanies it.

I believe that this concept of the burden of wealth explains the *mishnah* in *Pirkei Avot* that says, *marbeh nesochim marbeh deagah*—"one who increases his possessions increases his worries." Do we really need the *mishnah* to explain to us that the more we acquire, the more we worry? Isn't it obvious that along with cars, houses, businesses, and jewelry come care payments, insurance, mortgages, maintenance fees, and a host of worries? Or is the *mishnah* suggesting that we would be better off limiting our holdings in order to avoid worry?

I think that the *mishnah* is instead trying to tell us that he who increases his possessions must increase his worry in the manner of Avraham, by adopting the Avraham *Avinu* attitude toward wealth and property: namely, that we should worry about our possessions on a spiritual and religious level. Like Avraham, we need to worry about how we are allocating our blessings. Are we using them selfishly or to benefit those around us? One must ask oneself: Am I utilizing all that *HaShem* gave me in the performance of *mitzvot*? Am I using my home for *hachnassat orchim*, my car to offer rides to those who need them? The more we are blessed with, the more we should be worrying! But our worry should not be directed toward increasing or preserving our wealth but, rather, toward making sure that we are using it to perform good deeds that benefit others.

As we read this week about Avraham *Avinu*'s "burden," we should take inventory of all that we've been blessed with—resources, talents, and so on—and worry about whether we are using these blessings properly.

❖ CHAPTER 4 ❖

Vayera

Rabbi Hershel Becker

Young Israel of Kendall, Florida

Although we find a description of the life experience of Avraham *Avinu* in the *midrash*, the Torah text itself is not explicit regarding his biography. Yet, in *Parshat Vayera*, we find great detail concerning every move as Avraham *Avinu* entertained his guests. The Torah's message to us is readily apparent: *Chesed*—kindness to others—and *Hachnosat Orchim*—hospitality—require attention to detail. The greatness of our patriarch, Avraham, was that his closeness to *HaShem* was not an interpersonal relationship without connection to the world at large. Additionally, his great love of others stemmed from his desire to emulate the Creator and the fulfillment of the *mitzvot bein Adam lechaveiro*—between man and his fellow man.

The *midrash*, in *Kohelet*, *perek* 7, states, "If one denies the importance of kindness to others, it is as if he denies the Almighty. Piety is nonexistent if one is concerned only with oneself." *HaShem* created the world with kindness; it is our task to pursue the traits of *HaShem* and to perpetuate kindness as well.

In *Bereishit* 18:4, Avraham begged his guests to benefit from his hospitality: "Please take some water." Avraham asked that water be brought for the guests to wash their feet. Rashi notes that because Avraham did not go himself to bring water but rather relied upon a messenger, so, too, did the *Bnei Yisrael* have to rely upon a messenger for water in the desert, generations later. Rather than receiving water directly from *HaShem* in the manner in which the manna was given, Moshe was assigned the task of supplying water through a rock.

Our reaction to the above incident might be to think that the action of Avraham was insignificant; the guests were taken care of, if indirectly. Let us examine the resulting situation to gain a proper assessment of *chesed*. Had Avraham himself brought water to the guests, *HaShem* would have supplied water in the desert; Moshe wouldn't have hit the rock; *Bnei Yisrael* would have entered Eretz Yisrael under Moshe's leadership and complete *geulah*—

redemption—would have been at hand. As we look back upon all our suffering in the many years of *galut*, we can truly understand that there are major ramifications to our acts of *chesed*.

In *Bereishit* 18:7 we learn that Avraham ran to the cattle and gave a choice tender calf to the young lad to prepare. Rashi tells us that the youngster mentioned was Yishmael. Why didn't Avraham prepare the meat himself? If this was an error, why is there no mention of a reaction as there was by the water? Rashi states that the task was given to Yishmael to train him in the performance of *mitzvot*. With this goal in mind, not only was it permissible to give the task to another; it was, indeed, the parental obligation of Avraham toward his son. At times, a parent might set different standards for the *mitzvot* he performs and the *mitzvot* his children perform. True *chinuch* and guidance demand that children be incorporated in the fulfillment of commandments at the highest level. By having a child take part in the actual performance of *mitzvot* at an early age, by apportioning responsibility according to the child's capabilities, the *mitzvot* and *chesed* become part and parcel of his being.

As the *parshah* continues, we read of Lot, living in S'dom infamous for its cruelty. Lot chose to live in this society and was even appointed a judge. Yet, on the day of his appointment, when we know he was concerned with making a good impression on his constituents, we see Lot urging two guests to come to his home. Lot's wife would not even give salt to strangers. The society in which Lot lived was the very antitheses of *chesed*. Why did Lot risk all for the sake of guests? Rashi explains in *Bereishit* 19:1 that Lot learned, in the house of Avraham, to seek guests. The practices of his youth made an indelible imprint upon his being that no external circumstances—neither wife nor community—could erase.

In *Yalkut Shimoni* (*Bechukotai*), we read of an individual, together with his family, who was afflicted by famine. The prophet Eliyahu approached him and asked, "From what family are you?"

He responded, "From family Ploni."
"How many were you?"
"Three thousand."
"How many remain alive?"
"Only me."
Eliyahu then asked, "Would you like to say a statement and live?"
"Yes!" the man responded.
"Say, *Shema Yisrael* . . . and you will live!"
The man shouted in despair, "I can't. I won't. This is not what I learned in my father's home!" He embraced his idol and perished.

The importance of the home environment cannot be overemphasized. Our children will long remember how things were done in their home. The *chesed* we involve our children in *now* will become ingrained in their souls to be demonstrated in their future actions. Parental responsibility demands the realization that the manner in which we perform *mitzvot* will, in all likelihood, be the pattern our children will follow. The *chinuch* of the house of Avraham was enough to save Lot even from the perils of S'dom. Such is the lasting power of *mitzvot* and *chesed*.

The Jewish community of Kendall has been beneficiary to *chasdei HaShem*—the kindness of the Almighty—having been spared from bodily harm during Hurricane Andrew. We, at the Young Israel of Kendall, also recognize the great *chesed* of our family at the National Council of Young Israel. As our situation became known, the National Council of Young Israel mobilized to assist us in every way possible. We were contacted by many branches with offers of help and greatly appreciated words of encouragement. The kindness bestowed upon us has indeed had great impact on our community. We are grateful and proud to be part of Young Israel!

Rabbi Dov A. Brisman

Young Israel of Elkins Park, Pennsylvania

UNWELCOME GUESTS

> "And his wife looked behind him and became a pillar of salt." (Gen. 19:26)

Rashi comments, "With salt she transgressed and with salt she was punished. Lot would ask his wife to give salt to the guests, and she would reply 'Do you also wish to introduce this evil practice?'"

It seems that guests were invited into Lot's house and were served meals. This did not concern Lot's wife at all; she only commented and criticized when it came to the salt. How do we understand this?

In the manuscripts of my great-grandfather and namesake, the *Rosh Bet Din* of Kolno, Poland, I found the following interpretation:

Lot had grown accustomed to the *mitzvah* of *hachnasat orchim* (welcoming of guests) in the house of his uncle Avraham *Avinu*. Even in S'dom he did not part easily with this *mitzvah*. However, Lot's wife strongly disapproved of this practice and attempted to abolish it entirely. Knowing that Lot would never discontinue welcoming guests, Lot's wife devised a clever plan. She allowed the guests into her house and served them bland meals. Even salt was not provided. Thus, guests would feel most unwelcome and unwanted in Lot's home, and eventually word would spread that guests were not truly welcome there but were just brought into the home as a matter of habit. Eventually, nobody would frequent Lot's home, and *hachnasat orchim* would become a thing of the past.

I only pray that *HaShem* instill in us such tact and cunning in our outreach endeavors. Success would surely be guaranteed.

PRE-CONCEIVED ACCIDENTS

As we examine the incident of Sarah's "abduction" by Avimelech, and the intense wrath of the Almighty toward Avimelech, several issues beg clarification. Why was this considered a heinous action? Avimelech was totally unaware of Sarah's marital status, and had he known that she was married, he would never have "taken" her. Furthermore, Avimelech immediately returned Sarah to her husband. Why is Avimelech faulted so gravely for having acted innocently based upon misinformation?

Avimelech attempts to exonerate himself before the Almighty by declaring (Gen. 20:4), "Will You also execute a righteous nation?" Rashi explains that Avimelech implied that the Almighty "wiped out" righteous people during the flood and Tower of Babel periods. This comment requires elucidation, for how can Avimelech—a prophet—even entertain a notion that the aforementioned were righteous? Was he unaware of the evil of the peoples of these periods?

In the *vidui* (confession) service of Yom Kippur, we state "for the transgression that we have transgressed before You by accident and willingly." HaGaon Rav Dovid Kronglas, *zt"l* (*Mashgiach* and *Ram* of Ner Israel–Baltimore, MD) was bothered by this statement. The *Gemara* constantly states that the Torah exempts us from punishment for accidental violations. Why, then, is it necessary to confess for an accident?

The *Mashgiach, zt"l,* explained the *vidui* on the basis of a remark by Ibn Ezra. In *Parshat Naso* we learn about the *nazir* who makes a vow to lead a life in which he is precluded from consuming grape derivatives and from defiling himself with the dead. If there is sudden accident in which he becomes defiled by a dead body (*tumatmeit*), the *nazir* must bring a special sacrifice that consists (in part) of a *chatat*—a sin offering. Ibn Ezra explains that this atonement is necessary because the occurrence of an accident is indicative of a sin that was previously committed. Had no previous iniquity occurred, then one's "spiritual guard" would not have been "lowered," and, hence, no accident would have taken place.

In this light, the *Mashgiach, zt"l,* explained the significance of the *vidui*. Our confession to accidental violation(s) refers to the fact that we have sunk spiritually to the extent that accidental violations can actually occur. If our overall spiritual performance would have been superior, the Almighty would never have allowed a situation of accidental transgressions to occur.

Perhaps this is what is meant in Psalms (79) and in the *Tachanun* service: "Do not remember for us the original iniquities," for the initial violations may have caused a spiritual decline that lead to situations beyond our control. Therefore, we request that such a responsibility be lifted from our shoulders.

It seems to me that the case against Avimelech was not primarily for the "abduction" of Sarah. That was indeed an accident based on misinformation. However, only base behavior and an immoral lifestyle can lead to such errors. This is what Avraham *Avinu* meant when he explained to Avimelech that a guest should first be indulged with matters of comfort (that is, food, lodging, and so on), not interrogated about his wife. If an "innocent mistake" results from an immoral approach, surely the perpetrator must assume the responsibility. For this reason, Avimelech (especially as a king and leader) was indeed to be faulted.

Now we can understand the seemingly incomprehensible charge of Avimelech that the Almighty sought retribution for naught against the generations of the flood and the Tower of Babel. Avimelech understood that these were generations of base and corrupt people. However, his claim was that there inevitably must have been a great many individuals that were pressured by forces in the environment to transgress. They had no evil intentions, he argues; so how could You punish them with the real villains and perpetrators of evil? So, too, I was a mere victim of circumstances and, thus, Your wrath against me is unjust.

However, the flaw in Avimelech's reasoning can be understood with the *Mashgiach*'s explanation of the Ibn Ezra. It is true that we mortals cannot judge or punish others who sin by accident, but the Almighty knows which situations were precipitated by previous negligence and lack of prevention. The Almighty obviously understood that each and every individual in those generations was not a total "innocent." An ounce of prevention might have extricated them from difficult situations.

Let us hope that the Almighty spare us from all errors, so that we may serve Him to the maximum.

Rabbi Chaim Wakslak

Young Israel of Long Beach, New York

Avraham *Avinu* dedicated his life to the task of teaching the world about the existence of one God, Master of the Universe. An understanding of the importance of this mission to Avraham will provide us with a better understanding of several events that we encounter in the *sedrah* this week.

The *sedra* begins by describing how Avraham *Avinu* is eagerly hoping to receive guests on the third day after his circumcision. Avraham, we know, was famous for his hospitality. His tent had openings on all four sides, so that a stranger would always be welcome. Yet, now, during the period of his most painful recuperation, he has not had guests, and he is increasingly distressed. *Why* was Avraham so despondent at not receiving guests, just at this particular time? Surely he did not spend every moment of his time welcoming guests; certainly there were other activities that occupied him. Couldn't he have rested or engaged in other worthwhile activities? Yet his disappointment was so intense that God sent three angels disguised as men to satisfy Avraham's need for guests.

To understand what took place, we need to realize that Avraham's concern for this particular *mitzvah* of hospitality was directly connected with his circumcision. Avraham realized that the significance of the physical act of circumcision, for himself and all his descendants, was radical; from that time onward his race was a race set apart, with special duties, responsibilities, and status. The *Chiddushe HaRim* explains that Avraham feared that the gulf now dividing him from the rest of humanity might prove unbridgeable. He worried that now, when he had so much to communicate, he would no longer be able to communicate—that his whole mission in life might be frustrated by his own new status. He feared the development of an isolation that would prevent him from sharing with all mankind the joy of serving God. It was at this critical time that Avraham needed guests to reassure him that, in spite of his new closeness with God, he had not lost his old closeness to humanity.

A similar fear, say some commentators, haunted Avraham as he prepared for the *akedah*. Not only was Avraham asked to give up his only son but, in addition, he was asked to jeopardize his life's work: Who would continue to adhere to the philosophy of a man who had killed his own son? Here he was, a man who preached *chesed*, kindness and mercy, performing such a barbaric act. Who could doubt that the world would consider him the worst hypocrite?

Later in the *sedra*, following the birth of Yitzchak and before the trial of the *akedah*, there appears to be an interlude involving Avraham's alliance with Avimelech following a dispute regarding the seizure of a well of water by the servants of Avimelech. Why was this seemingly trivial episode placed between the birth of Yitzchak and the story of the *akedah*?

Once again we find that the Torah wants to stress Avraham's mission to influence the world. The story is not about digging wells at all! Rather, Avraham used the digging of wells as a technique to spread the name of *HaShem*. Avraham was aware that all humanity is dependent upon water. Thus, Avraham would dig wells but would give them names that included the name of God, and the people of the world would have the name of God included in their vocabulary. It was this clever technique to which Avimelech and the Philistines objected. While Avraham was alive, their resentment of this technique was expressed only in verbal disputes, but after his death, the Torah relates, the Philistines violated the covenant established between Avraham and Avimelech and stopped up the wells. Therefore, the Torah reports the victory of Yitzchak by relating, "And Yitzchak dug anew the wells of water which they had dug in the days of Avraham his father . . . and he called them by the same names by which his father had called them" (Gen. 26:18).

We, the descendants of Avraham *Avinu*, have always striven to emulate his model of *hachnasat orchim*, extending hospitality and welcoming guests into our home. However, if we are to truly emulate our forefather, we must also use our efforts and resources to influence and encourage peripheral Jews to join the ranks of the Torah-observant.

Rabbi Evan Shore

Young Israel of Syracuse, New York

> "And his wife looked behind him and she became a pillar of salt." (Gen. 19:26)

Why was salt used to punish and kill Lot's wife, Irit? Lot's wife was killed because she looked back to see the destruction of the cities of S'dom and Amorrah. But why did she become a pillar of salt? Our Rabbis tell us that when Lot invited the angels into his house for a meal, Irit said to her husband, "It is one thing to give matzah [according to Rashi it was *Pesach*] to our guests; however, it is another thing to give them salt as well." Irit was telling Lot that such acts of friendliness and charity were unacceptable in S'dom. As a result, one could postulate that Irit received a punishment that fit her transgression, in other words a *middah k'neged middah*; measure for measure. To support this theory, Rashi tells us, "With salt she sinned, and with salt she was smitten."

On the surface Rashi doesn't appear to make sense because, if she had not turned back, she might not have been punished. Let's first understand why Irit turned back. The Torah tells us, "And it was when they took them out that one said, 'Flee for your life! Do not look behind you. Do not stop anywhere in the plain.'" (Gen. 19:17). The Malbim explains that the Torah is informing us that Irit did not believe the words of the angel who said, "Do not look back." She looked back to see the death and destruction, and the plague caught up with her, and her body was turned into a pillar of salt. She had no right to look back because, as we learn from Rashi, "You were wicked together with them, and it is only through the merit of Avraham that you will be saved. As a result, it is not proper for you to see the punishment of S'dom." In spite of this warning, she still turned back.

The Ramban tells us that Irit looked back and felt pity for her two daughters who were left back in S'dom. The Ralbag tells us that, since these two daughters did not believe or have faith to do *teshuvah*, Irit had no right to feel compassion toward them; especially if they were recipients of the anger of *HaShem*, they deserved to be destroyed because of the lack of any decent human compassion or sensitivity.

Aznaim L'Torah says that she was, in fact, worse than the people of S'dom. The people in S'dom were killed instantly by the sulfur and fire. Whatever was left of their bodies was swallowed up by the earth. In a very crude way, the inhabitants of S'dom and Amorrah suffered death and burial, which are necessary components for *kapparah*, atonement. Irit, on the other hand, suffered a far worse fate. There is no doubt that she died. However the pillar of salt inhibited the decomposition of her body. As a result, she never attained a complete atonement.

It is here that we can now understand why a pillar of salt was used. The Talmud tells us that *tzedakah*, charity, is called salt. When one gives tzedakah, it preserves one's possessions. By definition, salt is a preservative that prevents things from decaying. When Irit showed herself to be so parsimonious that she did not possess any traits of charity, she became a pillar of salt as a sign to all generations of the ways we should be charitable to others. Her insensitivity has been preserved for all time, and her wicked acts will go unforgiven.

We learn from two sentences in *Mishlei*, "Charity delivers from death" (10:2) and "He that gives to the poor shall not lack" (29:27)—that *tzedakah* delivers us from a fate in which death is devoid of atonement. In other words, the *tzedakah* we give in life insures a place in *olam habah*. Irit, by virtue of not being a charitable person, lost the chance to have her *neshamah* preserved to merit the World to Come.

❖ CHAPTER 5 ❖

Chayei Sara

Rabbi Michael Whitman

Young Israel of New Haven, Connecticut

The last major accomplishment in the life of Avraham *Avinu* is finding a wife for Yitzchak. But, though we can understand and perhaps relate to Avraham's concern and desire for input into this choice, the specific guidance he gives is, on the surface, hard for us to comprehend. He commands his faithful servant Eliezer, "Do not take a wife for my son from the daughters of the Canaanim, among whom I dwell. Rather, go to my birthplace and my family to select a wife for my son, Yitzchak" (Gen. 24:3–4). And Avraham requires Eliezer to swear that he will heed this command.

But why is Avraham so set against a local *shidduch* (marriage) for Yitzchak? Why was everyone from Canaan automatically disqualified? Couldn't there have been someone who met Avraham's standards? In fact, according to the *midrash* that Avraham and Sarah engaged in developing righteous converts, there must have been numerous religious girls from which to choose for Yitzchak.

And what was available back in Aram, Avraham's birthplace? Avraham's family were idolaters! Rivkah was raised in a home suffused with idol worship. In what way was this preferable to a person raised as an observant Jew in Canaan?

Rabbi Samson Raphael Hirsch provides us with a fundamental concept with which to answer this difficulty. There may have been observant women in Canaan; however, the nature of those people was base, corrupt. They had terrible *middot,* as the Torah repeatedly records. On the other hand, Avraham's family in Aram, though they were idolaters, had excellent *middot* of kindness, hospitality, and compassion—like Avraham and Sarah. Idolatry is a sin, a terrible sin, that results from a mistake. A person mistakenly thinks, "This is how I should worship." If you enlighten that person and explain the nature of the mistake, it is possible for the person to change and forsake the sin of idolatry. But a fault in *middot* is much deeper. The *middot* of a person expresses his or her very essence. If a person's *middot* are faulty, they are much more difficult to change. Avraham had to choose between an observant person with bad *middot* (who would learn good *middot*) and a non-observant person with good *middot* (who would learn observance)—and he insisted on choosing the latter for Yitzchak. Eliezer's experience certainly showed the wisdom of Avraham's advice because Rivkah immediately displayed the sterling *middot* of her family, whereas she later developed a uniquely high level of *yir'as Shamayim* and *dikduk b'mitzvot*.

This concept can help us understand one of the central difficulties in the Torah's narrative of Bnei Yisrael's years in the desert. Two major failings take place during these forty years. Two sins stand above all the others in their seriousness: the *eigel*, the golden calf; and the *meraglim*, the spies.

Almost immediately after hearing *HaShem* speak at har Sinai, Bnei Yisrael appear to ignore one of the *Aseres HaDibros* they just heard, and they build a calf of gold to worship. And yet, in spite of the seriousness of their sin (and its subsequent impact on Jewish history) *HaShem* forgives them. In fact, this forgiveness culminates in Yom Kippur and the building of the *Mishkan*, which set the pattern for *teshuvah* and *kapparah* throughout our history.

Before entering the Land of Israel, however, Bnei Yisrael send spies to report on the conditions of the land, and the spies bring back a bad report. *HaShem* is furious, and He swears, that generation will never enter the Land of Israel. And they will have no chance to repent. But was the sin that serious? Let them go in and see they were wrong. As soon as they enter the Land of Israel they will see how wonderful it is. Why is this sin treated harshly, especially when compared with the "lenient" treatment after the sin of the *eigel*, which appears, *prima facie*, to be so much more serious?

Here too, Hirsch's concept is enlightening. The sin of the *eigel*, which in itself is hard to understand, was a mistake. Bnei Yisrael mistakenly thought this was how they should serve *HaShem*. It was a terrible mistake, but they could learn their lesson and survive to enter the Land of Israel. On the other hand, the sin of the *meraglim* was a lapse in *middot*. It was a lack of gratitude to *HaShem* for the gift of the Land of Israel and a lack of trust in His protection. If Bnei Yisrael had faulty *middot*, they had a fault in their essence and were not worthy to enter the Land of Israel. Only the next generation, who overcame the shortcoming of their parents, merited entering the Land of Israel.

Rabbi Elias Schwartz

Young Israel of Bensonhurst Bathbeach, New York

THE REBBE: INSPIRATION—TOTAL INVOLVEMENT

When Avraham *Avinu* is about to send his trusted servant Eliezer to choose a wife for his son Yitzchak, the Torah refers to Eliezer in these words: "And Avraham said to his servant, the eldest of his house, he who rules over all that belongs to him, . . ." (Gen. 24:2).

In *Gemara Yoma* 28:b, Rabbi Eliezer comments, "Since the Torah says that Eliezer ruled over everything that Avraham had, it means that Eliezer even shared in the learning and Torah that his master had. This means that Eliezer, the servant of Avraham sat with his master, in the *yeshivah* and learned with him."

This is the inspiration we expect from great people. If Avraham had become inspired to follow the ways of God and to preach the ways of God as a guide to daily living, then even his servant, who came in daily contact with him, had to become inspired as well. Avraham's way of life had to be a total involvement of everyone who came near to him, so that they, too, should become inspired with the way of life. Otherwise, he could not become the great Avraham *Avinu*, the first of the forefathers of *Klal Yisrael*. Avraham became the role model of his generation, so that the *nefesh* that he influenced in Charan followed him to *Eretz Canaan* (*Eretz Yisrael*).

Isn't this what we hope for and expect from any rabbi who teaches in a *yeshivah*? He is not just another teacher: he is a *rebbe*; he is a guide and mentor; he is a role model to all his students—to all his *kinderlach*. The *rebbe* inspires the student to learn Torah with dedication and love.

The Rebbe implants within the heart of his students the basic of character growth—*middot tovot*—that will guide the young students and remain with them throughout their adult lives. What an awesome responsibility one carries when you realize that youngsters watch your action, copy you, and try to emulate you!

THE HEREAFTER

When Avraham had to bury his wife Sarah, he went to the children of Cheit (*Bnei Cheit*) to buy a burial plot for her. He wanted to buy the *Meorat Hamachpelah*. Herein were already buried Adam and Eve. (Avraham and Sarah, Yitzchak and Rivkah, Yaakov and Leah were later buried there.)

We find the words *Bnei Cheit* ten times in *Bereishit*: eight times in this portion of the buying of the plot, a ninth time in *Chayei Sara* (Gen. 25:10, when Avraham dies), and a tenth time at the end of *Bereishit* (Gen. 49:32, when Yaakov dies).

The *midrash* tells us that the ten times we find the words *Bnei Cheit* in the Torah are equal to the Ten Commandments. Yet, after all, the Ten Commandments are the cornerstone and foundation of our Torah. How can we equate them with the tenfold repetition of the words *Bnei Cheit*?

The Malbim answers very beautifully: When Avraham went to buy a family plot, the *Bnei Cheit* were the owners of that plot. They said to Avraham, "We also believe in burying, in a common burial hill outside of town. Choose any place you want." But they buried their dead only for humane and practical reasons. They did not want people walking in the streets, stumbling over dead bodies.

Avraham *Avinu* wanted to teach them one of the basic foundations of *Yiddishkeit*. Avraham wanted to show them that we believe in the everlastingness of the soul, that there will be a time of *techiyat hamaytim*, when the dead will become alive again. We bury our dead in the ground because this is the commandment of the Torah: "From dust hast thou been taken and to dust thou shall return."

The *mitzvah* of burial is so great that even a *Kohein Gadol* (a High Priest serving in the *Beit Hamikdash*), who is not allowed to go to the funeral even of his own mother or father, had to take care of a *meit mitzvah*; if he were walking in the desert and found a dead person, and there was no one else to do the burial, he would have to make himself "spiritually unclean" and attend to the entire burial himself.

The concept of *techiyat hamaytim* is as important in our philosophy of Judaism as our belief in the Ten Commandments. Within the Ten Commandments, we find incorporated all the *mitzvot* of the Torah: the concepts of the *mitzvot aseh* and *mitzvot lo taaseh, mitzvot* between man and God and *mitzvot* between man and man. Therefore, the *midrash* says that the ten times we find the words *Bnei Cheit* in the Torah are equal to the Ten Commandments. These ten occurrences of the words *Bnei Cheit* refer to the family burial plot that Avraham *Avinu* bought to show that he believed in a hereafter, in the eternity of the soul.

The *Gemara* tells us that a person should spend every penny that he has to buy a burial plot for the family. We believe that there is a hereafter. We say goodbye to our dear ones only in the physical sense, but we believe that their *neshamah* is in *Gan Eden* above with all the other holy souls of Israel. We believe the time will come when these souls will yet live again and be reunited with their bodies, when *Mashiach* will come speedily in our time.

Parshat Chayei Sara has always been set aside as a *Shabbat* wherein we speak of The National Council of Young Israel Benevolent Association. The *mitzvah* of proper burial is a holy one. Our Rabbis tell us it is a *segulah* for long life to buy a burial plot (to be used after 120 years). I have personally witnessed the grief and anguish of a family that did not have a burial plot and had to run around the day of the funeral to make these arrangements. This is adding untold aggravation to what is already a very trying time.

Join your community Benevolent Association *now*. Spare your family unnecessary hardships and problems. Take care of this most important *mitzvah* and live long and happily.

Rabbi Herschel Kurzrock

Young Israel of Kensington, New York

The *Sedrah Chayei Sara* discusses two of the most emotional and affecting experiences in the life of every person, the traumatic occurrence of a loved one's death and the joyful occasion of marriage.

At the outset we read about the death and internment of Sarah, who was Avraham's beloved partner in life and in all his spiritual endeavors to spread the belief in *HaShem*. Her death caused him profound grief and sorrow. Our Sages tell us, "No one feels the death of a woman more than her husband" (*Sanhedrin* 22b)—especially in the case of Sarah, a truly saintly woman and eminent prophetess (*Megillah* 14a). Even before the Almighty, the demise of a *tzaddik* is considered an enormous loss, as the *midrash* states: "More severe is the departure of the righteous before the Almighty, than all the curses mentioned in the Torah" (*Midrash Rabbah Aichah* 1:37).

After this morbid experience of heartrending bereavement for Avraham, which occurred immediately after the most onerous of the ten trials that he had to endure—the near sacrifice of his beloved son and spiritual heir Yitzchak—the *sedrah* dwells upon the exhilarating episode of the betrothal and marriage of Yitzchak. He married a veritably pious woman, in consonance with the traditions imbued in him by his mother, Sarah.

The person privileged to acquire a suitable spouse has reached the apex of happiness. Our Sages tell us, "He that lives without a wife lives without *simcha*—joy—in life" (*Yevamot* 62b). How great was Avraham's rejoicing at this fitting marriage for his most worthy successor—the son who will continue to transmit Avraham's spiritual teachings and traditions to future generations with the help and support of the most appropriate mate! What greater joy is there for a father than this *nachas*—pleasure!

These two episodes in this *sedrah*, portraying the abyss of tragedy and the peak of happiness, are connected by a very interesting verse: "And Avraham became old and advanced in days and *HaShem* blessed Avraham with everything" (Gen. 24:1). Commenting on the word for old age—*Zakein*—which also denotes wisdom and scholarly attainment, our Sages tell us (*Yoma* 28b) that Avraham was always involved with a *yeshivah* and Torah study! Even in old age, he was *zakein v'yosheiv b'yeshivah*—a Torah scholar studying in a *yeshivah*! What type of *yeshivah* did Avraham maintain? The Rambam says that until the advent of Avraham, the generations were constantly developing and spreading the teachings and worship of idolatry. When Avraham was born, and at an early age perceived and comprehended the "true way"—monotheism; belief, faith, and trust in *HaShem*—he proceeded to teach and propagate the faith to all. The *Gemara* tells us (*Avodah Zarah* 14b) that Avraham's tractate dealing with idolatry encompassed four hundred chapters! This tractate he fervently taught to all who would listen. Avraham developed and sustained a *yeshivah* that disseminated Torah values pertaining to faith, belief, trust, and confidence in *HaShem*—A *yeshivah* for the concepts and teachings of *emunah* to a world steeped in idolatry! Of course, Avraham himself reached the ultimate heights of performance of all the *mitzvot*, the ethical and moral precepts of our holy Torah. We might call him the first *Rosh Yeshivah* and one to be truly emulated in every aspect of life.

The Torah, through the above-mentioned verse, depicts the Torah involvement of Avraham throughout his life as connecting episodes of tragedy and happiness. It thus relates to us, in a symbolic fashion, the basic ingredient in the life of a Jew that enables him to weather the turbulent storms of tragedy in life and to control headiness and the propensity for self adulation and irreverence during the sublime moments of profound joy in life. In the midst of both extreme adversity and exalted joy, Avraham was able to accept them, act rationally, and maintain his ideals and goals in life with a level head. His strong, tenacious faith and persistent and constant adherence to ethical and moral Torah values served properly to guide and stabilize his actions in these extraordinary moments of a person's life; it mirrored the general approach of Avraham to all the activities, occurrences, and manifold vicissitudes of life.

Ma'asei Avot siman lebanim (*Midrash Tanchuma Lech Lecha* 9). Deeds and actions of the Patriarchs are to be seen as a sign and omen to their progeny: This teaching stresses our sacred duty to emulate the *Avot* by nurturing the basic component in the life of a Jew—steadfast adherence to faith in *HaShem* permeated with involvement in all aspects of "Torah"—viewpoint, study, support, practice, and dissemination to future generations—throughout life.

A life with this *hashkafah*—outlook—at its core, will serve truly to ennoble a person and enable him to endure the many trials and tribulations of both adversity and success that are prevalent in every aspect of life.

Rabbi Raphael Wizman

Young Israel of Commack, New York

This *parsha* begins with the death of Sarah and ends with the passing of Avraham, "in good old age, mature and content" (Gen. 25:8). Several popular questions are asked about this *parsha*:

1. Why did Sarah merit to have a *parsha* named after her, whereas Avraham, who also died in this *parsha*, did not?
2. Why is this *parsha* called *Chayei Sara*—the *life* of Sarah—when it talks only of her death?
3. Why did Avraham merit to live 175 years and Sarah, only 127 years?
4. Why is the story of Yitzchak's engagement repeated in such detail, twice?
5. Why is Sarah the only woman in the Torah whose age is recorded, and, moreover, in such an unusual manner, with the word "years" repeated four times?
6. When Avraham came to eulogize Sarah, why does the Torah not record what Avraham said at her eulogy?

The popular answers to the above questions, given by several commentators, can be summarized simply by the name of the *parsha: Chayei Sarah*.

The fact that Yitzchak's engagement is told twice indicates that Sarah was still living in her son's life: "Tzaddikim, even after their death, are considered alive." Thus, the story of her death is in essence a reflection of the years of her life. When she was 100 years old, her life was as sinless as when she was 20. And at 20, she was as beautiful and wholesome as she was at the age of 7. It is not the same to sin at the age of 100 as at the age of 20; Sarah, even at the age of twenty, was sinless. And just as a girl of 7 is not concerned about her beauty, Sarah was unconcerned even at the age of 20.

This is not something that can be said about Avraham, whose real life did not begin until the age of 48, when he discovered *HaShem*, since "a convert is like a newborn child." (*Yevomoni* 22a) Therefore, Avraham's real lifespan was the same as Sarah's (175 – 48 = 127).Similarly, the *gematriah* of *vayihiyu* is 37, which stands for the years of the real, fulfilled "life" that Sarah lived, which occurred only after she gave birth to Yitzchak (at the age of 90). As *Chazal* tell us, "One is not considered alive unless he/she has children." (Talmud *Nedarim* 64b) Our children are our legacy and continuation of life.

Sarah was greater than Avraham in prophecy (see Rashi *Bereishis* 21:12). Sarah's life was greatly misunderstood because she dealt harshly with Hagar and then drove her and her son, Yishmael, away from their home. These seemingly bad qualities that Sarah exuded turned out to be for the benefit of Jewish continuation, not for her self esteem. As a prophetess, she saw that Yishmael simply would not or could not live with Yitzchak, as is proven even to this very day in Eretz Yisrael. And regardless of the fact that the purchase of *Meorat Hamachpelah* is recorded here in detail, the Yishmael of our generation still contests it. As King David put it so well, "I am peace, but when I speak, they are for war." (Psalms 120:7) In her keenness, Sarah, a long time ago, foresaw that the Arabs would never live in peace with the Jews.

Abraham recognized the greatness of Sarah, who died only after the *akedah*—when she took pride and joy that she succeeded in raising a son who was willing to sacrifice his life for the service of *HaShem*—but did not need to tell of her greatness. Avraham came to eulogize Sarah but did not, for her son, Yitzchak, was her legacy and greatness. He was a living testimony that Sarah did not die and does not need a eulogy. Yitzchak married Rivkah and brought her to Sarah's tent so that Sarah might continue to live.

Perhaps her eulogy is what Rashi says: "All her years were equally good." Sarah suffered much agony in her lifetime: childless till the age of ninety, exiled from place to place, captured twice, and so on. Yet, in her greatness, she accepted her lot in life without complaint. "This too is for the good," she would say continuously, and, indeed, in her eyes, life was good to her.

❖ CHAPTER 6 ❖

Toldot

Rabbi Nosson Fromowitz

Young Israel of Monsey and Wesley Hills, New York

The *parshah* of *Toldot* describes the birth of Jacob and Esau and their ensuing rivalry. Of their relationship with their parents, Isaac and Rebecca, we are told, "And Isaac loved Esau and favored him, for his game was a source of food (*tzayid befiyv*) but Rebecca favored Jacob" (Gen. 25:28). Rashi and midrash comment that the word *befiyv*—literally, in his mouth—means that Isaac was "captured" (from the word *tzad*) by the slyness and cunning of Esau.

To explain the differences in Isaac's and Rebecca's outlook regarding their children as merely favorites would be a gross oversimplification. Surely Isaac knew what the Torah tells us, that Jacob was "a tent dweller" who pursued the study of Torah and self-perfection, whereas Esau, by contrast, is described as "a man of the field" who pursued the art of capturing game (Gen. 25:27). Couldn't Isaac see what any parent would be capable of seeing? And why would Rebecca take an opposing view regarding this crucial matter?

Rabbi Yisroel Lipkin of Salant (Reb Yisroel Salanter, 1809–1883) in his book *Be'er Yosef*, explains this dilemma with the words of Maimonides in his work entitled *Shmona Perokim*. Maimonides presents the view of philosophers who assert that a person who is by nature and inclination good is greater than someone who must always control his or her natural tendencies to do evil. The opposing view, which is the opinion of Maimonides, is that it is more praiseworthy to fight the battle with the *yetzer hara*—evil inclination—and overcome it than never to have to fight the battle at all.

There is, however, a stipulation that Maimonides adds. When dealing with *mitzvot*—laws that can be understood through the intellect alone (for example, not to steal or murder)—then one whose nature would not permit the tendency toward such an evil is on a higher plane. Nevertheless, in dealing strictly with those laws of the Torah that human beings can derive by logic, then it is preferable to have to overcome your natural tendencies.

Therefore, according to Maimonides, the preferred attitude toward the eating of non-kosher food is not to say you have no desire for it but, instead, to say how wonderful and tasty it must be. It is only because the Torah forbids such food that we are not permitted to consume it.

With this approach, we can understand Isaac's appreciation for Esau and his constant battle with his evil inclination. This appreciation for battle with the *yetzer hara* is expressed in the words of King Solomon, who tells us *sheva yipol tzaddik vakam*—"seven times does the righteous one fall, only to get up after each fall" (Prov. 24:16). Rav Yitzchak Hutner, *zt"l,* in a letter to a student who bemoans his spiritual state and constant battle with his *yetzer,* explains the words of King Solomon in a unique and enlightening fashion. According to Rav Hutner, *zt"l,* the meaning of *sheva yipol tzaddik vakam* is not merely an appreciation of someone who falls seven times and is still able to arise—an indication that the person is a *tzaddik.* Rather, the individual becomes *tzaddik* through the experience of falling short and then arising despite the setback. This explanation of the battleground of life as an elevating experience would certainly give someone like Esau an advantage over his brother Jacob.

Rebecca, however, had understood from her inquiry of the "House of Study of Shem and Ever" that "two nations will come forth from you"—an indication that they would take divergent paths from birth. Jacob would be the righteous son and Esau, the evil son. Nachmanides further explains that Rebecca never divulged her prophecy to Isaac; therefore, he could not share her view. This, then, explains their divergent view regarding their children.

The *parsha* then proceeds to tell us of the sale of the rights of the firstborn by Esau to Jacob in exchange for the lentils Jacob had prepared. Esau's rationale is expressed in the words, "And Esau said, behold I am going to die, so what value does the right of the firstborn have for me?" (Gen. 25:32)

Rashi, quoting from the Talmud tractate *Sanhedrin,* tells us that Esau depreciated the value of being the firstborn because of the grave consequences entailed by falling short in the performance of the firstborn's obligations. Esau reasoned, Why place oneself in such jeopardy?

It is understandable that Esau would negate the privilege of the firstborn when he weighed it against the immediate gratification of the lentils that Jacob would feed him. This is the power of the *yetzer hara*! What is difficult to understand is the concluding verse regarding this incident—"And Esau shamed the right of the firstborn" (Gen. 25:34). Sforno tells us that the *pasuk* is saying that *even after* the fulfillment of Esau's desires he remained firm in his conviction that he had received the greater value in the sale. Why continue this self-delusion when the object of your desire is no longer there to confront you?

The message that Sforno is telling us, through his interpretation of this *pasuk,* is that man cannot cope with his failure. The charade must continue even after the pleasurable taste has long faded. The human spirit is such that we sometimes compound our wrongdoing in order to rationalize our behavior. We sometimes build castles in the sky in an attempt to cover up our failures. This being the case, we must be ever vigilant in questioning our motivations in order to arrive at the absolute truths that should govern our lives.

Rabbi Dovid S. Plaut

Young Israel of Greater Buffalo, New York

Esau, the Wicked One, is one of the most enigmatic characters of TaNaKh. Despite his enormous influence on *Klal Yisrael* even to this day, he is a hard person to categorize. On the positive side, we find that Yitzchak loved him more than he loved Yaakov; from this fact, we conclude that Esau had some good qualities. *Chazal* also tell us about the devotion of Esau to Yitzchak and his unsurpassed performance of *kibbud av va'em*–honoring one's father and mother. Furthermore, we find that he cherished the blessings of his father dearly—additional evidence of his closeness with his father and his appreciation of spiritual values. Nevertheless, just from a simple reading of the *pesukim*, we are revolted by Esau's crass, vulgar behavior; then, after learning of all the *averot*—sins—that *Chazal* attribute to Esau, we are totally perplexed about who he really was. An often-quoted character trait of Esau is found in Gen. 25:27: "And Esau was a man of the field." *Targum Yonatan ben Uziel* explains the phrase as implying that Esau was a lazy, unproductive, unmotivated person. Somehow, this explanation is not consistent with the picture of an evil, wife-snatching, hairy hunter.

The Vilna *Gaon* explains, speaking about the beginning of *Parshat Bereishit*, the difference between *beriyah*, creation; *yetzircah*, forming; and *assiyah*, completing. *Beriyah*—creation—refers to the development of something with intrinsic, immutable, ever-present qualities. *Yetzirah*—forming—refers to giving a creation a definite form with specific dimensions and parameters. The final stage, *assiyah*—completion—refers to the addition of external components that are needed for the sustained and efficient function of that creation. In addition, the completion of an item allows it to blend harmoniously with the rest of the environment. For an example of this all we have to do is look at a person. The heart, mind, and free-will are considered creation (*beriyah*), since these are intrinsic qualities that make a person what he is. The existence of two arms, two legs, two eyes, and so on, is an example of *yetzirah*—forming. A person's *assiyah*—completion—occurs after his birth with the development of such things as hair, nails, and teeth. These are non-vital extensions of the person that aid in his survival. Objects such as food and clothing are part of the complete man, since they are necessary for his continued survival and define his relations to the rest of the environment. The Vilna *Gaon* cites an example in Genesis 3:21, *Vayaas HaShem Elohim LeAdam ul'ishto Kotnot*—and *HaShem* made for Adam and his wife garments of skin—for making clothing is indeed *assiyah*. A somewhat more abstract example is the *pasuk* that says, *yotzer or uvorei choshech oseh shalom* . . . (Isa. 45:7). "[I am the One] Who forms light and creates darkness, who makes peace. . . ." The essential creation is darkness; if we do nothing, we always will have at least darkness. Light, therefore, is one step above darkness, being a form that is used to observe and define other things, and *shalom*, peace, is something that is found only at the end stage, when everything else is complete and in harmony.

Concerning the phrase *V'acharei-chen yatza achiv* (Gen. 25:26) Rashi says that Yaakov was formed (*notzar*) first, whereas Esau was formed (*notzar*) second. Since Esau was second, he was more to the outside than Yaakov and, therefore, emerged first. Yaakov tried unsuccessfully to stop Esau from emerging from the womb first (paraphrasing Rashi). We see from Rashi that Yaakov was the brother who had traits that relate to *yetzirah* (and probably *beriyah* also). Esau, therefore, came out with the character traits that relate to *assiyah*. Moreover, Yaakov and Esau were a twin birth—that is, they were really one unit, not two distinct ones. Therefore, what one has, the other lacks, and what the other has is lacking in the first. This situation leads to the conclusion that if one brother wants to have all the important character traits, he must get them from his brother, for they share one existence. (This explains why Esau was not satisfied with a *brachah* almost identical to the one that Yaakov received, for his new *brachah* was not one that belonged to both of them; it was one specific to him.)

With this in mind, we see that the reason Esau was completely covered with hair (including a beard) at birth and, according to *Targum Yonatan ben Uziel* (Gen. 25:26) also a full set of teeth, is that his whole nature came from the concept of *assiyah*—completion. Therefore, everything that normally develops in time and is taken to be a sign of physical maturity was present with Esau at birth. The name says it all; Esau—the one who is complete (except for food and clothing—the additional items that a person needs to live).

Immediately after man's creation (Gen. 1:29), *HaShem* declares, "Here I have given you seed producing grasses and fruit producing trees for you to eat." This is written here not because Adam, the first Man, was created hungry but because food is necessary for his survival; without it he is incomplete. Therefore, it is no surprise that right after Noah emerges from the ark, after the flood that ravaged the whole world, and is ready to begin the world anew *HaShem* says (Gen. 9:3), ". . . all living creatures are for you to eat like the grass." *HaShem's* reason for mentioning this right away is that in the post-flood world mankind's food changed from vegetable to meat. Therefore, the preoccupation of Esau with hunting animals and eating them is just a natural outgrowth of his essential nature—and the post-flood world. He is a man who focuses on those things that contribute to completion, a man who has no connection to that which is intrinsic and lasting.

His desire for clothes also becomes logical if we pay attention to what the Torah says immediately after the episode of the sin of Adam, the First Man. "And *HaShem* made for them coats of skin, and he clothed them." As mentioned earlier, without clothes a person is incomplete; therefore, Esau displayed an unusual penchant for clothes. In this way, I would suggest, we can understand why Esau is characterized as unproductive, lazy, and unmotivated. Esau was interested only in doing that which served to complete something else. He did not have his own identity. That would have come from *yetzirah* and *beriyah*, which Yaakov lay claim to. On the basis of this understanding, we see how profound the insight of *Chazal* is. Rashi, quoting *Chazal* on Genesis 25:27, says that Esau had a preoccupation with tithes (*maaser*). He asked his father how one tithes salt or straw. The *mitzah* of tithing is closely related to the character of Esau. Tithing is required only after the processing of the grain is complete; this tells us that tithing is a *mitzvah* of completion, rendering the grain edible by all, and it does so by sharing a part of the grain with the *kohein* and *levi*. This is Esau's specialty—finishing something. Thus, tithing attracted him more than other *mitzvot*. Furthermore, the examples he asked about—salt and straw—are also significant. Salt is a substance that has no value by itself. Its purpose is to enhance the flavor of other foods. Straw, too, is not a product by itself but, rather, serves to hold and nourish the wheat kernels. Both of these objects are consistent with the nature of Esau.

Finally, we can understand what the *Baal Haturim* writes about Esau. He says that in *gematriah* (numeric equivalences), Esau is *shalom*—peace. Since Esau represents the concept of *assiyah* and, as we explained before, *assiyah* is identified with *shalom oseh shalom bimromav*, the connections are now clear. Esau is not quite as enigmatic and perplexing a character as we first thought.

Rabbi Mordechai Terebelo

Young Israel of Lawrenceville, New Jersey

"And Yitzchok prayed to *HaShem* opposite his wife, because she was barren, and *HaShem* listened to him, and Rivkah his wife became pregnant" (Gen. 25:21).

Although the *posuk* mentions that both Yitzchok and Rivkah prayed to *HaShem*, it states that it was because *HaShem* heard Yitzchok's *tefillah*, not Rivkah's, that Rivkah became pregnant. Rashi explains the reasoning for this. Since Yitzchok's prayers were those of a *tzaddik ben tzaddik* (a righteous individual, the child of a righteous individual), in contrast to Rivkah's lineage as that of a *tzaddik ben rasha* (a righteous individual, the child of a wicked individual), *HaShem* listened to his *tefillah* more readily than to hers. However, why Rivka's *tefillah* was less worthy of being answered still needs further clarification. Is it not to Rivkah's credit that she who came from a house of wickedness (surrounded by such heinous individuals as Lavan and Besuel) was still able to remain righteous? Should not her *tefillah* be of greater merit and more worthy to be answered than that of Yitzchok, who was raised in Avrohom's house and did not have to face such spiritual tests?

The *Gemara Berachos* 32a says that after the sin of the golden calf, *HaShem* wished to destroy *Bnei Yisrael* and begin anew with Moshe *Rabbeinu*. Moshe pleaded, "If a chair with three legs cannot survive Your anger [a reference to *Bnei Yisrael*'s having the support of the three *Avot* (patriarchs), Avrohom, Yitzchok, and Yaakov], how can it be expected that a chair with only one leg will be able to survive Your anger?" We learn from Moshe's analogy that the three *Avot* are the support and foundation of *Bnei Yisrael*.

The Mishnah, in *Pirkei Avot*, chapter 1, *Mishnah* 2 says, "Shimon *Hatzaddik* said, "On three things the world stands: on Torah, *avodah* [service of *HaShem*], and *chesed* [acts of kindness]." These three pillars are the support of the world. We can logically assume that, just as the world needs the support of these three pillars in order to exist, so, too, the Jewish people needs these three pillars of support. Each one of the *Avot*—Avrohom, Yitzchok, and Yaakov—was unique. The *posuk* says, "Give truth to Yaakov and kindness to Avrohom," telling us that Avrohom was unique in his pursuit of *chesed*. The Torah elaborates, at the beginning of *Parshat Vayera*, concerning Avrohom's conduct with the visiting angels; his actions show us what true *chesed* should be. When Avrohom fed the angels and showed his dedication to *chesed*, we were shown that true *chesed* is an act that is performed with no hope of reciprocation. His generosity with complete strangers exemplifies what a true *baal chesed* is.

Our *Av Yitzchok* was unique in his *avodah* (service) to *HaShem*. It was Yitzchok who was brought as a *korban* in order to test Avrohom's faith in *HaShem*. Although the test was Avrohom's, it is the potential ashes of Yitzchok that remain as a reminder of Yitzchok's willingness to be sacrificed. The ashes are a constant reminder to *HaShem* for our merit. It is here that we see Yitzchok's dedication to serving *HaShem* with all his heart and life. It is this dedication to the *avodah* of *HaShem* that serves us as the pillar of *avodah* that Bnei Yisrael rests on.

The third pillar that *Bnei Yisrael* rests upon, which Yaakov represents, is Torah. Yaakov is described as "a perfect man who dwelled in tents." Rashi explains that "dwelled in tents" refers to the tents of Shem and Ever, in which Yaakov dwelled. The Maharal explains that, although the *Gemara* says that Avrohom fulfilled the entire Torah, learning and delving into Torah was a trait unique to Yaakov. Yaakov showed further evidence of his total immersion in learning Torah by not sleeping while learning during his fourteen years in Shem and Ever's *yeshivah*. This total dedication to learning was unique to Yaakov.

Each of our *Avot* had a unique way of serving *HaShem*—Avrohom with *chesed*, Yitzchok with *avodah*, and Yaakov with *limud haTorah*. It is interesting to note that, just as each had a uniqueness in his service of *HaShem*, so too, did *HaShem* deal with each of them uniquely. Avrohom, whose trait was *chesed*, was told only after the incident with the angels that Sarah would bear a child. It seems that only after Avrohom participated in the act of *chesed*, of welcoming guests, did *HaShem* find it proper to notify Avrohom of his forthcoming son.

Similarly, Yitzchok was granted his future family only after displaying to *HaShem* his trait of *davening*, which is one aspect of *avodah*. It was important that each *Av* use his perfected trait before he was answered. It was only through each *Av*'s achieving his ultimate level of perfection in his unique trait that each was able to have his prayers fulfilled by *HaShem*.

We find that the *Avot*, even in *tefillah*, had different approaches. The *Gemara* in *Brachot* says, "*Tefillot* were instituted by the *Avot*." Avrohom, Yitzchok, and Yaakov instituted *shacharit*, *mincha*, and *maariv*, respectively.

It is noteworthy that Avrohom's *tefillah shacharit* was a *tefillah* for the benefit of S'dom; Avrohom utilized his *tefillah* as an act of *chesed* to help others. Yaakov's *maariv* was *davened* after his total immersion in Torah in Shem and Ever's *yeshivah*. These are further examples of each *Av* using his perfected trait in other areas.

Now we can understand Rashi's explanation of the beginning of this week's *parshah*. It is true that a *tzaddik* who is the child of a *rasha* has made tremendous strides in life; yet, it is even a greater accomplishment for a *tzaddik* who is the child of a *tzaddik* to develop on his or her own. It would have been easy for Yitzchok to remain and learn from Avrohom. He could have lived his life as a mere copy of Avrohom. Instead, Yitzchok chose to develop into a unique pillar of *avodah*. It was not enough for Yitzchok to rest on Avrohom's accomplishments; rather, he carved out accomplishments of his own. It is for this reason that Yitzchok's *tefillah* was even greater than that of Rivkah.

Rabbi Michael Whitman

Young Israel of New Haven, Connecticut

This *parshah* can be approached through several questions based on the *perush* of Rav Samson Raphael Hirsch and the Malbim:

1. What does Yitzchok really think of Esav? He clearly knows that Esav is no *tzaddik* when Esav marries a woman of whom his parents disapprove (Gen. 26:35). Why is he still willing to give Esav the *brachot*?
2. Obviously, Rivkah sees it differently. Why does she not persuade Yitzchok that Yaakov should receive the *brachot*? Why does she need to resort to the encounter she sets up?
3. It seems that the disguise would never work. Does goat skin really feel like the arms of Esav? And even if it works, Esav will return soon, and Yaakov's deception will be known. It's almost as though Rivkah wanted Yitzchok to know he had been fooled.
4. When Esav returns and Yitzchok realizes what has happened, we would expect Yitzchok to be very angry and attempt to nullify the *brachot*, since Yitzchok did not intend for Yaakov to get them. But instead he says, "The *brachah* will remain his" (Gen. 27:33). Why?

Surely, Yitzchok knew what Esav was. But he also knew of the *brachah* of Avrohom, and he wanted his two sons to share that *brachah*. Yitzchok envisioned a kind of partnership, such as Yissocher and Zevulun would develop years later, with Yaakov in charge of the *ruchaniut* (spiritual) and Esav caring for the *gashmiut* (physical needs). Yitzchok considered Esav the appropriate one for this precisely because he knew Esav's nature, but he believed Esav would live up to this partnership, because Esav presented to his father a façade of integrity if not spirituality. He heard Esav asking questions regarding tithes, and so on.

Rivkah saw that Esav's religiosity was just a façade. She realized that not only would a partnership between Yaakov and Esav not work practically; it was philosophically faulty. In this world there needs to be a combination of *ruchaniut* and *gashmiut*. *Ruchaniut* must be grounded and played out in *gashmiut*, and *gashmiut* must be used for the higher purpose of *ruchaniut*; the two cannot be separated. Yaakov's spiritual nature was *more* of a reason for him to receive the *brachot* from Yitzchok, not less. Rivkah probably tried to persuade Yitzchok, but he didn't understand. Yitzchok couldn't imagine that his own son, Esav, could present a false image. He didn't believe he could be tricked.

And *that* is what Rivkah needed to demonstrate. Yitzchok was an incomparable *tzaddik* and *chochom*, but Rivkah saw that her vision needed to prevail. So she told Yaakov to dress up in the clothes of Esav and to cover himself in a very crude disguise. Yaakov did so, and Yitzchok was fooled. And when Esav walked in with the food he had prepared, Yitzchok trembled in fear. But he trembled not only because of the *brachah* he had just given. Yitzchok trembled with the realization that all along he had been fooled. All along Rivakah had been right. And Yitzchok trembled with the realization that the *brachah* he had just given was not a mistake but that, in fact, it was Yaakov to whom the *brachah* had to go; therefore, Yitzchok said, "The *brachah* will remain his [Yaakov's]."

This approach sets the stage for a powerful lesson to be learned from the behavior of Yitzchok. We can well understand Yitzchok's anger in learning what had happened. He might well have felt humiliated to have been proven wrong about so important a matter. However, Yitzchok's reaction is to recognize the truth whenever and however it comes. For Yitzchok *Avinu*, this complete self-control is expected. For us, it remains a goal toward which we strive. How often does it happen that someone criticizes us in a nonconstructive manner (that may happen quite often!) that does contain some truth? But because we have been made to feel uncomfortable, we feel we must reject everything the speaker is saying. In his eulogy of Rav Moshe Feinstein, *zt"l*, his Talmid Rav Gershon Weiss, *shlita*, relayed how, when Rav Moshe received harassing phone calls, he would listen to the whole discourse pleasantly and then say goodbye politely. And he often told others that there is a commentary of *Tiferes Yisroel* on *Mishnayot* that says that when someone curses you, you should listen calmly, because maybe there is some valid point mixed in with the insults.

❖ CHAPTER 7 ❖

Vayetze

Rabbi Baruch Sufrin

Young Israel of Sunny Isles, Florida

The Torah recounts how, after Yaakov awoke from his dream, he built a *matzevah*, a monument, from the rock that he had used to protect his head; he then promised God that he would give Him one-tenth of everything he earned. This promise, however, came with a stipulation. "If God will be with me and protect me on this trip upon which I am about to embark and if He gives me food . . ." (Gen. 28:20). Yaakov's request is strange, since God had already promised him in his dream, "I will watch over you wherever you go" (Gen. 28:15). Did Yaakov not believe that God would fulfill a promise He made to him just the night before?

Chazal, our Rabbis, also tell us that "the actions of our patriarchs are a sign for their descendents," which Ramban interprets as meaning, "Anything that our forefathers did during the course of their lives is not only a sign but also the strength that will help future generations go through similar events in their lives." What is the sign for the generations that evolves from this particular event?

When we take a closer look at God's promise to Yaakov in his dream and the request Yaakov made when he awoke, we also find some slight differences in the wording: God says, "I will guard you *wherever* you go," whereas Yaakov says, "Guard me on *this* trip"; he did not say, "*wherever* I go." God says, "I will return you to the land," meaning God will make sure he, Yaakov, returns specifically to the *land*. Yaakov says, "*I* will return in peace to my *father's house*"; the return is not dependent on God but rather on Yaakov himself, and he requests to return not to the land but rather to his father's house.

The *Keli Yakar* uses these above-mentioned differences in language to prove that, in actuality, Yaakov believed and accepted the promise given to him by God in his dream. He *would* be protected, *would* return to Israel, and so on. Yaakov, in his request, was not doubting God's blessing from the previous night, but, rather, was making an additional request from God.

Yaakov had received a blessing from God that God would protect him from material/physical damage, that God would bless him in material fortune, and that God would bring him back physically to *Eretz Yisrael*. But what about Yaakov's spiritual needs? He was about to go to Lavan's house—a house in which idol-worship was the norm, in a community in which the whole moral and value system was corrupt, a community in which his mother, at the age of three, was a rose among thorns not only among adults but also among her peer group (three-year-olds!).

HaShem, "Guard me on *this* path." Yaakov requested only to be helped in one particular road—the road of morality and good deeds. God had blessed him in the many paths of life and therefore said in the dream, "wherever you go," but Yaakov requested help in the *one* path of spiritual success and therefore used the singular: "in *this* path." God had blessed Yaakov with a promise that He would protect him physically and bring him back to the land (physical), but Yaakov asked for God's help in returning specifically to his father's house. "When I return from Lavan's house of idol-worship and immorality, please, God, bring me back to my father's house while I am still imbued with the Torah values of Yitzchok and the *chesed* of *Avraham*, my *zeide*."

Since the one thing God says He leaves up to the individual is the choice between good and evil, Yaakov states his request in a manner that denotes that he (Yaakov) will bring himself back: "I will return . . . to my father's house"; this, Yaakov knows, is dependent on his freedom of choice and, therefore, he himself needs to take the necessary precautions to ensure that he does not leave the ways of Torah and *mitzvot* even when he is in Lavan's environs. However, even though this is a human choice, because of the extreme conditions of immorality he would be exposed to, Yaakov still felt the need to request God's help in this matter. King David in Psalms also requests from God spiritual help when he says, "Turn my eyes away from seeing evil," (Psalms 119:37) for, even though it is man's choice that ultimately determines whether he is going to be good or bad, it is still necessary to receive God's guidance and help in these matters. That is also why the *Ethics of Our Fathers* says, "Do not believe in yourself until the day you die."

From this approach given to us by the *Keli Yakar*, it is clear what the *siman labanim*, sign for generations, is. When the Jew finds himself/herself in a society where Torah and *mitzvot* are not necessarily the values that are deemed important, he/she must be prepared to withstand the test of society. For this we need, not only our own strength, but also the help and guidance of God and His Torah. Now, since Yaakov *Avinu* already went through this situation in Lavan's house and withstood the tests of his times, this in turn gives us the strength to know that we can also succeed in this area; and, please God, through our successes in being strong and living a life of Torah and *Mitzvot*, we can help bring the ultimate redemption through *Mashiach*.

Rabbi Martin Rosenfeld

Young Israel of West Hartford, Connecticut

In this week's *parshah,* we are immediately introduced to a significant event in the life of Yaakov—his dream. The Torah tells us that Yaakov saw a ladder that was firmly planted on earth and whose top reached toward the heavens. There are many beautiful explanations of this dream which are found in the *midrash* and in various commentaries. I would like to focus on one school of thought in explaining this verse. This insight is inspired by the commentary of Ibn Ezra.

Ibn Ezra explains the ladder as a source of connection which unites the affairs on earth with the affairs in heaven. *V'divrei Matah Teluyim B'elyonim Uk'eilu Sulam Beineiyhem*—things of lower (sphere) are connected/dependant in the upper (sphere), as if there was a ladder between them. This comment can be understood in many ways. It could refer to the fact that a *mitzvah,* which is a spiritual act, is nevertheless, in its origin, a physical act performed by a finite human being. The purpose of a *mitzvah* is, therefore, to take the physical, mundane acts of life and turn them into spiritual occasions (an obvious example of this comment would be the recitation of a *brachah* before one begins to eat a food). Another possibility is that the ladder "connects" human conduct and spirituality. The Rabbis teach us that "proper ethical conduct must precede ritual activity." The ladder reaches toward heaven, but it is rooted firmly on earth. Not only must we practice the *mitzvot* that are between God and man; we also have the obligation to firmly "plant" ourselves on the "ground" of exemplary behavior between and man.

A third approach presents itself that goes to the core of our lives as observant Jews, committed to Torah. The "ground" in Yaakov's dream is a reference to secular pursuits and activities. The heaven is a symbol of Torah. Yaakov, who is the symbol of Torah learning ("Jacob was a pure man who lived in the tents [of Torah]"), saw in his vision that there must be some connection between one's religious life and one's secular. In essence, Yaakov saw the vision later articulated by Rabbi Samson Raphael Hirsch, who advocated the need for *Torah im derech eretz*—Torah learning merged with secular achievement. The test for the Jew, as Rabbi Hirsch explained, is to *raise* society to the norms of Torah. Most of us live in a secular environment. There is no need to feel apologetic about this circumstance. As Jews, however, we must take our secular knowledge and activities, firmly rooted on earth, and point them toward heaven.

The *Ktav Sofer*, in his Torah commentary, explains why we have the custom of slightly lifting our cup of wine whenever we recite *kiddush*, lead *birkat hamazon*, and so on. He states that wine is symbolic of the physical world and its pleasures. By lifting the cup of wine, even slightly, we are showing our intent to sublimate physical activities toward a heavenly purpose. We act on earth, but we must direct our actions upward.

A story is told about an acquaintance of Rabbi Yehezkel Abramsky, *zt"l*, an acknowledged leader of Israel's *yeshivah* movement in the mid-twentieth century. Rabbi Abramsky inquired of the individual as to the well-being of his son. The acquaintance conveyed to Rabbi Abramsky, with some sense of sheepishness, that his son was not involved in communal service but was a doctor living in Israel. To this, Rabbi Abramsky responded, "Israel needs religious doctors, too." The fact that Yaakov gave each of his twelve sons a different, unique blessing, indicates the acceptance of the need—and desirability—for different personalities and occupations within the Jewish camp. The secular domain is not inherently holy, but it may become so if we turn our actions heavenly. As the late Rabbi Joseph Breuer, *zt"l*, once reminded his audience, "In addition to being *Glatt Kosher*, we must also strive to be *Glatt Yosher* [ethically proper]." We cannot all be Torah scholars, but we can all strive to be holy people who can link heaven and earth with our daily activities.

There is a talmudic discussion (*Berakhot* 35b) which sheds some light on the link between secular and religious pursuits. The Talmud, in discussing the words of the *Shema* that describe the rewards for loyalty to the Torah, states the following:

> The Rabbis taught: "And you shall gather your grain." Why is it necessary for this to be taught? Since it says: "And the words of the Torah shall not depart from your lips," I might think these words are to be taken literally. Therefore it says, "And you shall gather your grain"—conduct yourself in the ways of the land [*minhag derech eretz*]. This is the opinion of Rabbi Yishmael. Rabbi Shimon ben Yochai, who states, "Is it possible that a man will plant, sow, harvest, thresh, and winnow in the appropriate times? What will happen to Torah? Therefore, in the time when Jews will do the will of God, their work will be done

for them. . . ." Abaye said, "Many have followed the opinion of Rabbi Yishmael and they succeeded. Many who followed the opinion of Rabbi Shimon ben Yochai did not succeed."

The commentary of the *Maharsha* sheds light on this discussion. He suggests the following: A truly righteous person may follow the opinion of Rabbi Shimon ben Yochai and spend no time with secular pursuits. But since such righteous people are scarce, a person should not rely on this opinion and state that he is a righteous person who "need not put forth the effort." Most people cannot attain the righteous standard described by Rabbi Shimon ben Yochai.

Clearly, the ideal of "Torah only" is appropriate for certain select individuals. However, there is no reason to fail to acknowledge the contribution of those who actualize the dream of Yaakov and link "heaven and earth" by introducing the sacred into their secular lives. Furthermore, there must be a partnership between those Jews who participate in secular society and those who opt for an exclusive Torah environment. In the words of many commentaries, this is precisely why we bless our children with the hope that they will be like Ephraim and Menashe. These brothers represent Torah and secular achievement, respectively. The Jewish community depends on "Ephraims" who dedicate their lives to Torah, and "Menashes" who devote their energies to support of a Torah society.

Rabbi Meir Shapiro, founder of the famous *yeshivah* in Lublin, was once asked by a potential donor why he needed a *yeshivah* with five hundred students. The man questioned whether Europe could possibly need five hundred *yeshivah*-trained rabbis. Rabbi Shapiro responded by saying that perhaps no more than two of his graduates would become rabbinic leaders. It was his hope, however, that the other 498 would be able to give the proper support and encouragement to the select few Torah leaders. There must be a bond between the Torah community and Jewish laity. This bond exists when there is harmony of purpose and when both "brothers" direct all their actions toward heaven.

The discussion above is illustrated by an anecdotal experience. As a *yeshivah* student in Israel, I spent a *Shabbat* at *Yeshivat Kerem b'Yavneh* with three fellow students from the Chofetz Chaim Yeshivah. The *Rosh Hayeshivah*, Rav Chaim Goldvicht *z"l*, invited us to his home. He asked us to identify ourselves and to tell him of our future plans. Three of us told the *Rosh Hayeshivah* that we were planning to return to America to continue *yeshivah* learning. The fourth student was more reticent in telling the *Rosh Hayeshivah* that he planned to return to his accounting practice in America after his year of study. The *Rosh HaYeshivah* reassured him by saying, "Whatever you do, make sure to sanctify the name of God."

We can labor on earth, firmly planted in secular society, if, and only if, we direct all our actions to heaven. This is the ladder that Yaakov was approvingly shown. Not everyone can merit the status attained by Yaakov as "a simple man who dwelled in tents"—a Torah scholar. However, we all must endeavor to lead a life that links heaven and earth through the sanctification of life itself.

Rabbi Raphael Wizman

Young Israel of Commack, New York

In this *sedrah*, Yaakov's dramatic life begins with his running away from his brother, Esav, who is plotting to murder him.

After learning in the *yeshivah*, of Shem and Even for fourteen years, Yaakov resumes his journey to fulfill his father's command—namely, that of finding a wife at his Uncle Lavan's house in Haran, outside *Eretz Yisrael*. On the way to Haran, Yaakov dreams of angels ascending and descending a huge ladder to and from Heaven. In this dream, *HaShem* promises him that the land on which he lies will be inherited by his descendants, who will become a great nation. Yaakov, in return, promises to contribute one-tenth of whatever *HaShem* will give him.

Arriving at his uncle's house, he meets Rochel and offers to work seven years for her father, Lavan, to gain Rochel's hand in marriage. Lavan, seeing that *HaShem* has blessed his house because of Yaakov, grasps this opportunity and agrees to the deal. At the end of the seven years, however, he fools Yaakov by giving him Leah instead of Rochel. Lavan proposes another seven years of work for Rochel's hand, and Yaakov accepts. Eleven boys and one girl are born to Yaakov in this *parshah*, after which he decides it's time to go home.

Rashi comments on the words "ascending and descending" (upon the ladder in Yaakov's dream)—"ascending" first, then "descending." Obviously, Rashi is concerned with the fact that, since angels dwell in heaven, they should be descending first and then ascending. As an explanation for "ascending and descending," Rashi says that the angels who were with Yaakov until that point were the same ones who accompanied him until the border of *Eretz Yisrael*. These angels were not permitted to leave *Eretz Yisrael* and, therefore, ascended to heaven, while others came down to accompany Yaakov on his journey outside *Eretz Yisrael*—hence, "ascending" first. Similarly, upon Yaakov's return, other angels came to accompany him to *Eretz Yisrael* while the others left (see Gen. 32:2–3—the last two sentences of the *sedrah*).

What is difficult to understand is why the angels of *Eretz Yisrael* are not permitted to leave the land and why the others are not permitted to enter the land. We may understand this by the Rambam's ruling (*Melachim* 5:9) that one who lives in *Eretz Yisrael* may not move to dwell in another land. The Rambam makes three exceptions for which one may leave *Eretz Yisrael*: (1) to find a wife; (2) to learn Torah, and (3) to escape danger. Yaakov, then, was not only permitted to leave *Eretz Yisrael*; for all three reasons he was actually obligated as well. He was requested by his mother to escape and by his father to find a wife. He was bound by his parents' wishes and, therefore, had to fulfill the mitzvah of *kibbud av va'em*—honoring of one's parents. Thus, it is essential to understand that had the same angels accompanied him from beginning to end some would have claimed that without the angels' help, Yaakov would not have been able to fulfill his parents' wishes. It is not that the angels were permitted or not permitted to leave the land. It is only that these particular angels were not permitted to lend any further help to Yaakov. He had to show his willingness to continue even without the help of angels. When he showed his determination to continue, *HaShem* sent other angels to speed him on his way. "[For] one who comes to be 'purified' [that is, to do a *mitzvah*] *HaShem* comes to his aid." For this reason, *HaShem* led Yaakov to a place where he met our pious matriarchs.

The *midrash* (also cited by Rashi) relates that Yaakov, not trusting his uncle, gave Rochel a sign (a password) so that he couldn't be fooled by a substitute for Rochel. When Rochel learned of her father's evil plan to give Leah in her place, she immediately became concerned about how embarrassing it would be if her sister could not present Yaakov with the sign. She therefore decided to give Leah the sign to save her embarrassment.

This unselfish and pious act paid off later on in Jewish history. The *midrash* relates that when the Jews were being sent into exile after the destruction of Jerusalem, *HaShem* refused the pleading of Avraham, Yitzchok, and Yaakov, and even that of Moshe. It was only after Rochel began pleading with *HaShem* to remember her unselfishness and piety towards her sister that *HaShem* responded in kind: "There is reward for your accomplishment (unselfish act). They (your children) shall return from the enemy's land (to their land [the gathering of exiles])." (Yirmiyahu 31:15)

My *rebbe*, *Hagaon Rov* Shrage Moshe kalmanowitz, *shlita* of the Mirrer Yeshivah in NY, used to say, "If a small deed like that of Rochel was able to accomplish such great things and bring about the gathering of exiles and even the coming of the *Mashiach*, how much more is the reward of every other *mitzvah*." Indeed, "some may acquire *Olam Habah* with but one hour"—one small deed, one small act of kindness.

Rabbi Eli Stern

Young Israel of Dayton, Ohio

As the Ramban and other *meforshim* explain, Rivkah's subterfuge in last week's *parshah, Toldot,* is to insure that Yaakov *Avinu* receives the blessings of *gashmiut* (material well-being) in addition to those of *ruchaniut* (spiritual well-being, which Yitzchak was prepared to bless him with and which Esav was more than willing to cede). However, for Yaakov to successfully lay claim to both *brachot* and win grudging acknowledgment from Esav of this reality, he must demonstrate in today's *parshah* and in the beginning of next week's *parshah, Vayishlach,* that there ultimately is no dichotomy between the physical and spiritual worlds. As the patriarch who represents Torah, he also symbolizes the unity that Torah represents—that is, the sanctifying of the mundane aspects of the physical world under the rubric of Torah.

At the very beginning of today's *parshah* we see these themes dramatically played out, albeit in a rather oblique format. After spending fourteen years learning in the *yeshivah* of Ever, Yaakov now is poised to plunge directly into the material (and corrupt) world of Lavan and to rely upon the *brachot* of Yitzchak to come out unscathed on all fronts. But *HaShem* forces him to detour from this direct road by making the sun set early (Gen. 28:11; Rashi), and he winds up sleeping on *Har Habayit* (the Temple Mount), receiving prophecy from *HaShem* and then going back to sleep (Gen. 28:18, "Yaakov woke up early in the morning"—apparently after sleeping again).

In next week's *parshah,* Rashi (quoting the *Gemara* in *Chullin* 91b) provides us with a provocative insight into this forced stop-over of Yaakov. The number of minutes the sun sets prematurely to force Yaakov to sleep on *Har Habayit* is equal to the time that the sun rises prematurely for Yaakov to help him defeat the guardian angel of Esav (who must return at dawn) and be healed from the wound inflicted on his thigh (Gen. 32:27, 32). Somehow, there is a direct causal nexus bridging these two pivotal moments in the development of *Klal Yisrael.*

The guardian angel of Esav comes to contest the *brachah* of *gashmiut* (material sustenance). Yaakov has amassed a great deal of wealth during his sojourn with Lavan. Yet he is victorious in getting Esav to confirm the *brachah* that Esav had so bitterly opposed for twenty years only because, during this interlude, Yaakov had implemented the lessons he had learned twenty years earlier on *Har Habayit* when the sun set prematurely.

What are these lessons? First, we see the imagery of a ladder that figures prominently in Yaakov's dream. The ladder bridges the gap between the dichotomous worlds of *ruchaniut* and *gashmiut*.

Second, Yaakov decides to lie down to sleep—"he lay down [specifically] in this place" (Gen. 28:11) which Rashi tells us is the first time he actually slept in fourteen years (while in the *yeshivah*, he just fell asleep on his *Gemara*, so to speak, without consciously planning to sleep). My *Rosh Hayeshiva*, Rav Reuvein Feinstein, *shlita*, explains that Yaakov is still thinking in a dichotomous mode at this point. When he is ensconced in the spiritual world, he deprives himself of all physical comforts. However, when he leaves that world, he can now afford to change his mode, however subtly. Thus, it is a tremendous shock to Yaakov to find out that this place where he has "switched gears" is none other than *Har Habayit*, the holiest spot on earth! (See Gen. 28:16; Rashi on Yaakov's "regret.") Yet we see by inference from *pasuk* 18 that Yaakov goes back to sleep on the same spot now having internalized the lesson that there are not two dichotomous worlds but only one harmonious continuum requiring constant sanctification.

Furthermore, we see this "unity" played out in Rashi's statement that all the stones under Yaakov's head when he went to sleep, united into one stone (Gen. 28:11). Yaakov is also the one to whom the twelve tribes said the *Shema*, ending with *HaShem echad* (God is One), bringing out the unity to *HaShem*. Also, the word *makom* (place) is used here to denote his rendezvous with *HaShem*. This is the same name of *HaShem* that is used to comfort mourners ("May the Place comfort you . . ." Here, too, we reaffirm that despite the tragedy of our seemingly being bereft of *HaShem*, He is present everywhere and nothing in this material world is devoid of His *hashgachah* (Divine Providence) (Rabbi Yochanan Zweig, *shlita Rosh Hayeshiva*, Miami Beach, Florida).

Yaakov learns these lessons well. He promises to give *HaShem* one-tenth of all that he earns, thus sanctifying the mundane (Gen. 28:22). The very first encounter that he has after fourteen years in *Yeshivah* and the night of prophecy on *Har Habayit*, is in *shmoozing* with and assisting the shepherds of Charan (clearly not the kind of people he had associated with previously). At the same time, he demands their strict adherence, to the laws relating to *gezeilah*, stealing time from their employers (Gen. 29:4–8).

Throughout the twenty years with Lavan—the epitome of duplicity and mendacity in the material world—Yaakov never wavers in his fidelity to the Torah's principles of honesty. In fact, he goes way beyond the letter of the law to show that he truly merits the *brachah* of *gashmiut*. The *parsha* ends with the symmetry of Yaakov dreaming again, this time not of angels but of sheep. He has succeeded in sanctifying the world of Lavan and using it to grow closer to *HaShem*.

The last hurdle for Yaakov to clear is the aforementioned encounter with Esav's guardian angel. It is only because Yaakov goes back for small jars that he is left alone to do battle. The *Gemara* (*Chullin 91a*) explains that since *tzaddikim* are scrupulously honest in obtaining all their possessions, they guard them even more zealously than their own bodies. Everything in this material world that Yaakov acquired had been obtained through his meticulous observance of the halachic standards of honesty and, therefore, must have intrinsic meaning and purpose; nothing is ever expendable. It is precisely at this moment of sanctification that Yaakov can once and for all defeat Esav's claims to the *brachah* of *gashmiut*, with the help of those minutes of sunlight reserved for him from twenty years earlier.

Thus, when Yaakov encounters Esav, Esav says, "I have a lot," and tries to encourage Yaakov to retract his gifts. Yaakov responds, "I have everything"—that is, everything I have acquired was obtained through sanctifying the mundane and thus has a deeper purpose; nothing is superfluous. With this sense of *shleimut*, completion, Yaakov and *Klal Yisrael* have finally defeated Esav within Esav's own world of the material.

One of the more incongruous passages in today's *parshah* is the discussion between Yaakov and his wives (Rochel and Leah) about the need to return to *Eretz Canaan* (Gen. 31:3–16). Even though Yaakov has been given an explicit command by *HaShem* to leave, he withholds this critical information and instead recites a litany of plausible reasons why they should leave, based upon Lavan's duplicity and the fear that he might harm them. Only in the end does he slip in that *HaShem* commanded them to leave. Likewise, in responding to Yaakov, Rochel and Leah first assert how cruelly Lavan, their own father, has treated them and only after this do they say "Whatever *HaShem* has said to you, do." How do we reconcile these two approaches with the concept of our *Avot* and *Imahot* teaching us to obey *HaShem* at all costs, even if we don't understand the reason?

Rav Eliyahu Lopian, *zt"l*, one of the great *mussar* teachers of this century, in his book *Lev Eliyahu* provides us with a very profound answer. Yaakov is inculcating a vital lesson in his wives (and by extension in us). Listening to *HaShem* (and observing His Torah) is not inimical to our best interests (as it may superficially appear to be at times) but in fact is quite compatible with our best interests (and, thus, Rochel and Leah respond in a similar vein, as though they, too, had been cognizant of this fact). When Yaakov first lists all the reasons for leaving, he is setting them up for the recognition that what *HaShem* wants is in their best interests.

In a similar fashion, *Kohelet* tells us in eleven *p'rakim* how everything that the world strives for in the realm of success is all vanity, illusory, vacuous, and futile. All the glory, honor, pleasure, and wealth cannot help one attain inner peace, equanimity, and happiness. Only after we have been intuitively convinced of the folly of the secular, non-Torah values does *Kohelet* zero in on the punchline: "The sum of the matter when all has been considered is to fear *HaShem* and keep His *mitzvot,* for this is man's whole duty" (*Kohelet* 12:13).

Unfortunately, this very basic principle of Torah Judaism is sometimes obscured even for Orthodox Jews. To buttress our observance, we sometimes employ inappropriate concepts such as "suffering for God in this world," "sacrificing" for religion, and the old standard, "*Es shvere tzu zein a Yid*"—"It's hard to be a Jew." Apropos of the latter, my *Rosh Hayeshivah,* Rav Moshe Feinstein, *zt"l,* said that this mantra was responsible in many ways for the horrific assimilation of American Jewry at the time of the great immigration from Eastern Europe seventy-five to one hundred years ago. Parents who were observant gave their children this masochistic message—and, not surprisingly, their children rejected the Torah way of life *en masse.*

We sometimes need to convince ourselves, as *Kohelet* did, that the secular ways of the world lead only to a dead end. Rather than "sacrifice" (that is, give up) something for Torah, living a true Torah lifestyle in *hashkafah* and observance places one in a veritable city of refuge, a *tumah* fallout shelter from the wholesale moral anarchy and turmoil that is evident in the secular world around us today. In fact, even many Gentiles recognize this; their awareness has catapulted William Bennett's *Book of Virtues* to the top of the best-seller list with two million hard copies sold. Yet, rather than deriving these values from places ranging from Aesop's *Fables* to Charles Dickens, we, *lehavdil,* have the greatest source of wisdom and guidance in the world—if only we used it to its maximum benefit. When we follow Dovid *Hamelech*'s advice in *Tehillim,* "Taste and see that *HaShem* is good, praiseworthy is the man who takes refuge in Him" (Psalm 34:9) and compare that with what the secular world offers us, we see, in fact, that there is no "sacrifice" involved at all—not even a contest.

The true joy that would ensue in our lives as a result of seeing just how compatible Torah is with our best interests should be so infectious that not only our children but all of our non-observant neighbors should, by osmosis, pick up on just how fortunate a Torah Jew is in this world and be inspired to emulate us.

❖ CHAPTER 8 ❖

Vayishlach

Rabbi Shmuel Greenberg

Young Israel of White Plains, New York

This *Shabbat*, we read of the encounter between Yaakov and Esau. The confrontation of these brothers is a constant battle, as the *pasuk* (Gen. 25:23) states, *ul'om mil'om ye'ematz*, the might shall pass from one regime to the other, these two powers will be at constant odds with each other. There will be no peaceful co-existence—rather, an ongoing war between Yaakov and Esau and what they represent. *Chazal*—the Sages—say, "When one will rise, the other will fall." These two value systems can not be reconciled.

Yaakov was full of fear at the prospect of having to face Esau. It was only after the birth of Yosef that Yaakov felt he could survive meeting and, possibly, clashing with Esau. The *pasuk* states, "After Rachel gave birth to Yosef, Yaakov said to Lavan, 'let me leave, I would like to go home'" (Gen. 30:25). Why was the addition of the young child, Yosef, sufficient to overcome the fear of a defeat at the hands of Esau?

As the meeting between Yaakov and Esau drew closer, Yaakov continued to reiterate that he feared "my brother, Esau." Bothered by the wording—after all, we all know who Esau is—Rashi (Gen. 32:12) comments that Yaakov was expressing the feeling that Esau does not act like a brother but, rather, like "wicked Esau." One must ask why this point is emphasized time and again.

At the beginning of Chapter 33, while awaiting the anxious moment of Esau's appearance, Yaakov should have been exhibiting a maximum show of strength. Instead, all he did was to place the various branches of the fledgling Jewish community on display. Where was the show of strength one would have expected?

The understanding of the power of Yaakov and the weakness of Esau is expressed in the *haftarah*: "The house of Yaakov will be fire, and the house of Yosef a flame, and the house of Esau straw" (Ovadiah 1:18). The key word of this *pasuk* is *beit*—house or, more accurately, home. The strength of the Jewish people lies in the greatness of its family unit. The courage and fortitude emanating from the *Beit Yaakov*—Jewish home, "*a Yiddesha shtub*"—is what has enabled the Jews to survive countless enemies over thousands of years.

Near the end of the *parshah* we are told of the passing of Rachel and her being buried "on the road of Efrat." Rashi, in *Vayechi* (48:7), explains that Rachel was buried on the road that the Jews would pass *en route* to *galut*—exile. At that time, Rachel would cry for her children. Rachel is the mother figure of the Jewish people. She is referred to by King David (himself a descendant of Leah) as the mainstay of the home. The Jews, thrown out of Israel, will pass a landmark grave as they are forced into the Diaspora. The good-bye to the land will be a tearful farewell to their mother—Rachel who is weeping about the fate of her children. It is this occurrence that will give the Jews strength and perseverance wherever they are dispersed. Although Rachel is dead, she is still our mother. If there is a mother, their is a home. The Jews should not despair despite the destruction in the land; their home has been spared. They always have a home awaiting their return.

Yosef was the heir to Rachel's legacy. Rachel named Yosef with a double meaning—on the one hand, to add, to expand, to spread out, and, on the other, to gather. Yosef was imbued with both these qualities. It was Yosef who took the Jews to Egypt, and it was Yosef who guaranteed their return. Yehoshua, an offspring of Yosef, fulfilled his "grandfather's" promise by leading them back to Israel. One can feel comfortable going beyond the confines of his home if he possesses the capability of gathering his family to return home.

Therefore, we can understand the action of Yaakov *Avinu*. After the birth of Yosef, he realized that the *Beit Yisrael* he had built with Rochel would be perpetuated. Now he can stand before Esau with the ultimate exhibition of strength—the family structure of Israel. It was this spectacle that caught Esau's eye and softened him: "And he saw the women and the children" (*Chazal* fault Yaakov for failing to utilize his full strength of family when he hid Dina).

Yaakov was frightened by the unbecoming attitude of Esau. He saw, in Esau, a distortion of family. Esau is referred to as "my brother Esau"—one who is a brother but does not act like one. Yaakov was not afraid that Esau would kill him. The *pasuk* states, "I fear he will afflict mother and child." Yaakov was afraid that Esau would inflict injury to the beautiful structure he had built of mother and child.

Now we can understand the relationship between the beginning of the *parshah* and its conclusion. The *parshah* ends with what seems to be the insignificant tale of the family tree of Esau. However, when we look closely, the Torah is describing the flaws in the house of Esau. As the list of the family unit is presented, Rashi comments that the various individuals were *mamzerim,* born from illegitimate unions. The house of Esau is built on a weak foundation of disgrace and impurity; therefore, it must ultimately collapse. The house of Yaakov, however, rests on pillars of holiness and respect; therefore, it shall endure.

Today, more than ever, we must seek to remove any "Esau" influence from the house of Yaakov. Our strength lies with the love and unity that must exist in the *Beit Yaakov.* As was the situation with Yaakov, our structure must be multi-tiered, bridging the generation gap of grandfather, child, and grandchild. If we support each other as brothers, fulfilling the meaning of the word *achi,* we will be worthy of the ultimate redemption "The house of Yaakov will be fire, and the house of Yosef a flame, and the house of Esau straw."

Rabbi Nosson Fromowitz

Young Israel of Monsey and Wesley Hills, New York

The encounter between Yaakov and Esau, described so vividly in the *parshah*, is more than just a description of a critical event in the life of one of our *Avot*. It is, as is the entire *Chumash Bereishit*, to be understood using the rule of *ma'ase; avot siman lebanim*—"The events that occurred to our forebears indicate what is in store for their children." At the same time we discover our future, we are to learn from the *Avot* what was the proper reaction to the events in their lives and then to apply it to our own experiences.

Yaakov understood what was meant by "Esau hated Yaakov"—namely, the concept that Esau would eternally threaten the Jewish people because of his inbred hatred towards them. No delusions of reconciliation were possible—only preparation to confront this threat. As Rashi tells us, "Yaakov prepared himself in three ways: bringing gifts to appease Esau, praying for Yaakov's salvation, and preparing to do battle if the appeasement failed."

The *pasuk* tells us that "Yaakov was very much afraid and was pained by this fear." The *Daat Zekeinim* explains the fear as stemming from the realization that he lacked two merits that Esau possessed—first, *kibbud av va'em*, respect for father and mother, and, second, *yishuv ha'aretz*—living in *Eretz Yisrael*.

Imagine the accomplishment of Yaakov during the twenty years he spent in the house of Lavan. He built the house of Israel through the *shevatim*, the twelve tribes and was able to withstand the test of living in an environment so corrupt that Yaakov had to tell Esau, "With Lavan I lived, but I still kept all the commandments." Yet Yaakov felt insecure because he lacked the merit of *kibbud av va'em*, which Esau fulfilled with such perfection, and because he had not lived in the land of Israel, whereas Esau had. From this we can see the enormous *zechut* of these two *mitzvot*.

Though Yaakov was pained by his fear, he had a guarantee from *HaShem*.

He rallied and overcame the momentary lapse, kept the fear from debilitating him, and continued his preparation for war, not relying on miracles alone. Yaakov, together with his wives and children, was going to do battle against Esau and his four hundred armed men!

In Yaakov's preparation through prayer, he beseeches God by saying, "Save me, please, from the hands of my brother, from the hands of Esau." Why the double reference to Esau? The text should have said either "from Esau" or "from my brother." The *Beit Halevi* explains that Yaakov foresaw two possible dangers in his encounter with Esau: either he would be killed in battle or there would be a reconciliation and Esau would want the two of them to live together in peace. Yaakov feared both of these possibilities. He certainly didn't want to perish at the hands of Esau, and he was terrified of living together with someone so evil. Therefore, according to the *Beit Halevi*, the double fear: that Yaakov was very much "afraid" and "pained" by this fear; he was afraid of death at the hands of Esau, and he feared living with him. This explains the double prayer: *miyad achi*—save me from Esau's brotherly love—*miyad Esau*; and save me from his evil intent. It is interesting to note that *miyad achi*—the threat of Esau's brotherly love—is stated before *miyad Esau*—the threat of his evil intent—for Yaakov feared living in close quarters with Esau even more than death itself. Fear for one's spirituality should be greater than fear of physical destruction.

As the *parshah* continues, we see that Yaakov's prayer regarding the physical danger is answered first as Esau embraces Yaakov. Then Esau offers, "Let's get going and move on; I will travel alongside you." To this Yaakov responds, "Please pass before me, my master." Yaakov's second prayer, regarding his spiritual danger, is also answered as Esau agrees to part ways.

Another dimension of the battle between Yaakov and Esau takes place when Yaakov does battle with Samael, guardian angel of Esau. This battle symbolizes the struggle with evil that the descendants of Yaakov would face from that time forward. The *pasuk* tells us that when the angel of Esau "saw that he could not defeat Yaakov, he touched his thigh and dislocated it" (Gen. 32:26). The Sforno explains that, during the entire night of struggle, the angel could not inflict injury on Yaakov because of Yaakov's constant clinging to *HaShem* in thought and speech. The angel of Esau was able to distract Yaakov momentarily by informing him of the sins the leaders of our people would eventually commit. My *rebbe, Harav* H. Liebowitz, Shlita pointed out in one of his discourses that the angel of Esau could have shown Yaakov any one of the many tragic events of Jewish history. All these tragedies were not powerful enough to distract Yaakov from his high spiritual state. The one thing Yaakov could not countenance was the failure of Jewish leadership. How can our people survive without leadership committed to high ideals of Torah? This is the only tragedy that could have caused Yaakov a moment of distraction, allowing the angel of Esau to gain the upper hand.

The lesson that Yaakov taught us in dealing with Esau is relevant to our own time. We should not delude ourselves by thinking that, somehow, we can coexist with the modern-day Esau. We must be as wary of the embrace of Esau as we are of his threat to our existence. Above all, we must be *mitpallel* that *HaShem* give us the leadership necessary to bring about a true and final peace in our time.

Rabbi Chaim Wasserman

Young Israel of Passaic–Clifton, New Jersey

Yaakov's nerve-racking encounter with his estranged brother, Esau, needed serious contemplation and preparations for disaster to be averted. Those preparations have become a paradigm for all times, for *Chazal* identified and established them as the preferred manner of dealing with the nations of the world: *doron* (lavish gifts upon the adversary), *tefillah* (yearn for Divine protection), and *milchamah* (prepare for war in the event that life-threatening hostilities erupt). *Chazal* also assume it to be axiomatic that what happened in such situations in the days of our founding *Avot* would inevitably recur in the lives of their descendants generations later (*ma'aseh Avot siman labanim*). Since the destruction of the both *Batei HaMikdash,* how capable have we been implementing this three-part strategy in the face of the belligerence and hostilities of Esav's descendants and, for that matter, Yishmael's?

We find two views stated in the commentaries on this encounter. The first represents, understandably, the view dominant for millennia; the second was advanced only within the last century. Rabbeinu Bachya (ben Asher) writing at the end of the thirteenth century (1291), explains with regard to Genesis 32:8:

> So do we have to do following in our forefathers' ways: (1) be prepared to greet them with gifts and in a dignified manner and (2) with prayer to our exalted God. But as far as war is concerned, that is impossible, since we were made to swear that we would not go to war with the nations of the world, as it says: "I made you take an oath, daughters of Jerusalem, that you not stir up . . ." (*Shir Hashirim* 2:7)

Of course this oath to which Rabbeinu Bachya refers is the captivating topic of conversation of the *Gemara* (*Ketubot* 111a) already recorded at the close of the third century C.E., when, even in Babylon of *Talmud Bavli* days, Rabbi Yossi ben Chanina determined that Jews could not rise up to revolt against their host nations or to retake Yerushalayim from the ruling power by force. The same discussion quotes Rav Zera later as saying that the Jews had accepted as many as six oaths restricting them not only in matters concerning armed revolt but also in the manner by which they were to treat eschatological happenings in the end of days (*acharit hayamim*). This is the same Rav Zera, the *Gemara* tells us there, who actually defied his *rebbe*, Rav Yehudah, and left *Bavel* to settle in *Eretz Yisrael*.

In any event, the concept of *shalosh shevuot* (three oaths) was a given throughout Jewish history even though it was entirely logical to argue that, on the basis of the *pesukim* from which the Talmud derived them, these restrictions applied only to the generations following the destruction of the first *Beit Hamikdash*. Nonetheless, the *Tosafot* indicate, Rav Yehudah, quoted in this *Gemara*, insists that the three oaths even applied after the destruction of the second *Beit Hamikdash* just as they did after the destruction of the first *Beit Hamikdash*.

It is not until the publication of the NeTZiV's commentary on the Torah, *Ha'amek Davar* (1879), that we find, probably for the first time in history since the Bar Kochba revolution, another position maintaining that all three strategies employed by Yaakov *Avinu* are to be considered as inseparable. Readiness for war is as fundamental for the Jewish nation as the gifts of appeasement and calling out to God for His protection. This, according to the NeTZiV, is the lesson to be learned from the Torah relating the struggle between Yaakov and the angel. ". . . It is possible to say that this comes to teach us for all future generations that what occurred to our forefathers is a sign unto the children." A careful reading of what the NeTZiV means in this statement leads one to the clear conclusion that Yaakov and all his descendants will have to be prepared for war despite their feelings of revulsion toward such strife. (*Ha'amek Davar, Bereishit* 32:26.)

The NeTZiV's youngest son, Rabbi Meir Berlin (later to become Meir Bar-Ilan), stated the perception of his father, the immortal *Rosh Hayeshivah* of Volozhin, in matters concerning Jews at war:

> It is impossible to separate the worthiness of the study of Torah from the need of the nation to go to war. When the enemy lurks you don't only sit in the halls of Torah. We [also] don't fight with armaments of war alone and as a result ignore the study of Torah. Jews go to war differently from all other nations. We fight with sword and spear when necessary, but at the very same time we engage in the ideological war of Torah study; the fiercer the war the more intense does the Torah study have to become. This was my father's perspective on Jewish history . . . as seen in his commentary, *Ha'amek Davar*. His view stands singularly unique in our Torah literature. . . . (Quoted from Rabbi Meir

Berlin's introduction to the revised edition and printed in back of *Ha'amek Davar, Sefer Bereishit.*)

Of course, one can argue that the NeTZiV meant to say that there is a need for two distinctly separate armies, those who fight on the battlefield and those who battle in the *beit midrash* pursuing *milchamtah shel Torah*. To so conclude would distort the position of the NeTZiV as set forth in his *Ha'amek Davar*. Throughout the entire commentary he insists that the nation at war to secure the borders and safety of its covenantal homeland do so with a united force joined to fight both wars concurrently. There is one organizing principle for any Jewish fighting force: in one hand is the *safra*, the book, Torah, while in the other hand, *sa'yefa*, the sword and any other weaponry necessary to protect that living Torah.

Elsewhere, the NeTZiV derived a pivotal lesson concerning national security from the first two *parshiyot* that mention *tefillin* (*Kadesh li kol b'chor* and *V'hayah ki y'viacha* at the end of *Parshat Bo*, Exodus 13:2, 11). Three times we find the phrase *b'chozek yad* or *b'yad chazakah* ("with a strong hand") mentioned here. This teaches that every nation needs three things in order to withstand external aggression, as well as to overcome internal disunity. *Bnei Yisrael* was taught at the inception of its nationhood that it can survive only with (1) a kingdom and its flag as a rallying symbol of sovereignty, (2) an army and its officers, and (3) effective weaponry with which to fight. So much for the *sa'yefa*. But there is also the *safra*'s war, which Jews must fight concurrently by (1) the acceptance of God's dominion (*kabbalat ol malchut shamayim*), (2) providing a veritable army of leaders to inculcate Jewish spirituality, whether they be the *b'chorim* (first born sons) or the tribe of Levi or other *talmidei chachamim*, and (3) carrying aloft the Torah, for only it is the ultimate source of Jewish national power. That having been said, it bears repetition that in the opinion of his illustrious son the NeTZiV was advocating a radical perspective: the mechanism by which all original three strategies of Yaakov *Avinu* are supported.

Twentieth-century realities have transformed Jewish living—it is to be hoped, for all times. For the first time since the days of Rabbi Akiva, Jews have accepted full responsibility for Jewish national aspirations by returning to the ancient homeland, defending its inhabitants, and taking active concern for the safety of Jews worldwide who are not in a position to defend themselves. Our century has seen the living reenactment of Yaakov *Avinu*'s strategy in three dimensions. In our times, we have merited the beginning of the fulfillment of the schema as the NeTZiV envisioned it.

But what about the long-standing restrictions of the three oaths? How can the position of Rabbeinu Bachya, an opinion that dominated our lives for nearly eighteen hundred years, be reversed so suddenly? In 1922 (5682),

Rav Meir Simcha Hakohen of Divinsk, author of *Meshech Chochmah*—yet another highly original commentary to *Chumash*—published a pronouncement concerning the validity of those three oaths once the San Remo Conference of Nations (April 1920) assigned a mandate to Great Britain based upon the conditions previously outlined in the Balfour Declaration (November 1917). He wrote:

> Divine Providence is such that with the assembly in San Remo of the enlightened nations an order was issued that the land of Israel shall be for the nation of Israel. Now that the fear of [violating] the three oaths has passed and kings have granted us this right of return, the priority of settling Israel returns to its glorious status—being equal to all the *mitzvot* in the Torah. (Printed in Avraham Y. Slutki, *Shivat Tziyon*, Jerusalem 5745 edition, last page.)

Still, the question begs to be asked: What do classical *poskim* say about these three oaths? Nothing, notes the saintly *Sochatchover Rebbe* in his *Avnei Nezer* (454). "None of the *poskim* record the three oaths that the Jews accepted as a *din*, since this is not a halachic issue (*ayn zeh aysek b' halachah*)." Indeed, there is no mention of these oaths in any of the halachic works of the Rif, Rosh, Rambam, or Tur, or in the Shulchan Aruch. There is, however, one mention that Rambam does make concerning the oaths at the end of his *Epistle to the Jews of Yemen* (*Iggeret Teman*), where he counsels that downtrodden community not to do anything hasty as a result of the tribulations they were then facing. Perhaps this constitutes the best argument for supporting the idea that the three oaths, which for millennia restricted the Jew from any form of organized self-defense, are, as the *Avnei Nezer* asserts, not a halachic issue, for, if that were not the case, the Rambam, of all people, would have addressed the halachic dimension of these oaths in his *Yad Hachazakah*.

Having raised the issue of the nature of the three oaths and *halachah*, how then can we account for such definitive arguments and extensive Torah literature maintaining its validity even today—or, better yet, *especially* today with the advent of a state in Israel? Both the *Minchat Elazar* of Muncacz and the *Vayoel Moshe* of Satmar, two of the finest authorities of *halachah* of our century, argue unyieldingly that they remain fully valid even now. How so?

Perhaps the question can be raised again, when we reach *Matot* (*Bamidbar* 32). See page 520.

Rabbi Yosef Goldberg

Young Israel of Wavecrest and Bayswater, New York

"And Yaakov sent *malachim* before him. . . ."

Onkelos, the primary Aramaic translator of the *Chumash*, understands the word *malachim* here to refer to human messengers or agents. Rashi, in contrast to Onkelos, takes the midrashic view that the word *malachim* here refers to actual heavenly angels. The *midrash* is based upon the fact that the previous *parshah*, *Vayetze*, concludes with Yaakov's meeting with a camp of *malachei Elohim*—angels of God—and his giving the name *Machanayim*—(Two) Camps—to that place of meeting. Since the last and very proximate usage of the word *malachim* referred to actual angels of God, so here, too, at the beginning of our *parshah*, the word *malachim* refers to actual angels of God.

I would like to suggest that, perhaps, there is not much conflict between the respective approaches of Onkelos and Rashi. Rashi, commenting on Hagar's encounter with the angel by the well in *Parshat Lech Lecha*, mentions that Hagar was accustomed to seeing angels in Avraham's house. One might assume that, just as angels appeared to Avraham as he was recovering from his *brit milah*, so, too, on other occasions not recorded in *Chumash*, Avraham was visited by heavenly angels. Yet, perhaps, there is another possible way to explain the *midrash* upon which Rashi bases his interpretation. This explanation would also serve to explain why Yaakov was so severely punished for hiding his daughter, Dinah, from his brother, Esav.

Anyone with the slightest spiritual sensitivity who has ever had the privilege of spending time with a genuine *tzaddik* knows that in the presence of a *tzaddik* even an ordinary person feels elevated and transported to a higher spiritual plane. One feels the Godly goodness of the *tzaddik* permeate oneself, and one feels oneself transformed into a better person. One could not dream of sinning or acting improperly in the presence of a true *tzaddik*.

A passage from one of my favorite S.Y. Agnon short stories, "Tehillah," illustrates the incredible ability of a *tzaddik* or *tzaddeket* to affect even a brutal heart. "Tehillah" is the moving story of an elderly *tzaddeket* who lives in Jerusalem. (As is typical of Agnon, the *tzaddeket* herself is a symbol of the Holy City.) At one point, the narrator of the story depicts the following scene (please pardon my poor translation of Agnon's superb prose) which unfortunately, in many ways, is relevant to the Israel of today:

> I found for myself a small spot near the *Kotel*. At times I stood there praying, and at times I stood there in wonderment. I was wondering about the nations of the world. It is not enough for them that they displace us from all of their lands, but they must also displace us within our very own home.
>
> As I was standing, I was pushed from my place by a Mandate police officer, who struck out with the lash in his hand. What angered him that he was so enraged? A sickly elderly woman had brought with her a stool upon which to sit. The officer jumped forward, kicked the stool out from beneath the old woman, knocking her to the ground, and snatched the stool away, for the woman had been in violation of the Mandate law that forbade Jews to sit while praying by the *Kotel* [Jews were not permitted to sit in prayer by the *Kotel* because that infuriated the Arabs]. Those praying saw and kept silent; for who can contend with someone stronger than himself? The elderly woman [Tehillah], whom I had met, came and stared at the officer. The officer lowered his eyes and returned the stool to the sickly woman.
>
> I approached her [Tehillah], and I said to her, "The power of your eyes is mightier than all the promises of England. For England has given us the Balfour Declaration but has sent her officers to nullify it. And you, my dear old woman, merely glanced at that evil man and nullified all of his evil intentions."
>
> "Do not say that," she responded, "He is a good Gentile, for he saw my distress at his behavior and he returned the stool to that unfortunate woman."

Therefore, one might say that the angels Hagar saw in the home of Avraham *Avinu* were not heavenly angels but men who had been transformed into angelic beings because of their exposure to the incredible spiritual personality of Avraham. In the presence of Avraham an ordinary man was remade into an angel. This concept fits beautifully with Rashi's comment, in *Lech Lecha*, on the phrase *hanefesh asher asu becharan*—"the souls that they had acquired [literally, "made"] in Haran" (Gen. 12:5); according to Rashi, this phrase refers to the converts whom Avraham and Sarah had brought under the wing of the *Shechinah*—the Almighty.

Perhaps the *malachim* that Yaakov had sent out to greet Esav were indeed ordinary mortal messengers, in accordance with the translation of Onkelos. Yet, at the same time, in accordance with the commentary of Rashi, they were men who had been transformed into Godly beings through their association with Yaakov. I would now offer a new translation to the final *pesukim* of last week's *parshah*. Instead of the usual translation, "And Yaakov went on his way, and angels of God encountered him," I would venture to translate, "And Yaakov went on his way, and those who encountered him became angels of God. And Yaakov said when he saw them, 'This is a camp of God' and he called the name of the place "Camps.'"

The ability of the *tzaddik* to transform an ordinary man into an angelic being is predicated upon the ability of the *tzaddik* to see the angelic goodness that resides deep within the psyches of even ordinary men. When a man sees that the *tzaddik* is perceiving him as somebody special with unlimited potential for spiritual greatness, than that person does indeed rise to the challenge and is indeed transformed.

With this in mind, we can now understand why Yaakov *Avinu* was so severely punished for hiding Dinah in a box to keep her from Esav, his brother. Under the constant exposure to a righteous person of the stature of the daughter of Yaakov, Esav might have been profoundly influenced. His personality and nature could have been radically transformed. But, in fairness to Yaakov, had not Esav spent the early years of his life in the presence of *tzaddikim* of the stature of Yitzchak, Rivkah, and Yaakov, himself, and Esav had not been so influenced?* The answer lies in the fact that Yaakov hid Dinah away from the *sight* of Esav. In the same way that Dinah was hidden from the sight of Esav, Esav was hidden from the sight of Yaakov. Had Yaakov struggled harder to uncover the small kernel of goodness that resided even within the dark heart of a *rasha* such as Esav, had he attempted to see through the evil until he uncovered the good, then Esav, too, might have been redeemed.

As we sit in *shul* this *Shabbat*, let us look to our neighbors on the right and left, in front and behind, and attempt to see ourselves, not in the presence of our usual friends and neighbors, but in a camp of angels of God.

---

*I would venture to state that Yitzchak's affection for Esav had no beneficial effect upon Esav because it was largely based upon Esav's constant deception, as *Chazal* point out in the *midrashim* to which Rashi refers. Rivkah's outlook concerning Esav was affected by her experience in pregnancy and the resulting prophecy that "the elder would serve the younger." Therefore, it was up to Yaakov, who was unfettered by any preconception, to attempt to find that essence of genuine good that lay dormant within Esav.

❖ CHAPTER 9 ❖

Vayeishev

Rabbi Yaakov Feitman

Young Israel of Beachwood, Ohio

YOSEF AND YEHUDAH. BROTHERS. *SHEVATIM*. FATHERS OF *MASHIACH*

On the surface, two separate stories are told in our *parshah*. One is the saga of the brother who is sold into slavery, undergoes tests and tribulations, and emerges triumphantly into monarchy and dominion, preparing the way for the later exile in Egypt. The other is the tale of the brother who appears to sin, nobly confesses his action, and sets into motion the chain that results in the Davidic dynasty—*malchut Beit David*.

Rashi alludes to the primary connection between the two narratives. When the brothers see the profound distress of their father, Yaakov *Avinu*, they blame Yehudah: "You said to sell him. Had you told us to return him, we would have heeded your words." Rav Mordechai Gifter, *shlita*, *Rosh Hayeshivah* of Telshe in Cleveland, Ohio explains that Yehudah was already considered a king among the *shevatim*—the twelve tribes—and, therefore, his decision would have been followed. The *shevatim*'s temporary "demotion" of Yehudah from his position of grandeur was a reflection of his greatness and the esteem in which he was always held. "The king's heart is the heart of the nation" (Rambam, *Hilchos Melachim*); and that great, majestic heart should have anticipated the deleterious result of such an action, no matter how exalted the motivations. My *rebbe*, Rav Yitzchok Hutner, *zt"l* often spoke of another sibling pattern that I believe sheds light on the events in the *sedrah*.

There are two eternal strains of redemption in the history of *Knesset Yisrael*—the Jewish people. There is the way of our matriarch Rochel, and there is the way of our matriarch Leah. Leah came into the house of Yaakov through subterfuge. Her entry embodies all future concealment (*hester*), those cosmic events that are essentially inscrutable, seeming to defy logic and good sense.

Rochel, on the other hand, personifies the open manifestation of God's sovereignty over the world: "A voice is heard on high" (Yirmiyahu 31:14). Her voice and the voices of her descendants are heard clearly and unmistakably. When her presence is felt, a slave can become a king in an instant and overpower the most evil of inclinations. But when the trait of Leah is what is instructing the Jewish people, sacred developments may appear as lowly sins, and the righteous are placed in positions of seeming compromise. To the untutored eye, nothing good can emerge from these episodes, but, in reality, what is being created is the ultimate perfection, the *summum bonum*.

The *midrash* reveals to us the secret of what is happening "behind the curtain" of our *sedrah*: "The *shevatim* were involved in the selling of Yosef. Yosef himself was involved in fasting and mourning. Yaakov, too, was in sackcloth and was fasting. Yehudah was involved in taking a wife for himself. *And Hakadosh Baruch Hu was involved in creating the light of Moshiach*" (*Bereishit Rabbah* 85:1). There is a Messiah from the House of David and a Messiah from the House of Yosef. Both must come into this world and travel their singular paths. The matrix of each will set in motion the forces and powers that will provide for the elements of *geulah*—redemption. Each must contribute to the *nitzchiyut*—eternity—of *Knesset Yisrael*. In the end, however, they herald a single redemption. They, too, are one: "Ephraim shall not be jealous of Yehudah and Yehudah will not trouble Ephraim." Says the *Gaon* of Vilna: "This means that Ephraim shall not be jealous of Mashiach ben David and Mashiach ben David will not trouble Mashiach ben Yosef" (*Aderes Eliyahu*). Not only the light of Mashiach ben David is being created in this *sedrah*, but that of Mashiach ben Yosef as well. And, in the end, one will come to the other: "And Yehudah came near to him" (Gen. 44:18).

Says the Holy *Zohar*: "Yehudah and Yosef must be joined into one, for Yosef is the *tzaddik*, and Yehudah is the king. For, when they are joined together, they bring much good to the world and peace to all the *shevatim* and cause the spirit of Yaakov *Avinu* to live" (*Zohar Bereishit* 206b; see also, Rabbi Matis Weinberg's vol. 8 *Patterns in Time*, chapter 12, Feldheim Publishers 1988). Indeed, what seem to be separate stories are truly one. It is the story of the coalescing of the "one people" into the unity that is its apotheosis. It is a oneness that blends disparate elements and diverse vantage points, but, as the *Gaon* of Vilna (commentary to *Safra*, *Vayikra* 26:42) points out, although there is a covenant for Sarah and a covenant for Rivkah, there is one covenant for Rochel and Leah, for, at the end of time, we shall see that they—and, through them, all of us—were truly one.

If the light of the two Messiahs shines through the *sedrah*, it is all the more incandescent when *Parshat Vayeishev* ushers in the Chanukah flames, for Yosef's holy beauty (Gen. 49:23) is the antidote to the distorted seductiveness of Greece's corporeal beauty, and Yehudah's quintessential gratitude is the remedy for Hellenistic denial of God's beneficence (see Rambam, *Hilchos Avodas Yom Hakippurim* 1:7 and *Pachad Yitzchak, Chanukah*, no. 10 and 13).

It is, thus, not surprising that, when Yaakov finally sends Yehudah to Yosef, the Torah records that he sent him *Goshna*—literally, "to Goshen" but, as the *Bnei Yissachar* points out, "to the letters on the Chanukah *dreidel*, which spell nes godal hayah sham—a great miracle happened there." Yaakov sent Yehuda to *Goshna*: *Gimmel, Shin, Nun Heh*.

That event is not just the miracle of Chanukah. It is the miracle of the reunification of the *shevatim*, the renewal of the oneness of the Nation of Israel, and the triumph over evil. It utilizes the special Chanukah illumination to distinguish the true inner beauty from the false appeal of that which captivates and enthralls but, in the end, is merely destructive. And it is the miracle that will soon restore the great primordial light that shone for thirty-six hours when the world was young and will be returned through the *mitzvah* in which thirty-six candles are lit by all of Israel (see *Yerushalmi Berachos* 8.5).

Rabbi Yaacov Wasser

Young Israel of East Brunswick, New Jersey

SURVIVAL STRATEGIES IN *GALUT*

The *parshah* deals primarily with the sale of Yosef into slavery in Egypt, his trials and tribulations in the house of Potiphar, and his being thrown in jail for rejecting the advances of Potiphar's wife.

The story of Yosef's travails is the story of the Jews in *galut*. As the *Zohar* says; "Come and see that because of *HaShem*'s love for Israel, He draws them near and causes them to be hated by the nations of the world. . . . And come and see that because of the special love of Yaakov had for Yosef, 'And they conspired to kill him. . . .'" The root of anti-Semitism is the same as the source of the brothers' hatred of Yosef—the jealousy of the special relationship between father and son. (Parenthetically, it is important to explain that the jealousy of the brothers must be understood in light of their lofty level. It was not outright hatred, but, in the eyes of *Chazal*, their jealousy clouded their judgment, and they should not have acted as a *Bet Din* Jewish Court of Law to judge Yosef. They are called *Shivtei Koh* (the Tribes of God) even after this episode.)

Yosef's reaction to this plight guides our behavior in *galut*. Some of the lessons we learn from Yosef's reactions are:

1. Not to hide our identity; when Yosef came to the house of Potiphar he made no secret of the fact that he was Jewish. Potiphar's wife refers to him as a Hebrew (*ish ivri*, Gen. 39:14). For this, Yosef was rewarded and was buried in *Eretz Yisrael*. (The *midrash* contrasts Yosef with Moshe, who is referred to, in Yitro's house, as an Egyptian (*ish mitzri*, Exod. 2:19) and was *not* buried in *Eretz Yisrael*.)
2. To rely on our own internal strength and fear of God to protect us; as Yosef says, "I fear God" (Exod. 42:18)! This knowledge, rather than

direct confrontation, is our best weapon, as the *Gemara* in *Yevamot* relates in a tale about Rabbi Akiva: "Rabbi Gamliel said: I was once on a boat and I saw a shipwreck. I worried about Rabbi Akiva, who was aboard that shipwrecked ship. When we reached port, Rabbi Akiva came to discuss *halachah* with me. I asked how he survived. He responded that he had found a plank in the water and bowed his head as each wave approached." Our Rabbis derive from this the principle that "if evil people attack, one should lower his head."

There is a fascinating *Gemara* that relates how a sage was traveling on a boat that was stranded on an island. The shipwrecked travelers came ashore and made themselves comfortable. After a while, they started a fire, at which time they learned they were on a large fish. The fish rolled over and, if not for a boat that was nearby, they would have all drowned.

The story is a parable about our experience in *galut*. Time and time again we move from country to country. We make ourselves comfortable and rise to positions of power within the government and business sectors (as, for example, in Spain before the Inquisition and in Germany before the *Shoah*). We consider it our home. Eventually, our making it our home *itself* is a cause of irritation to the country, and we loose our haven. In the parable, the boat symbolizes the Torah. If not for our observance of Torah and *mitzvot*, we would be lost.

3. Adherence to our traditions. When Potiphar's wife tried to seduce Yosef, we are told, "And he refused" (*vayemaein*, Exod. 39:8). The musical cantilation *trup* on the word is a *shalshelet*, a long-drawn-out sound. Our Rabbis say that this indicates the intense internal struggle of Yosef to overcome Potiphar's wife's advances. What finally allowed Yosef to refuse was, according to *Chazal*, that he saw "the vision of his father [Yaakov]." He could not give in. What would his father say? When we are enticed by the lure of the "good life" in *galut*, we should bring to mind our glorious heritage and the *mesirat nefesh*—sacrifice of our ancestors to transmit *Yiddishkeit* to us.

Even when Yosef rises to power, he does not shed his *emunah* or his Jewish pride. As the *Bereishit Rabbah* tells us regarding the *pasuk*, "and slaughter [an ox] and prepare it (Genesis 43:1b) . . . prepare means for *Shabbat*." In this merit, Yosef was rewarded at the time of the dedication of the *Mishkan* (Tabernacle). The Prince of Ephraim brought his gifts on the Seventh Day—*Shabbat*.

We should also have the ability to learn from our experiences in exile. The Marharam M'Lublin, in his book, *Nitzutzei Ohr Hameir*, asks, "Yaakov said, 'I lived with Lavan,' and, as Rashi says, 'I kept all the *mitzvot* and did not learn from his wicked ways.' What was so great about the fact that Yaakov was not influenced by Lavan? Rather, Rashi says, he should have learned a lesson from Lavan's devotion to his *teraphim*, his idols, as to the extent of *mesirat nefesh* one should have for *HaShem*."

Yosef remembered this when he observed the behavior of Potiphar. The day Potiphar left Yosef alone in the house with his wife was a holiday devoted to their *avodah zarah*. His wife claimed she was ill and could not attend. Potiphar was so involved in his *avodah zarah* that he had not compunction about leaving his sick wife alone at home. Yosef learned from this and was able to withstand her advances.

Let us follow these tactics, which will allow us to survive in *galut*. Let us hope the duration will not be long, as we anxiously await the arrival of Mashiach, *Bimiheirah B'Yomeinu*. Amen.

Rabbi Pesach Lerner

Executive Vice President
National Council of Young Israel

> "And Reuven heard and he saved him [Yosef] from their hands. . . ." (*Bereishit, Vayeshev* 37: 21)
>
> "And Reuven said to them [his brothers], do not shed blood, throw him [Yosef] into this pit . . . in order to save him from their hands to return him to his father." (*Bereishit* 37:22)
>
> "The flowers gave off a fragrance, and at our doors are all types of choice fruits . . ." (*Shir Hashirim* 7:14)

The *midrash* (cited in *Divrei Agadah L'Chanukah* of the Chasam Sofer's commentary on the Torah) explains that the *pasuk* in *Shir Hashirim*, "The flowers gave off a fragrance," refers to Reuven, who saved Yosef from death, and that "and at our doors are all types of choice fruits" refers to the *mitzvah* of lighting lights on Chanukah—that the *mitzvah* is to light those lights at the entrance of one's house, visible to all passersby. What is the connection between Reuven's efforts to save his brother Yosef and the *mitzvah* of lighting lights on Chanukah?

We read from the Torah this *Shabbat* that, when the brothers saw Yosef coming in their direction, they conspired to kill him. Upon hearing this, Reuven reacted and attempted to save Yosef from all harm; he was unsuccessful. Reuven then attempted, at least, to prevent the brothers from killing Yosef; throw Yosef into the pit, said Reuven; the pit is very deep, and Yosef will not be able to escape. We will leave him in the wilderness, no one will hear his cries. The Torah then tells us that, although Reuven advised his brothers to cast Yosef into the pit, his true intentions were to return at a later time, rescue Yosef, and return him to their father, Yaakov.

The *mitzvah* of *hadlakat nerot*—lighting the lights—on Chanukah is unique among other *mitzvot* in that it has a special requirement of publicizing the miracle. This requirement of *Pirsumai Nisa* demands that even a poor person must borrow money and/or sell one of his possessions in order to fulfill the *mitzvah* of *hadlakot nerot* for Chanukah. This requirement also demands that the time for lighting the lights be at that time of the evening that will have maximum public exposure and, if one lights them too early or too late, he may not have fulfilled the *mitzvah*. And this requirement to publicize the miracle qualifies the location of the *menorah*—that it must be placed at a height from which the lights will be clearly visible and that the *menorah* should be placed on the outside, at the entrance of one's home.

We can now understand the *midrash* concerning "The flowers gave off a fragrance"—that it refers to Reuven, who saved Yosef from death. The fact that the Torah publicly acknowledged Reuven's noble intentions and actions in his attempt to save Yosef teaches us that it is proper to publicly acknowledge and record the good deeds and *mitzvot* of those who perform them.

And it then follows that we—mankind, and specifically the Jewish people—must publicly acknowledge the miracles that God performs on our behalf. "And at our doors are all types of choice fruits": This refers to the lighting of Chanukah lights—to be lit by all, at a specific time and place, on the outside of our front doors, so all can see and be thankful for God's special miracles "in those days at this time." (It is interesting to note that, based on the *pesukim* quoted above, that God acknowledged Reuven's good intentions, the Rashba states that it is most worthy to publicize the good deeds of individuals within the community.) In the *zechut*, merit, of the *mitzvah* of *nerot Chanukah* and our appropriate publicizing of the miracle, may we see God's continued miracles and experience true peace in Israel, the return of the Israeli soldiers missing in action, and the coming of *Mashiach* speedily in our days. Amen.

Rabbi Moshe S. Gorelik

Young Israel of North Bellmore, New York

The portrayal of the conflict between Joseph and his brothers evokes sad feelings. Yaakov is the tragic figure. His life was filled with conflicts. He fled from Esau and, at a later time, contended with the treacherous machinations of Laban, from whom he eventually attempted to escape. Even within his household, before the birth of Joseph, he suffered the tensions between Leah and Rachel. Yaakov, himself, also experienced inner conflicts. A study of the dreams and the subsequent struggle with an unknown figure in the darkness of the night will bear this out.

Following the series of conflicts, the death of Rachel, and the violation of Dinah, Yaakov desired a life of peace and contentment. Alas, this was not to be his destiny. *Shalom* continued to elude him. A conflict between Joseph and his brothers erupted. Yaakov's hope for a normalized life was shattered.

Yaakov was partially at fault for the disruption of the short-lived tranquility. Since Joseph was the favored son, the distance between him and his brothers widened. This relationship was exacerbated by the boundless ambitions of Joseph. The two dreams recorded in the *sedrah* reveal his drive and energy for expanded success and glory. Unfortunately, at that stage in his life, he failed to take cognizance of the feelings of others. Since dreams reflect inner thoughts and suppressed emotions, the brothers deduced from them that his ambitions included plans to dominate them. In their eyes, the coat of colors symbolized authority and, furthermore, his apparent boastfulness smacked of raw arrogance. Even Yaakov reprimanded Joseph for his tactless behavior. However, it was too late. The brothers reacted with hatred and envy. They were no longer able to relate to him.

The situation became untenable. They departed from the area. Since grazing grounds were available elsewhere, the brothers felt it would be better for them to sever ties rather than engage in constant confrontation. At this point, the *Chazal* add an intriguing insight about the brothers' behavior. Commenting on the *pasuk* "And they could not speak peacefully to him" (Gen. 37:4), they declared, "From what is stated to their discredit we may infer something to their credit. They did not speak one thing with their mouth, having another thing quite differently in their hearts."

The *Chazal* had mixed reactions. The brothers are applauded for their honesty. They did not mask their feelings. On the other hand, however, they are criticized. They refused to speak to Joseph. Though Joseph stirred up their emotions with his brashness and enormous ambitions, the brothers should have transcended their anger and envy and preserved the relationship by refusing to communicate with him. Unable to discipline their emotions and repair the fissures in the family relationship, they widened the chasm that lay between them. In the absence of communications, emotional hurts fester and painful rifts are irreparable. It is truly to their discredit that they copped out and fled from mature responsibility.

The brothers should have remained and made the attempt to repair the rupture or, at the very least, learned to coexist. By not governing their emotions of anger and envy, they almost committed murder. The sale of Joseph remained an embarrassment to Jewish history. This is attested to by the reference to this unforgivable act in the eulogy about the ten martyrs recited on Yom Kippur. The Romans said to the sages, "You are guilty for selling your brother into slavery. Did not the Torah declare that the penalty for this heinous crime is capital punishment?" That the brothers were unable to communicate with or relate to Joseph because their hatred was all-obsessive.

Communication is the vehicle for the establishment of harmony among people. Familial relationships are often destroyed because the sides are unwilling to communicate feelings in a rational and quiet manner, or are incapable of doing so. Irrationality overtakes the antagonists. The results are deleterious and stunt the well-being of families. "They were unable to speak" is a curse frequently afflicting the relationships of spouses, parents and children, siblings, relatives, and friends. The message of Joseph and his brothers is too often unheeded. The brothers are credited for their honesty but are discredited for failing to transcend their feelings of anger, hatred, and envy and to communicate with Joseph.

❖ CHAPTER 10 ❖

Miketz

Rabbi Gershon C. Gewirtz

Young Israel of Brookline, Massachusetts

FIRST IMPRESSIONS

> "There was a young Hebrew man with us, a slave of the captain of the guard." (Bereishit 41:12)

Rashi states, "Cursed be the wicked for their goodness is not complete. The butler mentions Yosef in a derogatory manner," implying that he is "a fool and not worthy of authority" and that "he is not even familiar with our language."

The *Machazon Elivah* is troubled by the apparent premise of the butler's presentation. Clearly, Yosef was not a fool; the butler had to anticipate Pharaoh's interest in meeting Yosef and his own inevitable exposure. Why should he lie so blatantly when he would be readily discovered?

The *Machazen Elivah* answers that, in reality, the butler never uttered an untruth at all. He simply reported that Yosef was a Hebrew slave—which was entirely accurate. His statement was nevertheless insidious, as it created the impression that Yosef was a fool; he was necessarily a fool because he was a slave.

It is well established that first impressions are lasting. In fact, it is almost impossible to dislodge any initial impression.

This lasting impact of an uncomplimentary remark emerges as the foundation of the Torah's displeasure with *lashon hara*—slander. In *Tehillim* 120:4, Dovid *Hamelech* (King David) writes, "The arrows of the mighty are sharpened with coals of *rotem* wood." The Sages explain that *rotem* coals burn for inordinately long periods. On this basis, the *midrash Sachar Tov* teaches that one should never presume to view *lashon hara* as something temporary or even as an expression that may be readily withdrawn. As the *midrash* elaborates, a sword may be returned to its scabbard without inflicting harm, but an arrow can never be recalled once it is released from the bow. *Lashon hara* takes on a life of its own, a life that often appears eternal.

Rabbi Doniel Frank

Young Israel of Westport/Norwalk, Connecticut

OF DREAMS, ADVERSITY, AND INTROSPECTION

At the outset of *Parshat Miketz*, Pharaoh has a disturbing dream and summons all the wise men of Egypt in search of its meaning. The Torah tells us that "there was no one who could provide an explanation to Pharaoh." Although it would appear from the verse that these sages were dumbfounded and silent, Rashi understands it differently: They were interpreting, but not to Pharaoh, because their voices did not enter his ears; he was not satisfied with the interpretations that they would tell him: "seven daughters you will have and seven you will bury." And so it was not until Pharaoh was introduced to Yosef and heard his version of the interpretation that he was satisfied.

1. What was unique about Yosef's interpretation that impressed Pharaoh to the extent that he, in effect, chose to degrade himself and his country by rejecting the wisdom of Egypt's elite for that of a "lowly" Jewish slave?
2. Furthermore, from Rashi it appears that several efforts were made by the wise men of Egypt to offer a plausible explanation. The selection of the words "that they would tell him," rather than, "that they told him" indicates that they continuously repeated the same message. If they saw that Pharaoh was not receptive to what they were saying, why did they not think of alternatives that might have pleased him?

For Pharaoh, the essential difference between the interpretations was how the dream would reflect on him and how it would force him to react. If the wise men were correct in suggesting that he was to suffer a personal misfortune, he might be compelled to recognize personal faults and search for ways to improve himself in an attempt to avert the tragedy. This was a responsibility he preferred to avoid. Accordingly, with his defenses up, Pharaoh favored Yosef's message. By indicating an impending national disaster, this interpretation afforded Pharaoh's conscience relief by enabling him to blame his people for bringing it upon themselves.

The wise men suffered from this weakness as well. Their insistence on understanding the dream as a personal message to Pharaoh indicated their own denial of guilt and shifting of responsibility. Only Yosef, with the help of God, was able to settle the standoff.

These same defenses are the major stumbling blocks for the fulfillment of the following Talmudic dictum:

> Rava, and some say Rav Chisdah, says: If a man sees that sufferings visit him, let him examine his conduct, for it is said, "Let us search and try our ways, and return unto God." If he examines and finds nothing negative, let him attribute it to the neglect of Torah study, for it is said, "Happy is the man whom You afflict, and teach out of Your Torah." If he did attribute it to this, and still did not find this to be the cause, let him be sure that these are sufferings of love, for it is said, "For whom God loves He corrects." (*Berakhot*, 5a)

When the Talmud encourages us to seek the roots of our troubles, it does so knowing full well that we are not prophets who can pinpoint the actual cause of any particular event. Rather, I believe the requirement is that, to the best of our abilities, we search out a weakness that we may reasonably assume as having been the cause. The virtue in this activity is that we react and change in response to the events that surround us, and acknowledge that they are arranged by God on the basis of our behavior as part of His elaborate system of reward and punishment. In short, we must accept responsibility for our actions. The Talmud continues that, should one engage in careful introspection and find no faults in himself, he should assume he was lax in Torah learning; and if, even in that area, he is sure he has been proficient, only then may he assume these are afflictions of love.

Logically, this Talmudic passage would apply to groups that experience misfortunes, as well as to individuals. In such a scenario, the group would have to engage in introspection and see what they might have done wrong as a whole to warrant such treatment. When we consider that God is the ultimate and perfect judge whose judgments incur no reckless damage, everyone who is affected must assume responsibility. Pharaoh's comfort in the words of Yosef is unjustified. He has no more right to fault others in a national event any more than if the event had been uniquely his, for the event affects him as well as others.

Rabbi Jacob Rubenstein

Young Israel of Scarsdale, New York

Parshat Miketz is a very interesting and mysterious portion. It contains the dream of a king and the interpretation of a Hebrew slave. The two are related because the dream needs an explanation, and the king needs the slave. But the world needs to hear the story. As it says in the *midrash*, "The dreams of a king belong to the entire world" (*Bereishit Rabbah* 9:4). It was more than Pharaoh's dream; it was a lesson to all humanity throughout history.

The *Parsha* begins with *vayehi miketz shenatayim yomim*—"And it was at the end of two years of days." The Hebrew is awkward. The passage speaks of *shenatayim*, the two years since Joseph was last heard of in the story, but the passage stresses *yomim*, days. Why days? A number of commentaries explain that Pharaoh's dream of famine was related to two particular cosmic days in the creation of the world: The third day of creation, when food and sustenance were created; and the sixth day, when the essence of the human spirit was created.

Pharaoh's dream of the seven healthy cows and ears of grain allude to the third day of creation, which deals with needs of the body, to the abundance of food and nurture, to the physical world; whereas the seven thin cows and grain refer to the sixth day of creation and the needs of the heart and soul to the spiritual world.

These two days and the two dreams also refer to the two festivals that came about as a result of a king's sleep and dream—the holidays of Purim and Chanukah, which were not commanded by *HaShem*, as were our other holidays, but happened because of a king and his relationship to the Jews.

The first day and first dream speak of the festival of Purim, which represents a challenge to the body, as this was when the physical welfare of the Jewish people was threatened. For this reason, the celebration of Purim is mostly physical, with festive meals, *shalach manot*, and *matanot lievyonim* (gifts to the poor). On the holiday of Purim, our happiness is expressed in the joy of, and with, the body to remind us of the physical challenge to our lives.

But there is the other day and dream. These refer to the holiday of Chanukah, which was really a war against the soul of the Jewish people and its spirit, when our faith was in danger and the Torah (our *tzurat haadam*) challenged. As in the dream, we—the few and the weak—overcame this threat because of our spirit and not because of our physical superiority. Our celebration of Chanukah is, therefore, more spiritual. The emphasis is on blessing the lights, on the prayers of *Hallel* and special Torah readings. It is a holiday in which we celebrate the spiritual life of the Jewish people through Torah, *mesorah*, and *mitzvot*.

Throughout our history we have known danger to our people's physical existence and our spiritual welfare. *Parshat Miketz* comes to teach us *vayehi miketz shenatayim yomim*. At the end of these two days—after the experience of these two events of Purim and Chanukah in our history—we should be able to understand the needs of our people, both of body and of soul.

Pharaoh and Joseph taught us of these two days in two dreams, with two challenges that famine can bring upon us. The Great Codifier, Rav Yosef Karo, in his *Derashot*, reminds us that each of our Patriarchs suffered famine. In time, their descendants would also suffer famine, and they would learn that famine of the spirit is far worse than the famine of the body. As the prophet Amos said, "Behold, God has said that days will come when I will send famine in the land. It will not be a famine of bread or water, but to hear the words of *HaShem*."

For this reason, the *haftarah* of Chanukah declares, "Not by might, and not by power, but by My spirit, said *HaShem*." Without the word of *HaShem*, and without His spirit to propel us, we cannot endure. This Joseph taught to Pharaoh, and this is what Chanukah teaches us even today.

The dream continues to unfold.

❖ CHAPTER 11 ❖

Vayigash

Rabbi Eli Stern

Young Israel of Dayton, Ohio

YOSEF'S REBUKE

> "I am Yosef; is my father still alive?" (Gen. 45:3) The Torah describes Yosef's brothers as being terribly frightened when they heard these words. The *midrash* takes this a step further, informing us that this, the rebuke of Yosef to his brothers, is, in microcosm, the paradigm of the rebuke we will encounter, *chas vesholom,* when we face *HaShem* after leaving this world; *Oi Lanu Miyom Hadin Oi lanu Miyom HaTochacha*—woe to us from the day of judgement woe to us from the day of rebuke.

Besides endeavoring to understand why this was such an awesome rebuke, we need to answer several basic questions. Yehudah had just mentioned to Yosef that Yaakov would experience terrible grief if Binyamin were to be left behind in an Egyptian prison. Obviously, Yaakov was still alive! Furthermore, the brothers had explicitly assured Yosef just before this (Gen. 43:28) that Yaakov was still alive. And why did Yosef stress *avi—my* father—and not *avinu—our* father—if he truly wished to reconcile himself with his brothers?

In order for this reconciliation to take place, Yosef's brothers had to recognize the full depth of their transgression. They forcibly separated Yosef from his father—*avi*—at this most crucial stage in the spiritual interaction of father and son. All the Torah that Yosef could have learned from Yaakov during this unique period of time—ages 17 to 39—had been lost forever.

Moreover, Yosef exposed the hypocrisy of his brothers. The *Beis Halevi* explains that Yosef removed the veneer of righteousness that the brothers hid behind. They expressed such great concern over their father's fate (both now and when they came down the first time) if he would be bereft of Binyamin. What a sham! If they really cared about their father, how could they have forcibly separated him from Yosef all these years (after deciding not to kill Yosef), deceiving their father with the story of Yosef's "death"? For twenty-two years, Yaakov had been haunted by Yosef's absence; yet they piously proclaimed that they couldn't leave Binyamin behind for fear of upsetting their father!

This *midrash* on rebuke extrapolates this to our everyday lives. Do our actions later in life belie the excuses that we gave for not keeping the Torah earlier? We had no money for *tzedakah*, but perhaps later we were profligate in spending for luxuries.

Furthermore, the brothers' rationale for selling Yosef was that they *paskened*—decided as a court of law—that he was a *rodef*—a potential murderer. They were afraid that he was duping his father into rejecting his brothers and accepting Yosef as his only rightful spiritual heir (similar to Esav's deception of Yitzchak). Again, if they really cared about their father's spiritual welfare, how could they have been so callous? *Hasgacha Protis*—Divine Providence—now clearly showed them that they had been mistaken all along about Yosef. And thus their "concern" for their father that incited this whole tragedy was revealed retroactively to be insincere.

This is why Yosef chose his language so deliberately; for their *teshuvah*—repentance—to be complete, they had truly to comprehend what this unbelievable *hashgachah*—Divine Providence—was telling them. In our own lives, we need to keep an open eye as to what *HaShem*'s *hashgachah* is telling us about the assumptions we have made in our lives and paths we have followed on the basis of these assumptions. This intellectual honesty will help us re-evaluate our paths to see if they are truly leading to valid goals.

THE SYMBOLISM OF *MILAH*

"Come near me, please." (Gen. 45:4)

In the very next verse, Yosef attempted to reassure his brothers by showing them that he was circumcised (Rashi, quoting the *midrash*). Thus, they would be sure it was Yosef. But this was precisely what they were frightened of—that he *was* Yosef!

The *Maharal* (*Tiferes Yisroel* chapter 6) explains that *bris milah* represents the power of rising above nature—*mimaalah min hatevah*. We are created with an *orlah* only to find ourselves commanded to remove it on the eighth day of our lives. Eight represents rising above nature (seven days makes one week) just as man rises above his animalistic nature when he sanctifies his reproductive organ. Man is enjoined to perfect himself spiritually by rising above the hedonistic temptations of life.

Yosef's natural tendency would have been to exact revenge on his brothers for what they had done to him. He reassured them by pointing to his *milah;* he had dedicated himself as a Jew rising above the natural inclinations of life, and thus he could never harm them.

On a deeper level, Yosef pointed out to them that the *hashgachah* at work here was above nature. It is rare indeed in the pre-Messianic era that one sees the curtain rise, revealing the secrets of the vicissitudes of Jewish history, demonstrating how every event was designed by *HaShem* for our ultimate benefit. All the evil turned out to be a facilitator for good. The ability to snatch such a perspective on the secret workings of *HaShem* is above *tevah*—nature. *HaShem* created this world with the name *Elohim* (Gen. 1:1), which equals the *gematriah* of *hatevah* (to do good) (86). It is only in the messianic era that we will be granted this insight into the inner workings of *HaShem*.

Here Yosef showed them that all the evil that had befallen them since they first came down to Egypt to buy food was in reality good, since it effected a reconciliation with Yosef (through their newfound willingness to do *teshuvah*). In fact, the whole tragedy of the initial conflict of Yosef and his brothers (which culminated in his being sold) was now revealed, in one fell swoop, to be good, saving the family from starvation. Ultimately, this whole episode was a necessary fulfillment of *HaShem*'s promise to Avrohom (Gen. 15:13), which formed the basis of how we would merit to receive the Torah at Sinai. Thus the brothers were told, in effect, to rejoice at this rare, supernatural, glimpse into *HaShem*'s *Hasgachah Pratis*. And, certainly, now Yosef would not harm them when they had revealed that this was all part of *HaShem*'s master plan!

CHANUKAH AND GOSHEN

> "And [Yaakov] sent Yehudah before him to Yosef to show the way to Goshen." (Gen. 46:28)

Rashi tells us that Yehudah was sent ahead to establish a *yeshivah*, in Goshen, the ghetto where the Jews were to live. It is impossible for us to survive in *galut* without the ability to maintain our identity. We need to live apart from the Gentiles and to establish Torah learning (*yeshivot*) as the fulcrum of our society.

The *Bnei Yissachar* (a nineteenth-century *chasidic* master) takes a deeper look at the word *Goshnah* in light of the fact that this *parshah* always occurs around Chanukah. The letters of this word are identical to the letters of the *dreidel: gimel, shin, nun, heh*. They symbolically represent the four exiles that

Klal Yisrael underwent. *Gimel* is for *guf* (body)—the exile of Persia (hedonism). *Shin* (*sih*) is for *seichel* (mind)—the exile of Greece (Hellenistic thought). *Nun* is for *nefesh* (soul)—the exile of Babylonia (idolatry, affective emotions). *Heh* is for *hakol* (the amalgam of all three)—the exile of Rome.

Updating these concepts, Western (secular) humanism is the *seichel*; the Christian Church is the *nefesh*; Western materialism is the *guf*, and the totality of our tribulations of the past two thousand years can be summed up by *hakol*.

The antidote to all of these adversaries is *Goshnah*—Torah. This is what Yehudah foresaw when he set up the first *yeshivah*–in *galut*. But there's more. The *dreidel* spins on a tiny point, analogous to the letter *yud*. This refers both to *HaShem*'s name and to the *pintele yid*—the spiritual essence of the Jew within all of us. The nations of the world think they can "take us for a spin," but, in reality, *HaShem* is the One who is spinning them. In addition, He awakens the dormant Jewish soul to fight all these alien cultures, through the medium of *Goshnah*—Torah. Ultimately, the power of *Goshnah* will defeat all our spiritual enemies and will herald the coming of *Mashiach*, speedily in our days; amen. This is only fitting, since *Goshnah* and *Mashiach* both share the same *gematriah* of 458!

Rabbi Elias Schwartz

Young Israel of Bensonhurst/Bathbeach, New York

WHEREVER YOU ARE, BE A STEADFAST JEW

> "The brothers of Yosef came to Yaakov, their father, and exclaimed the good news: *Od Yosef chai,* Yosef is still alive, and he is the ruler of the entire land. Yaakov's heart stood still, for he did not believe them." (Gen. 45:26)

Yaakov did not believe them! Why not?

Yaakov had not seen Yosef for twenty-two years and had, perhaps, given up hope that he was still alive. He did not know what had happened to Yosef. His children had come back and told him that Yosef was still alive. Hurry up. Drink a *l'chaim*! Let's celebrate! Give a *kiddush*! Let us rejoice!

Yaakov did not believe them. He was still as despondent as before.

The next sentence is, "The brothers repeated all the words of Yosef's message, and Yaakov also saw the wagons, the *agalot*. Then the spirit of Yaakov, their father, became revived and uplifted" (45:27). He believed them.

The message of the wagons we can understand. When Yaakov told Yosef to go to Shechem to look for his brothers, Yaakov taught him the *dinim* of *egla arufa*. He taught him the following *din*: When somebody leaves you, you are supposed to walk with him out of the city for a little bit to fulfill the *mitzvah* of *levaya*. The wagons were a sign to his father that Yosef remembered his father's teaching. This we can readily understand.

What were "*all **the words** of Yosef*" that made such a difference that they revived Yaakov's spirit? Let us go back to the exact words that Yosef told his brothers in his message to his father. They were a little different from the original message to Yaakov. These are the exact words of Yosef: "This is what *your son* Yosef is telling you" (45:9).

The brothers left out the word *bincha,* your son. All they said was *od Yosef chai,* Yosef is still alive. The major difference here is that Yaakov was not interested only in the fact that Yosef was alive. Yaakov was not interested in the fact that Yosef was a ruler, that everyone knew him and acclaimed his greatness. Yaakov wanted to know if he was *still his son*. Is he still Yosef, the *tzaddik*, or did he become assimilated in Egypt? When they repeated *all* the words of Yosef, they carried a *clear* and *meaningful* message: "I am still your son. No matter where I was, even though I was all alone in *Mitzrayim* (Egypt), I did not change."

What does the word *bincha* mean? It means that he was still Yaakov's son; he did not become assimilated; he did not lose his *Yiddishkeit* even though he was alone in a foreign country.

Yosef also said: "*God made me* a ruler."

The full message was: Tell my father that Yosef is *still his son* and that it was the *hashgochoh pratis* of *HaShem*; this was God's way of personally watching over him.

"*God made* me a ruler in Egypt."

"Nothing happened by chance. In Egypt my dreams came true." Then Yaakov believed his sons, and he became revived and happy again.

A Jew must speak about *Klal Yisroel* in the same way Yosef *Hatzaddik* speaks. "Do not worry! What *HaShem* demanded of me, I did."

Yosef's message was beautiful: "I know that the entire world belongs to *HaShem*. I know that I was sent to *Mitzrayim* by *HaShem*. God watched over me. He made my dreams of 'being a ruler' come true. God took care of me all the years that I was in Egypt. I am *still* your son. I did not change."

This is what every person must understand.

No matter where one is living, no matter what one does in life, one can be, and should be, a God-fearing Jew. An individual must know that *HaShem* is watching over him his entire life.

If you live in a neighborhood where you are the only Jew, you cannot and must not say, "If I lived in Brooklyn NY, I would be a better and more observant Jew." Yosef was the only Jew in Egypt and remained *bincha*, a son of Yaakov.

I once spoke to a class in a *yeshivah* about their future hopes. The answers varied considerably. Some said that they wanted to be a *rebbe* in a *yeshivah*, a *rosh yeshivah*, or a rabbi in a community. Some chose to be professionals: a doctor, a lawyer, an engineer, or an architect. I do not care what their choice in life will be, but I do want each student to be a *talmid chochom first*, a *yorei shamayim*, a practicing Jew, doing and fulfilling all the *mitzvot*, and a *baal middot*, displaying a beautiful character in trying to help their fellow man.

First be a *talmid chochom*, then a doctor. First be a *talmid chochom*, then a lawyer. First be a *talmid chochom*, then a professional.

Realize that *HaShem* is always with you and watching over you. Remain true to *HaShem* and to all Israel.

Rabbi Yitzchak M. Goodman

Young Israel of Far Rockaway, New York

WHAT WAS YOSEF'S COMPLETE ORIGINAL PLAN?

"And Yosef could no longer control himself. . . ." (Gen. 45:1). This opening phrase implies that Yosef's original intention was not to reveal himself at this point, but that he lost control. Isn't this illogical? After all, haven't the brothers now passed all his tests and shown a complete *teshuvah*? What would Yosef have had in mind by remaining disguised further?

Rav Yosef Salant (*Be'er Yosef*) offers this analysis: As explained by Ramban, all Yosef's actions with his brothers since their first meeting in Egypt were directed toward one goal: the fulfillment of the dreams. Yosef understood that he was shown these dreams by God in order that he, Yosef, might arrange their implementation. Otherwise, there was no reason he had to know his life's story in advance! This is why he schemed to force his brothers to bring Binyamin down to Egypt to bow before him, since the dream specified eleven stars. But there remained the sun—his father, Yaakov. How could he expect his own father to bow before him? Apparently, this meant that Yaakov would bow to him not knowing his identity. Therefore, Yosef presumed that he must now hold Binyamin captive and tell the brothers that they could attain his release if they brought their father down to Egypt to plead for him! For this reason, he tried to control himself even now. He did not succeed only because Yehudah frightened him with the thought that the moment Yaakov did not see Binyamin with them, he would die! At this point, Yosef finally revealed himself and left it to God to contrive how the "sun" would bow to him. Rav Salant feels that it took place when they met (46:29), although not mentioned there specifically. He theorizes that Yaakov did not immediately recognize Yosef in his royal dress and bowed before the man he thought was an Egyptian officer sent to accompany him. The crying of Yosef in that verse would represent Yosef's sorrow that he was somehow responsible for Yaakov's bowing to him. (This analysis of the events recorded in *Vayeshev* my be unnecessary, however, since the Torah describes Yaakov bowing to Yosef in 48:31!)

THE REBUKE OF HUMANS/THE REBUKE OF GOD

> "And Yosef said to his brothers, 'I am Yosef; is my father still alive [*Haod avi chai*]?' And his brothers could not answer him, for they were startled before him" (Gen. 45:3).

The Talmud (*Chagigah*, 4) remarks: "Rabbi Elazar would break out crying over this verse" when he contemplated that, if this is the reaction to a reproof of a human, how much more frightening will be the reproof of *HaShem*. A similar comment is found in *Midrash Rabbah*, here (93:10) by Rav Abba Bardela: "Woe unto us on the day of judgment . . . when God will reprove each one according to what he is [*L'fi mah shehu*]." In an elaborate analysis of Rav Abba Bardela's statement, the precise text of his remark, "Woe unto us on the day of judgment [*miyom hadin*], woe unto us on the day of rebuke [*miyom hatochachah*]" is examined. The "Alter of Slobodka" asked, Doesn't the rebuke precede the actual judgement? Shouldn't these phrases be in reverse order?

The betrayal of Yosef is not what it seems to be on the surface. Just as deep halachic matters are reviewed briefly in the Torah but expanded immensely in the Talmud, so, too, the *aggadic* parts of Torah often hide much deeper ideas. When the brothers saw the special love and attention that Yaakov showered upon Yosef, they concluded that Yaakov was preparing to choose him as the exclusive heir of his great spiritual legacy and that they would be sent forth into the world like Yishmael and Esav before them. This would be Yaakov's revenge for having been fooled into his marriage with Leah (Sforno follows this approach too). Hence, they justified their action as a matter of self-defense. This is the meaning of the *midrash* quoted in Rashi on the verse "let us go to Dosan [*nail'cha Dosaenah*]" (Gen. 37:17): "to seek plots [*nichlei*] of legality [*dasos*]"—that is, they considered their plan legally justified.

(On the other hand, Yosef's tattling to this father about his brothers (Gen. 37:2), and his recital of his dreams to them, are understood by many *meforshim* on a higher level as well. His reports to Yaakov were meant so that Yaakov could teach them and improve them in their moral shortcomings. His recital of the dreams was meant to inform them of his obvious destiny and to let them know that they might as well recognize the fact. Nowhere is there any hint in the text that Yosef did not love his brothers.)

Therefore, we may conclude that the most serious aspect of their deed was that they did not take Yaakov into account in their plans. Once Yosef was disposed of, they caused their father deep anguish for twenty-two years. Had they fully considered this aspect, they could not have carried out their plan. However, the act itself, removed from this consideration, was in their eyes legally justified.

They themselves had declared that they deserved to remain as slaves in Egypt. Now, Yehudah faces Yosef and appeals to him to go beyond the law and consider mercy for the sake of a suffering father. This appeal to consider other ramifications so as to bend the law gives Yosef the perfect opportunity to point out how vile their action had been—and on the same basis, the effect on Yaakov. "I am Yosef—[is] my father still alive?" becomes one phrase that implies, "Did you consider our father in your treatment of me? Why didn't you do 'beyond the law' then, for his sake?" What do they now realize? That, in fact, it was more than "pure legality" that led them to their deed; there was an additional element of jealousy and hatred that blinded them to the ultimate truth and the proper way of dealing with their problems. Subjectivity distorts "law" and leads people with powerful emotions to deal falsely, and lawlessly. Thus, the brothers were stunned into shamed silence, until Yosef spoke again with forgiveness and love.

So, too, when we appear at the Throne of Glory for our accounting, all the smug justifications we give ourselves in this world, as we squander precious moments and opportunities for *mitzvot,* will be exploded in our faces. For this reason, the "day of judgment" precedes the "day of rebuke." Once we recognize the proper, objective judgments we should have made, and how we duped ourselves, only then will we understand how deserved is the rebuke we will receive.

Rav Dovid Buonich *hy"d,* as quoted in the book *Gevilei Eish* explained the thought of the Alter of Slobodka and I have expanded on Rav Budnich's explanation. Rav Budnich was a *Talmid* of the Alter, founded numerous *yeshivot* in Latvia and taught much Torah until he and his *talmidim* were murdered by the Nazis *ym"s.*

❖ CHAPTER 12 ❖

Vayechi

Rabbi Eli Stern

Young Israel of Dayton, Ohio

At the end of today's *parshah,* Yosef gives a very enigmatic response to his brothers when they fearfully express their contrition to him now that their father, Yaakov, has passed away. They feel their very lives are hanging in the balance now that Yosef is free to exact revenge. Yosef's response, "Am I in *Elohim*'s stead?" (Gen. 50:19), is found in one other place in the *Chumash.* In *Parshat Vayetzei,* Rochel confronts Yaakov over her barren state: "Give me children" (Gen. 30:1), for, if not, she says, it is as if she is dead. Here, too, we see the same puzzling response (this time by Yaakov), "Am I in the place of *Elohim?*"

In effect, these two responses frame our impotence vis-à-vis the two poles of life, birth and death. Only an inscrutable *Elohim* (the *Midat Hadin* of God) can determine why and when someone enters and leaves this world; it is presumptuous for us to even claim to fathom His logical imperatives.

(In fact, Rav Samson Raphael Hirsch points out an interesting contrast between the first *mitzvah* given to all mankind—"Be fruitful and multiply"—and the first *mitzvah* given to *Klal Yisrael*—sanctifying the new Moon. The former points out the frailty of man; the latter is indicative of the spiritual greatness invested in the Jewish people. No matter how hard a person may try to have children, the ultimate success rests with *HaShem*. Yet, when it comes to proclaiming Rosh Chodesh, the new moon, *Chazal* tell us that even if the *sanhedrin* erred in certifying the testimony of the witnesses, their decision created a new reality of Rosh Chodesh. The days of *Yom Tov* would thus be adjusted accordingly, with the concomitant emanations of *HaShem*'s *ruchaniyut* [even a woman's monthly menstrual cycle would then be "compelled" to adjust to this new reality].)

Our *Avot* (patriarchs) are telling us that the awareness of our futility in these areas has a tremendously liberating effect on ourselves and those around us, and not just in regard to the "blame game" we play in reference to failure in these two areas as the ends of life or our insecurity in the face of death.

Our society today is fixated on man's arrogation to himself of the right to begin and end life whenever he so pleases. Along with the "right" to abort fetuses and the "right to die with dignity" (read "suicide") comes a new, frightening terminology of "quality of life" and "wrongful birth lawsuits" ("If only we had known that this child would be born 'handicapped' in some way, we certainly would have aborted it").

It is interesting to note that it was a handicapped (deaf) grandson of Yaakov—Chushim ben Dan—who played a heroic role in today's *parshah* (according to the *midrash*) in killing Esav, thereby facilitating Yaakov's burial in the *Meorat Hamachpeilah*. And, at the other end of life, *Chazal* tell us that Yaakov is the first person to be *mitpallel* for illness at the sunset of his life ("Your father is sick," Gen. 48:1). He wants to take advantage of the final throes of life to enable him to gain a deeper perspective of his life and to contemplate *teshuvah* for anything that his twenty-twenty hindsight might detect.

If, in fact, man cannot pretend to master birth and death, where then should his effort reside? Rav Hirsch explains elsewhere that it is precisely the areas of life in which we claim impotence—our exercising of moral autonomy, the ability to control our hedonistic passions and transcend our nature and "orientation"—to which man should be devoting the sum of his energies. All the emotions, behaviors, and desires that society likes to claim are inborn or inevitably absorbed from the surrounding milieu are fair game for overcoming through our moral power.

Thus, Yosef takes credit for only one thing in his life: "Only *Elohim* do I fear" (Gen. 42:18). *Yirat Shamayim* (fear of Heaven) is that critical ingredient that enables us to reach this level of self-control. Yosef exemplifies this many times in his life (for example, the episode with Potiphar's wife) but no more so than in today's *parshah*. Yosef, the omnipotent viceroy, could easily have exacted revenge from his brothers for their conspiracy against him—but he refrains, out of his perfected *middot*, in accordance to the verse that we quoted at the outset.

But Yosef now takes this one step further. *HaShem* does not only control life and death; His *hashgachah* extends ultimately to all the events of our life. "All is in the hands of *HaShem* except the fear of *HaShem*" (that is, moral autonomy; *Berakhot* 33b). In the very next *pasuk* (Gen. 50:20), Yosef tells his brothers that all the hatred and pernicious *middot* cannot succeed unless *HaShem* so decrees. "So why bother trying your machinations or mine—it's all mission impossible!"

This is an even greater message of liberation than ceding birth and death to *HaShem*. Now Yosef is giving us the key to mastering control over our *middot*—all our schemes to get ahead by harming others are doomed to failure anyway! All his brothers' efforts to destroy him actually facilitated the fulfillment of his dreams, rather than thwarting them as they had intended. In *HaShem*'s grand scheme of history, *Klal Yisrael* would have to spend 210 years in Egypt (in accordance with the prophecy given to Avraham *Avinu*) and nothing could change that. Certainly, Yosef could not expect any more success by plotting revenge against the brothers if *HaShem* didn't will it. So why bother having the jealousy or the bitterness and anger in the first place if I can't act upon it? It is this liberating realization that a Jew lives with when he truly and viscerally internalizes the far-reaching *hashgachah* of *HaShem* in every aspect of his/her life.

Yaakov *Avinu* refers to the land of the Emori (Esav) that he conquered "with my sword and my bow" (Gen. 48:22). Rashi tells us these two weapons are, in fact, wisdom and prayer. The true strength of the Jew is that which his mouth—the *Kol Yaakov* that Yitzchak alluded to—achieves through Torah learning and *davening* to *HaShem*.

It is interesting to note that, in every place in the Torah in which the Jewish people conquer their enemies with the sword, the Torah uses the phrase *lefi cherev* ("at the 'mouth' of the sword"). This is an allusion to these two powers mentioned above. Our victory is attained because of our spiritual prowess, not our military skills.

There is only once place in the Torah where our victory is described as *becherev—with* the sword—not at the mouth of the sword. That is in *Parshat Matot*, when the Torah describes our killing of Bilaam (*Bamidbar* 31:8). Rashi there explains that it was precisely Bilaam—who came against us with our own weapons (the mouth of prophecy and prayer)—who has to be killed *b'davka* (specifically) with our sword. All our other enemies come against us with the sword, and our riposte is with our mouth.

Similarly, Yaakov denounces Shimon and Levi in today's *parshah* (Gen. 49:5) for using weapons of violence, weapons of war, which Rashi says are appropriated from Esav and are thus a "stolen" skill. We see that they eventually used this trait of violence not just against Shechem but against Yosef *Hatzaddik* as well.

Finally, *Chazal* tell us that the one letter of the alphabet that is missing from Yaakov's blessing to Yehudah is the *zayin*. The word *zayin* means "weapons" or "arms." *Mashiach* will be a descendant of Yehudah and, through his spiritual charisma—his mouth of Torah and *tefillah*, the world will be transformed from a place of violence to a place of peace. Thus the *zayin* has no place in his blessing.

It is unfortunate today that, because of our collective spiritual lacking (the weaknesses of our mouth—our Torah and *tefillah*), we have been forced to resort to Esav's weapon to defend ourselves. We should never forget that, ultimately, this is not our true strength, nor is military prowess the garland we wish the world to bestow upon us.

Let us be *mitpallel* that the day shall come that the *peh* of Yaakov's descendants once again defeats the *cherev* of Esav's offspring, heralding the coming of the *Mashiach*, speedily in our days. Amen.

Rabbi Chananya M. Berzon

Young Israel of Chomedey,
Quebec, Canada

SIBLING RIVALRY

Let me please pose a question to you: Is it fair for a parent to love one child more than the other? Can I assume that I would hear a resounding response of "Absolutely no"? And, yet, there are times that I have a suspicion that the opposite is true; that some parents do really care, love, and take pride in one child more than his/her siblings. Although they might express themselves in terms of all their children being equal, we can observe favoritism in their treatment. Is this justified? Doesn't this encourage hatred and jealousy among siblings? If it does, then that in itself should be a warning that special treatment of one child is unhealthy. What does our tradition say about this sensitive subject? Can we receive direction and insight from the Torah and the Rabbis?

Throughout the Torah, there are episodes of sibling rivalry. As soon as Adam and Eve are cast out of the Garden of Eden, we are told of the conflict between Cain and Abel. Once the Torah begins to relate the tales of our Fathers, we read of Isaac and Ishmael and then of Jacob and Esau. Finally, we read of Jacob's preference toward Joseph, the jealousy of his brothers, and then of his kidnaping and being sold into slavery in Egypt.

At this juncture, one would assume Jacob had finally comprehended that a partiality to one son is not a fitting method of treating siblings. It fosters enmity and, eventually, trouble. Yet, once again, Jacob, in his twilight years, shows an overt preference for one brother above another. Evidently, he is well aware of the possible danger; yet he does not hesitate to favor one child above another, even in the blessings, which clearly was considered by our forebears as the ultimate as a gift and legacy.

Although Menasheh is older that Efraim, Jacob, the grandfather, mentions Efraim before Menasheh. "Efraim and Menasheh should be unto me as Reuven and Shimon." Then, once again, he blesses Zevulun before Issachar, although Issachar was the elder. Why? What prodigious message did our father, Jacob, intend to relay to his children and to all of Jewry throughout the oncoming years? Why was he willing once again to risk a conflict between brothers?

An answer to these questions is found in the NeTZiV's commentary on the Torah. He actually conveys his message twice in the *parshah* of *Vayechi*. The gist of his explanation is as follows:

Efraim and Menasheh were special grandchildren to Jacob. Each had a unique character trait. Efraim symbolized Torah study and scholarship, whereas Menasheh became a national and communal leader. One would have considered that *Derech eretz kodma laTorah* and, thus, Menasheh would precede Efraim. However, Jacob insisted on giving preference to Efraim. Why? Because Menasheh's leadership, as important as it was, was not the cause of Efraim's Torah. *Derech eretz,* which enhances Torah, which encourages and sustains Jewish scholarship, is of great value but pure Torah learning is greater.

When Jacob blesses Zevulun and Isaachar, he behaves differently. Zevulun was the prosperous businessman, and Isaachar, the Torah scholar. Why here did Jacob actuate the Torah adage *Derech eretz kodma laTorah*? Clearly, Zevulun used his earthly affluence to support Torah. He was the one who directly enabled Issachar to consecrate his entire day and night to the study and pursuit of Torah. Therefore, Jacob, the simple person, dweller of tents, *ish tam yoshev ohalim,* gave priority to the Torah supporter, his son Zevulun.

This message was clear to Jacob's children. They understood it well. There was no room for misinterpretation. A father, at times, has to exhibit partiality to one child above the others. Everyone, including all the siblings, appreciates the message. Joseph's brothers, however, did not understand why Jacob displayed a favoritism to Joseph. They speculated that it was a continuation of his singular love for Rochel above Leah, Bilhah, and Zilpah. Therefore, they were jealous of Joseph and responded the way they did.

However, the treatment of Zevulun above Isaachar and Efraim above Menasheh did not evoke any dissension. Its message was clearly understood by all. It was respected, and it impelled the tribes of Israel to work in unity, to strive together, and to respect *Torah im derech eretz.*

Jacob, as a father and a grandfather, understood that which we all intuitively know: Jealousy amongst siblings is not healthy. At times, however, when the preferential treatment is obviously warranted—nay, demanded—when the message is clear and objective, there is no other choice. We must communicate to the other siblings, loudly and clearly, that there are priorities within the life of a Jew. There is nothing inherently wrong with their proficiency, nor with their father's ability to demonstrate love and appreciation to all his children. The message is not to be jealous of your brother. Endeavor to reach the heights toward which he is striving, as the top of the mountain can be shared by many. All will receive their just reward. Siblings may excel in diverse spheres, but as long as they work together, as long as they share and have mutual respect, rivalry will be a moot issue.

Rabbi Zvi Teichman

Young Israel of Los Angeles, California

Yaakov *Avinu* prepares for his imminent departure from this world by bestowing his unique blessings upon the *shevatim*, the Twelve Tribes. The first to be summoned are Menasheh and Efraim. As they appear before Yaakov, a strange discussion ensues. Yaakov, surprisingly, asks, "Who are these?" This is a strange inquiry, since Yaakov was evidently already acquainted with them! Rashi explains that Yaakov was not questioning their identity but, rather, their worthiness for a *brachah*. Rashi quotes the *midrash* that states that the *Shechinah* departed from Yaakov when it was prophetically revealed to him that the wicked Achav and Yeravam would descend from Efraim and Yehu and his sons, from Menasheh. Yaakov was, therefore, reluctant to bestow his blessing upon such progeny. Yosef's respone to this, Rashi further explains, was the displaying before his father of his marriage documents and exclaiming, "These are my children that *HaShem* gave me with *this*"—"this" referring to the marriage documents. Upon hearing Yosef's answer, Yaakov agreed and proceeded to bless the children. The question remains: What relevance did the marriage documents of Yosef have in prevailing on his father's reluctance to bless them because of their unworthy descendants? In what way did the documents placate the concerns of Yaakov?

Dialogues recorded in the Torah are not merely historical records. Our sages have taught us that these discussions and disputes are virtual *machloket haposkim*—disputes based on each one's understanding of the principles of the Torah. That being the case, what then was the *shakla vatariya*, the "give and take," between Yaakov and Yosef?

An almost identical dialogue is recorded in *Mesechtos Brachos, Daf* 10, that can help shed light on our dilemma. The *Gemara* tells of Chezkiyah the King, who suddenly took ill, and how the Prophet Yeshaiah was dispatched to tell the king that he would not survive his illness. Chezkiyah then inquired concerning the reason and was told by the Prophet that he was being punished for not having fulfilled the *mitzvah* of *p'ru ur'vu*, begetting children, for Chezkiyah was yet a bachelor at that time. Chezkiyah proceeded to rationalize his behavior by telling the Prophet that, since he knew prophetically that he would have a wicked son, Menasheh, he had therefore refrained from performing this particular *mitzvah*. The Prophet Yeshaiah then reproached the King with the now famous line, "In the secret ways of *HaShem*, what is your interest? What you have been commanded to do is what you must do."

Chezkiyah wanted to refrain from fulfilling his Divine obligation, just as Yaakov wanted to refrain from fulfilling his fatherly duty. They were both reluctant to beget or bless unworthy descendants. But the Prophet taught an important principle of Torah: we must do *mitzvot* without questioning or second-guessing the intentions of *HaShem*, and we must leave the "secrets" of the world to Him. It is not our right to compromise the commandments of *HaShem*.

This was the response of Yosef as well. By showing that he had complied with the traditions of the *Avot*, the Patriarchs, Yosef was stating that he had done what was commanded of him. With his marriage documents in hand, Yosef was exclaiming, in other words, "In the secret ways of *HaShem*, what is your interest?" Upon hearing this, Yaakov acceded to fulfill his parental obligation to bless Menasheh and Efraim, their unworthy descendants notwithstanding, ignoring the "secret ways of *HaShem*."

The book of *Bereishit* appropriately concludes with this legacy of Yosef. It was Adam who was the first to rationalize and second-guess the directive of *HaShem* when he observed "that the tree was good to eat and desirable to the eyes" (Gen. 3:6). Surely, Adam thought, *HaShem* couldn't possibly have meant to prohibit so enticing and delicious a fruit. The rest is history; man stumbling over his rationalizations and excuses, time and time again. Yosef *Hatzaddik*, on the other hand, is portrayed as the master of discipline, one who taught the world uncompromising adherence to the words of *HaShem*. As a young interpreter of dreams, Yosef declares, "It is not by my own power," refusing to claim any credit for his talents despite the obvious benefit and resultant fame such a claim would have brought him. So, too, Yosef refused to submit to the enticement of the wife of Potiphar, despite the dire consequences that awaited him. Surely, Yosef could have excused and rationalized his behavior had he submitted to temptation. Yet Yosef remains the paradigm of unswerving dedication to principle, a truly fitting contrast to the sin of Adam.

May we be granted the strength to maintain the legacy of Yosef *Hatzaddik*, to fulfill our responsibilities without seeking excuses and to leave the "secrets" of the world to *HaShem*.

Chazak Chazak Venitchazek!

PART TWO

❖

Exodus

❖ CHAPTER 13 ❖

Shemot

Rabbi Herbert W. Bomzer

Young Israel of Ocean Parkway, New York

> "And she called his name Moses; because she said: I have drawn him from the water" *(*Exodus 2:10*)*.

A student once asked me why the name of the redeemer of Israel, given by the Egyptian princess, was made eternal by the Torah and retained, as we learn, according to the *Midrash Rabbah* (Leviticus 1:3), "God said to Moses: of all the names that you were called by, I will call you only by the name given you by Batya, daughter of Pharaoh; 'and she called him Moses'."

Indeed, his mother, Yocheved, had bestowed many names upon Moses at his birth, according to *Talmud Bavli Sotah* 12a. Rabbi Meir said she called him Tov; Rabbi Judah said she called him Tuvia. The *Midrash Rabbah* (Leviticus, ibid.) states that he was given ten names. Yet only the name chosen by Batya was connected to him. Why?

Furthermore, since Moses was drawn from the waters, he should have been known as one who was drawn out (*Mashui*) (see Ibn Ezra, ibid., and see also *Midrash Hagadol*, quoted by *Torah Shelemah*, vol. 8, p. 69).

The first question is answered by the *Midrash Rabbah Shemot* 1:31:

> From here you [may] learn the reward of those who perform deeds of loving kindness. An eternal tribute is paid Batya and she is remembered whenever the name Moshe is pronounced. Our gratitude for her goodness which caused her to violate her father's decree that every male child shall be cast into the river is unending.

But Batya called him Moshe and not Mashui because, in addition to compassion, Batya also indicated by the name she chose that she was a wise person (see *Torah Shelemah*, vol. 8, p. 62) as well as a truly righteous person. She chose his name to project a goal for his future personality development.

"Mashui" would have forever reminded Moses that he was a recipient of someone else's charity. The name "Moshe" set the tone for his life by implying that he must draw others out of trouble. Sforno comments (on Exodus 2:10), "He would save and pull others out of afflictions." The *Torah Shelemah* (ibid.) also quotes the *Midrash Hagadol* with this view. The rest of Moshe's life would be devoted to helping others. The *parshah* gives us illustrations of his personality—manifestations reflecting Moshe, the one who draws others out.

Moshe defends his fellow Jew against an oppressing Egyptian; he intervenes when Jews fight; he protects the daughters of Yitro; he is merciful to a little lamb; he is chosen to be the shepherd of Israel and for a lifetime of service and love.

Moshe Rabbeinu teaches us, even today, two invaluable lessons. The first is that the reward for doing good is inestimable and eternal. The second is that one's life should be spent giving and not only receiving, in saving others even as we are saved. Both points are illustrated by a short anecdote that tells of a little boy who was saved from drowning by a stranger. "How can I thank you, sir?" asked the youngster. "Just be sure to make you life worth having been saved," answered the man.

Kant wrote, "beneficence is a duty; and he who frequently practices it and sees his benevolent intentions realized at length, comes to love him to whom he has done good."

"His daily prayer, far better understood in acts than in words, was simply doing good," said Whittier.

"Real goodness does not attach itself merely to this life—it points to another world," concurred Daniel Webster.

An old legend tells of the soul that was escorted by the angel and shown both Paradise and Hell. In both places he could see a festive table set with delicacies and men and women seated on both sides. The angel indicated that the souls could not bend their elbows. "What is the difference between the two places?" asked the soul. "The difference is that in Hell none could enjoy the feast because they could not put the food in their mouths, since their elbows were stiff. But in Paradise the souls were reaching with their outstretched arms and feeding the souls facing them across the table," said the angel.

Certainly, generosity, in terms of giving charity, is central in Jewish responsibility. Social awareness is mandated by the commandment to support the underprivileged, the handicapped, the poor. The commitment to share our possessions graciously and sympathetically is a basic, sanctified tradition. But this is not only a Jewish trait. When Aristotle was censured for giving alms to a bad man, he said, "I did not give it to the man; I gave it to humanity."

The unique view of Judaism transcends the obligation to give only because we are our brothers' keeper; and only in his hour of need. In Judaism we are always referred to as brothers (Leviticus 25:26, 35, 39, 47). The crowning climax of the *mitzvah* "to give" is expressed in gentle and warm words even to a stranger, in a smile and in the offering of a kind word of thanks or congratulations. There is a well-known story of a poor man who asked a rabbi for charity, but the rabbi was embarrassed because he did not have any money with him. "My brother," said the rabbi, "I wish I could do something for you, but I cannot." "You already have helped me," said the man, "you called me 'brother.'"

How about the little girl who asked her mother one morning, "Mommy, are you happy?" "Yes," said her mother. "Then why don't you tell your face," said the bright daughter.

The Kotzker Rebbe said that we are privileged and obligated to create heaven on earth and we can do it by following the excellent example of Moshe *Rabbeinu*.

Rabbi Moshe S. Gorelik

Young Israel of North Bellmore, New York

The dialogue between *HaShem* and Moshe at the site of the burning bush is intriguing and fascinating. At the outset, *HaShem* instructs Moshe to return to Egypt and lead the people to freedom. *HaShem* ensures him that He will be at his side protecting him from harm, and still Moshe declines the invitation. Notwithstanding *HaShem*'s insistence, Moshe refuses to yield. Not once, not twice, but five times he informs *HaShem* that he is unwilling to assume the leadership of the people of Israel, and each time he offers reasons for his refusal. Although each argument is shot down, Moshe remains adamant. After the fifth refusal, however, *HaShem* advises him that he has no option but to return to Egypt and prepare them for redemption.

At first glance Moshe's refusals smack of arrogance. The arguments that he presents do not add up to a valid justification for his obstinacy. The key to the understanding of Moshe's motive lies in Sforno's explanation of why he led his flocks of sheep to the wilderness. Sforno writes, "He [went] alone to seclude himself and to pray." The *midbar* (wilderness) is a dramatic, uninhabited, overpowering world. It is untouched by human hands and unaffected by the creations of society. It is a barren land with an occasional bush and a lonely figure searching for meager vegetation for his flock. At times, the landscape yields an oasis, but the view is predominated by the sand dunes and rolling hills and mountainous peaks jutting heavenward. It is nature in the raw, revealing the unadorned mysteries of the Divine Presence. The wilderness is an inspiring setting for reflection and contemplation.

Moshe's soul was in a spiritual turmoil. He was born of Israelite parentage but raised as a prince in the Egyptian royal family. Notwithstanding the youthful years spent at the royal court, his Jewish blood stirred within him. He stepped into the universe outside the royal court and discovered his people, who were reduced to abject slavery. Upon witnessing an Egyptian taskmaster mercilessly beating a Jew, he kills the Egyptian. However, when Moshe attempts to make peace between two Jews, he is rejected. When Pharaoh is informed of the death of the Egyptian, Moshe flees to Midian. There, he marries and names his first child Gershom "because I am a stranger in a foreign land." The name is significant and telling. He experiences alienation: frowned upon by Jews, pursued by Egyptians, and estranged in Midian.

Moshe enters the wilderness to ponder his destiny and to determine his identity. His argument with *HaShem* is his attempt to find spiritual certainty and human meaningfulness. He faces the ultimate challenges: Who is he? What is he? And whither is he heading? Only after a process of spiritual striving does he evolve into the *ish Elohim*—man of God. One cannot attain ultimate spiritual or religious fulfillment unless one confronts moral and spiritual challenges head on.

The *Chazal* long ago suggested this truism by declaring that a *tzaddik* is not the equal of a *baal teshuvah. Teshuvah* indicates a person who is in a state of progress. A *baal teshuvah* is not spiritually complacent but grapples with life's challenges and strives to climb to even greater heights. A *tzaddik* may simply be the individual who observes the *Shulchan Aruch* and is smug. He is content with the routine and does not wish to advance. On the other hand, the *baal teshuvah* is spiritually restless. He is aware that, to satisfy the yearning for deeper spirituality, one must look honestly inward and grapple with moral dilemmas and religious concerns; otherwise the *Shulchan Aruch* becomes a sterile catechism. Moshe was that quintessential *baal teshuvah* who ascended the mountain of challenges to become Moshe *Rabbeinu*.

To become an *ish Elohim*, one must meet the challenges. *Yahadut* will then become that much more significant. Torah will not merely be letters inscribed on a parchment; it will be a *Torat chaim*, a well-spring of spirituality infusing the heart with godliness, the soul with religious joy, and the mind with new religious dimensions.

Rabbi Harry Greenspan

Young Israel of Long Beach, California

One of the sources of merit through which our ancestors left Egypt was that they did not give up their Jewish names. In fact, the book of *Shemot*, dealing with the redemption, begins with "And these are the *names*." It seems worthwhile, therefore, to inquire into the significance of names in Judaism.

One premise is certain. We do not hold of Shakespeare's view: "What's in a name? A rose by any other name would smell as sweet" is not the philosophy of Torah. Names are very important, but why?

Adam was considered very wise in that, when *HaShem* paraded all the world's creatures in front of him, Adam was able to give each creature a name in *Lashon HaKodesh*, in Hebrew. What really is implied in this wisdom? Couldn't we combine random syllables into words and apply these word-labels to the various animals?

The answer is, "No!" A name in Hebrew is much more than a label. It is, rather, a definition of that person or creature or object, a way of capturing the essence and basic attributes in a word. The universe was created, according to *Chazal*, with the letters and syllables of our Holy Tongue. Consequently, a name in Hebrew defines and perfectly describes that individual. Adam's wisdom, therefore, was amazing. His intimate knowledge of God's creations was such that he could define the essential qualities of all God's creatures in the syllables of *Lashon HaKodesh*.

We can now truly understand a dialogue in the week's *parshah*. After Moshe *Rabbeinu* is charged by God to speak to the Jews in His name, Moshe asks, "[When] they say to me 'what is His name?'—what shall I say to them?" *HaShem* responds, "I shall be as I shall be." The difficulties are obvious. What kind of question is this, and what is its answer? Rav Zevin, *zt"l*, in *Letorah Ulemoadim*, explains that the people would be fascinated to hear that Moshe spoke to God and would ask, "Describe the God who spoke to you!"—that is, "Tell us His name." God tells Moshe that it is impossible to describe His essence to a human being. The only thing we can know about Him is that He is beyond time ("I will be . . .").

Again our *parshah*, Rav Zevin *zt"l* sees another illustration of the significance of names. Moshe *Rabbeinu* names his firstborn son Gershom to commemorate that "I was a stranger [*ger hayiti*] in a strange land." Does this not contain a superfluous phrase? "A stranger" implies that he was "in a strange land," and vice versa!

To answer this question, we must begin with another question, from *parshat Lech Lecha*, in the Covenant between the Sections, that critical treaty between God and Avraham *Avinu*. Avraham is told of the eventual servitude in Egypt: "your children will be strangers in a strange land." The same question needs to be asked! The two phrases are the same!

Rav Zevin, *zt"l* answers as follows: *HaShem* was promising Avraham that, although his children would live in a foreign land for hundreds of years, they would always be aware of its being a "land not theirs." *Klal Yisrael* would never forget that its only true home is *Eretz Yisrael*. "Your children will be strangers and they'll know it."

Similarly, Moshe realized that it was critical for his children to remember their roots. How could those born and bred in Midian of a father who grew up in Egypt, feel that only *Eretz Yisrael* is their true homeland? Moshe, who knew the secret of Jewish names, guaranteed just that! His son, Gershom, by virtue of his name, would always feel himself a stranger—except in *Eretz Yisrael*.

The Kabbalah tells us that there is a spark of Moshe *Rabbeinu* in every generation. Consequently, by imbuing his son with this special connection to Israel, perhaps he did the same for us all.

We now reach another level. A name is not only a definition of essential qualities; it can even imbue that named individual with attributes and potentialities that he would never otherwise have had! Esau, for example, knew this very well. "Is he not rightly named Yaakov? For he has supplanted me. . . ." (Genesis 27:36). How could the "simple" Yaakov, the man who grew up in the four cubits of the *beit midrash*, fool the master cheater himself? Sforno explains: Only because he was given a name that imbued him with the ability to trick others—even Esav.

In this week's *parshah*, we see a further illustration. Batya, daughter of Pharaoh, finds a child in the Nile. Possessed with Divine inspiration, she names him Moshe, which means "pulled out" (of the Nile). Sforno again comments on this naming: that he could now pull others out of dire straits. In other words, how could this man, a humble stutterer, become the redeemer of Israel? How could he "pull out" his nation from Egypt? Because he was given a name that imbued him with such an ability!

Finally, we reach a third level. Not only does a name define, not only does it grant spiritual attributes to a newborn child, but it can grant a renamed individual a new destiny. Avram and Sarai were barren. Avraham and Sarah were the parents of the Jewish nation.

Let me derive a further proof to this from an ancient custom of our people, that of giving an additional name to one who is deathly ill. I used to wonder about this *minhag.* Does the Angel of Death have a little notepad (*kvittel*) with a name, and by our changing it slightly, he misses his mark? It makes no sense. Perhaps now, however, we can understand. A baby is born. He is given a name that implies a certain potential. Years later, the *malach hamavet* comes for him and, perhaps, it's found that he hasn't lived up to his potential. Or maybe the opposite is true, and he has completed his life's mission. Either way, the Angel of Death is at his bedside.

What do we do by adding a name? We grant that sick person *new midot, new* potential, and a *new* destiny. The name change is a *tefillah*. Please allow him time, *HaShem,* to live up to his *new* destiny!

To sum up, a name is *quite* significant. We understand why the *Bnei Yisrael* left Egypt through the merit of not changing their names. This does not mean only that they used the names of the *Avot* and Tribes to name their children. It also means they maintained those unique spiritual characteristics of their forefathers, those special *midot* that made them who they were. Therefore, they merited to be redeemed.

❖ CHAPTER 14 ❖

Vaera

Rabbi Jeffrey Bienenfeld

Young Israel of St. Louis, Missouri

When Moshe is commanded to announce the advent of the first plague upon Egypt, *HaShem* instructs him to stand by the river's edge to greet Pharaoh: "And you should stand where you will meet him on the bank of the Nile" (Exodus 7:15).

On this phrase, the Talmud in *Zevachim* (102a) comments in the name of Rabbi Yochanan, "He is a king, and you must show him reverence." Similarly, the Midrash *Tanchuma*, quoted by Rashi (Exodus 6:13) maintains that Moshe was commanded to give *kavod*, honor, to Pharaoh. In *Melachim* I (18:46), we also find *HaShem* directing Eliyahu Hanavi to run before the wicked King Achav as a show of respect (see Rashi, ad. loc.). The question is rather obvious: Why show deference to a *rasha* (an evil person)? To answer merely that the honor bestowed in both cases was to their kingly rank and not to their person only begs the question; doesn't such flattery undercut and compromise the moral-religious rebuke of the Prophet?

I would like to suggest an answer based upon a fascinating discussion in *Sanhedrin* 101b. There, Rabbi Yochanan asks why Yeravam ben Navat merited sovereignty over the Ten Tribes. The answer: because he chastised Solomon concerning his marriage to the daughter of Pharaoh. If so, then, asks the Talmud, why was he punished? The answer: Because Yeravam rebuked the king publicly.

The question is plain: Why not let the good simply neutralize the bad? Why reward Yeravam and then punish him? Rabbi Yehuda Ginsberg, in his *Mussar Haniviim* (*Melachim* I, 11:27), answers the question by quoting the *Sifrei* on *Devarim* 33:6:

> One never exchanges: not merit for demerit and not demerit for merit. Rather, one gives reward for [doing of] *mitzvot* and punishment for [doing] sins.

Contrary to what we might commonly assume, our Sages, in the *Sifrei*, established the principle that the Almighty does not exchange merit for sin and vice versa. A person is rewarded for a *mitzvah* even as he is punished for an *averah* (trespass). The one does not cancel out the other.

This principle is further strengthened by the Talmud's discussion of the opening verse in II Samuel, 21: "And the Lord said: It is for Saul and his bloody house, because he put to death the Gibeonites." In *Yevamos* 78b, the Talmud asks how Saul can be rewarded with a praiseworthy eulogy while, at the same moment, his descendants are to be executed for Saul's crimes against the Gibeonites. Resh Lakish explains that such are the ways of the Almighty.

> As it is written (Zephania 2:3), "Seek out *HaShem* all you humble of the land (and who have fulfilled His law . . .)." Where there is His judgment there is also His good deeds.

God will independently reward a person for his many good deeds (*paalo*) and, yet, He will hold accountable the very same person for all transgressions committed (*mishpato*).

There are, I believe, two powerful messages that emerge from this rather perplexing manner with which the Almighty relates to man's actions. The first is pointedly made by Sforno in his comments on the phrase in *Devarim* 10:17, "And [the Almighty] takes no bribes." Sforno explains that God will simply not reduce the punishment for a sin no matter how meritorious another *mitzvah* performed by that person may be. "A *mitzvah* shall not extinguish a transgression," declares the Talmud in *Sotah* (21a). Consequently, if we sin, we cannot rely upon any merit to save us from retribution save perfect repentance.

There is a second lesson we can learn, as well, from God's independent treatment of man's good and bad deeds. The *Yalkut Yehudah* comments on Ramban's well-known analysis of Pharaoh's successful attempt to beguile the Jewish people into slavery in Exodus 1:10. He claims that, despite all of Pharaoh's wickedness, there was a sufficient shred of moral decency to prevent him from openly persecuting the Israelites. That the Almighty sees fit to warn him before many of the plagues suggests, says the *Yalkut Yehudah*, that Pharaoh surely had the capacity to reverse his monstrous ways. And, in fact, according to the *midrash*, Pharaoh *does* ultimately repent and becomes a charismatic spokesman for the word of God (see *Yalkut Shimoni* 550:3, and *Pirkei d'Rabbi Eliezer* ch. 43, both on *Yonah* 3:6). And so, indeed, why should Moshe not see fit to honor Pharaoh? Without forgiving a shred of Pharaoh's iniquities, Moshe can still show him a respect based upon a prophet's very real insight into the soul of a king that yet contains sparks of spiritual goodness. (A similar argument can be made for Eliyahu Hanavi's show of honor to Achav. See the comments of Radak on 18:41 in I *Melachim*.)

All too frequently, we are put off by another's offensive behavior. We make judgments quickly and fail to appreciate the profound observation of our Sages on *Avos* 1:6 that we are enjoined to judge *Kol Haadam*, the *entire* man. We need not fear compromising in the slightest any of our moral-religious standards by complimenting a person on some genuinely fine action, however small that action might be in the sum total of that person's behavioral repertoire. If the Almighty Himself is alert to a good deed performed by an otherwise unsavory character, we ought not to be any less charitable in our treatment of others. We might even discover that in our noble pursuit of the *emet* (truth) of Torah, adherents will more readily gather if we preface our preachments of truth with an honest measure of *chesed*—a *chesed* whose kindness is demonstrated when we take notice and appreciate the small acts of goodness that, it is to be hoped, grace each of our lives.

Rabbi Charles Weiss

Young Israel of Greater Pittsburgh, Pennsylvania

The recent *parshiyot* stress the importance of humankind's being aware that God runs the world. Many people, when wealthy and prosperous, take good fortune for granted. *HaShem*'s unobtrusive system of governance allows people to be unaware, even to forget about God's role, until one is ill or one goes to a funeral. So we see in this *parshah* that getting the Jews out of Egypt would have been a simple task for *HaShem*, except that the prerequisite for redemption was that the Jews and Egyptians should both acknowledge God's dominance and then act accordingly; stiff opposition from both sides had to be overcome. People who are set in their ways and practices, in an inertia mode, are hard to convince that change is the way to go. As Moshe complained, "If my constituency doesn't back me, what can I say?"

Our *parshah* opens, "I revealed myself to Abraham, Isaac, and Jacob," and Rashi says "to the Avot-patriarchs." Seemingly Rashi's comment is redundant—for, were not Abraham and Isaac and Jacob the *Avot*? For our purpose here, it is sufficient to say that *HaShem* did not reveal himself to Abraham, Isaac, and Jacob *only* because they were sensitive, special types (which they were) but also rather because they were *Avot* who would have descendants sensitive to *HaShem*'s presence and mastery. When Moshe came to Egypt as the Redeemer of Israel, he was armed with tools (*osot*—literally, signs) to reawaken the Jews' awareness that God does reveal Himself.

The elders, having been misled previouisly, checked out Moshe's credentials with Serach bat Asher. She asked them, what was his expression of *geulah* (redemption)? When they responded, *Pakod Pakadite Etchem*—"I have surely remembered you" (Exodus 3:16), she said, "He is the one; follow him"—but they did not. In a situation in which *HaShem* sent a *sheliach* (messenger), where our own authorities endorsed him, where the people were desperately seeking a savior, Moshe and Aaron had to face Pharaoh alone, unsupported by the very people they were trying to rescue.

The theme of acknowledging revelation is basic to the action throughout the *sedrah*. When Moshe and Aaron displayed the Divine *osot* to Pharaoh, the response was that they were merely a human manifestation: since Pharaoh's magicians were able to duplicate these feats, Moshe and Aaron could not have been sent by God.

When the rivers, ponds, and so on, all instantly became blood, a suprahuman event, Pharaoh denied God's presence because his magicians could also produce blood.

When Aaron called forth the frogs, the magicians did so as well. When the sheer volume of frogs showed the plague to be supernatural, Pharaoh agreed that *HaShem* was indeed controlling the situation—but this realization did not prevent him from recanting his promise.

When the ground became lice, the magicians were at a loss. Powerless to replicate this plague, they were forced to admit that the swarm of lice did constitute a minor revelation of *HaShem*—a finger of God, they called it. Still, Pharaoh would not bend to *HaShem*'s will; the magicians were no longer players in the process.

The Divine Revelation quality of *arov* (wild animals) was obvious. Moshe and Aaron only issued a warning; no one even waved a hand or a rod to cause Pharaoh to think there was a human participation, in attracting these animals. Only when it was obvioius to all that *HaShem* brought about the plague of the wild animals did Pharaoh seek to strike a deal—but, still, one favorable to himself. When *he* could set the terms, he felt confident, in charge; if the other side couldn't meet his terms, too bad! The revelation had not had the desired impact.

The plague affecting cattle was, again, a Divine action—and yet it affected property only, not Pharaoh's person. But, when boils were the plague—initiated by Moshe and Aaron (and the magicians sought to again become players in the process)—the magicians could not stand before Moshe, for their very persons were afflicted and involved. Moshe and Aaron's action are the subject of much comment in the commentaries. Rashi describes Moshe and Aaron's fistfuls of soot—four handfuls being compressed in Moshe's right hand as a *nes*, a miracle—and Moshe's flinging the light soot all over Egypt being *nisea nisim*, miracles upon miracles. Did Moshe's handful of soot really cover the entire land? Did the soot cause the boils? The commentaries disagree. All do agree that Moshe's gesture was symbolic; his futile effort, though miraculous, proved *HaShem*'s role in the process, for a small amount of soot became a blizzard affecting all; harmless soot became a source of terror. In the face of open actions by God, no one could stand or resist, and all knew that *HaShem* was truly the power.

Water is necessary but is external. The frogs were a pain, but external. The lice were a disgusting, external, nuisance. The wild animals were a physical danger—and the Jews stayed indoors safely away. The plague of *dever* affected only property; wealth is not personal. Boils are a personal violation; now we first wake up and realize that God is running the world and He is in complete control of the situation. Good morning! So the whole shebang *must* have been Divine revelation! Why didn't we see it before it hit us personally?

Were our people more sensitive to the Divine hand and presence than the Egyptians? The commentaries disagree on whether the plagues that didn't specifically exclude the Jews affected them or not. They had stopped working; the slavery had ended, but, from the plague of darkness, when many of the Jewish nation died, we can see that even the descendants of Abraham, Isaac, and Jacob became assimilated and lowered to the level of their environment, not having learned from miracles staring them in the face.

The final redemption will be patterned after the first redemption. Thus, the ingredients are prepared: the *noshim tzidkoneot*—righteous women—who raised proper Jewish children and, *nebich*, those who didn't; those who are ready and those who are not ready for the redemption, or don't want, or don't need, or are against, and so on. *Then*, 80 percent of *our* people died in Egypt (see Rashi, 13:10, *Shemot, Beshalach* 13:18)! Now, *all* are to join the *geulah*. We pray that their personal involvement and awakening and sensitizing will be *bechesed uv'rachamim*, with kindness and mercy.

Rabbi Evan Shore

Young Israel Shaarei Torah of Syracuse, New York

There is a famous midrash from *Shemot Rabbah* (9:10) that explains that, during the first plague, if a Jew and an Egyptian were drinking water from the same container, the Jew would be drinking water while the Egyptian would be drinking blood. The *midrash* further states that if the Egyptian purchased the container from a Jew, the contents would then be water even for the Egyptian! Apparently, *HaShem* performed this miracle for the Jewish people to enrich them financially after years of rigorous slave labor.

If the only way for an Egyptian to get water was to buy it from a Jew, how, then, do we explain the following *pasuk* (Exodus 7:22): "and the Egyptian magicians did so with their arts"? Where did the Egyptians get water to perform this trick? Apparently, the water was not bought from a Jew; this conclusion is based on the reasoning that Bnei Yisrael would not want to help give credence to the Egyptian black magic and be part of proving that *HaShem* wasn't the only true power.

The Malbim, quoting Rav Saadiah Gaon, tells us that when *HaShem* changed the water in Egypt to blood, only water that was fit to drink was changed. He based his premise on the fact that, when the word *meimei* is used in the Torah, it is used in the context of water fit for consumption. The word *mei* is used for bitter or salty water that a human being would not be able to imbibe. According to the Malbim, since the Torah states, "And all of the Egyptians dug round about the river to drink, for they could not drink from the water of the river." The *meimei hayeor* was water that was able to be consumed and, as a result, it was affected. Other water that might be contaminated, making it unfit for human consumption, was not affected.

The *Or Hachaim* also asks the same question: Where did the Egyptian magicians find water to turn to blood? He feels that, when the waters of Egypt were turned to blood, the plague affected only standing water or water that was exposed and was able to be seen. However, water that was below ground was not affected at all. He bases his conclusion upon the *pasuk* in Exodus 7:24 as well. The Egyptians dug for fresh water because any water that was at ground level was unfit for consumption. It made no difference whether the water was in the Nile River, ponds, canals, or reservoirs. However, if it was below ground, then it was fresh water that was *not* affected.

The Chizkuni has a very interesting interpretation of this problem. He feels that the plague of blood, in fact, only lasted a very short time and not the usual plague duration of one week. He bases his theory on the *pasuk*, "The fish that are in the river shall die and the River shall become foul, Egyptians will become weary of trying to drink water from the Nile" (Exod. 7:18). The Chizkuni theorizes that the water turned to blood long enough for the fish to die as a result of lack of oxygen. After the fish died, the Nile turned back to water. Even though the Nile was water again, the Egyptians could not drink its water because of all the dead fish that were floating around in it.

Oznaim Letorah adds one more explanation to this discussion. He maintains that the Nile River received its water from Ethiopia. The Egyptian magicians could not use the water once it flowed into the boundaries of Egypt because, once in Egypt, the water was turned into blood. Instead, the magicians traveled outside the borders of Egypt and returned with the water in an attempt to duplicate the plague. Since this water was not part of a natural collection of water, even when it was brought into Egypt, it remained unaffected.

Last but not least, why was the plague of blood brought upon the Egyptians? Rabbi Samson Raphael Hirsch postulated that the plagues were meant to be a punishment in terms of "measure for measure." Rabbi Yehuda Nachshoni explains Hirsch in the following manner: During the years of slavery, the Jewish people were wrested away from the source of our very being, *HaShem*. During our slavery, we descended to the lowest depth of impurity possible without being totally destroyed. To punish the Egyptians for pulling us away from *HaShem*, they in turn were torn away from their deity, the Nile River. As a result, the spiritual support they gained from the godlike Nile was destroyed. No matter which opinion discussed above, we find that are all in agreement that the Nile River, a god of Egypt, was "slain." To the Egyptians, their lesson was fully to learn about the existence of a true, real God and, at the same time, understand that their gods were useless and powerless.

Rabbi Fabian Schonfeld

Young Israel of Kew Gardens Hills, New York

In the beginning of this week's *parshah, HaShem* speaks to Moshe and reminds him that "I appeared to Abraham, Isaac, and Jacob." Now, we all know that these were the Patriarchs of our people. Thus, there is no reason to explain their relationship to us. Yet, we find Rashi saying *el haavot,* which means, to "the forefathers." Many of the commentators raise the question of why Rashi found it necessary to describe Abraham, Isaac, and Jacob as "our forefathers." After all, it is such a well-known fact that the commentary of Rashi seem completely superfluous.

As many questions as there are regarding this difficulty, there are as many explanations.

It seems to me that Rashi here describes the basic relationship between the nation of Israel and its Founders, on the one hand, and us, on the other. When, for example, we speak of the Founding Fathers of the American republic, we do not really regard them as our ancestors. We do respect and pay homage to them because they established the true democracy that inspires the American people to this very day. When we speak to Americans and ask them about their fathers, they will think in terms of Irish, Italian, Norwegian, or British ancestry. The Founding Fathers, as great as they were, have no direct personal link with the American people.

With the Jewish people it is a totally different story. Abraham, Isaac, and Jacob were not only the Founding Fathers, they were also, and are to this day, the real fathers of the nation of Israel. What Rashi wishes to emphasize is that we are not dealing with names, revered as they may be, of mere historical figures in the history of our people. When we mention Abraham, Isaac, and Jacob we think of them as real fathers who are our direct ancestors. They were not the Jeffersons and Washingtons of the Jewish people but true ancestors whose blood runs in our veins and whose soul breathes in our bodies.

It is for this reason that Rashi tells us that Abraham, Isaac, and Jacob were, indeed, our fathers. As such, our relationship to them is based on the *mitzvah* of respect for one's [actual] father (*kibbud av*), and not merely as those who established the original nation of Israel. We obey the *mitzvot* because, as children of our forefathers, we have an obligation to do so in line with our traditional observance of Torah.

When the Almighty wanted to destroy S'dom and Amorah and consulted with Abraham, He gave as a reason, the fact that Abraham would "command his children to follow him to walk in the ways of *HaShem*." To us, the Torah is a family heirloom, a real inheritance and heritage (*yerushah umorashah*). It is in this spirit that Rashi makes the comments that he does.

Finally, the land of Israel, *Eretz Yisrael,* was promised not to those who established the Jewish nation but, literally, to our fathers, to be handed down from generation to generation. Our loyalty to the land and our love for it are based, not on political or geopolitical reasons, but on the fact that it is *Eretz Avot*—"the land of our forefathers."

❖ CHAPTER 15 ❖

Bo

Rabbi Shaul Chill

Young Israel of North Woodmere, New York

Rav Richonon Sorotzkin, *zt"l*, asks why we celebrate the first days of Pesach with both full Hallel and the Pesach Seder, whereas the last days, when true independence was achieved with the drowning of the Egyptians in the Red Sea, are commemorated merely with the recitation of partial Hallel. Shouldn't the end of Pesach have been the correct time for the Seder and full rejoicing?

The essence of *Yetziat Mitzrayim* (the Exodus from Egypt), responds Rav Sorotzkin, was to achieve spiritual redemption rather than physical freedom. Thus, each time Moshe demands, "Let my people go that they may serve Me," the message is clear: the *raison d'être* of *Am Yisrael*'s deliverance from bondage was to become servants of God.

The *parsha* appropriately begins,

> "Come to Pharaoh . . . so that I can put these signs of mine in His midst, and so that you may relate to the ears of your son and your son's sons that I made a mockery of Egypt and My signs that I placed among them—that you may know that I am *HaShem*." (Exodus 10:1–2)

The object of the ten plagues was not primarily to punish Pharaoh and the Egyptians (if so, one plague would have sufficed). Rather, with each plague our faith in the Almighty increased as we witnessed His Omnipotence, and our gratitude to *HaShem* for being saved grew dramatically as well.

In this sense, the rescue corresponds directly to our suffering. The purpose of Egypt's enslavement of the Jewish people was not so much to physically enslave *Klal Yisrael* as it was to destroy us religiously. As Pharaoh—and every other anti-Semite in history—boldly declared, "Who is God that I should listen to His voice?" The ultimate lesson of the plagues necessarily has to be, "and you will know that I am *HaShem*."

We understand, then, why we observe Pesach to this day, although we are once again in *Galut*. *Yetziat Mitzrayim* achieved an eternal freedom of *ruchaniyut*; no matter how often we would be forced to return to the bitter exile, and regardless of its oppression, our faith would never be shaken.

The *parshah* concludes with the *mitzvah* of *tefillin*. Our faith in *HaShem* today isn't based upon seeing miracles but upon our commitment to Torah and *mitzvot*. Truly to see *hashgachat HaShem*, we focus upon the *tefillin*, which we place on our weaker hands, for it is not our strength that has saved us throughout history. Rather, it is the strong hand of the Almighy that has rescued each generation from the hands of those who would destroy us. As we recite Pesach night, "That in every generation they stand upon us to destroy us, and God saves us from their hands."

Rabbi Chaim Wakslak

Young Israel of Long Beach, New York

The first *mitzvah* that *Bnei Yisrael* were commanded to perform upon being redeemed from Egyptian bondage was the *mitzvah* of *kiddush levanah*—sanctifying the new moon; and, simultaneously, establishing the month of Nisan as the first month of the year. As Rashi explains, Moshe and Aaron joined together with the Almighty Himself to convene a *Bet Din*—a tribunal—which usually requires three participants. This unusual action on the part of the Almighty would be enough to mark this *mitzvah* as unusual, but its importance is further illuminated by the fact that Rashi, quoting from the *midrash*, tells us that the entire Torah should have commenced with the *mitzvah* of *kiddush levanah*.

What was so important about this particular *mitzvah*? There are several lessons we can learn. The first is the importance of Time. The definition of a slave is an individual who has no control over his (or her) own time, since he or she is completely at the mercy of the master's demands. In contrast, a free person is one who is in total control of his (or her) own time. *Bnei Yisrael*, after being slaves for so long, needed to re-establish the importance of time as a concept in their own lives.

Fortunately, they had never lost the more global unit of time in terms of a year, for Avraham had been told that his descendants would be slaves for four hundred years, and this tradition was transmitted to future generations. It was necessary, therefore, to start by teaching *Bnei Yisrael* about the next unit of time, which is a month. This was achieved by this first commandment of sanctifying the new moon. Once they learned about the month as a unit of time, they were then taught the next unit of time, which is a day, when they were commanded to count fifty days from the time they left Egypt until they reached Mount Sinai, where they received the Torah. Upon receipt of the Torah, they were taught the units of hour, minute, and second, since every single unit of time spent studying the Torah, regardless of how small, is considered a *mitzvah*.

The second lesson inherent in this commandment of sanctifying the new moon reflected the partnership formed between the Almighty and man. This joining of Moshe and Aaron together with *HaShem* to sanctify the new moon reflects the ideal relationship. Man must work to maintain his survival and achieve his goals on the basis of the principle of *ein somchim al hanes*—we do not rely exclusively upon a miracle. On the other hand, a person is forbidden to think that all that he has achieved is a result of *kochi v'otzem yadi*—"by the strength of my own hand." It is only through man's commitment and effort combined with faith in the Almighty that we are able to achieve anything in this world.

Another interesting explanation of this united sanctification by the Almighty, Moshe, and Aaron of that first month is offered by Rabbi Meir Don Ploski in his book *Kli Chemdah*. He explains that an individual who intentionally transgresses *Shabbat* is put to death because *Shabbat* is an "institution" that is completely Divine in nature. If one intentionally transgresses yom tov he receives lashes because ones observance of any yom tov is dependent on when a *Bet Din* establishes Rosh Chodesh. Pesach is unique because, on this holiday, aside from the lashes for which one can become liable, there is also a possibility of receiving *karet*—death before one's time—if one eats *chametz* during the course of the Pesach holiday. Reb Meir Don Ploski explains that the reason for this level of punishment, which is more severe than lashes but less severe than being put to death, is that the month of Nisan was sanctified through a partnership between the Almighty and man, and this first sanctification affects all subsequent sanctifications of the month of Nisan. (He also provides an explanation as to why there is a punishment of *karet* for anyone who eats on Yom Kippur.)

The third lesson we learn from this unusual sanctification of the new moon is the definition of *Bnei Yisrael*'s existence; by focusing upon the moon when we fulfill this first commandment, we become sensitized to the character of the moon. We well know that the moon in reality has no light of its own but, instead, reflects to earth the sun's light. It was important for *Bnei Yisrael* to recognize that, as a nation, their strength and very existence are a reflection of the Almighty's glory and radiant light.

Additionally, the destiny of *Bnei Yisrael* models the moon as described by the *midrash*. Just as the moon appears to become smaller and smaller during the course of a month, to the extent that it almost disappears, and at that point it once again reverses course and appears to become larger, so, too, *Bnei Yisrael* may be diminished by their enemies to the point of near annihilation, God forbid, but never are they destroyed, and they always return with greater strength and determination.

Rabbi Mordeche Young

Young Israel of Wynnefield, Pennsylvania

This *parshah* describes events pivotal to the history of our people. Yesterday there was slavery; now there is freedom. Yesterday there was sadness; now there is happiness. Yesterday there was mourning; now there is a holiday. Yesterday there was darkness; now there is great light. Yesterday there was subjugation; now there is redemption. We went from the depths of being slaves to Pharaoh to the heights of being subjects to *HaShem*, as it says in *parshat Behar*, "For the children of Israel are My slaves; they are My slaves that I brought out of Egypt" (Lev. 25:55).

We were on the way to becoming "a kingdom of priests, a holy nation." We began the process that would culminate after forty-nine days with the revelation at Har Sinai, where we received the Torah, hearing the first two commandments directly from *HaShem*. Indeed, *Yetziat Mitzrayim* is a cornerstone in our hsitory. But the Exodus is a cornerstone not only in our history but also in the faith and belief of every Jew. *Rabbeinu* Bachya writes that the first of the ten commandments—"I am the Lord, your God, that has taken you out of the land of Egypt, out of the house of bondage" is based on *Yetziat Mitzrayim*, not in the creation of Heaven and Earth, because the Exodus is something that we ourselves witnessed. Thus, affirmation of our belief and faith is based upon what hundreds of thousands of people saw with their own eyes, not on creation, which no human eye saw. *Yetziat Mitzrayim* is the basis of many other *mitzvot* as well, so that we constantly say *zecher Liyztiyat Mitzrayim*.

The Ramban, at the end of our *parshah*, is renowned for his characterization of a fundamental concept. The Ramban begins, "And now I will tell you a rule in the rational of many *mitzvot*." He explains that in the days of Enosh, people began to err in their beliefs. Some denied that there is a Creator; some acknowledged a Creator but denied that He knows what happens in this world; and some acknowledged that He knows what happens but denied that He cares and watches over this world (that is, there is no Divine Providence). Hence, when *HaShem* favors a group or individual and does a wonder for them, contrary to the ways of nature, He is showing that there is a Creator, that this Creator knows what is happening in this world, and that He is watching over it. And, if a *Navi* (prophet) foretold this wonder, then that would also show that God speaks to mankind. Consequently, the veracity of the Torah is proven. Thus, those great and wondrous miracles are trustworthy witnesses to the belief in a Creator and to the truth of the Torah.

Since *HaShem* will not do miracles for every generation and for every wicked person, He commanded us always to make a sign and memorial for what our eyes did see and to transmit this to our children after us, for all generations. So important is the obligation of *zecher letziat Mitzrayim* that *HaShem* declares *karet* as the punishment for one who eats *chametz* on Pesach or one who did not bring the *korban Pesach* when he could have brought it.

So, too, we are commanded to inscribe this in our *tefillin*, on our hands and heads. We write this belief on our doorposts; we say the *Shema* twice a day. We live in a *sukkah* every year, and so on—all those *mitzvot* are *eidot*—testimony to our faith and belief.

Thus, one who buys a *mezuzah* for a *zuz* (coin), affixes it to his doorpost, and understands the intent of the *mitzvah* has acknowledged that there is a Creator and that He runs the world. He has also acknowledges the veracity of prophecy, besides admitting to the great *chesed*, kindness, *HaShem* did by taking us out of *Mitzrayim*. Therefore, it says in *Avot*, "Be as careful with a 'minor' *mitzvah* as with a 'major' *mitzvah*." For every *mitzvah* that we fulfill, minor as it may seem in our eyes, is witness to our belief and faith in *HaShem*. And this is the fundamental purpose of all *mitzvot* and, indeed, of the very creation, for mankind to know and to acknowledge the Creator. This is what the Almighty wants from this world. This, too, is the purpose of lifting up our voices in prayer, of having *batei knesiyot*, *shuls*, of having public prayer, that there should be a place for people to gather and acknowledge the God who created them; and they should publicize this and say before him, "We are your creations!" So writes the Ramban.

To me this statement by Ramban defines the purpose of the Young Israel movement—to establish *batei knesiyot*, *shuls*, in which Jews will come together in unity and harmony and, as one, proudly proclaim for all to hear, "We are Your creations." We acknowledge and recognize that You have created and formed us. We acknowledge and recognize that You are the Master of the Universe, that miracles and nature are equally manifestations of Your Will. We acknowledge and recognize the veracity of the Torah, and that we are Your subjects, beholden to Your *mitzvot*.

Every Young Israel should strive to be a place where this message is heard, and it should be heard, not only in the echoes of the words of *davening* but in the *mien*, in the holiness, in the spirituality of the way we say the *tefillot*. It should be heard in the way we walk in *shul*, in the way we talk (or refrain from talking) in *shul*, in the awe with which we behave in *shul*. Our whole being must proclaim, "We are Your creations!" as it says, "All my being says, *HaShem*, who is like You?" This is the goal of the Young Israel *shul*. If we elevate our *shuls* to this level, then we can look forward to the fulfillment of the statement of the *Gemara* in Tractate *Megillah* 29, "Rabbi Elazar Hakapar says: In the future the *shuls* and study halls of Bavel will be re-established in *Eretz Yisrael*." May it come speedily in our time. *Amen*!

Rabbi Yehoshua Kaufman

Young Israel of Montreal, Quebec, Canada

The first *mitzvah* given to the children of Israel as a people—*Kiddush HaChodesh*—sanctifying the months—introduced a new era of thought and understanding in the history of the world. The Divine commandment relating to the consecretion of the calendar cycle represented a new determination of the place of man in the order of things.

Man, we have been told, is subject to and dependent upon external factors that mold the nature of his personality and determine the pattern of his behavior. This sociological view contends that man is a product of his environment, reacting to circumstances over which he has little or no control. The Torah tradition repudiates this environmental and behavioristic interpretation of man's conduct. The individual, the Torah teaches, is not the puppet of his environment, but rather the architect of his society, the master builder of his house. In the words of Rambam, "This species of man is unique in the world, and there is none like him in this matter, that he by himself, through his own mind and through his own knowledge, knows good and evil and acts accordingly, and there is naught that restrains him."

The deliverance from Egyptian bondage that the Almighty granted to Israel was not only an emancipation from an abject physical enslavement, but, above all, a redemption from a spiritual submissiveness to the immoral character of the Egyptian way of life. The fetters of the mind and spirit that were shattered by Israel's acceptance of the Torah way of life, heralded a new concept of freedom for all future civilization.

Throwing off the yoke of the times, Israel stood before God and man as a people that had discovered the inner soul of a man as a creation of God. Thus, the *Midrash Yalkut* comments on the verse in this week's portion, "Previously the setting of the times was in my hands; from this time forth I give it over to your hands."

This has been the historic role of Judaism—to mold the times, to shape the minds and hearts of man by the eternal verities expounded in the moral teachings of the Torah.

Rabbi Samson Raphael Hirsch interprets the admonition with which each Jew will be confronted by the heavenly tribunal, *kavata itim laTorah*? as meaning, "Have you set the times to the Torah, or have you, Heaven forbid, set the Torah to the times?"

The fact that we live in a period of crises in which man's understanding and sense of values have become distorted, pragmatic, and material in character, adds to the urgent need of a new orientation in the life of man, to give it purpose and direction. This direction can only come from the beacon light of Torah. The halachic way of life has always sought to liberate man from the chains of his environment and the evanescent standards that prevail.

Those who preach a Judaism based upon compromise and conformity represent a point of view that is unreal and, therefore, untrue to the faith of our fathers and the future of Israel. The Jewish philosophy of life cannot be synthesized with a society that boasts of the mind and worships the brute. The marriage of pragmatism with Judaism represents another endeavor to shape Judaism into the mold of the times. Such a union is untenable, for Judaism and pragmatic materialism are two philosophies of life that are irreconcilable in aims and goals.

We cannot perpetuate a living Judaism by rejecting its most basic concept, the supremacy of the Torah over the generation of man. The choice is ours, in our times, in our circumstances. It is in our hands.

We can mold our thoughts, our hearts, to bring about the fulfillment of a society that will bring the will of God into the affairs of man by "observing, practicing and fulfilling all the commandments of Thy Torah with love."

❖ CHAPTER 16 ❖

Beshalach

Rabbi Jacob Rubenstein

Young Israel of Scarsdale, New York

"And Moses grew up and went out to his brothers and he saw their affliction" (Exodus 2:11). The Rabbis comment that when Moshe saw the suffering of the Jews, he wept and cried out in empathetic pain, "I hurt for you. I wish I could die for you. He looked about and observed that there was no man" (Exodus 2:12); there was not one individual who was moved with indignation by the oppression. No one was shocked by the unspeakable horrors. Not one person would come forward even to condemn the evil.

Even after an impassioned plea to the elders of Israel to unite in pursuit of freedom, the Jewish leadership—the Jewish establishment—deserted Moshe. "They stole away furtively, singly and in pairs. . . . When Moshe and Aaron reached the palace of Pharaoh, not one of them was there. . . . The elders had slipped away" (*Midrash Rabbah* on Exodus 5:1). And the people continued to suffer.

The leaders made no effort to preserve their integrity and self-respect. They retreated into a fantasized sense of security, and they embraced the ploys and protocol of their tenuous political position. They accepted their status, which brought nothing but contempt, and they ran. The leaders—religious and political—fled the scene of confrontation rather than attempt to teach, to persuade, or to challenge. They were paralyzed with fear and ignored the call.

Nevertheless, this crime of desertion—of callousness, complacency, and insular reticence—was not repeated by the same generation. The decimation and deterioration of their people to one-fifth of their numbers had taught them well. When, as we read, the Jews crossed the Red Sea to safety, they were viciously ambushed by the Amalekim, and they reacted with a swift response. But the student of Torah may wonder how it was possible for the Amalekim to execute their attack when the Jewish nation was, as the Torah describes, Divinely protected by the pillar of cloud and the pillar of fire. The answer is that Amalek was not able to penetrate the Providential wall of protection; rather, Amalek had attacked the multitude of stragglers who followed far behind and could not keep up with the momentum of the Jews' journey. The Jewish camp viewed this nefarious attack with fury and indignation, and they left their protection to fight for and defend a people that shared their destiny. Moshe proclaimed, "Go out and fight Amalek." Rashi comments, "Leave the cloud of protection." At that moment, the Jews forsook their comfort and security and put themselves and their families in grave danger to save a life. They had tasted the bitterness of tyranny. They had the scars of suffering. They had the experience of abandonment, and they remembered—they responded.

FOOD FOR THOUGHT

The importance and meaning that we attach to food is fascinating. Our obsession with eating is worthy of attention. Equally important is the way we think and act when we're hungry and our disposition after we've eaten.

Parshat Beshalach expends much space on how we behave when we're hungry and our perspectives as to how much we can possibly eat! I'm referring, in particular, to an entire nation demanding food, being fed manna—the Bread of Heaven—then being told it's a test.

At first glance it's difficult to understand how this food from God could be a test. Not only did it come from a miraculous event but one of its unique features was that it took on any flavor the diner desired—a gourmet's dream in a desert devoid of spices.

Moreover, the portions were divided with exactly sufficient amounts for each individual's digestion and contentment. He that gathered much had nothing left over and he that gathered little had no lack. So what was the test? Rashi, the crown of commentators, explains: Would the Jew in the desert, given this food, be able to control the natural fear of not having enough for tomorrow and try to hoard? Would a person have the fundamental faith and confidence in God, who has been providing, to provide tomorrow? Intellectually and religiously, we know all good comes from God; but, if we do not have the comfort of a fully stocked refrigerator and money in the bank, will we be able to trust that God will provide for the next day? And even if all our material needs are provided for, with guaranteed sources of income, solid investments to keep even our grandchildren provided for, it's still possible for us to live as if we had nothing, constantly afraid of running out of things and grabbing everything in sight.

From this perspective, a full stomach and a content disposition must be measured not by what we have but by what we think we need!

When, wonders the Torah, can a person pass the test of knowing his needs, and not just his wants? We can't always get what we want, but, if we try and ponder, we can get what we need.

Two other commentators, Nachmanides and Sforno, interpret the manna test from diametrically opposite perspectives. Nachmanides explains that, since the manna did not grow from the ground and could not be planted, reaped, and stored, it was natural to fear there would be no more the next day. Since a person couldn't produce it, what would he do when there was no more? In other words, without money, job, or shelter, and with no guarantees or security, will a person still have faith in God, the provider, even though he doesn't know if tomorrow he'll have a job or food to feed his children? According to Nachmanides, will we believe in God when we are lacking and afflicted?

Sforno, on the other hand, sees the test not as a challenge to the poor but as a test to the rich. After all, the Jews in the desert were fortunate to be fed. They did not have to work much to accumulate the manna. They never had to go to the bank to withdraw money to shop for it, or peel, grate, fry, or bake it. With the manna they lived in the lap of luxury and the test was whether, with such a crowded lap, faith could even enter the picture!

Which one of these conditions is the greater threat to faith?

To have or have not? Is it easier to pray on an empty stomach or a full one?

Does one call on God when there is need and fear, a slump in the economy, or does the fat of the land inspire one to look Heavenward, when it comes so easy?

When we gather around the *Shabbat* table with the two challahs representing the two portions of manna gathered in the desert every Friday, it is time to ponder the nature of our faith and needs.

And then, when we're done eating, do we think in that moment of contentment of thanking God that we have what we need? Do we have the ability to pass this test of faith and make the blessing? Do we have the same desire to fill our spiritual reservoirs as we have to fill our physical ones?

That is a test we will take many times, and I pray we pass it.

Rabbi Yehoshua Wender

Young Israel of Houston, Texas

At the end of this week's *parshah* we read how *Bnei Yisrael* were attacked by Amalek. Yehoshua was appointed as general, and he led the Jews into battle. Moshe, together with Aaron and Chur, scaled a mountain that overlooked the battlefield. The Torah then tells us, When Moses lifted up his arms, the Israelites controlled the battle, and when he lowered his hands they faltered (Exodus 17:11).

The last *Mishnah* in the third *perek* of *Rosh Hashanah* (3:7) questions this story: "Can the hands of Moshe win or lose a war? Rather, the moral to be learned is that, when the Jewish people look upward and subjugate their hearts toward their Father in heaven, they win, but when they do not, they weaken."

Where, then, do the hands of Moshe fit into the picture?

The *Tosfot Yom Tov* on the *Mishnah* explains that Moshe's hands were a symbol. By looking at his hands reaching upward, Moshe was able to remind the Jewish army to lift their hearts toward Heaven. Just as a *mezuzah* or a pair of *tzitzit* remind us of our Creator, so, too, Moshe was supplying a visual aid to bring his soldiers to contemplate their ultimate General.

This *Chazal*, at first glance, is most puzzling! Why here? The Jewish people would be involved in countless battles throughout the ages. Faith in *HaShem* was always a requirement. Yet, we never see a repetition of this type of incident. Why, in this particular case, did *HaShem* give instructions to evoke the trust of the Jewish people?

The answer to this question lies in timing. This, after all, was the first "hands on" battle for *Bnei Yisrael*. Until now, *HaShem* had done all of the fighting. In Egypt, the Jewish people did not need to lift a finger. At the Red Sea, they were instructed to do nothing. As stated in Exodus 14:14, "*HaShem* will fight for you." Now, with the attack by Amalek, the people themselves were forced onto the field of battle. It was the first Jewish army. As a newly formed nation they were now responsible for joining in their own defense.

With this new experience also came an inherent danger. True, *HaShem* would be on their side and they would win, but would the Jewish people recognize their Divine assistance? The danger of believing, "My own strength has given me this great victory" (Deut. 8:17), had now become a constant threat to our people. This battle was, therefore, a crucial transition event. Would the Jewish people, who until now had been the beneficiaries of undeniable miracles, be able to see the hand of God even in the midst of a normal battle? Or would they fall prey to the lurking dangers of conceit?

With this in mind, *HaShem* gave His people a symbol. To focus the minds of the soldier on his dependence on *HaShem*, Moshe reached toward the skies. When this dependence was acknowledged, we triumphed; however, if even just for a moment we saw only our own efforts as essential, the tide of battle turned against us. *HaShem* was trying to teach a lesson for posterity during the first war of our history—"Some rely on chariots, some rely on horses, but we trust in God" (Psalms 20:8). Only when we have faith in God will we triumph.

Another important lesson from this episode is the need to prepare psychologically for major changes in our lives. The Jewish people were now, seemingly, on their own. Consequently, it was necessary for them to adapt to their new situation. To accomplish this change, they needed special help.

By teaching the lesson of faith the first time around, *HaShem* was weaning His people from their previous experiences. Do we do this in our own lives? When we are about to enter a stage in our lives in which God is not as obvious, do we adequately prepare for this test? When our children leave a Torah environment, do we assist them with a period of adjustment? When a young man or woman leaves *Yeshivah*, is it always necessary for them to go "cold turkey"? Wouldn't they prosper from an adjustment period during which they would have an hour or two daily of Torah study inside a Torah atmosphere to assist them in finding the presence of God in their new environment?

Let this model of *Chumash* be a lesson for us all. If we plan our spiritual welfare with wisdom, our chances to triumph are much greater. Who is wise? He who plans for the future (*Tamid* 32a).

Rabbi Doniel Frank

Young Israel of Westport/Norwalk, Connecticut

No sooner had *Bnei Yisrael* sung praise to God in response to the life-saving miracles performed for them at *Yam Suf* (the Red Sea), then they are faced with yet another challenge to their faith. Waterless for three days in hot desert conditions, they arrive at Marah, where the waters are too bitter to drink. They complain to Moshe, who, in turn, prays to God on their behalf. God instructs Moshe to throw a specific tree into the water to sweeten its taste. The people are pacified.

For a full appreciation of this *parshah*, several questions should be addressed.

1. Aside from playing host to this distasteful situation, Marah was also the place where certain *mitzvot* were introduced (see Exodus *Beshalach* 15:25 Rashi on *Shom som lo chok u'mishpat*). These two happenings are linked not only by their common locale but by the Torah's summary of the events of Marah (Exodus 15:25): "There He established for the nation a decree and an ordinance [referring to the *mitzvot*] and there He tested it [referring to the test of the bitter waters]" (see Rashi). What, then, is that connection?
2. Why did HaShem present any *mitzvot* at all prior to the Sinai revelation?
3. The concept of causing *Bnei Yisrael* to be without drinking water is not unique to the challenge of Marah. The Jews encountered a similar trial several times during their desert experience. However, what makes the Marah incident different is that they *did* have water; only, it was too bitter to drink. Why, then, did God introduce this twist on this particular occasion, rather than withhold water from them completely, as He had done in other cases?
4. According to Rashi, the test at Marah was to see how *Bnei Yisrael* would react to a water shortage. Had they asked for the water respectfully,

> they would have passed the test. Instead, they complained bitterly and failed. Although we can understand the value of such a test, why was this the time to give it?

Considering the above, one might arrive at the following conclusions: Clearly, the events at Marah were interrelated and, by their timing, were necessary in order to teach *Bnei Yisrael* a lesson immediately before receiving the Torah. And, the method by which these waters were prepared for consumption helped convey this critical message too. Allow me to elaborate.

Before entrusting *Bnei Yisrael* with His precious Torah, God wished to introduce them to selected *mitzvot* and their desired effects. The combined experiences at Marah were to demonstrate that the ultimate success of Torah involvement is measured by the degree to which that Torah positively influences the character of its adherents. There is a direct correlation between a Jew's pursuit of Torah and spirituality and the way that he or she behaves after having experienced it. Hence, it could be concluded that the demeanor by which one conducts himself at a sumptuous *kiddush* following *musaf* would accurately reflect the degree to which he or she succeeded in that morning's prayer and Torah reading.

In this light, the unique manner by which God tested the Jews can be appreciated. In *Mishlei,* Torah is compared to a tree of life, as it proclaims: "It is a Tree of Life for those who grasp it." (*Eitz chaim hi la'machazikim ba.*) Utilizing this analogy, one can view the sweetening of bitter waters by means of a tree as a symbolic illustration of the intent of the test. The Torah is portrayed as the sweetener of a bitter substance. The as-yet-unrefined nation needed to retain this image as it embarked on the final leg of its journey to Sinai, where it would accept God's Torah. Only with this awareness could it meaningfully proceed to accept the responsibility for living the life of a Torah Jew.

❖ CHAPTER 17 ❖

Yitro

Rabbi Yehoshua Weber

Young Israel of Windsor Park, New York

The Sages say, "A convert who converted is like a newborn"—that is, he assumes an entirely new identity. (*Yevamot* 23a) Yitro, our prototype convert, seems to have flouted this very basic rule.

The *Gemara* in *Yoma* 83b relates how Rav Meir deciphered names. It seems that precise character portrayals can be culled by expounding upon a person's name. We see a similar sentiment expressed by the Rambam (Maimonides) in *Halachot Teshuvah*; he states that it is customary for penitents to change their names to help promote a change of identity. The Ramban (Nachmanides) in his commentary on Exodus 2:16, declares, in a similar vein, that Yitro, upon his conversion, was transformed into Chovav—a complete change of name to help actualize a complete change of identity.

Rashi disagrees and says that conversion modified Yitro's name only slightly, from *Yitro* to *Yeter*. Accordingly, the *Shem Mishmuel* notes that Yitro's spiritual change was obviously only as monumental as his change of identity. Seemingly, conversion only effected a partial metamorphosis. Why?

Yitro, as the saying goes, was a riddle wrapped in a mystery inside an enigma. On the one hand, Rashi quotes the *Mechilta,* which tells us how Yitro experimented with every form of idol worship known to man. On the other hand, Rashi, commenting on Exodus 2:16, cites how Yitro's townspeople excommunicated him because he had rejected their idol. Was he or was he not an idol-worshiper?

A logical conclusion would be that Yitro was a tireless seeker of truth, methodically experimenting with and rejecting idol after idol. In essence, Yitro had, to a large degree, undergone the arduous process of rejecting falsehood even before he accepted the Torah. This process might have eased his conversion and made his transition and, hence—according to Rashi—his name change less drastic than it might have been. A large part of the process had already been accomplished.

This approach helps clarify some of this week's portions' most difficult issues. The *Gemara Zevachim* 11b debates whether Yitro joined the Jews in the desert before or after the giving of the Torah. Rashi (as explained by *Sifrei Chachinamin*, Exodus 18:1, footnotes 1 and Exodus 18:13, footnote 4), states that Yitro came after the giving of the Torah. Yet, the Torah's narration of Yitro's arrival precedes and serves as a prelude to the receiving of the Torah. The question begs to be asked. Why does the Torah preface our introduction to *Yiddishkeit*, the giving of the Torah, with a chronologically misplaced recapitulation of the arrival of a non-Jew (Yitro wasn't even Jewish at the time!) at the Jewish camp? The Ramban addresses some of these issues by assuming that the sequence of events is chronologically correct. Yet, difficulties remain. Let us recall that the Ramban's position is that Yitro's name was changed to Chovav upon conversion. Isn't it ironic that the portion that tells us how to be Jewish is titled after the non-Jewish past of a convert?

I think it is obvious that the Torah wanted us to learn from Yitro's past before *we* accepted the Torah. We must first clearly and emphatically reject all our personal, financial, egotistic, and materialistic idols, just as Yitro did. Disillusionment with the falsehood within each of us is already a major accomplishment. Only then can we properly appreciate the Torah.

This train of thought might help us address yet another set of problems. The *Gemara* asks in *Zevachim* 11b, concerning Yitro: "What did he hear that induced his coming [to join the Jewish people]?" The *Gemara* offers one of three possibilities: the battle with Amalek, the giving of the Torah, or the splitting of the Red Sea. Rashi combines two of these possibilities into one and says that the war with Amalek and the splitting of the Red Sea were the events that attracted Yitro. The *Klei Yakar* states the obvious by noting that the question is not what had Yitro heard; he might very well have heard everything. Rather, the question we actually need answered is which of the many events that Yitro heard about prompted his coming. Why did these specific events galvanize Yitro more than the ten plagues?

A proper understanding of the Egyptians and the Amalekites might shed some light on Yitro's motivations. How did the Egyptians gather the courage to commit yet another act of foolishness by pursuing the Jews into the Red Sea? Were not the ten plagues convincing enough? And why did the Amalekites follow in the illogical footsteps of the Egyptians by attacking the Jews?

It seems that the Amalekites, at least, knew in advance they were fighting a doomed battle. The *Tana Bei Eliyahu* tells us that when the Jews left Egypt, Elifaz called his son Amalek and told him that, if he wanted to benefit both in this world and the next, he should help the Jewish people. Amalek categorically refused and went on to proclaim that he would destroy himself and the whole world rather than help the Jews. Amalek, it appears, was motivated by hate; and hate, as we all know, is irrational.

What motivated this tremendous hate? Amalek, surprising as it may sound, was a child of respectable lineage. His great-grandfather was Yitchok. Amalek's father, Elifaz, who was Esau's son, must have imbibed much of Yitchok's *weltanschauung*.

Rashi, commenting on Genesis 29:11, tells us that Esau sent Elifaz to kill Yaakov but, "because Elifaz was raised by Yitzchok, he held himself back." *Tanchuma* is more explicit: "Because he was raised by Yitzchok, he became righteous and merited Divine revelation."

Concerning Genesis 36:12, Rashi tells us that Amalek's mother was a princess in her early years. She was so determined to associate herself somehow with Yitzchok's family that she resigned herself to being Elifaz's concubine. Amalek saw the beauty and truth of *Yiddishkeit* from his very own background, and yet he still chose to reject it. The only way for Amalek to justify such disassociation was by turning the Jews and *Yiddishkeit* into something vile, by growing to despise them and everything they stood for. Amalek was too close to the Jews, too involved in our destiny, to remain neutral. The Egyptians were as well; after all they had witnessed, they could not remain on the sidelines. They could have admitted philosophical defeat and joined the Jewish nation but they didn't. Therefore, the only path for them to take was to counter their own growing awareness of our righteousness by learning to revile us. Once they learned to hate, they were poised for the most foolish, self-destructive acts.

This is what shocked Yitro. He had wanted to maintain a balanced neutrality, maybe even to sympathize from a distance with the Jews, only to realize that a man of his era, who had seen all the miracles, could either join with the Jews or learn to oppose them. He saw how the Egyptians and Amalekites had consumed themselves in their own frenzy. He saw how hate had driven them insane and he feared for his own sanity.

The lesson is here for all of us to see. Our emotions, unfortunately, exercise greater control over us than we over them. As in the case of the Amalekites, passivity toward the Torah will slowly but surely degenerate into hostility. May we learn to save ourselves from the Amalek within each of us.

Rabbi Moshe S. Gorelik

Young Israel of North Bellmore, New York

While I was attending Brandeis University Graduate School, a professor asked me to write a comparative study of two classical codes, namely the Torah and the Babylonian Code of Hammurabi (which will be referred to as CH). The CH is a remarkable document of ancient law reflecting a civilization that was progressive in its outlook on human affairs. Immediately upon its discovery, it became a favorite academic pastime for semitists to engage in comparing the contents of the CH with that of the Torah and to ask the question, "What is new and different in the latter?" Phrases, case histories, terminologies, and decisions often coincided. Since the CH was supposedly older, many scholars reached the conclusion that the Torah borrowed from its predecessors (see Rav Kasher's *Torah Sheleimah*, vol. 17, pp. 217–224). Outward appearances, however, do not necessarily reflect identical views or moral values. Laws reflect philosophical stances, religious perspectives, and ideological positions. A legal code can best be understood when the context is cast within its moral framework.

I undertook the challenge and proceeded to explore all relevant materials and sources. My study included analyses of the two texts, a survey of rabbinic commentaries and midrashic sources, and the perusal of secondary works on the CH. The conclusion of the study was inevitable. The moral outlook of the CH is relativistic, pragmatic, and economically motivated. Members of different social classes do not stand as equals before the bar of justice. The philosophical consequences of its outlook is that morality, ethics, and justice are determined and defined by circumstances and societal bias. In modern parlance, this approach is called situational ethics.

The Torah, on the other hand, does not brook any intrusion by sociological, political, or economic forces to govern the definition of moral principles. *HaShem*'s Torah represents His ethical will; consequently, the application of *halachah* must be grounded in the universality of justice and morality.

In view of the foregoing, the remarks of Hagaon Harav Yosef Dov, *zt"l*, of Soloveitchik, *zt"l*, are especially meaningful. The *Aseret Hadibrot* are introduced with the words, "And *HaShem* spoke all [*kol*] the words saying. . . ." (*Shmot* 20:1). At first glance, the word "all" (*kol*) appears unnecessary. Were it omitted, the passage would not be diminished in meaning. However, in Rashi's reference to this word, "all" (*kol*), he comments, "This statement tells us that the Holy One Blessed Be He said all these words in one utterance, something that is impossible for a human being to do." Rashi's comment is pregnant with profound meaning. The *Rav zt"l*, points out that the *Aseret Hadibrot* encompass *mitzvot* relating directly to *HaShem* (*bein adam l'Makom*) and those relating to fellow human beings (*bein adam l'chaveiro*). The simultaneous utterance teaches us that all commandments emanate from *HaShem*. *Emunah* in *HaShem* and commitment to moral and ethical integrity are indivisible. "I am *HaShem* your God" is the basis of our faith and religious behavior. If a person dismisses ethical and moral imperatives, his *emunah* is wanting.

This message is reiterated by Rashi in his commentary on the opening passage to *Parshat Mishpatim*, which follows on the heels of *Parshat Yitro*. The main thrust of *Parshat Mishpatim* are *mitzvot bein adam l'chaveiro*. It begins with a *vav* ("and"), thus linking *Parshat Mishpatim* with the preceding *parshah, Yitro*. Rashi declares that this implies that *mitzvot bein adam l'chaveiro* were transmitted from Sinai in conjunction with *mitzvot bein adam l'makom*. Our commitment to all areas of Torah must be unconditional; we do not negotiate with *HaShem*. The Divine imperative is the criterion for our behavior; otherwise, the integrity of *Torah Yahadut* is compromised.

In light of the aforementioned thesis, the following extract from the classic work *The Main Institutions of Jewish Law* (vol. 1, p. 381) by the late, saintly *gaon*, *Harav* Isaac Halevi Herzog, *zt"l*, is enlightening.

> In every civilized society governed by a definite legal system there is the consciousness of a certain gap, more or less wide, sometimes existing between the law as actually enforced by the courts and the categoric imperative of ethical duty. The most advanced systems of law and legislation are ever striving to fill this gap, but it is not always found possible to fill it completely. Owing to certain causes and factors inherent in the law as an agency compelling obedience to duty, it sometimes cannot help falling short of the highest ethical standard and here Jewish law, to an appreciable extent, offers an exception. This peculiarity of Jewish law is due, in no small measure, to its specifically religious character. In Judaism what would generally be described as civil law as an integral part of the Jewish religion. . . . Jewish law . . . is therefore bound to advert to the ethical or higher aspect oftener and with

> greater emphasis than purely secular legal systems. . . . It is part of Torah, in the widest signification of the term, and the Torah is meant to be read and studied by the entire people of Israel. Its scope is therefore not limited by what the courts, for one reason or another, will or will not enforce, but by what is intrinsically right or wrong.

Harav Herzog, *zt"l*, put into bold belief the religious, philosophic view of halachic morality. A commitment to *HaShem* is a commitment to the entirety of His will as embodied in the Torah. The Jewish moral and ethical response to life's situations is spontaneous. A Jew's religious personality strives to the highest standards of moral and ethical behavior; otherwise he betrays the covenant of Sinai, and the covenant of Sinai begins with the declaration, "And *HaShem* spoke all (*kol*) the words saying . . ."

Rabbi Yehoshua Wender

Young Israel of Houston, Texas

There is a famous *midrash* in *Parshat V'zot Habrachah* that relates to the Jewish people's receiving the Torah on Har Sinai. The *midrash* says that, before we received the Torah, *HaShem* went to the children of Esav and offered them the Torah. They asked, "What is in it?" "Thou shalt not murder!" answered *HaShem*. They responded, "Our father built his reputation on murder. How could we leave his ways?" And, so, they refused the Torah.

HaShem then went to the descendants of Yishmael. *HaShem* informed them that stealing was forbidden. They, too, would not abandon the ways of their ancestor.

The children of Amon and Moav also rejected the Torah. Their problem was the prohibition of adultery. After all, their birth was a product of immorality.

Finally, *Bnei Yisrael* were approached and offered the Torah. The *midrash* tells us that the Jewish nation's immediate response was *Naaseh V'nishma*—"we will do and we will listen." They didn't even bother asking what was in the Torah, for they had total trust in *HaShem*. Therefore, the Torah became our legacy forever.

One can assume that *HaShem* offered the Torah to those nations so that in the future they would not be able to come back and complain that only the Jews were given the Torah. The opportunity was there, and they can only blame themselves.

It is important to note that *HaShem* challenged each nation with the law which would present it with the greatest difficulty. It is possible that they could have lived with the other 612 *mitzvot*. Yet, each group failed the overall test.

It would seem that *Bnei Yisrael* never actually had that test. Since they never asked concerning the contents of the Torah, *HaShem* never tempted them with a similar challenge. If this is true, it would be most interesting to know with which *mitvah* would we have had the greatest problem. Would we have been able to pass the test, or would we have failed like the others?

In actuality, there is a deeper understanding of this *midrash*. Our *baalei mussar* (teachers of ethical thought) tell us that the greatest *yetzer harah* (evil inclination) of the Jewish people is in the realm of philosophy. As a people, we are always questioning, always doubting, and often straying. After all, the episode of the golden calf came only forty days after *Matan Torah*. This is the meaning of our being a "stiff-necked people."

It has often been pointed out that the non-Jewish world seems to have much less of a problem with belief. Watching preachers at work, we can see an endless sea of believers. "I believe" seems to come so easily for the rest of the world. The ranks of agnostics, humanists, and atheists always seem to have a large percentage of Jews. Throughout history we have always been among the first to conceive of or embrace new philosophies. Indeed, it is within the realm of the mind that the Jew has always had its stiffest tests.

In the light of this explanation of the *baalei mussar* let us examine the *midrash*. Our response of "we shall do, and we shall listen" seems totally out of character. How unlike our people to accept something on blind faith! One would think that, of all the peoples of the world, we, the Jews, would be most unlikely to react in this way. But, at least for the moment, we reached the level of angels and trusted *HaShem* implicitly. It was our greatest moment. This was, in fact, our greatest test, and we passed it with flying colors, for the "people of the mind" were willing to subjugate their thoughts to those of their Creator. Esav had rejected the Torah because of his people's weakness. Yishmael, Amon, and Moav had done the same. But we had triumphed!

What follows? The first commandment. Belief in *HaShem*. The foundation of our faith—but often the loose brick that gives way. Not murder, not stealing, not immorality. Just plain simple belief. Simple for others; so difficult for us. We now see that we, too, were treated like the others. The hardest came first. The difference is, we said yes!

It is important to note that, like all the other *mitzvot*, belief in *HaShem* has many levels. The older we are, the wiser we grow, the greater should be our *emunah*. This commandment is one of the six *mitzvot tadirot* (constants), and it should therefore attract our special attention. Unfortunately, for many of us, it does not. We are often left with the juvenile understanding of *HaShem* and His universe that we had growing up.

Na'aseh v'nishma came at a moment of great inspiration. Regrettably, it didn't last. The stiff-necked people were soon back in philosophical trouble. We must learn from their error. We must solidify our faith with Torah study that speaks to the issue. The First Commandment isn't first by accident. It deserves our highest priority!

Rabbi Elias Schwartz

Young Israel of Bensonhurst/Bathbeach, New York

BEYOND AND ABOVE NATURAL ORDER

> "And Yitro heard everything that *HaShem* had done to Moshe and to Yisrael, His nation" (Exodus 18:1).
>
> "What hearing did he hear and [then] come? The splitting of the Red Sea and the Battle of Amelek."

He heard of two events—The splitting of the Red Sea and the battle with Amalek. Why does Rashi pinpoint these two events to the exclusion of all the miracles and plagues that were visited upon Egypt?

Rashi also quotes another word within the context of his question. Rashi adds the word *uva*—"and he came." This extra word imparts a tremendous lesson to each and every individual Jew, as we shall soon see.

Miracles and Wars

The splitting of the Red Sea and the war with Amalek were two great miracles beyond and above the natural order of events.

Yitro realized that Israel was different from all other nations. Wars are generally won by people, by efficient and well-armed forces. Miracles are made by *HaShem*, not by man.

These two events placed Israel on a different plane, the opposite of how general and natural causes affect world history.

The greatest miracle of all time, the splitting of *Yam Suf*, was not initiated by God. Not until Nachshon jumped into the raging waters did the sea recede and dry up so that Israel could cross on dry land. This great miracle was made by man. It caught Yitro's imagination.

The war with Amalek was another major difference that Yitro saw. This war and its victory was a result of God's intervention. "When Moshe held up his hands, then Israel prevailed" (Exod. 17:11). When Moshe held up his hands in prayer to *HaShem*, then the enemy was defeated; Yisrael conquered Amalek.

Yitro saw that man created a miracle and *HaShem* won the war.

Rashi had quoted the word *uva*, "and he came," in his original question.

There are two implications in Rashi's explanation.

The first part of this sermon dealt with the greatness and uniqueness of *Klal Yisrael.* We will not live, exist, and thrive like other nations of the world. Our nation is a miraculous one. We can create miracles, and God will take care of us in winning wars.

The Six Day War in 1967 was truly a miracle for Israel. In six days we defeated armies and air forces that could have annihilated our fledgling state of Israel. Before the Six Day War erupted in 1967, graves were dug in all the major cities. Preparations were made for the very worst calamities. Ambulances and *chevrei kadisha* were put on the alert.

On the first day of the war, the Israeli air force destroyed the Egyptian air power. Israelis flew under the radar and bombed and destroyed the Egyptian airplanes, which were sitting ducks, never even getting off the ground. On the second day, the same thing happened to the Syrian air force. The skies were free and clear and not to be feared.

Jordan had joined the Egyptian forces. The battle for a United Jerusalem was a most difficult one. During that fateful week, many American *yeshivot* planned to go by bus to Washington to plead with the United States government to intervene.

The day chosen was Thursday. We in Yeshiva Toras Emes (Brooklyn, New York) went by bus. We said *Tehillim* all the way. When we arrived on Thursday afternoon in Washington, we were greeted by the astounding news that Egypt and Jordan had surrendered. I told all my students that the war was finally won when the enemy *heard* that *yeshivah* students, with their prayers and Torah learning, were beseeching God for help.

Many statements were made by army people and by our coreligionists that this war was won because of the invisible hand of God fighting for us. Many felt that God had won the war for us.

There were some people who couldn't reconcile themselves to the fact that *HaShem* had intervened and made possible an unexpected and miraculous Israeli victory. Some even said that the miracles came from the *sitra acher*—from a negative, impure, destructive force.

Reb Yaakov Kaminetsky, *zt"l,* made two statements at that time. He did not believe that any miracle could be manifest unless *HaShem* willed it to be. Miracles could come only from *HaShem*. He also said that it was remarkable that so many rabbis, distinguished laymen, and army personnel who were in Israel all spoke about miracles. They were upon the scene and active participants in the events of the week. They recognized immediately that there were miracles and that *HaShem* saved our people in 1967 against overwhelming odds.

Uva—*"and he came"*

The added word, *uva*, deals with Yitro as an individual and teaches us a most important lesson. If something extraordinary occurs, you must take notice of it. It must affect your life.

Yitro was captivated by these two events. He immediately reacted by coming to see for himself. He did something that changed his life. He was so inspired that he came to Israel and converted to Judaism. He gave up the wealth, position, and prestige that he had enjoyed in Midian. He gave all this up and came to live in the desert to join Moshe and all Israel.

In 1986 I met a Colonel Bar-On who addressed a group of Torah Umesorah principals in Jerusalem. He was brought up by the *Shomer Hatzair* group, without Torah and religion. When he came home from the war his first statement to his father was "Why didn't you ever teach me that there is a God in this world?"

He became a *baal teshuvah* as a result of what he felt was God's intervention in that fateful war. He was so inspired with the miraculous victory, *that* God wins wars for Israel, that he immediately fulfilled the word "*uva*" in the same way that Yitro did. He came back to God, all the way, and changed his life.

Let us place our hopes for the future of Israel in the hands of *HaShem*. I am sure that *HaShem* is watching over Israel. I put my trust in Him alone. Look about you, at your own personal life. If something extraordinary happens to you, think about its effect on your life. You must react. It must strengthen your belief and faith in *HaShem*.

Remember the impact of the word *uva*. Do something about it.

Look for *HaShem*. You will find Him. You will live a better, more secure and more enjoyable life.

❖ CHAPTER 18 ❖

Mishpatim
Shabbat Shekalim

Rabbi Alan Schwartz

Young Israel of Richmond, Virginia

The coincidence of *Parshat Mishpatim* with *Shabbat Shekalim*—a rather frequent occurrence—makes this a *Shabbat* permeated by *tzedakah*. The giving of *kesef*—money—for the purposes of *tzedakah* appears in the *parshah*, the *maftir*, and the *haftarah*.

OBLIGATORY CHARITY

The *parshah* presents the first of many *mitzvot* that emphasize our obligation to help those in need and to do so in a spirit of brotherhood and generosity.

Im kesef talveh et ami—"If you lend money to my people, to the poor among you, do not behave as a creditor and do not charge any interest" (Exodus 22:24).

Even though the word *im*—"if"—is used, Rashi quotes Rabbi Yishmael in the *Mechilta*, who asserts that the *mitzvah* is an obligation: You *must* lend money. Based on the emphasis the Torah places on providing for the needy in other places, there can be no question that the Torah requires us to lend money and to do so without acting cruel and without charging interest.

Why, then, does the Torah use the word *im*—"if"—making it appear that the loan is discretionary? According to the Malbim, *im* is used because the circumstances may never be right. It is possible that a person may not have money to lend or may not come into contact with a poor person who could use a loan.

Even though this *mitzvah* is contingent on there being an opportunity, no one is exempt from giving *tzedakah* at some time each year, according to one's ability. The universal tradition among Ashkenazic Jews is to give *maaser kesafim*—one-tenth of one's income—for the support of the poor. One may devote up to one-fifth of his income for *tzedakah*.

THE HALF-SHEKEL AND COMMUNAL OBLIGATIONS

The reading for the *maftir* discusses the donation of a *machtzit hashekel*—half-shekel—for communal obligations. Rashi explains that the Israelites leaving Egypt actually were assessed twice. The first tax was to provide the silver needed for building the *Mishkan*. The second tax, which was repeated annually, was to provide for the communal sacrifices. Unlike *tzedakah*, which is contingent on ability, this assessment was equal for rich and poor alike. It was paid by men aged twenty and above.

Today, we follow a custom of re-enacting the ancient half-shekel by donating a half-coin of local currency (in the United States, a half-dollar), before reading the *Megillah* on Purim. This relates to the *Gemara*'s statement that Haman's plan to kill the Jews was foiled by the *mitzvah* of the half-shekel. Haman planned to pay the king for the right to annihilate the Jews, but the Jews were saved through the merit of their own payment of half a shekel (*Megillah* 13b).

I would suggest that the merit of the half-shekel is the support of the Jewish community. The purpose of the payment was to provide for communal institutions and sacrifices. In forming the community, everyone is equal, but, at the same time, individuals are incomplete. Half-shekels must be joined together to form a whole, and, when this is accomplished, God abides among the people, forgives their sins, and protects the nation from harm.

[Many *Poskim* follow the opinion of the *Rama* (*Yorah Deah* 249) that one may not use money set aside for *maaser kesafim* to pay for synagogue obligations. Just as the *mitzvot* of *tzedakah* and *machtzit hashekel* are separate, our charitable obligations are also different. Support of the community's institutions is like the half-shekel—an independent monetary obligation. Just as we pay our individual employees and we buy oil and electricity to use in our homes, so, too, we pay for the people who serve us by maintaining the synagogue and for the oil and electricity we use whenever we enter the building. On the other hand, the tithe for the needy is strictly money given to benefit others. (Many *Poskim*, however, do allow funds from *maaser kesafim* to be used for all charities if the donor is of limited resources.)]

THE FREE-WILL DONATION TO THE TEMPLE

In addition to obligatory offerings, the *maftir* alludes to the free-will offerings that the Children of Israel brought for the construction of the *Mishkan*. (This brings the number of donations mentioned in the *maftir* to three. Consequently, the custom is for everyone actually to give three half-shekels on Purim.) Similar contributions, brought to restore the *Beit Hamikdash* in the time of King Yehoash, are the subject of the *haftarah*.

Rabbi Mendel Hirsch (son of Rabbi Samson Raphael Hirsch), in his commentary to the *haftarot*, compares the account in II *Melachim* (II Kings 12) with the account in II *Divrei Hayamim* (II Chronicles 24). Yehoash asked the *Kohanim* to collect donations from the people, particularly from their closest friends, to finance the restoration. He encountered reluctance on the part of priests, now relegated to the role of tax collectors, and of the people, who saw the Temple as a symbol of holiness.

Rabbi Hirsch comments: "It is just so infinitely characteristic of the Jewish Sanctuary of the Torah that . . . it depended solely on the free-willed devotion of its children. Apart from the above-mentioned half-shekel . . . there was no sort of 'tax' or gift for the Sanctuary which did not rest on completely free-willed undertaking."

Yehoash's solution was to establish the first *pushke*, a chest with a hole in its lid, set in the Temple for offerings. Left on their own, the people duplicated the enthusiasm of the Israelites who built the *Mishkan*, filling the chest with donations on a daily basis.

Rabbi Asher Schechter

Young Israel of Merrick, New York

Many *mitzvot* and *dinim* of *Parshat Mishpatim* are repeated in *Parshat Ki Tetzeh* in *Sefer Devarim*—also known as *Mishneh Torah* (the repetition of the Torah). It is an interesting study to analyze, for each particular topic, the minor differences of presentation between these two sources and the lessons to be learned from them. Let us zero in on two specific *mitzvot*.

In *Parshat Mishpatim*, the *mitzvah* of *hashavat avedah* (returning lost objects to their rightful owner) is immediately followed by the *mitzvah* of helping an owner with his fallen animal. In describing these two *mitzvot*, the Torah picks a scenario in which you find a lost object that belongs to your enemy and/or you see the animal, of someone you hate, fallen in the road. The Torah demands your assistance even though you don't care for either individual as a person. These same two *mitzvot* are repeated in *Parshat Ki Tetzeh*, in the very same order. However, there the Torah describes the *mitzvot* with the word *achicha* (your brother). If you find something that belongs to your brother, you must return it; and if you see your brother's animal fallen, you must help him. Why the change? What is being added by the second version of these *mitzvot*, requiring us to help our brothers and friends? If we must help enemies, surely we must help friends?

The *Gemara Pesachim* 113b asks another pertinent question. Why does a Jew have an enemy? The *Gemara* assumes that the Torah is talking to an observant Jew. How is he permitted to hate his fellow Jew? The *Gemara* answers that one is allowed to hate a fellow Jew who knowingly and willfully transgresses the Torah. According to Rav Nachman bar Yitzchak it is even a *mitzvah* to hate him. Thus, according to the discussion in Talmud *Pesachim*, the *pasuk* in *Mishpatim* demands that we help people whom we are permitted to hate, with their lost objects and fallen animals.

Tosafot ask a question from a statement made in the *Tosefta* quoted in the *Gemara Bava Metziah* 32b. Normally it is considered more important to help unload a fallen animal than to help reload it. This is because of the concept of *tzar baalei chaim* (pain for living creatures), since the fallen animal is in pain under its load. However, the *Tosefta* states, if you have a choice between helping a friend unload his fallen animal or helping an enemy reload his animal, one should choose to help the enemy despite the *tzar baalei chaim*. The reason given is *kidey lachuf et yitzro* (translated simply: "in order to conquer his *yetzer hara*" (evil inclination), which doesn't want him to help the enemy altogether). *Tosafot*'s reason that this *Tosefta* makes a lot of sense if the enemy is hated for the wrong reasons; there is a need to conquer this *yetzer hara*. However, if the Torah sanctions the hatred of such a person—as the *Gemara* in *Pesachim* indicates—then what *yetzer hara* is there to conquer? He is fully justified and even commended for this hatred. Thus, it appears that the *Tosefta* understood the enemy as one who was hated because of the *yetzer hara*, which must be conquered, but the *Gemara* in *Pesachim* understands it as the transgressor who should be hated.

Tosafot answer with a profound thought. Hatred that is sanctioned by the Torah can lead to additional animosity that is *not* permitted. There still is room for conquering the *yetzer hara* and limiting the hatred to the issues pertaining to the transgressions of the Torah and preventing the hatred from spreading and becoming personal in nature. Hence, the *Tosefta* requires us to compromise *tzar baalei chaim* in order to conquer this *yetzer hara*.

I would like to offer an alternate answer to *Tosafot*'s question. The words *kidey lachuf et yitzro* in the *Tosefta* can be understood to be conquering the *yetzer hara* of *the sinner*, not the *yetzer hara* of the one commanded to help. Imagine a Jew who knowingly and willfully transgresses the Torah. The God-fearing, Torah-observant community hates him for his actions, as prescribed in the *Gemara Pesachim*. We can imagine that the feelings are mutual and that the sinner hates the religious community as well. Now, the sinner is traveling the road with his donkey, and it falls under its heavy load. Suddenly, a God-fearing Jew appears and offers to help him reload even before helping his fellow God-fearing Jew whose animal is fallen and still in pain under its load. The sinner can't help being impressed by the power of Torah observance. No other set of laws could dictate such devotion against emotions and better judgment. This experience should so deeply impress the sinner that he should be able to conquer *his yetzer hara* and return to Torah observance. Thus, the *Tosefta* was compromising on *tzar baalei chaim* in order to help bring back the *neshamah* of a forlorn sinner.

We can now understand the reason for the change from the enemy in *Mishpatim* to the brother in *Ki Tetzeh*. The word *achicha* is understood throughout the Talmud to refer to a Torah-observant Jew, *achicha bemitzvot* (your brother in *mitzvot*). The first time you chance upon a man with a donkey fallen over, or you find his lost object, he may be a sinner. Therefore, the first discussion of the *mitzvah* in *Mishpatim* refers to the enemy whom you are permitted to hate for his bad deeds. However, if you treat him warmly and fairly and you show him how caring the Torah is, then the next time you meet him on the road and he needs your assistance he will already be *achicha*, your fellow God-fearing, Torah-observant Jew. Thus, the second mention of the *mitzvah* in *Ki Tetzeh* calls him your brother—who was transformed by your kindness and beautiful actions.

This lesson is most important for us who live in a society full of non-religious Jews. We must make a strong effort to show them that the Torah maintains a higher standard and brings out the best in people. We must do everything in our power *kidey lachuf et yitzro*, to help them return to authentic Torah *Yiddishkeit*.

Rabbi Sholom Steinig

Young Israel of Bayside, New York

Parshat Mishpatim introduces us to the idea that the *mitzvot* between man and his fellow man are more than just the societal or moral teachings that the world presumes them to be; they are religious precepts. The opening words of the *parshah* serve to complete the overview of Jewish life and law that was begun in last week's *parshah, Yitro*. Receiving the Ten Commandments at Mount Sinai was the acceptance of *Torah*; the *mitzvot* at the end of *Yitro* describing the building of the altar in the Temple represent *avodah*, service; today's reading, with the interpersonal *mitzvot* that it contains, is the embodiment of *gemilut chasadim*, kindness; together they complete the cycle of the three values upon which the world's existence is predicated, as we are taught at the beginning of *Pirke Avot*, the Ethics of the Fathers.

The opening *mitzvah* in this *parshah* is that of the Jewish bondsman, the case of the thief who was punished by being sold into servitude to pay for his crime. This, obviously, is considered to be the most appropriate of the *mitzvot* between man and his fellow man with which to open the *sedrah*, for the mention of slavery reminds us of our slavery in Egypt. Just as the Ten Commandments open with the reminder that *HaShem* took us out of Egypt, so, too, do the moral laws begin with such a reminder. The mention of work also helps us remember the wonderful Divine gift of *Shabbat*, when we are mandated to take a break from our labors.

The concept of the Jewish slave seems somewhat foreign to us. The idea, though, of having a thief work off his debt does seem to make a lot of sense. By forcing the thief to become part of a family, living with them, working with them, and eating with them, we hope to show him the importance of societal interworkings, as well as the importance of trust and selflessness. As a slave, the former criminal does not suffer. He may not be assigned embarrassing work, nor may he be given work that is too physically taxing. The master is constantly reminded that the example of Pharaoh as a slave master is the antithesis of that which a Jew may follow. When there is only one comfortable bed, or if there is only enough fine-quality food for one, it is the slave who must receive them; this is the master's obligation. This is why our Rabbis tell us that slavery involves more obligations on the part of the slaveholder than on the slave himself. When the slave sees his superior give over his best possessions to him, the slave begins to learn how human beings can relate, and hopefully he begins to learn how to live an honest life.

We are also told that it can happen that the slave's new lifestyle becomes attractive to him and that he may not wish to leave. (This, by the way, is the reason why only slaves who are already married may be given wives while in servitude; it is hoped that at the end of the slaves' six-year term of duty they will want to go back to their original families. Slaves who have no families are not given the opportunity to start one while still in bondage because we do not want them to feel comfortable that they stay on with their new families after they are freed.) In these cases, we are told that the master shall take the slave to court and that the slave shall make a declaration of his wishing to stay on as a slave. The master then brings the slave to the doorpost, takes an awl, and drills a hole in the slave's ear. The symbolism of this act is important. The doorpost represents the opportunity for freedom which the slave is forfeiting. His opting to accept his master "forever" (until the Jubilee year) requires that his ear, which heard at Mount Sinai that only God is his master, must be punished. The master, and no one else, must carry out this punishment, to serve as a reminder that he remains as much in the slave's obligation as the slave does in his. The drilling of his slave's ear is as much a drilling of his own because his obligations in caring for the slave even outweigh his own personal needs.

The Talmud additionally teaches that the drilling of the slave's ear is also a punishment for not hearing the commandment "You shall not steal." This view, however, raises the question of why we wait six years before carrying out this part of the punishment. The thief was originally sold as a punishment for stealing; his ear should have been drilled then, rather than six years later when he decides to remain a slave in perpetuity. Perhaps we can answer that his original sale caused a deferment of the drilling and that it stood temporarily in place of the drilling. Six years later, when the slave does not wish to claim his freedom and when he imposes, as it were, an extended slavery and obligation not only himself but on his master as well, we belatedly punish the ear that did not listen to the command "You shall not steal." And it is his master, who is now also a slave, who must carry out this punishment and feel it as though it was his ear that was now being pierced.

The Torah text describing the slave's claim to remain a slave is as follows: "And if the slave shall surely say, 'I love my master, my wife, and my children; I will not go free . . .'" (Exodus 21:5). The words "shall surely say"—*amor yomar* in the Hebrew text—are understood to mean that the slave must repeat his request to remain a slave for life. Rabbi Elchanan Wasserman, *zt"l*, quoting his teacher Rabbi Chaim Brisker, *zt"l*, applies this teaching to the final request of Moshe *Rabbeinu* to be admitted into the land of Israel. "I love my master"—this is *HaShem*; "and my wife"—this is *Torah*; "and my children"—this is the People of Israel; "I will not go free"—I do not wish to be separated from them. *HaShem* answered Moshe at this point,—"Do not continue to speak to Me further regarding this matter." Rabbi Yehoshua Leib Diskin, *zt"l*, explains that *HaShem* was not going to allow Moshe to use his complete understanding and comprehension of the Torah to trick his way into *Eretz Yisrael*. Had Moshe said the formula one more time, as according to *amor yomar*, *HaShem* would have had no choice but to allow him to remain a "slave in perpetuity" and continue living in this world. God's choice of words, "Do not continue to speak," indicates that He saw what Moshe's plan was and put a stop to it before the fateful formula could be repeated. Had Moshe *Rabbeinu* repeated those words, the Torah itself would have mandated that *HaShem* permit him to continue to live and enter *Eretz Yisrael*.

❖ CHAPTER 19 ❖

Terumah

Rabbi Kenneth Stein

Young Israel of Baychester,
New York

HOLY SEPARATIONS

The opening passages of this week's *sedrah* have puzzled and tantalized commentators for generations. The problems with the text are many, some subtle and some obvious.

For one thing, the Torah uses the expression *veyikchu li terumah*, "and they shall take unto Me a *terumah* offering" instead of the more common *veyitnu li*, "and they shall give Me." In addition, the Torah enumerates the list of required materials even before it is clear what *Bnei Israel* would be expected to build.

In a beautiful analysis of the first portion of this week's *sedrah*, Rabbi Zvi Kanotopsky, *zt"l*, the much-loved Rosh Yeshivah and Young Israel Rabbi, notes that the *Bnei Yisrael* were asked to perform two separate and distinct tasks: first, to separate and dedicate a portion of their wealth to God's purpose and, second, to build the *Mishkan*.

The stages of the *mitzvah*, according to Rav Kanatopsky, directly parallel the more common form of *terumah*, the farmers' annual offering to the *kohein*. In the *halachah* of *terumah*, we learn of several stages in the process of preparing a holy gift. At first, the farmer's crop in its original state is called *tevel*. It is forbidden to the farmer until he has performed the next step. This step is called *hafrashah*, the separation or designation of the *terumah*. At this point, the crop is permitted, even though the *terumah* has not been physically removed. Lastly, *nesinah*, the actual presentation of the gift to the *kohein*.

We can deduce from the *mitzvah* of *terumat Kohein* that there is a distinct procedure that must be followed in order to create *kedushah* in the human sphere. The essence of this process is a form of *havdalah* in which the Jew seeks to create a division between the sacred and the profane. The farmer creates *terumah* and all the accompanying restrictions merely by the act of *hafrashah*, separating. Throughout the Torah, holiness is created through the act of separation. The first step of the construction of the *Mishkan*, therefore, was an act of separation.

Rav Kanatopsky points out that even the materials of the *Mishkan* closely parallel the forms of *havdalah*—separation—we invoke every Saturday night:

Oil for the lamp corresponds to the *havdalah* between light and dark.
The stones of the breastplate listing the names of the tribes correspond to the *havdalah* between Israel and the other nations.
The anointing oil (used to dedicate articles for holy use) corresponds to the *havdalah* between the sacred and profane.
The labors in constructing the *Mishkan* (the source of all our *Shabbat* laws) correspond to the *havdalah* between *Shabbat* and the rest of the week.

At Mount Sinai, the *Bnei Yisrael* experienced God's Holiness as it descended to them. How were they to maintain such levels of *kedushah*? God's answer came in ordering the construction of the *Mishkan*. The *Mishkan* was meant to teach the people that they could create holiness in their own midst—*veshachanti betocham*. How? By *taking* the *terumah*. Not *giving* it. Holiness is born of a separation.

I recall a story of a beleaguered rabbi of a small Orthodox synagogue whose membership were tempted by the lure of mixed seating. In one of the many debates on the issue, the rabbi dramatically drew a line on the ground behind the last pew and declared "*ad kan beit haknesset*—up to this line the sanctity of the synagogue will prevail." The rabbi was making a *havdalah* without candle or spices. He was delineating the power of the Jew to create a place of *kedushah* on earth. He was also cautioning his community that in order to maintain a holy atmosphere, we must create an immovable boundary against the encroachments of secularist ideas and fads in the house of *HaShem*.

We of the Young Israel movement are blessed to enjoy the spiritual treasures of the traditional Orthodox *shul*. However, lest we take for granted the holiness of our lives, let us always remember that we remain holy only to the extent that we perform *havdalah* and take *terumot*.

GOD'S DONATION

The *midrash* tells us that *HaShem* took part in the donations toward the building of the *Mishkan*. According to the *Targum Yonasan*, the Heavenly clouds brought the gemstones for the *ephod* and breastplate from the Garden of Eden.

In order to understand this *midrash*, we must remember the purpose of the stones in the priestly vestments. According to the Torah, the stones were engraved with the names of the twelve tribes of Israel. Whenever a dispute between the tribes arose, the matter was brought before the *Kohein Gadol.* By gazing at the stones, the *Kohein Gadol* was able to see some of the letters of the names on the stones light up, which indicated to him a message. This led to a correct and, most important, peaceful resolution of conflict.

This marvelous gift of *shalom bayis* in the house of Israel and, especially, in the House of God was God's donation to us.

Sometimes, in our zeal for the betterment of our beloved synagogues, we carelessly and foolishly cause hurt feelings and damage the mutual love that is the cornerstone of public worship. Many of us have noticed that at the very beginnings of many *siddurim* there is a reminder that we must accept the principle of *V'ahavta le'reyacha kamocha*, "you shall love your neighbor as yourself," before beginning to daven. Yet, how often we trample on each other's feelings through an unfortunate word.

We must remember the gemstones from Paradise that were God's gift to us.

Rabbi Herschel Kurzrock

Young Israel of Kensington, New York

"And they shall construct a Tabernacle for Me and I shall dwell in their midst" (Exodus 25:8). The Almighty commands the Jewish people to build Him a *Mishkan* (Tabernacle) so that He may dwell among them.

Rebbe Mendel of Kotzk deduces from the expression *besochum* ("in their midst") that the building of a physical *Mishkan* for *HaShem* is to be accompanied by the construction of a "spiritual" Tabernacle in the heart of every Jew; and the *Shechinah*—Divine Presence—will dwell, literally, *besochum*—in them, in the heart of each and every Jew (*Shaloh, Shaar Haosiyot*). In conjunction with this profound concept, a favorite saying of Rebbe Mendel, when asked by any layman, "Where is the veritable dwelling place for the Divine Presence?" was *Vu men lust Im arayn*—"Where He is 'invited' in"! If the innermost recesses of the mind and heart of a good person are permeated with love and reverence for *HaShem* . . . then *V'shachanti besochum*—"And I shall dwell among them"—spiritually.

Extending the above thought, one can learn by symbolism that the structure of the *Mishkan* and its appurtenances, aside from the "actual" construction adhering to the command of *HaShem*, serve also as a sacred model for each and every Jew's spiritual structure (see *Klei Yakar*, Abarbanel). "Just as I show you the form of the *Mishkan* and the form of all its appurtenances, and so shall you do!" (Exodus 25:9). The last words of this verse, "and so shall you do," in addition to the halachic interpretation (*Sanhedrin* 16b), symbolically allude to the building of one's own spiritual structure (see *Imrei Shefer* and *Divrei Shaul*).

In accordance with the measurements of the sacred vessels of *HaShem*'s Sanctuary, one should establish his own spiritual measurements, in a sincere effort to become a true servant of *HaShem*—a veritable receptacle for the Divine Presence. Thus, the dimensions of the *Mishkan* and its sacred vessels are also the specifications for the building and developing of the spiritual architectural achievement—the Jewish ideal: a Torah-true Jew, one whose very being is permeated with a reverence for Torah Judaism, with a passion for the study of Torah in all its ramifications, and with a heartfelt desire for practical observance, at every opportunity, of all its precepts.

Appropriately, the first object of the *Mishkan* to be discussed as to its proper construction and dimensions is the Ark. It contained the *Luchot* (Tablets) and is the symbol of Torah, which is *Klal Yisrael*'s most sacred treasure. Torah must represent to every Jew values that are eternal and that neither time nor any power on earth can surmount.

"And they shall make an Ark." The command to build an Ark was expressed by the Torah in plural form, "And they shall make." This is the only object of the *Mishkan* in which the command is expressed in words that depict Torah as the "possession" of every Jew, and the basic components in the life of every Jew are his commitment to and involvement in all its aspects—viewpoint, study, support, practice, and dissemination to future generations throughout life.

The measurements of the Ark are incomplete ones, not full figures. The length was two cubits and "a half"; the breadth, a cubit and "a half," and the height, a cubit and "a half." Figuratively these broken measurements represent the basic truth that no one, not even the greatest of *talmidei chachomim* can reach perfection in Torah learning, the heights of a "complete" Torah personality—saintliness. One must seek fulfillment by constantly striving to attain greater excellence in Torah learning and to reach spiritually richer and loftier levels of piety throughout life.

These broken dimensions seem also to allude to a famous saying of our Sages in the *Gemara* (*Brakhot* 8a)—"From the day that the *Beit hamikdash* was destroyed, the Almighty has in the world only the four cubits of *halachah*—Torah (as a dwelling place for the Divine Presence)." The dimensions of the length (2½ cubits) and the width (1½ cubits) of the Ark which represent Torah, equal "four cubits by four cubits" for all the sides of the Ark, thus implying the profound saying of our Sages that the Almighty considers only the four cubits of Torah as His dwelling place—for the Divine Presence in this world.

The *Baal Haturim* states that the letters of the word *aron* (Ark) can be composed to spell the word *oran* (light) and also *nura* (blight or fire). One might say that this symbolizes a profound thought that Torah, when studied and adhered to properly, is the guiding light for a nobler spiritual life; and if, Heaven forbid, Torah is studied with ulterior motives and practiced with distortion, this type of adherence to Torah leads to ultimate spiritual self-destruction. This concept is in consonance with the saying of the Rabbis in the *Gemara* (*Taanit* 7a), "For he who is engaged in Torah learning and practice, *lishmah*—for Heaven's sake—the Torah becomes a life-giving drug," but "anyone who is engaged in Torah learning and practice *shelo lishmah*—not for Heaven's sake, with ulterior motives in mind—for him the Torah becomes a deadly poison."

The Torah is also likened to fire (*Kiddushin* 30b; *Taanit*, ibid.). It is written (Jeremiah 23:29), "For My words are like fire, sayeth *HaShem*." Fire can be a source of light and warmth to a person if he keeps the "proper distance," but fire becomes a means of destruction when it gets out of control or when one comes too close to the flames!

Likewise with Torah; he who studies sincerely, *lishmah*—for the *mitzvah*—will realize and appreciate his proper "place" in relation to Torah and Torah scholars. When among greater scholars than he, he will keep silent and "drink with thirst their words of Torah" (*Avot* 1:4). However, when he is the best educated in Torah among a group, he will realize his responsibilities and guide the others. Thus Torah, likened to "fire," will be for him, and all coming in contact with him, a source of "light and warmth"—intellectual attainment coupled with fervent performance. On the other hand, he who seeks undeserved honors and recognition and studies with ulterior motives and to be disputatious (see *Tosafot Taanit* 7a) is not recognizing his proper "place"—role—in regard to Torah. He is coming too close to the Torah "fire" and for him, Heaven forbid, Torah becomes ultimately a death potion!

As our Sages say (*Avot* 6:6), one of the forty-eight qualities that a sincere Torah student must acquire to reach the heights of a true Torah scholar is to be a "*makir et mekomo*"—that is, someone who recognizes his place in the Torah world.

The above thoughts depict possible symbolic meanings inherent in various aspects of the first article of the *Mishkan* discussed in *Parshat Terumah*—the Ark, representing the Torah, the eternal shared treasure of the Jewish people.

May we all be *zocheh*—worthy by dint of Torah study *lishmah*—for the *mitzvah*'s sake—of reaching great heights in Torah learning and being able to deduce and comprehend the hidden, symbolic meanings and spiritual treasures represented by the Tabernacle and its sacred vessels, as well as in every letter of the Torah. Torah will then truly be a source of "light and warmth" for us all, ennobling and exalting every facet of our lives and making us deserving of a speedy redemption.

Rabbi Jordan Hoffman

Young Israel of Patchogue, New York

"Speak to the Children of Israel and let them take Me a portion . . ."

Imagine entering a marketplace or a retail store. You wish to make a purchase—say, for example, a multimedia 250-megahertz Pentium computer to put in your home office. You purchase the item. The owner gives you the sales receipt and places the computer in the trunk of your car. That's very nice. It is rare for the owner to place the computer in your car.

You drive home, excited about your purchase. When you arrive, you are greeted with a pleasant surprise. The owner has driven to your home to help you unpack the computer. Shocking. This is no longer merely rare, it is unheard of.

But wait, that is not all. The owner sits down with you and shows you the subtleties of Windows 98. He guides you step by step in how to get the most out of every application that is loaded into your computer. He then transfers your previous files into your new Pentium. He spends the entire day with you. The next day he comes in and trains your secretary. In fact, he now comes in every day. You sit in amazement at this economic impossibility, jaw agape. Finally, you ask him why he is doing this. He answers, "When you purchased the computer from me I came along with it."

Sheer fantasy? No.

The *midrash* in *Shemot Rabbah* (33:6) states:

> "And let them take Me a portion." It is written, *Ki lekach tov natati Lachem, Torati al taazovu*—"For I have given you a precious gift, My Torah do not forsake" (*Mishlei* 4:2). Said Rev Brachyah *Hakohen*: . . . Ordinarily, when one buys an article in the market, is he then able to acquire its owner too? But the Holy One, Blessed be He, gave the Torah to Israel and said to them [if it can be said]: "You are acquiring Me!" Hence, "And let them take Me a portion."

This is the beauty of Torah. The previously described scenario is an actual reality when it comes to Torah. When we study Torah, we are actually (if it can be said) acquiring *HaShem* Himself. This means that the nature of Torah study is such that we are acquiring both a relationship and a direct link with *HaShem*.

How? The study of God's *mitzvot* allows us to emulate *HaShem*'s nature. The *Gemara* in *Shabbat* 133b states, "*Ma hu rachum af Atah rachum*. . . . Just as He is merciful, so, too, should you be merciful." An example: In this week's *parshah*, *HaShem* tells us, "And you shall make the boards for the Tabernacle of acacia wood" (Exodus 26:15). Asks the *midrash*, "Why of acacia wood?" Surely, one of the other woods would have been much more suitable. The *midrash* explains that *HaShem* set an example for all time: When a man is about to build a house from a fruit-bearing tree, this initial tabernacle serves as an example. If *HaShem* Himself, the supreme King of Kings, commanded that the Temple be erected and yet stipulated that only non–fruit-bearing trees be used, how much more so should this be the case when man builds a house! By studying this, *HaShem*'s Torah, we begin the process of self-improvement through emulating Him.

By exploring this idea a little further, we can better appreciate the importance of providing everyone with a proper *yeshivah* education: it brings one closer to God. Conversely, we can also see the effects of denying someone a *yeshivah* education.

The Chofetz Chaim was known as the greatest *tzaddik* of his generation. He most assuredly fulfilled the *Pirkei Avot*–based dictum to greet everyone *besaiver ponim yafot*—with a smile and good cheer. Yet there was one instance when, in fact, he did not. It was approximately the year 1920, after the massive upheavals of the Russian Revolution. A rabbi came to see the saintly Chofetz Chaim. Knocking on the door, the man was shocked that the Chofetz Chaim gave him a quick glance and decided not to receive him. "I don't wish to see you, please go away." What? Is this how the Chofetz Chaim is responding to me? The man knocked again, only to receive the same response. Finally after seeing the man's persistence, the Chofetz Chaim let him in.

"You are 'Rabbi So and So,' are you not?"

"Yes . . ."

"You have been in charge of the *Yeshivah Ketanah* in that community for the past thirty years. Is that correct?"

"Yes . . ."

"Well, do you remember Lev Bronstein?"

"Bronstein? No . . ."

"Think hard!"

"Bronstein . . . Bronstein . . . Hmm . . . I seem to vaguely recall a young boy with that name. . . . But he was just with us for a short while. . . ."

"Well, why was that?"

"He was unable to pay any tuition, and we just couldn't keep him. . . ."

"Do you realize what you have done—what you could have averted if you had but kept that boy in *yeshivah*?"

"No. What do you mean?"

"Don't you realize," answered the Chofetz Chaim, "that Lev Bronstein is Leon Trotsky?"

Leon Trotsky—political agitator instrumental in the overthrow of the Czarist Russian regime. Imagine once again. Had the young Lev Bronstein stayed in *yeshivah*, seventy-five years of the absolute repression of Jewish study could possibly have been averted. Entire generations of Jews, now lost, could have yet been retained. "Let them take Me a portion."

Is this an example? Does the *yeshivah* education of just one child really make that much difference? Yes, because it is not just that child that we are dealing with. It is also his or her children, grandchildren, and all those who would have come under his or her sphere of influence. And often the effect is not immediate. If we look around we can see the astounding effects that a *yeshivah* education has, often after many many decades. A woman in the late 1930s works every day in other people's homes to earn the money to send her son to *yeshivah*. The child attends *yeshivah* but later joins the army and assimilates into American society, forgetting Torah and *Yiddishkeit*—or so it seems. Twenty years later, he spends two and a half hours ferrying his children and other children to *yeshivah*, and thirty years after that he has grandchildren in *yeshivah* in *Eretz Yisrael*.

Another case in point. A young, entirely unaffiliated kindergarten girl living with her entirely unaffiliated grandparents and attending public school learns that her Catholic classmate is leaving school to attend a Catholic school. The young girl demands of her grandparents that they find her a Jewish school, since she is Jewish. They do. Fifteen years later the grandparents are a veritable bastion of Torah and *mitzvot*.

It is said that the true Rosh Hashanah for many children is not the first of Tishrei but, rather, the day that it is decided whether a child will or will not be enrolled or accepted in a *yeshivah*.

Let us reflect upon the beauty of the gift that is Torah, truly a gift without parallel. Let us also think of ways that we can assist in providing this most precious gift to others by encouraging them to seek out a *yeshivah* education or by providing them with one.

❖ CHAPTER 20 ❖

Tetzaveh

Rabbi Yehoshua Weber

Young Israel of Canarsie, New York

The colors we use, whether in dress or décor, say a lot about us. Businesslike gray projects a certain type of image, whereas brighter shades project another, very different one. Pastel tints calm, whereas brighter shades agitate. Light colors lift us up; darker shades can pull us down.

What is true of people is even truer of the Divine. The materials, textures, and colors used in the *Beit Hamikdash*—the Sanctuary—were not, *chas veshalom*, chosen by chance. There must be philosophical underpinnings to the sanctuarial color schemes; let us attempt to decipher them.

"And they shall take the gold, the sky blue, the purple and the red wool and the [white] linen" (Exodus 28:5).

In *Aichah* (4:7), we read, "Her princes were purer than snow. . . . Their appearance ruddier than rubies." In *Shir Hashirim* (5:10), we read, "My beloved is pure and reddish." Red seems to be the color of exuberant, possibly even undisciplined, vitality. This vitality can be dangerous. It is entirely possible for this raw, red, human dynamism, if not properly harnessed, to become the blood-red of malignancy and murder.

Commenting on *Toldot* (Genesis 25:25) Rashi quotes the *Bereishit Rabbah*, which states that Esav's ruddiness at birth was a harbinger of his proclivity for spilling blood. A clearer indication of crimson's devastating potential can be culled from the *pasuk* in *Yeshaiah*, Isaiah 1:18, "If your sins are as red wool, as snow shall they whiten"—red being clearly synonymous with guilt. The *Mishnah*, in *Shabbat* 86a deduces from the aforementioned *pasuk* that a crimson string was attached to the *Azazel* goat of Yom Kippur; that string would whiten when the community was forgiven. Here, too, forgiveness is white, whereas sin is red.

Rabbi Samson Raphael Hirsch, in his collected writings, draws a similar conclusion from his remarkable analysis of the very structure of color and light. He notes that when a ray of light is beamed through a prism, it separates into the spectrum of colors. Among the rainbow of divergent colors angling away from the prism, the red ray is closest to the unbroken light absorbed by the prism. It seems that light, in its "initial fusion with terrestrial matter," is tinged red. Red might symbolize Divine light just beginning to peek through the earthly matter that we are. Red might also symbolize someone or something that has not yet reached its full potential.

Rabbi Samson Raphael Hirsch discerns the etymological root of *adam* (earthy man) in *hadom* (footstool), and *eden* (the base of a column). A footstool and a base both exist only to support what is above them. It seems, then, that both words refer to someone or something beginning to propel itself toward ever-greater heights. *Adom* (red), the etymological cousin of *adam* (man), alludes to the same process—red climbing its way into the spectrum of more spiritually advanced colors, colors more distant than red from the original ray of light divided by the prism.

These insights are in perfect resonance with other interpretations of *adam*. The Radak draws a parallel between *adam* (man) and *adamah* (earth)—a clear emphasis on man's lowly beginning. The Netziv also relates *adam* to *adamah*: "I can and will become similar to the Almighty; inasmuch as man was created in God's image, that within man, as like within Earth, are all the potential strengths of creation." Here, too, *adam* seems to describe someone striving toward his potential rather than someone who has reached it. *Adamah* implies, "I will become similar, although I have not as of yet." It is reasonable to postulate, is it not, that what is true of *adam*, man, in relation to *adamah*, earth, is true of *odom*, red. Red is the initial color of our spiritual quest, just as a base is the initial support of our soon-to-be-erected structure.

If red is the color of humble inception, what then is the color of perfect, unadulterated spirituality? Is it not *techelet*—sky blue, as in "The sky blue [of *tzitzit*] is like the sea, which is like the sky, which is like *HaShem*'s throne." The Ramban, in his discussion of *tzitzit*, in *Bamidbar*, correlates *techelet* with the word *tachlit*—goals met and results achieved. The Ramban continues, "Also, in colors, [blue] is the ultimate vision, for at a distance everything is seen as this color." The *Meor v'Shemesh* crystallizes the Ramban's idea by noting that all objects seen from an extreme distance take on a bluish tinge.

Rabbi Hirsch seems to concur. He notes that only the Ark, the utensil of extreme spirituality, was covered on the outside with a blue cloth during its travels through the desert. So, too, the individual of extreme spirituality, the *Kohein Gadol*, was clothed in a blue mantle. Blue is at the distant end of the spectrum of light we mentioned before—far removed from the original light that entered the prism; blue is the polar opposite of red in this segmentation of light. This also manifests itself spiritually; here, too, red and blue are polar extremes.

If so, what, then, do you think *argaman*, purple, indicates? Isn't purple simply the mixture of red and blue? The Raavid, in *Hilchos Hlei Hamikdosh*, divides *argaman* into *arug min*—"woven from" [a variety of fibers]. Purple's very identity seems to be the mixture of, or the level between, red and blue. Might not purple symbolize that physical/spiritual level between the red of *adamah*, earth, and *hadom*, footstool, and the blue of *techelet*—the ultimate? Is it not logical to say that these three colors are emblematic of these distinct levels of our service to *HaShem*—the initial red, the striving purple, and the celestial blue?

The text also mentions *shesh*—white linen. Needless to say, white is the color of cleansing and purity. The necessary prerequisite for anyone attempting to approach the *Beit Hamikdash* is a thorough spiritual cleansing. Only then can we ascend from the red to the purple and on to the blue.

"And they shall take the gold, the sky blue, the purple and the red wool and the [white] linen."

Rabbi Martin Rosenfeld

Young Israel of West Hartford, Connecticut

Moshe's name does not appear in this week's *sedrah*. Various answers are given to explain this fact.

BAAL HATURIM

The *Baal Haturim* states that this deletion was actually brought about by Moshe's own words. When Moshe beseeched God to forgive the Jewish people for the sin of the golden calf, he stated that if there would be no forgiveness, he would prefer to be "erased from the Book that You [God] have written" (Exodus 32:32). Even though Moshe's request was meant to gain forgiveness for the Jewish people, the negative impact of his words came true. Thus, according to the *Baal Haturim,* Moshe's name is absent from an entire portion of the Torah in accordance with his stated wishes.

ABARBANEL

Abarbanel poses a question similar to that of the *Baal Haturim*. He points out that if we view *Terumah* and *Tetzaveh* as one unified *parshah,* we note something unique. The familiar phrase, "And God spoke to Moses" appears only once in the two *parshiyot*—at the beginning of *Terumah*. The phrase appears only at the introduction to the construction of the Tabernacle, the *mishkan*. Abarbanel gives a lengthy analysis of the symbolic meaning of the Tabernacle. He concludes with the following summary:

> Do not believe the description of the building of the *mishkan*—its vessels, its erection, the sacrifices, the work of the Princes and *Kohanim,*

> and other historical matters—have no contemporary relevance. . . . The essential intent of these matters is to include Divine wisdom and knowledge, which can be studied by religious thinkers so that they can attain perfection in knowledge and achievement. Therefore, that which we know regarding the Tabernacle and its vessels, with its symbolism, assists us today as it did when it first occurred. Therefore, it may truly be said, that neither the sacrificial worship nor the laws of purity have been abolished, even though the practice has been discontinued. Their insights have not ceased and man attains, by their remembrance, a sense of humility before God.

The words of Abarbanel are quite inspiring but do not necessarily answer the question of Moshe's "disappearance." We will return to this discussion after introducing the Vilna Gaon's explanation.

THE VILNA GAON

The Vilna Gaon points out that the *yahrzeit* of Moshe (7th of Adar) often occurs during the week that *Tetzaveh* is read. Since this week marks the calendar date of Moshe's departure, it is marked symbolically by the absence of Moshe's name. While this comment is fascinating, one can surely question why it would be deemed appropriate to mark the *yahrzeit* of Moshe *Rabbeinu* by an omission of his name in the weekly *Sedra*. This comment, as well as that of Abarbanel, suggest an answer that goes to the essence of the character of "our Teacher Moses."

THE HUMILITY OF MOSHE

One of the signs of the greatness of Moshe is that he was able to prepare the Jewish people for a future when he would no longer be able to lead them. He had to give the Jewish community the confidence and courage to continue their loyalty to the *mesorah* (tradition) even when he would no longer be present to inspire them. Moshe wanted the Jews to be loyal to his teachings, but he eschewed the trappings of leadership and authority. This thought is expressed in one of the essays of the Ran, a talmudic commentator. The Ran asks why it was decreed that Moshe be a congenital stutterer. He answers that this defect helped ensure the fact that when Moshe rose to power, people would be inspired by the message of Moshe's teachings and not by any external, charismatic mannerisms. *What* Moshe said would be the focus, not the *way* he said it. This was the only way to guarantee that Judaism could flourish even after the demise of Moshe.

According to *midrash Shmuel* on *Pirkei Avot* 1:1, the teaching, "Raise up many students," refers to the obligation to allow students to attain self-sufficiency. An effective teacher is one who will prepare his students for their future role in life when they will have to stand up on their own. By his personality the teacher can create future leaders and not life-long followers.

Applying this thought to the comments of Abarbanel and the Vilna Gaon, we may conclude the following: The Mishkan does not require that the name of Moshe be associated with it. Holiness is something all can attain and personally experience; we can reach this plateau even in the absence of our great leader Moshe. In like fashion, when the *yahrzeit* of Moshe approaches, his name is absent from our Torah reading. This is a remarkable tribute to "our Teacher Moshe"—a teacher so prescient that he "raised" all future generations to carry on the message of Judaism even at times of concealment and doubt. In a word, one of Moshe's greatest achievements was to teach us how to live as proud Jews even at a time when there is no Moshe.

This thought is reinforced by a comment in the *Sefer Shvilei Chaim* written by Rabbi Chaim Elazari, *zt"l*. Rabbi Elazari was asked by a congregant why it is that on the joyous day of Simchat Torah we read the Torah portion of Moshe's death, since this obituary injects a sad note into the joyous *yom tov* spirit. Rabbi Elazari responded that this choice of reading shows the great wisdom of the Torah. The Torah is teaching us that even with the passing of our greatest leader, Jewish life and Torah are destined to continue. The Jewish quest for spirituality will never cease. Moshe has raised all Jewish generations to higher levels of spirituality by dint of his dedicated and self-effacing transmission of Torah. He is therefore given the greatest title of respect—"our Teacher Moshe" (Moshe *Rabbeinu*).

The Jewish people can live without a Moshe, but never can we survive without his greatest legacy—the transmission of the Torah. An occasional omission of Moshe's name reminds us of our greatest teacher's mission—to "raise" us all to be worthy recipients of the Torah (Numbers 9:23), "by the word of God, through the hand of Moses."

❖ CHAPTER 21 ❖

Ki Tisah

Rabbi Elias Schwartz

Young Israel of Bensonhurst/Bathbeach, New York

WHERE DO *YOU* STAND? ARE *YOU* ALWAYS FIRST?

In *Ki Tisah*, the word *pesol* is used in a positive sense. It occurs in God's instruction to Moshe, "Carve out two tablets of stone like the first, and I will write on the Tablets the [same] words that were on the first tablets, which you broke" (Exodus 34:1). Here, the word implies, carve out something lasting and beautiful. Carve out a second set of the Ten Commandments.

In *Yitro*, however, Exodus 20:4 and 5 we find the same root letters—*peh, samech, lamed*—referring to the worst transgression a Jew can commit. There, the word *pesel* refers to idol worship: "Thou shalt not make a graven image . . . of anything in [this world]. Thou shalt not prostrate yourself to them nor serve them because I am *HaShem*, your God" (Exodus 20:4–5).

Pesol is something *positive*, everlasting, that refers to the foundation of our people. *Pesol* causes us always to remember the Revelation on Mount Sinai: to *carve* out, to hew out of stone, two tablets so that we will always remember and fulfill the Ten Commandments.

Pesel, however, refers to idol worship—to *carving* out a false god, a *pesel*. A *pesel* must never be made and, if found, must be destroyed. It is used in a *negative* sense.

The Rizhiner Rebbe resolves these different connotations of words derived from the same root letters, the basic meaning of which is "to carve out." According to him, the meaning depends where the word "*you*" is placed. It depends on where *you* are and where *you* place yourself.

In *Yitro, l'cho*, the *you*, is put first, before the word *pesel*: "You shall not make unto *you* a *pesel*, a graven image"—that is, do not make of yourself a graven image. If you put *yourself* above all, if you always put *yourself* first, *l'cho* is followed by *pesel*—a graven image. People who are proud and arrogant, who think they are superior and believe that only their orders are to be followed and fulfilled, have established attitudes that create graven images *out of themselves*. Such individuals believe they are lords and masters over others.

In *Ki Tisah*, however, we see the opposite effect. *P'sol l'Cho*: "carve away the *l'cho*"—that is, chop away the idea that *you* are the only one who counts. When the *l'chow* is not first but last, the letters *peh, samech, lamed* present an entirely different thought. When you put the *you* last, when you carve away a little bit of the *you*, you are creating two tablets of stone, and upon the *you*, there can be inscribed the Ten Commandments.

A person who is sincere, humble, and modest, who has destroyed the *you*-effect in his way of life, will live the way *HaShem* has prescribed for us. This person will set an example for others to follow. It is important to learn the difference between arrogance and humility. When you are modest and put yourself last, you are creating greatness; you are creating a touch of godliness; you are creating everlastingness.

We find this same idea expressed in the sentence, "You shalt not make *unto you* a monument" (Deuteronomy 16:22). The *Kedushas Levi* says, "The pleasures of this world are represented by the word *l'cho*—'unto you.'" These are the things that man works for, without thinking of their future worth. Sometimes man forgets that the purpose of this world is a preparation for a glorious future. Therefore, the Torah commands us, "Do not make *unto you* a monument." Do not make the things that are important to you (the pleasures of this world) a monument—something that you think will last forever. Rather, whatever you do, even in material things, do as a preparation for your future in *olam haba*.

My Rebbe, Rabbi Shraga Feivel Mendlowitz, *zt"l*, said, "This is the problem of our world. Man is composed of *body* and *soul*. His *body* must labor so that he should be able to take care of his daily food and daily needs. The *soul* must devote itself to higher matters. The *soul* must worry about the spirit, the *neshamah*. The *soul* must worry about the future, and about following and fulfilling the *mitzvot* of *HaShem*. If body and soul *together* work and worry *only* about the piece of bread, the physicial needs of man, and the soul forgets about the primary purpose of life, the result will be the downfall of man."

In our *musaf* prayers on Rosh Hashonah and Yom Kippur, just before *kedushah*, we find the words *b'nafsho yavee lachmo*—that man uses even his *nefesh*, his *soul*, to bring him his bread. In this prayer, we ask forgiveness of God because we are misusing the *neshamah* aspect of life.

Let us give the body what the body needs. Let us give the soul what the soul needs. When the soul will be triumphant over the body; when *mitzvot* and *maasim tovim* will be the primary ideals of our life; when *midot tovot* will assert themselves in our dealing with our fellow man; then we will be on the road to human greatness; we will have created and reached the Torah ideal—the Torah Man.

Rabbi Meir Sendor

Young Israel of Sharon, Massachusetts

> "And I shall remove the heart of stone from their bodies, and I will give them a heart of flesh. . . ."

According to the *Gemara Shabbat* (87a), when Moshe *Rabbeinu* smashed the Tablets in response to finding the people worshiping the golden calf, *HaShem* agreed with Moshe's decision. Rav Shimon ben Lakish infers that God even congratulated Moshe. The *Gemara* explains the logic of Moshe's reaction: If the non-Jewish stranger is prohibited from eating the *Pesach* sacrifice and that is only one of the 613 *mitzvot* of the Torah, then certainly the Tablets, which represent the whole Torah, should be denied to those who have rebelliously estranged themselves from the essence of Torah

With all due respect, however, one could argue that, on the contrary, what the Jewish people needed at that moment was not less Torah but more Torah. If the goal was to wean the nation from idolatry and put it back in direct connection with *HaShem*, then to destroy the Tablets, a stone-etched revelation by the Finger of God, seems counterproductive.

Rav Meir Simcha Hakohen of Dvinsk explains that Moshe's decision to smash the Tablets was based on his sharp insight into human nature. Had he presented the Tables to the people at that moment, they would merely have switched their allegiance from the golden calf to the Stone Tablets and have learned nothing in the process. In their obsessive longing for concrete certainty in life, they would have turned the Tablets, and Torah itself, into an object of idolatrous worship (*Meshekh Chokhmah*). Moshe broke the Tablets to teach the people that their connection to *HaShem* should be a direct, living relationship, without reliance on intermediaries. Holiness comes from our observance of *HaShem*'s will through Torah, not from any created object.

This lesson has to be learned in new ways in every generation—in fact, every day. Rav Bahya ibn Pakudah, in his *Chovot Halevavot*, praises those people of true spirit who "do *teshuvah* anew every day on account of their increased awareness of the greatness of God, and [their recognition of] the narrow way they served Him in the past" (3:3). Throughout our lives, we must endlessly expand and deepen our sense of *HaShem*. The awareness we have of God today makes our limited conceptions of Him in the past seem like infinite idols of the mind, and the awareness we will mature to in the future will make our sense of Him today, in turn, seem narrow and limited. This is the process of spiritual growth, as our minds and hearts continually deepen and reach to connect with His infinitude.

The challenge to our generation, in particular, is to grow beyond limited, narrow views that reduce Torah to a mere book of rules to be followed in an externalized, rote way. The danger of our times, conditioned by technology and the computer revolution, is not just the turning of the Tablets or Torah itself into inanimate idols. The danger is taking the machine as a model for the human being and halachic life, turning our Torah practice into something inanimate and mechanical—precise, perhaps, but heartless: a cybernetic caricature of living humanity.

The goal of Torah is not to become narrowly tracked, sleep-walking halachic androids but to awaken ourselves to our full, living, spontaneous potential as human beings halachically attuned to *HaShem*'s will. A Torah Jew is not merely one who is absorbed in the outer minutiae of weights and measures, important as they are, but one who absorbs and internalizes Torah values.

Rav Bahya ibn Pakudah expressed the true model of Torah spirit this way: "One should attain the highest level of the levels of righteousness . . . to see without eyes, to hear without ears, to speak without a tongue, and to feel things without the senses. . . ." (*Chovot Halevavot*, 8). Ever since Moshe broke the stone Tablets, we have been on the way toward learning to see with depth and insight, with Torah intuition that penetrates beyond the idols and virtual realities of every generation; on the way toward a true life, fulfilling *HaShem*'s promise, "I will remove the heart of stone from their bodies, and I will give them a heart of flesh. . . ."

Rabbi Moshe Teitelbaum

Young Israel of Lawrence/ Cedarhurst, New York

Moshe's presence on *Har Sinai* afforded *Am Yisrael* the most direct transmission of *HaShem*'s guidance and teaching. *HaShem* spoke with Moshe as one would converse with a fellow man. The first set of Tablets was, similarly, the handiwork of the Almighty Himself, presented to Moshe upon the completion of the forty days and forty nights that he devoted to the receiving of the Torah, and during which he neither slept nor ate nor drank. *Har Sinai* was, therefore, another worldly event in the life of Moshe *Rabbeinu*—a time of unparalleled holiness, far removed from the rhythms of everyday life.

It was also very distant from the turbulent encampment of *Am Yisrael*, where they anxiously awaited Moshe's return and created an oracle to replace him when he failed to return as expected. The creation of a golden calf by the people stood in stark contrast to their exalted leader's rise in holiness while on *Har Sinai*. At the very moment that the Tablets were presented to Moshe, his people was preparing to commit idolatry.

This chasm between Moshe and *Am Yisrael*—which had grown during the forty days and forty nights of separation between Moshe, the leader, and his people—can be blamed for the creation of the golden calf. It was not only the miscalculation of the day of Moshe's expected return that caused panic among *Klal Yisrael*. That alone could not explain the radically unacceptable reaction of idolatry, even on the part of the panic-stricken. But the lone spiritual advancements of Moshe while his people were left behind, stagnating—this *does* begin to explain how such a tragedy unfolded. The relationship between teacher and student, between master and disciple, demands a near-perfect affinity between the height attained by the master and that held out within reach of the disciple. If the master enters a realm in which his students cannot even perceive his wisdom and spirit, they will surely be incapable of following his example.

If we imagine two friends attempting to climb the side of a mountain, we can envision how difficult and slow each step would be if, after ascending a few feet, the lead climber disengaged the piton or chock that he had wedged into the rock to climb on, forcing his fellow climber to repeat the very same procedure for himself. It would be a great deal easier to attach a stirrup ladder to the piton and help his fellow climber up to the next station on the rock-face. For a weaker climber, such a helping hand might make all the difference between making it up to the top (or at least close to it) and sliding down the slippery slope (or even experiencing a back-breaking fall). This parable is apt, since Moshe's spiritual ascent was clearly meant to be followed by that of his people. A certain unique greatness is expected of Moshe, but a leader's distance from his flock can be very dangerous as well. While personally rising ever higher, the careful leader maintains the "ropes and wedges" of his rise, leaving them behind to assist and guide others who would seek to follow.

When setting out to return to the troubled encampment where the golden calf had been created, Moshe is told *lech reid ki shicheit amcha* (Exodus 32:7). *Lech reid* means, "Go forth, descend." Because of the obvious redundancy—"go forth" would have sufficed, without the additional "descend"—Rashi tells us that the word *reid* was a command that Moshe diminish his own level of personal greatness, that he humbly assume the posture of a leader whose discouraged and alienated people requires his time and involvement in their basic challenges and struggles of faith: "Descend from the lofty heights of your own perfection in order to address the corruption that besets your people." The personal pronoun of *amcha—your* people, is meant to remind Moshe of his duty to remain firmly attached to the people in his charge, at all times, to look back and below, even to the uncouth and crass amongst "his" people, and restore their unswerving loyalty to Torah and service of *HaShem*.

An understanding of Moshe's reaction to *HaShem*'s wrath sheds a great deal of light on the "descent" of *lech reid*, with which Moshe was instructed. *HaShem* threatened to destroy *Am Yisrael* entirely and to rebuild the nation from Moshe alone. In response, Moshe pleads with *HaShem*, as we read, *Vayekhel Moshe et pnai HaShem Elohav* (Exodus 32:11). Tractate Berakhot 32 comments upon the word *Vayekhel*, "Moshe stood prayerfully before the Almighty to the point where he was seized by a fire that seemed to burn in his very bones." Rabbi Meir Simcha Hakohen of Dvinsk, in his commentary on the Torah, *Meshekh Chokhmah*, Shmos 32:11 explains that Moshe was struck by the perception of the very same weakness for idolatry within his own family that had occurred among *Am Yisrael* with the golden calf. The fire "burning in his bones" would one day erupt in the idolatrous service of *Pesel Micah* by Moshe's grandson, Yonatan. The bones of our children are the contribution of the male parent, *Chazal Niddah* 31 teach us. It was, therefore, even within Moshe's own makeup that some reprehensible proclivity to idol-worship could be found. Once Moshe found this awful, destructive fire within himself, he argued that there would be no benefit from rebuilding the nation of Israel using Moshe as a new beginning. Even within Moshe one found the antecedent of *avodah zarah* (idol worship)! With this awareness of a fire of such destructive power within a *tzaddik* such as himself, Moshe was able to rebut *HaShem*'s suggestion of solving the problem of idol-worship by destroying the would-be worshipers. Moshe was, in effect, saying, "Then you'll have to destroy me as well."

According to this commentary of the *Meshekh Chokhmah*, we gain a new insight into the meaning of *lech reid*, the descent *HaShem* commanded Moshe to begin. It was a call to self-examination and introspection that would enable Moshe to identify fully with the errant *Bnei Yisrael*, who had created a golden calf to worship. To facilitate such an ability to understand the nature of their sin, Moshe would have to come down to a base level of thought in which he could conceive of the sin of idolatry among his own descendants. *Lech reid* was a commandment that presented Moshe with firsthand experience of the fires that can rage within us, thereby enabling him to ward off *HaShem*'s plan for wholesale destruction of *Am Yisrael*. The ultimate fulfillment of this imperative, *lech reid*, took place when Moshe stood in prayer, contemplating the terrible sin of the golden calf until he felt the consuming flames burning within his own bones. Having reached that point, Moshe's descent was complete.

To rehabilitate and to defend *Am Yisrael*, Moshe had to be keenly aware of the awesome spiritual challenges facing each Jew in his or her everyday life. Such awareness by our leadership is absolutely critical in the contemporary era, in which numerous golden calves are craeted and re-created to constantly distract the Torah nation from its assigned tasks of Heavenly service. The *rebbe*, *manhig*, and *menahel* of today must be attuned to the moral and ethical dangers faced by those of *Klal Yisrael* for whom he bears responsibility. He must recognize the "fire within his bones" that could allow even himself to fall victim to the same negative and destructive passions that mislead and misdirect us. By identifying with the sources of our ills, the leader is better able to approach his fellow Jews and students with the solutions and rememdies that his knowledge and expertise provide.

To the extent that parents and grandparents assume leadership positions within their families, it is equally important for each of us to be attuned to the kinds of spiritual challenges our children and grandchildren have to face. By showing our interest in their concerns, we achieve both a watchfulness that helps us ward off negative influences in their lives and the ability to know how our guidance and leadership might help them develop into vital *Bnei* and *Bnot Torah*.

❖ CHAPTER 22 ❖

Vayakhel

Rabbi Yitzchok M. Goodman

Young Israel of Far Rockaway, New York

Vayakhel Mosheh: Rashi tells us that this great convocation of *Klal Yisrael* took place on the morning after Yom Kippur. There are many interpretations of this point and its significance. Several *meforshim*—commentaries—emphasize the point that it is not what we practice on the Day of Atonement that counts most. Of course all Jews pray and repent, and strive to become like angels. The real test is what they do the day after.

The *Pninim Yekarim* develops an intricate thesis: When the Torah praises Moshe as the greatest *anav*—the most modest of all humans—it spells the word *anav* without the *yud*. This omission led certain *meforshim* to conclude that in later history there was indeed one exception—Shmuel Hanavi, who is recorded as having gone from town to town all over Israel to judge the people where they resided, whereas Moshe would summon the people to come to him and gather when he wished to speak to them. But now the question arises: Why, indeed, did the humble Moshe not do as Shmuel did? The answer given is that we are taught in the Talmud (*Kesubos* 17) that a king may not forgo his honor. Hence, whereas Shmuel, as a prophet, could yield in this matter, Moshe, who was seen as a king (*Va-yehi bishurun melech*, Devorim 33:5, see Ibn Ezra) could not.

Nevertheless, we find that in one instance Moshe did go to the people (and the *sedrah* is titled by that verb): *Vayelech Moshe*! We must answer that, since on that day Moshe died, and since Kohelet states, *Ein shilton b'yom hamavet*—"There is no power on the day of death"—Moshe was no longer viewed as king on that day.

However, after the transgression of the Golden Calf, Moshe was told by God, *Lech reid*. The *midrash* says that this means, "Go down from your high status." Thus, Moshe was no longer seen as king. Why then did he not go to the people? To answer this question our *Chazal* stated that the gathering in this chapter took place "the morning after Yom Kippur"—the day after they were entirely forgiven. Thus, Moshe was restored to his prior status as king and could not forgo this honor. Hence, the verse correctly states, *Vayakhel Mosheh*, "Moshe gathered the nation"!

THE WEEK'S WORK

The *sedrah* begins with the laws of *Shabbat*. We are told that "for six days work *should be done*, and on the seventh day it should be holy unto you (*lachem*)." In the Ten Commandments, the expression is "six days *you shall work*. . . ." Variouis Hasidic *rebbes* are said to have made this observation: The *Aseres Hadibros* speak to all Jews of all generations. It is, therefore, quite appropriate that we should be told to do work, for this is the standard life-pattern for the vast majority of people. Since we are busy all week, *Shabbat* is truly holy unto God, to separate it from the busy work week. However, the generation of the desert did not work at all: they were fed manna daily; their clothes never aged, and God's cloud hovered over them constantly. All their basic necessities were taken care of properly. Their main occupation, therefore was to come to Moshe to hear him expound the Torah. Like *talmidai chachamim* in later ages, they were told that, in order to make *Shabbat* different from the weekdays, *their mitzvah* for *Shabbat* was to enjoy better food and drink. This, then, is the deeper meaning of the verse. It speaks to those who, like the *midbar* generation, have the blessing of not having to work themselves. "*For six days the work shall be done*"—that is, by others; hence, such people spend the week studying Torah and performing *mitzvot*. How, then, will *Shabbat* be different for them? The answer is that "the seventh day will be *lachem—for you*—holy"—that is, through the *Oneg Shabbat* of special, good food to mark *Shabbat* off as different from the rest of the week.

STUDYING THE *MISHKAN*

Rabbeinu Bachaya strongly encourages us to study, as deeply as possible, the entire system of the *Mishkan*, the Tabernacle—the dimensions of all its vessels and so on—for there is great advantage in this pursuit. He states that, whether or not we reach the higher plane of discovering some of the secret meanings in these items and their measurements, or even if we determine little more than the mathematical computations involved, our *zechut* in showing such dedicated interest in the *Mishkan* will contribute to God's restoring the *Mishkan* to us. This is the deeper meaning of the Psalm that we read on Mondays (Psalm 48), which concludes with these verses: "Surround Zion, count its towers, note carefully its courtyards" [that is, study well its dimensions]. For what purpose? So that the day will come that you can say, "*This is God, our God*" (that is, the *Shechinah* will once again be present and felt in the rebuilt *Mikdash*).

THE WOMEN'S CONTRIBUTION

The opening chapter emphasizes the work of the women, who wove the materials needed for the *Mishkan*. The phrase, "each woman who was *wise of heart, wove with her hands*" offered Rav Shlomo Kluger an opportunity for a halachic analysis: The Talmud (*Kesubos*, 59) teaches that, though, according to the original *halachah*, the work/wages of a married woman is her property, the Rabbis instituted that, in return for the husband's providing all his wife's basic necessities of food, clothing, and shelter, her earnings go to him. On this basis, Rav rules that any woman has the right to declare, "I waive my rights to his provisions for me, and I wish to keep my earnings for myself." Since, in the desert, the men did not provide to their wives any of these basic needs—all of which came from God—the labor of the women, called, in the Talmud, *maasei yadeha*, the product of her hand, certainly remained her own. This is the special emphasis in our verse: "each woman who was wise of heart" (that is, she knew the *halachah* that in this situation her labor belonged to her) "wove *with her hands*" (that is, with hands that belonged exclusively to her).

Rabbi Daniel Yormark

Young Israel of Eltingville, New York

"And Moshe gathered all the people of Israel and he said to them: These are the things that *HaShem* has commanded, to do them" (Exodus 35:1). Rebbe expounds on this *pasuk* and relates: "This refers to the thirty-nine prohibited labors of *Shabbat*" (*Shabbat* 97).

The basis of *Shabbat* observance, as far as the prohibitions (*shemirah*) are concerned, is to refrain from performing any of the thirty-nine constructive activities that were integral parts of the construction and proceedings of the *Mishkan*. By way of example: the *Mishkan* was erected. Consequently, construction is not allowed. The curtains of the *Mishkan* were sewn. Therefore, we do not sew. The dyes were cooked, and that is why all types of cooking are forbidden.

Apparently, there is a connection between *Shabbat* and the *Mishkan*. In order to understand this, we need to raise an intriguing question concerning the basic concept of *Shabbat*. In *Parshat Yitro*, the Torah tells us, "[On the day of *Shabbat*] You shall not perform any labor, you, your son and your daughter, . . . *because* [in] six days God made the heavens and the earth, the sea and all that is contained in them, and He rested on the seventh day . . ." (Exodus 20:10–11). Simply stated, the Torah is telling us the basis for *Shabbat* observance: "Follow My example. Mirror My behavior. Just as I refrained from activity on the seventh day, so shall you."

However, the equation doesn't seem to add up. During the six days, the Almighty designed and fashioned the universe and brought it into existence. On the seventh day He rested—from *that* activity. We, on the other hand, abstain from the thirty-nine labors performed in the *Mishkan*. How, then, is *our* rest—from activities we may not even have done during the week—a reflection of His rest?

"In the beginning, God created the heaven and the earth" (Genesis 1:1). And, as the Prophet Yeshaiah tells us, All was created for *kavod Shamayim*

(Isaiah 43:7). Everything in the entire universe fulfills the purpose for which it was created when it is used to serve the Creator. For instance, the purpose of food is not merely to please the palate but, rather, to provide the eater with the strength to serve *HaShem*. It goes without saying that this is a lofty *madreigah* (level of devotion)—all the more so in a society in which indulgence in pleasure and self-gratification is the order of the day. Nevertheless, as the *Mishnah* tells us, "Let all your deeds be for the sake of Heaven" (*Pirkei Avot* 2:12). Everything in creation fulfills its ultimate *raison d'être* when it is used for this purpose, the sake of Heaven.

Viewing creation from this perspective, we see that the entire universe is nothing but a sanctuary, a place to serve the Creator. And on *Shabbat*, the Almighty refrained from engaging in further creative activity involved in making that sanctuary. Similarly, *Bnei Yisrael* also erected a sanctuary, the *Mishkan*. And, on *Shabbat*, they are enjoined to refrain from all the activities involved in the making of that sanctuary.

Furthermore, *Chazal* relate that the *Mishkan* was an *olam katan*, a minature replica of the universe. Every aspect of the design, materials, and vessels represent and symbolize a part of the Creation. For example, the upper and lower curtains represent heaven and earth, and the lights of the menorah represent the sun and the moon.

The correlation is now complete. The Creator refrained from activity involved in the creation of the sanctuary known as the universe. Likewise, the Jewish people, the epitome of *tzelem Elohim*—that which is fashioned in the image of God—reflect His conduct by refraining from the activities involved in the making of the sanctuary known as *Mishkan*, a microcosm of the universe. By abstaining on *Shabbat* from those labors that were performed in the *Mishkan*, *Bnei Yisrael* are truly elevated and uplifted as they emulate the One Above.

"Six days you shall do your work, and on the seventh day you shall rest" (Exodus 23:12). With slight variations, this *pasuk* appears several times in the Torah. Two issues are addressed here: the days of the week and *Shabbat*. The second half of the statement is clearly a directive: Do not engage in the prohibited activities on *Shabbat*. The first part of the verse also seems to be giving instructions by commanding us to work during the week. However, we know of no such *mitzvah*. What, then, is the intention of the phrase, "six days you shall labor"?

The Rambam as brought in *Rabbeinu Bachya* (Exodus 20:9) informs us that, with these words, the Torah is telling us not so much *what* we should do but, rather, the attitude we should have when we do it. During the six days of the week the Jew is enjoined to engage in all his toil, labor, and activity with the mind-set that everything he does is for the sake of Heaven. The imperative, "Six days you shall labor," tells us that in everything one does one should strive to have the Creator in mind. That being the case, we see that the two subjects addressed in the *pasuk*, the six days and *Shabbat*, are really based on one theme because it is only when creation is perceived as a sanctuary to serve *HaShem* that our abstention from the labors of the *Mishkan* mirrors the Creator's abstention from creating the universe. Only when all is viewed through the spectacles of "Let all your deeds be for the sake of Heaven" do heaven and earth attain their ultimate fulfillment as a sanctuary. And only then is the *Mishkan*, the sanctuary built by the *Bnei Yisrael*, similar to it.

The Prophet proclaims, "And you will call *Shabbat* a delight" (Isaiah 58:13). Clearly the *Navi* is conveying to us that *Oneg*, indulging in pleasure on *Shabbat*, is the underlying theme of the seventh day. "Call *Shabbat* a delight," because that is the essence of the day. If the entire basis for *Shabbat* is emulating the Creator, it follows that our *mitzvah* of *Oneg Shabbat* must have its roots in the *Shabbat* of the Master of the Universe.

In the Torah's narrative of the completion of the six days of creation, we find, in *Bereishit Rabbah*, "And God saw all that He had made and behold, it was very good" (Genesis 1:31). The *midrash* explains the meaning of the verse by means of an analogy. A king constructed a beautiful palace. Upon its completion, the king relished its magnificence and said, "The special charm and delight that my palace gives me should remain always." So, too, with the advent of *Shabbat*, the entire creation was a charm and delight, so to speak, for *HaShem*. "And behold, it was very good"; it is the *Oneg Shabbat* of God, and it is the source for the *Oneg Shabbat* of the *Bnei Yisrael*.

Shabbat is not merely a day off. Moreoever, it is not merely a day on which there are so many things that one cannot do. It is a day on which the Jew enters the realm of reflecting the One Above. It is a day where even our indulging in physical pleasure can be elevated and become an integral part of mirroring God. It is a day when concern for mundane and ephemeral pursuits is inappropriate. Verily, *Shabbat* is a *matanah tovah*—a very special gift.

In the merit of "those who keep *Shabbat* and call it a delight," may the entire nation of Israel enjoy "a rest of peace, tranquility, serenity, and security" (*Shemoneh Esrei, Mincha Shabbat* Afternoon Prayer Service) which will pervade, in the world to come, all days of the week.

❖ CHAPTER 23 ❖

Vayakhel/Parah*

Rabbi Dov A. Brisman

Young Israel of Elkins Park, Pennsylvania

WOMEN: CLOSEST TO THE SOURCE

> "And every wise-hearted woman spun with her hands." (Exodus 35:25)
>
> "And all the women whose heart uplifted them in wisdom, spun the goats' hair." (Exodus 35:26)
>
> "Greater is that which is written by the upper curtains than what is written by the lower ones, for by the lower curtains it is written, 'and every wise-hearted woman spun with her hand,' but by the upper curtains it is written, 'with wisdom they spun the goats' hairs.'" (*Shabbat* 99a)

The superior skill used in the spinning process of the upper curtains is described in yet another part of Tractate *Shabbat* (74b), which is mentioned by Rashi (passage 26). According to these sources, a special skill was utilized, for the goats' hair was spun while it was still attached to the backs of the goats. Needless to say, this involved great skill and is described in the Talmud as "extraordinary wisdom." However, this concept still remains unclear. Why was it necessary to utilize such a skill? Was not the purpose—the final product—the main objective? What purpose was served by incorporating such wisdom when the same goal could have been attained in a much simpler way? Furthermore, if such wisdom was vital, why was it applied only to the upper curtains?

---

*See the festival section, chapter 66, The Four Parshiot.

In his commentary on *Parshat Terumah* (Exodus 26:1) Sforno explains that the purpose of the lower curtains is inherent in the fact that the Torah refers to them as *mishkan*, or "dwelling place." These curtains served as an "enclosing case" for the utensils of the sanctuary, such as the table, *menorah*, altars, ark, and so on. For this reason, the cherubs were woven into the curtains, thereby conveying the information that this was a dwelling place of the Divine Presence on the earth.

Thus, we can concur that when the Torah speaks of the upper curtains (Exodus 26:7) as being "for a tent upon the *Mishkan*," and when Rashi explains that this means a tent upon the lower curtains, the meaning is that the purpose of the upper curtains was to protect and preserve the values inherent within the enclosure below.

To preserve values and to guarantee their survival, imbuing them with constant meaning, requires great wisdom. It is very easy to lose and forget that which we gain. Special effort must be exerted to achieve retention. Maintaining skill and wisdom would propel a nonstop inertia to accomplish yet more. Hence, greater wisdom was expended in the spinning of the upper curtains; for preservation, the mark of endurance, requires our maximum energies.

Sforno further explains, concerning our *sedrah*, that the significance of spinning the goats' hair while it was attached to the animal is "in order that the spun material should have additional luster, for many creations lose some of their quality when they are detached from their source of growth." This "additional" luster, the preservation of the natural state, is the role of the upper curtains, which cover and protect the *Mishkan*, the dwelling place.

Who were the initiators of this unique tapestry and spinning process? The women of *Klal Yisrael*. For they are the guarantors and protectors of the Jewish dwelling place, the home. It falls upon their broad shoulders to keep the home, and its commitment to *Yiddishkeit* and proper conduct, as near as possible to the source. *Mesorah*, tradition, is pure and undiluted. The legacy transferred into each generation must be as fine as the original source. All attainments and achievements must maintain consistency. They must remain unadulterated, uninfluenced by outer forces and alien motives.

This protection is the role of the woman. It is a role that requires great wisdom, to act and react as near to the source as possible. Only then can maximum results be realized. Only then can we be guaranteed survival. Who, then, can claim that the role of the Orthodox Jewish woman is so restrictive and severely limited? Women are, indeed, the entire essence of our existence! When the objective of the *Bat Yisrael* is to protect our *Mishkan*, her role transcends all boundaries, for she links herself with eternity (*nitzchiut*). However, if her motivation is redefining her role and if the protection of the *Mishkan* is not paramount, *tzniut* not prevalent, then the role of the Jewish mother becomes truly limited!

PARSHAT PARAH–THE FOUNDATION OF TORAH

When a person becomes spiritually defiled (*tameh*) through contact with a corpse, the Torah prescribes a purification process involving the slaughter of a red cow (*parah adumah*) and the sprinkling of its blood. It is then burned and its ashes are sprinkled onto the impure person on the third and seventh days following initial contact with the corpse (*Bamidbar* 19:12). It is noteworthy to point out that the Torah prefaces this *mitzvah* with the designation *Chukat Hatorah*, the statute of the Torah. This seems to be a very broad designation for a single *mitzvah* that has not been practiced for over one thousand years. Can it be that the ramifications of *parah adumah* are fundamental to our everyday observance?

Another point to ponder: It would seem more logical for the Torah to introduce us to *parah adumah* by presenting the problem—*tumaat meit* (defilement by a corpse)—and then describing the solution—*parah adumah*. However, the order seems to be reversed. First, the Torah tells us about *parah adumah*, and only afterward is the issue of spiritual impurity presented. Why is a solution offered before the actual problem is presented?

The Rambam (*Sefer Hamitzvot, Aseh* 113 and *Sefer Hachinuch, Mitzvah* 397) explain that the *mitvah* of *parah adumah* is to burn the cow in order that its ashes should be available for those who require cleansing from *tumaat meit*. According to this explanation, this *mitzvah* is not merely a solution to an already existing problem. The Torah is not telling us that we must prepare the ashes of *parah adumah* only when someone needs the purification. Rather, the Torah demands that we be prepared and forewarned. It is our responsibility to be ready for the inevitable emergency. Let us not be caught unaware and thus be compelled and pressured to find the proper cow. Such negligence could leave a person in limbo indefinitely. It would certainly prolong one's agony, for the remedy is not readily available.

Parah adumah teaches us a valuable and fundamental lesson that should govern our entire outlook on life. We must always be alert, not only to the obvious needs and necessities, but also to avoid or reduce imminent problems. Make sure that the means for purification are readily available. Let us make our homes, *shuls*, and *yeshivot* into dynamic bastions of Judaism and Torah not only for our families, but also for the broad community. If the apparatus are functional, there is always hope.

Hence, *parah adumah* truly represents *chukat Hatorah*, a statute that broadly defines the entire expanse of Torah, for alertness and preparation are always the keys to successful and imminent problem solving. It does not suffice to develop solutions only when problems arise. Know that there is a *parah adumah*; make its ashes available, and when the need arises, use them!

May *HaShem* strengthen us to develop the foresight and fortitude to be armed and ready in order to sanctify His Exalted Name!

❖ CHAPTER 24 ❖

Vayakhel/Pekudei

Rabbi Charles Weiss

Young Israel of Greater Pittsburgh, Pennsylvania

Together again—joined once more after a year of separation—unity and harmony reign. The *sedrahs* of *Vayakhel* and *Pekudei* endorse unity from beginning to end. "And Moshe gathered *all* the congregation" (*Shemos* 35:1). They were not gathered in order of position or importance but in a gathering; all together they became an *eidah*—a community. This community, formed by Moshe's invitation to be part of the gathering (see Rashi, *Shemos* 35:5), was given the laws of *Shabbat* and, since *Shabbat* represents *achdut* in the fullest sense—as in "If all Jews would observe two *Shabbatot*, then . . ." (*Shabbat* 118b)—success was assured.

Next was the appeal to the "giving hearts" of our people. Fifteen items were solicited with unexpectedly gratifying results—oversubscription. The *midrash* asks, "Why was not everything in the sanctuary made out of gold?" and answers that gold represents *tzaddikkim*; silver, *baalei teshuvah*; brass, . . . and so on; these varied components thus allow *every* Jew, from the woodchopper to the prince, to share in the building of the *Mishkan*. *All* were partners in it; all had a personal share and sense of participation. The *Mishkan* united our people: it was ours and it unified and united us. The desire to enable Divine Manifestation to enhance our lives joined all in a common effort, blessed with positive results.

The sanctuary was built of many parts; and, if one part was missing, the whole was found lacking. Our nation is composed of many individuals without whom the *Klal* is incomplete. The parallel is that *Yisrael* in Hebrew is an acrostic for *Yesh Shishim Ribo Otiyot Latorah*—"There are six hundred thousand letters in the *Sefer Torah*"—and, should one letter be imperfect—whether the *aleph* of the *anokhi* in the Ten Commandments (Exodus 20:2) or a letter in the name Mehetavel bat Matred, an Edomite queen (Genesis 36:39)—the whole *Sefer Torah* is *posul*. Similarly, each and every action that promotes the wholeness and *achdut* of our people rebuilds our *Mishkan* and repairs the *Sefer Torah*.

Combining and connecting all these separate parts requires someone special. Moshe *Rabbeinu* was well qualified for this task, since only he could erect the Sanctuary that would unite the strivings and efforts of all his people. Therefore, because of Moshe's unfailing interest, supervision, and encouragement, the credit for construction went to him.

The next step on the path to oneness came with accounting. Reckoning is a great leveler. Each unit is uniform, the same, equal to any other. The half-shekel made both the rich and the poor, the haughty and the humble, count equally. As we say in America, *E Pluribus Unum*. The work was done, the contracts completed, in record time. From the commandment on 11 Tishrei to the conclusion on 25 Kislev, the preparations were completed. Still, with all ready for assembly, with all the donors and the workers eager to view and enjoy the fruits of their participation in this holy project, a delay was required. *Be aware*, we were taught, that although alacrity is a fine trait, some things require *Hachanah*—contemplation time. The *Mishkan* was not to be a mission *accomplished* but a mission *begun*, a means of spreading light and sanctity throughout the world, a pipeline of holiness and edification to the entire creation. Therefore, proper thought and direction were needed to start this activity off, enthusiastically at a propitious time. Since this ongoing job is not always easy, the *sedrah* ends with *Chazak chazak venitchazek*. We are charged to continue the task; may we merit to do so.

❖ CHAPTER 25 ❖

Pekudei

Rabbi Harry Greenspan

Young Israel of Long Beach, California

The outstanding theme of the second part of *Sefer Shemot* is the *mitzvah* of building the *Mishkan*. Five full *parshiyot* are devoted to its details. The only other major event in these *parshiyot* is the sin of the golden calf. They are certainly related. Although the Ramban writes in his introduction that the *Mishkan* was a logical conclusion to the Exodus and *Kabbalat Hatorah*, there are many indications in *Chazal* and *Rishonim* that the *Mishkan* was an atonement for the above-mentioned, and not originally part of the Divine plan. It seems, therefore, that a logical way to approach the concept of the *Mishkan* is to analyze the golden calf incident and how the *Mishkan* rectifies that sin.

According to the Ramban, there was no conscious desire for idolatry in *Klal Yisrael*. Far from it! This *Dor Deah*, a generation enlightened and elevated by the miracles they had personally experienced, could not possibly have denied that *Hakadosh baruch Hu* is Creator of heaven and earth and actively involved in our lives. Rather, they erred in being too enthusiastic—so passionate to come closer to their Creator that they chose to undergo a dangerous "religious experience" in order to approach Him. Moshe, their link with the Divine, had surely perished. His death, they felt, was due to human frailty. . . . "For this *man*, Moshe . . . we know not what has happened to him . . ." (Exodus 32:1).

Therefore, they sought an alternative, another intermediary (but no longer a human one) to connect them with the Divine Presence. Their intentions were *leshem Shamayim*; they had pure motives, but they sinned in not conforming to the details of *halachah*. At the end of *Parshat Yitro* the Torah commands, "You shall not make with Me gods of silver and gods of gold" (Exodus 20:20). "You shall not make a representation of anything with Me. . . ."—which the Kuzari interprets to refer to *any* images associated with Divinity. Desiring to enhance their spirituality, they intentionally transgressed the *halachah*!

When man seeks spiritual growth devoid of *mitzvah* observance he is not fulfilling God's will. Rather than serving *HaShem,* he is worshiping his own intellect, feeding his ego, in the guise of religiosity. Convinced of his own sincerity, he is merely a pawn in the hands of the *yetzer hara* (the evil inclination), satisfying a very human passion.

In a similar fashion, the Netziv comments, at the beginning of *Parshat Shemini,* as follows: Moshe *Rabbeinu* tells his brother Aharon at the dedication of the *Mishkan,* Vayikra 9:6, "This is the thing that *HaShem* has commanded you to do, then the Divine Glory will appear to you." But what is the "thing"? The *midrash* in *Torat Kohanim* explains: Moshe tells *Klal Yisrael* that if they remove a certain passion from their hearts, they will be able to fear God and to serve Him in a unified manner.

But what "passion" is the *midrash* referring to?

The Netziv decodes Moshe's message as follows: Even in those days, there were groups of Jews whose "Love of God" extended to their advocating going beyond the limits that are clearly delineated in the Torah, for the sake of what they claimed to be a sincere desire to reach spiritual heights. This was the sin of the 250 great men in *Parshat Korach,* Bamidbar 16:17 who were willing to put their lives in jeopardy for the privilege of offering *ketoret* (incense), an exclusive service of the *Kohanim.* Consequently, the *midrash* quotes Moshe *Rabbeinu* as follows. "If you all act in a uniform and prescribed path serving God, you will then reach spiritual heights. If not, you will fail miserably."

Essentially, this is also the Netziv's approach to the sin of Nadav and Avihu, the sons of Aharon who yearned to become closer to the Holy One but utilized an *eish zarah,* a "strange fire." Symbolically, he says, this "fire" represents the "burning passion," the *yetzer hara,* to serve God in a manner inconsistent with the dictates of the Torah. Because of it, a "Heavenly" fire consumed them (according to the principle of *midah k'neged midah*—measure for measure).

Returning to *Parshat Pekudei,* we now understand a difficult phrase repeated over and over again in our *parshah.* The work was done, says the Torah: *kaasher tzivah HaShem et Mosheh* (as God commanded Moshe). These words recur many times, says the *Beit Halevi,* to emphasize *that* which was rectified upon completion of the *Mishkan.* Measure for measure, our sin of seeking to approach God while ignoring Torah law was forgiven by our performing *this mitzvah* with meticulous observance of every detail, and by our completing the most perfect edifice ever built by man.

Finally, the *midrash* points out that the phrase *kaasher tzivah* is repeated eighteen times, corresponding to the eighteen *brachot* of the *Shemonah Esrei.* What do the *Mishkan*'s construction and the *Amidah* have in common? Perhaps the answer (based upon all of the above) is as follows: There is, perhaps, no more maligned *mitzvah* (in terms of its being "rigidly structured") than *tefillah*. Some people contend that they can more easily approach *HaShem* by "doing their own thing" when they pray, by introducing "novel" and "fresh" approaches to Divine worship. The lesson of the *Mishkan* is that it's not so! If we sincerely desire to reach spiritual heights, to become true servants of the Holy One, we need to pray and perform all *mitzvot* precisely according to the details recorded in *Shulchan Aruch*. If we act in such a fashion, we can hope to receive (in our *shuls* and homes) that which our ancestors experienced upon completion of the *Mishkan*: "*HaShem*'s glorious presence filled the *Mishkan*" (Exodus 40:34) and thus was infused into *Klal Yisrael*.

Rabbi Shlomo Hochberg

Young Israel of Jamaica Estates, New York

THE *MISHKAN* AND REDEMPTION

Ramban, in his introductory remarks, describes *Sefer Shemot* as *Sefer Hageulah*—the book that focuses upon the saga of the first Jewish exile as well as the subsequent redemption therefrom. Yet, less than half of the book actually pertains to the exile and the redemption, and a substantial portion details the erection of the *Mishkan*. Why doesn't *Sefer Hageulah* conclude with the Exodus from Egypt or with the Divine Revelation at *Har Sinai*? What role does the building and completion of the *Mishkan* play in the conclusion of *Galut* and the arrival of *Geulah*?

Ramban explains that the *Galut* did not conclude with the physical exodus from Egypt, "until the day they returned to their place and were restored to the (spiritual) status of their ancestors." Even as *Bnei Yisrael* wandered through the wildnerness following their departure from Egypt, their exile continued. Only subsequent to their arrival at *Har Sinai* and the construction of the *Mishkan*, when the *Shechinah* dwelled in their midst, did they regain the status of their ancestors, serving as the vehicle of the *Shechinah* in this world.

God's presence at the Red Sea and the revelation of His Glory at *Har Sinai* were only temporary, isolated incidents, after which the *Shechinah* withdrew. True redemption, however, is characterized by the *continuous* presence of God's glory, which was realized only in the *Mishkan*, as indicated by the repetitive use of the present form, *U'chevod HaShem malei et Hamishkan*—"and the Glory of God *fills* (continuously) the Tabernacle" (Exodus 40:34–35).

At the same time, the Clouds of Glory facilitated the second component of redemption by leading the Jewish nation through the wilderness toward

Eretz Yisrael. Thus, *Sefer Shemot* begins by listing the Jews who descended into Egypt to begin the *Galut* and concludes with the description of the Clouds of Glory, which effected the two aspects of the *Geulah Shleimah.*

MELACHAH AND *AVODAH*

In reflecting on the construction of the *Mishkan,* the Torah refers to the completed work as both *avodah* (Exodus 39:42) and *melachah* (Exodus 39:43). According to the *Zohar,* whereas *melachah* describes the superb craftsmanship required to fashion the various components of the *Mishkan,* the construction of the *Mishkan* also involved spiritual *avodah.* The attribute of *Chachmat Lev*—wisdom of the spirit—that distinguished Betzalel, Ahaliav, and the other artisans who fashioned the *Mishkan,* does not refer merely to artistic skill. Betzalel was selected to oversee the construction because, in addition to his extensive understanding of architectural specifications, he possessed the critical capacity to comprehend the profound spiritual significance of each detail.

HaShem's evaluation of the work (*avodah*) reflects the spiritual dimension that He knew the artisans had invested in their mission to construct this *Mikdash.* Moshe looked at the beautiful edifice, and although he could deeply appreciate the meticulous physical labor (*melachah*) successfully completed according to God's specifications, he could only speculate regarding the inner spiritual thoughts of the artisans. Moshe thus blessed them most appropriately: "May it be *the Will* that the *Shechinah* dwell upon the work of your hands" (Rashi, *Shemot* 39:43)—expressing the hope that the spiritual dimension might complement their physical accomplishment, and that the pleasantness of God might be evident in the work of their hands.

KAASHER TZIVAH HASHEM

No fewer than eighteen times in *Parshat Pekudei* do we find the phrase *Ka'asher tzivah HaShem*—"as God commanded," underscoring the exemplary manner in which *Bnei Yisrael* completed the *Mishkan.* The Torah's concluding remark that "all the work was done as *HaShem* commanded" should have sufficed to inform us that *Bnei Yisrael* discharged their duty efficiently.

Harav Yosef Dov Soloveichik, *Shlita,* in elucidating this text, makes reference to the Gentiles' confusion when, upon entering the *Beit Hamikdash,* they discovered the *Aron* and the *Keruvim.* They could not comprehend this apparent breach of monotheistic practice and surmised that Judaism sanctioned a form of idol worship. The *Rav* explained that the difference between *avodat HaShem* and *avodah zarah*—between virtuous subservience to God and concession to paganism—is dependent entirely on these few, but compelling words: *Ka'asher tzivah HaShem et Moshe*—as God commanded Moshe.

A particular action might be prohibited; yet comparable activities mandated by the Torah are *mitzvot*. In fact, *Chazal* tell us that every prohibited item has a parallel item that the Torah permits. Had *Bnei Yisrael* fabricated a structure identical to the *Mishkan* without God's command, it would, indeed, have constituted *avodah zarah*, but, by subjecting their own sense of aesthetics and logic to *HaShem*'s command, they became true servants of *HaShem*, enabling the *Shechinah* to dwell in their midst.

Chazak Chazak V'nitchazek!

PART THREE

❖

Leviticus

❖ ❖ ❖

❖ CHAPTER 26 ❖

Vayikra

Rabbi Herschel Kurzrock

Young Israel of Kensington, New York

In contrast to the first two *Chumashim—Bereishis* and *Shemos—Sefer Vayikra*, except for two brief narratives concerning the death of Aaron's sons and the episode of the blasphemer, deals only with commandments. The first half of this *sefer* is mainly concerned with the rules and regulations pertaining to the various *korbanos* and the laws of impurity and purification.

It is interesting to note that the *midrash* (*Vayikra Rabbah, parshah* 7–3) states:

> Rebbe Ahsi said, "Why do we begin the teaching of the *Chumash* with *Toras Kohanim* [*Sefer Vayikra* is known by this title] and not with *Bereishis*? Because the children are 'pure' and the *korbanos* are 'pure'; therefore, let the 'pure'" [spiritually clean] children come and occupy themselves with the "pure" *korbanos*."

On the basis of this *midrash*, many Torah institutions have retained, over many generations, the custom of having children begin their study of *Chumash* with *Sefer Vayikra*. The *Klei Yokor* (1–1) adds a novel thought to this *midrash*: "The reason for the 'small *aleph*' in the first word, *Vayikra*, of this *Chumash*, can be seen as an allusion to the young children mentioned in this *midrash*, meaning that the young children should begin learning with *Vayikra*." Also, that children should begin their learning with *Vayikra* is implied by the *aleph* that is the first letter of the Hebrew alphabet. It seems to me that we might also infer a possible hidden reference to the teachings of Rebbe Ahsi in the *midrash* from a *Gemera* (*Berachos* 31b). Rebbe Elazer states that Shmuel Hanavi, who was only two years old at the time, was guilty of insubordination to his *rebbe*, Eli, the *Kohein Gadol*. Briefly, Eli had sent a messenger to seek a *kohein* to perform the ritual slaughter of a sacrifice, and the young Shmuel told the messenger that the law is that, for ritual slaughter, a *kohein* is not necessary. He was right, but had it not been for the heartfelt supplication of his mother, Chana, he would have been punished. Let us note that Shmuel was only two years old at the time and had just been brought to Eli, where he would remain to study; yet he already knew this *halachah*, which is derived from the study of *Vayikra* regarding the sacrifices. We can infer from here that even in Shmuel's time they started with the laws of the *korbanos* when teaching the children.

One can interpret the above *midrash* by understanding the essence of the *korbanos*. Basically, *korban*, as the meaning of the word implies, signifies "drawing near" to the Almighty (from the root word *korov*—"near") through the medium of the sacrifices a person offers to *HaShem*. This drawing near is effectuated by the understanding and realization on the part of the person that he is obligated to bring himself as a *korban*, and this understanding is actualized with the performance of *smicha*—his laying of hands upon the offering and confessing one's iniquities (*Yoma* 36a).

The elements of repentance and awareness of one's faults and inadequacies—that is, an attitude of "humbling oneself before the Almighty," are basic to the proper offering of a *korban*. A juxtaposition contained in the introductory words of the instructions for bringing a *korban*—"*Adam Ki Yakriv Mekem Korban*" (Leviticus 1:2), "a person who will offer from *you* [himself] a sacrifice"—implies this interpretation (*see* Sforno 1:2).

In this regard, the *Gemara* in *Sotah* 5 states, "At the time of the *Beis Hamikdosh*, when a person brought a *korban*, he had the reward for *that Korban*. . . . However, a person who is truly humble is considered as deserving the reward for one who has brought *all the possible korbanos*, and when the meek person beseeches the Almighty in prayer, he will not be turned away empty-handed."

True modesty and humbleness lead to, and are rewarded by, perfection in feeling the fear of and reverence for the Almighty (*Yerushalmi Shabbos* 1:3).

It is interesting that, by using the small *aleph* specifically at the beginning of the *sefer* dealing with *korbanos*, the Torah indicates symbolically the great humility of Moshe (*Baal Haturim* 1:1). Moshe's meekness is consonant with the principle underlying *korbanos*, since humbleness on the part of the person offering the *korban* is basic to *HaShem*'s acceptance of it and is greater than all sacrifices; here, therefore, is the proper place for the symbolic indication of the humility of Moshe. Thus, a humble person is ready for sacrifice in all its implied meanings; whether he brings an external or an internal *korban*, he is willing to sacrifice for his religious principles and convictions. By his sincerity of purpose while sacrificing, he draws nearer to the Almighty.

The *midrash* quoted above stresses the importance of inculcating, from a very early age, the concept of humbleness before the Almighty and readiness to sacrifice for one's religious convictions. Let the "pure"—children not yet exposed to and affected by the various negative influences of the outside world—occupy themselves with the "pure"—*korbanos* that will teach the humbleness that leads to proper fear and reverence for the Almighty. Thus, they will develop strength of character, ethics, and morals. Equipped with these attributes, the child will grow into an adult who can withstand the spiritually unhealthy way of life permeating the atmosphere of modern society to the point of *sacrifice*, in order to live as a truly Torah observant Jew. Our children are our real treasures, and they must be guided from an early age to a life of purity.

Rabbi Yitzchok Goodman

Young Israel of Far Rockaway, New York

In the *Sefer Torah*, the *aleph* (the last letter) of the word *Vayikra* is written in a small size. The great kabbalist Rav Nasan Shapira of Krakow wrote a book in which he gave one thousand interpretations of this small letter's meaning. Great scholars have testified that they saw and read parts of the hand-written manuscript, which, as far as I know, is now lost. (For those who find this hard to imagine, one of his other works, *M'galeh Amukos*, is easy to acquire and offers 252 interpretations of the brief dialogue between Moshe and God, in *Vaetchanan*, regarding Moshe's desire to cross into *Eretz Yisrael.*)

Alas, in the absence of Rav Shapira's volume, we must be content with the about twenty interpretations recorded by our *seforim*. Most of these interpretations are based on the concept of Moshe's extreme modesty. *Baal Haturim*, for example, claims that Moshe, in his humility, tried to write *Vayikar*, which would indicate that God "chanced" upon Moshe. This expression is similar to that used when God spoke to Bilaam (Numbers 23:4), but God instructed Moshe to write the full word, for the "call" of God indicates that Moshe is beloved. Remaining humble, Moshe managed the "trick" of writing the *aleph* in small size.

The discussion of Reb Simchah Bunim of Pshischah is intriguing. To understand Moshe, he suggests, picture two men on top of a tall mountain. The boaster thinks he is great, standing on top of the world. The humble one knows that he is the same size he was before; it is just that the mountain is tall. So, too, Moshe felt that his greatness was no more than God's gift to him; therefore he remained humble.

We say in our daily davening, in the *Ezrat Avoteinu*, "He lowers the proud down to the earth and raises the lowly up to Heaven." The obvious question is: once a proud person has indeed been lowered to earth, he becomes by definition "low," but then he is entitled to be raised by the power of the second phrase—that God raises the lowly! In that case, does the raising and lowering become an endless cycle? But the answer is that, when a truly wicked and haughty person is lowered to the earth, he does not change at all; he remains with his *gaavah* and boastfulness. Not feeling lowly, he is not entitled to be raised. So, too, the *tzaddik*, who feels humble even when God lifts him to the greatest heights, is not affected to the point of becoming boastful and, therefore, does not deserve to be lowered again. Thus, our phrase is telling us that even when God Himself calls to Moshe, Moshe remains the same humble person (symbolized by the small *aleph*) that he was before. Finally, the Torah testifies to us later that Moshe was, in truth, the most humble of all men on earth.

An interesting additional point is made in a *sefer* called *Matamim*. The *Midrash Tanchuma* states that the beams of light that filled Moshe's face when he descended from Mount Sinai resulted from a tiny bit of ink that remained in his pen, which God passed over Moshe's forehead. Can it be that God miscalculated precisely how much ink Moshe needed? But our verse provides the answer: Moshe wrote the *aleph* in small size, in his humility. The bit of ink he saved by that act entitled him to the reward of a shining countenance, so that, despite his modesty, all Yisrael could see the special love *HaShem* had for him.

We should also note, that within the science of "The Codes," this verse (Leviticus 1:1) is rather strange, since, instead of saying, "God called to Moshe," as is typical, it mentions God only in the second phrase. The code investigators found that this first verse hides the four-letter name of *HaShem*, from the first *yud*, in intervals of the mystic number 8; the pattern is repeated in the *sedrah Kedoshim*.

SYMBOLS OF A *KORBAN*

It is well known that, in bringing a *korban* (sacrifice), a man is supposed to feel that the animal is a substitute for himself, as though he had offered himself to God. On the highest level, this feeling was, indeed, attained. In later generations, however, many of *Klal Yisrael* fell to the level of seeing a *korban* as a gift (or bribe) to God that guaranteed them His love despite their evil actions. The Apter Rav, known by his *sefer Ohaiv Yisrael*, states that this idea can be read into the second verse of the *sedrah*:

According to the Apter Rav, [The true] Adam—*mentsch*—feels that he sacrifices of himself (*mikem*—from amongst you, Leviticus 1:12); therefore, this is truly a *korban* to God. Since such people are a minority, the statement is in singular (*yakriv*, brings an offering, Leviticus 1:12). However, for most people, who do not have these higher conceptions, the main point is that they donated their funds—by buying an animal—to God's Temple. For them the verse continues, "from the animal . . . the sheep, you shall sacrifice (*takrivu*—in plural form) your *korban*"—that is, all you will perceive is that the animal is sacrificed. This was the error of later generations that led to the decline of the *Beis Hamikdash* and its service, causing the ultimate *Churban*.

CHASIDIC INTERPRETATIONS

The Hasidic *rebbes* read countless meanings into all the acts and expressions dealing with the *korbanot*. They are found in massive numbers in all the collection-types of volumes on *Vayikra*. A typical example is the interpretation of the *Mishna*, "What is the location of the sacrifices? [regarding] the most holy offerings, their slaughter is in the '*tzafon*'—north [side of the courtyard]" (*Mishna Zevachim* chapter 5 Mishna 1) ". . . the offerings of lesser holiness. Their slaughter is anywhere in the courtyard" (*Mishna Zevachim* chapter 5 *Mishna* 7). This means (since *tsafon*, "unworthy," also means "hidden") that most-holy Jews are not vulnerable to "slaughter" by the evil inclination except in the most hidden ways—that is, only in occasional private "thoughts" (*hirhurim ra'im*), whereas those who are less holy can be enticed into sin ("slaughtered" by their *yetzer hara*) anywhere and anytime!

TO TELL OR NOT TO TELL

The Torah demands (Leviticus 5:1) that we tell what we know and admonish those who sin, for our silence is our own sin. But, the Talmud also says, if you are certain that someone will definitely not listen, don't increase the person's sin by telling him or her, thereby making the person more of a *maizid* (who commits the transgression with full intent and understanding). *Meforshim* say that is why the negative word *lo*—usually spelled *lamed, aleph*—is spelled curiously, with a *vav* in the middle—*lamed, vav, aleph*. This hints that sometimes telling "him" *lo* normally spelled *lomed, vav* is itself the sin; for he will not listen anyway.

Rabbi Edward Davis

Young Israel of Hollywood/ Fort Lauderdale, Florida

Commentators disagree as to the purpose of bringing a sacrifice. Rambam (*Guide for the Perplexed* 3:32) writes that God commands us to bring sacrifices in order to take us away from the world of idolatry. Ramban (commentary to *Vayikra* 1:9) rejects Rambam's idea and suggests instead that the donor realize that he is substituting the animal for his own body, which should be sacrificed as a result of the sins he committed. The sacrificial ritual is a spiritual act designed to impress upon the people the seriousness of each deed they commit and each word they utter. The author of the *Meshech Chochmah* wants to embrace both opinions. According to him, the purpose of the private altars that were prevalent in Israel prior to the building of the Holy Temple in Jerusalem was to keep the people away from idolatry. Once the Holy Temple was built, the private altars were prohibited, replaced by the one altar on the Temple Mount. With the Holy Temple in existence, idolatry should have been uprooted from the hearts of the people. The purpose of the Temple sacrifice was to instruct the people, individually and collectively, in proper spiritual conduct—as Ramban points out.

Five kinds of sacrifices are discussed in this *sedrah*:

The ***olah*** (burnt offering) is a free-will offering entirely consumed by the altar.

The ***minchah*** offering is made of flour and oil mixed with incense. There are five types of *minchah* offerings discussed, differing in the type of pan used, if any, and whether the portion to be burnt was removed before or after the *minchah* was baked. Neither honey nor leavening was permitted in any offering.

The ***shelamim*** (peace) offering is a free-will offering by an individual, but only part of it is sacrificed on the altar. The rest is divided between the *kohanim* and the donors.

The ***chatat*** (sin) offering is an obligatory sacrifice brought by a Jew who inadvertently transgresses a negative *mitzvah* for which the punishment is *kareit* had this sin been done deliberately. Three special kinds of *chatat* are brought for certain errors committed by the *Kohein Gadol*, the *Sanhedrin*, or the king. There are also specific sins for which a *chatat* varies (whether an animal, bird, or flour offering), according to what the transgressor was able to afford.

The ***asham*** (guilt) offering was brought for certain sins, two of which are specified in the *sedrah*. If someone *may* have committed a sin for which a *chatat* is brought, he must bring an *asham* called *talui* (pending). If he later ascertains that he did commit the sin, he brings a *chatat*. (The *asham talui* atones, not for the sin itself, but for the carelessness that allowed it.)

For animal sacrifices, the donor was required to "lean" with all his might, with both hands, on the animal's head. He confesses his sin while he does so and, in the case of a peace offering, he utters praise to *HaShem*. When a non-Jew brings an offering, he does not lean on the animal because the non-Jew is classified as an idolater, and he does not consider the sacrifice to be a refutation of his other faith. The Talmud further restricts the leaning on the sacrificial animal to men, not permitting women to observe this law. Since the ritual is connected to the elimination of any idolatrous thinking, the Talmud is in essence saying that women are not prone to idolatry, as men are. This was evident from the fact that women did not contribute their gold jewelry to create the golden calf. Furthermore, the donor did not lean on the head of his sacrifice if he brought a bird. The leaning was to remove any belief in the animal as a god and, according to the Rambam, idolators did not bow down to birds in those days. This uprooting of idolatry could have been just as effectively linked to the *shechitah*—the slaughtering of the animal—but the *kohein* usually did the slaughtering though the donor was technically permitted to slaughter the animal.

All the sacrifices required salt (2:13). Salt draws the blood from the meat. This teaches us that, just as salt draws out the blood, so should we, when we stand in prayer, purify our thought and our minds, thereby enabling our prayers to ascend to the Almighty. Another way to understand the requirement to add salt is to note that salt adds flavor to the meat. Without salt, meat would not be served to royalty. Similarly our *mitzvot* must be performed with good taste and smell—that is, we should perform them with spirit and dedication and not as if they were burdensome. The requirement to add salt is introduced to us when the Torah is discussing the *minchah*—meal offering. This offering is brought by a poor person, who might not feel spirited and elated at bringing such an offering at a time when wealthier people are bringing the more expensive animals. Hence, the Torah teaches us to add salt, thereby elevating the poor person, who now knows that his offering is richly seasoned for the Almighty (Rabbi Moshe Sternbuch).

The Torah changes its terminology when it identifies the different people who sin. With the general assembly and the anointed *kohein*, the Torah employs the term *im*—"if"—implying that it might occur and this is what to do if they sin. When speaking of an individual sinner, the Torah uses the word *ki*—"whereas"—implying that it is quite probable for an individual to err. But, when referring to a ruler, the Torah uses the word *asher*—"when"—as if to say that he, the ruler, will most assuredly sin, as the *Zohar* states: "The ruler will definitely sin." Rabbi Yitzchak Karo states that honor and pride will bring a person to sin even against his will. Sforno writes that wealth and power will indeed bring an individual to sin. Homiletically, our Sages comment that *asher* is related to *ashrei*, meaning, "Fortunate is the generation whose ruler brings a sin offering." This is because it demonstrates to all that one should repent for one's sins. A leader who has sinned and repented will be a more compassionate and understanding ruler.

When a person sins and commits a misappropriation offense against God by lying to his neighbor, he is liable both to his neighbor and to God. For example, if a person finds a lost object and denies finding it, he has sinned. He must return the found article and, because he swore falsely, he must add one-fifth to its value as a punishment. Furthermore, he must bring a guilt offering (Leviticus 5:20–25). The *Or Hachaim* remarks homiletically on the verse, "If a person will sin and commit a treachery against *HaShem*" (Leviticus 5:21), he injures his friend as well. Since all Jews are responsible for each other (since our covenantal relationship with God is based upon God's relationship with *all* of us, not just a few), a sinner damages not only his own personal relationship with God but also damages all of Israel's relationship with *HaShem*.

Rabbi Yehuda Melber

Young Israel of Sunny Isles, Florida

There is a custom that, when a boy starts learning *Chumash*, the first subject matter is *Vayikra*. Question: Why is *Vayikra* so important to the very beginning of Torah study? The answer is, because in the one word *Vayikra* is implied the entire sacred principles of the eternity of Torah.

In terms of today's Jewish life, "sacred Principles" is the basic difference between Orthodox Judaism and non-Orthodox. The Orthodox view is that the Torah law is unchangeable and immutable. Its validity is expressed in all times and under all conditions. Why so? Because it was God-made, not man-made. However, the non-Orthodox maintain that every law, including the Torah law, is subject to conditions and circumstances. Hence, just as life changes from time to time and from place to place, so too the law. There is no exception to that rule.

Therefore, when the little Jewish boy starts his Torah study, right at the beginning we impress upon him this most important tenet: *Vayikra*. Know that you are going to study a law that is unlike any other law because this law comes directly from the Eternal Lawgiver. Consequently, it is, likewise, eternal and immutable, not allowing any change, alteration, or modification.

But how do we learn this from the one word *Vayikra*? Answer: The Rabbis said, "There is a difference in the Hebrew between *Vayikar*, meaning, "He happened to meet fortuitously," and *Vayikra*, "he called deliberately." *Vayikar*—"he happened to meet"—means that the heavenly voice happened accidentally to reach the man but the man remained where he had been earlier; he did not become elevated to a higher level through this call. This was the case with Bilaam. With Moshe, however, when the heavenly voice called him affectionately to teach him the laws of the Torah, Moshe was so highly inspired by that call that he reached near heaven; each time he was elevated to a higher level of exaltation and enthusiasm. That made the tremendous difference between one call and the other call. Therefore, the entire Torah became an extraordinary volume of Law, being absolutely eternal and infinite, unchangeable and immutable. No amendment is valid in view of that rule.

The same idea comes to the fore this year when we have the combination of *Parshat Zachor* and *Parshat Vayikra*. In *Parshat Zachor*, again we see the extraordinary fate of the Jewish people. Why were the Jews suddenly attacked by Amalek? There was no reason for any hate between the two people! The Jews peacefully went their way out of Egypt, not causing any harm to anybody. What triggered the animosity on the part of Amalek? Answer: the exception of the Jewish outlook. Amalek, grandson of Esau, did not want to allow any exception in the structure of human society. He thought the Jewish law, and with it the Jewish lifestyle, should not be different from any other law and lifestyle. That ignited the first attack against the Jews, and their Torah.

Therefore the Torah exhorts us: *Zachor*. Remember what happened in the past, and apply it to the present. Remember the principle of *Vayikra* and the implication of Amalek's attack. That will strengthen your faith in Torah, so that at the end you will be the victor over all the evil forces, and truth will prevail throughout the world for the best of all mankind.

❖ CHAPTER 27 ❖

Tzav/Shabbat Hagadol

Rabbi Shlomo Hochberg

Young Israel of Jamaica Estates, New York

SHABBAT HAGADOL

The Purpose of the Exile in Egypt

In the Covenant between the Sections (Genesis 15), *HaShem* promised the land of Israel to Avraham. He subsequently reconfirmed this promise to Yitzchak and then to Yaakov. Yet, the fulfillment of this promise was contingent upon the sojourn of their descendants as bondsmen and sojourners.

There are two terms in *halachah* that define such a conditional relationship: *Im* and *al menat*. For example, a man may betroth a woman under specified conditions: He may say, "Behold, you are betrothed to me *if* you give if me 200 coins (*zuz*)," or he may state the condition as "Behold, you are betrothed to me you give me 200 coins (*zuz*)." In the first case, the *kiddushin*-betrothment takes effect only after the two hundred *zuz* change hands, thus fulfilling the condition. In the latter case, however, the use of the term *al menat* mandates that once the two hundred *zuz* change hands, the *kiddushin* takes effect retroactively.

The Rav, Rabbi Joseph B Soloveitchik, *zt"l,* explained that, at the Covenant between the Sections, *HaShem* promised the Land of Israel to *Bnei Yisrael;* yet, until the bondage in Egypt, the land was not completely theirs. Jewish ownership of the land was not consummated until after the enslavement, so that Avraham had to buy the gravesite for Sarah, as did Yaakov for Rachel.

What would be accomplished during the Egyptian slavery to prepare *Bnei Yisrael* to receive the land? The Rav, *zt"l,* noted, that *Bnei Yisrael,* when exiled, were always exiled to very technically advanced civilizations, including Egypt, Babylon, and Rome—the centers of civilization. (One might wonder whether the United States and former Soviet Union, among other countries, could be included in this list.) The Torah thus guides our destiny—teaching us skills that will help us later in the land of Israel. God sent the Jews to Egypt to secure agricultural training ("and with all kinds of work in the field," Exodus 1:14). *Hashgachah* [Providence] sends the Jew where he will obtain the technical training he needs. The Torah includes so many agricultural *mitzvot* (a full one-sixth of the Oral Torah discusses *mitzvot hateluyot b'aretz, mitzvot* contingent on (being done in) the Land of Israel.

Though *Bnei Yisrael* learned the technique of farming in Egypt, the ethic of farming they learned from the Torah at Har Sinai. Each type of economy has its own ethic, and the Torah prescribes the *halachot* of each economic system. Throughout our history, then, *HaShem* has placed us geographically in countries that would contribute to the technical knowledge necessary for life in Israel. Paired with the parallel Torah ethic, we are thus prepared to be a light, in our land, to the nations of the world.

A Lesson from Enslavement in Egypt

How can we arouse ourselves to empathize with those who suffer? As we sit in the comfort of our homes, surrounded by the luxuries we take for granted, can we actually imagine the hardships endured by Jews in Yehudah, Shomron, Golan, or Beer Sheva, or in Aleppo, Cracow, or Warsaw, or in the countries of the former Soviet/Communist bloc? Can we actually picture ourselves relegated to virtual slavery, unable to move freely, unable to use our skills, unable to get training, unable to extricate ourselves from a life of hardship, cruelty, and suffering?

Rav Joseph B. Soloveitchik, *zt"l,* asserts that one of the purposes of our enslavement was to instill in us *rachmanut* (compassion), the distinguishing characteristic of the Jewish people. Subjected to ruthless and inhumane treatment for 210 years as strangers and slaves in Egypt, the Jewish people emerged as free men, sensitized forever to the plight of the downtrodden, *rachmanut* indelibly inscribed in our national consciousness.

The *rachaman* is compelled by the very fiber of his being to act mercifully. He does not merely act kindly; the very nature of the *rachaman* is one of kindness and mercy. *Chazal* mandated that at the Passover seder we experience the conflicting feelings of bitterness and sweetness, suffering and relief, slavery and redemption, subjugation and freedom, so that we may be moved to fully appreciate our many blessings and accept our responsibility in the community at large as *rachmanim bnei rachmanim,* empathizing with and responding to the needs of others.

PARSHAT TZAV: THE VESTMENTS OF THE *KOHEIN GADOL*

Among the vestments of the *Kohein Gadol,* the *Tzitz* (headplate) and the *Choshen* (breastplate) are singled out by the Torah in relation to the unique mission of the *Kohein Gadol.* The Torah directs "You shall make vestments of sanctity for Aaron your brother . . ." (Exodus 28:2) "You shall make a headplate of pure gold . . ." (Exodus 28:36) ". . . and it shall be on his forehead always . . ." (Exodus 28:38) "and Aaron shall bear the names of the Sons of Israel on the breastplate of judgment . . ." (Exodus 28:29) ". . . and Aaron shall bear the judgment of the Children of Israel on his heart, constantly, before *HaShem.*" (Exodus 28:30). That the *Tzitz* be constantly on the *Kohein Gadol's forehead* before *HaShem,* and that the *Choshen Mishpat* be constantly upon his *heart.*

The *Tzitz* is "*kodesh Lashem*"—"totally sanctified to *HaShem*"—words that appear right upon the *Tzitz;* it atones for *tumah* and is placed upon Aharon's *forehead* near the brain, the core of Torah *intellect* and *knowledge.* The *Choshen,* on the other hand, includes the names of all the tribes and rests upon Aharon's *heart,* the very center of love and affection for all fellow Jews, and is referred to as the *Choshen* of *Justice.*

The Rav, Rabbi Joseph B. Soloveitchik, *zt"l,* proposes that the *Tzitz* decided all issues of pure *halachah,* such as *issur* and *heter, tumah* and *taharah, agunah* and other marital issues, *kashrus* and *niddah.* The *Choshen* (with the *urim v'tumim*), however, would determine issues of much different nature, questions of how to respond to an enemy, for example; or whether or not to attack, whether and how to protest a nation or group that had wronged *Am Yisrael*—in short, how to respond practically to the national crises that face our people, to find the correct words, deeds, and pronouncements. These issues could be determined only by one with a heart, like Aharon's, filled with love for the nation and individuals of *Am Yisrael,* a heart that aches with the pain of fellow Jews, and that is tormented by any national misfortune.

Of course, it is the *Kohein Gadol* who must wear both the *Choshen* and the *Tzitz*—that is, the same *kohein* who is versed in the intricacies of *halachah* can discern, through *ruach hakodesh,* Divine inspiration, the appropriate response to diverse political and contemporary issues. The same principle remains intact today: True Jewish leaders are those imbued with the highest level of *kedushah* and intellectual *halachic* expertise, as well as with the purity of heart to perceive the complex nuances of each contemporary political and ethical dilemma and to conceive and effectuate the suitable response.

❖ CHAPTER 28 ❖

Tzav

Rabbi Dov A. Brisman

Young Israel of Elkins Park, Pennsylvania

GOOD TIMING

The *Shulchan Aruch* (*Orach Chaim* 428,4) states, "[We] always read *Parshat Tzav* before Pesach except during leap years, when we read *Parshat Metzorah*." The *Eliyahu Rabbah* explains the reason for this arrangement, saying that *Parshat Tzav* introduces the concept of *kashering* utensils in the Torah; therefore it is appropriate to read this *parshah* immediately before Pesach. *Parshat Metzorah* discusses the inability to *kasher* earthenware and, thus, also relates to the Pesach holiday.

Allow me to expand upon the explanation of *Eliyahu Rabbah*. Even in a leap year, when *Parshat Metzorah* and not *Parshat Tzav* is read immediately before Pesach, *Parshat Tzav* does not lose its connection to the Pesach *yom tov*; it is still most appropriate and within the spirit of the upcoming holiday of Pesach to read *Parshat Tzav* right after Purim. The *halachah* dictates (ibid. 429,1): "[We] deliberate and consult in the laws of Pesach thirty days before Pesach." Some *poskim* state that this time-frame begins on Purim. The *Mishnah Berurah* concludes that, though on *Shabbat Hagadol* the Rav speaks publicly about the *halachot* of Pesach, every individual should, on his own, begin to study *hilchot Pesach* on Purim.

On the basis of this reasoning, during a leap year we read *Parshat Tzav* after Purim to show that we are beginning the process of studying *hilchot Pesach* at the beginning of the thirty day period, and we read *Parshat Metzorah*, which discusses the inability to *kasher* earthenware, right before Pesach.

SERVICE WITH ROYALTY

The first *mitzvah* discussed in the *parshah* is *terumat hadeshen*—the removal of the ashes of burnt *korbanot* (sacrifices) from the *mizbeach* (altar). *Terumat hadeshen* is a service that requires a *kohein* to be dressed in the *bigdei kehunah* (priestly garments). *Rabbeinu* Bachya writes that from *terumat hadeshen* comes the concept that even a relatively degrading duty, when done in the service of the Almighty, must not be belittled; as we see that even this supposedly "janitorial service" of *terumat hadeshen* is performed in *bigdei kehunah* and not in street clothes. *Rabbeinu* Bachya furthermore states that we should apply this lesson to our everyday lives; whenever we perform a *mitzvah* that can bring us closer to *HaShem*, we must glorify Him by humbling ourselves for His honor.

Rabbeinu Bachya's lesson seems to say that a person who wears *bigdei kehunah* while performing an apparently degrading service comes to the realization that the *bigdei kehunah* are not an end in themselves, for one's own self-aggrandizement, but, rather, a medium with which to serve *HaShem*. Just as *HaShem* requires *bigdei kehunah* to be worn "for honor and glory" (Exodus 28:2), so, too, He instructs that these garments, which represent glorification, shall be worn while doing an obviously inglorious task—removing the ashes. Thus the *terumat hadeshen* service teaches us humility, that the glory with which we appear to be endowed is really only for the sake of *kevod Shamayim*. And for *kevod Shamayim* no duty is too lowly a deed.

Rabbeinu Bachya, though, goes much further than this. He explains that, in order to be considered an *eved*, or true servant, one must have a master. The title "master" is appropriate only if there is a servant. These two terms are intertwined and dependent upon each other. If one serves *HaShem*, his service is incomplete if one does not actually accept upon himself the conditions of servitude—humility and subordination. In this way, our *parshah* contains the essence of *avodat HaShem*—royalty embellished with humility, readiness to serve our Master under all conditions.

In the light of the above, perhaps we can explain why the word *mokda* (firewood) in the second *pasuk* (Leviticus 6:2) is written with a tiny *mem*. The Torah states, "This is the law of the *olah* (burnt offering), this is the *olah* on the firewood on the altar the entire night . . ." (Leviticus 6:2). The *Midrash Rabbah* homiletically interprets this phrase to mean that one who is haughty is punished through fire. The word *olah* literally means "rising"; hence, if one raises himself, his "law" (judgment) is "firewood"—to be burnt.

One can also interpret the *pasuk* to say, "This is the law of *olah*, the rising and elevating of oneself." How? By *mokda*; when a person is humble and realizes that all material things will eventually be "burnt" instead of enduring forever, he is then able to rise. The *korban*, which is termed "elevation," is implemented through a burning process. Humility causes us to realize that we are not entities unto ourselves, that our material existence was not meant to be self-serving. These are the thoughts and intentions that must be felt when an *olah* is offered before *HaShem*. Even its remnants, mere ashes, must be gathered with deference.

Therefore, the Torah hints to us that it should not suffice to sacrifice the *olah* perfunctorily. Even as it is consumed upon the altar, as we see it engulfed by flames, as the firewood—*mokda*—takes over, we must absorb the lesson of the *olah* and see the small *mem* of *mokda*. We must observe that this large firewood diminishes to mere ashes and note that this is not a process of disintegration but, rather, an elevation—a *korban olah*. In the same way, by humbling ourselves, by diminishing our material being, we are actually experiencing an *aliyah* (a rising—from the word *olah*) of the *neshamah*. Only after absorbing this lesson will the true bond of servant and master—*eved v'adon*—between man and *HaShem* materialize.

ORDER OF PRIORITIES: THE PROPER WAY TO EAT

"The *minchah* (flour offering) shall be baked as leaven, their portion (that is, of the *kohanim*) I have given them from my fire-offering . . ." (Leviticus 6:10).

The *Torat Kohanim* derives from this *posuk* that the portion of the *minchah* allotted to the *kohanim* is permitted only following the sacrifice of the *kometz* (a fistful of flour) portion. The *Torat Kohanim* then indicates that the same principle applies to all *korbanot* (sacrifices). It is incumbent upon the *kohein* to sacrifice; only after he has fulfilled his *mitzvah* is he then permitted to partake of his portion.

The *Talmud* (*Pesachim* 59b) states that, by having the *kohanim* eat their portions (from the *korbanot*), the owners of the *korbanot* are presumed to have done—or at least begun—the process of atonement. This, too, is based upon a *pasuk*.

If this eating can serve as a catalyst for atonement, it is apparent that the *kavanah* (intent) of the *kohein* at the time of that particular eating must be pure. The meat of *korbanot*, categorized as *kodshei kodshim* (sanctified of sanctified), as well as the flour offering, are eaten only in the *Beit Hamikdash*. Levity was not permitted in the entire Temple Mount; even more so in the *Beit Hamikdash*. Therefore, it is evident that proper behavior was required when feasting in the *Beit Hamikdash*, especially if the meal was to serve for the purpose of atonement.

For this reason, the Torah directed the *kohanim* to eat from the *korban* only after the sacrifice was offered on the altar. After such intense service to *HaShem* and such great *kavanah*, it was truly appropriate to partake of a meal, for then there could be a guarantee of proper behavior and attitude, which also had the result of converting a mundane act of eating the meat into one of spiritual fortitude.

Rabbi Abraham Union

Young Israel of Beverly Hills, California

LESSONS IN FIRE

Fire plays a prominent role in the opening verses of our *parsha*. After instructing the law of the burnt offering, the Torah continues, "A lasting fire should be kindled on the altar, it should never go out" (Leviticus 6:6). This *posuk* presents two distinct *mitzvot*. It commands us with a positive precept to maintain the fire on the altar at all times and also issues a negative prohibitioin forbidding an action of extinguishing even a portion of the altar's fire (see Rambam, *Hilchot tmidim U'musafim*; *Sefer Hachinuch*). Examination of these *mitzvot* reveals timeless applications even in the absence of the Temple and altar.

The *Talmud Yerushalmi* (*Yoma* 4:6) derives an interesting halachah from this *posuk* (Leviticus 6:6), "Even when the Sanctuary was traveling, the fire on the altar had to keep going." This was accomplished, the *Talmud Yerushalmi* tells us, by placing a metal dome over the altar so that movement and the natural elements would not put out the flame. What can we learn from this?

The history of civilization is dynamic and changing. Society is always in transition, and, especially today, it is moving so rapidly that some believe we are suffering from "future shock." With life in constant flux, there is a danger of running ahead and leaving our spiritual ideals behind. We may preserve the outward trappings of Torah observance and piety, but lose the "fire"—the inner warmth and dedication that was the hallmark of the Sanctuary and the *Batei Hamikdash*.

Folklore tells of a great sage who was asked how he would react if his house caught on fire. What would he try to save first? The cash, the food, the clothes? None of the above, he replied. His first priority would be to save the fire. Without fervor and enthusiasm, our Torah lives are bland and unexciting. If there is no fire, our prayers are dull, and our *mitzvot* are rote. Our *Avodat HaShem*, in and out of the synagogue, should be alive and vibrant.

Lamentably, the age-old Jewish custom of *shuckeling*, swaying to and fro during prayer, has become an object of derision among some. Yet the *Zohar* explains this practice as profound and beautiful; the outward movement of the body mimics the flickering of a flame, to which the soul is compared (heard from Harav Dov Schwartzman, *shlita*). Rav Kook *zt"l* wrote in his study of the *siddur* (*Olot Reivan*) that the *neshamah* is constantly in a state of song and that we should view *tefilla* (prayer) as an opportunity to express that song externally. Obviously, this does not mean we all have to jump around during *davening*. We should, however, take it as a call for greater depth and feeling.

Fire also represents dedication and devotion, which go hand in hand with the task of sacrifice. The *Midrash Tanchuma* on our *sedrah* gives a marvelous portrait of the circumstances leading to the selection of Aharon and his sons for the priestly services enumerated in *Tzav* (Leviticus 8:2). At the time that the complaining Jews fell victim to the plague sent by *HaShem* (Numbers 17), Moshe told Aharon to take the incense holder and immediately place fire upon it to halt the decimation.

> "Aharon said to him, 'My master Moshe, are you trying to kill me? My sons [Nadav and Avihu] were burnt with fire precisely because they brought fire that *HaShem* did not command.' . . . Moshe said to him, 'Go and do what you were told, quickly. While you are standing around talking the people are dying!' . . . Upon hearing this Aharon exclaimed, 'Is it not fitting that I should die for the Jewish nation' and immediately went to take action."

This, says the *midrash*, is why God appointed Aaron in our *parshah*, as Kohein Gadol.

Aharon assumed that Moshe's order to ignite incense was a death sentence for himself. He nevertheless rushed to obey when he realized that the welfare of Klal Yisrael was at stake. His personal ardor and conviction propelled him to offer his own life for the salvation of others. He was inspired with the flame of selfless service.

But fire can be dangerous as well, in both the literal and figurative senses. Rashi comments on the above-mentioned verse (Leviticus 6:6) that the Torah requires that the fire of the altar must be used in lighting the menorah. Rabbi Samson Raphael Hirsch elaborates: "There is only one place where the Divine Torah allows its fire to shine, from where and whereon all other fire in the *Mikdash* . . . receives its origin and existence."

Our people in general, and in this century in particular, bear awesome witness to what can happen when fire and zeal run out of control and are not connected to the "altar," the center of sacrifice and devotion to *HaShem*'s will. It was true "religious" zeal that fueled the torture chambers and *auto da fè*'s of the Spanish Inquisition. The Bolsheviks exhibited enormous enthusiasm in their desire to build a utopian society; unfortunately, the crimes they committed in pursuing their aims were equally enormous. Similarly, the knife-wielding Islamic fanatics of Hamas have ample fervor for their cause. These tragic examples underscore the grave danger of fire and enthusiasm that do not originate with the holy altar. Misguided fire can burn and destroy.

Even in the context of Torah, there are times when it is appropriate to "cool it." The Talmud in *Zevachim* 91b discusses how the voluntary wine libations could be sprinkled on the altar. However, sprinkling the wine over the fire would partially extinguish it, which we have learned is forbidden. The *Gemara* ventures the answer that dousing the flame for the purpose of a *mitzvah* is permissible. Therefore, the wine could be poured without concern, since this, too, was a *mitzvah*.

Perhaps we may understand this as an allusion to the principle that, despite our strong emphasis on keeping the flame alive, there are circumstances in which it is proper, even a *mitzvah*, to lower the temperature.

This week's *haftorah*, the selection for *Shabbat Hagadol*, speaks of the eventual return of Eliahu Hanavi. This prophet, whose ascension to Heaven in a chariot of fire constitutes one of the most remarkable episodes in the entire *Tanakh*, is the herald of the final redemption. That redemption will also arrive amidst a conflagration. "Behold, a day shall come which is fiery like a furnace" (Malachi 3:19) which will consume all evildoers and perpetrators of wickedness. Fire, we see, is like nuclear power. Depending upon how it is harnessed and utilized, it can fuel the altar or devour what is flawed and imperfect. Eliahu left this world in fire and will return to us in fire, teaching us the power and energy the Almighty has placed in creation for us to channel and use. Keeping the fire glowing within its proper boundaries is part of our task until we realize the ultimate promise of our *haftorah*: "And He will turn the hearts of fathers to their sons and the hearts of sons to their fathers."

Rabbi Shlomo Hochberg

Young Israel of Jamaica Estates, New York

ZRIZUT IN *MITZVOT*

Rav Moshe Chaim Luzzatto, in his classic *mussar* treatise *Mesilat Yesharim* (*Path of the Just*), delineates the importance of the trait of *zrizut*, zeal, based on the Mechilta's comment, "You shall watch over (safeguard) the *matzot* (Exodus 12:17); if a *mitzvah* presents itself to you, don't let it grow stale." Rav Luzzatto lists various obstacles or excuses that may prevent one from accomplishing the *mitzvah* at hand.

Rashi's first comment on *Parshat Tzav* underlines the significance of *zrizut* as it relates specifically to the *mitzvah* of bringing the *korban olah*. He quotes from the *Sifra*, which notes that the verb *tzav* (to command) is singled out to begin our *parshah*, rather than the more commonly used verbs "to say" or "to speak," which are employed throughout the Torah when Moshe *Rabbeinu* transmits the word of *HaShem* to *Bnei Yisrael*. The *Sifra* cites two opinions to explain this choice of verb: "Whenever the form *Tzav* is used, it implies the need for zeal immediately, and for future generations. . . . Rav Shimon, however, says that zeal is especially needed when the performance of the *mitzvah* may potentially cause a monetary loss."

We are thus told of three common rationalizations presented when we want to delay our performance or completion of a *mitzvah*. First, it's a *mitzvah* for now; the *mitzvah* is important only for the immediate future but will make no long-term difference. Therefore, I need not expend my effort for something of only fleeting consequence. Second, it's a *mitzvah* for the coming generations. Therefore, it's not important if I do the *mitzvah*, as long as I pass it on to my children. Third, the *mitzvah* involves *chisoron*, his loss of money. Valuable resources must be expended to fulfill the *mitzvah*. Perhaps other expenditures have a higher priority. So the Torah tells us in the strongest possible terms, *Tzav*! Tell *Bnei Yisrael* that, despite any rationalizations, obstacles, or excuses, the *mitzvah* is not to be postponed but should be accomplished immediately and with zeal.

The *Chidushai Harim* adds that the *mitzvah* under discussion, the *Olah* sacrifice, is brought for sins of the heart. Regarding other human organs, such as the ears and eyes, the *kis*—the pocket, or covering—enables the person to escape from sin, as the eyelids can cover the eyes, and the earlobe can cover the ear, when needed. But in the case of the heart, the *kis*—the covering—leads to sin, as it prevents the proper feelings from being expressed. In the case of the heart, having a *kis* is the greatest *chisoron*—detraction from doing a *mitzvah*. Therefore, special *zrizut* is necessary to facilitate the proper fulfillment of the *mitzvah*.

HAFTARAH: YIRMEYAHU

Yirmeyahu Hanavi counsels us not to glorify ourselves because of our wealth, wisdom, or power.

> Thus says *HaShem*: Let not the wise man glorify in his wisdom, nor the powerful in his strength, nor the wealthy in his wealth. But only, with *this* (*zot*) should one glorify—in comprehending and knowing Me, for I am *HaShem*, Who, with lovingkindness, does justice and righteousness in the land, for it is these things that I desire, says *HaShem*. (Yirmeyahu 9:22–23)

Reb Shlomo of Redomsk, author of *Tiferet Shlomo*, expresses shock at Yirmeyahu's exhortation. Are we then foolish children, he asks, who need to be told something so elementary as not to be arrogant because God blessed us with specific gifts or talent? He explains, therefore, that Yirmeyahu's remarks are directed at a higher level of character development. Yirmeyahu speaks to the wise person who does learn, and to the wealthy person who, in fact, gives *tzedakah*, and to the powerful person who uses his influence to help others. But, he does so for his own private goals, such as personal growth in Torah. He does not have others in mind. Hence the verse refers to his wisdom, his power, his wealth. Yirmeyahu challenges this self-centered individual and proclaims, this is not *HaShem*'s way.

Rather, he instructs us to utilize our talents and resources in the context of *HaShem*'s desire to benefit the world. The essence of Torah learning and of accumulating and distributing wealth wisely is to benefit others, and so, too, with the use of power. One who does so demonstrates a true knowledge of *HaShem* and of how He uses His infinite power, wealth, and wisdom to do "lovingkindness, justice, and righteousness" . . . for this is what He desires for our sake.

In *gematriah* (numerology) the word *zot* has a value of 408, which equals the sum-total of *tzom, kol,* and *mamon* (fasting, voice, and money), each of which numerically equals 136. These three are parallel to the three elements that can avert a bad decree, as recorded in the *Machzor* for Rosh Hashanah and Yom Kippur: *teshuvah, tefillah,* and *tzedakah* (repentance, prayer, and charity) which, in turn, are manifestations of the three pillars of the universe: *Torah, avodah,* and *gemilut chasadim* (Torah, worship, and lovingkindness), which are the proper applications of our *chochmah, gevurah,* and *osher* (wisdom, power, and wealth). These, then, are the basic tools for serving *HaShem*. It is *with* these tools that the *Kohein Gadol* approaches *HaShem* and enters the *Kodesh HaKodashim* on Yom Kippur: "*Bzot*—With this shall Aaron come into the sanctuary. . . ." (Exodus 16:3)

And it is these same tools that enable us daily to become closer to *HaShem*. Yirmeyahu Hanavi tells us that only if we utilize these gifts correctly and if our intent is to emulate *HaShem* and benefit those around us, are we truly worthy of praise.

"But only '*bzot*' with this should one glorify"

tzom fasting	*kol* voice	*mamon* money
teshuvah repentance	*tefillah* prayer	*tzedakah* charity
Torah Torah	*avodah* worship	*gemilut chasadim* lovingkindness
chochmah wisdom	*gevurah* power	*osher* wealth

❖ CHAPTER 29 ❖

Shemini

Rabbi Pesach Lerner

Executive Vice President National Council of Young Israel

> "You shall not make yourselves disgusting [by eating] any small creature that breeds; do not defile yourselves with them that it will make you spiritually unclean. For I am the Lord, your God; you shall sanctify yourselves and you shall be holy; and do not defile yourselves [by eating] any small creature that creeps on the earth. For I am God, that brought you up out of the Land of Egypt to be for you a God, and you shall be holy, for I am Holy."
>
> (Leviticus 11:43–45)

We find in the Talmud (*Bava Metziah* 61b): Raba said, Why did the Torah mention the Exodus from Egypt in connection with not lending with interest, the wearing of *tzitzit*, or the use of honest and fair weights and measures (see Leviticus 25:36–38; Numbers 15:38–41; Leviticus 19:35–36)? The Almighty declared, "I, who in Egypt differentiated between a firstborn and a non-firstborn, will exact punishment from someone who ascribes his money to a non-Jew and lends it to a Jew with interest or one who steeps his weights in salt [which makes them heavier] or one who attaches to his *tzitzit* an imitation of blue *Techelet* and maintains that it is the genuine blue *Techelet*." (These fraudulent actions may escape the notice of man but not God.)

The Talmud then relates that Ravina happened to be in the city of Sura, which was on the Euphrates River. Rav Chanina, an inhabitant of Sura, asked Ravina, Why does the Torah mention the Exodus from Egypt in connection with *sheratzim*, creeping things? Ravina responds, "The Almighty is telling us, I, who in Egypt differentiated between a firstborn and a non-firstborn, will exact punishment from someone who mixes the entrails of an unclean fish and a clean fish and sells them to a Jew as kosher." Rav Chanina then asked, "What is the significance that specifically with regard to the prohibitions of eating *sheratzim*, creeping things?" The Torah writes, ". . . for I am God, *that brought you up out* of the Land of Egypt."

Ravina responded, the *pasuk* refers to that which was taught by the school of Rabbi Yishmael: *If God had taken the Jewish nation out of the land of Egypt just for the sake of this, that the Jewish people not defile themselves with the eating of creeping things, it would have been sufficient and worthwhile.*

Rav Chanina then questioned: And is the reward for not eating creeping things greater than that of not lending with interest or the wearing of *tzitzit* or the use of honest and fair weights and measures? (With regard to these commandments the Torah mentions the Exodus from Egypt but does not use the specific wording "that brought you up out of the Land of Egypt.") Answered Ravina, even though their reward is not greater, it is more loathsome to eat the creeping things.

It would seem that less emphasis, not more, should be placed on the commandment not to eat *sheratzim*, specifically for the reason that Ravina gave: we would not eat creeping things, bugs, and insects anyway because they are loathsome and disgusting to eat!

The last *Mishnah* in Tractate *Makkot* says: "Rabbi Chanania ben Akashia says: The Almighty wished to confer merit upon Israel; therefore he gave them Torah and *mitzvot* in abundance, as it is written, '*HaShem* desired for the sake of Israel's righteousness that the Torah be expanded and strengthened.'"

Rashi explains this *Mishnah*: The Torah states many admonitions against eating abominable creatures, crawling things, and so on, and there is no person who is not disgusted by them. God's purpose was to increase their reward; since it is a *mitzvah* to abstain from eating these things, they are rewarded for keeping the *mitzvot*.

Once again the question arises, why do *Bnei Yisrael* merit reward when people abstain from eating these bugs in any case? True, people do not normally eat *sheratzim*, bugs, and insects, but now that *HaShem* has commanded us not to eat (in fact there are numerous commandments against the eating of *sheratzim*) the Jewish people perform the mitzvah without incorporating in that performance and observance any personal interest—only to fulfill God's will. And that is clearly what the teaching of the school of Rabbi Yishmael says: "the Jewish people do not defile themselves with the eating of creeping things." It is the defilement, the impurity, that prevents their eating of *sheratzim*—the spiritual cause and effect, *not* the physical disgust and abomination of eating insects.

To return to the passage in *Bava Metziah*, "the school of Rabbi Yishmael taught . . . it would have been sufficient": This is the greatness of Israel, a trait for which they merited being taken out of Egypt, that they rise up above their natural tendencies of disgust in the eating of *sheratzim*; rather they abstain *only* because of the commands of *HaShem*. God took us out of Egypt because He knew that our actions would be dictated by His commandments and not by our personal needs and sensitivities. Our deliverance from Egypt was in merit of our true *avodas HaShem*—service of God.

Rabbi Asher Bush

Young Israel of Stamford, Connecticut

THE DEATH OF NADAV AND AVIHU

The punishment received by Nadav and Avihu is unique in the Torah. It is unique not just in the manner in which they died (that a fire consumed their souls, leaving their bodies intact) but also in the very fact that they died. While there are a number of other individuals whose punishments are recorded in the Torah, in each of these cases, they had either violated a stated law of the Torah, as in the case of the blasphemer (Leviticus 24) and the gatherer of wood who desecrated the *Shabbat* (Numbers 15:32), or they received a specific warning to stop, as in the case of Korach or the *meraglim* (spies).

However, Nadav and Avihu were killed without any apparent warning. Moreover, despite the fact that the Torah spells out that their deaths were a result of their having brought an inappropriate offering (*eish zarah*—strange fire) this does not seem to be the full story. Rashi quotes a debate as to whether their primary sin was the fact that they entered the sanctuary while intoxicated or that they had the *chutzpah* to rule on matters of *halachah* in the presence of Moshe, their teacher. Apparently, our Sages felt that this story could not be understood at face value; something was missing. This story becomes even more difficult in light of the words that followed their death, as Moshe told Aharon that this is what God had previously explained to him, that *B'krovai ekadeish* ("through those who are close to Me, I will be sanctified" (Leviticus 10:3)), implying that Nadav and Avihu were righteous and not at all sinful; these words reinforce the question, why were they not warned or even given the chance to do *teshuvah*, as their own father Aharon had at the time of the golden calf?

It seems that our Sages could not explain this story at face value because, throughout the Torah, God does not administer severe punishments for sins without a prior warning. What made their sin so bad and necessitated their deaths was not the gravity of the sin but the likely results and implications of their sin. It was not just a private failure but one that could well affect the future of the new *Mishkan* (Tabernacle) and of the Jewish people.

According to either of the above-mentioned explanations for their punishment, the main point of the story remains unchanged. The Jewish people had just spent significant amounts of time, effort, and wealth in fulfilling God's command to build a sanctuary. It would soon become a regular feature in the lives of the people; it would be their primary manner and location to commune with God. The process of inaugurating the *Mishkan* and using it had just begun; the nation had begun its formal service of God.

It was precisely at this moment that the greatest danger existed. There were only five *Kohanim* in the entire nation, and now two of them had begun to conduct themselves in God's Sanctuary in a manner not very different from that of the pagan priests of the other nations. It is well known that many pagan cults utilized drunkenness in their services, as it led to the frivolity, debauchery, and licentiousness that attracted so many of their adherents. For this very reason, God was compelled to deal harshly with Nadav and Avihu, to kill them in this most unusual manner, to teach the Jewish people in the strongest terms possible that the *Mishkan* was never intended to be a Jewish version of a pagan temple but, rather, to be a House of God.

A similar logic holds for the explanation that their great sin was that they had the *chutzpah* to rule on matters of *halachah* in the presence of Moshe and Aharon. From the end of *Parshat Yitro* through *Shemini*, the overwhelming majority of the laws of the Torah have dealt with the building of the *Mishkan* and the laws of *korbanot* (sacrifices); the Torah speaks of these matters in great detail, seemingly repeating itself as it states that the commands were indeed followed as given. After all this, Nadav and Avihu entered the *Mishkan* ignoring all these many laws, simply following their own ideas and not the laws that they had been taught.

This was not just a simple matter of having the brazen *chutzpah* to rule on a matter of *halachah* in the presence of their teacher; they were negating the entire Torah, which devoted so much attention to each detail of the laws of building and serving in the *Mishkan*. At this moment, the entire *Mishkan* and all that it stood for was in jeopardy of being lost. It was to be a House of God, where, if one followed the path laid out in the Torah and came with the proper dedication, it was the ideal way to come close to God. Nadav and Avihu, however, had come and ignored all of this, possibly treating an environment in which each person would do whatever he pleased and not follow the *halachah*. Therefore, this most unusual act of Divine intercession was required to teach the people that the true path to God is to follow the Torah and not to follow our own impulses.

Rabbi Aaron S. Tirschwell

Director of Synagogue Services, National Council of Young Israel

As *Parshat Shemini* opens, *Bnai Yisrael* are elated from Aharon's blessing the Jewish people with the very first *Birkat Kohanim* and the placing of *HaShem*'s *Shechinah* on the Tabernacle through a fire He sent to the *mizbeach*. As the *pasuk* states, "The people saw and sang glad songs and fell upon their faces" (Leviticus 9:24).

Then, tragedy strikes. Two of Aaron's sons, Nadav and Avihu, in a display of what they considered gratitude and joy toward *HaShem*, decide to bring their own offering—without prior authorization from God (literally, they brought a foreign fire, or *eish zarah*). As a result of their actions, *HaShem* strikes them down with fire, the result being their deaths (Leviticus 10:3).

Upon the discovery of the bodies, Moshe adopts a threefold plan of action in order to deal with this tragedy: (a) he successfully comforts Aharon by explaining that "[the deaths of Nadav and Avihu are] exactly what *HaShem* meant when He said, 'I will be sanctified among those close to Me, and I will thus be glorified'"; (b) he tells Aharon's cousins, Mishael and Elzefon, to take the bodies out of the Sanctuary and out of the camp (to be buried); (c) he instructs Elazar and Itamar not to go without a haircut and not to rend their clothes—two signs which would indicate that they were in mourning.

These three directives from Moshe seem out of the ordinary. One could question each one of Moshe's statements:

1. How does Moshe's rationalization of Nadav and Avihu's deaths comfort Aharon (the *pasuk* says, after Moshe's explanation that *Vayidom Aharon*, "and Aharon was silent—or comforted)? What solace does Aharon find in the statement that *HaShem* will be sanctified by those close to Him?

2. Why did Moshe call upon Mishael and Elzefon to carry out the bodies? Granted, Aharon couldn't do it because a *Kohein Gadol* cannot defile himself, even for a close relative, but why didn't Elazar and Itamar (Aharon's other two sons), who were ordinary *kohanim*, do it?
3. Why does Moshe instruct Elazar and Itamar not to mourn for their brothers? It seems as though Moshe instructs them to disregard the fact that Nadav and Avihu died.

I believe that, through this tragedy and Moshe's responses to it, one can understand the very essence of *Bnei Yisrael* and their relationship with *HaShem*. Mark Twain, in his famous literary piece from *Harper's Monthly Magazine* entitled "Concerning the Jews" (September 1898), questions the "staying power" of the Jewish people. Twain writes

> . . . The Egyptian, the Babylonian and the Persian rose, filled the planet with sound and splendor, then faded to dream-stuff, and passed away. . . . other peoples have sprung up and held their torch high for a time, but it burned out and they sit in twilight now, or have vanished . . . all things are mortal but the Jew; all other forces pass but he remains. What is the secret to his immortality?

The answer to Twain's question is quite simple: a Jew is not immortal; *HaShem* and His Torah, however, are everlasting. Leaders may come and go; the Jewish people may experience a golden age in one generation or, *chas veshalom*, a Holocaust in another; but, after all is said and done, the Torah remains intact—serving all generations. One needs only to look at the other nations of the earth, both past and present, to corroborate this point: nations can be made or broken by a leader's death; eventually, they just fizzle. The Jewish people has had its leaders throughout time, and the loss of even one leader seems to leave us devastated and unable to move forward; yet, Judaism continues to thrive and the Torah remains the mainstay of our religion's existence.

Moshe recognized the fact that man is mortal and that the only thing that carries on throughout the generations is Torah. Therefore, his response to the tragic deaths of Nadav and Avihu (which could have potentially broken the spirit of *Bnei Yisrael* at that time) recognizes the fact that, no matter what tragedy any given situation may offer, the Torah needs to remain the prime objective. Now, we can understand Moshe's seemingly out-of-the-ordinary directives regarding this tragedy:

(a) Moshe's attempt to explain the deaths of Nadav and Avihu was meant to be an awakening to Aharon in order to have him refocus on the main goal, which was to continue with the *avodah* and to have *Bnei Yisrael* continue to celebrate the inauguration of the *Mishkan*, rather than to comfort him.

Moshe's explanation that *HaShem* will be sanctified by those close to Him may mean that God will sanctify His presence throughout time immemorial by any means He sees fit—even through the deaths of two of the leaders of the Jewish people. Moshe's answer helps Aharon deal with the loss by putting him on a different train of thought. Therefore, after hearing Moshe's words, Aharon becomes silent—*Vayidom Aharon*. (As Ramban explains, Aharon was crying before this; now, with this explanation, Aharon becomes silent, meaning that he stopped crying.)

(b) Ramban comments that on the day of the death of Nadav and Avihu, even an ordinary *kohein* was not allowed to defile himself because of the celebration of the consecration of the *Mishkan*. That is why Moshe asked Mishael and Elzefon (both *Levi'im*) to carry out the bodies. Even though Elazar and Itamar may have wanted to show their dead brothers proper *kavod* by taking care of the removal of the bodies, Moshe instructs them to remember their responsibility to serve *HaShem* and the Jewish people by remaining in the *Ohel Moed*.

(c) Moshe instructs Elazar and Itamar not to show the normal signs of mourning because, even though this tragedy affects them personally, it cannot disrupt what *HaShem* has commanded. That is why Moshe, after telling them not to go without a haircut and not to rip their clothes, states that your brothers, all *Bnei Yisrael*, shall bemoan the tragedy. This is why *halachah* mandates that when a great *Talmid Chacham* passes away, everyone shall mourn for him; yet, the nation must, and will, go on.

❖ CHAPTER 30 ❖

Tazria

Rabbi Emanuel Quint

Vice President, Council of Young Israel Rabbis in Israel

TAZRIA IN CONTEMPORARY TIMES

The opening theme of the *Sedrah Tazria* is the fruitfulness of Jewish women; it consists of three phrases: (1) the giving birth, "when a woman conceives and gives birth to a male child" (Leviticus 12:2); (2) the circumcision of the boy, "And on the eighth day the flesh of his foreskin shall be circumcised"; and (3) the bringing of a sacrifice to the Holy Temple, "she shall bring a lamb of the first year for a burnt-offering, and a young pigeon, or a turtle dove, for a sin offering."

It is written in the *midrash* that the Jewish people will be redeemed because the women are fruitful and multiply (*Tanna Devai Eliyahu Zuta*, chapter 14, paragraph 6). Thus, this *sedrah* represents the coming of the Messiah because of children born to the Jewish women.

A story is told about a young woman, Mrs. Chana Goldstein, who gave birth to a son in a concentration camp during the Holocaust years. Very soon thereafter, she and her newborn son were sent off to a death camp. As she was marching to the gas chamber with her infant in her arms she saw a German soldier holding a knife in his hand. She grabbed the knife from the soldier and ran away, still carrying her infant. Everyone thought that she was going to kill herself and her infant son; instead she used the knife to circumcise him. She then went into the gas chamber carrying her circumcised Jewish infant son (see a similar story in *Hasidic Tales of the Holocaust* by Yaffa Eliach, page 152).

What induced Mrs. Goldstein to exhibit such *mesirat nefesh*, such an overwhelming desire to abide by the word of her Maker, with Whom she and her son would soon be united?

The *Torat Kohanim*, the classical Tannaic work on Leviticus, commenting on the opening words of the *sedrah*, "Speak unto the children of Israel," states that the laws of this *sedrah* dealing with childbirth refer only to Jews, not to non-Jews (a notable exception is the Noahide laws, which apply specifically to non-Jews). I think the reason is that these laws are unique in that they are centered on the very fabric of the existence and perpetuation of the Jewish people. True, *Shabbat* has preserved the Jew more than the Jew has preserved *Shabbat*. But the observance of *Shabbat* does not bring another Jew into the world; it merely sustains the Jewish people after they are born into this world. This *sedrah* deals with the laws that perpetuate the Jewish people, for without childbirth there cannot be a people.

What is the source of the concept that a Jew is commanded to perpetuate the race (see Maimonides, *Sefer Hamitzvot*, Positive Commandment 212)? Citing a verse from the Book of Isaiah ("He created it not a waste, He formed it to be inhabited," Isaiah 45:18), the *Mishnah* states that the world was created only for propagation (*Mishnah Eduyyot*, chapter 1, *Mishnah* 13. See also Tractate *Yevamot* 62a).

Who is obligated to perform the *mitzvah* of perpetuating the Jewish people? There is a difference of opinion in the *Mishnah* that states (Tractate *Yevamot* 65b): "A man is obligated to fulfill the command of propagation but not a woman. However, Rabbi Yochanan ben Beroka holds that both a man and a woman are commanded, as it is written: 'And God blessed them, and God said unto them, "Be fruitful and multiply"'" (Genesis 1:28).

The *halachah* is that the command to multiply applies only to the man and not to the woman (see Maimonides, *Laws of Women*, chapter 15, law 2). Thus, although Mrs. Goldstein was not under the command to propagate, since she did, she helped bring the redemption that much closer.

The laws of this *sedrah* dealing with childbirth are sandwiched in between the laws of the last *sedrah*, dealing with types of animals that may be eaten and the laws that follow in this *sedrah*, dealing with plagues. The *midrash* tells us that the former represents the distinction between pure and impure that God has prepared for the Jews to eat, whereas the latter represents the Jew being punished with plagues for violating the laws of God; these two groups of laws indicate that man can rise to great heights or sink to great depths. Chana Goldstein rose to the heights foreseen by this *midrash*; she was capable at this moment when her life was about to be extinguished, of realizing that she could still perform the greatest *mitzvah* of all, the creation of a Jew. At that moment, Chana Goldstein was able to scale heights reserved for very few in every generation.

There is a story related in the Talmud that the Prophet Isaiah went to visit the King Hezekiah, who was ill (Isaiah 38:1). The prophet said to the king, "Thus said the Lord, 'Set thy house in order, for thou shalt die and not live.'" When the king inquired why he was being punished, he was told that it was because he did not have children. When King Hezekiah replied that he was able to see by *Ruach Hakodesh*—Divine insight that his children will be sinners and therefore he did not have any children. The Prophet replied that Hezekiah had to have children and that it was up to God what shall become of those children. Chana Goldstein brought her child into the world as a Jew and left the rest to God, just as was stated by the Prophet Isaiah (it is also Isaiah's statement that forms the basis for propagating the world), and what would become of this young Jew whom she had just circumcised was for God to decide.

The heights that can be achieved by bringing another Jew into the world is seen in another *midrash* that tells us that the angels came to God and asked why He had to create man, since He already had angels. God replied that the Jew would be able to fulfill the laws of childbirth, something that the angels could not do (*Midrash Tanchumah* on *sedrah Bechukotai*, chapter 6).

This is not the first time a mother circumcised her son in a desperate situation. Moses was on his way to redeem the Jews from Egypt and took his wife, Zipporah, and their two sons (Exodus 4:24–25). When they stopped in an inn to spend the night, an angel appeared, to slay one of Moses' sons, who was not yet circumcised. (This is the view of Rabban Shimon ben Gamliel. Rabbi Yehuda ben Bizna said it was Moses who was about to be slain by the angel. See Tractate *Nedarim* 32b.) Zipporah circumcised her son and saved the redemption process for the Jewish people. We are taught that her name, Zipporah, is derived from the fact that she was as swift as a bird—*zippor*—to perform the *mitzvah* of circumcision (*Midrash Lekach Tov*). On the basis of this incident, the Talmud (Tractate *Avodah Zarah* 27a) quotes Rabbis who hold that a woman may perform a circumcision, and this is incorporated in the *halachah* (Maimonides, *Laws of Circumcision*, chapter 2, law 1).

Rabbi Yehoshua ben Karcha said, "Great is the *mitzvah* of circumcision, for all the great and meritorious deeds of Moses did not save him when he showed laxity in not circumcising his son" (Tractate *Nedarim* 31b). At every circumcision there is a special place preserved for Elijah the Prophet. This custom is based on the fact that Elijah was zealous to protect the laws of the Torah when circumcision was prohibited by Jezebel (see I Kings 19:10; and commentary of Radak). Because of this zealousness, Elijah participates in every circumcision and because of this he is the harbinger of redemption (see *Pirkei De Rabbi Eliezer*, end of chapter 29).

The story of Chanukah also beings with it a story of martyrdom involving circumcision. It is recorded that Antiochus prohibited the Jews from practicing circumcision. Two women who had circumcised their sons were led around the city of Jerusalem with their babies bound to their breasts and then cast down from the wall (II Maccabees 6:10).

At the time of the Holy Temple in Jerusalem, a woman who gave birth brought offerings, including a sin-offering. Nowadays there is a special prayer that is uttered by an individual who accepts a fast upon himself. This prayer, recited at the end of the *Shemonah Esrei,* includes words to the effect that when the Holy Temple existed and a sin-offering was brought, the only part that was placed on the altar was its fat and blood. The person who accepts the fast asks of God that diminution of his fat and blood resulting from the fast be considered as if he had offered a sacrifice on the altar.

What greater sacrifice can there be than the sacrifice of Mrs. Goldstein, who died in sanctification of His Holy Name? Those of us who have the privilege of living as Torah-true Jews can perpetuate the memory of all of the Chana Goldsteins, bring the redemption to actuality, and, once again, practice the laws of *Tazria,* with the laws of all the other *sedrot* and the accompanying *Torah Sh'ball peh.*

Rabbi Nachman Kahana

Young Israel of the Old City, Jerusalem, Israel

The *parshah* deals with a spiritual malady that expresses itself through physical distress. The appearance of a white blemish on the outer skin, and the paling of the hair within the area of the blemish, is *nega tzaraat* (the plague of *tzaraat*), and, when it is declared as such by a *kohein*, the sufferer becomes *tamei* (spiritually unclean). Under these circumstances, he may not reside within a walled city in Eretz Yisrael and must live as a recluse as prescribed in the Torah.

Within the over-all mysteries surrounding any and all of the *mitzvot* of the Torah, there is a particular detail in the laws of *metzorah* that seemingly defies all explanation. The Torah states in Leviticus 13:12–13: "And if the *tzaraat* breaks out on the skin and the *tzaraat* covers all the skin from head to feet as far as the *kohein* can see: then the *kohein* shall look and, behold, if the *tzaraat* has covered all his flesh, he [the *kohein*] shall pronounce him clean; it has all turned white, he is clean."

We see here that if the blemish is limited to a part or even several parts of the body, the person is considered a *metzorah*, with all the halachic implications, but, if the blemish spreads to cover his entire body, he is declared "clean" and may return to his home. This is surely a dilemma.

However, the matter may be explained by an event that occurred in the period of the kings of Israel. According to II Kings 14:23–27:

> In the fifteenth year of Amaziah, son of Joash, King of Judah, Jeroboam, son of Joash, King of Israel, began to reign in Samaria for 41 years . . . and he did that which was evil in the sight of the Lord; he did not depart from all the sins of Jeroboam, son of Nevat, who caused Israel to sin: He [Jeroboam ben Joash] restored the border of Israel from the entrance of Hamat to the sea of Araba . . . for the Lord saw the affliction of Israel, that it was very bitter . . . neither was there any helper for

> Israel: And the Lord did not wish to blot out the name of Israel from under heaven. And He saves them through the hand of Jeroboam ben Joash.

We have here a king who rejected the Torah and is even compared to the arch-evil Jeroboam ben Nevat, who, according to the *Mishnah* in *Sanhedrin*, is one of three kings who do not have a place in the World to Come. Nevertheless, Jeroboam ben Joash was victorious in all his military campaigns, extending the boundaries of Israel to their fullest.

How is it that such a total denier of Torah succeeded in his reign as king? The answer is stated in the verses, "For the Lord saw the affliction of Israel, that it was very bitter . . . neither was there any helper for Israel. And the Lord did not wish to blot out the name of Israel from under the heavens."

Jeroboam ben Joash lived in times in which the spiritual situation of the nation was so neglected that, according to the strict lettter of the law, the people were worthy of the harshest treatment. However, since the Lord did not wish to destroy His chosen nation of Israel, He had no choice (so to say) but to condescend to their human frailties and with compassion aid them in victory.

This, in effect, is the principle behind the cleansing of the *metzorah* whose entire being became afflicted with *tzaraat*. This man had reached a spiritual level so low as to make *teshuvah* almost impossible. According to the letter of the Torah, he has lost the privilege of remaining alive; however, since for reasons known only to the Almighty, Judge of the world, this individual must still remain alive, *HaShem* must "go out" from the *midat hadin* (the quality of pure justice) and adopt toward the sinner a compassionate attitude, the expression of which is the revocation of the severe laws of *Metzorah*.

In our times, beginning with the *Haskalah* and the denial, not only by individuals but even through movements, of Torah from Sinai and the authority of our Sages to interpret and impose halachic decisions, the Jewish nation has reached a low point in our spiritual mission in this world. We do not have the benefit of a prophet or a judge, and we flounder through mediocrity and reject the status imposed upon us by *HaShem* as His chosen nation. Nevertheless, the establishment of *Medinat Yisrael* three short years after the Holocaust was a repetition of the manner in which *HaShem* reacted to the generation of Jeroboam ben Joash twenty-seven hundred years ago.

Today, more than fifty years after the Holocaust, one cannot deny the great advances made in the Torah world, but neither is one permitted to deny the enormous weaknesses of our generation. When intermarriage is running at the rate of 50 percent in New York and 80 percent nationwide, when *Eretz Yisrael* thirsts for the mass *aliyah* of Torah-dedicated people who can fight the assimilating tendencies of secularists who have infiltrated into the leadership of the Jews in *Eretz Yisrael*, we cannot deny that there is a spiritual *tzaraat* within us.

But perhaps our weakness is also our strength. Perhaps the absence of giant Torah leaders, the mediocrity of our accomplishments, and the ferocity and cruelty of our enemies will "force" the Almighty to have pity on His nation Israel. As the verse says, "For the Lord saw the affliction of Israel, that it was very bitter . . . neither was there any helper for Israel: And the Lord did not wish to blot out the name of Israel from under the heavens. . . ." (See also the last *Mishnah* in Tractate *Sota*.)

❖ CHAPTER 30 ❖

Tazria-Metzora

Rabbi Reuven Stein

Young Israel of Patchogue, New York

The *Midrash Rabbah* 19:3 quotes Rabbi Shmuel, the son of Yitzchok, who states that the laws that are found in *Tazria-Metzora* such as those concerning *zav*, leprosy, plagues, and *niddah* seem both distant from religion and improper to discuss publicly. *HaShem*,, however, tells us that to Him these laws are very pleasant. We see from this that all elements of life are in the realm of Torah and *halachah* and that we can gain valuable insight from studying them.

Rambam in *Mishnayos Negaim* explains that *tzaraas* and other plagues mentioned here are not natural sicknesses but were spiritual diseases. He proves this from the fact that if the disease spreads out (completely) white over the entire body (Leviticus 13:12) the sufferer then becomes pure. If this were a sickness, this would be the most contagious and dangerous stage. Rabbi Samson Raphael Hirsch brings other proofs that this leprosy has no connection with a physical illness.

1. The first physical leprosy, called Egyptian leprosy, would not make someone impure.
2. Healthy flesh is a sign of impurity.
3. The *kohein* does not have to examine every fold methodically.
4. During holidays and festivals, no exams for *tzaraas* took place.
5. Items with which the person had previously come in contact before he had been declared impure were not impure even though we discover he had the "disease."
6. Only Jews would be impure.

If we understand these afflictions as spiritual, we can learn ethical lessons from them.

What is the connection between *Parshat Shemini*, which talks about *kashrus*, and *Parshat Tazria* which deals with *tzaraas*? Rabbi Yisrael Salanter (founder of the *mussar* movement) explains that, according to *Chazal*, *tzaraas* is caused by speaking *loshen hara*. The Torah is hinting to us that, although so many of us are extremely careful about what goes into our mouths—it must be *glatt kosher* with a good *hechsher*—we also need to be exceedingly careful of what comes out of our mouths. We should not speak *loshen hara* and cause ourselves to be punished with *tzaraas*.

The Torah says that the *metzorah* must stay outside the camp, totally alone, even separate from other lepers. The *Sifsei Cohen* explains that if the *metzorah* were together with others who had sinned and were stricken like himself, he would justify his actions and not repent. We, who have mass media and can see and read constantly about the worst elements of society, have to be careful that this exposure does not prevent us from improving ourselves and reaching heights greater than those around us.

Vayidaber Moshe explains the double expression used in the Torah to describe that which the impure person says, *Tamei, tamei, yikra*. An impure person complains and calls out about the impurity of others; those who constantly disparage others and point out their shortcomings are revealing their own deficiencies.

In the year 1848 there was a terrible plague that hit the city of Vilna. The Jews prayed and did a great amount of soul-searching to try to discover the reason for this punishment. Somebody came to Rabbi Yisrael Salanter and told him that in a certain house grave sins were being committed. Rabbi Salanter explained to him that the sin of *loshen hara* applies even to a true statement. The reason that *loshen hara* is wrong is that one must not seek out the faults of others. One who speaks is punished by getting *tzaraas* and being sent to live alone. If he must find faults, then let him find them in himself.

The "impurification" process is dependent on the *kohein*'s seeing the plague and pronouncing it impure. The *Dubna Maggid* explains the reason why the impurity is dependent totally on the *kohein*. The one who speaks *loshen hara* against others does not feel he has done a great crime. After all, it was only words. Now he will learn the power of a few words—for with one word the *kohein* can change his status and drastically affect his life.

The *Meshech Chochmah* explains why it says twice in one sentence that the *kohein* will see the leprosy (Leviticus 13:13). There are two things the *kohein* must see. He has to look for signs of impurity in the plague and he has to look at the person and time period to see if it is possible to declare the person impure. If it is during a holiday or if the person recently married, the *kohein* does not declare him impure. So, too, one who decides halachic issues must always take a double look—not only at what the *halachot* are but at the person and situation to determine whether they affect the *halachah*.

Why is the *kohein* the one to decide impurity? It is said in the name of Rabbi Chaim of Volozhin that one who engages in *loshen hara* is usually talking about the religious leaders, and this is why he must go to the *kohein*. The *kohein* can also advise the person how to do *teshuvah*. It is also consistent with the role of the *kohein* to bring peace to this fellow who creates arguments by speaking against others. Aaron was the *kohein par excellence*, and his role was that of peacemaker. So, too, the *kohein* would administer the waters of *sotah* to bring peace between man and wife. Here the *kohein* who brings peace between man and his Maker will help this *metzorah* come back to society.

After the plague disappears, the *metzorah* must cut his hair and bring his sacrifices. The *Klei Yakar* points out that he must shave his hair in three places; his head, to atone for his arrogance and for holding his head up too high; his beard, which surrounds his mouth, which spoke against others; and his eyebrows, for the sins that he committed with his looking down at others and degrading them.

The Chofetz Chaim (Leviticus 14:21) comments that when the *metzorah* must bring his sacrifice, the Torah says that if he is poor he can bring a less expensive sacrifice of birds. Only a poor person can satisfy his obligation with a lesser sacrifice. We must remember that, as far as spiritual matters are concerned, we cannot satisfy our obligations with the minimum davening and a class a day if we are capable of doing much more. We must always strive to do the maximum.

❖ CHAPTER 32 ❖

Metzora

Rabbi Bernard Weinberger

Young Israel of Brooklyn, New York

Last week's Torah portion, *Tazria*, detailed laws concerning a man afflicted with leprosy. The Torah, this week, deals with the purification process. Our Rabbis taught that the "disease" of leprosy comes as a result of an evil tongue, and they treat the Hebrew word *metzorah* as a fusion of *motzei ra*—"he who brings forth an evil tongue."

We must view the disease of leprosy as a gift of God in that what is an internal and spiritual disease in its source—a form of a psychosomatic condition—is revealed externally and becomes treatable. We all know the horror of serious diseases that remain concealed within the body and are discovered only after they have corroded and destroyed vital organs needed to survive. It was, therefore, a testimonial to the spiritual health of *Klal Yisrael* that a malignancy such as an evil tongue was immediately detected and treated with isolation.

The Torah requires that "all the days wherein the plague is in him he shall be unclean, he is unclean, he shall dwell alone, without the camp shall be his dwelling" (Leviticus 13:46). Rashi asks why this uncleanliness is treated with the requirement of dwelling totally removed from the camp of Israel. The answer is that, because this sinner came between man and his neighbor or man and wife with his evil tongue, therefore, he shall dwell alone. The disease of *tzaraas* should not be viewed simply as a punishment, as *midah keneged midah*; rather, it must also be understood as therapeutic. Living in total isolation, the leper learns through contemplation and experience the reality of loneliness and the effects of a schism between humans. Since leprosy is of benefit to the gossiper, it therefore requires a *kohein*, not only for the purification of the leper but also for its diagnosis. Until such time as the *kohein* pronounces the word *tomeh*—"unclean"—the leper remains clean, even if the condition is clear to a layman.

It is only in this light that we can understand what the Torah bids us: "Remember what the Lord thy God did unto Miriam by the way as yeh came forth out of Egypt" (Deuteronomy 24:9). Imagine; the remembrance of Miriam's leprosy becomes one of the remembrance (that some recite daily) required by the Torah and equated with *Shabbos, Kabbolos Hatorah, Amalek,* and so on. Why? Because at one time we had the blessing that a spiritual malfeasance was revealed to us and we were afforded an opportunity to mend our ways and be healed. We have lost that gift, and our maladies lie hidden beneath the skin and cause untold damage. This loss of the gift of *tzoraas* requires the jogging of our memory.

You may wonder why the Torah associates the remembrance of Miriam's affliction with the location "as ye came forth out of Egypt." What significance is there to the fact that she became leprous then? In the case of *Amalek,* where the identical words are used, we understand that "when" is crucial to the gravity of the attack, but of what importance is the "when and where" as it relates to Miriam? My suggestion is that it is crucial because the essence of freedom, which is first and foremost a freedom of speech, should not become a license for unbridled and unchecked speech. Indeed, the Exodus celebrates freedom and, as the Ari *Hakodosh* was wont to say, Pesach means *peh soch,* the mouth speaks, meaning that in the Exodus Jews regained their power of speech. It would be a shame if this power led to anarchic speech as freedom of speech so often becomes. Speech is the definition of the human being, and it must have parameters and limitations.

The gift of leprosy, though, extends beyond the body of the Jew and goes to his home and to his clothing; thus, we have *nega begodim,* affecting clothing, and *nega batim,* affecting houses, as well as *nega haguf* (see Rambam *Yad Hilchot Tumas Tzoraas* 16:10, where the sequence is detailed). A Jew's spirituality extends to his body, his home, and even his clothing, as evidenced by the daily experience of three fundamental *mitzvot* of *mezuzah* (houses), *tzitzit* (clothing), and *Tefilin* and *milah* (body).

In the purification process of the bodily leper, the Torah requires "then shall the priest command to take for him that is to be cleansed, two living clean birds . . ." (Leviticus 14:4). We read further how the priest cleansed the leper by dipping the living bird in the blood of the slaughtered bird. However, we are given no hint as to why two birds are required, and we must turn to the *Zohar,* which teaches that the birds are to atone for "*lishnah tova* and *lishnah bisha*"—good speech and bad tongue. We all know at close range the devastation caused by an evil tongue—the enmity, jealousies, and even hatreds that it can cause. That is obvious to us. But we learn from the *Zohar* that we need to be cautioned against the failure to use good speech and the ill effects that can result from withholding good speech. The man or woman who fails to express appreciation to a spouse who has shown selflessness or devotion will evoke an air of latent hostility in the home. A parent or teacher who does not recognize the special efforts of a child or student will do damage equal to if not greater than those who indulge in the evil tongue. The sins of omission of good speech require, according to the *Zohar*, the same atonement as the sins of commission by the leper—and that is why two birds are needed.

I once heard a story in the name of a famed *rosh yeshivah* who came home after a trying day of fund-raising for his *yeshivah*, during which he not only accomplished little but also suffered abuse. He was asked how to explain that a man like himself, who should be busy teaching Torah, spends such a wasteful day and suffers abuse besides. His answer was, "You know, when I say my *shiur* I am sometimes interrupted by a student who does not understand my teaching and asks a silly question. I get impatient with him, and so I brush him aside with a sharp retort. It could well be that in so doing I have killed that boy's appetite for learning; he may have been so embarrassed as to want to withdraw from learning entirely. I might even have ended his career in Torah. And a person guilty of an accidental killing is required to go to *galus*. That is why I have to run around and suffer for the *yeshivah*."

How many people realize the effect of their failure to encourage and appreciate the efforts and yes, the kindness, of others? In our day it is considered wimpy to say to someone, "I appreciate what you've done," or, "Keep up your good work," and the like.

It can be said that the meaning of *Shabbos Hagadol*, the Great Sabbath, the *Shabbos* preceding Pesach, is simply that our concept of the Sabbath has been enlarged and become greater. Until now, we understood *Shabbos* as a testimony to God in that He created the world, the heaven and earth, in six days and rested on *Shabbos*, as is written in the first *Aseres Hadibros* (Exodus 20:11). With the Exodus, our vision and perspective was enlarged to recognize that not only did God create the world; He also directs its sustenance and changes its natural course at will—as He did in freeing the Jewish people from bondage in Egypt. This is the *Shabbos* of the second *Aseres Hadibros* (Deuteronomy 5:15).

In that spirit of greatness on this *Shabbos*, we must also enlarge our perspective to recognize that we need to atone, not only for the evil tongue, but also for the good tongue that we withhold from those who deserve it. Like the leper, we need to bring two birds, for *lishnah tova* as well as for *lishnah bisha*.

❖ CHAPTER 33 ❖

Acharei Mot

Rabbi Yosef Goldberg

Young Israel of Wavecrest and Bayswater, New York

> *Bzot*—"With this shall Aharon enter the Holy of Holies" (Leviticus 16:3).

I

Rabbeinu Bechaye says that the *gematriah* (numeric value) of the word *b'zot*—"with this"—is 410, the number of years of the *Bayit Rishon*, the first *Beit Hamikdash*. It was only in the first *Beit Hamikdash* that the Holy of Holies was in its complete form. The *aron*, the *kaporet*—the special covering of the *aron*—and the *cheruvim*—the cherubs—did not exist in the second Temple (see *Yoma* 21b). Thus, the *pasuk* in our *Parshah* is hinting at the fact that the First Temple, with the Yom Kippur service of the *Kohein Gadol* in the Holy of Holies in its complete form, would last for only 410 years. (For other hints in the Torah concerning the duration of the First and Second Temples, see the *Baal Haturim* in the beginning of *Parshat Terumah* regarding *veshacanti betocham*—"And I shall dwell in their midst"—where it is pointed out that the word *vesachanti* can be broken down into "And he shall dwell 410" and rearranged into "And the second 420" [the Second Temple existed for 420 years]. See also the *Baal Haturim* in *Parshat Ki Tisa*, where it is noted that (*shemen*) *katit* stands for 420 and 410 [with and without the *yud*]. *Rabbeinu Bechaye*, on the first *pasuk* in *Parshat Pekudei*, derives a hint of the 420 and 410 years from the words *mishkan* and *hamishkan*. Apparently, it was part of the Divine plan from the beginning of creation that the Temple service of Yom Kippur would not continue throughout Jewish history.

It was the special service of the *Kohein Gadol* on Yom Kippur that provided for the atonement of the Jewish people. However, even if one considers the years of the existence of the *Mishkan* in its varioius locations and combines them with the 830 years of the Holy Temples, one finds that more than two-thirds of our history has been without this special service. What filled this glaring void on all of those Yom Kippurs throughout the millennia?

The beautiful poetic prayer *U'Nesana Tokef*, recited before the *kedushah* of *musaf* on Rosh Hashanah and Yom Kippur, mentions that three things can overturn an evil decree: prayer, repentance, and charity. In the *Machzorim*, above each of these words, respectively, is cryptically printed: *kol* (voice), *tzom* (fast), and *mamon* (money). The numerical equivalence of each of these words is 136, which, when multiplied by three, equals 408—the *gematriah* of *zot*. Thus, in the merit of prayer, repentance, and charity, it is as if Aharon still comes into the Holy of Holies every Yom Kippur, even without the existence of the Holy Temple, may it be speedily be rebuilt in our lifetime.

II

Although Aharon's sons, Nadav and Avihu, died in *Parshat Shemini*, *Acharei Mot*, the *parshah* that details the Yom Kippur service of the *Kohein Gadol*, begins: "And *HaShem* spoke to Moshe after the death of the sons of Aharon." What does the death of the two sons of Aharon have to do with the service of Yom Kippur?

We know that Aharon's reaction to the death of his sons was, "and Aharon remained silent." In the section entitled "The Laws of Yom Kippur" of his major halachic work the *Sefer Rokeach Hagadol*, Rabbi Eliezer Rokeach of Worms (1160–1238), cites a very beautiful *midrash* from the *Pesikta Rabasi*. The *midrash* states as follows:

> The Holy One Blessed Be He said to His ministering Angels: "Come, and I will inform you of the righteousness of my children. I have so often burdened them in their world with all kinds of troubles and suffering, which they have undergone in every generation and at all times. Yet they have not resented me, for they publicly proclaim themselves as evildoers—*rashaim*—and Me they call righteous—*tzaddik*. And they declare in this language: "But we have sinned and transgressed; and You have acted truthfully, whereas we have acted wickedly. . . ."

Perhaps the Rokeach is hinting to us that *B'zot yavo Aharon el Hakodesh* (Leviticus 16:3) signifies that, as a result of the very trait of *vayidom Aharon*—"and Aharon remained silent," does Aharon merit to atone for all Israel on Yom Kippur. So, too, the ability to remain silent in the face of suffering and even to find fault in ourselves and not in *HaShem* is the trait of the Jewish people that enables us to find complete atonement on Yom Kippur even without the Temple service of the *Kohein Gadol*.

Rabbi Naphtali Burnstein

Young Israel of Greater Buffalo, New York

The Yom Kippur service in the *Beit Hamikdash* is the highlight of *Parshat Acharei Mot*. Traditionally known as the *Avodah*, this special service, done completely by the *Kohein Gadol*, is the highlight of all services at the *Beit Hamikdash* throughout the year. People waited anxiously all year to witness this special activity. Through the *Kohein Gadol* and his role in the *avodah*, the Jewish people hoped to achieve forgiveness for their sins and to receive the blessings of health and prosperity for the year to come.

We follow the *avodah* in great detail in a section in *musaf* called "The *Avodah*." Because of various differences of opinion among the commentaries as to the exact sequence and other particulars of the *avodah*, two different versions have been accepted and inserted into the Yom Kippur *machzor*. Most *nusach Ashkenaz machzorim* include the versioin called *Amitz Koach*, whereas most *nusach Sefarad machzorim* include the version called *Atah Konnantah*. Both versions are based on Tractate *Yoma* (chapters 1–7).

The *parshah* begins (Leviticus 19:3), *B'zos yavo Aharon el Hakodesh* ("with the following shall Aharon come into the Holy Place"). The *midrash*, commenting on the word *b'zos*, says that with the *zechus* (merit) of *Shabbat*, the *Kohein Gadol* will enter into the *Beis Hamikdash* on Yom Kippur. What is the connection between the *Avodah* of the *Kohein Gadol* on Yom Kippur and *Shabbat*? Rabbi Shlomo Yosef Zevin, *zt"l*, attempts to connect the two in the following manner: The day of *Shabbat* is special not only in terms of its own holiness but also because of what must go into preparing for *Shabbat* and the effect *Shabbat* has on the week to come. Our Rabbis phrased it simply: "He who prepares before *Shabbat* will eat on *Shabbat*." This is true both physically and spiritually. Only one who prepares for *Shabbat* can truly appreciate it. This, then, will also relate to what lasting effect *Shabbat* will have on the coming week. *Shabbat* is, in fact, connected to the rest of the week, and the greater the connection, the greater the spiritual effect of that *Shabbat* on the days that surround it.

Looking at the *avodah,* we notice that during the Yom Kippur service the *Kohein Gadol* changed his clothes five times, switching from his street clothes to his special gold set of clothes to his special white linen clothes and then from one set to the other until, finally, he changed back to his regular clothes at the end of the day. His white linen clothing was worn for those activities known as *avodas pnim* (inner service), whereas the set of gold clothing was worn for *avodas chutz* (service done outside the actual temple building). With each switch from one form of service to the next, the *Kohein Gadol* had to immerse in a *mikvah* (ritual bath) and also had to sanctify his hands and feet: *kiddush yadayim v'raglayim.*

Now, it may be understandable to require the *Kohein Gadol* to immerse and sanctify himself when switching from the outer garments to the inner ones. After all, that would seem an appropriate and necessary step when going from a less holy activity (outside) to a seemingly holier activity (inside). Why, however, would it be necessary for him to go through the same purifying process when going from an *avodas pnim* to an *avodas chutz*?

To ask this question is to assume that the *avodas pnim* was a holier form of service than an *avodas chutz.* The truth is, however, that to take the holiness of the Temple into the outside world, as was exemplified with the *Kohein Gadol*'s service *outside* and, then, actually to retain that degree of holiness that he achieved *inside,* takes an even greater degree of strength and commitment than the contrary. To remain strong and dedicated when removed from the source of holiness is not a simple feat. The *Kohein Gadol* purified himself upon *leaving* the *Kodshei Kodoshim* to remind him to hold on to the *kedushah* within and to put it to use outside.

With these two thoughts, relating to both *Shabbat* and the *Kohein Gadol,* we can better understand how the *midrash* connects *Shabbat* and the *Avodas Kohein Gadol* on Yom Kippur. Just as *Shabbat* can and should have a lasting effect on its surroundings, the *avodah* of the *Kohein Gadol* on Yom Kippur can and should also leave a lasting impression on himself as well as all those who surround him.

May we merit the *zechus* of reliving and truly experiencing the *Avodas Yom Kippur* very soon.

❖ CHAPTER 34 ❖

Acharei Mot—Kedoshim

Rabbi Herschel Kurzrock

Young Israel of Kensington, New York

There is an interesting connection between *Parshiyot Acharei Mot* and *Kedoshim*. Most of *Parshat Acharei Mot* is read on Yom Kippur, the holiest day of the year (the latter part of the *parshah*, dealing with the practical laws of sexual morality, is read at *mincha* on Yom Kippur). In fact Rashi, commenting on *Kedoshim*, quotes the *midrash* that states, "Whenever you find mention of prohibitioin of sexual immorality, there you will find reference to *kedoshim*—holiness." Thus, on Yom Kippur toward evening, we read about the laws pertaining to sexual immorality; so that, on this holy day when we seek to repent and merit a blessed year, we are reminded of the basic step to lead us to *kedushah*—holiness, morality!

The *Sedrah Kedoshim*, linked to *Acharei Mot*, could veritably be called a manual of ethical and moral instruction. Of the fifty-one precepts contained therein, thirteen positive and thirty-eight negative, a very healthy majority (over 70 percent) directly emphasize a Jew's duties and obligations toward his fellow men; and these culminate with the "*klal gadol batorah*"—"great principle in the Torah," as it was called by Rabbi Akiva, "Love thy neighbor as thyself" (Leviticus 19:18; see *Yerushalmi, Nedarim* 9:4). The motivation for these laws is the recurring theme with which the *sedrah* begins: "Sanctify yourselves and be holy, for I, the Lord your God, am Holy." This stamp of *kedushah*—holiness—with which the *mitzvot* of *sedrah Kedoshim* are labeled, dispels a common notion regarding sanctity in Jewish life held by the general public. Whereas the average person identifies holiness only with being erudite in Torah and being saintly in the pious observance of *mitzvot Bein Adam L'Makom*—between man and God, our holy Torah has stressed another point of view in regard to *kedushah*.

Man's proper *kosher* and honest performance in his financial monetary dealings deserves the appellation of *kodosh*—holy. Rabbi Yisrael Salanter, father of the *mussar* movement, says that in the *sedrah* of *Kedoshim* we find the conditions for holiness outlined by such *mitzvot* as "You shall not steal; neither shall you deal falsely," and "You shall not oppress your neighbor or rob him" (Leviticus 19:11, 13). All these injunctions deal with monetary matters. The Torah specifies, "You shall be holy because I, the Lord your God, am Holy" (Leviticus 19:2). Whereas God's holiness abides in Heaven, the human being must be holy on earth. Reb Yisrael explains this to mean *b'inyonim artzei'im*—earthly affairs—such as business, work activity, and all areas of one's relationship with his fellow man. People do not realize the many *mitzvot* involved in everyday mundane activities and interpersonal relationships with other people in daily life.

There is an interesting story told about a particular *shochet* (ritual slaughterer) who was a great *talmud chochom* and Godfearing man. He came to Reb Yisrael Salanter and told him of his desire to leave the position of *shochet* in a certain town because of the awesome responsibility he had of providing ritually slaughtered meat for the populace. Reb Yisroel asked him, "What do you plan to engage in to earn a livelihood?" The shochet answered, "I will open a store and be involved in business activities." With a look of sincere wonder and apprehension of not correctly slaughtering an animal, which only deals with one *mitzvah*—*shechitah*—leads you to contemplate leaving the post of *shochet*, then opening a store, which is linked to so many warnings and prohibitions including not to steal, deceive, lie, and cheat and to give correct weights and measures, and so on, should surely arouse in you greater feelings of trepidation and inadequacy!

Reb Yisrael's type of "businessman" would definitely merit the title *kadosh*. The Kotzker Rebbe says on the verse in *Mishpatim* (Exodus 22:30), *V'anshei Kodesh tihiyun li*—Holy people shall you be unto Me, *Mentschlich haylig zolt ir zaiyn*—That a human holiness, one that pervades regular earthy activities natural to mankind, is required. "Angels," he says, "God has enough of them in Heaven."

Rashi's first comment on the *sedrah* mentions, from the *Sifra*, that this *parshah*, *Kedoshim*, was said to the whole assembly of men, women, and children because the majority of the essentials of the Torah are summarized therein! Only at the giving of the very first *mitzvah* that the Jews received—the command for the *Pesach* offering (Exodus 12:3)—do we find the order to announce the law to the whole community of the Children of Israel.

Apart from these two places, this form of command is not to be found in any other paragraph of the Torah. In connection with our explanations of holiness as including the implanting of sanctity into every earthly activity in life by proper, sincere performance of the pertinent *mitzvot*, the admonition to *kedushah* can well be addressed expressly to every individual of the nation. No one can be excluded from this call to *holiness—that is, ethics and morality in man's daily life.*

The *Baalei Musar* state explicitly that holiness does not mean merely performance of duty or the punctilious observance of *mitzvot*. Holiness requires a personal consecration and dedication to the service of God and man. It denotes purity of thought and of action. In this manner, a person can reach the heights of *kedushah*—holiness—and, as expressed in the *Gemara* (*Yevamot* 20a), "achieve the holiness of yourself in the realm of that which is permitted to you." The Ramban, commenting on our *sedrah*, discusses this concept in a most illuminating and beautiful fashion:

> In all areas of permissible activity such as eating, don't gorge yourself; cohabitation, don't overindulge; idle talk, don't become involved in such discussions, and so on. A person must exert self control and act in an ethical, moral manner. He must not sink to the depths of spiritual depravity and, Heaven forbid, be labeled a *naval bershut Hatorah*—an ignoble person within the permissible confines of the Torah.

Only intensive and assiduous Torah study is the proper means to prepare and guide a person toward a life permeated with *kedushah*—holiness. Though few people ever attain the lofty peak of true *kedushah*, everyone on his own level is commanded by the verse in the Torah, *Kedoshim Tihiyu*," to have this basic ingredient permeate all his activities in leading a Torah-true way of life.

Rabbi Dovid Plaut

Young Israel of Greater Buffalo, New York

Parshat Kedoshim contains the fundamental concepts of the Torah (Rashi, *Vayikra* 19:2). Among thse important but often overlooked *mitzvot* between man and his fellow man is the *halachah* "Do not seek revenge; do not harbor ill-feeling [against someone who mistreated you]" (Leviticus 19:18). The *Gemara* in *Yoma* 23 explains this *halachah* in very practical, down-to-earth terms. To paraphrase the *Gemara*, what is considered revenge? If a person (for example, Reuven) asks another person (for example, Simon) to lend him a scythe and Simon denies the request, and then the next day Reuven refuses to lend Simon his ax, saying "I will not lend you my ax, just as you did not lend me your scythe," this would be considered taking revenge.

What would be considered bearing a grudge? If Reuven asks Simon to lend him his ax, Simon refuses and then, the next day, when Simon asks that Reuven lend him some clothing, if Reuven replies, "I will lend you the clothes in spite of the fact that you would not lend me your ax," Reuven would be bearing a grudge.

I would like to clarify three points regarding the *halachah* of "Do not seek revenge; do not harbor ill-feeling."

1. How literal is the example given in the *Gemara*? Does "Do not seek revenge; do not harbor ill-feeling" apply in other cases as well?
2. Is it necessary actually to verbalize one's feelings in order to violate the *issur* of "Do not seek revenge; do not harbor ill feeling," as the *Gemara* seems to imply?
3. Is there any significance to the fact that the revenge mentioned in the *Gemara*'s example occurred on the day after the provocation?

The *Gemara* in *Yoma* 23 says clearly that the law of "Do not seek revenge; do not harbor ill-feeling" applies only when the provocation and the revenge involve issues of money or property. If a person is personally insulted or his character defamed, he is permitted to avenge his honor and harbor ill-feeling toward the perpetrator. This distinction is accepted by *Rabbeinu* Yonah in *Sefer Sharei Tshuvah* (13:38), and the *Sefer Yereim*. The logic behind this distinction perhaps can be explained by the Rambam's explanation of "Do not seek revenge; do not harbor ill-feeling." In *Hilchot Deot*, Chapter 7 Halacha 7, the Rambam explains the reason for the *issur* "Do not seek revenge; do not harbor ill-feeling": "To those who truly understand, everything material in this world is worthless, and there is no justification in avenging its loss." It would seem from the Rambam's explanation of "Do not seek revenge; do not harbor ill-feeling" that this *halachah* may apply only to material possessions in this world. One could argue that a person's honor and dignity cannot be termed worthless and that, therefore, it would be justified to take revenge.

The Chofetz Chaim in *Shmirat Haloshen* (Introduction: *Lav* 8:9) points out that according to this distinction it would be forbidden to take revenge, even using non-monetary or non-property means, as long as the provocation came through some sort of financial mistreatment. So, for example, if Reuven refuses to lend Simon his ax, it would not be permitted for Simon to speak badly of Reuven in retaliation since Simon should not view Reuven's refusal to lend him something as a justification for revenge. However, the Chofetz Chaim is unresolved whether revenge would be permitted in a case where Reuven insulted Simon and then Simon avenges the insult by not lending Reuven a desired object.

It is noteworthy that the Chofetz Chaim cites other commentators who disagree with this distinction and say that it is forbidden to take revenge even in cases of insult. The Chofetz Chaim concludes that, since we are dealing with an *issur* of the Torah, we should follow the more strict opinions of the Rambam and the Chinuch.

For the second question—whether it is necessary to verbalize one's feelings to violate the *issur*—again *Rabbeinu* Yonah sets the record straight. *Rabbeinu* Yonah writes, "The punishment does not come because of what was said; rather, for the resentment that is felt inside." Therefore, when a person acts on the basis of his resentment, he violates the *issur* of "do not seek revenge," and if he feels ill-will toward a person who wronged him, he violates "do not harbor ill-feeling" even without saying anything.

The reason the *Gemara* used an example in which the revenge took place on the next day is that there is a difference between an immediate response and a reaction after time has elapsed. The *Sefer Chinuch* says that an immediate response is not considered to be revenge. In *mitzvah* 338 the author writes, "However, it appears to me that if a Jew wrongs his fellow Jew by insulting or antagonizing him, he is allowed to answer back his attacker; for a person cannot be like a stone without feelings. The Torah would not command a person to react identically to a person who curses him as he would to a person who praises him." Therefore, the illustration of the *Gemara* is very precise in setting the revenge on the next day.

*Regarding the second half of the *posuk*, "you should love your friend as yourself," Rashi quotes Rabbi Akiva, who stated that this is an important principle in the Torah. The Chasam Sofer says that this seems to contradict what Rabbi Akiva says in *Bava Metziah*—that one's own life takes precedence over the life of his friend. How, then, could he maintain that one must love his friend on an equal level with himself? The Chasam Sofer answers that this is exactly what Rabbi Akiva alluded to when he said that this is an important principle in Torah. In matters pertaining to this world we give our life precedence. However, when it comes to Torah and *mitzvot* we must treat our friend as an equal. *Kol Yisrael arevim zoh lazeh* means that all Jews are responsible for each other's Torah observance.

❖ CHAPTER 35 ❖

Kedoshim

Rabbi Eliyahu Rabovsky

Young Israel of Boca Raton, Florida

"Speak to the entire community of the sons of Yisrael."
(Leviticus 19:2)

The *baraisa* in *Eruvin* (54b) explains the method of Moshe's teaching of the Torah to the Jewish people. First, Moshe called Aharon and taught him privately on a profound level of comprehension. Then Aharon's sons came to learn and received the Torah according to their understanding. Following them were the elders, and then the rest of the men of *Bnei Yisrael*, each being taught the instructions of *HaShem* on a level commensurate with his spiritual standing.

Rashi tells us that such was not the case with *Parshat Kedoshim*. It was taught to everyone, even the children, and it was taught to all at the same time.

Several reasons are given for this variation in communal transmission. *Parshat Kedoshim* contains many fundamental Torah precepts. In fact, the view of Reb Levi is that the entire Ten Commandments can be found in this *parshah* (*Vayikra Rabbah* 24:5). The Almighty's desire was that every member be present together at a national assembly so that these critical tenets would be imbibed by all. Additionally, the Mizrachi explains that *HaShem* wanted all to be present simultaneously so that, if there was any question as to Moshe's teachings, it could be clarified easily. If these lessons had been taught in small classes, perhaps a particular class would have an understanding of a certain point. They might reject clarificatioins offered by another class, contending that "what was told to you was not told to us." With the entire nation gathered together, all hearing the same identical teachings, this barrier to learning was removed.

KEDOSHIM TIHEYU—"YOU SHALL BE HOLY"

What is meant by this holiness that the Torah demands of us?

The Ramban explains that the Torah here issues a call to arms to each and every one of us. Notwithstanding the prohibitions placed upon us regarding our physical involvement in this world, we still are given much latitude. Exercising the freedom that latitude implies can lead us to a place far distant from that which the *Ribono shel Olam* desires for us. For example, the guidelines of *kashrus*, as demanding and pervasive as they may be, still do not preclude one from becoming a glutton and a drunk. There is an abundant array of foods from which to choose, some of the gourmet variety, all with the fineset *hechsharim*; not to mention the kosher wine list, which is long both in quantity and quality.

Says the Torah to us, "Sanctify yourselves even in that which is permitted to you." Recognize that the spiritual mission of the Jew can be attained only with a personal system of restraints and limits that take over where the Torah's legislated barriers leave off. If there is overindulgence in any area of our physical lives, one can be involved in the most kosher activity or organization in the world but, at the same time, be devoid of anything spiritually meaningful. However, when both the intellect rules and we keep within certain limits, true holiness can then be attained.

Rav Moshe Feinstein, *zt"l*, addresses the mandate of *Kedoshim tihiyu* from another perspective by first asking this question: "Why does this call for holiness and the listing of all of the interpersonal *mitzvot* that follows it come between the warning about forbidden relationships that occurs at the end of *Acharei Mot* and the specifically enumerated punishments for these violations mentioned at the end of this week's *sedrah*?" It appears that the first part of *Kedoshim* interrupts the flow between the end of *Acharei Mot* and the end of *Kedoshim*.

Rav Moshe sets out to explain the order of the text by first clarifying the Torah's concept of criminal punishment. Other peoples certainly have criminal codes that may even, on occasion, prescribe a more severe punishment for misconduct than the Torah. Yet the Psalmist still exclaims, regarding the nations, "And of His laws—they know them not." This is because of an essential difference between the secular system and that of the Torah.

The secular system's laws punish in order to protect society against the menace of evil doers. The effect that such a system has on criminals is to motivate them to "*beat the* law." *HaShem* does not need any system to protect the innocent. He can watch over His children in many ways. The desire of the Torah in punishing the criminal is to raise his consciousness and make him see the disgrace of sin. But to raise consciousness, there must first be a developed conscience—that is, an inherent desire in the individual for the spiritual.

This is the meaning of the Torah's "interruption" of *Kedoshim tihiyu*: Change yourselves from physical beings, governed by selfish wants and needs, into creations of the soul that long for the holy and the Divine. Embrace the interpersonal *mitzvot* such as fearing parents and giving the preordained gifts to the poor, commandments that require holiness (selflessness) if they are to be done properly. Now, after the entire Jewish people have been imbued with the desire and need for holiness in all facets of their lives, the Torah can detail its punishments for illicit relations, knowing that even the wayward sinner might now see their justice and rise to the lofty station of *Kedoshim tihiyu*.

Rabbi Yaakov Feitman

Young Israel of Beachwood, Ohio

THE PERSPECTIVES OF RASHI AND THE RAMBAN

It is well known that Rashi and the Ramban (Nachmonides) appear to have significantly different understandings of the *mitzvah* of *Kedoshim tihiyu*—"You shall be holy." Rashi is of the opinion that this commandment relates to the avoidance of specific sins. The Ramban teaches that the Torah here introduces the new concept of sanctifying acts that are neither inherently sinful nor *mitzvot*. Being holy relates to the ostensibly optional acts of eating, drinking, sleeping, and other natural human functions. One can perform these no differently than do the animals, or one can consecrate them and infuse them with profound *kedushah*.

DOES "IMATATO DEI" INCLUDE BEING HOLY?

Whichever perspective one uses, an issue arises concerning the need for a commandment that we be holy. There is a *mitzvah* in the Torah that we emulate *HaShem*—"and you shall go in His ways" (Deuteronomy 28,9). The Rambam (Maimonides) in *Hilchot Deiot* 1,5 sees this *mitzvah* as the mandate to do all good and Godly things that are not otherwise specifically enumerated in the Torah. The question is, therefore, what about holiness itself? Does the *mitzvah* of emulating *HaShem* include the charge to be holy, just as God is holy, or is being Holy different from being kind, visiting the sick, comforting the depressed, and so on?

My *rebbe*, Rav Yitzchok Hutner, *zt"l*, alludes to this query but does not resolve it (*Haskamah* to *Sefer Mitzvot Habayit*; *Igrot*, page 139, no. 76 in that particular letter; to my knowledge, the *Rosh Yeshivah* did not return to the topic in any printed work). However, I believe an interpretation by Rav Shimon Shkop, *zt"l* (introduction to *Shaarei Yosher*), although not addressing this problem directly, goes to the heart of the matter.

EMULATING *HaShem* AS CREATOR

Reb Shimon quotes the *midrash* (*Vayikra Rabbah* 24), "You may have thought you could be as Holy as I am, therefore the Torah states, 'Because I am Holy, my holiness is greater than your holiness.'" "We might have thought that we must attempt to emulate *HaShem* totally in the matter of holiness. The Torah, therefore, specifies that *HaShem*'s Holiness is unique and inimitable in its loftiness."

What does this *midrash* mean? What would it have meant to imitate God completely, and why the admonishment not even to make the attempt? In answering these questions, Reb Shimon Shkop examines the seemingly abstruse enigma of what exactly we mean when we declare that God is holy. Without resorting to Kabbalah or terms that would be meaningless to most of us, Reb Shimon offers a simple and classic definition of *kedushah* and our ability to emulate this quality. The essence of *HaShem*'s relationship with this world, he teaches, is that all that God does is for others. There is no act, indeed no word or statement, emanating from *HaShem* that flows from any need of His own, so to speak. God's every act, by definition, is altruistic, and that is the essence of His holiness.

Following this approach, says Reb Shimon, both Rashi and the Ramban's interpretations can be understood in context. At first it seems strange to assert that avoiding that which is prohibited, as well as excess in that which is permitted, can be considered ways to emulate *HaShem*. Surely God Himself has no prohibitions, nor is the concept of excess remotely applicable to Him. However, if we understand all matters prohibited to us and immoderation in those things that are permitted as wanton self-indulgence, then we can begin to comprehend the *mitzvah* of *kedoshim tihiyu* in the sense of emulating God. Just as God does nothing except for the good of others, so should our every act be free of prodigality and self-gratification. Any action that contributes to our physical or spiritual dissipation is a negation of holiness because it leaves out the "other" in the human equation and isolates the self and its ego. Conversely, one who measures every deed to make sure it contributes only to physical need and spiritual well-being is emulating the most basic trait of God, that of Creator in order to provide benefit for His creatures.

A LIMITED EMULATION

But this is where the *midrash* warns us not to try to imitate God too closely. Remember, say our Sages, God cautions us, "Your holiness will never be exactly the same as Mine." The *Shaarei Yosher* explains: Human beings dare not ignore their own needs entirely. Do not seek to suppress your ego and personal needs entirely, as this is unhealthy and unnatural. On the contrary, expand them to include as wide a net as possible. Instead of your "I" being a limited and restricted one, intensify your "self" to embrace an ever-widening group. At first your "I" may incorporate your family. As you gain in *kedushah*, you may encompass your entire community in your purview. If you blossom further in your quest for holy godliness, your range of personal concern will be all of *Klal Yisrael*. Eventually, your sphere of influence may become all of mankind.

We may now return to the problem of whether the *mitzvah* of imitating God includes the trait known as holiness. With the help of Reb Shimon Shkop, *zt"l*, we can suggest that unquestionably becoming godly must include the requirement to become holy as well. The insight of *Parshat Kedoshim* is that the holiness demanded of us is a particularly human endeavor. We are to enage in uniquely human activities. We are to retain a healthy and stable sense of ego and self. And yet, it is our obligation and our mandate to invest these traits and ventures with *kedushah*.

THE MARRIAGE OF TWO MITZVOT

Perhaps the inclusion of the *mitzvah* "Love your neighbor as yourself," the "great rule of the Torah" (Rashi) in this *parshah* may now be understood in a fresh light as well. The premise of *kedushah* is not self-absorption but caring for another. Furthermore, as the Ramban points out, the Torah commands *l'reacha* ("*to* your friend") not *et reacha* ("your friend"). One is not expected to love another exactly as one does oneself; rather, one must *act* in as loving a way with others as one would for oneself. With the teachings of Reb Shimon Shkop, we can add that all involvement with others derives from the expanded sense of self; thus, *l'reacha* reflects not a new foreign love but the realization that we are each a part of something much greater and more important than the narrow appearance that greets us in the mirror.

In many ways it is appropriate that we read this *parshah* during the days of *sefirat haomer*. The *Gemara* (*Yevamot* 62b) teaches that the disciples of Rabbi Akiva died during this time of year because they did not give each other the proper respect. Rav Aharon Kotler, *zt"l* (volume 3, page 19), points out that we have little understanding of the incredible greatness of these holy beings and why they were punished so severely. But this much is clear. On the highest levels of holiness, one must consider each act, word, and gesture and test it carefully for any ill effect on another. For the students of Rebbe Akiva, holiness was indeed measured by concern and, ultimately, caring for another. In the famed European Talmud Torah of Kelm, even the *havdalah* candle was not extinguished in the *beit hamidrash* for fear that the momentary smoke would sting someone's eyes or throat.

Perhaps, if we carried the joint message of *kedoshim tihiyu* and *V'ahavta l'reacha kamocha* with us through *sefirah* to *matan torah*, we would achieve the kind of holiness that *HaShem* truly wants from us—a compassionate, loving *kedushah* that affects all with whom we come in contact and brings glory to *HaShem*, His Torah, and His nation.

❖ CHAPTER 36 ❖

Emor

Rabbi Elias Schwartz

Young Israel of Bensonhurst/ Bathbeach, New York

WHO ARE YOU? DO *YOU* KNOW WHO YOU ARE? REMEMBER *WHO YOU ARE*!

The first *pesukim* in *Parshat Emor* teach ritual and ritual purity laws (*tumaat meit*) that relate only to *kohanim*, who are in a class by themselves. Because of their service (*avodah*) in the *Beit Hamikdash*, their laws of *tumah* and *taharah* far surpass these same *dinim* for non-*kohanim*.

The introductory sentence to all of these laws is very thought-provoking: "*HaShem* told Moshe: *Say* (*emor*) to the *kohanim*, the children of Aharon; and *say to them* (*v'amarta aleihem*): they are not to make themselves spiritually impure (*tamei*) when dealing with *tumah* relating to death."

This sentence repeats the word *say* (*emor v'amarta*) twice. It seems there are two messages that Moshe is to give to the *kohanim*. The second occurrence of *say*, *v'amarta*, is easily understood from the concluding words of the *pasuk*—do not become *tamei*. This is clearly the second message of the *pasuk*. But what message does the word *emor* bring? What does the first *say* mean to tell us? And why does the *pasuk* include the words *bnei Aharon*? Everybody knows that all *kohanim* are descendants of Aharon.

In reality, these opening words to our *parshah* are the foundation of all the laws referring to *kohanim*, and their message is most important.

Say to the *kohanim*, say to the priesthood of Israel, tell them: Remember at all times: Who you are! Remember at all times: That you are *Bnei Aharon*. Be identified as a son of Aharon. It isn't enough for you go know that you are a *kohein*. You must at all times carry the title with you, wherever you go. "I am a descendant of Aharon." You must stand out in your life activities as an individual who remembers his heritage and is mindful of his past and his future.

"Hillel said: Be of the disciples of Aaron, loving peace and pursuing peace; be one who loves his fellow man and draws them near to the Torah" (*Pirkei Avot* 1:12). Always carry in front of your eyes a true role model, a visual picture of Aharon, our first *Kohein Gadol.* Whenever you are confronted with a problem, perhaps you could say to yourself, "How would Aharon tackle this problem? How would Aharon act?" Study the way Aharon lived—how he loved every Jew, how he made *shalom* (peace) between people.

One of the *meforshim* says: Aharon was not deserving to be involved in the sin of making of the golden calf. He did everything possible to stop them. The title of *Kohein Gadol* was not taken away from him for this transgression.

We must realize the purity of the mind of Aharon. He was completetly *kadosh* (holy). He felt only complete happiness and joy when he realized that his younger brother, Moshe, would become the leader of *Klal Yisrael.* There wasn't a speck of jealousy in him at all.

Aharon was involved in the sin of the Golden Calf *only* so that he would feel the remorse of a sinner. He was also involved in this sin but was completely exonerated and remained in his high position.

Aharon would be responsible for bringing forgiveness to every person who brought a sinner's sacrifice. He would be responsible for bringing forgiveness to all of *Klal Yisrael* on Yom Kippur.

Now he was *personally* involved in a sin, although *superficially,* he felt and tasted the remorse of a sinner. In *Parshat Shemini,* Moshe had to plead with him to draw near to the altar. "Bring the *korbanot* of this day of dedication of the *Mishkan,*" and Rashi says: "You were chosen to be the *Kohein Gadol* *because* of this feeling of shame, *because* of the remorse of being a sinner yourself, *because* you went through the feelings of repentance and forgiveness." Now, Aharon could transfer these feelings of repentance and plead for forgiveness for all Israel. He could show all Israel that they, too, could and would be forgiven for wrongdoing.

Now, on Yom Kippur, Aharon could feel the impact of transgressions and plead before God for complete forgiveness for every Jew. This is what every *kohein* should feel—that he is a son of Aharon.

We find this idea of a role model in another area as well. *Kohanim* also see and feel and react to the Aharon aspect in their service when they bless us on all holidays (and *Shabbat* and daily in Israel).

In the blessing that the *kohein* recites before the *birchat kohanim*—the blessing of the congregation by the Mohanim—a few words are added, words not usually found in a regular blessing. "Blessed are You *HaShem* . . . *Asher kid'shonu bikdushoso shel Aharon* (who has sanctified us with the *Holiness of Aaron*) *V'tzivonu L'voraych et amo Yisroel b'ahava* (and has commanded us to bless His nation Yisroel with love). Why isn't the regular language *asher kid'shonu b'mitzvosov v'tzivonu* (who has sanctified us with His commandments and has commanded us . . .) sufficient. After all, in this blessing, we find inserted the words "with the holiness of Aharon." Whatever the *kohein* does, the complete holiness of Aharon must be involved. When a *kohein* blesses us, he must feel the sanctity of that moment as if he were Aharon, the *Kohein Gadol,* with the inherent sanctity and holiness that stems from Aharon. He must transfer his psyche to the highest elevation of *kedushah* that a *kohein* can attain.

This *brachah* also would be complete without the word *b'ahavah,* "with love." Why do we say *yasher koach* to the *kohein* after *birkat kohanim*? It is a *mitzvah* that he *must do,* just as *tefillin* is a *mitzvah*. Do we say *yasher koach* to each other when we take our *tefillin* off? We say *yasher koach*—may your strength be increased—to the *konanim* because of the word, *b'ahavah*. We know how pleased they are to bless us. We feel that they do this *mitzvah* with total love; therefore, we thank them and say *yasher koach* as they leave the *bimah*.

"Say to the *kohanim,* the children of Aharon . . ." All *kohanim,* remember who you are! All *kohanim,* remember your role model! All *kohanim,* remember to try to emulate your first *Kohein,* Aharon *Hakohein Hagadol*!

We can extend this thought to all Israel. When a Jew does something wrong, all Jews, all of *Bnei Yisrael,* are held accountable. *Remember who you are. Remember you are a* Ben Yisrael. *Act like one; think like one. This is a great responsibility.*

This same principle is surely also true of a *talmid chochom*—of *bnei Torah*. Remember the badge of greatness that you carry. Remember that you are on a higher rung than most of our people. Remember that you are a *ben Torah*. Remember that you are a *yeshivah bochur*. Your *middos,* your character traits, must be finer and on a higher plane than those of others. Think like a *ben Torah*. Act like one.

Perhaps this is our problem with Russian Jewry, particularly in America. The *refuseniks* who upheld and fought for their *Yiddishkeit* when in Russia all emigrated to Israel. Many have successfully made their personal transition into Orthodox Torah Jewry. They rose step by step, higher and higher, prouder and prouder, in serving *HaShem* properly in the Holy Land. As new Russians come to Israel, there are many role models for them to emulate. From their own people, there are *bnei Torah*—truly Orthodox scientists, doctors, and so on. Every new immigrant has somebody to look up to. "That person made it in Israel as an Orthodox person; I'm going to be like him."

Alas, in America, there are very, very few role models. We are constantly sending our children to *yeshivot,* but their homes are still untouched spiritually; their home life is not the way we would like it to be, the way their children are being taught in the *yeshivah*. They desperately need role models. They need to look up to Orthodox Russian doctors, lawyers, businessmen who have made their way up the ladder in America and who also learned to live as proud Orthodox Jews.

Let us not give up on them. Perhaps the next generation will set the right road and bring their parents along with them. We will then see our Young Israel motto take effect: "And He will turn the heart of the fathers to the children, and the heart of the children to their fathers."

Rabbi Doniel Frank

Young Israel of Westport/Norwalk, Connecticut

In *Parshat Emor,* the Torah recounts the brief yet infamous story of the *mekaleil,* the individual who blasphemed God's name while fighting with a fellow Jew.

The product of an Israelite woman, whom the Torah identifies as Shlomit bat Divri, and an Egyptian man, this crossbreed was temporarily imprisoned for his offense while Moshe inquired of God as to the appropriate punishment for such a crime. Subsequently *HaShem* told Moshe that a *mekaleil* must be put to death through stoning. However, before these Divine instructions were to be transmitted to the rest of *Klal Yisrael* and implemented, God presented Moshe with several additional laws (see verses 15–22) that were also to be taught.

For a full appreciation of this *parshah,* several questions must be answered.

1. For what purpose did the Torah identify the name of the Israelite woman who was the *mekaleil*'s mother? (See Rashi for one explanation.)
2. Why was it necessary for God to introduce the series of laws that He did at this time when all Moshe asked for was the one governing a blasphemous person?
3. Rashi explains that the reason the Torah identifies the tribe of the *makaleil*'s mother is to teach the lesson that an evil person causes embarrassment to himself, his family, and his entire tribe. Why is that lesson especially appropriate to this *parshah*?

In an effort to resolve these questions, we should begin with an insight of the Ramban in his commentary to *Parshat Nitzavim.*

When the Jews stood before God, prepared to enter into His covenant, they were told that the oath they were about to take was to be taken not only on behalf of themselves but also on behalf of "those who are not yet here with us today." (Dueteronomy 29:14) It was essential, the Torah continued, that no one harbor any feelings of rejection of God in his/her heart, and referred to these feelings as roots that can produce rotten fruit. (Deuteronomy 29:17)

Elaborating on this analogy, the Ramban explains that parents are likened to roots and their children, to branches and fruit. Any traits or thoughts, be they good or evil, latent or expressed, will be transmitted to the children, where they may then germinate and sprout. Recognizing this reality, the Torah warns that anyone with a trace of heresy in his/her heart should first eradicate it before entering into any covenant with God, for, if the heresy is merely suppressed, it will be passed on to future generations, where it may ultimately find expression.

With this insight as our basis, we can assume that the Torah's purpose in implicating Shlomit bat Divri is to encourage us to draw a parallel between traits that she may have demonstrated with those of her son and to identify what may have motivated the *mekaleil* to sin the way he did.

Throughout the Torah, God refers to us as His children. Since He is the King of Kings, we can reasonably conclude that all Jewish men are princes and all Jewish women, princesses. As such, when Dovid *Hamelech* says, "The *entire* glory of the daughter of a king is her modesty" (Psalms 45:14), he is teaching us that the majesty of a Jewish woman is through her achievements in humility, a theme that is clearly underscored throughout Judaic literature. In other words, while *tzniut* is important for a Jewish man, it is the very essence of the Jewish woman.

Shlomit bat Divri was verbose and flirtatious. Rashi (*Vayikrah* 24:10) explains how her very name suggests that about her. It was in this manner that she stepped out of her royal mold. Through her immodest behavior, Shlomit rejected her Jewish identity and no longer exhibited the virtues of a king's daughter. We can understand her punishment accordingly. Rashi (*Vayikrah* 24:10) tells us that she was the woman who was assaulted by the Egyptian that Moshe eventually killed while in Egypt. By being forced to mate with a Gentile, she was made to realize that her behavior was no longer in accordance with her Jewish character and made her a suitable match for a non-Jew.

Just as roots blossom, Shlomit's son took his mother's behavior one step further. It is well known in Jewish thought that the difference between man and animal is the human capacity for speech. When the *mekaleil* utilized *his* speech for blasphemous purposes, he lost his advantage over animals (see *Sefer Hachinuch*). And so, while his mother rejected one aspect of her identity, namely her Jewishness, he rejected his entire humanness.

Having answered our first question with this approach, we can now deal with the other two.

The *mekaleil* showed how man can sink to the level of an animal. Therefore, in an effort to reinforce the superiority of man, God taught Moshe, along with the instructions on how to deal with the *mekaleil*, a series of laws that reveal the important distinction between man and animal. One who carefully reads these additional laws will see how they each demonstrate this difference.

Concerning Rashi's comment that one who behaves improperly dishonors his family and his tribe, we can explain that such dishonor is not merely an embarrassment caused by association. On a more profound level, they are dishonored because that person expressed a negative trait that is likely to be present, though perhaps latent, in all of those from whom he descends. And we have seen that in our *parshah* in the case of Shlomit and her son.

The sins of Shlomit and her son, though different in degree, were similar in nature. They both rejected their self-worth. They were both unable to live up to the honorable positions into which they had been born. Perhaps we can say that they preferred, consciously or subconsciously, to forfeit their prominence in order to shake off the responsibility that always comes along with it.

Behaving like a person—a *mentsch*—is not easy. Behaving like a Jew—a *ben Torah* (a disciple of the Torah)—is all the more difficult. But for one who has any moral convictions or, more accurately, for one who is God-fearing, is there any other way to live?

Rabbi Dov A. Brisman

Young Israel of Elkins Park, Pennsylvania

SEFIRAT HA'OMER: BRIDGE OF OUR FAITH

> "And you shall count from the day after *Shabbat*, from the day that you bring the *omer*. . . ." (Leviticus 23:15)

This season, commonly known as *sefirah*, connects Pesach and Shavuot, creating a cohesive unit of spiritual elevation. We begin with *Yetziat Mitzrayim* (the Exodus from Egypt), our inception as a nation, and culminate the season with *Matan Torah* (the giving of the Torah), the consummation of our nationhood.

It is interesting to note that the Torah refers to Pesach as *Shabbat*. What is the significance of this designation?

The Berditchiver *Rebbe, zt"l* (*Kedushat Levi*) explains: *Chazal* relate that the world was created for *Klal Yisrael*. Although the physical creation was completed with *Shabbat*, the true purpose of creation was manifest in Pesach, for then the Almighty portrayed His love for *Klal Yisrael*. Therefore, in essence, Pesach is *Shabbat*, for the theme of *Shabbat* reached fruition on Pesach.

According to this interpretation, we can explain the reason that the *mitzvah* of *emunah* (faith) in *HaShem* is described by its relationship with *Yetziat Mitzrayim*. The beginning of the *Aseret Hadibrot* (the Ten Commandments) states, "I am *HaShem*, Your Almighty, *who has taken you out of Mitzrayim*." Why did the Torah not state that faith is based upon the fact that *HaShem* created the universe? Why is it necessary to relate creation to *Yetziat Mitzrayim*? (See Ramban, Sforno, and so on.)

On the basis of *Kedushat Levi*, we can suggest the following explanation. Creation itself culminates with *Yetziat Mitzrayim*. The declaration that the Almighty has designated a nation as His own and its people as His adherents clearly clarions the message that the purpose of creation has been achieved. By proclaiming our faith on the basis of *Yetziat Mitzrayim*, we are reaffirming that creation was Divinely designed for a purpose. *Yetziat Mitzrayim*, our inception as a nation, defines the objective of creation. Hence, in basing our faith in *HaShem* on *Yetziat Mitzrayim*, the Torah implicitly indicated to us our role in creation as the basis of faith in *HaShem*.

The *Sefer Hachinuch* (*mitzvah* 306) writes that the *mitzvah* of *sefirat ha'omer* is to prepare for *Matan Torah*. Counting every day between Pesach and Shavuot indicates our awareness that we are gradually coming closer to *Matan Torah*. Our nation's essence is the Torah, and we were redeemed from Mitzrayim in order to receive the Torah at Sinai. The ultimate goal, *Matan Torah*, is more significant than the actual redemption from slavery. Therefore, we were commanded to count every day until Shavuot in order to express our tremendous desire to approach the day of *Matan Torah*. Counting days expresses a person's desire to reach a lofty goal. This can be achieved only by gradual progression.

This concept of gradual progression strongly manifests itself in another part of our *parshah*, which states, "When an ox, sheep, or goat is born, it shall be seven days under its mother; but from the eighth day and onward, it shall be accepted as a sacrifice to *HaShem*" (Leviticus 23:27). Why is it necessary to state that the newborn will be under its mother for seven days? Would it not suffice merely to state that the animal is fit for a sacrifice when it is eight days old?

The *midrash* explains with a parable that the first seven days are also a necessity. Once a king imposed a decree throughout his kingdom that any person who wished to have an audience with the king must first appear before the governor. So, too, states the *midrash*, an animal is not fit to come before *HaShem* until it has lived in the world for seven days and has spent a *Shabbat* in this world. Upon being imbued with the spirit of *Shabbat* (the governor), the animal is then ready to be received by *HaShem*.

The Taz (*Yoreh Deah*, chapter 255) points out that for this reason we celebrate the *Shalom Zachar* on the *Shabbat* (Friday night) preceding the *brit milah* of the newborn baby boy. The child is not ready to absorb the sanctity inherent in the *brit milah* until he first experiences a *Shabbat* in the world.

Indeed, no individual can climb the rungs of spirituality immediately. It requires much exertion and toil to ascend gradually to high levels of scholarship and sanctity. So, too, a nation cannot rise immediately from bondage and submission to become a Nation of Torah. Preparations must be undertaken over a period of time. Only through proper reflection and adjustment to the new situation can we evolve into an *Am Hatorah*.

It is, therefore, incumbent upon us to utilize the period of *sefirat ha'omer* as a time of reflection. Gratitude for being chosen as *Am HaShem* must be cultivated as a preparation for *Matan Torah*. As our forefathers did, we must prepare ourselves to receive the Torah with great participation and enthusiasm. I can think of no more practical way than to devote more time to learning or to upgrading our present learning. May we be granted a meaningful *Matan Torah* this year with only *simchah*!

❖ CHAPTER 37 ❖

Behar

Rabbi Jacob S. Rubenstein

Young Israel of Scarsdale, New York

THE *SHEMITTAH* SOUL

When the Torah speaks of the original *Shabbat* it says, ". . . it is a sign forever that in six days *HaShem* created the heavens and the earth, and on the seventh day *shavat vayinafash* (Exodus 31:17). The conventional translation of *shavat vayinafash* is "He rested and was refreshed." Even accepting the limitations of anthropomorphic terms, however, it would be untenable to say *HaShem* had need to rest and to be refreshed. The more precise rendering of *shavat* would be "He desisted." *Vayinafash* clearly comes from the word *nefesh*—the soul or the essence. This definition adds dramatically to the meaning and explains the thrust of the statement and its implications for us today.

For six days, *HaShem* was an architect, a designer and creator, builder and molder—a force that related to the created—but on the seventh day, *HaShem* ceased being *something* and retreated to who He is, returned to His essence. *HaShem* mandated man to be *domeh l'otzro 'yotzro*, like his Creator; we are to emulate His ways to discover our own unique essence. He tells man, "All week long you are creators and workers with labels and titles. You have professions; you are doctors, lawyers, merchants. But, on the seventh day, return to your essence: restore your soul! On *Shabbat*, search for the soul that is intrinsic to you and discover your real identity outside your worldly profession."

We serve a purpose that is greater than our profession, and that is what we are charged to discover on *Shabbat*. Only by ceasing our work are we free to discover the essence that is unique to our existence, and that parallels *HaShem*.

This was, after all, the ultimate purpose of *shemittah* the sabbatical year; to afford *Am Yisrael* the opportunity to be preoccupied with the *nefesh* and rediscover its national identity as defined by *HaShem* in creation. Sforno speaks to this issue when he explains, "Then shall the land keep a *Shabbat* to *HaShem*" (Leviticus 25:2). "The entire year, which will be free of any agricultural labor, will instead be one devoted to serving Him, as was the intention of the *Shabbat of Bereishit*, as it says, '*Shabbat* to *HaShem*, our God' (Exodus 20:10). By resting during the year, landowners will be moved to seek *HaShem*."

Enslavement to work and the toil of the soil are liable to lead to spiritual poverty and estrangement from *HaShem*. This was indeed the contention of Rabbi Shimon bar Yochai. "If a man continually plows in the ploughing season, sows in the sowing season, reaps in the harvest season, threshes during the threshing session and winnows when the winds blow, what will become of the Torah?" (*Berakhot* 35b). The questions Rabbi Shimon bar Yochai didn't ask but perhaps should have were, "What, in these circumstances, will become of the human being? What will become of the nation of Israel?"

We, who have abhorred the mere thought that *Arbeit Macht Frei*, ironically live with the mistaken impression that work will give us the opportunities we seek. But, as Rabbi Shimon bar Yochai implied, there is always a "season" that seems to require our attention. If *Shabbat* did not impose the "season" to rest, we would lose sight of the spiritual splendor of the divine soul.

In the same respect, Rav Kook wrote in his *Shabbat Ha'aretz*, "What the *Shabbat* achieves in its impact on the individual, the *shemittah* achieves in its impact on the nation as a whole. . . . During the year the character of the nation manifests itself." The soul of the individual, that of the nation, and even that of the land function together in realizing the full potential of the longing and yearning that emanates from the depths of their holiness. It is only then that the chosen people in a chosen land blend in the harmony of a *Shabbat* to *HaShem*.

A PROPHECY OF *GEULAH*

Two personalities from two distinct historical periods and cultures, living sixteen hundred years apart, used strikingly similar language to describe *Eretz Yisrael*. The first wrote, "The further we went, the hotter the sun got and the more rocky and bare, repulsive and dreary the landscape became. . . . There was hardly a tree or shrub anywhere . . . desolate country whose soil is rich enough, but is given over wholly to weeds—a silent mournful expanse . . . desolation is here that not even imagination can grace." The year was 1867 and the writer, Mark Twain. "Of all the lands that are for dismal scenery," Mark Twain writes, "I think Palestine must be the prince. It sits in sackcloth and ashes. . . . it is a hopeless, dreary, heartbroken land."

In using the expression "heartbroken" and not "heartbreaking," Mark Twain ingeniously sensed the sentiment expressed centuries earlier in our sources—statements that endow the Land of Israel with a living personality of its own. Rabbi Yehudah, in *Pirkei D'Rabbi Eliezer* 34, declared, "From the day when the Temple was destroyed, the Land of Israel is *broken down*. . . . like a man who is sick and has no power to stand, so is the land broken down and is without power to yield her fruits."

From the time the Jews were driven from *Eretz Yisrael*, the land suffered utter desolation. It became a dismal wasteland, occupied and abused. In one of the harshest biblical admonitions, *HaShem* warns that if we do not follow His ways, "I will lay your cities in ruin. I will make the land desolate so that even your enemies who settle it will be appalled" (Leviticus 26:31–32). The Rabbis in the *Sifrah* saw a positive note in this dreadful prophecy. They understood that the land would be so devastated that no one would want it afterward. And so it would be till the beginning of the redemption.

One sign the Rabbis give that the *geulah* is arriving is that the trees in the land bear fruit (Tractate *Sanhedrin* 98). As Rashi states, "When the Land of Israel will clearly bear fruit, then the Redemption is near, and you have no clearer indication of the Redemption."

For centuries the land lay barren and wasted, and the people who conquered it over the centuries allowed it to remain desolate. Political rhetoric and ideological debate often blurs the fact that up till *Aliyah Aleph* "Palestine" was a neglected piece of land in the Ottoman Empire, with malaria-infested swamps and with desert and rocks that supported only meager vegetation—a far cry from a land flowing with milk and honey. The famed archaeologist Robinson records that in 1838 only two palm trees stood in Jericho, a city known in the Torah as *Ir Hatemarim*—the City of Palm Trees. Twenty years later, another scholar visited Jericho and reported that there were no palm trees at all.

Only after two lovers—the land and the people—came together did we see the land bloom. We never abandoned the land, and the land never abandoned the Jewish people. Many conquered and occupied the land, but not one made anything of the land, built the country, or shaped a nation. The land simply did not respond to them. It waited, as the Torah revealed, for its people to return.

The land is now fertile; the earth bears vegetation; the trees bear fruit. Can the Redemption be far behind?

CREATION, *SHABBAT*, AND *SHEMITTAH*

"My ***Shabbatot*** you shall observe and My sanctuary you shall revere; I am *HaShem*" (Leviticus 26:2).

The use of the plural for *Shabbat* beckons interpretation. To which *Shabbat* is the text referring when it speaks of the *Shabbat* of *Shemittah?* In exploring the notion of *Shabbat* in the Torah we discover three types of *Shabbat*—three concepts and directions that are alluded to in the plural expression *Shabbatot*. The first *Shabbat* is ***Shabbat Bereishit***, the *Shabbat* of *HaShem* and creation. It is the *Shabbat* of the past and, from our vantage point, is totally retrospective. Then there is the ***Shabbat of shamor v'zachor***, the *Shabbat* of man and the sanctity of time. Including the *chaggim*, this *Shabbat* commemorates the history of *HaShem*'s encounter with man and speaks of the historic dynamics that flow from our relationship to *HaShem*; within it, we move from the past to the present. Then there is the ***Shemittah* and *Yovel***, the *Shabbat* that blends creation and earth, man and history, time and place, belief and trust, in a movement that is future oriented. It is a *Shabbat* that, according to the Ramban (Levitucus 25:2), points to the "End of Days," the messianic dream and the fulfillment of **the day that is completely *Shabbat***. "My *Shabbatot* you shall observe," therefore, becomes the ultimate direction for mankind—to discover, by observing *Shabbatot*, the prophetic vision of the great *Shabbat* of peace and harmony, as individuals and as a nation.

Rabbi Dovid Simpson

Young Israel of Kingsbay, New York

Behar. What's in a name? Whether or not we think a name, in and of itself, has any significance, when we speak of the *parshiyot hatorah*, surely there are relevant and meaningful lessons to be learned.

The names of the *parshiyot* are an integral part of Torah. We see this first from the fact that they are mentioned and quoted extensively in all of halachic literature, and, second, *Klal Yisrael*—including *Gedolei Yisrael*—have used them for many centuries. As such, the names by which we identify each *sedrah* have entered the category of a *minhag Yisrael*, of which the Tosafot in *Menochot* 20b states, "The custom of our ancestors is [part of] Torah."

The name of this week's *parshah, Behar* (on the mountain), is a difficult one to understand. The Torah begins by stating that the Almighty spoke to Moshe *Behar Sinai*—on a *specific* mountain, namely, Mount Sinai, the mountain upon which the Torah was given to *Klal Yisrael*, and not just *Behar*—"on *a* mountain." If the idea in the name of this *parshah* is to emphasize Mount Sinai, the *parshah* should have been named *Sinai* or, at the very least, *Behar Sinai*.

To be sure, we do find one notable exception to the custom. The Rambam (*Ahavah, Seder Tefillot*), in listing the order of *parshiyot* and their *Haftarot*, uses the title *Behar Sinai*. However, the majority of texts and sources uses only the title *Behar* for this *parshah*.

Furthermore, the Talmud (*Sotah* 5a) states that *HaShem* chose Sinai over all the other mountains upon which to give the Torah to *Klal Yisrael* because of its humility. Sinai did not seek honor and glory but, rather, shied away from being the choice for *Matan Torah*, and was subsequently chosen precisely for this reason. *Behar* alone doesn't make the point.

As we examine this *Gemara*, another question becomes obvious. If Sinai was chosen for the site of *Matan Torah* because it demonstrated the important trait of humility, why didn't the Almighty choose a more appropriate place for which to illustrate and emphasize this point, such as the valley or flatland?

In trying to understand this, let us first take a closer look at the very name *Har Sinai*. We can suggest that *Har* and *Sinai* represent two distinct, even opposite, character traits in human nature. *Har*, a mountain, symbolizes greatness and self-assertion. *Sinai*, on the other hand, symbolizes humility and self-effacement; as the Ramban (*Devarim* 1:6) explains, the name *Sinai* is derived from the word *sneh*, "bramble," the lowest of all trees in the world, indicating humility.

The reason for this paradox is to teach us that it is necessary for a Jew to possess both elements—humility *and* pride. There are times that we need humility, and pride would be a fault; and there are times that we need pride, and to behave humbly would be a fault.

Throughout the Torah, in passages dealing with the character traits that Jews should attempt to develop, it is humility that is praised and encouraged. The *Mishnah* (*Avot* 4:4) states, "Be of an exceedingly humble spirit," and, in many places, the Talmud equates pride with idolatry. However, in regard to *HaShem* and the observance of His holy Torah, a Jew must possess a measure of self-esteem and pride—albeit the type of pride that should be utilized for the sake of Heaven. This is the type of pride that is needed in order to enable one stoutly to face spiritual trials and challenges. The *Mishnah* (ibid., 5:20) charges us, "Be bold as a leopard . . . and strong as a lion in the service of *HaShem*." The Remah, in his first gloss on the *Shulchan Aruch*, instructs: "Do not be ashamed before the scoffers in your service of *HaShem*," and in *Divrei Hayomim II* (17:6) we find, "He prided himself in the services of *HaShem*."

Perhaps it is only for this reason that this week's *parshah* is called only *Behar*, not *Sinai* or *Behar Sinai*, for this week's *sedrah* deals with the *mitzvot* of *shemittah* as well as other *mitzvot* given to us on Mount Sinai. When fulfilling *mitzvot*—especially those that require a significant measure of *emunat HaShem*, belief in God—the *Behar* must be emphasized. There is no room for weakness or self-effacement. We must have true "Jewish Pride" in the fact that we are the *Am Segulah* and *Am Hanivchar*.

In this vein, the Baal Shem Tov (quoted in *Toldot Yaakov Yosef*) explains that, although humility is an indispensable Jewish trademark, it must nevertheless be accompanied by some pride and satisfaction from the fact that the Torah one learns and the *mitzvot* one performs make a positive and indelible impact on the physical world. This satisfaction will serve as an incentive for further good deeds.

There is another lesson to be learned from *Behar Sinai*. During these weeks, we are studying *Pirkei Avot*, the *Ethics of the Fathers*. The first *Mishnah* begins by tracing the *Mesorah*, the origins of Torah, and states, "Moshe received the Torah from Sinai." The commentator Rav Ovadia Bartenura wonders why specifically the *Mishnah* in *Avot* finds it necessary to trace the *mesorah* and indicate that Torah was given at Sinai, a point that is not mentioned in any other *Mishnah*. The Bartenura explains that *Avot* is unlike any other tractate of the *Mishnah* because it deals exclusively with *mussar* and *midot*, ethical conduct. The Gentiles, however, also have moral codes, and we must therefore realize that our teachings of *mussar* originate at "Sinai" and are not the product of human perception.

From this perspective, *Behar* (a mountain), which is of a tangible essence, represents obvious and substantial human logic that can be "felt" and appreciated. *Sinai* represents that which we accept with humility and subservience, God's will. "*Behar*-Sinai" would suggest that there must be a feeling of *Sinai*—humility and reverence for God's will—permeating even those *mitzvot* that are *Behar*, common-sense *mitzvot* that human logic would dictate, such as the laws of ethics.

We must realize that it is the Almighty Who decides what is ethical and moral and what is not. In *Bereishit* (18:13), after notifying Avraham and Sarah about the upcoming birth of Yitzchak, *HaShem* told Avraham of Sarah's saying, "Shall I in truth bear a child though I [Sarah] have aged?" Whereas, in truth, Sarah had actually said ". . . and my husband [Avraham] is old." Do we have any difficulty with the fact that the Almighty changed the truth—although one can argue that this seems "unethical"? No! God saw it fit to do so for the sake of peace between husband and wife, and that makes it ethical.

Conversely, Torah teaches us that it would be foolish to think of actions that some in the secular world consider "compassionate," such as euthanasia ("mercy" killing), as true kindness and compassion.

Concerning the laws of ethics—as with the laws in the entire Torah, it is only God, in His infinite wisdom, as He dictated in the Torah, who can decide what is truly ethical and moral.

One last thought. This week, we celebrated *Pesach Sheini* (thirty days after the beginning of the *Pesach* sacrifice—an opportunity for those who were spiritually unclean or far from the temple on that day—to bring the sacrifice they missed). During the holiday of Pesach we are forbidden to enjoy even the smallest amount of *chametz*, it is *assur b'mashehu*. On *Pesach Sheini*, however, we eat *matzah* together with the *chametz*, as the Talmud (*Pesachim* 93b) states: On *Pesach Sheini*, one has bread and matzah with him in the house. The words of our Sages are replete with the theme that *chametz*, leaven (which "rises") represents pride and arrogance, whereas *matzah*, "the bread of affliction," symbolizes ultimate humility. On Pesach, in order to remedy the negative effect that Mitzrayim had on *Klal Yisrael*, it is necessary to train ourselves in the extreme: not one crumb of *chametz*, not one iota of pride. For eight days we refine our character and eat only *matzah*, impressing upon our hearts and minds the importance of humility. Extreme measures are sometimes necessary; as the Rambam in *Hilchot Deiot* explains, that when one suffers from an extreme negative character trait, the only way to remedy it is by behaving in the extreme opposite fashion.

On *Pesach Sheini*, however, as a result of the Pesach observance followed by a month of refinement through *sefirat ha'omer*, we are capable of striking the perfect balance: The *chametz* and the *matzah*—that is, pride and humility—coexist peacefully, each, in fact, complementing the other. Once again, an illustration of the aforementioned idea of *Behar Sinai*.

Chazal often advise that we travel along the *shvil hazahav*, literally the "golden path," meaning that we should seek to find a synthesis in all our ways, reconciling apparent contradictions. At the time of our redemption, this will be the ultimate state of worldly perfection, when everything will naturally coexist in harmony. The Prophet Yeshaiah (11:6) prophesies, "The wolf will dwell with the sheep and the leopard will graze with the kid." May we merit to see these days very soon.

❖ CHAPTER 38 ❖

Bechukotai

Rabbi Nachman Cohen

Young Israel Ohab Zedek of North Riverdale/Yonkers, New York

The Talmud (*Megillah* 30b) states: Ezra decreed that the *berakhot* and *kelalot* (blessings and curses in *Bechukotei*) be read before Rosh Hashanah and Shavuot, so that the year ended with its curses. The *Gemara* goes on to explain that Shavuot is also considered a Rosh Hashanah.

Exodus (24:7) reports, "And Moshe took the book of the covenant (*Sefer Habrit*) and read it to the nation." Rav Yishmael asserts that the *Sefer Habrit* was the portion of the Torah beginning with *Behar* and ending after the *tochachah* (the admonishments in *Bechukotai*). This is because *Behar* is the only *sedrah* in the Torah that begins with the words, *Vayedaber . . . behar Sinai* (God spoke to Moshe *on Mount Sinai*). These words indicate that it was this *parshah* that was read before Revelation.

This section, referred to as "*Sefer HaBrit*," which might be thought of as God's *tennaim* (conditions of marriage) with Israel, is encapsulated in Exodus 19:5 as follows: "And now, if you listen to My voice, and heed My covenant, then you shall be special to Me from all of the nations, for the land is Mine."

Mekhilta explains that *briti* ("My covenant") refers to *Sefer HaBrit*; while *ki li ha'aretz* ("for the land is Mine") hints at the essence of *parshat Behar*. The main *mitzvah* in *Behar* is that the *shemittah* (sabbatical) year be observed. At the root of the *mitzvah* of leaving one's field fallow is the belief that the Earth belongs to the Lord, and that all man's efforts are successful only if this is God's desire.

Mekhilta explains the phrase, *veheyitem li* ("and you shall be to Me") as meaning, "all your attention shall focus upon Me"—that is, you must be involved in the Torah and not in other pursuits. This notion is the essence of *Bechukotai*.

IS THIS WHAT YOU TELL YOUR BRIDE BEFORE THE MARRIAGE?

This explanation is not without its difficulty. A study of *Behar/Bechukotai* reveals that, aside from the statement of positive rewards which will accompany compliance, the Torah is very explicit about the punishments for transgression. If a person does not observe *shemittah,* the progression of the laws stated in *Behar* foretells what will befall him. If he does not repent, he will be forced to sell his chattel and homestead, borrow at high interest rates, and, finally, sell himself into bondage. In brief, *Behar,* which is written in the singular, stipulates that for violating the principle of "the Earth is the Lord's," a person will, eventually, go into personal exile. *Bechukotai,* which is written in plural, details the tragedies that will befall those who cease Torah study and observance. Here, too, the ultimate punishment is exile.

Given that these *parshiyot* were recited to *Klal Yisrael* before Revelation, one must wonder why the Almighty found it necessary, wise, and/or prudent explicitly to state all the negatives. We must seek to understand the motivation for this strong admonition at the moment that Israel stood at the foot of Mount Sinai and willingly called out, "we will observe," before "we will understand."

THE PRECIPITANT WAS THEIR ACTIONS BETWEEN PESACH AND REVELATION

The *Sefer HaBrit* must not be seen as a theoretical set of conditions. Rather, the *Sefer HaBrit* was in direct response to the actions of Israel from the time they left *Yam Suf* (Red Sea). In order to show this correspondence, we first need to examine the contents of *Bechukotai* more closely.

In the *Bechukotai* section of the *Sefer HaBrit,* the Torah traces the seven steps of those who cease to study Torah. The progression is as follows (see Rashi):

1. Diligent study ceases
2. *Mitzvot* are no longer fulfilled
3. Animosity is developed against those who perform *mitzvot*
4. The Rabbis are detested
5. Attempts are made to prevent others from performing *mitzvot*
6. Denial of the authenticity of *mitzvot*
7. Denial of the existence of God

The *parshah* then goes on to enumerate the catastrophes that will befall the nation if it does not repent. After each admonition, God says, "If you simply consider what has befallen you thus far as happenstance (*keri*), then I will heap tragedy upon you sevenfold."

We are now ready to show the correlation between the *Sefer HaBrit* and the occurrences before the nation of Israel reached Mount Sinai.

ISRAEL HAD DEGENERATED THROUGH THE SEVEN LEVELS

Most people believe that the first major sin that *Klal Yisrael* committed after they left Egypt was that of the golden calf. In fact, a careful reading of *parshat Beshalach* shows that they degenerated, step by step, in accordance with the pattern outlined in *Bechukotai*, starting right after they crossed the Red Sea.

Immediately after the Jews sang *az yashir*, the Torah relates, *vayas Moshe et ha'am* ("Moshe caused the nation to journey from there," Exodus 15:22). *Keli Yakar* explains that Moshe had to force the Jews to leave *Yam Suf*. Despite their knowing that they would receive the Torah as soon as they reached Mount Sinai, they, nevertheless, could not tear themselves away from the Egyptian spoils. Thus, **they were not interested in learning Torah.**

In Marah they fell to the second level—**they did not observe *mitzvot***. They were instructed by Moshe that "no man shall leave it (the *man*) until morning." (Exodus 16:19) However, in the very next verse we are told, "and they did not listen to Moshe, and people left it over. . . ." Not only did they transgress, but they **detested others who observed**. The sinners tried to weaken the conviction of other Israelites by showing that Moshe's predictions were false. Thus, on Friday night they put out pieces of *man* in order to disprove Moshe's pronouncement that no *man* would remain on *Shabbat* morning. It is well known that their plot failed because the birds ate up their *man*.

In Refidim they fell one more degree—**they showed their contempt for Moshe**. So upset were they with Moshe that they wanted to kill him. **They renounced the one *mitzvah*** they were given—that is, going to Israel—saying, "Why have you taken us from Egypt to die in the desert," (Exodus 17:3) and they eventually **renounced God**, proclaiming, "Is God among us or not?" (Exodus 17:7).

The consequence of this spiritual descent is found immediately in the next event—the war of Amalek. In *Ki Tetzeh* the Torah ascribes the reason for Amalek's coming as, *asher korcha baderekh*. (Deuteronomy 25:18) Rashi interprets *korcha* to mean "happenstance"—that is, Amalek is the nation that made you feel that all that befell you was happenstance.

THE *SEFER HABRIT* WAS READ AGAINST THIS BACKGROUND

Given the above occurrences, it is no wonder that God insisted upon inserting all the conditions listed in *Behar-Bechukotai* in the *Sefer HaBrit* (that which was read before Revelation). Through the *Sefer HaBrit*, the Almighty pointed out to Israel that it was the sins of the previous six weeks that brought Amalek and that the attack by Amalek was not just *keri* (happenstance).

LESSON FOR SHAVUOT

With the approach of Shavuot, we must be mindful of the two conditions necessary for our union with the Almighty:

1. That God is in complete control of the economics of the world; He determines mankind's sustenance
2. That we must dedicate ourselves to Torah study

Shavuot encompasses both of these themes. It is known as both *Chag Habikurim* (the Festival of First Fruits) and *Zeman Matan Torateinu* (the time of Revelation).

Every year, the time-properties of a particular time period are rekindled. Ezra decreed that we read *Behar-Bechukotai* during this part of the year to remind us of what had occurred during this part of the year in the past. If we do *teshuvah*, then *tichleh shanah vekileloteha* ("let the year and its curses end") will truly be fulfilled.

Let us hope and pray that through our *teshuvah* we can reverse the conditions of the days of mourning and have them become days of joy, to the extent that *Mashiach* will come and we will be ushered into *Eretz Yisrael*.

Rabbi Meyer Fendel

Rabbi Emeritus of Young Israel of West Hempstead, New York
Executive Member, Council of Young Israel Rabbis in Israel

In the *sedrah* of *Bechukotai*, in the midst of the sea of terrible tidings of the *tochachah*, we find an island of hope and comfort: "I will bring desolation upon the Land, and your enemies who dwell therein will be desolate as well" (Leviticus 26:32). Rashi there comments, "This is good tidings for Israel, that her enemies will not find happiness in the Land, and she will remain forever barren from her inhabitants."

The question that may be asked is, how will Israel benefit if her enemies will also be unable to inhabit the Land? Let us look at the explanation of Ramban, who concurs with Rashi, but adds something more: "This is also a great proof and promise, for in the whole inhabited world, one cannot find such a goodly Land that was [once] inhabited and yet is as ruined as she is today, for since the time that we left her, she has not accepted any nation or people, and though they all try to settle her, their efforts are in vain."

The Ramban is telling us that, in effect, the Land "went into *galut*" together with the people: she could not produce; she could not give forth its blessings to strangers on her soil. Herein lies the good tiding in which *Chazal* found a source of hope: the Land would never produce for *strangers*—but for *Klal Yisrael* returning home, she would! Eretz Yisrael lay dormant for two thousand years, as it were, simply because she was awaiting the return of her children.

Paradoxically, the Land was *so* barren and *so* desolate that one could not fail to see this as a fulfillment of the biblical *tochachah* "I will lay waste to the Land." In the very midst of the rebuke, *Chazal* saw the hope and dream of the Return: The Land will wait and remain desolate, as a sign of both the sins of Israel and its guaranteed return.

The *Gemara* in *Sanhedrin* (98a) vividly captures this vision and promise in the extraordinary words of the Prophet Yechezkel: "Therefore shall you prophesize regarding the Land of Israel, and say to the mountains and the valleys . . . you, the mountains of Israel, shall sprout forth your branches, and your fruit shall blossom, for my people Israel, for they are coming." Commenting on this verse, the Gemara cites the words of Rabbi Abba: "There can be no more manifest sign of Redemption than this [the physical blossoming of the Land]."

Rav Kook, *zt"l*, had this vision of Yechezkel and the prophetic words of Rabbi Abba before his eyes when he wrote so stirringly of the events of his day: "Yes, the beginning of the Redemption is certainly appearing before us. Indeed, this process did not begin today, but from the time that the mountains of Israel began to shoot forth their branches and to yield their fruit to the nation of Israel coming home" (Letters 545). In the new rebirth of Palestine, in the deserts and swamps turned into fertile fields producing magnificent fruit, he saw the beginning of the *atchalta d'geulah*, the beginning of the Redemption. There was no greater sign than this that, indeed, the Land was preparing to welcome home her returning children. As Rashi comments there so poignantly, "When the Land of Israel will give forth her bounty, then the Redemption will be at hand."

In the great *sefer em habanim se'meicha*, May the Lord Revenge His Death, by Rav Yissachar Teichtal, we find a fascinating thought on this theme. On page 102, the revered author quotes the *Gemara* in *Megillah* (17b): "Why did the Men of the Great Assembly, when formulating the *Shmoneh Esrei* prayer, place the blessing of the Ingathering of the Exiles after the blessing of the Land? Because such will be the order of events in the days preceding the Messiah: first the Land will give forth her bounty, and then the Ingathering will take place." This would be the sign that the Land is beckoning our return: The spreading of her warm green carpet welcoming our homecoming. And in fact, the Ingathering of the Exiles has taken place in front of our eyes, beginning a half-century ago, and gaining steam ever since.

However, we must ask ourselves this question: Is this process continuing in our time, even now? Or do we detect a slowing down, even a reversal, of the glorious events of the establishment of the State, the Six Day War, and the Reunification of Jerusalem, Eternal City? True, millions of Jews have come home in the last few decades, and over a half-million from the former USSR in the last four years alone; but recent events cause us to wonder: Somewhere along the road to Redemption, could we have taken a wrong turn?

Rav Kook, *zt"l*, recognized that there would be periods of great ups and downs throughout the *geulah*: "We have a tradition in the Land of Israel and among the People of Israel during the time that part of the Nation will begin to arouse themselves to return."

He quoted the following passage in the Jerusalem Talmud (*Berchot* 4): "Rav Chiya and Rabbi Shimon ben Chalafta were walking before daybreak in the valley of Arbel when they saw the first rays of the sun straining to break through the pitch-black darkness. Said Rav Chiya, 'So will be the *geulah* process—at the outset it proceeds ever so slowly, and gets stronger as it continues." Rav Kook explained that the sunrise betrays the secrets of our Redemption. It is to be a slow, gradual process, sometimes appearing bright and filled with hope and, at other times, dark and gloomy. Just as the sun often appears about to break through, only to recede disappointingly into the mist, so, too, we sometimes appear to be on the brink of Redemption, only to veer off course with the End nowhere in sight.

The *geulah* itself is, of course, guaranteed; the *course* of the *geulah*, however, is not automatic or irreversible. Our actions play a major role: we can speed it up or, *chas veshalom*, we can cause it to come to a grinding halt. Rav Kook felt it imperative for every Jew to realize his place in the process and to attempt to do all in his power to help it along. He was once confronted by one of his many detractors who did not understand the critical role that *Klal Yisrael* plays in aiding the *geulah* process. We say every day in *birkat hamazon*, "The All-Merciful will lead us upright to our Land." Rav Kook was asked; so who are we to "help" the All-Merciful along with His job? Rav Kook countered immediately that we also say, "The All-Merciful should help us earn an honorable living"—yet no one hesitates to try with all his might to "help" the All-Merciful along with *that* job! Just as there must be *hishtadlot* (major efforts) on our part in that area, so, too, does *HaShem* ask for our participation in the *geulah* process.

Our generation has not yet lived up to the challenge that *HaShem* has placed before us. We have failed, so far, to develop a deep-seated desire to build, defend, and return to the Land. The Kuzari quotes the *pasuk* in *Tehillim* Psalms 102:14 that reads, "You will arise and show mercy upon Zion, for it is time to favor her, the set time has come." When is this time? the Kuzari asks, and explains that the answer is found in the next verse: "When thy servants hold her stones dear, and cherish her very dust." When we show that *Eretz Yisrael* is important to us, the ball of *geulah* begins rolling—but our apathy, God forbid, accomplishes the opposite.

It would be a terrible crime against our *emunah* (faith) if we were to disregard the cataclysmic events of our time because of what appears to be a temporary decline. How tragically ironic it would be if the turning of part of the nation's back on the holiness of the Land were to cause the rest of us to do the same thing! How can we fail to see that *Eretz Yisrael*, which did not give solace to strangers throughout its long millennia of desolation, opened itself up in our generation to millions of our brethren from all over the world? This, a phenomenon that defies rational explanation, comes upon the heels of the reunification of Jerusalem, the reclaiming of the holy biblical cities of Chevron and Beit El, and adjoining areas, and nothing less than the establishment of the first sovereign Jewish state in over nineteen hundred years! Sometimes we forget that all this has happened in our very own generation—"The recipient of a miracle does not always recognize the miracle." We must constantly remind ourselves of what *HaShem* has shown us and respond in kind.

Today, more than ever, Diaspora Jewry must heed the call of Jewish history and respond to the miracles that *HaShem* has wrought for us. Many Jews have come over the past decades to build and contribute to a vibrant Torah society in *Eretz Yisrael*; but it is not enough! Let it not be said that as a direct result of the failure of the masses of Jews to respond to these extraordinary times, this generation missed the chance for Redemption! It is up to us.

"Speak to the Jewish people and they should proceed." (Exodus 14:15)

Chazak Chazak Venitchazek!

PART FOUR

Numbers

❖ CHAPTER 39 ❖

Bamidbar

Rabbi Daniel Yormark

Young Israel of Eltingville, New York

The Jewish people stand at Mount Sinai and, among the awesome sights they witness, they perceive myriads of angels with *degalim* (banners), surrounding the *Shechinah*. Upon seeing this, the *Bnai Yisrael* express a desire for *degalim* of their own, whereupon *Hakadosh baruch Hu* grants their request and instructs Moshe Rabbeinu to arrange the *degalim* as they desire (*Midrash Rabbah* 2:3).

Evidently, the *degalim* possess great significance and importance. As we are told in the *parshah*, the setting of the *degalim* was such that three tribes camped on each side of the *mishkan* with the *aron* (ark) in the center. In so doing, the encampment took on the appearance of a unit. Even multitudes can become one by means of formation. That the concept of oneness is a basic ingredient in *Klal Yisrael* has its roots at *Har Sinai*. As we learned in *parshat Yitro*, "and there Israel encamped before the mount" (Exodus 19:2); according to Rashi, the encampment preceding the giving of the Torah was unique in the feeling of unity that prevailed.

Acceptance of the Torah is based on acceptance of God as King. For, in order to obligate oneself to adhere to the commandments, one must first accept and recognize the authority of the commander. And, as the Torah explicitly states, "And there was a king in Yeshurun, when the heads of the people were gathered, all the tribes of Israel together" (Deuteronomy 33:5). Rashi comments, "When is *HaShem* King? When there is peace and harmony among the Jewish people." To accept *HaShem echad* (one God), there must be an *am echad* (one nation).

More. At *Matan Torah*, the *Bnei Yisrael* climbed the spiritual ladder and achieved the quintessence of the human being: for man was fashioned in the mirror image of the Creator, *tselem Elohim*, and his goal and purpose in life is to emulate his Maker. In order to reflect *HaShem echad* (one God), *Klal Yisrael* needed to attain cohesiveness as an *am echad* (one nation).

The oneness that the Torah fosters actually encompasses more than just the Jewish people. This becomes apparent by means of the following illustration. In order to build a house, a person gathers all the supplies which he will need. He procures brick and cement, and lumber and nails. Upon completing the structure, he is anxious to show the fruits of his labor to his friend. When shown the new house, the friend remarks, "This is really something. I see thousands of bricks, approximately a ton of cement, hundreds of beams, and countless nails." The builder responds, "You have missed the point. True, originally I had large amounts of various materials. However, now that the work is completed and the house is ready to be inhabited, the bricks and beams take on new meaning. They are all joined together, united in purpose, to provide a home, a shelter for the inhabitants."

Similarly, until the giving of the Torah, there were many unrelated, independent parts of creation. With *Matan Torah,* however, a dramatic and sweeping change took place. For, as our Sages tell us, the entire universe was brought into existence only for the Torah. *Bereishit,* "in the beginning," is explained to mean, "for the sake of *Bereishit,*" which refers to Torah, "God created heaven and earth." Also, with regard to "on *the* sixth day" (in the verse "And it was evening and it was morning, the sixth day"), Rashi quotes the *midrash* that states that the entire creation was hanging in the balance until the sixth day of Sivan (Shavuot) to see if the Jewish people would accept the Torah. With the arrival of Torah, the goal, purpose, and intention of creation was realized. All became one. Everything joined together to play some role in facilitating the observance and recognition of Torah.

Yet a further illustration of Torah as a unifying force is mentioned in the *parshah.* We read, "And these are the children of Aharon and Moshe on the day *HaShem* spoke to Moshe on Mount Sinai" (Numbers 1:3). The next verse proceeds to mention only the children of Aharon. Rashi explains that Aharon's children are to be considered as Moshe's, in line with the principle that teaching Torah to the child of one's friend is considered tantamount to giving birth to him.

The Ramban, in the beginning of *Parshat Terumah,* points out that the *Mishkan,* in a sense, is a continuum of the revelation at Sinai. The glorious public display of the *Shechinah* at Sinai continued in a relatively reserved manner in the *Mishkan.* The Ramban draws parallels and demonstrates the similarities between the revelation at Sinai and the *Mishkan.* Concerning *Maamad Har Sinai,* the Torah states, "Behold, God has shown us His glory and His greatness." Corresponding to this, we are told in reference to the *Mishkan,* "and the glory of God filled the *Mishkan*" (Exodus 40:34,35). This verse occurs twice in *Parshat Pekudei,* once to reflect His glory and a second time for His greatness. Just as, at Sinai, "His words you heard emanating from the fire" (Deuteronomy 4:36), so, too, in the *Mishkan* (Numbers 7:89), ". . . he heard the voice speaking to him . . . from between the two Cherubim. . . ." The Cherubim were made of gold to have an appearance similar to fire. The *Bnai Yisrael* understood the need to maintain the unity of Sinai and to carry it over throughout their journey in the wilderness as they camped around the *Mishkan*. Indeed, it was at Sinai that they saw the angels utilizing the *degalim* formation and then and there yearned for the same to preserve the Sinai experience for the duration of their stay in the desert.

One difficulty remains. The *Bnai Yisrael* desired the *degalim* of *Matan Torah* but were not granted them until the second year. Why? Rabbi Yaakov Kaminetzky, *zt"l*, offers a profound solution to this query. He explains that each of the twelve tribes possessed an inherent uniqueness that distinguished it from all the others. This is evident from the individualized blessings (see Genesis 49:1–28; Deuteronomy 33:1–29) that were bestowed upon them by Yaakov *Avinu* and Moshe Rabbeinu. Had each tribe been given its own banner immediately, the differences would have been emphasized and magnified. However, the *Mishkan* (which was erected before the *degalim* would be granted), situated in the center of the camp, brought with it a message that there was one address to which all of the tribes directed their attention. It was the place where everyone came together and the *avodah* (service) was performed on behalf of the entire nation.

As we approach Shavuot and prepare for a reacceptance of the Torah, let us recognize the need for a renewed sense of understanding and cohesiveness among our people. Uniting under the banner of Torah, we will relive the beautiful lyrics of the *Shabbat* song: Zemirot for the Sabbath Day, "Yom Shabbason," 3rd stanza: "And they entered into the covenant together as one, 'We shall do and we shall adhere,' they said as one, and they proclaimed 'God is One,'" thereby meriting to be worthy of the accolade. Divrei HaYomim (I 17:21), "Who is comparable to Your people Israel—one nation on earth!"

Rabbi Yosef Goldberg

Young Israel of Wavecrest/ Bayswater, New York

According to Ramban, *Chumash Bereishit* is, in essence, the story of the *Avot*—the patriarchs and matriarchs of the Jewish people—culminating in the descent of Yaakov and his sons to Mitzrayim. The purpose of *Chumash Bereishit* is to explain the selection of the *Avot* by the Creator and, thereby, to justify the right of their descendants to the Land of Israel. Again, according to Ramban, *Chumash Shemot* is the story of the servitude of *Bnei Yisrael* in, and their subsequent redemption from, Mitzrayim. *Chumash Shemmot* ends with the greatest redemption of all—the residing of the *Shechinah*—the spirit of God—in the midst of *Bnei Yisrael. Chumash Vayikra* is *Torat Kohanim*—the book of sacrificial law and other laws pertaining mostly to *kohanim*. The essence of *Chumash Vayikra* is the attainment of *kedushah*—sanctity—resulting in a closeness to the Creator. The fifth book of the Torah, *Chumash Devarim*, is the *Mishnah Torah*—a review of the Torah and a preparation for both the death of Moshe Rabbeinu and the imminent entry of *Bnei Yisrael* into the promised Land of Israel

The essence of *Chumash Bamidbar* is harder to define. The Netziv (Rav Naftali Tzvi Yehudah Berlin, nineteenth-century *Rosh Yeshivah* of Volozhin), in his commentary to the Torah, *Haamek Davar*, explains that *Bamidbar* is a transitional *sefer* that marks the beginning of the transition from the supernatural and openly manifested Divine Providence of the wilderness existence, to the seemingly more natural and concealed Divine Providence of life in the Land of Israel.

I would like to offer a different perspective on *Sefer Bamidbar* based on an analysis of several *mitzvot* that are introduced in this *chumash*. The word *midbar* here means a wilderness. A wilderness is an area that is savage and untamed. It is overspread with rustic, undomesticated flora and fauna. Its denizens run savage and wild, mostly hidden from the eyes of passersby. Primitive and feral impulses dominate such a place. In this *midbar* we find the *Bnei Yisrael* approximately one year after their exodus from *Mitzrayim*, and slightly less than a year after their participation in the greatest moment in human history—the giving of the Torah. Now they are to be counted and then molded from what was a horde of ex-slaves into a camp whose hub is the holy *Mishkan*, and whose members march and rest in a carefully defined and disciplined fashion.

It is in this wilderness that we find the *Bnei Yisrael* constantly succumbing to their worst and wildest impulses—cowardice, insecurity, lust, jealousy, distrust of Moshe and Aharon, and distrust of (*lhavdil*) *HaShem* Himself. We find the *sefer* running in an almost staccato pace from the tragedy of the *meraglim* (spies) to the revolt of Korach to the debauchery at Baal Peor. After that debacle, we find a second command to count the *Bnei Yisrael*. In that second command for a census lies, in my opinion, the crux of *Chumash Bamidbar*—that in the wilderness of life there is a second chance for a new beginning even after great and tragic failure.

The initial passages of *Chumash Bamidbar* deal with the first census, the arrangement of the camp, the consecration of the *Leviim*, and the specialized tasks of the various Levitical families during the transport of the *Mishkan*. There are no *mitzvot* that apply to future generations in *Parshat Bamidbar*. In the second *parshah*, *Parshat Naso*, the first two *mitzvot* that apply to future generations still pertain to the theme of the sanctity of the *Mikdash* within a holy camp.

The first *mitzvah* mentioned that departs from the theme of the disciplined environment is the *mitzvah* of *teshuvah* with confession (*viduy*). This, according to the Rambam in *Sefer Hamitzvot*, is the quintessential *mitzvah* of *teshuvah*. It appears to me that *Chumash Bamidbar* is the *sefer* that deals with life at its worst moments. When even the holy and disciplined environment of the Torah society is not sufficient to stifle the wild and primitive impulses of the *yetzer hara*, when life breaks down into the "wilderness" existence, when one has succumbed to the most base and demeaning human impulses—then the strategies and insights of *Chumash Bamidbar* must be used, the first being *teshuvah*.

The insights of *Bamidbar* involve two themes: (a) how to recover from human failure, and (b) how to attain new spiritual heights. Therefore, immediately after the *mitzvah* of *teshuvah*, we have two extraordinary *mitzvot*: *sotah* and *nazir*. With the *mitzvah* of *sotah*, a woman who has violated her husband's warnings against fraternizing with other men is given an opportunity to cleanse herself of suspicion and to begin life anew with a fresh and closer relationship with her husband. With the *mitzvah* of *nazir* the ordinary man or woman is given the opportunity to attain a new level of sanctity.

It should not be surprising to us that in the book of second chances we find the *mitzvah* of *Pesach sheini*, with its second chance to do the precious *mitzvah* of *korban Pesach* for one who was unclean or far from the *Mikdash* in the month of Nisan.

Nor should it be a surprise to us that we find in this *sefer* the *mitzvot* of *challah* and *parah adumah*. With *challah*, grain that has already been fully tithed and is now totally *chulin* (non-holy) is given a second chance for the attainment of *kedushah* by the mixing of its flour with water, a process that creates the obligation to take *challah*. With the *parah adumah*, the reattainment of purity after defilement with the dead is made possible.

The *mitzvah* of *tzitzit* fits well into *Chumash Bamidbar*. Man's garb is one of the symbols that separate him from the animals. With the *mitzvah* of *tzitzit*, the Torah recognizes the fact that when one is beset upon by the call of the wild, be it lust or desire for the seeming freedom of the idolater, even the civilizing veneer of clothing is not sufficient. A man must be constantly surrounded by stimuli that will serve to remind him of the 613 *mitzvot* and of the Divine throne of glory.

Parshat Bamidbar is always read before the holiday of Shavuot, with *Parshat Naso* following immediately after. Perhaps the reason is that, with *Kabbalat Hatorah*, we must realize that though we may, on occasion—or even often—fail horribly, the Torah always offers us the opportunity to return and to achieve even greater heights.

Rabbi Aaron S. Gelman, z"l

Young Israel of Santa Barbara, California

Parshat Bamidbar is almost always read on the *Shabbat* before Shavuot. There are manifold references by *Chazal* as to why this is so. To quote but a few: Commenting on the *pasuk* of *Shirat Habe'er* ("Song of the Well," Numbers 21:18) that contains the words *umimidbar matanrah* ("and from the desert [the Israelites went] to Matanah," a gift from the wilderness—the *Midrash Rabbah* teaches us:

> Why was it [the Torah] given in the wilderness? Because if it had been given in the Promised Land, the tribe in whose territory it was given would have said, "I have a prior claim to it." Therefore, it [the Torah] was given in the wilderness so all should have an equal claim to it. Another reason why [the Torah was given] in the desert: As the wilderness is neither sown nor tilled, if one accepts the yoke of Torah one is relieved of the yoke of earning a living. Another reason why it was given in the wilderness: Who preserves Torah? He who makes himself like a wilderness and segregates himself from everyone [and spends his time only learning Torah].

Another famous *midrash* is quite explicit as to the relevance: "Why in the wilderness of Sinai? Our Sages infer from here that the Torah was given in the accompaniment of three things, fire, water, and wilderness. Why was the giving of Torah marked by these three features? To indicate that as these are free to all mankind, so also are the words of Torah free."

Surely the above midrashic references and many of those not repeated here should indeed suffice as proper rationale for the positioning of *Bamidbar* to be read before *Matan Torah*. It is interesting to note, however, that this relationship (reading of *Parshat Bamidbar* before Shavuot) is conveyed to us by halachic sources as well. It is within these halachic inferences that a distinct personal message vis-à-vis *Kabbalat Hatorah* (the receiving of the Torah) appears to be embodied.

In *Shulchan Aruch, Orach Chaim* (428:4) we are taught, "One always reads *Parshat Bamidbar* before *Atzeret* (the rabbinic name for Shavuot).

The *Shulchan Aruch* then proceeds to present a catch-all phrase to facilitate the augmentation of this practice, the sign being, "*Minu v'itzu*—first count, then observe." The *Shulchan Aruch* is referring to the first theme found in the Book of *Bamidbar*; counting—namely, that of the census taken of *Bnei Yisrael*!—the allusion being that this accounting is to be read before the observing of Shavuot. In rabbinic literature these verses are referred to as *Parshat Hapekudim*, the Chapter of the Count. It appears quite clearly that the delineation of the word *minu*—"take the count"—and all that it might signify is relevant to *Kabbalat Hatorah*.

What is most intriguing, however, is that, in the *pesukim* in *Parshat Hapekudim*, the word *minu* does not occur. As is widely known, we Jews never count human beings as objects or as things. Instead of the word *minu*, in this context, we find two other terms:

1. *Se'u*, translated as "take a census"
2. *Tifkedu*, translated as "you shall count them"

As understood by the commentators, these two terms thus provide a fitting dichotomy that precedes and prepares us for Torah acceptance and Torah study.

The term *se'u* arises from the root *nun, sin, aleph*, which connotes elevation. Rabbeinu Bechaya (*Bamidbar* 1:2) cogently points out this dimension of aggrandizement: "The People of Israel arises only through conformance to Torah. Thus, perforce, the text employs the term *se'u*, which suggests elevation."

The term *tifkedu*, on the other hand, alludes to the opposite: to deficiency, or what is lacking. Rashi clearly expresses this in his comment on Numbers 31:49, *v'lo nifkad* (they were not counted) *loshon* (a language terminology of) *chaser* (missing deficient)—that the underlying meaning of the root *peh, koph, dalet* is to take stock of what is or what is not missing.

Every year, on the *Shabbat* before Shavuot, we are accordingly reminded by the Torah reading that we must cognitively re-evaluate ourselves and properly ready ourselves for a renewed vigorous reacceptance. We must engage in a qualitative assessment of the prescriptions and proscriptions of the Torah way of life, and of our present society. *Se'u*—we must raise our sights and reaffirm that it is Torah and the transcendence of Torah above all systems that we accept, and we must engage in a qualitative assessment of ourselves—*tifkedu*—being conscious of what is lacking in our own inner selves. How deficient we may yet be in Torah study and more so in *middot*!

How pertinent and eternal is this message of *Chazal*. We live in a technological milieu in which discovery and achievement is the *summum bonum*. The *Shulchan Aruch* reminds us that an annual probing of one's inner self and a striving toward spiritual attainment are priorities that must take precedence over all other preoccupatioins. May this new generation be conscious of the necessity of this humbling evaluation. May we together accept the Torah with *ahavah*—with love—and with innate sensitivity.

❖ CHAPTER 40 ❖

Naso

Rabbi Kenneth Auman

Young Israel of Flatbush, New York

THREE KINDS OF PEACE

The concept of *shalom*, peace, is explicitly mentioned once in *Parshat Naso* and is implied, possibly, twice. The explicit reference is in *birkat kohanim*, where the Torah concludes the blessing with "peace." Implied references are:

1. The case of the *sotah*, the suspected adulteress, concerning whom the Torah states that a portion of the text of the Torah is dissolved in the water that she must drink. Our Rabbis, in explaining this procedure, comment that marital peace is so precious that even the name of God (found in this section of the Torah) may be erased (into the water) in order to reunite the couple involved (should she be found innocent).
2. The *nessi'im*, the leaders of the tribes, brought offerings on the first twelve days of the establishment of the *Mishkan* in the desert. These sacrifices were identical to each other, and yet the Torah painstakingly records their content over and over, twelve times. Perhaps this was done to teach us to what extent the Torah will bend over backward to refrain from arousing feelings of resentment on the part of these *nessi'im*, lest an impression of favoritism be conveyed.

These three contexts of *shalom* represent three different areas in which peace is needed:

1. Within the family (*sotah*)
2. Within the nation (*nessi'im*)
3. Universally, among all peoples (*birkat kohanim*).

Unfortunately, one type of peace is often achieved at the expense of another. For example, war is often a unifying factor within a nation. The lesson of the three types of *shalom* is that all must exist together.

IS THE *NAZIR* A ROLE MODEL FOR US?

Rabbi Elazar Hakappar's opinion, quoted by the Talmud in a number of places, is that a *nazir* is a *choteh*, a transgressor, because he needlessly deprives himself of permissible worldly pleasures. This opinion is accepted by Shmuel with regard to one who fasts a great deal. Rabbi Elazar (not the Rabbi Elazar Hakappar just mentioned), however, disagrees and states that one who accepts voluntary fast days upon himself, if he is in the physical condition to so do, is a *kadosh*, a holy individual. His opinion is also based upon the model of the *nazir*, for the Torah speaks about the *nazir* as being *kadosh*.

It seems, therefore, that we have two very different opinions about the *nazir*. Is he a truly holy person who should be considered an ideal to attempt to emulate or, at least, to admire, or is he considered one who improperly shuns the pleasures of this world?

I would like to suggest that, perhaps, the difference between these two points of view is not as great as it appears to be. Rabbi Elazar Hakappar's opinion that the *nazir* is a sinner is difficult to accept at face value. After all, doesn't the Torah itself describe the individual who takes the vow of *nezirut* as being done "to God"? And, indeed, why would the Torah provide the option of becoming a *nazir* if it is always a negative? In order to understand Rabbi Elazar Hakappar's position, we must focus in on his words very carefully. He states that the *nazir* is a sinner "because he caused himself to suffer by refraining from wine." What he is telling us is that, indeed, for the average person, who enjoys worldly pleasures, *nezirut* is not acceptable, for the person may not suffer needlessly. However, there are unique individuals who have risen to great spiritual heights, people who have developed their characters and personalities in such a manner that worldly pleasures mean very little to them. For these people, a period of *nezirut* can be of great benefit for their further edification. And, for them, abstaining from wine causes no suffering. Rabbi Elazar, therefore, holds that, though for the ordinary individual *nezirut* would be inappropriate, for a unique minority it would be praiseworthy indeed.

We can therefore conclude that the point of contention among our *chachamim* regarding the *nazir* relates to the average Jew who, though he or she does have significant spiritual aspirations, has not divorced himself or herself from living a normal worldly life. However, even Rabbi Elazar Hakappar would agree that, for some individuals, *nezirut* is a valid and praiseworthy path to follow. The Torah does not expect identical behavior from all people. Though there are basic *Shulchan Aruch* laws that all Jews must accept, certain forms of behavior might be entirely proper for some Jews but totally inappropriate for others.

BIRKAT KOHANIM: SELECTED *DINIM* BASED ON OUR *PARSHAH*

1. From the fact that the Torah places the *parshah* of *birkat kohanim* immediately following the *parshah* of *nazir*, we deduce that, just as a *nazir* is prohibited from drinking wine, so, too, a *kohen* who wishes to participate in *birkat kohanim* must not drink wine. (See *Orach Chaim* 128:38 and *Mishna Brurah* there for a discussion of the amount of wine and the *halachah* regarding other intoxicating beverages.)
2. Although certain of our required recitations may be performed in other languages, *birkat kohanim* must be recited only in Hebrew. This *din* is based upon the phrase, *ko tevarchu*—"thus shall you bless"—indicating that it must be recited exactly as it is written.
3. Another *halachah* is derived from *ko tevarchu* as well. Since the Torah directs this *mitzvah* to the *kohanim*—that they are commanded to bless the Jewish nation—if a non-*kohen* blesses them, he violates the commandment. Thus, non-*kohanim* may not join the *kohanim* on the *duchan* (platform) for the *birchat kohanim*.

From the fact that the root word *barech*, which is used here, is used in other contexts, we derive two *dinim*:

a. In *Devarim Parshat Ki Tavo* the Torah speaks of standing when the blessings on *Har Gerizim* were to be given (*Ve'eleh yaamdu levarech et ha'am* . . .). Therefore the *kohanim* must stand while blessing the people.
b. In *Vayikra Parshat Shemini* the Torah speaks of Aharon's raising his hands while blessing the people (*Vayisa Aharon et yadav vayevarchem*). Therefore, the *kohanim* must raise their hands while they bless the people.

A number of *halachot* are derived from the words *amor lahem*—"say to them":

a. The *kohanim* and the congregation must be face to face (just as a person normally conducts conversation in this manner).
b. The *kohanim* must recite the *brachot* in a voice that is audible to the congregation (as in normal conversation).
c. The congregation must call upon the *kohanim* to bless them; therefore, the *chazzan* says, *Kohanim*, in a loud voice. (This is derived from a different understanding of "say to them"—namely that the people have to speak to the *kohanim*.)

Rabbi Daniel N. Korobkin

Young Israel of San Diego, California

This week's *parshah* contains the *birkat kohanim*, the priestly blessing. Abarbanel explains that the purpose of this *brachah* is to protect the Jewish nation from an *ayin hara* and other types of metaphysical damage.

The last of the three sentences in this blessing is, "May *HaShem* show favor toward you and grant you peace." The Talmud (*Berakhos* 20b) relates that the angels had difficulty with this sentence:

> The ministering angels said to *HaShem*, "Master of the Universe, it is written in Your Torah (Deuteronomy 10:17) '[*HaShem*] will not show favor, nor will He take bribery,' and yet You show favor to the Jewish people, as it is written, 'May *HaShem* show favor toward you'!" Replied *HaShem*, "How can I not show favor toward them? I wrote for them in the Torah (Deuteronomy 8:10), 'And you shall eat, be satiated, and bless *HaShem* your Lord [that is, the Torah obligation to *bentsch* (say grace after meal) is only when one has eaten to the point of satiation].' Yet they oblige themselves even further, by *bentsching* after eating just a *kezayit* (the size of an olive) of bread!"

We need to understand a few things from this story:

1. Why did *HaShem* choose the *chumra* (stringency) of *bentsching* after eating a *kezayit* as an illustration of the Jews' devotion to God, rather than any other *chumra* that the Rabbis have placed upon us to strengthen Torah law?
2. Ultimately, the question of the angels is still unanswered. Granted that *HaShem* may have a good reason for showing favor to the Jewish people, but the contradiction in Scripture still stands: Why does it say in the other sentence that *HaShem* does *not* show favor?
3. In general, what does the Torah mean by "showing favor"?

Furthermore, the angels weren't the only ones bothered by this contradiction. The Talmud relates two other stories in which other parties raised this contradiction. In Tractate *Niddah* (70b) the rabbis of Alexandria asked Rabbi Yehoshua ben Chananya the very same question: Why in one passage does it say that *HaShem* does not show favor, whereas at the end of the priestly blessing it says that *HaShem will* show favor? Rabbi Yehoshua's answer was that it depends upon what point in the heavenly judicial process we analyze. Before God finalizes His decree against an individual, He will be inclined to "show favor." But once the decree against the individual is finalized, *HaShem* is unmoving regarding the judgment and will "not show favor."

Tractate *Rosh Hashanah* (17b) relates the story of a woman convert named Bluria who raised the very same contradiction.

> Rabbi Yossi the Kohen attended to her and said, "Here's a parable: A man lent his friend a *maneh,* and set a time—in the presence of the king—when the loan was due. The borrower swore by the life of the king to repay the loan at the allotted time. The time for payment came and passed, but the borrower could not repay the loan. He therefore went to the king in an attempt to appease him for having sworn falsely with his name. The king said, 'I forgive you for my disgrace; now go and appease your friend the lender.' The same is true here," concluded Rabbi Yossi. "When it comes to sins that are between man and God, God will 'show favor.' But when it comes to sins between man and his fellow man, God will 'not show favor.'"

Three different answers to the same question. Which one is the real answer?

Once we understand the meaning of "showing favor," we will be able to answer all the questions. At the end of the very same sentence in *birkat kohanim*, it says, "and grant you peace." What peace are we referring to? According to the *Kesav Sofer*, it refers to the peace that one experiences after defeating his *yetzer hara* (negative inclinations). We call the inner turmoil that the individual experiences when choosing between good and evil the *milchemes hayatzer*—the battle with the *yetzer hara.* When one has vanquished this internal enemy, he experiences true inner peace. This is the blessing with which we conclude *birkat kohanim*: may *HaShem* grant you victory over your *yetzer hara*, thereby granting you true inner harmony. But for the individual to accomplish this, he needs Divine aid. This is, then, the preceding phrase, "May *HaShem* show favor toward you"—that is, may *HaShem* be your ally in your war with the *yetzer hara*, thereby enabling your success.

This explains why *HaShem*, in His response to the angels, chose the *chumra* of *bentsching* after eating a *kezayit*. There are many proscribed foods that, if a Jew eats them, will "close up his heart" to spirituality. The Jewish people, explained God, are meticulous in their diet in order that they may fortify their spiritual strength better to combat the *yetzer hara*. Not only will they not eat any forbidden food; they will also be exacting in the amount of food that they eat to be elevated spiritually through the Grace after Meals! Since they show such initiative in their battle against the *yetzer hara*, argued God, how can I not come to their aid? The other verse, indicating that *HaShem* does not show favor, refers to other nations, who do not display such initiative in their battle against the *yetzer hara*.

The same explanation can be given for the answer that Rabbi Yehoshua ben Chananya gave to the rabbis of Alexandria. The reason *HaShem* helps us in our *milchemes hayatzer* is so that we will do *teshuvah* and avoid a harsh decree from Heaven, but if the decree has already been made, then it is already too late; the *yetzer hara* has already won this round of the war. There is now no reason for *HaShem* to come to our aid. This is what Rabbi Yehoshua meant in his response: Before the decree is finalized, *HaShem* comes to our aid in our fight against the *yetzer hara*, but, after the decree, *HaShem* no longer has a reason to "show favor."

So, too, we can explain the answer given to Bluria the convert. When it comes to offenses between man and God, *HaShem* is eager to break the barriers that the *yetzer hara* has placed between us and Himself, but when two of His children have strife between themselves (that is, sins between man and man), *HaShem* requires that the offender fight the battle alone. *HaShem*'s attitude is: If you offend Me, that's something that I can forgive, and even help you in your attempts to apologize to Me. But if you've hurt another of My children, then don't expect Me to come to your side in an attempt to reconcile with the offended party. I am jealous for My other child's sake as well, and so this is one battle you will have to fight on your own.

So, ultimately, no matter how we answer the contradiction between the verses, the key to an understanding of the answer lies in knowing the definition of "showing favor." Sometimes *HaShem* helps us in our *milchemes hayatzer*, and sometimes He does not.

To understand why three different answers were given, we need to examine the parties who were asking the question. Shlomo *Hamelech* said (Proverbs 22:6), *Chanoch lana'ar al pi darko*—"Educate the youth according to his path of reasoning." The nature of the asker, and his/her motivation for asking, can make a world of difference in the nature of an appropriate answer.

When *HaShem* was asked this question by the angels, their question was full of anger and contempt for man. The very same angels, when Moshe ascended to the Heavens to receive the Torah, derided him and his people by saying (Psalms 8:5), *Ma enosh ki tizkerenu?*—"What is man that You should bother with him?" (See Talmud *Shabbos* 88b.) The angels perceived mankind as an evil and imperfect portion of creation, unworthy of *HaShem*'s attention. In reply, *HaShem* needed to provide a lesson to the angels about man's greatness. That is why *HaShem* answered with an explanation of the Jews' meticulousness in religious observance.

When the rabbis of Alexandra asked their question, their intent was to find out about the inner workings of *HaShem*'s system of retribution management (see the Maharsha in Tractate *Niddah* there). They, therefore, received an answer that would satisfy their desire to discover more about this hidden aspect of *HaShem*.

When Bluria the convert asked her question, she was fascinated by the beauty that Judaism displays in its treatment of man's attitude and behavior toward his fellow man. This, after all, is what tends to draw Gentiles towards conversion, as is witnessed by the famous interchange between Hillel and the Gentile who sought to learn the entire Torah while standing on one foot. Hillel's response was, "That which is hateful to you, do not do to your friend" (see Talmud *Shabbos* 31a). It was this answer that drew the heart of the Gentile toward conversion. Rabbi Yossi the Kohen, seeing this sensitivity within Bluria, provided a fitting answer: when it comes to sins between man and his fellow man, God is much more demanding.

From all of this, we see the importance not only of knowing what to answer to the inquisitive but also of carefully determining the nature of the questioner so as to provide the most appropriate answer for that one individual.

Rabbi Elimelech Goldberg

Young Israel of Southfield, Michigan

Counting the Jewish people as a whole or as individual tribes appears as a preoccupation of the Holy One in the desert. Yet, *HaShem yitbarach*, the possessor of all knowledge, does not require a census for His own sake. The purpose of counting the Jews is to allow this people, who had known too well the feeling of being inconsequential slaves, to understand that in the eyes of Heaven they truly did count. To this end, the Torah utilizes the language of *Naso*, "uplift the heads," to describe the act of counting. By being counted by the Almighty we are, in act, being lifted to the task for which we were created.

As we begin again, this week, the first chapter of the *Ethics of the Fathers*, we are reminded that the Jew is defined by three elements: our "Torah, *avodah*, and *gemilut chasadim*." It is through these three foundations that we are to understand why we count in the eyes of *HaShem*. The learning of Torah determines our ability to look into our *neshamot* (souls). *Avodah*, the service of God allows us to focus the medley of individual impulses of personality to reach upward to our Creator. *Gemilut chasadim* is the standard of love and sensitivity that gives us the strength to drop the normal selfish exclusiveness of our outer shells to reach outward to our fellow man. By looking inward, upward, and outward, we construct the symbol of the triangle, the building block of the Jewish star, which the Maharal describes as a unique image.

The triangle, composed by the connection of three points, is unlike other geometric shapes. The rectangle still maintains its body if one of its outer points is removed; it becomes a triangle. The octagon becomes a septagon, and so on. The triangle is the geometric shape that cannot close when one of its points is removed. Thus, the Maharal suggests, the triangle is an excellent representation of the foundations of our existence. Unless the Jew is willing to reach upward, inward, and outward, he or she will be unable to be a "whole" person. The Magan David, composed of two distinct triangles superimposed one upon the other, represents the soul, personality, and body of the individual together with these three elements (of Torah, *avodah*, and *gemilut chasidim*) of the nation of Israel. As a people, we, too, are obligated to reach up to *HaShem*, inward to each other, and outward to the world.

The census that begins *Parshat Naso* is part of the separate counts of the three families of Levi. Each group of *leviim* had a different part of the *Mishkan* to carry. Even a cursory look at the setup of the Tabernacle suggests the three-part image of the triangle of our being. The innermost sanctum, the Holy of Holies, was hidden by a curtain. Within these covered walls was the Torah, the *neshamah* of our people. The *cherubim*, borrowed from the world of Heaven, stood guard within the Holy of Holies. The Tabernacle itself, outside the Holy of Holies, was the place of the *avodah*. Between the physical statement of the table and its breads and the spiritual light of the *menorah*, the golden altar was the platform for the incense to rise to Heaven. The mixture of the different types of incense describes the personality, or the combinations of nature and nurture of the individual, that, when mixed properly and directed upward, was a pleasing aroma to the Almighty. Outside the Tabernacle lay the courtyard of the people. This was the dimension of interaction of the masses, the corridor of *gemilut chasadim*. It is in this last, outer part that the physical expression of the body in God's service draws expression. The courtyard was the place of the outer altar on which the flesh of our sacrifices was offered on high.

The soul, personality, and body of the individual was also represented by the three coverings that lay on top of the *Mishkan*. The innermost one was woven of the pure linens and materials into the sevenfold strands of the intricate tapestry of the cherubim. The Talmud tells us that there are seven layers to the soul. This parallels the seven layers of the world of Heaven. On top of the *neshamah* level lay the coarser, darker goat's-hair covering. Here, the buttons of gold are replaced with the less pure brass as the purity of the soul is covered by the coarser persona of the individual. Lastly, the sealskins, the actual hides of the animal, cover the outermost level. The flesh is directed to recognize its importance as but the outermost covering of the soul.

Our *parshah* is not silent about the implications for a person who lives his or her life without a connective fiber that links our souls to the elements of personality and animal nature. Without "the Torah, *avodah*, and *gemilut chasadim*," our lives fall apart. The triangle becomes undone, unable to contain anything within. In the description of the *sotah*, the woman accused of infidelity, the *midrash* sees an indictment on her husband, as well, since that which he did, did not provide for his wife. (Numbers 5:12) *Ish, ish*, the repetition of "a man, a man" may be a significant negative description of the husband because only two of the vital three characteristics of a man are displayed. If the husband is not able to offer the element of *chesed* of love and sensitivity to uplift his wife, he, too, is an accessory to her crime. Perhaps he is a man only in regard to the Torah and its *avodah*. Lacking caring, he is not fully a complete individual who can maintain the proper focus of his family.

The *nazir*, who is discussed after the *sotah*, has three prohibitions. He may not cut his hair, drink wine, or come in contact with the dead. The Talmud indicates that this vow is a distinct means of redirection. The elements that the Torah emphasizes again focus upon the points of our Jewish star. One's outward appearance is important only to someone who cares how others see him. The *nazir* is told that his grooming is not the essential element in his relationship with the outside world; *gemilut chasadim*, real person-to-person interaction, is accomplished by his soul through the body, not by the lifeless strands of hair upon his head. The prohibition of wine speaks to the personality of an individual; *avodah* must be generated by the movements of one's soul, not by the mood-altering application of the vine. The true serenity of our being begins within and cannot be produced by anything from the outside. And, lastly, regarding the third prohibition of the *nazir*, Rabbi Samson Raphael Hirsch describes the anxiety of a soul in contact with a corpse. He suggests that a soul looks longingly upon death as a yearning to return home, unbounded by the shackles of life. The *nazir*, through this distance from death, emphasizes the important task his soul must still respond to in the course of his remaining life. Thus, the vow of *nezirut* reintroduces the individual who has lost his focus to the needs of conducting his soul, personality, and body to the concert of a Heavenly score.

Following the laws of the *nazir*, the *parshah* describes the *mitzvah* of *birkat kohanim*. Here, too, the threefold function of spiritual completion is uncovered in the context of this commandment. The first blessing is the simple three-word statement, "Let *HaShem* bless you and guard you." It is the physical, outer shell that seeks the blessing of being guarded and safe. The second stanza is one of enlightenment and inner wholeness: "Let *HaShem* illuminate His face to you and give you graciousness." *Chein*, grace, is a form of the inner serenity of an individual. All the bundled characteristics of the personality form a single descending column in response to the radiance of love from on high. (This five-word expression is the same symbol that the *heh* of number five represents to us throughout our Torah. As the Five Books of Moshe, *heh* points to revelation. Even the form of the letter *heh*, the Maharal contends, depicts a small opening above and a large one below. The image is akin to that of sunlight piercing through the clouds and spreading forth as it illuminates the ground below.)

The last phrase of the *birkat kohanim* is the seven-word intonation, "May *HaShem* lift up His face to you and grant to you, peace." The body and the outer, darker wrappings of the personality are already blessed. But when layer after layer is peeled away, the final *brachah* is the one for the soul. Only on the level of the *neshamah* may we hope to see the presence of *HaShem* as he lifts up His face to us. Only within the confines of the soul is true peace a possibility. Like the sevenfold strands of the interwoven threads of the curtains of the Holy of Holies and the first layer of the cherub-covered section of the Tabernacle, the last seven words transmit the blessing of our Priests to the inner sanctum of our souls.

Our Rabbis see great significance in the combination of phrases that form the fifteen words of the priestly benediction. They, like the fifteen parts of the "Song of Ascents" (Psalms 120–134), sung upon the fifteen steps of the Holy Temple, refer to the Name of God Himself (*yud-heh*) (*yud* numerically equals 10, *heh* equals 5 for a total of 15). This is the blessing of ascension that calls to the inner part of our very being from on high. This is the loving mirror that the Holy One holds up to the individuals of a glorified nation to see the foundations of our peoplehood and the roots of our personal identities in "the Torah, *avodah*, and *gemilut chasadim*" of our existence. This is the means to uplift our existence as we are counted one by one, again and again, so that we may truly recognize how much every one of us counts to our loving Father in Heaven.

❖ CHAPTER 41 ❖

Beha'alotcha

Rabbi Simcha Krauss

Young Israel of Hillcrest, New York

Parshat Beha'alotcha is replete with both narrative and *mitzvot*. A full analysis showing the conceptual unity of the narrative part of the *sedrah* and the *mitzvot* part is beyond the scope of this article. Still, I would like to point out one idea that does create a thematic whole, uniting various parts of the *sedrah*.

We are informed that "the multitude that was among them felt a 'lusting'; and the children of Israel also wept again, and said, who shall give us flesh to eat?" (Numbers 11:4). Listening to their complaints of the "good old days" in Egypt, with the ample fish and cucumbers and garlic, Moshe Rabbeinu almost loses control, and then turns to God.

God's response is as follows: "Gather unto me seventy men of the elders of Israel . . . and bring them to the appointed tent. . . . And I will come down and speak with them: And I will infuse from the spirit that is upon thee, and put it upon them. . . . And say unto the people sanctify yourselves, for tomorrow you shall eat meat for you have wept in the ears of God . . . therefore God will give you flesh and you shall eat" (Numbers 18:16–18).

A close analysis of these sentences will reveal a seemingly superfluous sentence. God responds by ordering the gathering of seventy elders (11:16) and then that they—the people of Israel—should prepare: "sanctify yourselves" for tomorrow ye shall have meat (11:18). The statement "I will infuse from your spirit unto them" (11:17) does not really belong here. It does not seem *prima facie* to add anything to the whole episode of the "multitude" that was murmuring and criticizing.

We are taught something about the psychology of a human being. A person makes demands. He complains, criticizes, and murmurs, and feels a "lusting" for meat. If only he would get that meat . . . if only he would make that financial "killing" then . . . if only he gets that piece of flesh, everything would be right, all problems would be solved.

But in reality, are all problems solved with the resolution of economic issues? Are human problems really reducible only to issues of distribution of wealth? Is the human condition assuaged by taking care of and distributing "flesh" alone? Do we not, in our everyday experience, see people and nations whose economic and material problems have been solved, more or less satisfactorily, yet they still are uneasy, still feel a sense of rudderlessness, are still overcome by anxiety and a sense of ennui? Somehow "flesh" alone is not the answer to the human condition. The basic hunger, the fundamental yearning of the human being is, as the *pasuk* states, "As the hart pants after the brook, so does my soul pant after thee, Lord" (Psalms 42:2). One day we will all know that our "hunger" and "thirst" are for the "word of God." Now, however, we do not openly see it. For now, this hunger and thirst come out in a "crooked" way and are manifest in the unrelenting and insatiable request for "meat."

This is the message of the *parshah*. The "multitude" expresses its frustrations, its superficial needs, in terms of the need for meat. And, says God, the meat will be provided in such proportion that they will get sick of it. Yet, in reality, what they really need, what they should be asking for, is spiritual fare. What will really help them is, "I will take from the spirit that is upon you." What they should be asking for is more spirituality.

When people ask and pray for spirituality, when this is expressed in a straight and forward manner, when it comes out of the depths of a soul yearning to find the good of the nearness to God, then God responds with abundance and grace.

Let us again look into the *sedrah*. ". . . There were people who were unclean . . . so that they could not do the Passover [sacrifice] on that day; and they came before Moshe and before Aharon and said, . . . We are unclean . . . why are we to be kept back from offering the sacrifice of God in its appointed season among the children of Israel?" (Numbers 9:6,7)

Moshe Rabbeinu relays their request to God and comes back with the *halachah* that indeed a person who was unclean on the first Pesach or "on a distant way" and unable to offer the Pesach sacrifice at its appointed time, will have a second chance; he will be able to bring a *Pesach Sheini* (Numbers 9:10–12).

Here we have one of the most promising, hopeful, and optimistic messages to humanity. A person has a second chance. One is not eternally bound by the events of the past. Yesterday's mistakes are not chains that bind and fetter a person forever and ever. God promises a *Pesach Sheini*, another chance, a second opportunity to free and purify oneself. There is one proviso, however; the initiative must come from ourselves. We must ask, "Why are we kept back?" We must demand the added dimension of spirituality. In truth, everything can be attained, everything worthwhile can be achieved when one has the attitude of "Why are we kept back?"—we, too, want to partake in enhanced spirituality.

One example is participation in the blessing of *Eretz Yisrael*. The Torah tells us in *Parshat Pinchas* that the daughters of Tzelofchad were, at first, not involved in the division of the land. They came before Moshe Rabbeinu and asked, "Why are we kept back?"—in their case, why should our father's name be lacking? Why should we be bereft of possessing part of the land? And God answered, "The daughters of Tzelofchad speak right"! Indeed, everyone can have a second chance, if the desire for betterment is strong enough and deep enough. (Numbers 27:7)

What is the purpose of Young Israel? What has been our aim as a movement, and what is still our goal? In addition to being a home for the committed Jew, for the *yeshiva bachur* and the Orthodox family, we are here to give a second chance to those hundreds of thousands of Jews—in America, in Israel, in the former Soviet Union, wherever Jews live—to participate in freedom in the joy, the sheer exhilaration, of Torah and *Yiddishkeit*.

Our movement, banded together under the aegis of the National Council of Young Israel, raised the banner of "Why are we kept back?" over eighty years ago. We were the ones to say that Jewry and Judaism in America needs, and deserves, a second chance. We are still active, and, with God's help, will continue to be here and to give the hope of a second chance to further generations of Jews everywhere.

Rabbi Mordechai Terebelo

Young Israel of Lawrenceville, New Jersey

Rashi begins his commentary on this week's *parshah* with the question, "Why is the *parshah* of the *menorah* placed adjacent to the *parshah* of the sacrifices of the *nesiim* (Princes of Israel)?" He answers, "When Aharon saw the dedication of the *nesiim* he was disappointed that neither he nor his tribe had a part in the dedication. To that *HaShem* answered, 'Your portion is greater than theirs, for you are responsible for the lighting and preparing of the lights of the *menorah*.'"

The Ramban takes issue with Rashi's interpretation of the *midrash* as referring to the everyday lighting of the *menorah*. First, the Ramban questions why Aharon was comforted specifically with the lighting of the *menorah* and not with one of the many other *avodahs* (services in the *Beit Hamikdash*) that were exclusive to the *Kohein Gadol*—for example, the *Ketores* incense offering brought every morning and evening, and the Yom Kippur *Avodah*, which includes the entering of the *Kodesh Kedoshim* and can only be done by the *Kohein Gadol*. Why were these not enough to comfort Aharon? Second, the Ramban points out that Aharon was, in fact, included in the dedication, for he also brought sacrifices during the days preceding the *nesiim*'s sacrifices. Therefore, the Ramban interprets the *midrash* as referring not to the everyday lighting of the *menorah* but, rather, in a prophetic manner, to the dedication and lighting of the *menorah* that would take place in the times of the Hasmoneans. *HaShem* is telling Aharon that the dedication of the *Beit Hamikdash*, to take place on Chanukah many years later, would take place through his children; the miracle of Chanukah would occur through the *chasmonaim* who were descendants of Aharon.

To understand Rashi's interpretation of the *midrash* as referring to the daily lighting of the *menorah*, as well as why Aharon was comforted by the *avodah*, we must first analyze both the *avodah* and the structure of the *menorah* and what the latter represents.

The *posuk* says, "toward the center of the *menorah* shall shine the seven lamps." (Numbers 8:2) Rashi explains that all the lights of the *menorah* should face toward the middle light. This means that the three lights on the right side and the three lights on the left side should all face inward toward the center light.

Sforno explains that the lights on the right side of the *menorah* represent those who are primarily occupied with spiritual endeavors (such as rabbis and teachers). The lights on the left side represent those who are primarily occupied with material endeavors. The right and left sides of the *menorah*, representing different groups and types of people, must both point in one direction—toward the middle light, which represents *HaShem*'s will. Thus, according to Sforno, the *menorah* represents the synthesis of the different components of Jewry into one harmonious group whose goal is the doing of *HaShem*'s will.

Sforno also explains this meaning as the reason for the *menorah*'s being made of one solid piece of gold. The *menorah* represents the binding of the spiritual endeavors with material endeavors in such a way as to elevate the material and inject it with spirituality. To take seemingly physical actions such as eating and inject them with spirituality (*Oneg Shabbat*, to be able to serve *HaShem*, and so on. See *Orach Chaim*, chapter 231) serves to uplift our material world and give it a sense of *kedushah*.

If we analyze the *menorah* further—specifically, the type of fuel used—we will find the same concept. Oil, the fuel of the *menorah*, when used as a food, serves the material needs of man; when used as a fuel in the *menorah*, it becomes elevated, enabling it to serve a spiritual function.

The *Gemara*, in *Pesachim* 68b, says that Rabbi Eliezer and Rabbi Yehoshua disagree as to the conduct of a person on *yom tov*. Rabbi Eliezer is of the opinion that a person should dedicate it either entirely to spiritual endeavors or entirely to physical endeavors (*oneg yom tov*), whereas Rabbi Yehoshua is of the opinion that the *yom tov* should be divided between both spiritual and physical endeavors. Shavuot is not included in their dispute; both agree that that time must be set aside for both material and physical enjoyment. The question is apparent. Rabbi Eliezer asks why Shavuot is the only *yom tov* on which physical enjoyment is required; the obvious requirement would seem to be just the opposite—that Shavuot, the day on which we received the Torah, should be spent learning and pursuing spiritual goals. It certainly should not be the day on which, all our *gedolim* agree, we must also pursue physical enjoyment.

The *Gemara* in *Shabbos* 88b says that at the time that Moshe was to receive the Torah, a dispute arose between the angels and Moshe. The angels wished that the Torah should remain completely pure and holy and *not* be given to mere mortals. Moshe disagreed, and put forth the following arguments: Can *HaShem* say to the angels, who were never enslaved in Egypt, I am *HaShem* Who redeemed *you* from Egypt? Can the commandment to rest on Shabbat be given to angels, who engage in no work anyway? Can angels, who have no parents, fulfill the *mitzvah* of *kibbud av va'em*? Finally, Moshe argued, do angels have jealousy or an evil inclination necessitating a prohibition against stealing? Immediately, *HaShem* decided to give the Torah to Moshe and not to the angels. It would seem from this *Gemara* that only with this last argument did Moshe prevail. What made this last argument more convincing than the previous ones? Moshe argued that the purpose of Torah is to enable man, *with* his physical limitations and desires, to become a spiritual being and serve *HaShem*.

Just as the Jewish nation contains both spiritual and material elements, as Sforno explained, so, too, each individual has within himself both material and spiritual elements that must be used to serve *HaShem*. This is man's task, and only man can accomplish this. It is for this purpose that the Torah was given to people, not angels. Therefore, on Shavuot, when we celebrate the giving of the Torah, all agree that we must serve *HaShem* through physical enjoyment. The lesson to be learned is that we must inject *kedushah* into the physical aspects of life. Our working, eating, sleeping, must all be done with the goal of serving *HaShem*. It is this concept of man's ability to elevate and infuse even material aspects of life with a sense of *kedushah* that the *menorah* represented. Because of this, Aharon found consolation in the lighting of the *menorah* more than in his other *avodahs*.

With this we can understand the words of the Maharal in *Nesivos Olam*: that man is greater than angels. Man can take even worldly objects and transform them into *kedushah*—something that angels cannot do.

Rabbi Raphael Wizman

Young Israel of Commack, New York

Parshat Beha'alotcha depicts the Israelites in their closeness to *HaShem* but ends with some disturbing episodes that bode ill for Moshe as well as for the Israelites.

It begins with kindling of the *menorah* by Aharon *HaKohen* and the purification and sanctification of the tribe of Levi for the worship in the sanctuary in place of the firstborn. Chapter 9 describes the strict observance of the second Pesach, though that year was probably the only time the Israelites observed Pesach in all their forty years in the desert. It goes on praising them: "According to the words of *HaShem* will they encamp and according to the words of *HaShem* will they journey, the charge of *HaShem* they would safeguard, according to the word of *HaShem* through Moshe."

Finally at the height of this glory, Moshe pleads with his father-in-law to remain with them and share the glory of *HaShem*. Although the Torah does not record whether or not Jethro decided to remain, the Ramban states that he and his children remained, whereas Sforno opines that only his children remained but he returned to the country Midian.

The Talmud (*Shabbat* 115) speaks of the two sentences, *Vayehi binsoah ha'aron*. . . . As a separate book, entirely separated by the reversed *nuns*, they then divide the Book of *Bamidbar* into three books—the first being before *Vayehi binsoa* and the third, after. This is done perhaps to separate this glorious time from the next few chapters, when this glory is lost.

It appears that this short fifth book of two sentences is the end of their praises. After this, we encounter the *mitonenim*—complainers—who kindled *HaShem*'s wrath and brought about fire that consumed the "edge of the camp," and the *assafsuf*—rabble-rousers—who craved the meat, fish, cucumbers, melons, leeks, onion, and garlic that, they claimed, they ate in Egypt for free. These complainers and rabble-rousers forced Moshe to plead with *HaShem* to relieve him of his responsibility. "I alone cannot carry this entire nation . . . and if this is how You deal with me, kill me now . . . and let me not see my evil." *HaShem* responds by instructing Moshe to appoint seventy elders to help him, by giving the people the meat they craved, and by striking a mighty blow against the people of Israel for this rebellion. For the next few weeks, as well, we will be reading about other rebels and other tragedies that will befall the wandering Israelites in the desert.

This *parshah* concludes with the evil talk against Moshe by his brother and sister, who were rebuked and punished by *HaShem* for speaking evil against Moshe—an individual whom the Torah describes as the most humble man on earth.

Several questions may be posed about the last two episodes. It is a known phenomenon that the manna that *HaShem* provided from heaven was miraculously capable of satisfying any desire or craving for any kind of food. If so, why then did these rabble-rousers not satisfy their cravings with the manna? The answer to this question is found in the sentence *hitavu ta'ava*. The Chofetz Chaim explains this to mean "craved for craving." Although they had no reason to crave, they wished for a craving. These ungrateful rebels craved for foods that would increase their appetite so that they might gorge themselves with meat, fish, and so on. This interpretation is confirmed by the name given to this particular town, *Kivrot Hata'avah*—the graveyard of craving—instead of *Kivrot Hamitavim*—of the cravers.

In the last episode, Miriam and Aharon were rebuked by *HaShem* for slandering Moshe. There is much misunderstanding as to exactly what took place and how Aharon, who was a *rodef shalom*—a pursuer of peace—could be involved in a slander, and of his brother, no less. Rashi explains that, at Mount Sinai, *HaShem* commanded Moshe to separate from his wife so that he might constantly be in a state of *taharah*—purity—so that *HaShem*'s words could come to him without advance notice. Moshe informed only his wife of this. Because of his great humbleness and humility, he refrained from notifying his brother and sister of this personal commandment lest he portray himself to them as a superior prophet.

Moshe's wife, however, was no longer able to contain herself and confided in Miriam, who, in turn, went to Aharon, the pursuer of peace, to save this marriage. She claimed that "We, too, are prophets, and yet *HaShem* did not command us to separate from our spouses. Why does Moshe hold himself superior?" Although this complaint about Moshe may have been well intended for the purpose of saving a marriage and for the benefit of Moshe's wife who was a "Cushite"—beautiful and well mannered (and, therefore, unworthy of this treatment)—*HaShem* still considered this to be slander because it was said against Moshe, who was "more humble than any man on the face of the earth."

HaShem, therefore, punished Miriam with *tzaraat* because she was the one to initiate this slander. Her punishment teaches us that slander is evil even if it is well intentioned. But the worst punishment, which they both received, was, "and *HaShem*'s anger was upon them, and He departed." There is no punishment worse than the departure of *HaShem*'s presence. As this week's Haftarah also confirms, "Sing and rejoice, daughter of Zion, for, lo, I come and I will dwell in your midst" (Zechariah 2:14). A true *simchah* comes only through *HaShem*'s presence.

HaShem suddenly appeared to Aharon and Miriam before they had a chance to purify themselves. Aharon and Miriam panicked and began searching for water to purify themselves. *HaShem* taught them a good lesson here: that Moshe indeed had to be pure at all times and that indeed he was a superior prophet. They, then, should not have passed judgment on a prophet who was *HaShem*'s faithful "servant" and who, as a *ben bayit*, was constantly in the presence of *HaShem*.

The Ramban adds that *HaShem* taught them another lesson: that he who is humble is worthy of God's intervention. *HaShem* will demand the respect of the humble from others.

Aharon pleads with Moshe, since they and Miriam were brothers and sister, all born from the same womb, not to allow part of their flesh to become a "corpse" (a *metzorah* is regarded as a corpse).

Moshe responds by offering a mere five-word prayer for Miriam so as not to seem to be favoring his sister with a long prayer (Rashi). It is interesting to note that Moshe was described as "more humble than any man," whereas King Solomon was "wiser than any man." Both of these qualities are intertwined. For a wise man cannot be wise unless he is also humble; and humility surely requires wisdom.

Rabbi Aryeh Ralbag

Young Israel of Avenue K, New York

Historically, as a people, we Jews move around a great deal. Especially in America, we no longer have a sense of neighborhood. When we move we erase all contacts and obligations to our former *shuls*. A *yeshivah bachur* changing *yeshivot* often "forgets" his former *yeshivah*. We rationalize this by saying that newer and more urgent responsibilities require our loyalties.

However, our Torah, as expounded upon by the *mussar* movement of Reb Yisrael Salanter, requires us to sensitize ourselves to our obligations vis-à-vis our former *shuls* and *yeshivas*. "When the Ark would journey, Moshe would say, 'Arise *HaShem*, and let Your foes be scattered; let those who hate You flee before You.' And when it rested, he would say, 'Reside quietly, *HaShem*, among the myriad thousands of Israel'" (Numbers, 10:35–36). In reality these verses should have been written in chapter 2 of *Sefer Bamidbar*, where the Torah discusses the tribal formations. Furthermore, the Torah separates these two verses from the rest of the Torah by placing inverted letters—*nuns*—before and after these verses.

The Ramban, quoting the Talmud (*Shabbat* 115–116), states that the inverted *nuns* were placed so as not to record three Jewish sins in succession. The recording of three sins in succession—without the verses of "When the ark would journey" (Numbers 10:35, 36)—would have foretold eternal damnation for the Jews. We would have evolved into a people doomed to eternal persecution (*Muchzakim B'Puroniyot*). Therefore, these verses (10:35, 36) were taken out of their proper content and placed here with inverted "runs" preceeding and following them, in order to avoid writing three sins in succession.

What were these horrible sins? The first, says the Ramban, is hinted at in Numbers 9:33, "They journeyed from the mountain of *HaShem* [Sinai]." The Torah offers no explanation. The second and third sins of the Children of

Israel, which follow "When the ark would journey," are those of the complainers and the rabble-rousers. Both of these sins occur shortly after the Children of Israel leave Sinai. The complainers despair of the desert and bemoan their terrible fate. They succeed in their intention of angering *HaShem*, and a fire burns them at the camps' edge (10:1). The rabble-rousers incite *Bnei Yisrael* to complain about their diet of manna. They not only crave meat (11:4), but they even have the audacity to declare "Why did we leave Egypt?" (11:20). Again, as in the previous incident, the instigators are punished; they die while eating the meat (11:33).

Though the second and third sins are explicitly stated, nevertheless, it is not clear from the Torah what the first sin entailed. The Ramban (commentary on Numbers 10:35) quotes a *midrash*: "that they fled Mount Sinai, like a child running away from school." The Ramban continues by stating that this sin was so severe that had they not "sinned" in this manner, *HaShem* would have brought them immediately into *Eretz Yisrael*, without their having to travel through the wilderness, for forty years.

This is difficult to comprehend. After all, they traveled in compliance with *HaShem*'s will. This is attested to in Numbers 10:34: "The cloud of *HaShem* was over them by day, when they journeyed from the camp." Even if the Children of Israel were not politically correct—even assuming they did not have the proper attitude when they departed from *Har Sinai*—nevertheless, why were they so severely punished for this wrong attitude?

The following explanation was offered in a *mussar* discourse delivered in Chevron *Yeshivah* in Yerushalayim by the *Rosh Yayeshivah*, my mentor, my teacher, *Harav Hagaon* Rav Simcha Zissel Broide, *shlita*, in expanding on a *mussar* discourse given by the Alter of Slabodka, *zt"l* (the founder of the *yeshivah* in Chevron in 1924).

The analogy to a child fleeing does not refer specifically to studies. Rather, it refers to the school itself. The child feels constricted by the school; therefore, he cannot empathize with this school that confines him. Running away from school means that no importance is attached to the school.

In a similar vein, it was expected the *Bnei Yisrael* would feel deeply pained by *HaShem*'s ordered departure from *Har Sinai*. Though *Har Sinai* no longer retained its sanctity, and though they continued to develop in Torah for forty years longer, the Jews should have been profoundly saddened that they were leaving the Mountain, where they had received and then learned the Torah. *Hakarat Hatov* (the trait of appreciating when good is done) required a deep sense of gratitude to *Har Sinai*. For this lapse they were severely punished, for it really meant that they attached little importance to the Mountain and all that occurred there.

For us too, *hakarat hatov* means an unbroken emotional bond—an eternal gratitude—to our former places of Torah and *tefillah*. *Hakarat hatov* is an ongoing relationship with all those who have helped us in the past.

This goes to the essence of our "self," and, through *hakarat hatov*, we enhance our relationships with our fellow Jews.

This is the lesson gleaned from the manner of our departure from *Har Sinai*; and true *hakarat hatov* among Jews will bring the *geulah*.

❖ CHAPTER 42 ❖

Sh'lach

Rabbi Asher Bush

Young Israel of Stamford, Connecticut

The Divine decree that fated the Jewish people to wander forty years in the desert and to have that generation never enter the Land of Israel was without precedent. It was not only without precedent in that it punished the entire generation; but, far more significantly, it was decreed with no chance of a reprieve. This is evident the very morning after the decree, when a group of *Bnei Yisrael* decides to enter Israel right away. They are told by Moshe that God is not with them and they will not succeed. There is no suggestion from Moshe about what they should do instead and there is no thought that, somehow, they might be allowed to enter Israel. Simply, he tells them that they cannot and will not be going to Israel.

The results of such a decree could well be catastrophic, as, without the chance of forgiveness, there is little hope or purpose for the future. This is an idea we are familiar with from the well-known verse from *Tehillim* (130:4) often recited in times of disgress, *Ki imcha haslicha lima'an tivarei*—"For forgiveness is with You, in order that You may be revered." Without the possibility of forgiveness, a person is prone to give up hope and to stop trying.

This was the problem now facing the Jewish people, who had been sentenced to wander for forty years until that generation all died out. How were they to spend the next forty years if all hope had been lost? How were they to pass on the Torah to their children, the generation that would be entering the Land of Israel? The entire second half of *Parshat Shlach* is dedicated to answering these critical questions, with each part of the *parshah* adding new and important details:

1. The laws of voluntary *korbanot* (sacrifices)
   The laws of the *korbanot* are introduced with the words, "When you will come into the land of your settlements that I am giving you." As Rashi observes, the very first message that God gave to the Jewish people after the decree of the forty years of wandering was to inform

them that the Jewish people would indeed be entering the Land of Israel. There was no need to give up hope for the future, although some patience would be needed while waiting.

2. Challah

The *mitzvah* to separate and give *challah* to a *kohein* is also introduced by the words, "When you come into the land to which I am bringing you." This verse is not needed to inform them that the Jewish people will be entering the Land of Israel, as they have already been told. Rather, it teaches the proper attitude toward Israel and its produce—the attitude that the spies did not have. The separation of *challah* teaches us to do what the spies sought to prevent—namely, properly to express our appreciation for God's gift of the Land of Israel and its produce.

The connection to *challah* goes one step further, as based on the word *b'voachem*—"in your coming." There is a *halachah* that the Torah obligation of *challah* applies only when the entire Jewish nation resides in Israel. If the spies tried to turn us away from Israel, the *mitzvah* of *challah* teaches that we *all* belong in Israel.

3. *Korban Chataoh* (sin offering) of the entire Congregation and of the Individual

In the aftermath of the decree to wander forty years, it became imperative to make clear to the people that this kind of predicament was not the norm. In general, even for the most severe sins, there always exists the opportunity and mechanism to do a full and proper *teshuvah*. This is true both for the individual who sins and for the entire nation, as can be seen from the institution of *korban chataoh*. The incident of the spies and the subsequent punishment of the Jewish nation should not prevent them from doing *Teshuvah*.

4. *M'koshesh eitzim*, the man who gathered wood on *Shabbos*

This is one of the very few incidents of the desecration of *Shabbos* recorded in the Torah. The fact that this incident was recorded in this *parshah* is no mere chance, as Rashi quotes an opinion that says that it really took place far earlier. However, it was necessary to write this incident here to teach that, even though a decree had been issued against the entire generation, that did not mean that henceforth their individual lives and deeds no longer mattered, that there was no more accountability. This individual desecrated *Shabbos* and is held responsible; so, too, is every other person.

5. *Tzitzis* (the Fringes of the Tallis)

The wearing of *tzitzis* serves as a constant reminder to perform the *mitzvos* that God has commanded us to do. In what may appear to be almost an afterthought, the Torah adds, "that you should not go about after your heart and after your eyes." Rashi points out that the word

> *sasuru*—"to go about"—is the same as the word *lasur*—"to scout out"—that was used in reference to the spies.
>
> The feelings and emotions that come from the eyes and the heart play a major role in deciding whether to follow the will of God or not. When the Jewish people accepted the report of the ten spies, their reaction was based on this raw instinct and emotion, completely lacking in both faith and logic. The *mitzvah* of *tzitzis* reminds us of the need to trust in God and in God's Torah; not to react on impulse and emotion alone.

If viewed by itself, the incident of the spies could well be a cause for despair but, when looked at through the eyes of the Torah, with the perspective of the rest of the *parshah*, it becomes a lesson for successful Jewish living. We are responsible for our actions; sin is not inevitable; if we do stray, we have the chance to return; and, ultimately, every Jew has a place in the Land of Israel.

THE LAW OF *CHALLAH* OUTSIDE OF ISRAEL

Even though it is clear from the words "When you come into the land" (Numbers 15:18) that the Torah law of *challah* applies only in Israel, the Rabbis enacted that it be taken by Jews living both inside Israel and *chutz la'aretz* (outside of Israel). They felt compelled to do this because, even in Israel—as mentioned above—the *mitzvah* of *challah* applies only when the Jewish people as a whole are settled in Israel. Unfortunately, this type of complete settlement has not existed since the days of the First Temple. Thus, the Rabbis feared that the very concept of separating *challah* would be forgotten by the Jewish people; therefore, they legislated that Jews everywhere should observe this *mitzvah*.

When the *mitzvah* of *challah* was extended to *chutz la'aretz*, certain leniencies were incorporated. The most noticeable one is the concept of *tevel*—forbidden; in Israel, until the *challah* has been separated from a dough or bread, the food is strictly forbidden to be eaten. Although this *mitzvah* of separating the *challah* still exists in *chutz la'aretz*, the food is *not* forbidden prior to the separation. In most cases this is of little consequence, as the baker or homemaker takes the *challah* during the process of baking. However, there is one case in which this law is of great significance. If a person baked *challah* for *Shabbos* and forgot to separate *challah* during the kneading, or purchased *challah* from an otherwise kosher bakery that does not happen to separate *challah* from its bread, the separation of *challah* at this point would involve cutting up the bread, thus disqualifying them for *lechem mishnah*, the two *Shabbos* loaves (we also have to remember that separating the *challah* on *Shabbos* (and thereby "perfecting" the God item) is a forbidden activity). In this situation, it is permitted to eat the bread as usual, leaving over a slice from which the *challah* can be taken after *Shabbos* is ended.

Rabbi Chaim Wasserman

Young Israel of Passaic-Clifton, New Jersey

THE MEASURE OF MEN

The *meraglim* chosen to scout the Land of Israel were twelve known, prestigious leaders among that generation (Rashi on Numbers 13:3, quoting Talmud *Sotah* 35). As to the particular qualities and strength of character that determined that they be chosen for this task, there are divergent opinions. The NeTZiV feels that they were highly skilled in scouting the terrain so as to guide the nation along the most appropriate route by which to come to the Land of Israel; they were not necessarily chosen for their piety and righteousness (*Ha'amek Davar*). Not so, claims Rabbi Yosef Karo. They were above all else chosen because of their greatness in Torah knowledge (*Maggid Mesharim*).

In any event, how was so prestigious a group of individuals capable of such a tragic error, after the mission, in reporting what they had done?

The *Zohar* offers a pointed explanation for their actions:

> "All of them, men" (Numbers 13:3). They were all virtuous, but they were misled by a false reasoning. They said: If Israel enters the land, we as leaders will be superseded, since it is only in the wilderness that we are judged worthy of leadership. And this was what caused their death and the death of all who followed them. (*Zohar Shlach* 158b)

The primary issue, then, for these ten leaders was to find a way to sustain their political influence, which, in their minds, was seemingly endangered once the nation arrived in Israel. Let the report show that survival could be attained only by securing the socio-political status quo: by remaining in the desert or perhaps even returning to Egypt, but surely not by pressing on toward Israel.

What could have been that in their minds that they felt not worthy of being leaders in the Promised Land? Of this we can only speculate. Was their style of leadership appropriate and effective only in a *galut* environment? Was it their language or accent or inflection? Could it have been their perspective on life—a result of having been reared in a host civilization in which Jews were always a minority? Could their leadership style work in a social structure that had to design a permanent system of living for a nation that had come home to its roots and natural habitat? Perhaps they may have sensed that all these issues would be on the minds of the rising generation, especially, and they feared being passed over in favor of other leaders, new blood. So they decided upon a campaign to insure that they would hold on to their ministerial portfolios, even at the cost of overturning the long-awaited promise that God had made to Avraham and to Moshe: the Jews would come back to their homeland.

(How strangely reminiscent this drama is of ten other Jewish leaders—all brothers, sons of one father—who had fought two centuries earlier to prevent the political dominance of a younger brother, Joseph, and also devised a horrendous plan by which they dispensed with him and rid themselves of his presence.) According to the *Zohar*, then, in these *meraglim* we have a lesson of "power tends to corrupt."

Can power corrupt the truly righteous? Seemingly, yes. That even the righteous are potentially corruptible is the lesson of this incident of the *meraglim*, according to Rav Chaim Yosef Sonnenfeld, *zt"l* the saintly Rav of Yerushalayim. Despite his strong antagonism toward the Zionist establishment in his time, Rav Sonnenfeld never missed an opportunity to express his unreserved love for the Land of Israel and for those who were then rebuilding it. As pained as he was by the desecretation of *Shabbat, yom tov*, and *kashrut* by so many of the early settlers in the new communities, he always reiterated his belief that their efforts on behalf of a rebuilt Land of Israel would, in and of itself, purify their hearts and get them to mend their ways.

At no time would he countenance any *loshon harah* concerning Israel. He would explain that the 17th of Elul, the date of death of the Torah's *meraglim*, is known as *Taanit Tzaddikim*. Why, wonders the Magen Avraham, should this day be associated with *tzaddikim* when, in fact, it is observed as a result of the *meraglim* who died? It is because the *meraglim* were nonetheless *tzaddikim*. To which Rav Sonnenfeld would add: This teaches us for all times that even *tzaddikim* can turn into *meraglim*.

But is criticism of Eretz Yisrael always *lashon hara*? Obviously not. There is criticism that is essential to human existence and criticism of another sort which is downright evil.

What the *meraglim* engaged in (*dibat ha'aretz*), speaking about the land (of Israel) was innately evil because of their motivation. As a result, ever since, Jews are hypersensitive over every bit of criticism that relates to Israel. For, if *tzaddikim* can err so horribly and be the agents of the demise of an entire generation, how exceedingly cautious must the average person be in such matters. And the acid test of determining whether criticism is *lashon hara*, in all cases, is to search for the underlying motive of the critic. Since the distortions that the *meraglim* presented about the Land of Israel were motivated solely by self-aggrandizement, their words were purely *lashon hara* despite their righteousness.

MODERN DAY *MERAGLIM*

Rav Yosef Eliyahu Henkin, *zt"l*, dean of American *gedolim* for a half-century, wrote extensively about such criticism of the State of Israel and its government.

> Israel and its Jewish population are surrounded by fierce enemies who wish to annihilate the government and the people. Our fate is tied to the support of enlightened countries, chief among which is America. [They support us] because all Jews are united behind the government and the State. Should we, however, denigrate the State and its government, why, then, should they continue to feel responsible for us? Such an attitude is unspeakable. Heaven forbid. . . . (*Kisvei Harav Henkin*, Vol. 2)

Rav Henkin branded those who were ambiguous toward the Land of Israel and its government as *malshinim*, slanderers who malign Jewish interests to foreign powers, similar to those in the times of the Roman Empire about whom a *bracha* was appended to the daily *Shmoneh Esrei*.

How then does one offer acceptable criticism? After having established the motives of the one criticizing as being pure, look, then, to the tone in which the critique is offered. Continues Rav Henkin:

> Should the government of the State of Israel conduct itself improperly on certain matters, let us remember how Eliyahu *Hanavi* finally learned to confront Achav, King of Israel. Neither amidst windstorms, nor deafening noise, nor fire and conflagrations will God's presence be felt, but only amidst the still, silent voice will the message of truth be heard.

Rabbi Evan Shore

Young Israel Shaarei Torah of Syracuse, New York

The ultimate goal for the human being is to achieve a certain level of *devekut* (connection) with *HaShem*. It is very clear that, since *HaShem* created the human being with a free will to do as he feels fit, some parameters must be set in order to keep man on track to achieve this goal. Unfortunately, there are many obstacles that we may face in our attempt to reach this level. Many philosophers think that action is the real culprit when in fact it is really the thought process. The mind and the desires of man develop a plan for the body to implement. We learn, concerning *tzitzit*, "And it shall be unto you for a fringe that you may look upon it and remember all the commandments of *HaShem* and do them, and "*vlo sasuru*," you shall not go astray after your own eyes and after your hearts" (Numbers 15:39).

The *Daat Soferim* tells us that there is both a command and a promise contained in this *pasuk*. On one hand *HaShem* is commanding us constantly to look upon the *tzitzit* as a reminder not to turn aside from Torah and *mitzvot*. The promise is that, through the performance of the *mitzvah* of *tzitzit*, we will develop and strengthen our connection with *HaShem*. The only way this is achieved is through the observance of *mitzvot* and avoidance of transgression.

It is important to point out that the same verb that is used in the *pasuk* quoted above is also found at the beginning of this *parshah*. "Send out men that "*VeYasuru*," they spy out the land of Canaan" (Numbers 13:2).

What is the basic difference between the usage of the verb in these two sentences? At the beginning of the *parshah*, there were no parameters set for the spies as to how they should report their findings. In fact, the spies were following Moshe's own command, for we learn, "See the land, what it is" (Numbers 13:18). The spies were supposed to determine whether the people were weak or strong, whether the cities and towns were fortified or not. They had to figure out for themselves what to do with the data they gathered during their spy mission. In other words, they had to map out their own strategy of thought and deed. In a very real way, the spies may have possessed a very high level of free will, in that no boundaries of right or wrong were set down in advance. When the spies came back with their report, it is very possible in their minds they felt they were doing the right thing. The sequence of events that followed tells us otherwise.

Now, however, we see that the sentence dealing with *tzitzit* shows that free will should not be left to chance. Rather, by mapping out strategy, *HaShem* shows us that He does not want us to forge ahead in unexplored territories of thought and deed on our own. The Torah is warning us that when we use our free will there will be pitfalls we must overcome. As a result, *HaShem* tells us how to deal with the situation before it becomes a problem.

Rashi tell us, (Numbers 15:40) "The heart and the eyes are the spies of the body. They are the agents for its sins: the eye sees, and the heart desires, and the body commits the sin."

The heart of man can be broken down into two distinct desires. On one hand man desires to do good. However, at the same time, the heart also craves for bad things. The *Mishnah* in *Berakhot* Chapter 9 *Mishnas* 9:5 tells us, "A person is obligated to bless the bad the way he blesses the good. As it says: 'And you shall love the Lord your God with all your heart.'" (Deuteronomy 6:5) It is written with *all* your heart [with two *bets*]; meaning, with two inclinations, the good and the bad." It is the hope of the *Gemara* that we can harness the bad inclination along with the good and that, together, they may be used in the worship of *HaShem*.

Our eyes also can place man in a difficult position. The eyes seek out the desires of the heart, whether they be for good or bad. It is this quality that the *Daat Soferim* says poses the greatest threat to us. The eyes have the ability to arouse the thoughts as well as the desires of the human being.

It is for these reasons that *HaShem* warns us about the power of the heart and eyes. But here we have the advantage the spies lacked. The Jew wears *tzitzit* as a daily and constant reminder to fulfill *HaShem*'s *mitzvot*, for they are the remedy and the path to keep the Jew away from transgression. When we see the *tzitzit*, our hearts should burn with a desire to come closer to *HaShem*. It is for this reason that our Rabbis tell us, "The *mitzvah* of *tzitzit* is equal to all the *mitzvot* in the Torah." Furthermore, it is no coincidence that the *Gemara* in *Menachot* 43b tells us, "One who is diligent in this commandment will merit seeing the Divine presence." With all said and done, what greater motivation can there be in harnessing our heart, eyes, and thought processes, especially when our doing so will lead us down the road to receive the Divine presence of *HaShem*.

Rabbi Chaim Wakslak

Young Israel of Long Beach, New York

Just prior to the scheduled entry of *Bnei Yisrael* into *Eretz Yisrael,* Moshe Rabbeinu was instructed by *HaShem Yisborach* to "Send men to scout the land of Canaan, which I am giving to the Children of Israel." Moshe chose for this important mission men of great stature, leaders of the people of Israel. Yet we know that the mission of these scouts (the *meraglim*) was a failure that ended tragically when they returned with a negative report about the Land. How was this possible?

Furthermore, they brought back this disastrous, erroneous report during a period of time in which there existed a miraculous relationship between *HaShem Yisborach* and *Bnei Yisrael.* The people of Israel had just been delivered miraculously from the Egyptian bondage. They had followed *HaShem* into the desolate desert, where there existed no viable means of survival. They witnessed the miraculous sustenance that *HaShem* sent down each day and enjoyed the protective benefits of the *Ananei Hakavod* (the Clouds of Glory). The Revelation of the Torah at Mount Sinai was supernatural and, without hesitation, the Children of Israel proclaimed, "We shall do!" and "We shall listen!"

The *meraglim* whom Moshe Rabbeinu sent on this mission were not only people personally familiar with the total, miraculous power of the *Ribbono shel Olam* to protect, defend, and deliver His people; they were the best of *Bnei Yisrael.* How could they, of all people, sabotage the glorious entry of the Children of Israel into *Eretz Yisrael* by returning with a report that the land was unconquerable? Did they suffer some monumental loss of faith?

The Chasam Sofer, in his preface to his monumental books of responsa, suggests that, to the contrary, it was because of their leadership positions, intense piety, and acclimation to a miraculous existence that they wanted to avoid the non-spiritual, non-miraculous, somewhat pedestrian existence that awaited them in *Eretz Yisrael.*

As the subsequent events indicate, this philosophy was found to be flawed in the eyes of *HaShem* and can be explained further by an insight of the Lubavitcher Rebbe, *zt"l*. The Rebbe questions the *midrash* that states that, on the night prior to *Kabbalat Hatorah*, the Jews overslept. Given the tension of this historic moment and the enthusiasm expressed by the Jews themselves, it is somewhat incomprehensible that the Jews should have overslept. The Rebbe explains that, on the contrary, they overslept because they wished to reach a higher spiritual plane, as happens when a person sleeps and his or her *neshamah* leaves the body and goes up to the heavens. Thus, uninhibited by their bodies, they could maximize their attachment to the Torah. The *Ribbono shel Olam* frowned upon this intention, as evidenced by the *midrash*'s implication that their oversleeping was perceived as a transgression.

In a similar vein, as well-intentioned as the *meraglim* may have been, the goal of a human being is not to be a *malach* (an angel), living a totally spiritual life unburdened by the needs of the human condition. The decision on the part of the *meraglim* to sabotage the entry into *Eretz Yisrael* was not consistent with the mission of man.

Years later, when Yehoshua sent spies just before the actual entry of *Bnei Yisrael* into *Eretz Yisrael*, they were able to complete their mission successfully, and *Bnei Yisrael* did enter the land. Why, when Moshe Rabbeinu was the greater leader, were his scouts unable to fulfill their mission? What was different about the scouts that Yehoshua sent?

The *navi* Joshua 2:1 refers to the *meraglim* sent by Yehoshua as *cheresh*—"potters." The *Yalkut Shimoni* explains that the *pasuk* is teaching us that they disguised themselves as pottery salesmen so they would not be detected. However, there appears to be a more significant message in their characterization as "potters." The Talmud, in Tractate *Berakhot* (57b) states that one who sees a pot in his dreams should anticipate peace. This is understandable, given the reality that a pot creates peace between two opposing forces of water and fire. The fact that the scouts sent by Yehoshua succeeded is directly linked to the fact that they were able to make peace between the physical aspects of man and his spiritual responsibilities. The lack of this accommodation is precisely where Moshe's *meraglim* failed.

The true goal of man is reflected in the commentary of the *Chidushei Harim* at the end of the *sedrah*. The Torah details three *mitzvot*: wine libations to accompany the sacrifices (*nesachim*), *challah* that must be given from bread, and *tzitzit* that must be worn on our clothing. The proximity of these three *mitzvot* to the episode of the *meraglim* is significant, according to the *Chidushei Harim*. In essence, he states that, while in the desert, *Bnei Yisrael* were sustained through the manna, flowing water, and clouds of glory. As they entered Israel they would no longer have these miracles, but the great spiritual endowment these miracles brought would be captured through the fulfillment of these three *mitzvot*. Specifically, the manna corresponds to the *mitzvah* of *challah*; the *mitzvah* of *nesachim*, to the *Be'er* (well) of Miriam; and the *mitzvah* of *tzitzit*, to the clouds of glory. Had the *meraglim* that Moshe Rabbeinu sent realized that it was incumbent on *Bnei Yisrael* to move from a realm of the overtly miraculous, which they had enjoyed till then, to the realm of fulfillment of *mitzvot*, as represented by these three *mitzvot* now being given them, they might not have arrogantly decided to resist the Divine plan, and *Bnei Yisrael* might have been spared the punishment that the sin of the *meraglim* led to.

❖ CHAPTER 43 ❖

Korach

Rabbi Neil N. Winkler

Young Israel of Fort Lee, New Jersey

An open rebellion. Certainly, Moshe *Rabbeinu* had faced challenges to his leadership before—malcontents who tried to appoint a new leader so that they could return to Egypt—but never before had such a large following been attracted to an attempt to undermine the positions of leadership held by Moshe and Aharon. And why this attraction? *Chazal* share with us in *Midrash Shocher Tov* that Korach did not make this a "one issue" campaign. Korach was clever enough to present to the people a distorted picture of Moshe Rabbeinu as an unfeeling, uncaring leader who was concerned only with amassing more wealth for himself and his family.

The argument centered on a poor widow with two orphaned daughters who possessed but one field. When they went to plow the field, Moshe told them that they could not plow with a mule and an ox together. When they went to seed the field, they were prohibited from mixing seeds. When it was time to harvest, they were told that they had to leave gifts for the poor. As they prepared the grain, they were told to hand over portions to Aharon's family (the *terumah*) and Moshe's tribe (the *ma'aser*). In frustration, this poor woman sold the field and bought two sheep, but as soon as the first lamb was born, Aharon came and demanded it (*bechor behemah*), and when she sheared the wool, Aharon also claimed the first portion (*reishit hagez*). When she decided to slaughter the animals, Aharon told her that he was entitled to certain portions of the meat. In frustration, she finally sanctified the animals and forfeited her rights to them; so Aharon claimed full ownership of the animals (*cherem*). This was a powerful argument that drew much support from a feeling and sensitive people. Yet it was, of course, twisted, distorted, and one-sided. Korach purposely ignored the many *mitzvot* demanding compassion to the widow and orphan; he omitted the great accomplishments of Moshe and focused only upon the negative. No wonder he was successful!

Chazal, however, were able to see through the guise and guile of Korach and reveal the core of the argument. *Vayikach Korach*—"and Korach took"—What did he take? "*Ben Yitzhar, ben Kehat ben Levi*," the verse Numbers 16:1 goes on to say: his lineage, his parentage, his *yichus*. Korach's true argument with Moshe was not one of ideas, of substance, but one of personality. Korach demanded the *kavod* and position due him as a result of who his parents were—not what he had accomplished. No wonder, then, that Yaakov *Avinu* prayed, *bikehalam al teichad kvodi* (Genesis 49:6)—"let my honor not be diminished in their uprising." Yaakov knew that Korach would use his ancestry as a reason to rebel—and, therefore, made sure that *he*, Yaakov—would have nothing to do with it (which is why his name is not included in the lineage of Korach).

Korach failed to realize that ancestry was meant to serve as an example to the new generation, that our ancestry is a challenge to live up to the standards and righteousness of our parents. In the words of our Rabbis, "A person should constantly ask himself: When will my deeds and accomplishments reach those of my parents?" It is in this light that we understand the statement in the *Gemara* (*Pesachim* 62), "From the day that the *Sefer Yuchasin* [Book of Ancestry] was lost, the power of the Rabbis was diminished." For, unless the spiritual leaders of each generation can point to the accomplishments of the past as a challenge for their children, their ability to influence and inspire is severely curtailed.

Korach began his argument in a most altruistic tone; yet, in truth, it was a personal and selfish rebellion. Note, the *Akedat Yitzchak* points out, how Dotan and Aviram purposely use Moshe's exact words to them, mocking him and turning the argument into a personal one. How much more chutzpah can there be than to call the Land of Egypt a "land flowing with milk and honey"—words identified only with *Eretz Yisrael*! No wonder that *Chazal* understood this rebellion as *Shelo leshem Shamayim*—a selfish argument that did not enhance God's glory. It was an argument that twisted fact and centered upon personal attack instead of substantive discussion.

The Jewish world stands at a crossroads. Both within the Torah world and within the general Jewish community, there are crucial decisions to be made and honest differences to be expressed. How tragic when we read of arguments that swerve from substance and center upon the personal! They become springboards for *lashon harah* and *sinat chinom* when they could become forums for understanding and cooperation. It is time that frank discussion—especially within the observant community—reflected the discussions of *Beit* Shammai and *Beit* Hillel, arguments *leshem Shamayim* that did not cause a breach in the Jewish world, rather than the arguments of Korach and his cohorts, personal attacks, *cherems* and malicious slander, that can only lead to destruction and tragedy.

Rabbi Feivel Wagner

Young Israel of Forest Hills, New York

Each of us has had *rabbanim, rabbeim,* and other teachers of Torah who have left their mark upon us. Our knowledge, our commitment to Torah and *mitzvot,* our *middot* and character have been furthered and formed by these mentors, and we are the richer for it. Sometimes there are ideas and lessons that touch us constantly, and we can still remember the first person who opened our eyes to them.

I can still picture a *vaad* (informal *mussar* class) led by the late *mashgiach* of my *yeshivah* (the Mirrer *Yeshivah* in Brooklyn, New York), Rav Hirsch Feldman, *zt"l.* Every Thursday night he would lead a class in *Chochmat Mussar,* a *mussar* text written by Rav Simcha Zissel, *zt"l,* the "Alter" of Kelm. We studied the *sefer* in order, slowly going through it chapter by chapter. Invariably, the chapter would touch on a thought that "happened" to be connected to the *parshah* of the week, a coming *yom tov* or fast day, or an event that had occurred that week. The *mashgiach* would always point out how thorough and complete the truth of *hashgachah pratis* (divine intervention) is. The *Ribbono shel Olam* controls the world; nothing is a coincidence. We just have to delve into everything around us to see His presence.

This thought comes to mind as I look at the confluence of *Shabbat Rosh Chodesh* and *Parshat Korach.* What connection is there between the two? Looking at the revolt of Korach and the *mitzvah* of sanctification of the new moon through the eyes of *Chazal,* I have come up with the following thought: The first *mitzvah* given to the Jewish people is the *mitzvah* of sanctification of the new moon. Witnesses would appear before the *Bet Din,* testify that they had seen the new moon, and the *Bet Din* would proclaim that day as Rosh Chodesh, the first day of the new month. It is based on this act of sanctification that all the *yomim tovim* are set, since they are tied to a specific day of the month, not a day of the week.

The *Gemara* of *Rosh Hashanah* (pg 25) teaches us a fundamental concept in understanding the role of the *Bet Din*. The *Mishnah* relates an incident in which Rabban Gamliel, the *Nasi*, had accepted witnesses and proclaimed Rosh Chodesh on the basis of their testimony. Rabbi Yehoshua claimed, rightfully, that the witnesses were obviously lying, since their description of what they had seen was a physical impossibility, and that, therefore, the next day should be Rosh Chodesh. Upon hearing of Rabbi Yehoshua's disagreement with his ruling, Rabban Gamliel sent a message to him. "I decree upon you that you must come to me with your staff and money on the day of Yom Kippur according to your reckoning."

Rabbi Yehoshua was severely troubled by this command of the *Nasi* until his student, Rabbi Akiva, reminded him of a lesson that he himself had taught: "The Torah uses the expression *Eileh mo'adei HaShem . . . asher tikre'u otam*— 'These are the festivals of *HaShem* . . . that you should proclaim them' (Leviticus 23:14). The spelling of the word *otam* (them) is the same as that of *atem* (you) to teach us that the determination of the new moon is totally dependent on *Bet Din*, and that even if they are fooled, mistaken or even purposely choose the wrong day, it is still valid."

Rabbi Yehoshua, hearing these words, did as Rabban Gamliel commanded and came to him with the money and staff. Rabban Gamliel stood up, kissed him on his head, and said, "Come in peace my master and disciple—my master in wisdom, and my disciple in that you accepted my words."

The authority of *Bet Din*, which has its fullest expression in *Kiddush Hachodesh*, is an important idea in all other areas of Torah as well. It is the teachers and those who decide the Torah who are our ultimate authority.

The story of Korach expresses this idea as well. Rashi quotes the *midrash*, which details the arguments of Korach and his cohorts. They asked Moshe whether a garment completely made of *techelet* (the blue wool used as part of the *tzitzit*) needs *tzitzit* and whether a house full of *sifrei Torah* needs a *mezuzah*. Upon hearing Moshe's answer in the affirmative, they mocked him: "If one strand of *techelet* can fulfill the requirement of *tzitzit*, how much more so if the entire garment is made of that material. If one small scroll on the doorpost can fulfill the requirement of *mezuzah*, how much more so if the house is full of *sefarim*."

What were they trying to say? What was their real argument? Korach claimed that there was no need for Torah authorities such as Moshe and Aharon. "*Ki kol ha'eidah kulam kedoshim*—" (Numbers 16:3). All of the members of the congregation are holy; each one can decide for himself. One does not have to defer to *talmidei chachamim* or *poskim* to deal with questions that arise; we can decide for ourselves. The response of *HaShem* comes quickly and, with it, guidance for future generations. It is to our Torah leaders that we must look for the answers to the questions, which become increasingly more difficult to answer.

American Jewry has been orphaned over the past decade with the loss of our great *poskim* and *rabbeim*. If we truly understand the qualifications for Jewish leaders, we must turn to true Torah authorities for answers to individual and communal questions, and we must also increase our support for Torah institutions to develop the leaders of tomorrow.

Rabbi Naphtali Burnstein

Young Israel of Cleveland, Ohio

In *Pirkei Avot* (5:20) we are reminded of the difference between "a dispute that is for the sake of Heaven" and "a dispute that is not for the sake of Heaven." In giving us the examples of each, the *Mishnah* chooses that of Hillel and Shammai as that of "a dispute that is for the sake of Heaven" and that of Korach and his entire community as that of "a dispute that is not for the sake of Heaven."

The question is asked, why are the two examples given in the *Mishnah* not comparable? In the first example, Hillel and Shammai, who disputed with each other, are cited as having disputes for the sake of Heaven, whereas, in the latter example, rather than Korach together with Moshe and Aharon, Korach and his community are cited. Did Korach indeed dispute with his followers, or with Moshe and Aharon?

Many suggestions have been offered; perhaps the best-known approach is the following:

The *Mishnah* mentioned above points out that a dispute for the sake of Heaven will have a constructive outcome, whereas a dispute that is not for the sake of Heaven will not. The basis of this quite striking difference is the motivation for each. A dispute for the sake of Heaven has truth as its ultimate goal. Under such circumstances, as in the case of Hillel and Shammai, both sides, seeking the ultimate truth, or *emet*, can have validity and permanence to their particular stance or view. In the particular case of Hillel and Shammai, the Ritva explains that, although presently the halacha follows Hillel, a time will come in the future when Shammai's opinion will be followed and practiced. Thus, ultimately the words used by our Sages to describe their disputes as these and these are words of a living God (*eilu v'eilu divrei Elo-him chayim*) will be fulfilled.

On the other hand, when *emet* is not the goal, and personal gain and honor are being sought, then not only do such disputes not endure, but even their adherents begin to differ and split apart themselves. The classic example of a dispute that is not for the sake of Heaven is not Korach and Moshe, but rather Korach and his community. Each member of Korach's community was fighting, but not necessarily for the same cause or goal. Each had his own particular interest and/or need in mind.

Along the same lines it may be suggested that our Sages in *Pirkei Avot* wanted to stress to us the tragic effects of *machloket* (division). Within Korach's followers there were two groups:

1. Those who were there to cause trouble
2. Those whose intentions were sincere but who were misled by others

By identifying the classic example of an inappropriate dispute as that of Korach and his community, our Sages teach us to avoid any form of division, whether it be one with the motives of a Korach (1) or with the motives of a member of his community (2). The Torah itself warns us to avoid both of these approaches to *machloket,* when it says "that he may not be like Korach and his community" (Leviticus 17:5).

Rabbi Moishe Silverman

Young Israel of Phoenix, Arizona

Parshat Korach contains actually two areas of complaints against Moshe. The first is the well-known dispute with Korach. In Numbers 16:21, we find *HaShem* instructing Moshe and Aaron, "Separate yourselves from among this congregation that I may consume them in a moment." In the following verse it states "And they fell upon their faces and said, 'O God, God of the spirits of all flesh, shall one man sin and You be angry with the entire assembly?'"

HaShem responded by instructing Moshe, "Speak to the assembly saying, 'Go up from all around the dwelling places of Korach, Dathan, and Abiram.'" The rest is history. They are gone, swallowed up, and Moshe and Aaron are vindicated by God.

The very next day, "The entire assembly of the Children of Israel complained on the morrow against Moshe and Aaron saying, 'You have killed the people of *HaShem*'" (Numbers 17:6). You would think that, after what they had seen the previous day they would have been a bit more inhibited in their complaints. In *this* complaint, the commentaries explain, the people thought that Moshe, on his own, told the two hundred and fifty rebels to offer the incense that would cause their death. They believed that Moshe should have chosen a test that would not have caused the rebels to die. Thus, they held Moshe accountable for the death of the people. The fact that the assembly, who now complained, were punished, is obviously intended to tell them that they should have trusted Moshe enough to know that what he said came from *HaShem*.

When *HaShem* is about to carry out the punishment, we read, "Get yourselves up from among this assembly, and I shall destroy them in an instant. And they fell on their faces" (Numbers 17:10). In the following verse it states: "Moshe said to Aaron, 'Take the fire-pan and put on it fire from the altar and place incense—go quickly to the assembly and provide atonement for them, for the fury has gone out from the presence of *HaShem*; the plague has begun!'"

Rashi offers two interesting thoughts on why incense was used. The first reason was that the Angel of Death had taught Moshe that incense stops the plague. The second reason was that the Children of Israel saw incense as an instrument of death, as Aaron's two sons Nadav and Avihu and now the two hundred and fifty rebels were burned to death because of the incense. Thus, Moshe used the incense to stop the plague so that the people would know that only sin is deadly.

There remain some unanswered questions in these two cases of complaints against Moshe. First, why, in the episode of Korach, does *HaShem* instruct Moshe and Aaron, "Separate yourselves," whereas later, during the people's complaint, *HaShem* says, "Get yourselves up"? Second, why do Moshe and Aaron, in the episode of Korach, "fall on their faces" (Numbers 16:22), whereas, during the people's complaint (17:10), they "fall on their faces" after *HaShem* instructs them, "Get yourselves up"? Finally, during the Korach episode, Moshe intervenes only on behalf of the innocent, and *HaShem* responds accordingly, waiting for those that are innocent to separate from Korach. However, at the time of the people's complaint, Moshe intervenes on behalf of *all* the people; yet *HaShem* immediately takes retribution, and 14,700 died. Why?

We know that the dispute Korach had with Moshe was "not for the sake of Heaven." The guilt of Korach and his community was clear; their actions were not innocent or due to poor judgment but were premeditated.

Moshe cannot save Korach. It is up to Korach to save himself by recanting. He does not, and he is swallowed up. However, Moshe can and does separate himself and the rest of the Jewish people. Thus, in the very next verse, he falls on his face and asks *HaShem* to exonerate the people. *HaShem* listens, and the people are spared.

In the second scenario, when the people complained they did not do so with malice. They believed that 250 excellent people died when they could have been spared. They thought, as the commentaries pointed out, that this was Moshe's doing. They did not know that it was from *HaShem*.

Thus, when Moshe hears God's plan, that he is being asked to "Get yourselves up from among this assembly, and I shall destroy them in an instant," in the very same verse "he falls on his face," showing *HaShem* he does not want to "get up" and remove himself from associating and guiding these people. Though the people are guilty of challenging Moshe, and, thus, the plague begins immediately, Moshe responds without delay by showing the people their error: the 250 rebels did not die because of the incense, as the people thought; rather, *HaShem* killed them because of their sins. The people then realized their mistake and regretted their actions, and the incense stopped the plague of death.

Again, it is interesting to note that Moshe immediately responded to *HaShem* when told to "separate" in reference to the death of Korach, whereas he did not immediately respond to *HaShem* when told, "Get yourselves up," at the people's complaint. Moshe is not even offended by their challenge; he is concerned only about preserving their well-being and showing them their error.

Perhaps this is what we should be looking at in life. Disputes that are based on error, not malice, need to be approached as Moshe our teacher did—first, by immediately showing concern about the party that is in error; second, by taking caring action to help show that party's mistake, and, finally, saving the party from further pain by putting an end to the specific situation that caused the error. If we can all take Moshe's approach to personal complaints that are made in error, I am sure we will again soon see Aaron, *Kohein Gadol,* and his descendants offering incense on the Altar in the Third Temple. May it be built speedily in our time!

❖ CHAPTER 44 ❖

Chukat

Rabbi Reuven Fink

Young Israel of New Rochelle, New York

This week's *parshah, Chukat,* opens with the law of *parah adumah,* the red heifer. This law concerns the purification of one who has become ritually impure by contact with a human corpse. The *kohein,* the priest, would sprinkle the person who is *tamei* with fresh water into which the ashes of the red heifer, cedarwood, and scarlet have been placed. This is done on the third day and again on the seventh day. After the process is completed, the person is *tahor,* purified. He may once again be permitted to enter the precincts of the *Beit Hamikdash,* the Holy Temple.

The *parshah* begins, "This is the statute of the Torah" (*zot chukat Hatorah*). *Parah adumah* has always been the classic example of a *chok,* a statute that defies human explanation. Even King Solomon, the wisest of all men, declared concerning this precept: "I said I would acquire wisdom, yet it, (the *mitzvah* of *parah adumah*) has eluded me" (Kohelet 10:23).

The rationale behind *parah adumah* presents a variety of problems. Why must the heifer be all red, a color that usually symbolizes sin? Why do we include a piece of cedarwood and some hyssop grass? Why is a red thread thrown in? Why is there a need for fresh water to be put into the entire mixture?

These questions are, perhaps, no different than those posed about many of the Torah's other commandments that are *chukim.* Why, for example, does meat need to come from an animal that has cloven hooves and chews its cud in order to be kosher? Why are we forbidden to wear garments containing linen and wool—the *halachah* called *sha'atnez*?

However, with *parah adumah,* there is a paradox within the fabric of the law itself. While the red heifer has the power to *purify the defiled,* it also, at the very same time, *defiles the pure.* How can the very same substance have two opposite effects on people?

Rav Ovadiah Sforno, the sixteenth-century Italian commentator, addresses himself at length to this topic of *parah adumah*. Though not presuming to be wiser than Shlomo *Hamelech*, he writes that, by carefully analyzing this law, we can discover something of its rationale and derive a profound lesson from it. He bases his analysis upon the doctrine propounded by Maimonides —that *HaShem*, God, wants man to conduct his behavior in accordance with the "*golden mean*." This doctrine states that man should always strive for a middle path in all his personality traits. For example, a person should be neither a miser nor spendthrift. He should seek a happy medium between these two extremes. The same applies to all man's characteristics.

The Rambam points out that a person who finds that he is guilty of inclining to any one extreme can get back to a state of equilibrium by leaning toward the opposite extreme. If a person is very stingy, he should, for a while, become a spendthrift. When he thus rids himself of his stinginess, he will then achieve a middle path in regard to money, "just as a needle that is bent," the Rambam says, "becomes straight when you bend it to the other side."

This is how Sforno explains the paradox of *parah adumah*. A person who has sinned has gone to an extreme. All the transgressions in the Torah are undesirable extremes. This is symbolized by the *parah adumah*, for red is the color that biblically represents sin. To do *teshuvah*, to repent, the person must incline himself to the opposite extreme of his particular area of transgression in order ultimately to achieve the happy medium, the "golden mean."

That is why cedarwood and grass are mixed in: the mighty and tall cedar tree, which symbolizes haughtiness, and grass, which grows close to the ground and bends in the breeze, are taken together. They represent extremes of the same type of trait, arrogance and self-effacement. The person seeking purity is reminded that he must now, for a while, choose the extreme that will bring him back to the desired stability. A red thread is also put there as a sign that usually all extremes are sinful. These symbols are then thrown into water mixed with the ashes of the heifer, which gives a middle state, in between a liquid and a solid. This is the purification process for one who has sinned. One who has not sinned, one who is *tahor*, has already achieved the "middle path" and cannot expose himself to extremes. What heals a sick person can be toxic to one who is healthy. What purifies the defiled can defile the pure. This is Sforno's analysis.

The difficulty, however, is that we are discussing the purification process of an individual who just happened to walk into the same room where a dead person was lying. We are not speaking about either sins or sinners!

I believe that if we go one step further in the analysis, we will find the answer to this question. When we *daven* at the home of a mourner, an extra psalm is added at the end of the prayers. In it, King David writes, "Man's inward thought is that he and his possessions will live on forever" (Psalms 49:12). We glorify life to the extreme of feeling that the outward trappings of power and wealth will outlast death. Therefore, we live our lives thinking that the joy of physical possessions is the antidote to our inevitable deaths. We fail to recognize the part of ourselves that is infinite. Man's soul transcends death.

Man, himself, is comprised of two extremes—the physical side and the spiritual side. To go to either extreme is sinful. To live a totally ascetic life, a life completely devoid of physical pleasure, is as wrong as living a completely hedonistic existence. Man must choose a middle path. This "golden mean" is the path of the Torah.

When man comes in contact with a dead person, his initial reaction is that all has ended with the biological death. He is repulsed and revolted by the mere prospect of his own death. This reaction is sinful and impure. It reflects man's awareness of only the physical dimension of himself. In order to deprogram man from the cult of materialism, the Torah demands that he go through the *parah adumah* experience. It shows him that man has a spiritual side that transcends death and that only by living a life of balance and equilibrium, not a life of excess—only by following the Torah—will he achieve a holy existence.

Now, when there is no *Mishkan* and the laws of ritual purity do not apply, the heart of man is the sanctuary—the *Mishkan HaShem*. Man must see to it that his heart remains pure. This is not an impossible task for, as our *Chazal* tell us, "If a Jew desires purity, *HaShem* Himself will assist him."

Rabbi Abraham Morduchowitz

Young Israel of Orangeburg, New York

Discontent is difficult to control. Sometimes it gives rise to open rebellion, but mostly it simmers beneath the surface, flaring up every now and then. Sometimes there are valid reasons for the unhappiness and justification for the discontent. Most often, however, it is merely a state of mind with a vague and intangible feeling of displeasure gripping the individual or society. The dissatisfaction that governed the mood of the Jewish people in the desert is the focus of *Parshat Chukat*.

Even after Moshe had settled the rebellion of Korach and his followers, who challenged Moshe's right to leadership, he still had to contend with the constant murmuring. It is noteworthy that the discontent described in this week's *sedrah* was directed neither against the right of Moshe to be the leader of the people nor solely against Moshe. The Jewish people were not denying that Moshe had acted in accordance with the will of God since the Exodus. Their complaint and discontent were also directed against God.

After the death of Miriam, when the Jewish people were camped at Kadesh, they suffered terribly from a lack of water. They came and complained to Moshe and Aaron, saying that they would rather have died in the uprising instigated by Korach than suffer a lingering death due to thirst. Their complaint was attended to by God, and Moshe was called upon to bring water forth from the rock without any prejudice, since their suffering was very great. Later, after the death of Aaron, when they traveled from *Har Hahor* by way of the Red Sea to pass around Edom, the people spoke out again against God and Moshe. This time they complained about the lack of water and their dislike for the manna. This time, they were punished for their discontent, and God sent poisonous snakes to bite the malcontents. After the snakes killed a great number of them, the people came to Moshe, saying, "We have sinned against God and against you. Please pray to God to remove the snakes from us." Moshe prayed for them, and God relented: "And God said to Moshe, 'Make for yourself a serpent, and place it on a flagpole. And whenever anyone is bitten, he will see it and live.' And Moshe made a serpent of brass and placed it on a flagpole, and it happened that whenever anyone was bitten by a serpent, he would look at the brass serpent and he would live" (Numbers 21:8–9).

The entire episode is very strange. When the Egyptians were smitten with a plague before the Exodus and asked Moshe to pray and intercede for them, God removed the cause of their distress directly rather than give them an antidote to their misfortune. Yet, in this case, God did not simiply remove the snakes. He gave the Jew who was bitten the opportunity to obtain an antidote to the venom by looking up at the brass serpent. Rashi questions the whole episode and, in essence, cites the *Mishnah* in *Rosh Hashanah*: "Surely the serpent had no power to either kill or preserve life. The point was that whenever the Jews would turn their eyes upward and subdue their hearts to their Father in Heaven, they would be cured; otherwise they would suffer harm." The problem still remains, however. Why did the snake have to be used at all? It would have been enough if those who were bitten had been required to raise their eyes to the heavens and pray to the *Ribbono shel Olam* for help so that they would be cured. Why did they need the snake to begin with?

The Ramban, commenting on this week's *sedrah*, explains that the purpose of the brass serpent was a manifestation of the concept of the *derech HaShem* showing itself through *neis betoch neis*—a miracle within a miracle, the miraculous cure being brought about through the very agent that caused the death threat. There is a popular belief that when someone is traumatized by a fright, as well as hurt physically, all references to or contact with the causative agent must be avoided for the mental health of the patient. Thus, if someone is bitten by a dog, it is thought that all contact with dogs or even seeing the picture of a dog can bring on anxiety attacks and can be very dangerous. In the case of the brass serpent, however, God commanded that the healing should come about by the very cause of the disease. The image of the snake that caused danger to life has now become the medium of the cure in order that Israel should realize that life and death are totally in the hands of God alone.

The relationship between what Rashi was telling us about the need to look up to God as the source of salvation and the *neis betoch neis* concept of the Ramban are now clear. By setting this image of the serpent, which is the common symbol of evil and death, high above the people, thereby forcing them to look upward when they looked upon it for their cure, God demonstrated an important lesson: There is no separate realm or domain for evil. Satan and the Angel of Death have no independent wills or caprices whereby they can plague mankind. Rather, they are the servants and messengers of God and act only with God's concurrence and permission. (This is also another area of major difference between Judaism and Christianity. Christian theology includes the concept of Satan revolting against God, but that can never be in Judaism. Interestingly enough, the snake on the staff became the symbol for healing and curing, as it was adopted by the medical profession as their logo.)

There is another important lesson we learn from this episode. The *midrash* explains the symbolism of the snake as that of the original snake—the snake that led Adam and Eve astray in the Garden of Eden. Adam and Eve lived in a perfect world. They had no need to struggle for a living or for food or clothing, as all of their needs were provided for them. The serpent aroused in them a feeling of discontent only because, in the vast Garden of Eden, they were not permitted to partake of the Tree of Knowledge, even though everything else was for them to enjoy. They became blind to what they had and could focus only on what they were denied.

This, too, was the situation of the Jews in the desert. They could not see what the *Ribbono shel Olam* was doing for them. Their clothing did not wear out; the manna dropped for them every morning; they had the squab for food, and they had the pillar of cloud by day to protect them from the sun and the pillar of fire to light their way at night. Their discontent with what they had became a fixation, and it resulted in tragedy. The brass serpent was to be an object lesson for all men for all times. When they looked up to heaven and saw the brass serpent, they would remember the original sin of Adam and Eve, instigated by the serpent, who blinded them to what they had and caused them to focus on what they did not have, thus fostering the discontent that leads to sin. When they looked up in prayer for help and healing from their affliction, they would remember that all they had was given to them by God and would truly repent.

This is a message all of us must be able to absorb and practice in our own lives, and in this *zechus* may we all be blessed.

Rabbi Chaim Wasserman

Young Israel of Passaic-Clifton, New Jersey

For a second time, we find Moshe Rabbeinu striking a desert boulder with his staff. The incident and its consequences, as related in *Parshat Chukat*, leave us with three gnawing questions:

QUESTION 1

What was so terrible this time about Moshe's striking the rock, especially since, at a similar prior scene (*Parshat Beshalach*), Moshe was specifically instructed to hit the desert rock with his staff? The act of striking the rock, therefore, was an appropriate action when water was desperately needed!

The first incident, in which Moshe is instructed to strike the rock, occurred on 22 or 23 Iyar (the year was 2448 since creation), only a short month after the Exodus from Egypt and the crossing of the Red Sea.

At that time, God instructed Moshe in fine detail how to solve the problem of the need for water: Pass in front of the people and take with you some of the elders, as well as the very same staff with which you smote the river. I (God) will be present in front of you on the spot where you are to strike the rock, so that, as a result, water will flow from that rock for the people to drink (see Exodus 17). God's instructions were meticulously followed, and water flowed forth from the rock, in sufficient quantity to convince the nation that, in fact, the very God who freed them from Egyptian bondage was carefully watching over the plight of His people.

Obviously, despite the lesson in faith they learned that fateful night when they left Egypt, which was reinforced for them a week later when they crossed *Yam Suf*, and despite what they witnessed as they stood round Mount Sinai, faith for that generation was very short-lived. Now, water was again scarce; so the people needed manifest miracles at the hands of Moshe and Aharon. And they demanded answers from them immediately.

God well understood the proclivity of His people for regression to a slave mental state. In Egypt, that generation was well indoctrinated and fully conditioned to react to the authority that Pharaoh's shamans (*chartumim*) wielded because of their magical sleight of hand. That is why, when Moshe Rabbeinu first came on his mission to the Jews, of necessity, he had to communicate with them in a manner that would attract their attention and that would then motivate them to listen to a new message from their God. This was the reason for the staff, which, when thrown before them would turn to a snake and then back to a staff. With this staff Moshe was commanded to smite the desert boulder; with the same staff he split the waters of *Yam Suf* so that the nation could march freely out of Egypt. With this staff, a faithful messenger of God was initially able to win the loyalty of a people to the God of their ancestors. And so, Moshe, this first time, I instruct you to hit the rock, to show My people wonders and miracles—from a rock you will be able to produce sufficient water to quench their thirst. In this way you will be able to teach them a supreme lesson of faith about Divine providence in a manner, appropriate to their new mental status as freed slaves, that they will be able to understand.

The incident in *Parshat Chukat*, the second time Moshe struck a desert rock, took place during the month of Nisan 2487, which was the beginning of the fortieth year after the Exodus from Egypt. Four decades have now passed, and the nation had indeed flourished. It is a new generation of Jews whom we are dealing with. The people are at this point on the brink of entering the Promised Land. Now their concern is not just to survive harsh desert conditions or a nomadic existence but to realize the fulfillment of a dream—a Divine promise—that their parents and grandparents did not merit to see. They were coming home to the land of Avraham, Yitzchak, and Yaakov.

But suddenly, there wasn't sufficient water, and the nation once again blames Moshe and Aharon for having gotten them into this appalling situation. Listen to the way they express their anguish: It would have been wiser, they screamed, had they remained in Egypt instead of following the lies they were handed—that they were headed for a land where grain, fruits, and water are abundant. How ironic: forty years pass, and the people sound as though their experience with Divine providence counted for nothing. The nation now regresses to the slave mentality, as though they were the same individuals who had left Egypt. The same accusations that were hurled at Moshe a month after leaving bondage are now again repeated nearly verbatim. (Compare Exodus 17:3 with Numbers 20:3–5.) Where was faith (*emunah*)? Where was trust (*bitachon*), backed by forty years of real life experience? It was as though *nothing* had changed!

Accordingly, God instructs Moshe *Rabbeinu* that this time what was essential was a demonstration of the power of prayer. This time, Moshe, talks to the rock for effective results. One thing is now certain: the old attention-getting methods that were employed with the previous generation of freed slaves could no longer be appropriate. And so we come to our second question.

QUESTION 2

Just what did God want Moshe *Rabbeinu* to say when speaking to the rock?

Moshe, this time, was simply being told to lift his hands in prayerful supplication and talk from the depths of his heart—a process he so well knew. Pray for water. Start, the way you always would do, with praise (*shevach*)—something, perhaps, along the lines of *kaddish*: "*Yitgadal, v'yitkadash sh'mei rabah. . . .*" Then, ask for water (*bakashah*). Yes, invoke the merit of Avraham, Yitzchak, and Yaakov. Ask for water in the merit of their children who crossed the waters of *Yam Suf* following you, Moshe, faithfully, believing firmly that I, God, was protecting them. (What a perfect moment it would have been to hear what Moshe Rabbeinu might have said as the very first version of *tefillat geshem*, as an example for later generations to recite each Shemini Atzeret!

Moshe Rabbeinu, master of prayer on behalf of the Jewish people, what a perfect moment it would have been for you yet again to publicly reinforce the efficacy of prayer for this generation and all generations to follow. You, Moshe, prayed so fervently on behalf of the Jewish people when I wanted to destroy them all for having made the golden calf; do it again this time. You, Moshe, begged for the well-being of your sister, Miriam, when she besmirched your good name and I smote her with a debilitating *tzaraat*. In five words you changed her life when you beseeched Me, *eil, na, refa na lah*, "Most Beneficent One, I beg You, heal her, I beg You." And I know you well, Moshe, soon you will stand and endlessly pray for a chance to enter the Promised Land. Over and again you will pray (*Va'etchanan el HaShem*) until I will stop you. I know already what I will tell you: Enough! Too much already! . . . *Rav lach! Al tosef daber aelei od badavar hazeh* (See Deuteronomy 3:23–26). Moshe, *now* was the time for prayer. In this way My name would have been sanctified in the eyes of this entire generation more than in any other way. And, tragically, such an opportunity was missed. Instead, you struck the rock, as you did once before. They needed a lesson in prayer, and they saw a sleight of hand.

QUESTION 3

Ultimately what was Moshe *Rabbeinu*'s terrible sin, for which he was denied entry to Israel?

There are at least a dozen suggestions as to what Moshe's precise sin was at this time; Abarbanel summarizes ten opinions before offering his own eleventh version. Among the better-known suggestions are:

1. Had Moshe talked to the rock at this time, God's name would have been greatly sanctified (Rashi).
2. Derision of the Jews over this incident was unwarranted.
3. Moshe's anger under the circumstances was totally uncalled for and inappropriate (Rambam).
4. Moshe stepped out of character when he boastfully challenged the Jews by asking, "Do you think that we—my brother and I—can produce water for you?" In fact he should have pointed to God's Omnipotence, upon which they could rely (Ramban and Rabbeinu Chananel).
5. Moshe unnecessarily struck the rock twice rather than only once.

Abarbanel goes on to suggest that the text itself delicately discloses Moshe's sin, namely: "Because you (both Moshe, and Aharon who was entirely in the background here) did not have faith in Me sufficiently to have sanctified My name in the eyes of the Jews. . . ." Had Moshe used his power of prayer at this time, what a lasting paradigm he would have offered the Jews when they had to confront situations of natural disaster. And, though Aharon was entirely blameless in this incident, he, too, is implicated in the same shortcoming—a missed opportunity. Why so? Abarbanel reminds us that Aharon also was presented with a once-in-a-lifetime opportunity to sanctify God's name at the time he fashioned the golden calf forty years earlier. He could have attempted to resist the mass hysteria.

Here, then, is the timeless lesson learned from this dramatic incident: Missed opportunities for doing great things prevented both Moshe and Aharon from leading the Jews into the Promised Land. Each of these two greatest Jewish leaders had only the one shortcoming. And every Jew needs to take the lesson to heart. Everyone is confronted with innumerable ways to do great things (*kiddush shem shamayim*). A missed opportunity to do so when the opportunity presents itself ("I should have . . . I would have . . . I could have . . .") may be the costliest transgression held against us. I hear Hillel's message in *Pirkei Avot* (1:14) reverberating over and again: "And if not now, then when?" (*ve'im lo achshav, eimatai?*)

❖ CHAPTER 45 ❖

Balak

Rabbi Edward Davis

Young Israel of Hollywood/ Fort Lauderdale, Florida

After Moshe led the *Bnei Yisrael* in a dramatic victory over the two strongest kings of the area, Og and Sichon, the people of the region displayed a great fear. On their behalf, Balak appealed to Bilaam to come and curse the *Bnei Yisrael*. The opening portion of the *parshah* is a bit perplexing: *HaShem* first commands Bilaam not to go—"You shall not go with them"; then *HaShem* seemingly changes His mind—Rise, go with them. As soon as Bilaam does go, *HaShem* is angry because Bilaam went. And then, finally, after the scene with the talking donkey, *HaShem*'s angel tells Bilaam, "Go with the men"—that he may go with Balak's men.

The key to understanding the seemingly shifting Divine orders is knowing the difference between the two Hebrew words that mean "with": *Imahem* and *Itam*. *Imahem* has a connotation that the two parties are equal; there is a partnership, in which both parties who go have the same intention. *Itam* on the other hand, is the term used when the two parties are going in the same direction but not sharing the same goal. *HaShem* tells Bilaam that he may not go with *Imahem* Balak's men—that is, with the goal they have of doing damage to *Bnei Yisrael*. Later, *HaShem* tells Bilaam that he may go with the men *Itam*—that is, go with them but not share the same intention. Bilaam, though, goes with *Imahem* them, sharing their intentions. Therefore, *HaShem* became angry with Bilaam. At the end, however, the angel tells Bilaam that he may go with *Im* the men if that is his desire. As Rashi states, "In the way which a person desires to go, in that way they lead him." And Bilaam will suffer the same consequences as those with whom he goes (Vilna Gaon).

As Bilaam travels to meet Balak, an angel of *HaShem* stands in Bilaam's way. Bilaam is incapable of seeing the angel; his donkey, however, has no problem seeing him. The donkey tries to detour to the side of the road and, in so doing, crushes Bilaam's foot against the wall. The road has a fence on both sides of it. Rashi feels it necessary to explain that the fence was made of stone; in so doing, he goes well beyond the definition of a fence, since the material of which the fence is made should not make any difference as far as we are concerned.

The *Tosefet Berakhah* explains that Rashi's point refers to something else. According to the *midrash*, Bilaam was the grandson of Lavan. Lavan and Yaakov had established a peace treaty when Yaakov left Lavan's house, physically completing the treaty by building a large mound of stones (Genesis 31:44–54). By virtue of this treaty, neither party was allowed to cause harm to the other. Now, however, by approaching *Bnei Yisrael* with the intention of cursing them, Bilaam was smashing against the stone wall, trying to break the existing treaty.

The Chofetz Chaim has an interesting comment on the verse "Let me die the death of the righteous." Bilaam did not want to live as a Jew, but he did want to die as a Jew. Life as a Jew is not easy; it is filled with prohibitions and restrictions. "This you may eat, this you may not eat. This is allowed; this is not." There are numerous commandments, obligations, and responsibilities that make the life of a Jew difficult. The faithful Jew, however, lives as a Jew and knows that his death is the gate to the eternal life of the next world. Believing in the immortality of the soul, in reward and punishment, he does not fear death. Bilaam desired only to die as a Jew without living as one.

The most famous of Bilaam's Divinely inspired statements is, "How goodly are your tents, o Jacob, your dwellings, o Israel" (Numbers 24:5). Rashi offers two explanations of "tents." One is that they refer to the physical tents of the Israelite encampment; Bilaam saw that the doors of neighboring tents were not directly opposite each other, thereby protecting each individual's neighbor from an evil eye and granting each a measure of privacy and modesty in his personal life. The second interpretation (in Rashi) applies the term "tent" to the Tent of Meeting—the Tabernacle: as if to say "How goodly are the tents of Shiloh and the Holy Temple when they are inhabited." Rabbeinu Bachya says that the simplest interpretation of the above passage is a prophecy by Bilaam that the *Bnei Yisrael* are to be settled in the Promised Land and will build a Tabernacle and Holy Temple.

Rabbi Dov A. Brisman

Young Israel of Elkins Park, Pennsylvania

A CASE OF MISTAKEN IDENTITY

"And Balak, son of Zipor, saw all that Israel had done to the Emori." (Numbers 22:2)

I strongly believe that this passage actually uncovers the root of the evil intent inherent in Balak's motivation to harm the Jewish nation. Balak saw what "Israel" had done to the Emori. He associated the victorious performance on the battlefield with the military superiority of one nation over another. Thus, he had failed to see the spiritual element included in the success of Israel. The *yad HaShem*, the hand of *HaShem*, prevalent in all facets of our nation, sinks into oblivion before the eyes of a Balak. For this reason, Balak and his fellow Moabites were confident that the stronghold of Jewish power would crumble before the curse of the prophet Bilaam.

However, even this resolve was shattered when Bilaam himself was forced to concede, "How can I curse if the Almighty has not cursed, and how can I show wrath if the Almighty has not shown wrath?" (Numbers 23:8). The Israelites are a nation whose destiny is intertwined with an Omnipotent Almighty who watches and actually supervises every breath of His nation. One cannot view Israel merely as a nation that enjoys military superiority, but rather as a nation sanctified by an ever-protecting God.

If only the Arab nations surrounding our small Israel would realize that our Protector in Heaven has stayed their hand far more effectively than military might! If only their evil schemes would be negated by experiencing feelings of sanctified love rather than murderous hate!

If only the above "if onlys" were realized, a true and ever-lasting peace would be achieved in our times!

LOOKING OUT FOR BILAAM

Known to all is the phenomenal occurrence in our *parshah*. A donkey is speaking to a person—and actually makes sense: an incident enjoyed by all who read, study, and merely hear the tales of the Torah. However, stories are not recorded in the Torah merely for entertainment. There is always a purpose, and a lesson to be learned. Why was it necessary for Bilaam to be rebuked by a donkey? What does this story teach us?

Sforno comments that the Almighty's purpose was to inspire Bilaam to repent "in order that a man of his stature not be destroyed." Bilaam, endowed with prophesy and certainly brilliant, had decided to live a corrupt and base life. He did not lack guidance or background. An accomplished and respected personality, Bilaam nevertheless opted for a place of honor among the wicked. The normal attitude toward such a person is to let him "dig his own grave," for did he not forfeit any consideration or niceties on our part? However, even such a person is constantly presented with opportunities to repent and to refine his character. Let no talent be lost! It was worthwhile for the Almighty to create *pi ha'aton* (the mouth of the donkey)—a supernatural phenomenon—solely for this individual person to be spared from spiritual decline and to be given another chance. So, too, we are also obligated to move mountains in order to help others utilize their abilities toward *avodas HaShem*. Let us never give up hope on any *neshamah*. Even nature is transcended in order to attempt to give proper guidance even to one individual.

A PROCESS OF REFINEMENT

As Bilaam traveled upon his donkey toward the camp of the Israelites, the Almighty was displeased and dispatched a *malach* to counter Bilaam's efforts. Upon seeing the *malach*, the donkey strayed from the path. Bilaam, unaware of the *malach*'s presence, struck the donkey. The *malach* stood in the path between the vineyards, which was "fenced in" on both sides. In deference to the *malach*, the donkey swerved and pressed Bilaam's foot against the wall. Finally, the *malach* proceeded to a narrow area where there was no way to turn to the right or to the left. Following the second and third appearances of the *malach*, the donkey's behavior was also rewarded with beatings.

The *Yalkut Shimoni* poses the question: Why was it necessary for the *malach* to appear three separate times? Explains the *Yalkut Shimoni*: the three appearances represent three messages that were being conveyed to Bilaam. Upon the first appearance, there was room for the donkey to proceed with comfort through the path. Later, the path narrowed, and the donkey could only stray to one side. Finally, the path was so narrow that no spare room remained upon either side.

Originally, Bilaam attempted to curse the descendants of Avraham *Avinu*, only to find the descendants of Yishmael and Keturah on "both sides." Upon attempting to curse the descendants of Yitzchak, his curse could prevail only upon the descendants of Eisav; so he was "pressed against the wall." The final attempt, to curse the descendants of Yaakov, turned up "empty": there was no room to turn right or left, for all Yaakov's sons were righteous.

We recite in the Pesach *Haggadah* that "from the onset our forefathers were idolaters, and now the Almighty has brought us nearer to His service." Our history and actual existence have been a long and arduous process of refinement. More improvement and embellishment do not suffice; change is required. Even subsequent to Avraham *Avinu*'s embracement of monotheism, constant upgrade and refinement were necessary. Yishmael, Keturah, and Eisav had to be weeded out. The morsel of grain had to be processed and sorted out. The ore was removed and melted until a finished product—descendants of Yaakov *Avinu*—emerged.

Bilaam's curses chopped only at the wedges, winnowing away the chaff. The grain, that staple which is *Klal Yisrael,* cannot be chiseled away. The end-product retains its vibrancy even when engulfed by "outer disturbances." By definition, *Klal Yisrael* is not a mere entity but a refinement process, an unalterable momentum that continually reaches higher. Let us rest assured that the schemes and devices of all Bilaams will not hinder the progress and vitality of *Klal Yisrael.*

Rabbi Chaim Wasserman

Young Israel of Passaic–Clifton, New Jersey

Scrutinizing all possible implications attributable to Bilaam's poetic words, *Chazal* arrive at a clear consensus that everything uttered by this scoundrel was intended to be his devastating curse upon the heads of the camp of Israel. Thus we learn in *Sanhedrin* (105b): "Rabbi Yochanan said: From every blessing of that wicked man one can learn his real intention." In fact, says Rabbi Abba bar Kahana, every one of the blessings turned out to be a curse upon Israel except the one passage of *Mah tovu* in which Bilaam refers to the Jew's schools and *shuls*. Rabbi Shmuel bar Nachmani concluded that, as strange as it may seem, though Jews have had their share of self-hating Jews, we have fared better with the most vicious curses of our own kind than with the blessings of this wicked Bilaam.

Moreover, should one have difficulty with such a conclusion on the basis of the loftiness of the words Bilaam spoke, Rabbi Eleazar assures us that they were spoken by an angel whom God sent to Bilaam; an angel actually said the words we thought we heard from Bilaam. Rabbi Yonatan opines that a hook was placed in Bilaam's mouth to control what came out of it. In any event, Rabbi Yonatan reminds us that our knowledge of this man should tell us that what he felt in his heart was certainly not what he uttered for posterity.

The fundamental question, then, that faces us here is: Can a person such as Bilaam, driven as he was to seek glory, be able momentarily to suspend his self-centeredness and admit to an existence of truth or beauty or greatness deserving of his admiration rather than his curse? In Bilaam's case, is it at all possible for the curses of such a self-aggrandizing opportunist ever to be recycled into glorious blessings when he was being paid royally to thwart the progress and advances of Israel by uttering his magical curses upon them?

With the passage of millennia since *Mah tovu* was uttered by Bilaam, the truth has been recognized in this singular "blessing": what has kept us alive and spiritually vibrant is indeed our schools [*mishkenosecha*] and our *shuls* [*ohalecha*]. Our intellectual quest within the halls of Torah study, rejuvenated by the outpouring of Jewish soul yearning to be touched by the Divine spirit through *tefillah* (genuine *avodah shebalev*) is the singular blessing that has sustained us through all adversity.

It would seem entirely fitting, then, to utter Bilaam's *Mah tovu* each time we enter a *shul*. This ancient *minhag* is already recorded in the times of the *Geonim* in *Siddur Rav Amram Gaon*, one of the earliest written *siddurim* we have.

Nevertheless, many years after the practice of reciting *Mah tovu* was firmly established, Rabbi Shlomo Lurie (the Maharshal) protested vociferously over its recitation. A curse is a curse, he claimed, and no matter what happened with the passage of time this utterance cannot be whitewashed. Additionally, and perhaps more critical for the Maharshal's argument, a personality such as that of Bilaam can utter only derision and contempt for *Bnai Yisrael*. Such a personality does not and cannot change his mind, even for a fleeting moment. Should this, then, be the manner in which we say our first "hello" to God?

Rabbi Elimelech Goldberg

Young Israel of Southfield, Michigan

Bilaam, the prophet of the nations, looks down upon *Am Yisrael* and exclaims, "I see it from the tops of cliffs, from the high places, I gaze upon it. It is a nation dwelling alone at peace, not counting itself among the other nations." Looking for some weakness in our people, Bilaam searches below to curse us. Instead of the hatred he so much wanted to invoke, words of blessing for the Jews fill his mouth. What image did he see that forced this change in direction? What armor did we own to repel this evil?

Rashi quotes for us the words of the *Midrash Tanchuma*: "I stare at their beginnings," Bilaam says, "and at the source of their roots. I behold them established and strong, as these rocks and high places. This is through their Fathers and their Mothers." Bilaam is unable to look upon the dwellings of the Jews without seeing the image of our ancestors protecting our camp. He is unable to pierce the armor of love of our *Avot* and *Imahot* for their children.

In his final attempt at cursing the Jews, Bilaam is forced to explain, in the form of a blessing, this connection between the generations: "How good are your tents, Yaakov, your dwelling places, Israel." The "tent," our *Chazal* tell us, is the symbol of Torah learning. Our home, our resting place, our source of nourishment, where we begin and end each day: that is our Torah. Through the medium of Torah, every generation introduces the next to the previous one.

Bilaam could not possibly have broken through the walls of this tent. The *Gemara* explains in *Berakhot* (7a) that Bilaam's power was to be able to discern that one cosmic microsecond of time in the day when the wrath of *HaShem* could be kindled even against His children. Bilaam was a master of that moment. But our secret is stronger. When we dwell in the tent of Yaakov, in the *Ohel shel Torah*, there are no "moments." *Hachodesh hazeh lachem*; "this month shall be for you" (Exodus 12:2), time belongs to us because we are greater than it. The Torah transforms our limited lives into the eternal. Our house becomes a tent where the generations of the past sit together and teach the generations that are not yet even here. The moment of the present pulls forward the past as the past continues to meet the future. With this we "dwell alone at peace, not counted among the other nations." In the tent of timeless Torah we have watched through the window of history every nation rise and fall, every other people come and go. Only the tent of Yaakov remains intact, unshaken by the harsh winds of time. Bilaam was only a master of the finite moment, and, therefore, his curse proved futile upon the nation of the infinite.

When Bilaam was confronted by the timeless nature of the Jews, he showed great understanding of our strength and power. "They are a nation that dwells alone" is preceded by the word *hen*. *Haketav Ve'hakaballah* associates this with the Hebrew word for benefit or pleasure, *hana'ah*. Thus, we read that "Israel will enjoy its reward alone." There is a hasidic principle, described in the *Degel Machaneh Ephraim*, that interprets this point as a statement of the security of the Jewish mind when we truly dwell in the tent of Yaakov. We take pleasure in our lives precisely because we are not obligated to seek the approval of others. Our strength lies within the values of good and justice that do not flutter in the passing fancies of movements and upheavals. Our models of behavior and our standards of right and wrong are eternal, not subject to the votes of the League of Nations. Our *Avot* and *Imahot* never become outdated as models of heroic response and just behavior. How can they, when they sit with us, every day, as we learn together from the Torah of *HaShem*? It is the pleasure of their company that allows us to reject the self-destructive pulses and pushes of the world around us. And as we continue to make our Matriarchs and Patriarchs honored guests in our homes, they continue to protect us from the curses of Bilaam.

Perhaps, this is also the theme that Bilaam expressed in his coerced praise of the layout of the tents of Yaakov. "How good are your tents, Yaakov." Rashi refers us to the statement in the *Gemara* in *Bava Basra* (60a) that Bilaam saw the care the Jews maintained not to face the opening of one tent toward that of another. On one level, this is a statement of propriety and modesty. It would not be correct to be able to look into some else's tent. On another level, however, this is a reinforcement of the same theme expressed above. We do not need to look into someone else's tent to define ourselves and assess our successes and failures. The Torah provides us all that we need, within our very own tent, to grow to be the type of individual that we are capable of being. When we recognize the greatness that *HaShem Yisbarach* placed within every one of of us, we are able to come together and be the dwelling place of Israel, the seat of *HaShem*'s throne on Earth.

❖ CHAPTER 46 ❖

Pinchas

Rabbi Elazar R. Muskin

Young Israel of Century City, California

IN THE SHADOW OF MOSHE

Few Biblical stories are as sad as this week's Torah account recording Moshe's destiny not to lead the People of Israel into the Promised Land. At this most traumatic and difficult time, Moshe humbly ignored his own fate and concerned himself only with the appointment of his successor. This altruistic manifestation received the highest adulation of our Sages when they declared, "To inform us of the praise of the righteous: When they are ready to part from this world, they put aside their own needs and concern themselves with the needs of the community." (*Yalkut*, 247)

Although our Sages praised Moshe's behavior, his successor, Yehoshua, seemed not to fare as well. The Talmud in *Bava Batra* (75a) remarks, "The elders of that generation said: The countenance of Moshe was like that of the sun; the countenance of Yehoshua like that of the moon. Alas, for such shame! Alas, for such reproach!" Rashi, in interpreting this talmudic passage, explained that the elders of Moshe's generation were depressed and frustrated because they realized that Moshe could not be adequately replaced. No matter how great Yehoshua was, he simply wasn't another Moshe; and in a short period of time, the elders witnessed the level of Jewish leadership decline, like the moon's light in comparison to that of the sun.

The nineteenth-century school of *mussar* went one step further and suggested that Yehoshua was only like the moon because he didn't reach his maximum potential. Actually, they claimed, Yehoshua would have truly replaced Moshe, but he never rose to the challenge and remained only like the moon, never as brilliant as the sun.

But not all commentaries agree with this critique of Yehoshua. Some of the greatest commentators felt that our Talmudic passage was a negative assessment of the elders. The "shame" and "reproach," they claimed, was due to the fact that the elders didn't give Yehoshua the opportunity to demonstrate his leadership qualities. So often, they note, the elders of a generation find it too difficult to encourage a younger leader, feeling that the new leader isn't worthy of their support. True, the elders missed Moshe, but Yehoshua deserved their help; and this they tragically were unable to offer.

If one were to read this episode accordingly, one would also conclude that Yehoshua, and not Moshe, was the correct leader at this juncture in history. As the children of Israel prepared to enter the Holy Land, they needed a leader equipped with the talent of communicating with the masses. The 19th-century commentator Malbim remarked that it was this very charisma that Yehoshua possessed, for everyone could identify with his warm, congenial, and dynamic leadership, whereas Moshe was an aloof personality that only the intellectual elite could approach.

Perhaps this is exactly what the Chasam Sofer meant when he explained our talmudic passage from *Bava Batra* as an expression of only "the elders of that generation." This statement didn't reflect the thinking of the populace but, rather, only the few special leaders who learned directly from Moshe and had a personal relationship with him. The masses, however, were afraid of Moshe, and it was Yehoshua, his pupil, to whom they turned for advice and guidance. All too often we are critical of our leadership, for we compare them to the leaders of a glorious past and see only their glaring deficiencies. And yet, we must always remember that each generation receives the leadership it needs. Yehoshua wasn't a failure at all, but the elders of his generation judged him harshly and incorrectly, for they hoped that he would be another Moshe. Israel, however, didn't need another Moshe. Rather, they needed Yehoshua, and in God's infinite wisdom, they received exactly what they desperately required.

Rabbi Yosef Goldberg

Young Israel of Wavecrest and Bayswater, New York

> "Behold, I now give to him my covenant of peace (*shalom*). And he and his seed after him shall have an eternal covenant of priesthood. . . ." (Numbers 25:12–13)

Haketav Ve'Hakabbalah, a nineteenth-century work on *Chumash* by Rabbi Yaakov Tzvi Meklenburg, is known for its very original and creative interpretations of words and phrases found in the *Chumash*. In discussing the "covenant of *shalom*," Rabbi Meklenburg translates the word *shalom* as being derived from *shaleim*—not peace but, rather, perfection. The perfection referred to is the attainment of priesthood that is discussed in the next *pasuk*. *Haketav Ve'-Hakabbalah* expresses the concept of human perfection in the following way:

> The intent of the Most High, Blessed be He, is that all of His creatures and, in particular, the human race, should perfect themselves. This means they must utilize every one of their physical and spiritual attributes to elevate themselves from the lowly status that they now have to a higher and more lofty status. When one has reached the level to which he was intended to rise, he has reached the level of perfection demanded of him.

Non-Jews reach their level of perfection by faithfully observing the seven Noachite *mitzvot*. *Yisraelim* reach their level of perfection by performing all the *mitzvot* that they are commanded to do. If a *kohein* performed every *mitzvah* which a *Yisraeli* is commanded to do, but had not performed all the *mitzvot* incumbent upon a *kohein*, he would be lacking perfection. *Haketav Ve'Hakabbalah* further states:

> The Lord of all has correlated and tailored the *mitzvot* to the stature and level of the individual soul. He knew that the souls of the descendants of Aharon are equipped with greater spiritual quality and potential than those of ordinary *Yisraelim*. That is why He separated them

for His service with more *mitzvot* than those of ordinary Jews. Thus, they can attain a level of perfection (*shleimut*) that corresponds to the enhanced status of their lofty souls.

Pinchas, prior to this event, had the soul of an ordinary Jew. Through his zealotry, his soul was elevated beyond that level. The quality of his soul was enriched so that it could attain the higher level of perfection that can be achieved only by a *Kohein*.

Most commentators, however, interpret the covenant of *shalom* as being one of peace, in one of two ways: (1) in the narrow sense of Divine protection for Pinchas from his enemies—in particular, the relatives of Zimri; or (2) in the broader connotation of a *brachah* of peace and tranquility that was granted to Pinchas.

It is in this latter connotation that I would like to borrow from another comment of *Haketav Ve'Hakabbalah*, found in *Parshat Noach* on the *pasuk*, "And I will establish my covenant with you" (Genesis 6:18). The classical commentators interpret the reference to covenant in this *pasuk* as alluding to: (1) the promise that Noach's food supplies will not rot and decompose (Rashi); (2) the covenant of the rainbow (Ibn Ezra); or (3) a guarantee of Noach's survival (Ramban). The author of *Haketav Ve'Hakabbalah* interprets the word *brit* ("covenant") here as a derivative of *beriyah* ("creation"). He interprets the *pasuk* as referring to the miraculous new development in creation in which a manmade ark of finite size will hold at least two of all of the animals of the world—a collective volume which is larger than that of any ark that could possibly be built by man. That the ark could hold all the animals was an incredible miracle in which the rules of nature are suspended. He states, "Anything that is distinguished and conspicuous by its being a departure from the ordinary dictates of nature is called a *brit* (covenant)."

With this new insight into the very meaning of *brit*, we can state that a "covenant of peace" in the sense of "peace of mind and tranquility" is something that is a departure from the ordinary.

Indeed, it is the very nature of a human being to be troubled. In existential terms a person could declare, "I am, therefore I am miserable." A *piyut* of the *Yom Kippur Machzor* refers to human beings as "forgetful of good, full of rage, sad of spirit." There is an often quoted insight of an aged caliph who described himself as having had unlimited wealth and power—all that his heart could desire—and, after having taking an account of the truly happy moments of his entire life, he calculated that they added up to a brief few days. Indeed, true peace of mind is a rare and unusual gift indeed. Thus, *HaShem*, by blessing Pinchas with a "blessing of peace," was bestowing upon him a unique and rare state of mind.

With the state of peace and tranquility being such an unusual commodity, we can readily understand why the final of the three priestly benedictions is a blessing of peace, and why the concluding *brachah* of the *Shemonei Esrei* is a prayer for peace.

A FORMULA FOR OBTAINING PEACE OF MIND: *ELOHAI NETZOR*

At the conclusion of the *Shemonei Esrei*, after the *brachah* in which we ask *HaShem* for peace, we have a paragraph that most of us, unfortunately, do not give much thought to, but which is a remarkable formula for the attainment of peace of mind.

The first sentence of this formula is a request for *HaShem*'s help in keeping ourselves away from lies and deception—a stress-reducer in and of itself. After all, a lie detector works by detecting the reaction of the body to the stress of lying.

The second sentence alludes to a psychological principle that teaches that no one can hurt our feelings or make us feel bad if we do not allow them to do so. It is our personal interpretation and reaction to the deeds and statements of others that causes our hurts and bad feelings. Now, note the second request in this prayer: "And to those who curse me, may my soul be still, and may my soul be like dust to all." This is a request of *HaShem* to make us invincible to and unmoved by the actions, insults, and spitefulness of others. It is a request for the ability to understand that most of the things that trouble us are *narrishkeit*—not from an arrogant or supercilious perspective but, rather, from an understanding of our own insignificance in the light of the infinite greatness of *HaShem* and His Torah. Thus, this prayer continues: "Open my heart to your Torah, . . ."

Truly to feel good about oneself, one must always feel that he is doing the right thing. The Jewish people were given at Sinai a detailed plan of how to do the right thing every single day of existence. The details of this plan, of course, are the *mitzvot*. Thus, this prayer continues, "May my soul pursue Your commandments."

But what about those things that are out of our control, such as the plots and machinations of evil-doers against us? In regard to this the prayer continues, "And may You nullify the counsel and destroy the plots of those who plan evil against me."

There is also a very basic principle of Torah: that true happiness and contentment come from being close with *HaShem*. The word *simchah* (happiness) is most associated with being in the *Beit Hamikdash*. The very act of attempting to approach closer to *HaShem* in prayer is, in and of itself, a great source of tranquility and peace.

I sometimes wonder how many of us utter this prayer three times a day without realizing the incredible gifts that it can offer, with of course, the help from *HaShem* that it so eloquently requests.

Rabbi Reuven Kruger

Young Israel of Ramat Peleg,
Netanya, Israel

PINCHAS AND THE LIMITS OF ZEAL

Pinchas, the paradigm of passionate revenge, shares the spotlight in this week's *parshah* with Joshua, the incarnation of steadfast service and unswerving loyalty. The Torah's juxtaposition of these two men offers an instructive basis for investigating the limits of leadership. In these troubled times, which style of leadership deserves our approbation and merits our emulation?

Pinchas earns the everlasting covenant of priesthood in a volcanic eruption of zealous indignation. For his summary execution of two illicit lovers, a Jewish man and a Midianite woman, he and his direct descendants are rewarded with the office of High Priest.

The roots of this pulsating revenge stretch back to the fear and trembling with which Balak beheld the advancing Israelites. Frantic for any scheme to undermine the march of Jewish conquest, Balak took counsel with the sorcerer, Bilaam. When the latter's intended curses were transmuted into copious blessings, a more insidious strategy was adopted. Israel's enemies now sought to destroy her from within, by corrupting sacred sexual mores. Pinchas's zealous vengeance was sudden, violent, and uncompromising.

Joshua, on the other hand, takes office, not revenge. Moses is directed in our *parshah* to anoint his successor in a Divinely ordained and dignified state ceremony. Whereas Pinchas emerges in a sudden blaze of zeal, Joshua steps to the fore only after a long and distinguished career, first as Moses' loyal aide-de-camp at Sinai and, later, as chief of staff in the battle against Amalek.

Yet despite its orderliness, Joshua's succession was hardly a foregone conclusion, at least in Moses' eyes. Following the successful claims of Tzelofchad's daughters to inherit their father's portion in Zion, Moses, too, attempts to bargain with *HaShem*: "This is the time for me to make my demands known. If these daughters have the right to inherit their father, than my sons, too, should inherit my greatness!" The *midrash* articulates a Divine reply:

> Your sons sat idle and neglected the Torah! Joshua was zealous to serve you and guard your honor; he came early and stayed late at your office; he set out the chairs and arranged the cushions. Since he served you with all his might, it is only fitting that he should serve Israel and not forfeit his merit. As it is said "He who plants a fig-vine will eat its fruit" (Proverbs 27).

Joshua earns the right to succeed Moshe because he "set out the chairs and arranged the cushions"; Pinchas earns the right to succeed Aharon because he wielded a flaming sword of vengeance. Yet the difference between these two men extends far beyond a dramatic conflict in leadership styles. The two leaders have different agendas and different sets of considerations that fundamentally affect their policies and priorities.

Pinchas, the priest and moral absolutist, is necessarily aloof from any consideration of social station. Fidelity to Divine imperative far outweighs any possible human or social considerations. The fact that Zimri was the son of Salu, the Simeon tribal chief, was irrelevant. Nor did Pinchas pause to consider the implications of attacking Kasbi, a woman with prestigious family connections in Midianite society.

Joshua, the leader of battalions, could hardly afford to be completely aloof from human considerations. On the contrary, in his petition to *HaShem*, Moses specifies that the future leader of the Jewish people have the special capacity to relate to the unique spirit of each individual Jew. Indeed Joshua is selected precisely because he is a "man of spirit"—that is, a leader who can relate to the different spirits that make up *Am Yisrael.*

The Sages well understood that Pinchas's act was a dangerous morality play for the masses. The Jerusalem Talmud goes so far as to assert that Pinchas was nearly excommunicated by his contemporaries (although their suit was ultimately rejected by the Heavenly Tribunal). Pinchas' zealotry, though correct in theory, is an unworkable model of practical leadership. While we can be educated by his inner rage, by his abhorrence of moral decay, we must restrict ourselves to admiring his motives while eschewing his methods. The pristine morale purity required of a would-be Pinchas is simply unattainable in our tainted times.

For guidance in the arts of practical leadership, we must rather turn to Joshua. Here we find a reassuring ethos of service rather than a volatile political ideology. Prosaic acts of public service like setting out the chairs and arranging the cushions are, perhaps, more reliable contemporary indicators of genuine concern for the commonwealth.

Even more reassuring is the fact that Joshua's duties as leader ultimately required him to evoke the leadership qualities resident in each member of society. The Torah notes that not only is Joshua required to "come and go" before the people but also to teach them, through his example, to "come and go" between the public and private realms.

Social life thus becomes charged by the aggregate of many individuals stirred by the ideals of service and sacrifice. The quest for leadership may begin with a search for a specific personality but, ultimately, the duties of leadership devolve on each member of the society. Thus, Hirsch notes, immediately following Joshua's appointment the *parshah* takes up the theme of communal sacrifices, since both the enlightened leader and the daily Temple rites endeavor to educate the public as to its higher responsibilities.

Despite their striking dissimilarity, Pinchas and Joshua share a remarkable sign of Divine grace; both men were "renamed." Joshua's original name, Hosea, was transformed with the addition of the Hebrew letter *yud*. Pinchas, too, was bestowed the gift of the Divine initial in an enlarged name, albeit in the form of a *yud zutra*, a downsized letter.

Here, perhaps, is a quiet intimation of the relationship between these two leadership paradigms. The *yud* in Joshua's name is prominently revealed; the *yud* in Pinchas's is virtually concealed. At present, God's presence is more readily transmitted to the world through the norms of leadership embodied by Joshua. Though the leadership model offered by Pinchas is also worthy of Divine recognition, its fullest expression has yet to appear.

When will the leadership of Pinchas again reappear? The Sages identify the spirit of Pinchas with the prophet Elijah, harbinger of the Messiah. At the end of the Book of Malachi, we read the surprising details of the Pinchas-Elijah mission: "Behold, I am sending to you Elijah the prophet on that great and terrible day of *HaShem*. He will incline the hearts of the fathers towards the sons and the hearts of the sons toward their fathers. . . ."

The passion of Pinchas holds the seeds of tenderness and intimacy. The flame of youthful rage will mature into a glowing ember. In those marvelous days, may they come soon, the same heat and passion for closeness to *HaShem* will no longer demand acts of cleansing catharsis but, rather, gently melt away all that still divides us.

Rabbi Jordan Hoffman

Young Israel of Patchogue, New York

> "Pinchas, the son of Elazar, the son of Aharon *Hakohen,* turned My wrath away from the children of Israel in that he was very jealous for My sake among them" (Numbers 25:10–11).

Rashi is bothered as to why the Torah felt a need to trace Pinchas's genealogy to Aharon *hakohein* here. Why did the Torah not merely state that "Pinchas ben Elazar *Hakohein* turned My wrath away from the children of Israel?" We all know who Elazar *hakohein* was.

Rashi answers that, in tracing the genealogy, the Torah is setting to rest certain charges and criticisms laid upon Pinchas by the tribes of Israel. Rashi explains that the tribes mocked him, saying, "Have you seen that son of Puti, whose mother's father [Yitro, called *Putiel,* literally "fattener for a god"] fattened calves for idolatry, who killed a prince of a tribe of Israel?" The Torah here is addressing the remarks of these critics, saying, in effect, "No! The motivation of Pinchas was not on account of his idolatrous forebear. . . . His lineage was to Aharon *Hakohein*—the seeker of peace. In killing Zimri, Pinchas sought to soothe My wrath against the children of Israel. He bore that same feature characteristic of his grandfather, Aharon, and was a seeker of peace."

What is perplexing about Rashi's words here is how these critics could ever have laid these charges in the first place. Our Sages tell us that this generation, the *Dor Deah,* was the greatest generation that had ever lived. Even the lowliest maidservant among them was privy to visions far beyond that of the prophet Ezekiel. If so, how is it possible that these holy members of the tribes of Israel attributed derogatory and degrading motivations to the righteous actions of Pinchas? We must further recall that Pinchas was the scion of the most illustrious family in Israel. He and his family members merited the ultimate honor of serving *HaShem* directly. How then could they dare view the driving force behind Pinchas's actions as anything but the pure impetus that it was?

We see from here the pernicious nature of our evil inclination. Man possesses an unremitting tendency to view the motivations of others pejoratively. The *yetzer hara*, or evil inclination, does its best to induce us to ignore the *Pirkei Avot*–based mandate of our Sages to judge our neighbors favorably. All are victim to this trap set by the *yetzer hara*, even the holy tribes of Israel. And no one is safe from our vicious assaults, neither a Pinchas ben Elazar, nor a Moshe *Rabbeinu*, nor our current Torah leaders.

The question now arises: Is the situation hopeless? Is there nothing we can do to safeguard ourselves from attributing unfavorable motivations to the actions of others? If these great men failed, how ever can we hope to succeed?

Within the answer to this question lies one of the most basic principles of *mussar* thought. Only when we are aware of what we are up against, are we prepared to deal with it effectively. The bravest of warriors will lose a battle to the weakest of opponents if he is taken by surprise. However, if we are aware of how strong and pervasive this tendency is within us, then we can know to watch for it when it begins to sow seeds within us. The spiritually elevated men of the *Dor Deah*, great though they were, were not fully cognizant of the ubiquitous and all-encompassing nature of this tendency of ours. Therefore, they failed. We, however, can succeed if we know to watch against it and if we constantly remember the words of our Sages, *Haveai dan kol Adam lakaf zechut*—"Judge *each* person favorably."

❖ CHAPTER 47 ❖

Matot-Maasei

Rabbi Yaakov Krause

Young Israel of Hancock Park, California

> "Moshe spoke to the tribal heads of the Children of Israel, saying, 'This is the word that God commanded. If a man makes a vow to God or makes an oath to obligate himself, he must not break his word; he must do all that he expressed verbally'" (Numbers 30:2–3).

The Rashbam, Ramban, and *Da'as Zekeinim* point to the unique wording of the *parshah*'s opening verse, "This is the word that God commanded." When and where did He command it? Where is the usual *Vayedaber HaShem el Moshe Leimor* that generally precedes chapters of such halachic nature?

The Rambam, in *Yad Hachazakah*, places the *halachot* pertaining to vows and oaths in the section of *Hafla'ah*. The origin of this title is the *posuk* concerning the *nazir* in *Parshat Haflach* that begins with *naso ki yafli* (Numbers 6:2) and, in accordance with the interpretation of Targum Onkelos, it means "to utter, to express." Ibn Ezra sees in the word *yafli* an element of *pele*, wonderment and amazement. What element of *pele* could possibly be attributed to the utterance of a vow? (See Ibn Ezra, *Bamidbar* 6:2.)

Rab Yitzchok Hutner, *zt"l* (*Pachad Yitzchok*, Pesach 15) offers a novel and penetrating insight that not only addresses the Torah's use of the word *hafla'ah* but also sheds light on the entire spectrum of verbal expression.

The Rama in *Orach Chayim* (6:1) offers the following translation of the concluding words of our daily morning *brachah*, *Birkat Asher Yotzar—Rofeh kol basar umafli la'asos*: "The 'wondrous act' of God expressed in this *brachah* is His synthesizing the spiritual and physical within the human body."

Man was created *afar min ha'adamah*—"dust from the earth"—with purely physical needs and functions commonly shared by all forms of life. The *brachah* of *Asher Yotzar* articulates these biological functions. However, man was also infused with a *nishmas chayim*, a *tzelem Elohim*, a spark of the Divine. This component of the human being is addressed by the *brachah* of *Elohai Neshamah*.

The transition from *Asher Yotzar* (*afar min ha'adamah*) to *Elohai Neshamah* (*nishmas chayim*) is *Umafli La'asos*—"and He acts wondrously" (*Mishnah Brurah* 6:12 and *Be'ur Hagra, Orach Chayim* 46 state that these two *brachot* are to be said in succession). The wondrous act is to unite the physical and spiritual components of the human body.

The Torah's description of man's creation reads, "God formed man out of dust of the ground and breathed into his nostrils a breath of life. Man thus became a living creature" (Genesis 2:7). Targum's definition of *nefesh chayah*—"living creature"—is *ruach memalla*—a talking spirit. In the view of Onkelos, the unique character of man, his distinguishing mark, the *mafli la'asos* of his creation, is his capacity for verbal expression.

If *koach hadibur*—the ability to express oneself—exemplifies the spark of Divine in man, if it represents the binding agent that fuses the spiritual with the physical, how careful one must be to maintain its integrity. Its abuse would be tantamount to the destruction of the *tzelem Elohim*.

In light of the above, it is evident why the Torah uses the word *pele* (*isho'ishah ki yafli*) in dealing with matters pertaining to verbal expression, and why the Rambam chose the title *Sefer Hafla'ah* for the section reserved for expounding its laws, for, in the words of Rama, verbal expression is the *mafli la'asos*, the wondrous act of creation.

Zeh hadavar asher tzivah HaShem—"This is the word that God commanded." The laws governing vows, that maintain the integrity of the ability to speak, require no prior Divine instruction, for speech represents the core of our existence; its roots can be traced directly to "and He breathed into his nostrils a breath of life."

Rashi quotes the *Sifri*, which contrasts the level of prophecy of Moshe with that of other prophets. Other prophets expressed their prophecy with *Ko amar HaShem*—"so said God"—whereas Moshe achieved a level of *Zeh hadavar asher Tzivah HaShem*—"this is the word that God commanded." Why was the chapter on vows selected to demonstrate the clarity of Moshe's prophecy? (See *Emes Leyaakov* by *Harav* Yakov Kaminetzky, *zt"l*.)

Chazal define Moshe's prophecy as *Shechinah medaberes mitoch grono*—that is, Moshe merely moved his lips; the voice that emanated was that of God, the unadulterated *Nishmas Chayim*, the purest form of *Ruach Memallah*—a talking spirit—the theme of the chapter on vows.

The portions *Matot-Masei* are read during the season of *Bein Hamtzarim*, the period of the Three Weeks, when *Klal Yisrael* notes with sadness the loss of the *Beit Hamikdash* and the ongoing exile of our people.

The *Gemara* in *Bava Basra* (74a) relates how Rabba bar bar Chana overheard a heavenly voice cry out, "Woe unto Me that I have taken an oath [to place *Klal Yisrael* in exile: Rashi]—and now that I am under oath, who will absolve Me of My vow?"

When Rabbi bar bar Chana related the incident to his colleagues, he was rebuked for not immediately responding, *Mufar Lach*—"Your vow is annulled." Some *meforshim* see in this *Chazal* a common theme between the chapter on vows and *Churban Habayis* (see *Pri Tzadik* of Reb Zadok Hakohen). On the basis of the above insights into the concept of *hafla'ah*, perhaps we can understand the correlation.

Our present exile is a result of serious deficiencies in *Bein Adam Lachavero*—"between man and his fellow man"—of which *sinas chinim*, hate, is but one symptom. In the opinion of the Chofetz Chayim, almost all sins of this nature find their roots in a lack of *shemiras halashon*—"watching one's speech."

When we resolve to adhere to the principle of *Lo yachel Devoro* by not desecrating the Divine spark of our talking spirit, which is the hallmark of man, then God will respond with the assurances of *Kichol hayotzei mipiv ya'aseh*—He will do all that we express verbally. Our words will then have the potency and efficacy to enable us to cry out, *mufar lach, mufar lach*, nullifying the oath that has stymied the collective prayers of *Klal Yisrael* for so many generations.

From *Matot*, which represents the perfection of our Divine capacity for speech, will come *Masei*, our nation's final homeward voyage to our long-awaited destination; speedily, in our time.

Rabbi Elimelech Goldberg

Young Israel of Southfield, Michigan

There is no prayer in our liturgy that is as profoundly moving as *Kol Nidrei*, nor is there any as controversial. That prayer, which is synonymous with the onset of the Day of Awe, is the subject of great criticism by several of our noted commentators. As a legal tool, serving to void our vows without the presence of a *Bet Din* (Jewish court), it leaves unclear whether future vows are affected or whether this prayer refers to vows of the past. Further controversy is stirred up by the question whether the prayer of *Kol Nidrei* must be remembered at the time of the vow for the *Kol Nidrei* prayer to be effective or, quite the contrary, whether the prayer of *Kol Nidrei* must be *absent* from thought when the vow was uttered. Lastly, the mistaken notion that vows could be so easily excused could constitute a significant stumbling block for the average Jew.

Why was the *Kol Nidrei*, whose effectiveness is so questionable, chosen to introduce the most moving moments of the Jewish year? The emphasis on *nedarim* ("vows") serves as a reflection on the godly qualities that *HaShem Yitbarach* has granted to His nation. The Talmud tells us that a *neder* is an "*issur cheftza*," a prohibition that we create on some object around us by consecrating it with our speech. The individual who makes a vow changes the target of his oath into another reality. That which was permissible has now been transformed into something prohibited through this verbal consecration. This is a godly quality. One would imagine that only the Creator of the universe could have the power to define the status of the objects in His world. Only *Hakodosh baruch Hu* should be able to designate those animals that have hooves and chew their cud as kosher and the others as not kosher. Yet, the Holy One has granted us the power of the *neder*—the creative capability of speech to consecrate and define the world around us as if we were its very creator.

The greatest impact of the moment of *Kol Nidrei* is not our remembrance of the wrongful deeds of the passing year. This prayer reminds us of much more. It speaks to us of the incredible godly power, represented by the concept of *neder,* that was at our disposal. It describes the worlds of good that we could have created had we maintained the proper focus to our lives and recognized the force of consecration that we were afforded. Thus, the *Kol Nidrei* serves as a profound lesson of what could have been rather than merely what was.

Parshat Matot begins with Moshe teaching the laws of *nedarim* to the princes of the tribes. The Rashbam questions why this *parshah* begins with *His* words, minus the usual statement, "God spoke these words to Moshe, saying. . . ." Furthermore, why were the laws of *nedarim* specifically directed to the heads of the Jewish tribes? Though our commentators debate the specific command from *HaShem* that is the basis of the laws of vows, no one denies that *HaShem Yitbarach* is the originator of this *halachah.* However, as we have already indicated, the realm of *nedarim* presents a distinct ontological message. It demonstrates the creative godly character that *HaShem* has bestowed upon us, granting us power over the objects of our world. Therefore, Moshe alone is given center stage in this *mitzvah,* as the leadership of the Jewish people are first targeted to hear it. This is a *mitzvah* that speaks of leadership and power. It has within its framework our obligation to use this God-given mastery over our world for the purpose of serving *HaShem.* When we have failed to focus this control in the proper direction, we repeat the theme of the *Kol Nidrei* and beg *HaShem* to pardon our misuse of our power, as well as our apathy in its application.

As we conclude *Sefer Bamidbar,* we find a similar theme in the opening words of *Parshat Maasei.* There, Moshe recounts the journeys of the Jewish people. "And Moshe wrote of their starting points to their travels commanded by *HaShem,* and these are their travels to their starting points." What is meant by their "starting points" and "travels"? Why is the order reversed at the end of the verse? Why is *HaShem*'s command invoked in the first part of the phrase and not the second?

The "*Klei Yakar*" sees within the travels and starting point of the Jewish people much more than a geographical statement. When the Nation of Israel was going from its starting place outward, it was "on the command of *HaShem.*" This represented the growth of spirit and commitment beyond the slavish insecurity of their Egyptian past. These were the forward movements of a people marching with our God. Those journeys, however, that were travels *to* their starting points were without the command of *HaShem.* They occurred as the Jewish people sinned and backtracked toward the idolatrous Egypt of their youth.

Why does the Torah bother with the journeys of our ancestors? What may we cull from their travels and their starting points? We, too, are on a trek. We, too, have the options of being enslaved by the non-godly movements that pull and sway us in the alien cultures in which we are found. These voices of assimilation call us to return to a time of non-commitment and spiritual apathy. On the other hand, we have the journey "on the command of *HaShem*." This travel propels us away from the natural weakness of the human condition and allows us to journey ever forward, accompanied by the Holy One.

To know that we have the ability to direct our travels in life and to understand that we have been granted the godlike quality of transforming the very universe into which we have been placed is the theme of this *sefer*. Therefore, as we conclude *Parshat Maasei*, the *parshah* of Jewish travels, preceded by *Matot*, which represents our power in the world, we are fully able to round the corner of the Jewish calendar and soon anticipate the responsibility and joy that is included in the opening sounds of the *Kol Nidrei*.

Rabbi Hershy Worch

Young Israel of Pawtucket, Rhode Island

If we all contain the same spark of infinity within our souls, how can we be so different from each other? If our *neshamah* is a piece so to speak, of God, how can we blunder so far from righteousness? How can there possibly be *tzaddikim* and *resha'im* in the world among us, when we are all fired with the very same impulse from the beginning?

This week's *sedrah, Maasei* is the last in the fourth of the five *Chumashim*. In a sense, it is the last portion of the Torah (the fifth book, *Devarim*, is a repetition of the Torah, *Mishneh Torah*). It is not a coincidence that it is always scheduled to be read at the beginning of the month of Av.

The forty-two journeys that the Children of Israel made are given names in this week's *sedrah*. If we translate them into English, we get sentences that read like this: "And they left the mountain of beauty, arriving in fear. They left fear behind them and gathered in crowds."

The names places are given are mostly fictitious, purposely so, to facilitate their use as projections, to make it easier for us to map our own journeys through life. Every Jew has the duty to learn this Torah for him- or herself, to look for the meaning of these journeys in his or her own life.

The most extreme example of this, the endeavor to personalize the Torah, to shift it out of the abstract into the concrete, is the last portion of this same *sedrah*, the end of the Book of *Bamidbar* (which, was we said before, is, in a sense, the end of the Torah). Daughters who, during the forty years of wandering in the wilderness, inherited land in Israel through their deceased fathers, were prohibited from marrying out of their tribe. There are few, if any, laws in the Torah with such a short lifespan, affecting so few people. What a way to end the Torah!

We are being given permission and encouragement to apply the Torah to ourselves in every personal situation—for instance, by learning lessons from these smart Tzelofchad women. The whole Torah is eternal, holistic, and deep. If we allow it to pervade our lives, imbuing all our actions with its color, the result is the solution and resolution of the most complex and painful of our dilemmas, to the smallest detail.

If there is ever an appropriate time to ask ourselves, "How did we get into this awful mess?" it has to be now, in the month of Av, between the rock and the hard place. How are we supposed to interpret the events in our own lives, the meaning in the challenges and suffering? Why has God thrown truth to the ground, only to have it trampled down before it can flourish and spread? When a Jew in despair cries out, "Help us, please," how does the world keep on turning?

This is the time of year when the world makes least sense. The wicked have declared a war against the Holy Blessed One, attacking us Jews as the only handy targets. When Gentiles should be stopping us on the street to ask, "Tell us again how you did it, staying so faithful and so close all the time?" they throw stones and insults instead. And we, with our mistakes, what sense can we ever make of it all?

The Torah, in its words to us, gives a clue to the mystery. It begins this *sedrah* with a curious phrase in the second *pasuk*: "Moshe recorded the outcome of the journeys of God's command, and these were the journeys to their outcome." You see, whether the outcome follows or precedes the journey depends on where you stand. When the *neshamah* becomes part of the world of flux, it is already destined to return to its place of origin. What could possibly change about a *neshamah*, about infinity? If we are destined to return whence we came, why then must we struggle so hard at life while we are here?

The truth is that God looks much deeper than our outside personality, deeper even than our actions and our struggle. For example, when we were leaving Egypt, all the powers of the world tried to demand our destruction, saying, "These are idol-worshipers, and these [the Egyptians] are idol-worshipers." The angels argued, "Why should You favor these and not those?" God refused to judge that way.

God does not look at the outside of people but into the hidden minds, where motives are secret; there God watches and knows. The story of Israel is God's testimony that at their source, in their very root, Israel is Holy. That Israel is unblemished is one of the fundamentals of faith. That we are blind to this truth as we live it, is equally fundamental.

To return to the *pasuk*, we see what Moshe meant: At God's command, the outcome was recorded before the journey. However, we experience life as, "These are the journeys to their outcome." What then is left of the struggle and the journey after it is all over?

This is how the Izbicy Rebbe explains it. There is no such thing as one Jew being greater than another; everyone has an infinite *neshamah*; everyone's existence is a portion of God from the same highest place. The purpose of human life is to be forced to go through the forty-two journeys and stops mentioned in this week's *sedrah*. The outcome of the journey is a story. We each end up with different stories of successes and failures, of joys and grief. In the unique shape of our lives are moments of grandeur, moments in which we rise above our impoverished selves and stand out, separate, distinct and triumphant; moments in which we fail. In the over-all scheme of things, these stories of our lives are the *gestalt* of our *neshamah*. At the level of *neshamah*, the People of Israel are distinguishable from each other only by our different histories. There will yet come a time when God will tell all these stories to the Gentile nations, and they will hear and understand how we were different. God will bear witness that we longed and trembled with our hearts to be joined with no one but God.

Rabbi Chaim Wasserman

Young Israel of Passaic–Clifton, New Jersey

We find Moshe Rabbeinu instructing his people, soon ready to enter the Promised Land, "Clear out [or "occupy"] the land and live in it, since it is to you that I am giving the land to occupy" (Numbers 33:53). At first blush, there could be two diverse reactions to this charge: First, that this is a *mitzvah* akin to the original Pesach, which was meant to be observed only once, in Egypt, for that generation exclusively. Then again, it may be that Moshe's instructions are a biblically mandated *d'oraita*, for all times, as compelling as eating *matzah* on Pesach or fasting on Yom Kippur.

Is it a *mitzvah* these days to conquer the land, clear it of its non-Jewish settlers, and do everything humanly possible to resettle the area with Jews? An imposing literature has amassed in answer to the question. What follows is a woefully brief summary of the major positions, tailored, of necessity, to the format of these shared lines.

THE RAMBAN'S POSITION

The Ramban, who disagrees in seventy instances with the Rambam's system of counting *mitzvot* in his *Sefer Hamitzvot*, considers the conquest of the land as biblically binding *d'oraita* for all times.

> According to the Ramban: we are commanded to occupy (*lareshet*) the land that God gave to our fathers, Avraham, Yitzchak, and Yaakov, and not to allow it to remain in the hands of other nations, nor allow that it be desolate. This is what is meant by "You shall occupy the land [*ve'horashtem*] and settle it because it is to you that I have given this land to occupy it." . . . [These words] denote that this is indeed a *mitzvah*, not a Divine promise. . . . This is what our Sages called a *milchemet mitzvah* [warfare that is considered to be a *mitzvah* when

> engaged in]. . . . In *Sifre* we find: "'You will occupy it and settle in it'—because you occupied it you will merit to settle there." . . . In my opinion this [occupying the land] is a *mitzvah* for all times even when we are dispersed in exile. . . . (*Hasagot Haramban l'Sefer Hamitzvot, Mitzvot Asei*, Standard Edition, p. 42.)

RAMBAM'S POSITION

Rambam, however, did not list in his *Sefer Hamitzvot* this particular *pasuk* of our *parashah* [33:53] as one of the 613 binding *mitzvot* for all times. Rabbi Yitzchak de Leon, author of the primary commentary to *Sefer Hamitzvot*, in defense of the Rambam's position, explains:

> It would seem to me that the reason for the Master [Rambam] not having included this in his list is that the *mitzvah* to occupy the land and settle in it was in effect only in the days of Moshe, Yehoshua, and David and [continued to be in force] so long as we were not exiled from the land. But once the exile from the land occurred, the *mitzvah* is not in force until the arrival of *mashiach*. . . . (*Megillat Esther to Sefer Hamitzvot*, Standard Edition, p. 42.)

His explanation notwithstanding, there is yet another plausible way of viewing the Rambam's position on the issue that can be derived from the fourteen introductory principles set forth by the Rambam himself; there, he sets forth his criteria for designating something as a *mitzvah d'oraita*. In his tenth principle, the Rambam writes that "acts that serve as preliminaries to the performance of other *mitzvot*, setting forth the procedure of how the *mitzvot* are to be performed, are not to be counted" among the 613. For this reason, for instance, what seems to be the most fundamental of all *mitzvot*, belief in God, does not qualify to be listed in the Rambam's system. For without the *a priori* presumption of belief in God, how could any other *mitzvot* be observed as Divine imperatives? Nonetheless, for the Rambam, belief in God is a preliminary act to all other *mitzvot* and, consequently, is not to be included in his list of 613. Very similarly, without the preliminary act of conquering and settling the land, how could any of the *mitzvot* connected to and dependent upon the Land of Israel be observed once we managed to arrive in Israel? Accordingly, it is not entirely clear that the Rambam would disagree with Ramban as to whether occupying the land is a *mitzvah d'oraita* for all times.

FROM HALACHAH TO AGGADAH

Witness a scene in Babylonia of the third century C.E. as is recounted in *Ketubot* (110b–111a). Rav Yehudah, a second-generation *Amora*, insisted that leaving Bavel at that time to go on *aliyah* was not a *mitzvah* but, ironically, to the contrary, was the very abrogation of a *mitzvah*. He maintained that only through Divine intervention could we return *en masse* to Israel just as we returned to Israel after the destructioin of the first *Beit Hamikdash*—by prophetic message. Until such time, we are prohibited from going on *aliyah*.

His eminent student, Rav Zeira, while disagreeing with his *rebbe* as to how exactly this restriction was derived from the *TaNaCH*, introduced into the conversation the notion that Jews, while in exile were bound by three ancient Divine oaths (*shalosh shevuot*):

1. They could not rebel against the nations who subjugated them
2. They could not insist on returning to Israel *en masse* before the appointed time
3. The third oath was the one God made the nations of the world swear, that they will not overly oppress the Jewish people.

The *Gemara* here then relates that Rav Zeira, the illustrious student, alienated himself from his *rebbe* over the issue of leaving Bavel to go on *aliyah* and left to spend the rest of his life in Israel. Elsewhere, the Talmud reports that, upon reaching Israel, Rav Zeira fasted one hundred days in order to forget the style of learning he acquired in Bavel. It is entirely plausible that, by fasting, Rav Zeira wanted not only to distance himself from the style of learning in Bavel but also, now that he was in Israel, to repent for any effects that his teachings about the three oaths may have had on others wanting to leave Bavel to go on *aliyah* (*Bava Metziah* 85a).

Amidst this discussion the *Tosafot* of twelfth- and thirteenth-century Franco-Germany recorded two reasons why living in Israel was no longer a *mitzvah*. First, it is too dangerous a trip to take, and, therefore, one is not required halachically to endanger his life in trying to arrive and settle there. (Recall that this was the era of the Crusades.) Second, opines Rabbi Chaim Hakohein, it is nearly impossible to observe properly the *mitzvot hat'luyot ba'aretz* (those *mitzvot* that are agricultural in nature and can be done only in the Holy Land of Israel), incumbent upon every Jew once arriving in Israel; better, then, that one does not enter into such a dilemma and stays away from *aliyah* (*Tosafot Ketubot* 110b s.v. *Hu omer la'alot*).

Rabbi Yosef of Trani, the illustrious Maharit, dismissed the statement attributed to Rabbi Chaim Hakohein as an unauthoritative footnote of some unworthy student, for to suggest such a position is preposterous.

But let us take a quantum leap in time briefly to touch upon how twentieth-century Jewry has reacted to all this information, and, most especially, the impact that this portioin of *aggadah* concerning these three oaths has had in modern times.

Curiously, the doctrine of *shalosh shevuot* has served as the textual energy for two disparate segment of Jews to be able to distance themselves from any modern movement of returning to Zion. Better known to most is Hungarian Torah Jewry's assault against the Zionist movement. The previous Satmarer Rebbe, *zt"l,* after World War II, was not the first to campaign relentlessly that Torah Jews totally disassociate themselves from all Zionist activity. He was preceded after World War I by the sainted Munkaczer Rebbe (the *Minchas Elozor*). Their fire and brimstone (a voluminous literature still in print) derived almost entirely from the strength of Rav Yehudah's position and the doctrine of *shalosh shevuot*.

But, *lehavdil,* two hundred years earlier, at the dawn of Jewish emancipation in Germany, Moses Mendelssohn cited the very same *shalosh shevuot* to assure his generation of Jews (and Germans) that "our hoped for return to Palestine . . . will come about for us only miraculously and supernaturally as indicated in our holy scriptures."

Well, then, how do halachic sources view the validity of these *shalosh shevuot*? It is essential to realize that no reference to these restrictive oaths is made by any of the major *poskim* as an issue of *halachah*—not Rif, nor Rosh, nor Rambam; neither the *Tur* nor the *Shulchan Aruch*. Likewise, major commentators on *Ketubot* (Ramban, Ritva, Meiri) all treat the three oaths as strictly a matter of *aggadah*. If so, how, then, in modern times, can a piece of *aggadah* gain such prominence as to outweigh *halachah* and probably a *mitzvah d'oraita*?

Moreover, with the appearance of the Balfour Declaration in 1917, at which time Britain supported the establishment of a Jewish homeland in Israel, one of the halachic giants of his time, Rabbi Meir Simcha Hakohen of Dvinsk (the *Or Sameach*), wrote that "the fear of these oaths no longer existed." Nonetheless, in time, some have tried to dismiss this position of Rabbi Meir Simcha as a forgery.

Additionally, the Chofetz Chaim's son noted that his father never once referred to the three oaths in any of his writings as having contemporary validity despite the fact that the Chofetz Chaim addressed all current issues facing the Jewish people.

The Sochatchover Rebbe (the *Avnei Nezer*), yet another halachic giant, definitively stated that the *shalosh shevuot* are not a matter of *halachah*.

Given the halachic position of the Ramban that conquest of the land is a *mitzvah* for all times, and given the Rambam's position (end of *Iggeret Teman*) that these oaths are an allegorical statement (*mashal*), how is it that the *shalosh shevuot* have come to be regarded as so inviolable?

PONDERING A SOLUTION

Could a key to understanding this curious submergence of a *mitzvah* be found in understanding the manner by which we react to history?

Perhaps the solution rests in realizing that despite the staunch faith we have in God's ultimate redemption, as a nation we have become pitifully jaded amidst this endless exile and dispersion. The only hope we ever had, over these last eighteen hundred years, of returning to our homeland was, understandably, to assign the task entirely to Almighty God's outstretched Hand. But suddenly, in our times, "miracles" have curiously started to be sensed. Is it possible, therefore, that amidst all this darkness we have lost the ability to discern a thin ray of Divine light? Have we despaired of being worthy to have "miracles" occur on our behalf? And so, the human mind being what it is, we immediately deny the existence of any miracle in our time. *Chazal* knew this well when they said that a person does not recognize that a miracle has occurred to him personally (*Niddah* 31a). (Some few do recognize the miraculous and respond appropriately. A dimly remembered incident occurred when, in 1947, the UN voted to partition the land of Israel and recognize an independent Jewish state. Upon hearing the news, the *roshei yeshivah* of Jerusalem's Chevron Yeshivah led the entire student body in the ecstatic recitation of a complete *Hallel*—with a *brachah*!)

Of course, once we invoke the possibility of "miracles," then we have to ask: Would God allow miracles to occur through the agency of those who are not loyal to Torah and even those who are outrightly belligerent toward it? But this particular question will have to wait for another time.

For now, here is what I should like to offer for your consideration as but a start to deciphering the quandaries we have faced as Torah Jews throughout this century. When one cannot deal with the stresses of profound and fundamental change, it is human to deny that changes occurred; it is human to distort what has actually changed; it is even human hysterically to relegate change to the work of the devil and his evil accomplices on earth. It is entirely within human frailties to want to remain totally safe by fantasizing that *Mashiach* will suddenly appear out of thin air to redeem us instantly and lead us to a new era; we only have to sit back and wait patiently, passively, endlessly. It is even human for Jews steeped in *halachah* to employ a piece of *aggadah* with which to suppress or shy away from an opportunity to observe a *mitzvah d'oraita*.

Yet, it is also very much human to hear God's call and accept His challenge (already sensed in the times of the Vilna Gaon and the Ba'al Shem Tov) to pave the highways and the byways of the Promised Land, occupy and settle the Land, so that when *Mashiach*, in due time, does emerge he will be greeted by a massive population of Jews who joyfully will follow him in a grand march up to Jerusalem to sing out their praise to God.

Chazak Chazak V'nitchazek!

PART FIVE

❖

Deuteronomy

❖ ❖ ❖

❖ CHAPTER 48 ❖

Devarim/Chazon

Rabbi Pesach Lerner

Executive Vice President, National Council of Young Israel

> Rav Yehudah, the son of Rav Shmuel Bar Shilas said in the name of Rav: *K'sheim* Just as when (the month of) Av begins we curtail joy so too when [the month of] Adar begins we increase joy (Tractate *Taanis* 29a).

We usually find the term *k'sheim*—just as used to connote an item and then its opposite; thus showing that one reason/rationale is the cause of the positive as well as its opposite, the negative. Therefore, *k'sheim* is generally used to indicate relative concepts, similar ideas. However, in the statement above, it would seem that the cause and effect of each are completely independent and entirely different; we curtail joy during the month of Av because of the destruction of the Holy Temple and the exile of our people from Israel while we increase joy during the month of Adar because of the miracles that took place during the time of Mordechai and Esther. Why is the terminology *k'sheim* used here?

> Rav Yehudah said in the name of Rav: What does it mean that which is written "Who is a wise man that can understand this and [who is it] that the Mouth of *HaShem* spoke to him and can tell it: for what reason was the land lost" (*Yirmiyahu* 9:11)?
>
> This matter was discussed by the Sages yet they could not explain it, it was discussed by the Prophets yet they could not explain it until the Al-Mighty Himself explained it—as it says 'Because they have forsaken My Torah which I put before them" (*Yirmiyahu* 9:12).
>
> Rav Yehudah said in the name of Rav: This means that when they studied Torah, they did not make a blessing on the Torah first (Talmud *Bava Metzia* 85a) [and Rashi explains, since they did not make a blessing first they demonstrated that, in their minds, the Torah was not, to them, a valuable gift].

The great commentator Rabbeinu Nissan, in Tractate *Nedarim* 81a, explains that the verse cannot be understood literally "that they abandoned the Torah." If this were to be true why were the Sages and Prophets unable to explain why the land was lost while only the Almighty was able to respond, "since they did not say a blessing on Torah study, the Torah did not receive the proper esteem and respect."

The question still remains, however, if the Jewish people did not recite the obligatory blessing before studying the Torah, why didn't the Sages and Prophets observe this lack of observance and comment on it?

> "The Jews had light and gladness and joy and honor" (Esther 8:16). Rav Yehudah said light refers to Torah . . . gladness refers to the Holidays . . . joy refers to circumcision . . . and honor refers to *tefillin* . . . (Tractate *Megillah* 16b).

The Sfas Emes questions the above statement. If the Prophet wished to tell us that the Jewish nation now had the opportunity to practice the study of Torah, the specialness of the Holidays, the ability to circumcise their sons, and the honor to wear *tefillin,* why does it not simply say the Jews had Torah, *Yomim Tovim,* circumcision, and *tefillin*? Why write it as a hidden meaning?

Perhaps the answer to all of the above is as follows:

Yes, the Jews did practice the *mitzvot* during the time of *galut,* but they did so, often from force of habit and not necessarily from inner conviction. The miracles of Purim showed them the Hand of God and, once again, they understood and realized the inner beauty and depth of each mitzvah. Once again Torah became "light"; "for the commandment is a lamp and the Torah is light" and they felt the "gladness" of celebrating *Yom Tov,* the "joy" of the mitzvah of circumcision and the "honor" of wearing *tefillin.*

That is why the Prophet tells us, "The Jews had light and gladness and joy and honor" because it was that deeper meaning and feeling that they regained.

And, perhaps, that was what God saw as missing in the Jewish people's learning of Torah and in their saying a blessing before that study. The Sages and Prophets saw Torah learning, heard blessings being recited. But it is only the Al-mighty Who can penetrate the hearts of mankind, Who was able to see that this Torah study was missing "the light of Torah"—the appreciation, sensitivity, and understanding that is required.

Now we have the explanation of *k'sheim.* We curtail joy during the month of Av as our lack of appreciation for God's Torah was the cause of the destruction of the Temple. Therefore we commemorate Tisha B'av. The miracles of Purim, however, enabled us to regain that appreciation of Torah that had been lacking and for that positive gain, we celebrate Purim and joy during the month of Adar.

May we merit to once again fully understand and appreciate the "light, gladness, joy, and honor" of Torah and *mitzvot* and merit to see the rebuilding of the *beit HaMikdash* speedily in our day.

Rabbi Shaul Chill

Young Israel of North Woodmere, New York

Rabbi Samson Raphael Hirsch (*Judaism Eternal*) describes Tisha b'Av night in 1828 Germany, when the rabbi of a newly formed Reform temple in Hamburg condemned the mourning for the *Churban*. After all, he argued, to cry over a Jewish homeland is treason against the Fatherland and will only bring hatred by the local population against the Jews. Rather, he states, Germany is our Palestine, Hamburg is our Jerusalem, and this temple is our Holy Temple

Rabbi Hirsch portrays the pain that all Torah-true Jews felt as they saw the publicity given to that incident by the local papers, encouraging "the awakening of a better Jewish consciousness." He then adds that now—28 years later—Germany has yet to become the "Palestine" that Reform rabbi hoped for. Paradoxically, everywhere else in Germany, relations between Jews and Germans were relatively good—with the exception of Hamburg, where overt anti-Semitism raged.

From the moment our people was first exiled, the cry of "If I forget you, Jerusalem, let my right hand forget [its skills]" (Psalm 137) has been on our lips. No matter how much loyalty Jews have ever shown to the country we find ourselves in, nonetheless, our prayers and yearnings have always been directed toward *Eretz Yisrael*. Lamentations for the *Churban Habayit*—Destruction of the Temple—are said not just once a year on Tisha b'Av, but every midnight at *Tikkun Chatzot*.

The Talmud (*Taanit* 30) assures us "that all who mourn for Jerusalem (the destruction of our *Beit Hamikdash*) will merit to see its rejoicing." It doesn't say *yizkeh* ("will see"), but *zocheh* ("present tense"). The Chatam Sofer explains that our continuous refusal to be consoled is the greatest reassurance that the hope to return has never ceased—and that itself guarantees our ultimate redemption.

The first time *Bnei Yisrael* cried on Tisha b'Av was when the *meraglim* (spies) returned with their *lashon hara* (slander) about the Land of Israel. Rashi (Psalms 106:27; also see Ramban Bamidbar 14:1) comments, "Tonight you cried for no reason, but in the future it will be for tragedy." The *Klei Yakar* explains that the concept of *sinat chinam* ("senseless hate") was ingrained within us that fateful night because we exhibited hatred for our land. Sadly, future years saw much *sinat chinam* among the Jewish nation, leading to the destruction of the First and Second Temples. Directly proportionate to senseless hate is senseless crying—our mourning for tragedy that could have been avoided.

This theme of the need to show concern for others, says the *Otsar Chaim*, explains something in *Parshat Devarim*. The *minhag* is to read the *pasuk Eichah esa levadi turchachem* (Deuteronomy 1:12) "How can I alone carry your contentiousness, your burdens, your quarrels?", to the tune of *Megillat Aichah*. People may think that the less responsibility in communal affairs one undertakes, the easier life will be for him. Not true; the result will be a disintegration of the Jewish community, and we will end up sitting on the ground chanting (Lementations 1:1) *Eichah yashvah vadad:* Alas—she sits in solitude (woe to us who sit in solitary punishment). Once again, the tragic consequence of *sinat chinam* demonstrates itself.

Chazal instruct us often: *ma'aseh avot siman lebanim*, the actions of our patriarchs are signs for the(ir) children—history repeats itself. What led to the original redemption from Mitzrayim is what ultimately will bring about the final redemption. What, indeed, saved us from Mitzrayim? Jewish identity (we didn't forsake our language, dress code, or Jewish names) and our refraining from *lashon hara* about one another. When Moshe *Rabbeinu* encountered Datan and Aviram fighting, he acknowledged the longevity of the *galut* by saying "indeed the matter is known" (Exodus 2:14) and as Rashi explains it now became known to Moshe why the Jews deserved to suffer, they quarreled and told tales. If we, in our generation, realize the severity of *lashon hara* and *sinat chinam*, the perpetuation of our bitter *galut* should not be a surprise, unfortunately. We can only *daven* for the day when contention will cease and unity will prevail—an attainable step toward the final redemption.

In July, 1942, as Field Marshal Rommel and the Panzer Division stormed through the Middle East, Nazi forces were poised to invade *Eretz Yisrael*. In Yerushalayim, a massive gathering was held on the Fast of the 17th of Tammuz. One of the *gedolim* of that time, Rav Zalman Sorotzkin, *zt"l*, addressed the crowd: The Talmud relates that Betar was destroyed during the Bar Kochba rebellion because they did not mourn sufficiently for the Jews of Yerushalayim during the Destruction of the Temple. Since 1939, the Jews of Europe have been persecuted and exterminated by the Nazis, may their names be blotted out; how many tears have we shed, and how much do our hearts bleed for them?

The Talmud tells us that since the destruction of the Temple, all the gates of heaven have been sealed, with one exception—the Gate of Tears. Emotions can be faked, but tears are genuine. *Hakodesh baruch Hu* responds to the sincerity of a person's pleas. This is our challenge of Tisha b'Av: to pour our emotions out to *HaShem* with heartfelt tears and prayer, bemoaning not only the destruction of the Temple but all the tragedies the Jewish people has suffered ever since in *galut*. If we all joined in such an effort, how could Our Father in Heaven not respond to His children's tears (indeed, how many people do we know who actually cry and shed tears on Tisha b'Av)?

Yirmeyahu *Hanavi* (chapter 31), in prophesying about the final redemption, tells us of our Matriarch, Rachel, pleading for her children. He does not say, "Rachel *cries* for her children"; rather *mevakah*—"will make others cry." When we will all heed the words of the *Navi* and join our Mother, Rachel, in her efforts to free us from *galut*, then we will merit with God's help to see the fulfillment of the end of that prophesy, promising our ultimate return to our land.

Rabbi Eliyahu D. Kaufman

Associate Rabbi, Young Israel of Staten Island, New York

The most solemn *Shabbat* of the year is *Shabbat Chazon*, the *Shabbat* that precedes the saddest of all days, Tisha b'Av—the Ninth Day of Av. It is on Tisha b'Av that each Jew becomes an *aveil*, a mourner. We observe on that day an *aveilut* as our fathers did, and their fathers before them, going back all the generations since the *Churban* (destruction of the *Beit Hamikdash*). We again sit on the floor, remove our leather shoes, and shed those tears as we recite for another year *Aichah* and *Kinot*. This is the way it has been for the generations, and we mourn this tragedy, as they did, with the same sincerity.

It is interesting to note that there is a stark contrast between this *aveilut* of Tisha b'Av and that of an *aveilut* of an individual, *aveilut yachid*. With the *aveilut* of a *yachid*, an individual, *halachah* has incorporated the important concept of *nechamah*, consolation. *Halachah* dictates limits to *aveilut*. As *Chazal* tell us in Talmud Tractate Moed-Katan 27b, *Shiva* is for seven days and *bechiyah* (crying) is for three. *Kaddish* is for eleven months for a parent, *aveilut* for twelve months. One may not sit longer, cry longer, say *kaddish* longer, mourn longer. In fact, the same *Gemara* relates a tragic incident of a woman who suffered the loss of a child and the dire consequences of her refusal to accept consolation because of her insistence on prolonging her mourning more than the prescribed time given to her by *halachah*. *Halachah* is very specific on the limits of *aveilut*; *nechamah* is a concept that must be the very essence of our being, even in the face of the most overwhelming tragedy.

How ironic, that this most important principle of *nechamah* is even expressed at the moment of an individual's ultimate personal pain and loss by the *kevurah* (passing) of a parent. It is at that time that an *aveil* recites the *kaddish* extolling and sanctifying the *Borei Ha'olam* in creating anew and in reviving the dead, to raise them to everlasting life. The concept of *nechamah* is expressed even at these most difficult moments.

In contrast, in the *aveilut* of Tisha b'Av, we find the complete lack of *nechamah*. On the contrary, the *halachah* dictates that *aveilut* of Tisha b'Av should not be softened in any way or manner, but intensified with every passing year. In fact, we are told by the *Chachamim*: All who mourn for Yerushalayim will merit to see her happiness and those that do not mourn for Jerusalem will not see her happiness (Taanit 30); that our very *Geulah* for the future is dependent on the intensity and sincerity of our mourning for the *Churban*. Although a distinction can certainly be made between the *Churban Habayit*—that catastrophe of an entire nation and world–and the loss suffered by a mere individual, it would be good for us to understand the reason for the lack of this integral and very important element of *nechamah* that is so blatantly absent from Tisha b'Av.

Let us mourn a hundred years, five hundred years, for the *Churban*. Why all this time? After all this time, where is the *nechamah*? I remember that my illustrious and esteemed father, *Hagaon Harav* Yehoshua Heshel Kaufman, *shlita*, the *Rav* and *Moreh D'Asra* of the Young Israel of Montreal, the *Chaver Bet Din* of the *Bet Din* of Montreal, observed that there is a comment by Rashi on *Parshat Vayeshev*, the story of the selling of Yosef into slavery by his brothers, that can help us understand. The *pasuk* (Genesis 37:35) states that all Yaakov's children attempted to console him, but the Torah tells us that Yaakov refused to be consoled or to accept solace. For twenty-two years he cried and mourned for Yosef. He could not accept *nechamah*. Why? How can we understand Yaakov *Avinu*'s refusal of this most integral element of Judaism, *nechamah*? Rashi answers, quoting the *midrash*, "No one can accept consolation for one who is still living and only thought to be dead," as Yosef was. Rashi continues the explanation of the *midrash*: Only for the dead is there the blessing that the pain of loss should be forgotten from the heart—that is, consolation, *nechamah*. This blessing is not bestowed on those who mourn for the living, as Yaakov did.

We mourn for the *Beit Hamikdash*. We do not forget. We are not consoled, and we cry with increasing intensity each year because "No one can accept consolation for the living."

When our enemies destroyed the *Beit Hamikdash*, what did they want to accomplish? They wanted to destroy the Jewish people, destroy our Torah, eradicate our spirit. We are not consoled. We do not forget because our spirit, our Torah, remains vibrant and alive. The moment that we begin to forget, it is then that we admit that they have, *Rachmana Litzlan*, won. They can put us in chains; they can put a star on our sleeves; they can place us in concentration camps, but the Jewish spirit lives on. Torah lives on. *Am Yisrael chai! David Melech Yisrael chai vekayam!* How true are the words of our

Chazal when they say that those who properly mourn Yerushalayim, who properly feel the pain, who shed the tears for this bitter and lengthy *galut*, will be rewarded by seeing the *simchah* of its rebuilding. Our *chachamim* understood that the more we mourn, cry, and refuse to be consoled, the more we make the powerful statement that we do not give up, that Torah and *Am Yisrael* live on forever.

This Tisha b'Av, let us remember, as we once again sadly join with our *Avot Hakedoshim* in intensifying our *aveilut*, feeling the pain of this horrible and lengthy *galut* and the suffering of all the generations, that in that *zechut* may we merit the *brachah* of our Sages, that we will be deemed worthy one day of seeing that wondrous day, the rebuilding of the *Beit Hamikdash*, enjoying its *simchah* and *nechamah*.

Rabbi Raphael Wizman

Young Israel of Commack, New York

Parshat Devarim begins the book of *Mishneh Torah*. This *Shabbat* is also known as *Shabbat Chazon*.

"On the fortieth year, on the first of the eleventh month" (Devorim 1:3) on the first of Shevat) a little more than a month before he passed away, Moshe reviews *HaShem*'s Torah and gives words of *mussar* to the new generation. Moshe was speaking, not to the *Dor Deah*, the generation of knowledge that experienced the Exodus; not to the generation that witnessed *Kriat Yam Suf* and *Matan Torah*. That generation was gone, perished in the desert, as *HaShem* decreed after the sin of the spies who doubted *HaShem*'s ability.

The generation Moshe speaks to is a younger generation that will soon be entering *Eretz Yisrael*. To this generation who did not *see*, but only *heard* of, the great miracles and the great revelation on Mount Sinai, Moshe had to give his best and last effort to give words of *tochechah* (reproof). And he did so at the most effective time, right before his death (see Rashi)—a time when no one could accuse him of any ulterior motive, a time when Moshe was standing between *shnei olamot*, this world and the world of truth. When speaking to this generation, it seems, one that had not actually seen miracles and revelations, Moshe had to be more convincing.

Moshe uses the word *Eichah*, (Devorim 1:12) which stands for *tzarot* and tragedies. *Eichah*! "How can I carry your burden . . . ?" Rashi comments on *masa'achem* ("your burden"), stating that they were *apikorsim*—heretics or non-believers. How does Rashi derive "non-believers" from the word "burden"?

Rav Nachman of Breslov explains this beautifully. He says, "It's much more burdensome to be a non-believer." An *apikoros* who doubts everything has the burden of explaining everything in his world, whereas a believer has only to say, "It is from *HaShem*."

This generation, which did not *see*, is probably more doubting than the previous generation, which did see. It is, therefore, more pertinent for Moshe to warn, reprove, and encourage them not to lose their *bitachon* in *HaShem* than it would have been for him to do the same for the previous generation, who did *see*.

It is interesting to note that this is one of only two occasions when Moshe spoke to *kol*—"all Israel"—the other being in *Parshat Vayakel*. Since *kol* has two meanings, *all* and *every*, the use of the word suggests that his message was meant for every one of us; not only was Moshe speaking to his generation but to *kol Yisrael*—to all future generations as well.

For a *tochechah*—a reproof—to be effective and meaningful, it must come lovingly. As the *midrash* says, "Reproofs should have come from Bilaam and blessings from Moshe. Why is it reversed? Had the reproof come from Bilaam, Israel would have said, 'It's just an enemy talking' [pay no attention to him]. Had the blessings come from Moshe, the other nations of the world would have said, 'they received a blessing from someone who loves them' [it's insignificant]. Therefore, said *HaShem*, 'let the reproof come from Moshe, who loves them, and the blessing come from Bilaam, who hates them.'"

In his love and respect for his people, Moshe did not embarrass them. He reproved them only through a *remez*, a hint. They understood what he meant and were not embarrassed.

In his reproof, Moshe reminds his people of their lack of faith, as demonstrated by the sin committed by the spies. He states, "And you retreated and cried before *HaShem*" (Devorim 1:45). This crying, as the *Gemara Sanhedrin* (104) says, took place in the month of Av. *HaShem* said to Israel, "Since you have cried for nothing, I will therefore establish this night as a night of crying for future generations." Crying implies that they cried at least twice; thus, future generations will also have to cry twice, as the destruction of both Holy Temples took place on this date.

Moshe hinted that one *Eichah*, one sin of *apikorsus* and the lack of belief about the Promised Land, will lead to future *Eichahs*—tragedies and destructions of *Eretz Yisrael*.

The Jerusalem Talmud (*Yoma* 1.1) states the following: "A generation that did not merit to see the Holy Temple rebuilt is regarded as if it itself destroyed it."

Rav Levi Yitzchak of Berditchev says that the reason this *Shabbat* is called *Shabbat Chazon* is that the word *chazon* means "seeing"; every Jewish soul "sees" the third Holy Temple and is awakened by this vision. Our souls long for the rebuilding of the Temple and for its glory. The Rebbe illustrated this through a parable of a father who had a beautiful suit made for his son, who promptly tore it. The father then made him a new one; but the son tore it again. The father then made a third suit and showed it to his son but would not give it to him until such a time when he would learn how to treat his beautiful suit properly.

We too are "shown" the third Holy Temple every *Shabbat Chazon*. All we need to do is earn the merit to have it rebuilt in our time.

Rabbi Evan Shore

Young Israel Shaarei Torah of Syracuse, New York

"If you will be willing and you will obey, you shall eat the goodness of the land. But if you refuse and rebel, you shall be devoured by the sword, for the mouth of *HaShem* has spoken" (Isaiah 1:19:20). When we read these two sentences from this morning's *haftarah*, should we be surprised that the Holy Temple was destroyed, not only once but twice? If we knew that our house would be burned, robbed, ransacked, or otherwise destroyed, wouldn't we take the necessary precautions to protect it? Apparently, the Jewish people have not been good learners, or, even worse, we have not taken seriously the exhortations of our prophets. If so, why should we have been taken aback when our national and religious home, the *Beit Hamikdash*, was taken away from us and destroyed?

In this morning's Torah reading we learn, *Eicha*—"Alas, how can I myself alone bear your contentiousness, your burdens, and your strife?" (Deuteronomy 1:12). Rashi tells us that *Bnei Yisrael* constantly questioned Moshe's decisions. It seems that they did not take seriously either his leadership or the punishment that would result if they continued to disobey the commands of *HaShem*.

Moshe was not alone in his frustration with *Bnei Yisrael*. The *midrash* tells us that, in addition to Moshe, the prophets Yeshaiah and Yirmeyahu also used the word *eichah*—traditionally defined as "alas." However, the Radak tells us that the word *eichah* denotes the feeling of "How did this come upon her?" In spite of all the biblical warnings, as well as the prophecies of the *Nevi'im*, we still did not take heed, and we did not listen. How did we ignore it then, and why do we still ignore the warnings set down by the Torah and by the prophets?

In *Parshat v'Etchanan* we learn, "When you will have children and children's children and you grow old in the land" (Deuteronomy 4:25). The

Talmud, in *Gittin* (88a) discusses this *pasuk*; we learn that the *gematria* (numeric value) of the word *noshantem* ("grow old") is 852. The number of years between Joshua's crossing over the Jordan and the destruction of the first Holy Temple is 852. The Jews grew old and became complacent with *Eretz Yisrael*. We seem to have taken for granted the gift of the land *HaShem* gave to us. In spite of all the warnings, we still did not listen or take heed, and the Holy Temple was destroyed.

This problem still remains for the Jewish people today, but with a slight difference. There is no question that we are still complacent—not with *Eretz Yisrael*, however, but, rather, with our own *galut*. Year after year Tisha b'Av comes and goes, and yet there is no change. Our attitude should not be only one of lamenting the fact that the *Beit Hamikdash* has not been rebuilt or that the *mashiach* has not yet arrived. Rather, we should look at our own actions and see what every one of us can do to change our present situation. Toward the end of *Eichah* we read, "Bring us back to you, *HaShem*, and we shall return; renew our days as of old."

Ibn Ezra tells us that contained in this *pasuk* is the desire to return to the place of the Dwelling Place of *HaShem*'s name so that we may once again serve *HaShem* as before. Do we really mean what we say, or are we just giving lip service by a mere recital of the Book of Lamentations?

In his commentary on *Navi*, Rabbi Samson Raphael Hirsch writes that this morning's *Haftarah* is unique. The emphasis for this morning's selections is not the actual destruction of the *Beit Hamikdash* but, rather, that the Holy Temple *had* to be destroyed. This idea is very important in that it should be a message to us on what we should be thinking about on this *Shabbat* that precedes the tragedy-stricken day of the Ninth of Av. Strangely enough, Rabbi Hirsch seems to hint that we should not dwell upon the past on this day but, rather, on the present and our future.

When we look at what the *Navi* Yeshaiah has to say, we will be better equipped to change our present as well as our future: "Go forth now, and let us reason together, says *HaShem*: If your sins will be like scarlet they will whiten like snow. . . . If you will be willing and you will obey, you shall eat the goodness of the land" (Isaiah 1:18–19).

Yeshaiah is telling us that we should not languish in our past or dwell upon grief. Rather, we should be comforted in the knowledge that in spite of our past, *HaShem* has not forsaken us. In other words, when it comes to Tisha b'Av, we should all undergo attitude changes. That is not to say that we should not mourn; on the contrary we must, as it says in the Talmud in *Taanit*: "Anyone who mourns for [the destruction of the Holy Temple] will merit and be able to see it in happiness."

The Talmud is telling us not to be complacent. To mourn properly, we *must* mourn, *must* feel the loss, *must* know there is a void in our lives. Let us realize that the feeling of emptiness of the present will continue into the future until we say: enough. This year we should shift from a *galut* mentality to a *geulah* mentality. Let us act as if we really mean it when we say this year will be the last year Tisha b'Av is observed as a day of mourning.

An interesting story is told about Reb Avrahom Kamai. He needed to buy *Kinos* for Tisha b'Av and started to dispute the price of the book with the storeowner. The owner asked Reb Kamai why he started to haggle about the price of a book, since for years the books the rabbi purchased were bought without any question as to the price. Reb Kamai replied that all the other *seforim* he possessed he would need once the *Moshiach* comes; however, *Kinos* would not be needed next year, since the *Moshiach* will have arrived and the Holy Temple will be rebuilt.

All we have to do is realize that our attitudes and actions do make a difference—so much so that we all possess the power that will be the catalyst to rebuild the Holy Temple, please God, speedily in our days.

❖ CHAPTER 49 ❖

V'Etchnan

Rabbi Peretz Zutler

Young Israel of Avenue U,
New York

In this week's Parsha, Moshe *Rabbeinu* appeals to *Bnei Yisrael* not to forget what they had seen and experienced at Horeb. He also points out to them how fortunate a people they are by telling them, "For what great nation is there, that has God so near them, as the Lord our God is whenever we call upon Him?" (Deuteronomy 4:7)

Pertaining to this statement, the midrash reveals to us a dialogue between *Hakadosh baruch Hu* and Moshe Rabbeinu:

> Moshe said to the Holy One, "Master of the Universe, whenever You see Your children suffering and there is no one who pleads for Mercy on their behalf, answer them immediately." [Thereupon] God said to Moshe, "I swear that at any time that they [*Bnei Yisrael*] will call upon Me, I shall answer them, as it is written '. . . as the Lord our God is whenever we call upon Him.'"

Upon close scrutiny of this *midrash*, several difficulties surface:

1. The words "answer them immediately" are inappropriate in the context of the *midrash*; the word "answer" is apropos only when there is another individual calling. In our *midrash*, it explicitly states, "there is no one that asks for mercy"; it is, therefore, not feasible to use the words "answer them." Perhaps, it would have been more applicable for the *midrash* to say, "immediately have mercy upon them."
2. The response of *Hakadosh baruch Hu* is not comprehensible at all. Moshe asked (of *HaShem*) that He answer and come to the aid of *Bnei Yisrael* even when they do not call upon Him for help. *HaShem*, however, tells Moshe, "whenever *they* will call upon Me," which clearly implies that if *they* will not seek mercy, He will not answer them.

3. How does the *midrash* deduce from the words "as the Lord our God is whenever we call upon Him" details of this dialogue between *Hakadosh baruch Hu* and Moshe?

The Ropshitzer Rebbe, *zt"l*, in his commentary on *Chumash*, *Zera kodesh*, interprets the first sentence of our *parshah* "And I prayed to God at that time," in his inimitable way, which gives us an insight as to how the Rabbis interpreted the sentence "For what great nation is there . . . ?" It is written in the Prophets (Isaiah 63:9), "In all their affliction He is afflicted": The *shechinah* (Omnipotent Presence) shares with us our pain in exile. This concept is also mentioned in the Talmud: "When man suffers, what expression does the *shechinah* use? My head is too heavy for Me; My arm is too heavy for Me." (Sanhedrin 46a)

Therefore the primary intent, or *kavanah*, during prayer should not be concerned with a person's individual needs but with the needs of *Hakadosh baruch Hu*—the fact that He is in pain, so to speak, and suffering with us in our exile. And this is the meaning of the sentence "And He answers His people Israel." When does He answer the prayers of His people Israel? "At the time that they pray on behalf of Him (God)." They pray about the pain and suffering that God experiences, so to speak, when His people are in exile. When a Jew prays in this manner, it is certain that all his prayers will be answered.

There are times when the Gates of Prayer are open, and there are times when they are closed. This, however, is the situation when an individual prays for his personal needs. But the Gates of Prayer are always open for the person who prays concerning the pain and suffering of the *shechinah*, so to speak.

This was the manner in which Moshe Rabbeinu prayed. "And I prayed to God": Moshe's entire *kavanah* and intent concerned the *Ribono shel Olam*—that we, His people, should not experience suffering so that the *shechinah* should not experience suffering. Therefore, it is written, "at that time." It does not specify a time—to teach us that when prayers are offered in this manner, the Gates of Prayer are always open.

Seeing prayer from this perspective, we can now understand how the Rabbis in the *midrash* interpreted the sentence: "For what great Nation is there . . . ?"

As the *Tiferet Shmuel* points out, there are two difficulties with this sentence:

1. Since the sentence begins with the words, "For what great Nation is there, . . ." the sentence should have concluded with the words "like the Jewish people" and not with the words, "as the Lord our God."
2. Why does this sentence contain the two names of God that indicate the Attribute of Mercy and the Attribute of Justice?

It is human nature that, when something tragic occurs in a person's life experience, he prays to God to both help and alleviate the pain and suffering. It is quite understandable that, when an individual offers his supplications to God, the Attribute of Mercy has no hesitations about helping the individual who is in need of salvation. It is, rather, the Attribute of Justice that begins to criticize the person and his actions and deeds, arguing that this individual does not merit any salvation. How does a person defend himself or withstand this vilification? The answer is to let him follow the advice of the Ropshitzer Rebbe, *zt"l*, that was previously mentioned. In his prayers let him concentrate on the pain and anguish that God, so to speak, experiences when His people are in exile. The Attribute of Justice would certainly not contest a prayer offered in or on behalf of God. Consequently, the Attribute of Justice would concur with the Attribute of Mercy in alleviating the pain and suffering of that individual, thus alleviating the pain and suffering of God as well.

Now we can understand how the Rabbis in the *midrash* interpreted the sentence starting with "For what great nation." The words "that has God so near them" refer to the Attribute of Justice. The sentence is telling us that even the Attribute of Justice is close to the Jewish people, befriends the Jewish people, as does the Attribute of Mercy. For the sentence states, "that has God so near them, as the Lord our God . . . , implying that "our God," Attribute of Justice, is difficult to differentiate from the Attribute of Mercy, "as the Lord our God": they are as one. The sentence then goes on to explain when this is so—"When we call upon Him," when the prayers that are offered pertain to the welfare of the *Ribono shel Olam*, so to speak.

It is with this interpretation of the sentence "For what great nation . . ." that we can now understand the *midrash* we mentioned at the very outset: "Moshe said to the Holy One, 'Master of the Universe' whenever You see Your children suffering and there is no one who pleads for Mercy on their behalf, answer them immediately."

The question raised was, why does the *midrash* use the words "answer them immediately" if no one did any asking? The *midrash* clearly states, "there is no one who pleads for Mercy." The answer to this question is found in the text of the *midrash* if we underscore the word "in their behalf." Certainly, *Bnei Yisrael* will pray to God, but their prayers will not be concerned with their own needs but, rather, with the needs of God, so to speak.

The *midrash* continues: "[Thereupon] God said to Moshe, 'I swear that whenever they [*Bnei Yisrael*] will call upon Me I shall answer them.'" God is saying to Moshe, I give you My word, that whenever *Bnei Yisrael* will offer prayers, they "will call upon Me"—that is, their prayers will be concerned about My welfare; I shall answer them. As it is written, "as the Lord your God is whenever we will call upon Him": whenever we call upon Him, the

Attribute of Mercy and the Attribute of Justice become one, and our personal needs are granted.

With this perspective of exile in mind, we can answer the well-known question that the commentaries ask pertaining to the *haftarah* that is read on this *Shabbat*, which is referred to as *Shabbat Nachamu*—the *haftarah* that begins with the words, "Comfort ye, comfort ye, My people, saith your God." Why, ask the commentaries, does the sentence start with the word *nachamu* repeated?

Perhaps the answer is that one *nachamu* ("comfort") refers to the Exile of the *Shechinah*, while the second *nachamu* refers to the Exile of Israel.

Let us hope and pray that the words of the prophet be fulfilled and we may merit to see perfect redemption speedily in our days. Amen.

Rabbi Aharon Simkin

Young Israel of Northridge, California

TWO SETS OF TEN COMMANDMENTS

The *Aseret Hadibrot*, the Ten Commandments, found in *Sefer Shemot* are different from the version we read this week in *Parshat V'Etchanan*. Regarding *Shabbat*, we are commanded in *Sefer Shemot*, "Remember the Sabbath day to keep it holy" (Exodus 20:8), but here in *V'Etchanan* it says "Observe the Sabbath day to keep it holy" (Deuteronomy 5:12).

The commentators give various explanations for this difference. Some explain that in *Shemot* the reason for "remember" is to remember that *HaShem* created the world. Here, however, in *V'Etchanan*, we remember when *HaShem* took us out of Egypt.

There is an old joke regarding two Jews who come to their *rav* for a *Din Torah*. The rabbi listens to the first person's arguments and responds, "You're right!" Then he listens to the second person's story and comments, "You're right!" The rabbi's wife, who had been listening to the exchange, burst out with, "They can't both be right!" And her husband, the rabbi, responds, "You're right too!"

But, in fact, the Ramban would agree with the logic of this story because he holds that both reasons are correct. *Shabbat* is based on remembering both *HaShem*'s Creation of the world and the Exodus from Egypt. In fact, *Chazal* teach us that when *HaShem* originally taught the Ten Commandments, He said both verses of this command *at the same time*, in a stereo effect, as it were. Therefore, we must conclude that "observe" and "remember" are not just two separate concepts; rather, they are a unified whole. In other words, *Shabbat* is both observed and remembered—at the same time.

According to the Ramban, "observe and remember" refers to the fact that *Shabbat* includes both negative and positive *mitzvot*. Many of the *meforshim*, however, argue with the Ramban. The Maharal points out that *Chazal* teach that, in general, when a *mitzvah* appears in the Torah and then is repeated in *Sefer Devarim*, the reference in *Sefer Devarim* is meant to add details to the *mitzvah*. *V'zachor* means to remember *Shabbat* orally, to say *kiddush*, but *shamor* means to observe *Shabbat* by refraining from work. This different word does not merely add details to the *mitzvah* of *Shabbat* but expresses a fundamental difference that is explained by *Chazal* as being both versions of the *mitzvah* uttered by God simultaneously.

There is one more approach that has special significance to us today. The best-known commentator of all time, Rashi, explains as follows: "*Zachor* means to remember *Shabbat* during the week by preparing for *Shabbat*—cooking special food, buying nice clothes, making sure the children have treats. 'Observe the Sabbath' refers to observing *Shabbat* on the seventh day itself. Even the Hebrew language supports Rashi's interpretation; how are the days of the week named in *lashon hakodesh*, the holy language of Hebrew? Not with names of days in honor of pagan gods or astronomical objects (Sunday is the day of the sun; Thursday is Thor's day, and so on) but rather, "Today is the first day of the week toward *Shabbat*, . . . the second day toward *Shabbat*," and so on.

We all know to work six days a week and rest on *Shabbat*. But are we actively anticipating and looking toward *Shabbat* every day of the week? Do we concentrate our daily activities merely to support our bodily needs, or are we remembering that all our work throughout the week is toward the goal of a spiritual experience on the holy *Shabbat*?

And when it comes to the seventh day itself, do we merely erase working or do we remember to fill in the void formed by the absence of *melachah* ("work") with *kedushah* ("holiness"), with the holiness of *Shabbat*, with spiritual creativity? Do we improve ourselves and advance spiritually on *Shabbat*, or, on Saturday, do we merely substitute discussing work for actually doing work?

The *midrash* teaches that *Shabbat* complained to God, "You gave a spouse to each day of the week except me." *HaShem* responded, "the Jewish people, will be your spouse." *Shabbat* complained to *HaShem* because, when it was set aside as a day of rest, it seemed that *Shabbat* was to be merely a day of absence of action. Each of the other days had *melachah* as its spouse, but *Shabbat* was left alone. When *HaShem* promised that Israel would be the spouse of *Shabbat*, that meant that our spiritual creativity would be expressed on *Shabbat* to contrast with our physical creativity, which is expressed during the week.

This, then, is our challenge with *shamor v'zachor*: We must anticipate and prepare for *Shabbat* all week long and culminate our week by climbing to new heights of spiritual creativity, *ruchaniyut*, on the seventh day itself. We must strive to be a good and faithful spouse to *Shabbat*, to live, learn, and teach all Jews the secret of *Shabbat*.

Rabbi Yoel Schonfeld

Assistant to the Rabbi, Young Israel of Kew Gardens Hills, New York

THE ART OF *NECHAMAH*

"Comfort ye, comfort ye My people, saith your God" (Isaiah 40). These are the opening words of the *haftarah* for this week's *parshah*, for the *Shabbat* appropriate known as *Shabbat Nachamu*.

The *midrash* (*Yalkut Shimoni*) on this *pasuk* proclaims, "May it be a comfort for those above and for those below, for the living and for the dead, for this world and the world to come." This *midrash* seems to be conveying an important message. Unless comforting or consolation is total, there is no real comfort at all. To comfort an individual or a people half-heartedly is no consolation. To offer a sympathetic word covering only half the situation is meaningless in the final analysis.

In fact, the *midrash* elsewhere states that when Yeshaiah first uttered the words, "Comfort ye, comfort ye," the Jews wanted to kill him. It is only when he completed his message with "saith your God" that they were assuaged. The Jews at the time were so distraught and in such despair that nothing short of a direct message of comfort from *HaShem* would do. Anything less would ring empty of meaning and speak poorly of the messenger.

When we as individuals are put to the challenge of having to offer *nechamah*, as on the occasion of *nichum aveilim* comforting mourners, we must be aware of the same hazards of offering incomplete *nechamah*. In essence, saying "the right thing" at the right time is an art. Unfortunately, all too often, we are all called upon to be artists.

In *Avos D'Rav Nasan* (chapter 14) we are told that when Rabbi Yochanan ben Zakkai lost his son, his *talmidim* came to offer *nichum aveilim*. One by one they entered, each suggesting that others before Rabbi Yochanan had suffered the loss of a child and yet overcame their tragedy.

Rabbi Eliezer pointed to Adam *Harishon*, who suffered the loss of his son, Abel. Others pointed to Aharon, who lost two sons; still others mentioned Job, and so on. However, not one of these *talmidim*—nor all of them together—were able to succeed in comforting their *rebbe*. In fact, he seemed quite annoyed by their remarks. "Am I not suffering enough over my own loss that you have to remind me of the loss of yet others?" he would respond.

Finally came Rabbi Elazar ben Azariah, who said to Rabbi Yochanan, "I will tell you what your situation is comparable to. It is comparable to a king who entrusts an invaluable treasure to one of his subjects. The person prays every day that all should go well so that he can return the treasure intact. The same is with your son. *HaShem* gave you a valuable treasure to maintain: a young man who studied Torah and was extremely pious. You are fortunate indeed to have returned this treasure intact."

To this Rabbi Yochanan responded, "Rav Elazar, my son, you have comforted me as a comforter should."

The difference between Rav Elazar and the others is that Rav Elazar focused on the deceased, whereas the others tried to sidetrack the conversation by discussing other tragedies. It was only the penetrating words of Rav Elazar that offered complete comfort.

Yes, *nichum* is an art; however, let us hope that we no longer need such comfort, that it becomes a lost art.

May *HaShem* comfort the mourners of Zion and the mourners of Jerusalem speedily in our days. Amen.

❖ CHAPTER 50 ❖

Ekev

Rabbi Herbert W. Bomzer

Young Israel of Ocean Parkway, New York

FEAR OF HEAVEN: AN EASY TASK

> "And now, Israel, what doth the Lord, thy God, require of thee "*ki im*" but to fear the Lord, thy God, to walk in all His ways and to love Him; and to serve the Lord, thy God, with all thy heart and with all thy soul." (Deuteronomy 10:12)

Our sages questioned the expression *ki im*, "but to," which indicates that feeling awe is an easy task to achieve. "Is then the fear of Heaven a small thing?" The Rabbis then answered, "Yes, for Moshe [literally "near Moshe"] it was a small thing." This can be compared to a person who is asked for a large utensil and he has [many]; he, therefore, considers the request insignificant. If he were to be asked for a small utensil and he has none, he would consider this difficult (T.B. *Berakhot* 33b/*Megillah* 25a).

The *Torah Temimah* questions the talmudic explanation that Moshe's saying that God requires *ki im*, "but only" to fear Him is inapplicable to most ordinary people, who do not have the "large utensils" that Moshe himself had. It may be simple for Moshe to fulfill what God asks, but Moshe was talking to the masses and, for them, it might be an unreachable goal!

In addition, why was it such an easy undertaking, even for Moshe, to have *yirat Shamayim*? Does not the Talmud declare, "All is in the control of Heaven except the fear of God" (ibid.)? Moshe was a mortal human being, and so the fear of heaven was his only area of choice, as with everyone else.

Parenthetically, our Sages comment on the verse, "And the Lord said: My spirit shall not always strive in Me for the sake of men, [*b'shagam hu vasar*] for that he is but flesh; and his days shall be a hundred and twenty years" (Genesis 6:3). The *midrash* relates this verse to Moshe in response to the enigmatic question, "From where do we derive Moshe from the Torah (the book of *Bereishit*)?" And the answer given is that the word *b'shagam* refers to Moshe (numerically both are equal). The verse then tells us that he will live for one hundred and twenty years. Was this an exercise in arithmetical novelty? No! They were telling us that Moshe was a mortal man of flesh and blood whose years were limited, and *nevertheless* he became the great Moshe *Rabbeinu* from the Torah!

Let us return to our theme. First, the talmudic answer that for Moshe—"*near* Moshe"—it was an easy task to fear God. He had so much fear that anyone near him had to be influenced. Moshe's *yirat Shamayim* overflowed (*shefa*) so that he was able to be a *mashpia*—one with influence. So it became a simple challenge for all the Jews, even the most ordinary of the masses.

Why was it a simple thing for Moshe? Because he was born into and nursed in an atmosphere of reverence for God. His mother and sister, according to our Rabbis, showed the fear of Heaven in defying the evil decree of Pharaoh. Shifra and Puah are identified as Yochebed and Miriam (see Rashi, Exodus 1:15) and the Torah tells us: "But the midwives fear God" (Exodus 1:16), and again, "And it came to pass, because the midwives feared God, that He made them houses" (Exodus 1:21). So Moshe grew up in that kind of spiritual atmosphere, and, therefore, for him it was natural to fear God.

The lesson to be derived is obvious. Fear of Heaven, reverence for the word of God; emulation of God's attributes of graciousness, kindness, love, mercy, patience, and tolerance, are character traits that must be learned *at home*.

> What is a home? A roof to keep out the rain. Four walls to keep out the wind. Floors to keep out the cold. Yes, but home is more than that. It is the laugh of a baby, the song of a mother, the strength of a father. Warmth of living hearts, light from happy eyes, kindness, loyalty, comradeships. Home is the first school and the first religion (or lack) for young ones, where they learn what is right, what is good and what is kind. There they go for comfort when they are hurt or sick. There joy is shared and sorrow eased. It should be where fathers and mothers are respected and loved; where children are wanted; where the simplest food is good enough for kings because it is earned; where money is not so important as loving-kindness; where even the tea kettle sings from happiness. That is home. God bless it. (Ernestine Schumann)

Jane Addams wrote, "America's future will be determined by the home and school. The child becomes largely what it is taught, hence we must watch what we teach it, and how *we live* before it."

I was at the *aufruf* (shabbos aliyah before a wedding) of a very wonderful young man to whom I told the following story (found in many places):

An artist wanted to paint a picture of the most beautiful scene in the world. He asked a rabbi, "What is the most beautiful thing in the world?"

"Faith," answered the rabbi. "It can sustain you in joy or stress."

A tired soldier said, "Peace is the most beautiful thing in the world for war is ugly."

A young bride was then queried and she responded, "Love. It builds lives, sweetens bitter moments."

"Faith, peace, and love! How can one paint these intangibles?" thought the artist for an entire day. Then he went home, and as he entered his door he saw faith in the eyes of his children; he felt so peaceful there, and he was elated by the love of his wife. So he painted the picture of the most beautiful thing in the world and called it "Home."

The important thing is to give our children the opportunity to absorb *yirat Shamayim* so that the call of God will be as easily answerable by them as it was by Moshe and so that, God willing, they will develop into the leaders of tomorrow from whom others, in their presence, can also be influenced to do good.

This is the goal and role—and not only of the physical home, which has broken down in modern times. The destruction of traditional family structures and traditional attitudes has undoubtedly contributed to the problems of violence, abuse, and societal conflicts. The loss of the Jewish (Torah) home has been accompanied by ignorance of Torah, desecration of *Shabbat, yom tov, kashrut,* and Jewish values, which include integrity, compassion, respect for Torah teachers (rabbis) and *mentschlichkeit*.

These obligations must be taught and practiced in the *yeshivot* and *shuls*. The Young Israel must be the best example of *yirat Shamayim*. We have the numbers, as well as the role models of erudite rabbis and responsible lay leaders. The rewards are the blessings of God.

Rabbi Hershel Kurzrock

Young Israel of Kensington, New York

> "And it shall come to pass, *ekev*—as the consequence of—your hearkening to these ordinances and carefully performing them, that *HaShem* will keep the covenant and loving kindness with you that He swore to your forefathers." (Deuteronomy 7:12)

On this opening verse of the *Sedrah Ekev*, Rashi quotes the *Midrash Tanchuma* (*Ekev* 1) wherein the word *ekev* is rendered as meaning "a heel," and the verse is interpreted in the following manner: "If you will hearken unto the 'light' precepts—commandments of minor importance—which man is prone to trample with his heels—that is, treat lightly—then *HaShem* will keep His covenant. . . ." (Rashi, Deuteronomy 7:12).

It is difficult to comprehend why Rashi, who at all times pursued the most literally simple and logical interpretation, should, in this case, offer an explanation seemingly not clearly stated or implied in the words of the sentence. In fact, the *Targum Onkelos* and *Yonathan* both render the word *ekev* by its simple meaning, *chalaf* ("in consequence of" or "because"), which is fitting for this verse.

Also, since, in the preceding verse, which is the last sentence of *Sedrah V'Etchanan*, the Torah clearly admonishes the Jewish people to adhere strictly to the "*chukim* and *mishpatim*" ("statutes and ordinances"), why, in the first verse of *Sedrah Ekev*, which discusses the reward, mention is only made of the *mishpatim* (ordinances)? (See *Klei Yakar* and *Meshech Chochmah*.)

The *Midrash Tanchuma* (*Ekev* 2) stresses the importance of striving to perform every one of the 248 positive precepts with equal devotion, care, and diligence. The measure of reward doesn't attest to the ease or difficulty in the performance of a particular *mitzvah*. Also, we cannot determine the importance of a *mitzvah* by ascertaining how easy or difficult it is to perform that *mitzvah*.

To prove this point, the *midrash* cites a saying of Reb Shimon ben Yohai, who says, "For observance of two *mitzvot*, the Torah explicitly reveals the reward; one is considered *kal shebakalot* [easiest to perform; when chancing upon a bird's nest one should first send away the mother and only then take the children—not difficult to perform and entailing no expenditure of funds, see Deuteronomy 22:6–7], and the other, *chamurah shebachamurot* [most difficult to perform properly; Honor your father and mother; see Exodus 20:12 and Deuteronomy 5:16], requiring constance viligance, awareness, possible loss of funds, and accepting shame and invective, and so on. See Talmud *Kiddushin* 31a, 32a], and yet the reward that these two *mitzvot* earn is exactly the same: 'that you may merit long life'" (Deuteronomy 22:7, 5:16).

We are admonished in *Pirkei Avot* 2:1, "Be as careful [in observance] with a minor *mitzvah* as with a major one, for you don't know the rewards given for *mitzvot*." In fact, although, in our vast talmudic literature we find *mitzvot* characterized as *kalot* ("light") in specific instances (for example, see Talmud *Avodah Zarah* 3a), there really are no clear, sharply defined rules given by our Sages that would enable us to label and categorize *mitzvot* as officially "light" or "weighty," "minor" or "major." No one actually knows how to make distinctions among different *mitzvot* and conclude which are truly "great" in the eyes of the Almighty.

However, in regard to those *mitzvot* called *mishpatim* ("ordinances"), which are also known as *Mitzvot Sichliut* ("dictated by reason"), a person may be inclined to use his own subjective judgment as a yardstick to evaluate the reasonableness and wisdom of a particular "ordinance precept" and then classify it as either a minor or major *mitzvah*. A person is more apt to take this approach with *mishpatim*, where we have reasons, rather that with "*chukim*-statutes", where no reason is given and it is understood that performance is based on the faith and belief in *HaShem* and His Torah (Deuteronomy 4:6). It seems to me that the above thought is strongly alluded to by the *Alshech Hakodesh* (*Tehillim* 19, 10:12) in a beautiful, lengthy discourse that ends with a strong admonisition: ". . . And it should not seem in the eyes of man that the reward for *mishpatim* (ordinances) is not that great since reason dictates their observance."

This tendency on the part of a person to assess and classify *mishpatim* ("precepts") often leads to laxity and apathy in the observance of those deemed trivial and to their eventual complete neglect and discard. Those *mitzvot* are literally *dosh b'ekeivov* ("trampled by his heels")!

If the above is kept in mind, a clear answer to the questions posed at the beginning becomes apparent. The very use of the word *ekev* instead of the simple term *im* ("if") [*Sefer Or Hachaim*] and this verse's reference to *mishpatim* only can be the basis for Rashi's using the midrashic interpretation. Rashi seeks to stress that the use of the extraneous word *ekev*, which can also mean "a heel," in conjunction with rational precepts, teaches us that a person must be particularly careful, vigilant, and alert not to deceive himself into believing that he has the right to evaluate and classify *mitzvot*. ("Deceive" is also a possible meaning for the root letters of the word *ekev* if they are pronounced *akov*, as in the verse *Vy'akveini* . . . ["and he deceived me"], Genesis 27:36.) Man must strive to perform every *mitzvah* in as perfect a manner as possible.

With this interpretation, a quotation by the *Midrash Tanchuma* on this first verse in *Ekev* becomes clear. The *midrash* (*Ekev* 1) quotes the verse from *Tehillim* 49:6 in which King David cries forth, "Why should I fear in times of evil [suffering], for the 'trivial' *akeivai* [*ekev*] iniquities surround me . . ." (see Alshech). King David laments that he may have been lax in observance of *mitzvot* that can be construed as trivial, and for this he feared the wrath of the Almighty.

True, no one is perfect or reaches perfection (*Kohelet* 7:20). As the Kotzker Rebbe said, "He that thinks he has attained spiritual perfection . . . this is his greatest imperfection." Yet, a person must be cognizant of his responsibilities and try to be alert and vigilant to perform all *mitzvot* with equal fervor and dedication. With this approach, man may, at times, temporarily transgress and be guilty of "stepping on a *mitzvah*" (as one may tiptoe on one's sole), but, never, can he be accused of "trampling on a *mitzvah*" (as one does on one's heel) by completely neglecting and rejecting its observance.

The story is told that when Reb Yaakov of Lisa accepted a call to become a Rabbi of the city of Stree, he was confronted by the elders of the city of Lisa. They asked him in bewilderment, "Rabbi, why are you leaving? What are you missing by being with us?"

Rabbi Yaakov answered, "I'll tell you what I miss here. Since I became Rabbi in Lisa, this is the very *first shailah* [question] asked of the rabbi. I seek a live, vibrant community interested in the knowledge of Torah and *mitzvot* with the viewpoint and desire for proper dedicated observances."

Yes! The arrival of Rosh Chodesh Elul heralds and initiates the days of *teshuvah*—repentance. A firm resolve to live by this principle of cherishing and appreciating the value of every *mitzvah*, where "light" or "weighty," will transform a perfunctory approach to the performance of *mitzvot* into a regular, consistent one (NOTE: the letters of *ekev* transpose into *keva*, which means "regular, continuous"!).

Living by these convictions guarantees that *HaShem* will keep His covenant and lovingkindness that He swore to our forefathers (Deuteronomy 7:12) and merit for us the blessings of a *Shanah Tovah*.

Rabbi Eliyahu Rabovsky

Young Israel of Boca Raton, Florida

The eighth chapter of *Sefer Devarim* relates a speech given by Moshe to the *Bnei Yisrael* to prepare them for their entry into *Eretz Yisrael*. The first three *pesukim* alone contain many critical fundamentals of Jewish thinking, and these ideas are certainly worthy of our consideration.

The first *pasuk* states, "The entire commandment which I enjoin upon you today, you shall keep to carry it out so that you may live and multiply and come in and take possession of the land that God swore to your fathers."

The *Klei Yakar* notes the inconsistency of the verse regarding the expression of the word "you." In the beginning, when Moshe is talking about the responsibility of abiding by the Torah, he uses *metzavcha*, "command you," with the singular form of "you." At the end, when reward for Torah adherence is mentioned, the plural form of "you"—*l'ma'an tichyun urevitem*, "so that you may live and multiply," is employed. The *Klei Yakar* derives from this mixing of singular and plural an insight into the power of an individual.

The Torah is saying that even if one single soul will accept the responsibility and perform a *mitzvah*, the greatest blessings of health, children, and material needs will be secured for and enjoyed by the entire community. In addition, the *teshuvah* of an individual can gain a pardon for an entire community.

How often do we find ourselves ready to do something positive but are deterred by the feeling, "What difference will it make anyway? I'm only one person." This sentiment is particularly felt when we consider undertaking projects that are designed to benefit others. We find ourselves saying, "I will work hard to craft a meaningful program and run around to implement it, but, in the end, only a few will care." We must resist this defeatist type of thinking in light of the *Klei Yakar*'s message that my sacrifice and commitment alone can mean so much in the grand scheme of things.

The second *pasuk* states, "Remember the entire path along which *HaShem*, your God, has led you these forty years in the wilderness, in order to have you live in want, to test you, to show what is in your heart, whether you will keep His commandments or not."

HaShem tests people for many reasons. One important dimension of these tests can be to publicize spiritual accomplishments to others. *Rabbeinu* Bachya interprets *lada'at*, "to know," in this verse as "to make known to the nations of the world."

Why is it important that all people know of our practice of Torah? *Rabbeinu* Bachya explains, "Let it be publicized so that it will illustrate to the world that Divine service is the basis for all of creation."

The Torah wants the world to see our service to *HaShem* amidst adversity after a history of birth, exile, slavery, and liberation. Then the world will realize that in Divine service lies the purpose of life. Moreover, when our service is put to the test and we respond positively and publicly, our own commitment is reinforced.

The third *pasuk* states, "He had you live in want, He let you go hungry and then He fed you with the manna that you did not know and your fathers did not know, in order to have you know that it is not by bread alone that man lives but by all that comes out of the Mouth of God."

The NeTZiV writes that the goal of our being sustained by the manna was to implant within us a sense of eternal hope, even in the face of a hopeless situation. When all seems lost, we can turn to our experience in the desert and see that *HaShem* can always provide our needs. The expression, "but by all that comes out of the Mouth of God does man live" refers to many different aspects of Torah living. The NeTZiV highlights the importance of *tefillah* and the recitation of *brachot* before we eat.

When we are mindful of *HaShem*'s presence in the most mundane settings, His ever-outstretched arm of assistance is always in our sight.

Rabbi Aaron Batt

Council of Young Israel Rabbis in Israel

In discussions of *parshat hashavuah* there are a number of options available and a number of approaches that may be taken. In the next few pages an attempt will be made to develop a central theme in this *parshah*. This concept is an extension of *smichoot haparshiyot*—juxtaposition of parshas—when one parsha is next to another. Not only are two adjacent incidents or commandments related, but the relationship may extend to a larger section as well. When searching for a general theme in a *parshah*, one must consider the circumstances surrounding the Jewish people at that particular juncture in history.

In Deuteronomy in general, Moshe is speaking to the people before his death. He has before him two tasks. He must give *mussar* (rebuke) to the people for the past. He reprimands *Am Yisrael* by reminding them of past misdeeds and exhorts them to improve their ways, not to repeat the mistakes of the past generation. In addition to this, however, he also performs another task: he prepares the people for the future.

Moshe, at this point, faces a whole generation that has lived forty years in the wilderness. This generation was brought up and developed under the protection of the clouds of glory, under the protection of the Divine "umbrella." They were immune to environmental dangers, to the vicissitudes of nature. This generation was the generation that ate the manna. The necessities of life were provided for them by God. In the wilderness they did not have to concern themselves with earning a living, with building and/or maintaining cities or farms. Their needs were met by Divine fiat.

At this point in history, the situation will change radically. They are getting ready to leave the "unnatural" state of the wilderness and enter the "land," the natural state of a nation that must fend for itself, of a nation that experiences a normal life. Perhaps, in searching for a unified theme, one should take cognizance of this particular situation.

Life is not static but dynamic and ever changing. How does one deal with the various episodes in life? We believe the Torah is a *Torat chaim,* a living Torah, and a Torah of life prepares man and informs man as to how he should react to the challenges of life. At times this preparation is exemplified by specific *mitzvot,* specific commandments that indicate a man's direction and guide him. At other times, the Torah provides man with a general attitude toward real situations, an attitude that serves as a guideline for the future.

We are accustomed to the idea that man must learn how to deal with misfortune. There are dangers involved to man's spiritual well-being when he faces a crisis brought about by misfortune. Man may lose faith; he may become discouraged and despondent and, as a result, his service to God and/or Torah learning may suffer. The Torah, in the large sense, has provided guidelines for the human response to these situations. These guidelines can help protect man from the dangers and forestall spiritual damage. To mention two of the traditional responses:

1. God is telling me something; let me analyze what is happening to me.
2. What have I done wrong, and how can I improve myself?

Life at times smiles on man, and he may experience good fortune and success. Such a happy situation can contain within itself a parallel, if not so evident, spiritual danger. This situation is given a halachic framework by the *s"mag* (*Sefer Mitzvot Gadol*). He formulates a commandment: "One should not become proud when God provides him with good and consider it as if his efforts brought it about but, rather, praise God for it. . . ." What are the possible dangers, and how does the Torah suggest protecting oneself?

There are a number of forms of good fortune, and our reactions to each may be different.

Man may receive good fortune without having worked for it. This is described in *V'Etchanan* 6:10–13 and in *Ekev* 8:7–11:

> For the Lord your God is bringing you into a good land, a land with streams and springs and fountains issuing from plain and hill; a land of wheat and barley, of vines, figs, and pomegranates, a land of olive and trees and honey; a land where you may eat food without stint, where you will lack nothing; a land whose rocks are iron and from whose hills you can mine copper. When you have eaten your fill, give thanks to the Lord, your God for the good land which He has given you.

If we concentrate on the second instance in our *parshah,* we find that the Torah provides a specific *mitzvah* as a protection. This *mitzvah* is *birkat hamazon* (Grace after meals). *Birkat hamazon* is one of the *brachot* (blessings) that are *min Hatorah* (commanded from the Torah). The *Mesach*

Chochmah on this section discusses the relevance of the fact that the *brachah* that is *min Hatorah* is after eating, not before. When man is hungry and he is given food, of course he will thank God. The more important task is to recognize and thank God when one is satisfied. After one has received the blessing of God, one must be ready to recognize and proclaim whence come all blessings. Such an attitude will protect one against the danger of haughtiness, a concern raised by the *s"mag*.

Our *parshah* postulates another scenario relating to good fortune. Man may feel that he has received a blessing because he has worked for it. In *pasuk* 8:17, this is expressed as, "and you say to yourselves, 'my own power and the might of my own hand have won this wealth for me.'" The proper response to this is given in the next *pasuk*, 8:18: "Remember that it is the Lord, your God, who gives you the power to get wealth." Man recognizes that, in the final analysis, his strength comes from God. It is true that I worked for what I received, but without the help of God all of my efforts would have been in vain.

Alternatively, man may feel that good fortune has come to him because of his righteousness. The situation is expressed in *pesukim* 9:4–6: "Say not to yourselves, 'The Lord has enabled me to occupy this land because of my virtues,'" and the answer is given immediately. "No, it is not your righteousness or saintliness that entitles you to reward but, rather, the punishment due to others and the promise of God to your fathers, Abraham, Isaac, and Jacob."

This concept may be applied to the spiritual realm as well. Man should never feel that whatever spiritual level he has reached has been through his own efforts. Even in this area, without the help of God, man could not have attained what he did.

We find the *nisayon* (test) of good fortune in another section of this week's *parshah*. In describing the manna, *pasuk* 8:16 says, *u-lema'an nasotecha*. In what way was the manna a *nisayon*, a test? The Ramban, commenting on Exodus 20:17, explains this by saying that "good" may also be a *nisayon*—good can also present man with a challenge. How do we accept this bounty of God?

The Torah has chosen to present this message, this challenge to the Jewish people, in *Parshat Ekev* as part of the preparation for entering *Eretz Yisrael*. Moshe repeats the great daily miracle that God performed for the people in the desert for forty years. They are in a period of transition; they are living a supernatural life of daily miracles and, at the same time, preparing to enter a natural life of "each man under his vine tree and each man under his fig tree." The challenge becomes greater upon entering the Land. They find homes filled with all good things, houses filled with plenty for which they did not have to lift a finger. Maybe they will begin to feel, "God is good to me because I deserve it." At the same time, there is another challenge waiting for them from the opposite point of view. They are about to enter the Land and to conquer it by force of arms. They may begin to feel, "My success is a result of my own strength, of my own ability."

It is not sufficient for the Torah to teach man what is the improper approach; it must also provide the framework for a proper appreciation of God's bounty to the nation upon entering the Land. In *pesukim* 9:4–5, we read, "Do not say, 'It is because of my righteousness.' . . . not your virtues," but why? "It is in order to fulfill the oath that the Lord made to your fathers, Abraham, Isaac, and Jacob." This is repeated again in 10:15: "Yet it was to your fathers that the Lord was drawn in His love for them so that He chose you, their lineal descendants, from among all peoples." You must (10:16) uproot from your hearts the incorrect notion, "I deserve it." You must be willing to bow your head and admit that it is not your own intrinsic strength that has provided you with all your victories.

The Torah is eternal, and its messages are eternal. These are dangers and challenges that existed for the Jewish people not only three thousand years ago, when they left the wilderness and entered the land that God had promised to the patriarchs. These are challenges that have faced our people over the generations and, perhaps to a greater extent than ever, in the past few generations. A generation that had to contend with the concept of the Shoah—the challenge of an inconceivable evil, of a destruction of a large portion of the nation—then witnessed a miraculous rebirth of the nation in its land. This generation has to learn from our *parshah* the proper response to the bounty of God. It is the unique responsibility of the religious community to formulate for itself and for the Jewish people as a whole the appropriate approach to historical events. Every historical occurrence demands its own response. The commentaries explain the first part of the *kohanic* blessing—"May the Lord bless you and protect you"—by saying that each *brachah* requires its own protection. Any blessing can present a danger and a challenge. This is true not only on the national, historical level but also on the immediate, personal level. Each individual is required by the Torah to develop his own response to God's providence to him. One who believes in Divine providence, one who believes that God is involved not only in national, historical events but also in the lives of everyone, must be prepared to analyze the path of his life. The Torah outlines the way; it is up to man to travel the path together with God.

❖ CHAPTER 51 ❖

Re'eh

Rabbi Mordecai Shapiro

Young Israel of Jackson Heights, New York

As Moshe *Rabbeinu*'s "words of admonishment" continue in *Parshat Re'eh*, the first half of this *sedrah* introduces us to a series of seemingly disjointed concepts. We open with the distinction between *brachah* (blessing) and *k'lalah* (curse) and then move immediately into a group of laws dealing with various aspects of *avodah zarah* (idol-worship). These include the injunction that requires total destruction of all forms of *avodah zarah*—the idols; their actual forms of worship and service; "the enticer and those that draw you away," and the wayward city. The *sedrah* then turns to the laws concerning the false prophet and concludes with the section on the laws of forbidden foods.

Certainly, each of these topics stands by itself with its own set of *mitzvot* and detailed laws. Yet, there is a common thread that binds them into a magnificent unit. All these injunctions are designed to emphasize the difference between the Jewish nation and the nations of the world. They are laws whose underlying purpose is to keep us separate from the non-Jewish world and to prevent assimilation and the disintegration of the Jewish people.

The portion of *brachah uk'lalah* serves as an introduction to the difference between good and evil and their consequences. It has often been pointed out that the human condition prevents us from seeing exactly what is a blessing and what is a curse. We grope for a definition and react instinctively to events without the objective analysis needed for a true understanding of what lies before us.

Sforno points out that in the blessings and curses there is only one or the other; there are no compromises and no shades of gray. Thus, with a faith in God there are also no compromises; therefore all forms of idolatry must be destroyed. Even the places where these services were performed must be obliterated from memory. It is only at this juncture of the *parshah* that we are told of the importance of the *Beit Habechirah*, the Temple, the one and only chosen place for full service to God.

The contrast drawn by the *pesukim* is emphatic in its attempt to differentiate between two distinct ways of life. This is further borne out by the warnings against all possible forms of intrusion, as evidenced by the laws concerning the "false prophet." Here is a person with the ability to perform miracles and truly test one's strength of faith and religious conviction. The Chofetz Chaim has pointed out that this *pasuk* tells us that the degree to which God is testing us is a direct corollary to the success of the false prophet. Of course, the false prophet need not be someone with a glib tongue or sleight of hand. He can take any form, spiritual or materialistic, outwardly religious or not—anything that stands to challenge faith in *HaShem*. Once again, "choice" is clear.

We find a similar thought concerning "the enticer and those that draw you away" and "the wayward city." Family pressure, peer pressure, mob rule, and group psychology can all entice us to an alien form of life. They must be resisted at all costs and with the gravest of consequences to those who submit to temptation.

The *parshah* then proceeds to the laws of forbidden foods. What more obvious mode of teaching us self-control and necessary social isolation is there than forcing us to be conscious of the foods we eat, where we eat, and with whom we eat? *Chazal*, our Rabbis, were so aware of this concept and understood the dangers so well that they expanded the laws of forbidden foods to cover even the staples of life—bread, milk, and certain beverages—as well as cooking by non-Jews. Each category is notable for special reasons of its own, but all have the common purpose of reducing social interactions that would lead to assimilation and its devastating result. History has proven time and time again that the more we attempt to assimilate and blend with society, the greater the hatred and ultimate destruction. As the *midrash* points out, when Yosef died, the people of Israel abandoned the *mitzvah* of circumcision in an attempt to be just like the Egyptians. As a result, God changed the love and acceptance of Israel by the Egyptians into hatred and, eventually, the devastating servitude.

In the latter portion of this *sedrah* we read of the *mitzvah* of *tzedakah*. *Chazal* tell us that nature calls for a world of haves and have-nots, as the *pasuk* says: "for the poor shall never cease out of the land." It is this very condition of inequity, perceived by humans as an imperfection in God's world, that creates the basis for the *mitzvah* of *tzedakah*. We ask, why did God create a cruel world where people must beg and scrounge for even the barest necessities of survival? God, in His infinite wisdom, gives mankind a hand in building and sustaining the world, and "the word is built with kindness."

It is only through the acts of *chesed* (kindness) performed by humankind that the perceived imperfection is erased and the world becomes whole. How beautiful is the story in the *Yerushalmi Sotah* about the student of Rabbi Yehudah, the Prince of Israel, who was a regular recipient of the generosity of his teacher because his assets fell below the minimum level which they allowed for such assistance.

One year, the Talmud tells us, some of the other students of Rabbi Yehudah sought to "help" their colleague by giving him just enough funds to make him ineligible for the stipend he had been receiving. When Rabbi Yehudah learned of this generosity, he devised a scheme to reduce his needy student's assets, thereby restoring his eligibility for the much-needed funds. At the same time, Rabbi Yehudah admonished his other students for failing to see the damage they had caused to their friend. In their veiled attempt to help him, they violated the concept, "and thy heart shall not be grieved when thou givest to him." They had "given" with an evil heart. *Tzedakah* given with *simchah* is the greatest fulfillment of this *mitzvah*, for it is only through joy that we can build worlds.

Avraham *Avinu*, the "pillar of righteousness," stands as our example *par excellence* of the attributes of *chesed* and *tzedakah* in all forms. In the throes of great physical pain, he searched in the hot blazing desert for opportunities to fulfill his mission. The *midrash* poses an interesting query. Why does the Torah wait until after the *mitzvah* of circumcisioin to describe the degree of self-sacrifice with which Avraham performed the *mitzvah* of *tzedakah*?

The *midrash* tells us that Avraham said, "Before my circumcision many wayfarers passed my tent; now that I have been circumcised they have ceased. Why?" Clearly, Avraham is giving us an insight into human nature. How often do we hear that "charity begins at home"? Surely, there is good reason to believe that family, friends, and neighbors may have priority, but philanthropy to this segment alone does not complete one's obligation to perform the *mitzvah* of *tzedakah*. Avraham's neighbors stopped coming because they thought he was now too different from them and that he would no longer be interested in helping them.

Avraham demonstrated that this was not the case. Though there are many reasons to separate people by geography, religions, or some other less-than-noble reason, we must realize that, when it comes to *chesed* (kindness) and *rachamim* (pity), there are no boundaries and no divisions. The Talmud in *Gittin* notes that we are obligated to sustain the non-Jewish poor together with the Jewish poor and that we are to visit the non-Jewish sick together with the Jewish sick, along with many other such statements of equality. Avraham *Avinu* points out that, though there are distinctions among people and valid reasons to maintain uniqueness, there is a practical need to be generous and helpful to all, not to mention the great "sanctification of God's name" that can result from such actions. Surely, through such commitment to *chesed,* we not only are partners with God in building the world but will also help hasten the redemption of our people and the restoration of Israel's glory.

"Zion shall be redeemed with judgment and those that return to her with righteousness" (Isaiah 1:27). "In righteousness thou shalt be established" (Isaiah 54:14).

Rabbi Kenneth Auman

Young Israel of Flatbush, New York

TOV VERSUS *YASHAR*

> "Observe and hear all these words which I command thee, that it may go well with thee, and with they children after thee forever, when thou doest that which is good (*tov*) and right (*yashar*) in the eyes of the Lord thy God."
>
> (Deuteronomy 12:28)

The *Sifre* records a strange dispute between Rabbi Akiva and Rabbi Yishmael concerning the connotations of the terms *tov* and *yashar* as used here by the Torah. Rabbi Akiva is of the opinion that *tov* is "in the eyes of Heaven," whereas *yashar* is "in the eyes of mankind." Rabbi Yishmael's position is exactly the opposite—that *yashar* refers to Heaven and *tov*, to mankind. It is difficult to understand the significance of the disagreement between the two.

Perhaps the issue can be understood in the following manner. The term *tov* has the connotation of absolute good, whereas *yashar* is a relative term. Rabbi Akiva's position is therefore clearly understood. When dealing with *Hakadosh Baruch Hu* our obligation is an absolute one. We have exact and precise definitions of both the *mitzvot aseh*, the positive commandments, and the *mitzvot lo taaseh*, the negative commandments. All Jews have the same basic obligations. However, with regard to *bein adam lachavero*, our obligations toward other human beings, there is a certain amount of leeway in our behavior. Our obligations, to some degree, are governed by the nature and personality of the other party. A certain type of action, for example, might be injurious to one party and yet be of no consequence to another. Hence the use of *tov*, the absolute term, with reference to God and *yashar*, the relative term, with reference to man.

Rabbi Yishmael's position, however, is more difficult to understand. Presumably, he, too, would agree with the above analysis. However, there is a perspective from which our relationship with God is more relativistic than our relationship with man. When it comes to man's being judged for his action, if God is our judge, He has a certain amount of leeway, so to speak, in meting out punishment and reward to human beings. He can take many variables into account, since He is the One who truly knows our innermost thoughts, intentions, and abilities. A human judge, on the other hand, lacks this ability. Therefore, he must judge on the basis of absolute criteria, and the verdict for any given crime will be the same, regardless of the nature of the individual involved. Therefore, Rabbi Yishmael says that *tov*, the absolute, refers to man, who must judge based on fixed criteria, whereas *yashar*, the relative term, refers to God, Who takes many different factors into His decisions.

MAASER SHENI AND *YIRAT SHAMAYIM*

The Torah gives us many rules concerning *terumot* and *maasrot*, the various tithes that are required on all produce grown in the Land of Israel. *Terumah* (generally 2 percent) was given to the *kohanim*; *maaser rishon* (10 percent) to the *leviim*, and *maaser ani* (10 percent, in the third and sixth years of the seven-year cycle) to the indigent. *Maaser sheni* (10 percent, in the first, second, fourth, and fifth years of the seven-year cycle) was different in that it was not given to anyone but, rather, was consumed by its owners. However, it could be eaten only in Yerushalayim. The Torah tells us that the purpose of this *mitzvah* was "in order that you learn to fear God all the days."

The obvioius question that arises is, how does the *mitzvah* of eating the *maaser sheni* in Yerushalayim inculcate in us a fear of God?

As we have noted, *maaser sheni* is unique among the tithes in that it was not given away. The concept of a required tithe is not a difficult one to grasp. That certain groups, such as those devoted to the service of God, or the needy, should be entitled to support from others is a concept that exists in many cultures and religions. However, the notion that that which is reserved for oneself is also subject to certain restrictions is a novel concept. That even what we own is subject to Divine rule is a basic approach in Judaism to *yirat Shamayim*. There is no separation of "that which is to God" and "that which is to man." All is under God's domain. Thus, the observance of *maaser sheni* truly instills *yirat Shamayim* in our beings.

SHECHITAH

In *Parshat Re'eh*, the Torah forbids us to eat the blood of animals with the rationale that the blood represents the life of the animal. In *Parshat Acharei*

Mot (Leviticus 17:11), the Torah gives us a somewhat more detailed explanation, stating that blood has been designated for use on the altar to effect the proper atonement of a sacrifice. These two sections of the Torah give us a very deep insight into the Torah's view regarding the slaughtering of animals for private use vis-à-vis the slaughtering of animals for sacrificial use. When an animal is sacrificed for purposes of human consumption, the act of shedding the animal's blood is viewed as a practical necessity. Though the *shechitah* of the animal under these circumstances is a halachic requirement, it is not a *mitzvah* in and of itself (that is, there is no *mitzvah* to slaughter animals if one is not interested in eating meat or in giving others the meat to eat). Therefore, the blood, which represents the life of the animal that was taken, may not be consumed. However, when *shechitah* is performed for sacrificial purposes, it is intrinsically a *mitzvah,* for it allows the blood to be put upon the altar, where it performs the crucial role of effecting the act of sacrifice and achieving atonement on behalf of those for whom the sacrifice was offered.

It is interesting to note that the eating of the slaughtered animal is also a function of the type of *shechitah* involved. Where the *shechitah* was *shechitat chulin,* done merely for purposes of private consumption, the eating of that meat, though entirely permissible, is not a *mitzvah per se* (it may be a *mitzvah* for other reasons, such as *oneg Shabbat* or *simchat yom tov,* but those are incidental to the issue we are discussing). On the other hand, when the *shechitah* was *shechitat kodoshim,* done for sacrificial purposes, the eating of the meat is indeed a *mitzvah.* If the shedding of the blood was a *mitzvah,* it is then a *mitzvah* to eat the meat as well.

Let us pray for the day when we will once again merit being able to fulfill the many *mitzvot* associated with the bringing of sacrifices and the rebuilding of the *Beit Hamikdash.*

Rabbi Nachman Kahana

Young Israel of the Old City, Jerusalem, Israel

YERUSHALAYIM—CITY OF PEACE AND STRUGGLE

> ". . . to *the rest* and to *the inheritance* which the Lord God gives you . . ." (Deuteronomy 12:9)

> "*The rest* is the Sanctuary in Shilo; *the inheritance*, the Temple in Yerushalayim." (*Zevachim* 119a)

"Yerushalayim"—the very word—is a symphony for the Jewish soul: Yerushalayim, the synthesis of *yirah* and *shalem*—fear of God, and perfection—qualities that the Holy City bestows upon those who love and who are devoted to her.

King David, the embodiment of *yirah* and *shalem*, prophesied in *Tehillim* 137:

> By the rivers of Babylon, there we sat and wept when we remembered Zion.
> There upon the willows, we placed away our harps
> for there, they that led us captive, asked of us words of song
> and our tormentors asked of us to be of joy:
> "Sing us one of the songs of Zion."
> How shall we sing the Lord's song in a foreign land?
> If I forget thee, Jerusalem, let my right hand lose its strength.
> Let my tongue cleave to the roof of my mouth if I remember thee not,
> if I set not Jerusalem above my chiefest joy.

Yerushalayim, in its various forms, appears over 650 times in the *TaNaKH*. Yet Yerushalayim is not mentioned, or even alluded to, in the Koran; and the Christian world abandoned Yerushalayim over fifteen hundred years ago to take up residence in Rome. A Muslim in prayer turns his back on Yerushalayim and faces Mecca; Yerushalayim is not part of Christian liturgy.

It is only we—God's chosen people—who relate to Yerushalayim. A Jew outside of Yerushalayim turns to her when in prayer, and we in Yerushalayim face the Temple Mount, the site of the Holy Temple.

The *Zohar* describes the process whereby a Jew leaves this world to enter the world-to-come. Upon leaving this world, the *neshamah* reports to *Ma'arat Hamachpelah* in the city of Chevron. There, an angel leads the *neshamah* to those who were closest to it in this world, in order to comfort the *neshamah* in its new dimension; and the *Zohar* continues to describe the process. The importance of Chevron is its status of a "border crossing," connecting the two worlds.

In the Book of II Kings (chapter 2), the *TaNaKH* relates how Eliyahu *Hanavi* departed from this world. Eliyahu and his protégé, Elisha, went down to Yericho (Jericho), and verse 11 states: "And it came to pass as they still went on and talked, that behold, there appeared a chariot of fire and horses of fire which parted them asunder, and Eliyahu went up by a whirlwind into heaven" (II Kings 2:11). The city of Yericho, too, is a border crossing connecting God's two worlds.

The major "border crossing" between the worlds, however, is the Holy City of Yerushalayim, for it is here, on Mount Moriah, that our father, Yaakov, saw in his dream angels passing from this world to the heavenly world. The Torah describes his state of mind when he awoke: "And he was afraid and said: 'How full of awe is this place, this is none other than the house of God, and this is the gate of heaven" (Genesis 28:17).

Today, in *Eretz Yisrael,* the major places of contention between the children of Yitzchak and the children of Yishmael are Chevron, Yericho, and, above all, Yerushalayim. We are witnessing today the beginning of the uncompromising struggle between the Torah and the Koran for spiritual supremacy; its outcome will be expressed in who will control Yerushalayim and, hence, the entire Holy Land. In this critical time in our history, no conscious Jew will be free from taking part. The conflict will strike at every Jewish home the world over, at every *beit knesset* and *yeshivah,* at every Jewish heart.

The Young Israel of the Old City, situated in the (so-called) Muslim Quarter, is at the forefront of the struggle. Our very presence here is a thundering statement to the Yishmaelites and to those among our brothers who would relinquish our dream of two thousand years of the return of Jewish sovereignty over the Holy City.

As with all things in life, Judaism does not relate to difficulties as "problems" but as opportunities for asserting one's devotion to God. The period we are now entering is the final test for our nation, a period that will eventually result in the establishment of God's kingdom in this world and restoration of the *Beit Hamikdash*.

"*The inheritance* is the Temple in Yerushalayim."

Rabbi Eliyahu Rabovsky
Young Israel of Boca Raton, Florida

"See! I am setting before you today, Blessing and Curse."

Rabbi Samson Raphael Hirsch views this opening verse of our *parshah* as a watershed in Moshe's presentation to the nation. To this point, the review of the law and the history in *Sefer Devarim* has been introductory and general. Now, a transition is made from the abstract "mission statement" to a specific charge to the generation that will enter *Eretz Yisrael*. Here are the laws necessary for those who will settle the land. The term "see" conveys a level of understanding that at this time should be apparent to the people—namely, that they are the ultimate masters of their spiritual destiny. Through the Torah they have learned and reviewed from Moshe, they can and should see that their conduct alone will determine whether their lot will be blessed or cursed. Moreover, this concept of spiritual self-determination is not based merely on belief in teachings from another person but on the personal experiences of the nation, which have just been reviewed. That history, shared by all, forms the basis for this abiding conviction in Torah.

In a similar vein, *Rabbeinu* Bachya learns from here a fundamental reference to the entire concept of *bechiras chofshis*, free will. Unlike the angels of the "upper world," who are compelled to serve God by virtue of their total intellectual makeup, or the creations of the "lower world" whose service and praise of *HaShem* is manifest through their nature and instinctive behavior, man has no such compulsion to service; because he is composed of both intellect and nature, a spiritual soul and a physical human body, he finds himself constantly confronting choices in life. On the one hand, there is the "physical" path, replete with options that are self-serving and uncaring toward others, and then there is the "majestic" path, full of choices that are spiritually driven, exhibiting kindness and compassion. The measure of life in the end are these choices that we must make. The more we opt for the Godly path, the more bountiful will be our blessing.

Sforno understands the Torah here to be calling us as a nation to a special charge. Recognize a major difference between you and the nations of the world. They act and they are rewarded in an *ofan beinoni*—as average. One might say that, in general, there is no great consequence in this world or in the world-to-come from their actions, whether positive or negative. Not so with *Am Yisrael*. "I have set before you today a blessing and a curse." This indicates extremes of both accomplishment and failure. "Blessing," says Sforno, means attaining more than is necessary. It implies an excess of good. "Curse," conversely, refers to a state of deprivation—not having enough even to achieve the basic standard. And both blessing and curse are "before you," to eat the fruits of plenty, or to be mired in a state of want.

Jewish life, in the fullest sense, does not know mediocrity. We may view others, and perhaps ourselves as well, from a painfully distorted perspective. We see a person living a typical "Orthodox lifestyle," and we deem it nothing special. Nothing could be farther from the truth! As we travel through life, encountering others and evaluating ourselves, we must always remember this fundamental message, that inherent in a life of loyalty to Torah is an excellence that has no parallel in human achievement.

The *Klei Yakar* points out a grammatical contradiction in this verse. The word *re'eh* (to see) is in the singular, addressed to the individual. *Lifneichem* (before you) is in the plural. He explains that the Torah here is hinting at the principle that the deeds of the individual can have a demonstrable impact on the community. As *Chazal* say, "A person should always consider the world and himself as completely balanced between merits and sins, with his new single *mitzvah* performance tipping the balance for good." How often do we find ourselves wondering, "What difference will my contribution, participation, prayer, and so on, make?" The Torah tells us here that even a small, single *mitzvah* can make the difference for us all. Knowing the power of our actions can be our greatest motivator.

❖ CHAPTER 52 ❖

Shoftim

Rabbi Yaacov Lerner

Young Israel of Great Neck, New York

A CORRECTIONAL SYSTEM THAT WORKS

Parshat Shoftim contains the law of the inadvertent killer. The example cited in the Torah is of an individual who goes into the forest to chop down a tree. An accident occurs; a passerby is struck and killed. The punishment for the crime is *galut*, exile. The inadvertent killer must flee to one of the six cities of refuge set up throughout *Eretz Yisrael*. There he remains until the death of the *Kohein Gadol*.

Why is the man punished if what happened was an accident? The *Gemara*, in the second chapter of Tractate *Makkot*, answers this question. The *Gemara* tells us that there are three categories of "accidents." The first is called "close to being forced." These are life's unavoidable tragedies, the "freak accidents" that could not have been foreseen and prevented. When such a tragedy strikes, the individual is totally blameless, and there is no punishment. At the other end of the spectrum are the cases that the *Gemara* terms, "as if on purpose," or "close to intentional." In such situations, there is a great deal of culpability. Although the individual did not intend to kill anyone, he displayed a wanton disregard for life. He entered a situation knowing that the risk to others was high. Perhaps a perfect example of this would be a drunken driver. According to the *Gemara*, this individual is also not sentenced to *galut*, but for a totally different reason: his guilt is too great for exile to suffice as expiation for his sin. Instead, he is condemned to spend the reset of his days as a fugitive, constantly on the run from the avenger of the blood, who is permitted to avenge his relative's death.

What, then, is the *parshah*'s case of the inadvertent killer sentenced to exile? According to the Talmud, it is limited to the narrow middle ground of accident cases in which there is some element of culpability but not gross negligence, instances in which a little forethought and precaution could have saved a life. In other words, the law of the inadvertent killer is a lesson in sensitivity. It conveys to us the high degree of respect that we must have for the value of human life and the lengths that we must be willing to go to protect and preserve it.

We can now better appreciate the sentence of exile and why this is a punishment which truly fits the crime. The same *Gemara* in *Makkot* tells us that there were not just six cities of refuge, but many more. In addition to the six mentioned in the Torah, there were forty-two others. All the forty-eight cities known as *arei haleviim*, the cities in *Eretz Yisrael* given to the tribe of Levi, simultaneously served as *arei miklot*. This link to the *leviim* exposes the true nature of the cities of refuge. The role of the *leviim* was, above all else, to be the teachers of Torah to the Jewish people. Moshe expresses this assignment in his *brachah* to the tribe of Levi at the end of the Torah: "They will teach Your laws to Yaakov, Your Torah to Yisrael." (Deuteronomy 33:10)

The *leviim* were there to be the educators, the conveyors of Torah values. Is there a more pre-eminent value of our Torah than respect for human life? The overriding importance of *pikuach nefesh*—danger to one's life—with its emphasis even on *chayei sha'ah*, a temporary saving of a life (that every moment of life is precious and worth saving), is but one example of a system of *halachah* that enshrines this ideal. Judaism preaches that life is a sacred gift from *HaShem* that we must cherish and preserve to the fullest extent possible.

For good reason does the Torah order the inadvertent killer to take refuge in those cities. It was not so much a matter of punishment as of rehabilitation. He who had shown callous disregard for life needed to be resensitized to its supreme value. The method—total immersion in a Torah environment where he could be surrounded by a community of scholars and role models of Jewish values.

Proof of this interpretation can be adduced from one further law found in Tractate *Makkot*. The *Gemara* derives from a verse in *Sefer Yehoshua* that if a city of refuge ever reaches a point at which there are so many inadvertent killers living there that they form the majority of the resident population, it forfeits its status as a city of refuge. Such a shift in demographics makes the *halachah* wary of the community's ability to carry out its mandate as a rehabilitative environment. Long ago, the Torah understood that you can't put a criminal with other criminals and expect him to be rehabilitated. Our American penal system still has a lot to learn.

Rabbi Sholom Tendler

Young Israel of North Beverly Hills, California

The President of the United States of America, undoubtedly the most powerful human in the world today, never leaves home without an aide carrying a certain famous briefcase. This briefcase reinforces his incredible power, for in it lie the codes which can unleash unimaginable forces bringing instant death, destruction, even obliteration, to the enemies of his country. Contrast this image with that of a King of Israel. The descendant of Dovid *Hamelech* never leaves home without the *Sefer Torah* that he personally wrote (Deuteronomy 17:18–20; *Sanhedrin* 21b). His briefcase carries within the codes that will always remind him of the purpose of his power and glory. This Torah will be a constant deterrent to arrogance and abuse of power. And this Torah will indeed channel his powers to make him the most powerful and influential human on earth. He will become a true light unto the nations, taking that other briefcase and harnessing its power of destruction for no purpose other than peace and the common good for all mankind.

We should remember this image when we pray thrice daily for the restoration of the monarchy of David. Yes, we who believe so firmly in democracy pray so fervently for a monarchy and theocracy. Dose this offend our sensibilities? Or are we not conscious of what our lips are uttering? If it does seem disturbing, it is only because of a lack of appreciation for what it means to be a King of Israel who never leaves the side of the *Sefer Torah*. It is not the Torah that follows the king, but the king who follows the Torah.

The Rambam (*Melachim* 11:1) writes, "and anyone who does not believe in him [the restoration of a duly anointed monarch of the House of David, popularly referred to as *Mashiach*] *or one who does not yearn for his coming*" is considered a heretic. The obvious difficulty with the Rambam's statement is his second category, "one who does not yearn for his coming." This person obviously believes in the concept, for, if he had been a nonbeliever, he would have already been classified as a heretic for his faulty theology. He just has no interest in the restoratioin of the monarchy. Perhaps he is a democrat. Why is this considered heresy? Granted, it is wrong, but why a heretic? The Rambam, with his deep insight, is teaching us that one who does not yearn for the monarchy of *HaShem*, the royalty of a Torah State wherein the ruler literally and figuratively follows the Torah, has a faulty understanding and lack of appreciation for the beauty and pleasures of a Divinely ordained Judaism. If there were not some heresy in him, the Rambam says, he would most definitely be yearning for the only true Utopia for all human beings, of all races and nations—not Marxism, not democracy, but a society led by a descendant of Dovid *Hamelech* who never lets go of his *Sefer Torah*.

The Torah provides checks and balances for this monarch through the *sanhedrin* and through specific restrictions, set forth in this *parashah*, obviously intended to protect against abuse of power. One of them is the prohibition against acquiring many horses (17:16). The Torah seems to give a reason for this restriction by saying that the king should never bring his people back to Egypt, which was the source for the best horses. The thinking, obviously, is that the king may give in to the pressure of obtaining the most and the best horses and transgress the law prohibiting Jewish settlement in Egypt. The *Klei Chemdah* explains that the concern is that, in order to obtain these horses, he may be willing to sacrifice the spiritual well-being of his people and allow them to return to the levels of impurity that we experienced as slaves in Egypt.

However, an analysis of this *halachah* raises an interesting question. The Talmud, in *Sanhedrin* 21b, states clearly that the prohibition against excessive horses applies only to the king's personal stable and chariot. He may not have even one extra horse. But the prohibition does not apply to horses for communal need, such as the army, public transportation, and sanitation. This King of Israel has (as an example) the obligation to provide his army with 200,000 of the heartiest and swiftest horses; public transportation with 300,000 of the strongest; sanitation with 150,000; and, let us say, six for his own use. He has the responsibility not to skimp but to create the strongest nation and most efficient society possible.

Imagine that the king hears of a powerful and beautiful Arabian stallion that he longs to own, but does not really need. This is clearly the intent of the Torah's prohibition. Are we really concerned that, if the king orders 650,007 horses instead of 650,006, something terrible is going to happen? Is he so untrustworthy that he is suspected of establishing a settlement in Egypt and endangering our spirituality just for that one extra horse?

Yes. *HaShem* has total trust in the monarch who never leaves home without the *Sefer Torah*. His values are derived only from sources of the Torah. He will consult with the *sanhedrin* and the *Kohein Gadol*, and he would never do anything to belittle the honor of his people or threaten their adherence to the values written in his Torah. He has the total trust of his Creator that, despite the enormous pressures of the responsibilities of running a nation, he will never do anything against the Torah. This monarch who figuratively and literally follows the *Sefer Torah* will stand up to any pressure regarding his acquisition of 200,000 horses for his army. He cannot be bribed, and he cannot be enticed to do anything unethical, either from a Torah perspective or regarding the laws of the nations with whom he is doing business. He is a walking *Kiddush HaShem* in all of his dealings. The pressure of obtaining an additional 450,000 horses for his public services, would never cause him to do anything even remotely questionable halachically. He is the King of Israel performing his duties. He is a descendant of the Sweet Singer of Israel and all his actions and statements are poetry in motion worthy of being incorporated into *Tehillim*.

But the moment he wants something extra for his own personal use he is no longer trusted. He is personally involved. He has lost his ability to be objective and, as great as he may be, he may sell the very soul of the nation just to get himself an extra Rolls Royce, or an additional Swiss bank account. The pressure of obtaining tanks and planes for his army? No worry! The state of the art public transportation system? No problem! But a yacht for the king? Every human being, when he can be tempted into subjectivity, is suspected of rationalizing and justifying acts that can bring the nation to its knees, right down to the depths of the impurities of Egypt.

This lesson is for all of us, not only those in leadership positions. It is, unfortunately, all too easy to become subjective. In order to ensure that our actions are indeed according to the Torah, we need good mentors and even better friends who can help us achieve at least a modicum of objectivity.

Rabbi Aaron Parry

Young Israel of Beverly Hills, California

> "It shall be that when he sits on the throne of his kingdom, he shall write for himself two copies of this Torah in a book, from before the *kohanim*, the Levites." (Deuteronomy 17:18)

Rashi cites the Talmud, which indicates that the king is to keep one copy of the Torah in his treasury and the other one with him most of the time. Likewise, the Rambam in *Hilchot Melachim* (chapter 3, *Halacha* 1) rules:

> At the time when the king assumes his throne, he must write a Torah scroll for himself in addition to the one bequeathed by his forefathers. He would allow the *Sanhedrin* to correct this Torah from the Torah [written by Moshe] that was kept in the *Beit Hamikdash*, as a standard. One was placed in his treasury . . . and the second would stay with him continuously except when he would enter the bathroom or attend the bathhouse, or any other place not suited for reading. . . . "It shall be with him, and he shall read it, all the days of his life.'" (Deuteronomy 17:19)

In *Sanhedrin* 21b, the text states that this second *Sefer Torah* that was to accompany him was actually worn as an amulet. The Maharshal omits this reading, which is also omitted in the Rambam, as quoted above. The Kesef Mishnah questions why the Rambam excludes this detail in *halachah* and since some authorities (for example, the Ridvaz) wonder as to how a Torah scroll could be written small enough to be worn as an amulet, the *Kesef Mishnah*'s query is not very problematic. (Incidentally, Rabbi Aryeh Kaplan, *zt"l*, in his writings, commented that he personally beheld a perfectly written Torah Scroll only two inches high!)

The Ridvaz's comments concerning the omission by the Rambam of this unusual practice of the king wearing the Torah scroll is based on his objection to the applicability of the rationale given by the *Gemara*, "I place *HaShem* before me always." As the Ridvaz writes: "Furthermore, this would not fulfill Dovid *Hamelech*'s proclamation, 'I place *HaShem* before me always. . . .' Perhaps the Sages are speaking metaphorically, that just as he would not likely divert his attention from a *kameah*, amulet, worn around the arm, so too should a *Sefer Torah* be kept at his side, never to be neglected."

Mori v'Rebbe Hagaon Harav Chaim Pinchas Scheinberg, *shlita*, in his *sefer*, Derech Emunah and Bitachon, cites the *Sifre*, which applies this regal law to commoners as well—namely, that it is forbidden for a person to divert his attention from *divrei Torah* that might prevent him from fulfilling the Divine command, "so that he will learn to fear *HaShem*, his God . . ." (Deuteronomy 17:19). (The context of this *Sifre* can be understood from the words of the *Mechilta* in *Parshat Beshalach*, "One who learns two *halachot* in the morning and two more in the evening, even if he is preoccupied with his labor the entire day, the Heavenly Tribunal considers it as if he has fulfilled *Kol Hatorah kulo*, the entire Torah.") The Torah informs us concerning the leader of Israel, however, that despite his myriad daily responsibilities, he must constantly possess a Torah Scroll and meditate on its message. Only this process will allow him to properly inculcate *yirat HaShem*, fear of God.

The question to ask is, just how does the *mitzvah* of possessing the *sefer Torah* facilitate *yirat HaShem* in the king?

On this, *Harav* Scheinberg responds with Sforno's comment on our *parshah*: "'In order to learn to fear' refers to the portion of deep reflection in Torah that teaches the profundity of the Almighty's *hashgachah* (Divine oversight). This knowledge of God's involvement in our daily lives engenders a natural awe of the Creator." This means to say, "I place *HaShem* before me always" is, as the *Moreh Nevuchim* interprets, "one's sitting in the presence of an ordinary person is nothing compared to sitting before a king." Rather, Sforno emphatically adds that it is only this portion of *iyun Hatorah* that can bring about a conscientious level of *moreh Shamayim* in a person's every act."

A Jewish king is enjoined to be vigilant by keeping a *Sefer Torah* perpetually close to his heart. May the Almighty give us commoners the strength and fortitude to follow His lead and find opportunities to delve ever deeper into our legacy of Torah.

Rabbi Moshe Bleich

Young Israel of Brighton Beach, New York

From a *pasuk* in this week's *parshah*, it is commonly understood that it is prohibited to engage in wanton destruction. The *pasuk* tells us that it is prohibited to destroy the trees of the field: "When you shall besiege a city for many days to wage war against it, you shall not destroy the trees by wielding an ax against them; you may eat of it but not cut it down. For is the tree of the field a man that it should be besieged by you?" (Deuteronomy 20:19). From the comments of the *Gemara* in *Shabbat*, it would seem that this prohibition is not merely quantitative but qualitative as well.

The *Gemara* in *Shabbat* (129a) relates that in the times of our Sages it was considered healthy to engage in bloodletting. After bloodletting, it was common to catch a chill, and people would light fires for themselves after the procedure to prevent serious illness. Rabbah, on one occasion after bloodletting, could not find any fire-burning wood and broke up his footstool for that purpose, whereupon Abaye said to Rabbah, "But you are infringing on the prohibition 'thou shall not destroy.'" Rabbah responded, "'Thou shall not destroy' in regard to my own body is more important to me." Abaye's question is somewhat problematic, for, after all, if Rabbah is using the wood of his footstool as firewood, it is being put to good use. It seems from the *Gemara* that when an object can be used in an optimum manner but is used for a lesser function, this lesser use is considered to be a form of destruction. Items that are not used to their full potential are also deemed to have been wantonly destroyed. Thus, Abaye asks Rabbah how he could use a footstool for firewood, since Rabbah is not maximizing the use of expensive wood and hence is violating the prohibition against destroying things needlessly.

It would appear that the prohibition against destroying things needlessly is not limited to material possessions. We all have unique human talents and spiritual potential. When we fail to utilize that potential, we are all guilty of spiritual waste. To be sure, when one goes on vacation or rests to recharge one's spiritual batteries and, at that time, does not engage in spiritual pursuits, that falls within the purview of Rabbah's answer, "Thou shall not destroy in regard to my own body is more important to me." Yet, at other times, one must engage in spiritual pursuits and cannot be satisfied with minimum standards, for, when we do not actualize our spiritual potential we are guilty of a spiritual violation of the prohibition against destroying things needlessly.

The question we have to ask ourselves is, Why do we not raise our standards and try to actualize ourselves more. The answer, I think, resides in a *pasuk* at the beginning of the *parshah*. The Torah prohibits a judge from taking bribes, "for bribes blind the eyes of the discerning and upset the plea of the just." The *Gemara* in *Ketubot* (105b) records that bribery is not merely financial; flattery is also a form of bribery—a verbal bribery. I would add that we are also guilty of a third form of bribery, that of complacency. As the Torah says, bribery blinds us; we are complacent in our lifestyles and thus blinded to the need to improve.

The month of Elul and the blowing of the *shofar* serve to remind us not to be complacent in our lives. The idea of the Rambam that the *shofar* is an alarm clock is well known. The Rambam writes, "Rouse you from your lethargy! Scrutinize your deeds and return in repentance. Remember your Creator, you who forgot eternal truth in the trifles of the hour, who go astray all your years after vain illusions which can neither profit nor deliver. Look well into your souls and mend your ways and actions; let each one forsake his evil path and his unworthy purpose and return to God so that He may have mercy" (*Hilkhot Teshuvah* 3:4). Thus, the *shofar* serves as an alarm clock and in the month of Elul it is sounded every day; thus, if you missed it this week or did not listen to its message, there is a snooze alarm to wake us, the rest of the month. The *brachah* that we recite on the *mitzvah* of *shofar* is *lishmoa*, to hear and understand its message, that we must be roused from our complacency and actualize our potential.

Perhaps this is why *Parshat Shoftim* is always read during the first week of Elul, when the *shofar* is blown and arouses us to remember not to be bribed by our complacency and to actualize our potential, thereby preventing a spiritual waste and thus a spiritual violation of the prohibition against needless destruction.

❖ CHAPTER 53 ❖

Ki Tetzeh

Rabbi Yosef Goldberg

Young Israel of Wavecrest and Bayswater, New York

"WHEN YOU GO FORTH TO WAR AGAINST YOUR ENEMIES . . ."

The arrangement of the annual cycle of Torah reading is such that the reading of *Parshat Ki Tetzeh* must inevitably occur during the month of Elul—the month in which we begin our arduous campaign of *teshuvah* (repentance). Because of the relationship between *Ki Tetzeh* and the month of Elul, it is very important that we delve into the *derush*—the homiletic level of interpreting the Torah—in regard to this particular *parshah*.

Rabbi Yitzchak Aramah, the author of the classical work on *Chumash*, the *Akeidas Yitzchak*, prefaces his remarks on the *parshiyos* concerning war that begin in last week's *parshah, Shoftim*, and continue into *Ki Tetzeh*, by pointing out that there are three types of wars that people are involved with: (a) physical wars between nations or individuals, usually involving disputes over territory or property; (b) physical wars fought within the body of an individual involving his physical health and welfare; and (c) the third type of war, more secret and more dangerous than the others; fought against the uprising of wicked character traits and evil needs; traits such as jealousy, lust, desire, wickedness, and selfishness as well as other vulgar characteristics that overpower an individual and force him to rebel against the King.

The *Akeidas Yitzchak* maintains that the Torah's teachings concerning military wars are actually meant to inform us of the real war that we must fight with the *yetzer hara* (the evil inclination) at all times. Just as certain proclamations are made before battle, so too, "Every year we must begin with proclamations a month before [Rosh Hashanah], in order to wake the sleeping and arouse the slumbering with the words of the Sages, who know what the people must hear in order to prepare them for this battle. We must also blow the *shofar* in order to frighten and arouse the people, because no one with any sense will ignore the clarion call of the *shofar* and not rush to save his soul. Our Sages have stated that the month of Elul was made special for this purpose from the time that Moshe went up on the first day of Elul to atone for the breaking of the first set of *luchos* by receiving the second set of *luchos*. So, too, will one with any sense rise with the best of intentions to repair the breaking of his first *luchos*—that which he has ruined of the purity of his soul."

The Dubbiner Maggid in *Ohalei Yaakov* discusses the unusual and problematic nature of the *mitzvah* of *yefas toar,* which permits the taking of a Gentile woman captured in war. Our Sages view this *mitzvah* as the Torah's concession to the *yetzer hara* during the heat of battle. The Dubbiner Maggid maintains that one's success against one's human enemies is equal to the degree of success that one has in his internal warfare against the *yetzer hara*. Thus, there are three types of people: (a) those who have already vanquished the *yetzer hara* and have total control over it. Such people need never go to war. Rather, their enemies will simply flee from before them; (b) those people who are in a constant struggle with the *yetzer hara*. They are the ones who must go forth to battle against their enemies, and *HaShem* will deliver their enemies into their hands, just as He will enable them ultimately to vanquish the *yetzer hara*; (c) those who are controlled by their *yetzer hara*. They will be easily conquered by their enemies. (Rav S.Y. Zevin, in his work *L'Torah ul'Moadim*, at the beginning of *Parshat Naso,* has a somewhat similar categorization of three types of people, built around the three Levitical tribes: Kehas, Gershon, and Merori.) The *mitzvah* of *yefas toar* is an allowance to those individuals who are involved in a constant struggle with the *yetzer hara*. So that they should not be defeated by the *yetzer hara* at a vulnerable time, *HaShem* permits them the *yefas toar* during battle.

"BLOT OUT THE MEMORY OF AMALEK . . ."

Parshas Ki Tetzeh begins with laws relating to a *milchemet reshut,* a voluntary war, and it ends with the *mitzvah* of destroying Amalek, which is one of three *mitzvot* that the Israelites were commanded to do once the Land of Israel was conquered and settled. If the beginning of the *parshah* contains a message to the individual regarding his own internal struggles with his evil inclination, so, too, does the end of the *parshah*.

The *Zohar*, in *Parshat Beshalach,* states that Moshe *Rabbeinu* saw Samael (the Angel of Death) coming to the aid of Amalek. Amalek is a force in the world that is in alliance with evil and death against godliness and truth. It is the nature of Amalek to attempt to deny that which is undeniable. After all the miracles in Mitzrayim and at the *Yam Suf,* Amalek still had the unmitigated audacity to attempt to undo, with one heinous attack, all the effects of the incredible signs and wonders that had all of the other nations of the world in fear and trembling of *HaShem* and His people Israel. Our Sages, of blessed memory, compared the attack of Amalek to the act of a madman who sees a boiling cauldron whose heat is intimidating, and who nevertheless undertakes to dive into it. Even though he comes out scalded and mutilated, psychologically he has reduced the heat of that cauldron in people's minds.

In his commentary on *Chumach, Ohev Yisrael,* the Apter Rav—the Hasidic rebbe, Rav Avraham Yehoshua Heschel—states the following concerning the *mitzvah* to blot out Amalek:

> One can say that the Torah is teaching every Jewish person the good and upright way; the most beneficial manner of escaping the snares of the evil enemy who is hidden within the heart of everyone. In truth, it is not only the nation of Israel that is commanded regarding the destruction of the nation of Amalek. It is also every single individual who is obligated to eradicate that portion of evil hidden within all of our hearts that goes by the name Amalek, and to totally uproot it so that there is not the slightest remnant of it left in the world. Since every human being is a miniature universe unto himself, there is in everyone that force of Amalek; that essence of evil which is attempting at all times to cause a person to sin. And this is the reason for the need to remember at all times the power of Amalek.

Indeed it is the power of Amalek that causes people to minimize or even forget the magnificent miracles that *HaShem* has wrought for us even in recent decades, whether in Israel's War of Independence, or the Six Day War, or most recently during the Persian Gulf War. It is the force of Amalek in the world that has evil individuals, no doubt the genuine seed of Amalek, maintaining that even the Holocaust was an exaggerated hoax.

It is our duty to realize that there is a little of Amalek within us all, forever attempting to challenge our belief in *HaShem* and His holy Torah.

In this time of the approaching Days of Awe, with all of their call for introspection and coming closer to the Creator, blessed is He, may we all merit to be victorious in our battles with all of the enemies of *Klal Yisrael,* the Jewish People, whoever they may be and wherever they may reside.

Rabbi Moshe Portnoy

Young Israel of Plainview, New York

YIBUM AND *CHALITZAH*: THE LEVIRATE OBLIGATION AND ITS DISSOLUTION

> If brothers live at the same time and one of them dies and has no child, the wife of the deceased shall not marry outside to a strange man. Her husband's brother shall come to her and take her to him as a wife and perform the Levirate's [from Latin *lever*, husband's brother, Hertz commentary] duty of *yibum*. (Deuteronomy 25:5)
>
> But if the man does not wish to take his sister-in-law, then his sister-in-law shall go up to the gate [the seat of the *Bet Din*] to the elders and state. . . . He refuses to fulfill his Levirate obligation. And she shall approach him in front of the elders and take off his shoe (*v'chaltzah*, hence *chalitzah*) from his foot and spit and proclaim: So should be done to a man who does not build his brother's house. (Deuteronomy 25:9)

HALACHIC OUTLINE

Perhaps one of the least understood mandates of Jewish family life, even among the Torah observing, is that of *yibum*. Very few of us know personally of cases in which this *mitzvah* was actualized. Even fewer have ever seen a *chalitzah*. Yet, this Biblical obligation applies to us at all times and anywhere in the world.

Some basic particulars:

1. *Yibum* is triggered only where the two brothers share a common father. Half-brothers who share a mother alone do not count as far as *yibum* is concerned. In fact, the living brother in this instance is *prohibited* from marrying the sister-in-law (*Even Ha'ezer* 156:1).

2. *Yibum* is possible only when the deceased brother does not leave behind any child or grandchild. If there was a child who died *before* the father, then *yibum* is actualized since, at death, there was no child (Tur, ibid.).
3. Even where the widow had children from a *prior* marriage but the deceased brother had no biological children of his own, *yibum* and *chalitzah* are triggered. Conversely, where the deceased had children from a prior marriage but not with the widow, then there is no *yibum* or *chalitzah* (ibid. 156:1, see *Pitchei Teshuvah*).
4. The age of the living brother does not matter for the purposes of *yibum*. Whether he is one day old or one hundred years old, the widow must be freed from the obligatioin of *yibum* by the ritual of *chalitzah*. In the former case, the widow would have to wait until her one-day-old brother-in-law reached Bar Mitzvah, obtain her *chalitzah* from him, and then be freed to remarry (ibid. 4; 167:3).
5. It does not matter whether the living brother is single or married. In both instances, *yibum* and its freeing ritual of *chalitzah* are triggered (ibid. 159:11 in Rama).
6. Where there are multiple surviving brothers, the primary obligation of *yibum/chalitzah* falls on the firstborn son, where applicable. If that is not possible or feasible—for example, if the firstborn son lives very far away or refuses to participate—then the primary obligation falls to the next older brother. Ultimately, if *any* brother gives the widow *chalitzah*, then she is freed to remarry (ibid. 161:4).
7. Today, we *do not* allow *yibum* (the marriage) to be performed under any circumstances. Only *chalitzah* (the freeing ritual) is done. This is based on a *baraita* in Tractate *Yevamot* (39b) that states that, according to Abba Shaul, a child born as the result of any *yibum* that was not solemnized strictly for the sake of perpetuating the deceased brother's memory is "close to being a *mamzer*." We are fearful that ulterior motives—inheriting the brother's estate, personal attraction, and so on—may play a role in the *yibum*. Certainly, in the last two hundred years only *chalitzah* has been done in the Ashkenazi tradition (Tur 165, see *Beit Yosef* and the *Shulchan Aruch*).
8. The *chalitzah* (as well as *yibum*) cannot be performed until at least 92 days after the brother's demise. This is similar to any woman's remarrying after she is widowed or divorced; she must always wait at least 92 days (ibid. 164:1).
9. Once a woman has undergone *chalitzah* she may not marry a *kohein*, as is the case with a divorcee (ibid. 6:1).
10. If a woman was remarried to an outsider while she was under obligation for *chalitzah* to free her, this is a complicated halachic question

and requires consultation with a qualified halachic authority. Certainly in cases in which *chalitzah* is mandated, both the living brother(s) and the widow should be urged strongly to go to their rabbi to see that *chalitzah* is given/received before the widow remarries.

THE *CHALITZAH* RITUAL

The ritual has many details that are beyond the scope of this dvar Torah.

At a very minimum, three judges are required. *Shulchan Aruch* (ibid. 169:3) discusses the almost universal practice that at least two others are added so that there is wide dissemination of the fact that a *chalitzah* took place. In most cases, more than two are added to the core *Bet Din*.

The ritual itself takes about one hour, and documentation is issued to certify that *chalitzah* was effected.

RATIONALE

Rabbi Samson Raphael Hirsch, in his commentary on *Devarim* 25:5, discusses the great concern the Torah felt for every Jew and his basic need to leave behind a spiritual memory and legacy. If the first *mitzvah* of the Torah is to be fruitful and multiply, then every Jew who was not afforded the fulfillment of this primal instinct must be given some modus to do so, even after death.

It is only a brother, who grew up under the same roof, had the same educational influences and shares the same values as the deceased, who can carry forth and establish the deceased's "home in Israel." Indeed, where this premise is not valid (people are people, brothers can grow up differently, and the Torah would not force dissimilar people to wed) then the Torah allowed for the inevitability of failure should that *yibum* take place, and granted *chalitzah*. As mentioned previously, we do not allow *yibum* today in any event.

Interestingly, the two most famous cases of *yibum* were really not that at all in a strict halachic sense. In the story of Yehudah and Tamar (*Bereishit* 38), when Er died and his widow, Tamar, married the brother, Onan, *that* was *yibum*. When Onan died, however, and subsequently, through a subterfuge engineered by God, Yehudah had a set of twins with Tamar, this could not be considered biblical *yibum*. This was before the giving of the Torah, however, and in the interest of perpetuating the lineage it was permitted at that time. One of the twins, Peretz, was a ninth-generation ancestor of King David.

The other case is that of Ruth and Boaz (Book of Ruth 4) wherein Boaz, a cousin of Ruth, wed her to establish for his "brother" (family) a home in Israel. Though halachically not mandated under *yibum*, the marriage was an act of sheer grace by Boaz. The child produced, Oved, was the grandfather of King David.

What wonderful things accrued to our people through the kindness of family who were concerned lest their "brother" perish without a legacy. The very Davidic dynasty, the only monarchy Jews recognize, could not have been established without this selflessness. The Torah truly does teach that we are our brother's keeper!

Rabbi Yehuda Melber

Young Israel of Sunny Isles, Florida

The *parshah* of *Ki Tetzeh*, interestingly enough, starts with war and ends with war. Yet, there are two differences between the beginning and the end: (a) In the beginning, the Torah deals with an optional occasional war, whereas, at the end, the Torah deals with a perennial mandatory enemy, "Amalek." (b) In the beginning, we hear the Divine promise, "The Lord will deliver the enemy into your hands," whereas at the end, the battle goes on and on from generation to generation, and we must continually blot out the remembrance of the enemy from our heart and mind.

Why was Amalek singled out from all the other enemies in our long history to be dealt with the toughest sharpness and poignancy? A remarkable comment was given by Malbim on this puzzle—that, researching and reviewing the history of mankind we find four causes of attacks of one people against another:

1. On a *geographic* ground; a people wants to expand its territory for whatever reason they feel it necessary. But here, concerning Amalek, the Torah says, *Asher Karcha*—he met you by the *way*. There was no question or problem of expanding territory.
2. On a *political* ground; there was a longstanding dispute between one people and another, dating back to a remote past. But again, here, the Torah emphasizes that this was not the case at all, because *Betzeitzchem Mi-Mitzrayim*—you just came out from Egypt. It was just a sudden attack without any history of previous disputes or wranglings.
3. On a *religious* ground; a people strongly attached to one religion cannot condone the adherence of another people to a different religion. But here, again, the Torah stresses that this was not the case at all, because *Velo yarei Elohim*—Amalek was not interested in religion and fear of Heaven.

4. On an *economic* ground; a people starts an economic competition against another that leads, finally, to a war. But here, again, the Torah focuses on *Ve'ata ayeif ve'yageia*—you were faint and weary, faint from thirst and weary from the way. Hence there was no problem of competition in any economic productivity.

In conclusion, according to Malbim, the sudden attack of Amalek was nothing but blind hatred and enmity without any kind of political, social, religious, or economic reason. Therefore, the call goes out: *Timche et zaicher Amalek*—blot out the remembrance of Amalek once and for all. Hatred for no reason whatsoever has no right to exist in a good society—or at any time, in any place at all, for that matter.

With this in mind, we must compare present and past events. There is no doubt that Hitler (*yimach sh'mo*) was the follower of Amalek. Hitler's attack against the Jews, like that of Amalek, emanated only from a blind hatred of and animosity toward Jews and Judaism, for *no* reason whatsoever. The fact that over a million Jewish innocent children were ruthlessly annihilated and brutally murdered by the Nazis is the best evidence that Hitler's devilish plot of the "Final Solution" of Judaism repeated the history of Amalek's attack after the Exodus in our present time.

Therefore, we must pray and say: As we have gone through the horrible recurrence of hatred for the sake of hatred, so may we see the final blotting out of the memory of today's Amalek—together with the salvation and consolation of Israel for the best benefit of all mankind.

❖ CHAPTER 54 ❖

Ki Tavo

Rabbi Elimelech Goldberg

Young Israel of Southfield, Michigan

There are two directions that accompany the *Shemoneh Esrei*. Before we address the Holy One, we must move forward, imitating the posture of the angels as we put our legs together and bow before Him. Prior to marching forward, however, we are asked to take three steps backward. Human beings cannot proceed from their everyday world into the corridors of *HaShem* without first stepping backward from the common and profane shadows of our minds. Only after those steps backward do we find ourselves capable of moving forward towards the Throne of the Holy One in the ultimate prayer of the *Shemoneh Esrei*.

Parshat Ki Tavo addresses the Jewish people as they are ready to march forward and claim the spiritual address of the Land of Israel. Preceding that forward movement is the *Ki Tetzeh*—"when you go out"—of last week's *parshah*. Here, too, there must be a statement of egress before the going in, a self-extraction from the affairs of human conflict and corporeal weakness, symbolized by the *yefat to'ar*—the "beautiful captive woman-slave"—to make possible the bringing forth of the first fruits of our vineyards to the Holy Temple. *Parshat Ki Tavo* speaks this message of the progress from the "beautiful captive woman-slave" to the bringing forth of the first fruits—a forward movement toward spiritual awareness.

The cornerstone of the farmer's recital of thanksgiving as he brings the bounty of his first fruits up to Yerushalayim is the phrase, *Arami oveid avi vayeired Mitzraymah*—"an Avramean nomad was my father, and he went down to Egypt." Despite the importance of these words to the opening of our *parshah*, as well as the central role that they play in the Pesach *Haggadah*, there is a great deal of controversy among our commentators as to its basic meaning.

Rashi's interpretation, as we read during the Seder, declares Lavan the Aramean the subject of this sentence. Thus, we translate, "an Aramean

(Lavan) sought to destroy my father (Jacob)." Ibn Ezra, on the other hand, poses many grammatical problems with this traditional understanding. He posits that the subject of the sentence was Jacob, who was "the *oveid*" (the nomad), ready to perish because of his poverty as he was visiting the land of Aram. The third interpretation is offered by Rashbam, who assumes the literal reading, "a wandering Aramean was my father (Abraham)."

What message is the farmer supposed to come away with as he makes this confusing declaration with his first fruits in hand? Why is the vital formula shrouded in the bewildering mystery of the undefined subject? All three of our commentators suggest the very same theme. All of them are correct. The farmer must remove himself first from his mundane work place in the present before he is able fully to absorb the lessons of the holiest place on earth. He must walk backward and see the struggles that preceded him. The Jewish people throughout our history have walked through many perilous paths. All of them are included in this declaration. We had an Avraham *Avinu* who wandered through a spiritual wilderness of idolaters, lonely and searching until he found the ultimate Truth. We had the afflictions of incredible poverty and homelessness as our father Jacob suffered within his world and the horrific chapters of relentless hatred and anti-Semitism embodied within the character of a Lavan. These three interpretations merge together the darkest corridors of both suffering and heroic endurance. From the strength of this past comes the bounty of blessing of the future. Therefore, the farmer can rejoice as he walks forward only after taken that step backward, intently focused upon the intrepid mettle that led to our having the blessing of producing the fruits of the Holy Land.

In this vein, Abarbanel cautions us to look at all the suffering that is offered up in the too-familiar annals of the *tochachah*—"the rebuke of the Jewish people." When our *parshah* informs us (28:65) that we will have no respose among the nations in which we find ourselves exiled and suffering, that is, in fact, a blessing. It is our response to that suffering and the intolerance of the nations around us that will serve to fortify our individual qualities and cement our communal spirit. The object is to understand, to remove ourselves from the profane so that we may open our eyes to the holy. Our awful tour through Egypt was guided by the strength of the past that led our *Avos* (forefathers), through the spiritual wilderness, the harrowing hungers and the hate-filled violence of our enemies.

It is with this in mind that we understand the message of Moshe *Rabbeinu* at the conclusion of *Parshat Ki Tavo*. Even though they have seen all that *HaShem* had done in the land of Egypt, it is only now that *Bnei Yisrael* have "the heart to know, the eyes to see and the ears to hear." Only after the conclusion of all the wanderings, trials, and tribulations, as they are ready to enter the Holy Land, are the Jewish people able to step backward to piece together the tattered pages of wonder and miracle, horror and grief. Only then are they able to fulfill the very last verse of the *parshah*: "In order for you to understand all that you do." That understanding, that enjoyment of the bounty of Heaven and the privilege of the land, requires us to step backward, garnering from our heroic past the strength of our enduring future.

Rabbi Hershy Worch

Young Israel of Pawtucket, Rhode Island

The *sedrah* begins with the *mitzvah* of *bikurim*, "First Fruits."

AN OUTLINE OF THE *MITZVAH*

When we settle in the land God has given us, we must take of the first of every fruit of the soil, put it in a basket, and take it on a pilgrimage to the Temple in Jerusalem. There we give the basket to the *kohein* to be placed before the altar, whereupon we say the following:

THE PILGRIM'S DECLARATION

> An Aramean (Laban) tried to destroy my ancestor (Jacob). He (Jacob) went down to Egypt with a small number of men, living there as an exile. It was there that he became a great, powerful, and populous nation.
>
> The Egyptians were cruel to us, making us suffer and imposing hard labor on us. We cried out to *HaShem*, God of our ancestors, and *HaShem* heard our voice and saw our suffering, our hard work, and our distress.
>
> *HaShem* then brought us out of Egypt with a strong hand and an outstretched arm, with great visions, with signs and miracles.
>
> He brought us to this place, giving us a land flowing with milk and honey. I am now bringing the first fruit of the land that You, *HaShem* have given me.

THE MEANING OF THE *HAGGADAH*

The *sedrah*, quoted above, gives us the kernel text of the Passover *Haggadah*. The four short verses (26:4–8), comprise the bulk of the Passover story.

We have a rule, though, that wherever the Hebrew word *haggadah* is used, the implication is of severity, judgments and unpalatable truths. In Torah literature, there are various forms of address used in dialogues. The gentlest form of address is *amar*, "to say." A more direct address is *dabeir*, "to speak." The least gentle address is *hageid*, "to tell." The Sages refer to *haggadah* as "words as tough as sinews." The root of the word *haggadah* is sinew, *gid*.

Now, when a farmer brings his "First Fruits" to the *kohein* to be placed before the altar, what is so difficult for the *kohein* to understand? Why is the act of bringing the "First Fruits" so hard for the *kohein* to hear that the Torah calls it *haggadah*?

The Rebbe of Izbicy explains thus: At the moment a person brings the "First Fruits" to the *kohein* in the Temple, the *kohein* becomes aware that the act—*avodah*—of farming and working a field is no less holy an occupation than serving as a priest in the Temple; that each type of work is done at the behest and will of God, and that each worker is serving in his own specific temple. This is no welcome truth to the *kohein*.

One might well have a question regarding the whole *Haggadah*: Why is Laban held so responsible for our descent into Egypt that the Torah mentions him in the retelling? Jacob and his family ended up in Egypt because of a famine in the land of Canaan. Furthermore, what is it about this story that so embarrasses us each year in the telling that we continue to refer to it by the name *haggadah* ("words as tough as sinews")?

To answer this question is to understand how we process our history. "We begin with our embarrassment, ending with our praise." (The Passover Seder.) Laban, father-in-law of Jacob, loathed his own daughters, his son-in-law, and his grandchildren. A hundred times he tried to cheat, rob, and ruin them. When there was famine in the land, Jacob and his family could not reach out to their own family in Mesopotamia for help, having instead to go to Egypt. There is little in this story to be proud of. Therefore, the story of our descent into Egypt begins, to our chagrin, with Laban. It ends in praise of the Jewish people, for now God has drawn us close.

The Izbicy Rebbe goes on to explain the connection between the bringing of the "First Fruits" and the reference to Laban. Laban was the great trickster, illusionist, and master of confusion. How can one be sure at any given moment that one's life is not being manipulated by someone like Laban? Perhaps we are just confused, thinking we are doing God's will, when we are really in the grips of a Laban?

The solution is to be in the habit of bringing "First Fruits." This guarantees we maintain an intimate relationship with God. We speak to God in the first person, saying, "I am now bringing the first fruits of the land that You, *HaShem*, have given me."

Jacob, too, was the first to bring "First Fruits." Before ever going to the house of Laban, he prayed for guidance and the ability to see through the tricks and wiles of Laban, promising: "Of all that You give me, I will set aside a tenth to You." It is said that Abraham served God with all his heart; Isaac served with all his soul, and Jacob served with all his money. He was willing at any moment to give it all back to God. This is the essential underlying principle in the *mitzvah* of "First Fruits"—returning everything to its source; it gives us clarity in confusing times.

Later in the *sedrah* a verse (28:60) mentions, "all the Egyptian diseases that you dreaded." Here Moses was hinting to us that with each of the plagues that befell the Egyptians, many of us were set trembling. When we looked to see what crime fitted the punishment that was being meted out to them, we began to see our own faults and how closely they resembled, at least in spirit, the actions of the Egyptians.

"Thunderbolts," say the Sages, "were created only to straighten out crooked hearts."

Each of the plagues that fell upon the Egyptians was accompanied by loud and persistent thundering. The thunder, you might say, was for our benefit. Here again we are given to see God's great kindnesses. Instead of having to go through the painful process of having our faults and character defects pointed out to us in no uncertain terms, God shows us these vicariously. We find ourselves among people with faults that are very similar to ours, albeit more severe or overt than our own, who are in the process of having them delineated.

For example, we can look at the collapse of the Soviet, communist bloc, and see clearly the flaws in their system. Dialectic materialism is devoid of worshipful principles. Its basic premise is the sharing of material wealth. On the surface, this might seem a noble sin, but it lacks aspirations to spirituality, holiness, or humility.

Our duty remains to apply these lessons to our own lives and be thankful.

In case all of this seems too far detached, we have only to look at the levels of chaos in this, our own society. Whether it is recession due to greed, racial tensions due to slavery, or rampant disease due to compulsive behaviors, all come under the banner of "All the diseases that you dreaded." This is why the story of the redemption from Egypt begins with our chagrin and ends in our praise. Historically, as Moses points out in this *sedrah*, we have well learned our vicarious lessons.

Rabbi Yeshaya Siff

Young Israel of Manhattan, New York

In today's *sedrah* we read of the special events to take place upon *Bnei Yisrael*'s entry into *Eretz Yisrael,* including gathering the entire people to receive the special Blessing and Curse at Mount Gerizim and Mount Eval. Six tribes ascended Mount Gerizim and six ascended Mount Eval. The kohanim, levites, and the *aron hakodesh* were below, between the two mountains. The levites turned to Mount Gerizim and recited the blessings, the opposites of those that are written in the Torah as a curse: "Blessed is the man who will not make a form or molten image and both groups answered Amen." They then turned their faces toward Mount Eval and began with the curse and said: "Cursed is the man who will make a form or molten image" (Rashi quoting Tractate *Sotah*). In this way they recited all of those curses written in today's *sedrah*.

The entire event was extraordinary! Firstly, why was the entire pageantry necessary—for the tribes to ascend two opposite mountains and for the levites to turn their faces to the various sides to recite the curses written in the Torah in a language of blessing, and why did the Torah itself articulate the curses and not the blessings?

Sforno explains that the curses were written because the main intent of *HaShem* was to place sole responsibility for the enumerated transgressions upon the sinners and not upon the rest of the people. But if that were so, why mention the blessings?

A possible answer to all the above is one that is as relevant and necessary today as on the day that the Torah was given.

We live in a world of moral and ethical relativity. More simply stated, our egalitarian society has taken to ruling out moral absolutes. The very term "abomination" is glibly used for every undesirable situation; but dare one use it for that which was once morally offensive, and the user is immediately castigated. Every form of sexual deviation and/or perversion is now given sanction and even formal acceptance. Even the sanctity of the family as a unit is no longer absolute. The "single parent" does not now connote an unfortunate situation; marriage is no longer a requirement for childbearing. A "religious" movement seeks spiritual values in premarital sex! In short, we have confused blessed with cursed, right with wrong.

The difference between acceptable and unacceptable, *kodesh* and *chol*, is what *HaShem* wanted to impress upon *Bnei Yisrael* as they entered a new land and a new era. No longer would they be clustered around the *Mishkan* (the Tabernacle), where any spiritual confusion would quickly be dispelled. They would disperse to all parts of *Eretz Yisrael*, to conquer and inherit the land. They would now become involved in a very material way of life, and *HaShem* wanted them to be sure to distinguish between right and wrong, between cursed and blessed. Therefore, the twelve tribes stood upon opposite mountains, to portray starkly the chasm between that which is permitted and that which is truly an abomination.

But *HaShem* also wanted to impress upon them that a person, if not guided by the Torah with absolute values and standards, could subconsciously descend into the worst depths of immorality and transgression. It is not sufficient merely to distinguish between good and evil; it is crucial to realize how blessed a person is who does not succumb to his or her base instincts. He or she must constantly be on spiritual guard. Thus the levites recited, "Blessed is one who will not lie with any animal"—the opposite of "Cursed is one who lies with any animal," which is written in the Torah. Why is he blessed? Because, if he will allow himself and follow only his lust, even that abomination can become acceptable—just as acceptable as male weddings, unmarried "partners," and "alternative" lifestyles.

And so, a striking event had to take place and be recorded for all time, a message for eternity. *HaShem*'s will is blessed and the opposite is cursed, and we have to know and appreciate the difference between them, to guard against spiritual slippage in order to bring to ourselves, to our families, and to all Israel only blessing.

"Blessed is the one who will establish the words of the Torah to do them, and the people answered, Amen."

Rabbi Yaacov Wasser

Young Israel of East Brunswick, New Jersey

In Moshe's farewell address to the Jewish nation, he tells them, "And *HaShem* has not given you a heart to know, eyes to see, and ears to hear until this day" (Deuteronomy 29:3). Many of the commentaries are puzzled by this statement and wonder what it was that *Bnei Yisrael* had perceived just now that was previously unknown to them. Rashi says that he learned that this refers to the day that Moshe gave a special *Sefer Torah* to the tribe of Levi (Deuteronomy 31:9).

> The other tribes came before Moshe and stated, "Our teacher, Moshe, we also stood at Mount Sinai and received the Torah, and it was given to us. Why are you entrusting a special Torah only to *Shevet Levi*? One day, they may claim it was given only to them and not to the other tribes." Moshe rejoiced and said, "Now you are a nation. Today I understand your devotion to and desire to serve *HaShem*."

My *Rosh Hayeshivah*, *Harav* Henoch Leibowitz, *shlita*, comments on this that *Bnei Yisrael* had shown their devotion to *HaShem* by clinging to their faith during their slavery in Egypt, by unconditionally accepting the Torah at Har Sinai, and by following Moshe in the desert for forty years. Yet it was only when he heard their absolute concern for the perpetuation of the Torah that Moshe was assured of their commitment. The litmus test, then, of commitment, is not personal devotion alone, but an appreciation of the need to safeguard and transmit this Torah to future generations.

Rabbi Yaakov Emden says to all who feel they need to witness miracles in order to have total faith in *HaShem* that the greatest miracle in Jewish history is the continued study of Torah and its transmission through the ages.

Similarly, we find in *Parshat Vayera* that *HaShem* feels He must inform Avraham of the impending destruction of S'dom and Amorah because "I know he will instruct his children and household after him to observe

HaShem's way" (Genesis 18:19). *HaShem* had many different reasons to confide in Avraham. Avraham had shown unswerving devotion to Him and his acts of *chesed* set the standards that we should all strive to meet. Yet it is the fact that Avraham will raise future generations to walk in the way of God that is the primary consideration in *HaShem*'s decision to make His covenant with Avraham.

As the *Rav*, *Harav* Yosef Dov Ber Soloveitchik, *zt"l*, points out in explaining that one of the primary roles of a parent at the time of the Pesach Seder is being a teacher to his/her children, parents are not only biological progenitors but also teachers, and they are traditionally referred to as *Avi Mori* ("my father, my teacher") and *Imi Morasei* ("my mother, my teacher").

The requirement to pass the *mesorah* (tradition) on to the next generations necessitates two commitments on our part. First, as parents, we must continually learn in order to teach. All professionals require continuing education and, in this critical area, we must constantly seek ways to teach both by example and by sitting down to learn with our children. Second, we must see that our children receive the most comprehensive Jewish education available. Yes, it isn't inexpensive, but the tuition we pay should not be looked upon as an expense but, rather, as an investment. Not only that, but this investment is guaranteed to rise in value and will pay dividends in the perpetuation of Judaism to future generations.

❖ CHAPTER 55 ❖

Nitzavim

Rabbi Yaacov Wasser

Young Israel of East Brunswick, New Jersey

The primary theme of *Parshat Nitzavim* is one that is most apropos to this time of the year—the concept of *teshuvah*, repentance. The ability of an individual to wipe the slate clean of previous transgressions is one of the greatest gifts that *HaShem* has given us.

Most of those commentators who list the *mitzvot* count *teshuvah* as one of the 613 *mitzvot*. They quote one of two *pesukim* as the source. Either "And you shall return to *HaShem*, your God" (Deuteronomy 30:2) or "They will confess their sins" (Numbers 5:7) is given as the source for listing *teshivah* as a *mitzvah*.

The Ramban and Sforno interpret the *pesukim* state, "For the commandment which I command you today is not yet beyond your understanding, nor is it far way. It is not in the heavens . . . but it is very close to you, in your mouth and heart that you do it" (Deuteronomy 11–14), as referring to *teshuvah*.

The Torah goes to great lengths to assure us that the ability to do *teshuvah* is in the grasp of each individual. Why are so many *pesukim* devoted to reassuring us of this? Why is the concept of *teshuvah* written seven times in this *parshah*?

The answer is that the concept of *teshuvah* is such a great act of kindness on *HaShem*'s part that we need to be convinced that He really means it. From a logical standpoint, a person should receive a full measure of punishment for doing an *averah* (sin). Imagine being hauled into court for a particular crime and being exonerated and given a totally clean slate when you express remorse and promise not to do it again!

In a letter to a student who was upset by his (the student's) struggles to do the *mitzvot* properly, Rav Yitzchok Hutner, *zt"l*, the *Rosh Hayeshivah* of *Yeshivat* Chaim Berlin, writes about the concept expressed in *Mishlei* 24:16,

"A righteous man falls down seven times and gets back up." We should not think that we are lacking just because our life is a constant battle against the *yetzer hara,* the evil will. Even *tzadikkim* have these battles. Rav Hutner writes, "Who knows what battles the Chofetz Chaim had with his *yetzer hara* in his fight not to speak *lashon hara* (evil speech)?" Nobody is exempt from this battle. The mark of a *tzaddik* is that he picks himself off the floor time after time to start anew after each battle. Fighting the battle draws one closer to *HaShem.*

Sforno commenting on the *pasuk,* "And you shall call to mind among all the nations . . ." (Deuteronomy 30:1) explained that this is not a vague reminiscence of past events but a deep introspection by every Jew into his subconscious to determine motivations for his deeds and establish whether they are in accordance with the Torah. This is the essence of *teshuvah.*

My *Rosh Hayeshivah, Harav* Hanoch Leibowitz, *shlita,* of *Yeshivas* Rabbeinu Yisroel Meir Hacohen explains Sforno as saying that we must constantly probe our subconscious and ascertain our true intentions, both good and bad, in all that we do. This honest approach to our life will allow us to be *baalei teshuvah.*

An important part of our day should be spent reading a *mussar-* (ethics-) oriented *sefer* such as *Mesilat Yesharim* or *Chovot Halevovot* to facilitate this honest introspection.

I would like to conclude with the definition given by *Harav* Yosef Dov Soloveitchik, *zt"l, Rosh Hayeshivah* of *Yeshivas* Rabbeinu Yitzchok Elchonon, *refvah shlemah,* of the word *teshuvah.* Rav Soloveitchik writes in his classic *sefer Al Hateshuvah* that one context in which the word *teshuvah* is used in *TaNaKh* is when the text (*1 Shmuel* 7:17) describes how the Prophet Shmuel would travel the Land of Israel throughout the year and would return home at the end of the year. "And he returned (*u-teshuvato*) to Ramah, for his home was there."

The Rav says that the concept of *teshuvah* is that of a cycle. Just as Shmuel, when he took the first steps from his house to start his journey, was also beginning his return home, so, too, an individual, even when he does an *averah,* can never move away from *HaShem,* since at the same time he starts on the road to do *teshuvah.* For some, the circle is larger than others, but we each have that *pintele yid* that keeps us attached to God. We all return home at the end of the journey.

Let us hope that this *Yomim Noraim* will enable us to bring ourselves closer to *HaShem* and allow us to sincerely do *teshuvah.*

A *ketivah chatimah tovah* to all.

Rabbi Edward Davis

Young Israel of Hollywood/ Fort Lauderdale, Florida

1. Moshe calls upon all the people to hearken to the responsibilities of the covenant now binding them to *HaShem*. This call includes the woodcutters and water-drawers. Rashi identifies these low-level members of society as Canaanites who came to Moshe to convert to Judaism; Moshe made them, in essence, slaves. In Joshua's time, Gibeonites came to convert (Joshua 9) and Joshua made them water-drawers and woodcutters because they came in trickery.

They had lied to Joshua and told him they came from far away. In King David's time, these converts were treated in the same fashion. From the text (II Shmuel 21) and from the Talmud (*Yevamot* 79; see *Tosafot*), we note that King David also had reason to degrade these Gibeonites; they were cruel people and wanted to kill seven of Saul's sons. But what reason did Moshe have to degrade these Canaanites? With what form of trickery did they approach Moshe? Rabbi BenZion Firer (contemporary, Israel) suggests that Moshe degraded these people because of what Moshe had learned from his sad experience with the *erev rav*, the multitude of non-Jewish slaves who accompanied *Bnei Yisrael* out of Egypt. They were a bad influence over the Jewish people, leading them to sin in the debacle with the golden calf. Therefore, Moshe felt it necessary to degrade these new converts in order to make sure that they would not be able to influence the Jewish people at all.

2. Upon entry into the Promised Land, the responsibility incumbent upon each Jew was no longer limited to him/herself. The new responsibility was *arevut*; each person was also responsible for his fellow man and for *Klal Yisrael* as a whole. Rav Shimon bar Yochai offered the famous story of a passenger on a boat who decides to bore a hole under his seat. When angrily questioned by his fellow passengers, he responded that they shouldn't care; he was boring the hole only under his own seat. All of *Bnei Yisrael* are in the boat together.

One Jew who transgresses *Shabbat* cannot claim that his actions have an effect only upon himself.

By the standards introduced in the Torah at the end of chapter 29, each person's actions have a profound effect on the general Jewish population. On Rosh Hashanah, we are judged both as individuals and collectively, as *Klal Yisrael,* a nation (when speaking of the nation of Israel living in *Eretz Yisrael,* this discussion can be enlarged to include the co-responsibility of the religious and the non-religious).

3. Our Sages tell us that *HaShem* did not reveal the reasons or the rewards for the *mitzvot* in order that a person would not decide to neglect the *mitzvot* that do not command much of a reward and decide to perform only highly rewarding *mitzvot*. For only two *mitzvot* does the Torah promise a specified reward: one is the *mitzvah* of honoring one's mother and father, the reward for which is "length of days"—long life. The second *mitzvah* for which the reward is length of days is sending away the mother bird before taking the chicks or eggs. Whereas the latter is an easy *mitzvah* to observe, the former is extremely difficult. Equating them with their relative rewards teaches us to treat equally the easy and the difficult *mitzvot*. Perhaps this is the proper interpretation of "the secret things" and "the revealed things" (Deuteronomy 29:28). The revealed things are these two *mitzvot*—one for us (taking the chicks) and one for our children (requiring them to honor their parents). All the other *mitzvot* are among the secret things, since we do not know the meanings or the rewards involved.

4. Moshe states that the time will come that *HaShem* will exile the Jewish people from their homeland to "the midst of all the nations" because of our neglect of the responsibilities we took upon ourselves. In the exile, we will begin to reflect upon the covenant; from the exile we will begin our return to *HaShem* and to *Eretz Yisrael.* I personally prefer the term "exile" to the modern term "Diaspora." From the latter, I infer a feeling that it is acceptable to live outside *Eretz Yisrael.* The term "Exile," however, makes it clear to me where it is religiously preferable for the Jew to live.

Commentators note that the exile will be to "all the nations." Other nations have been exiled from their homeland, but the fact that the Jewish exile carried the Jews to all parts of the world displayed the Divine origin to our exile. Abarbanel (in his comments on *Ki Tavo*) states that there is a blessing in this total dispersion of our people. When persecution and pogrom broke out against Jews in one part of the word, other Jews, who were elsewhere, prospered. From this ongoing phenomenon in Jewish history, we see evidence of the Divine blessing of the eternality of the Jewish people.

5. "Neither is it beyond the sea." There are those who do admit that the prescribed way of life of the Torah is necessary for Jews abroad—that it is there that one has to be concerned about assimilation or disintegration. They

are intensely concerned about the state of Jewish education in the United States or disturbed about the condition of Jews in the former Soviet Union. However, the same people will not do anything concerning the fate of education in their own neighborhood or about the fact that they have not seen the inside of a synagogue for years. It is to these people that Moshe cries out "neither is it beyond the sea." Torah is not only for those overseas. The way of Judaism and Torah is not "far off"; it is neither "in heaven" nor "beyond the seas." It is here and now. "The word is nigh unto thee, in thy mouth and in thy heart, that thou mayest do it" (Deuteronomy 30:14). Indeed, many may be ready to have the word of God in their mouths to give it lip service at conventions and public meetings. Many may even claim that it is well to be "good Jews at heart." Both are no doubt performing a good service for Judaism. Yet, in the final analysis, both the "mouth Jews" and the "heart Jews" are not enough. The real purpose of the Torah is "that thou mayest do it." It is the doing, the action, that assures the continuity of life.

Rabbi Yeshaya Siff

Young Israel of Manhattan, New York

Today is the *Shabbat* on which we should bless the new month of Tishrei. However, as the Baal Shem Tov explained, tradition has decreed that *HaShem* Himself blesses this new month for us, as *Parshat Nitzavim* is always read on the *Shabbat* before Rosh HaShanah.

And what is the special blessing that *HaShem* gives us on this *Shabbat*? "You are standing firmly today, all of you," from the greatest to the most insignificant. As long as you stand together, accept responsibility for one another, view each other with genuine concern, and take interest in the spiritual and material welfare of one another, then you will be meritorious in the coming judgment.

The Ramban explains that a new covenant is now being made with the generation entering *Eretz Yisrael*. The first covenant was made forty years before, at Mount Sinai, with the generation that eventually died in the desert, but the second covenant is being made with a new generation, as well as with all future generations—"For [with] the one that is here with us standing [here] today . . . and the one that is not here with us today." As Rashi explains: With the generations that will come in the future. The commentaries explain that the Torah means either that the souls of every Jew were there or, alternately, that a child is an extension of the parents and, thereby, bound by their acceptance.

But the *arevut* (co-responsibility) of *Parshat Nitzavim*, of this new covenant, is unique. Normally, when one becomes a co-signer or accepts responsibility for another, a wealthy individual accepts responsibility for a poor person, or an adult accepts responsibility for a child. Here, on the banks of *Eretz Yisrael*, each individual became responsible for every other person, no matter what their station. Not only are the leaders expected to correct or to encourage their compatriots, but even those of minor stature are obligated to accept responsibility for their superiors. In the *halachah* that derives from our accepting responsibility for one another, even a youngster can help a venerable sage fulfill his obligation of reciting blessings, of making *kiddush*, of sounding the *shofar*.

The co-responsibility of the second covenant means that our entire people—every member of *Klal Yisrael*, young and old, scholar and layman—has immense obligations and responsibility, as well as blessing. Whoever can correct the deeds of his family and does not do so is held accountable for the members of his family; whoever can correct the deeds of his city and does not do so is held accountable for the actions of his city; and the same for the entire world.

Our forefathers willingly accepted upon themselves this great obligation, as well as this great opportunity. The phrase "All Israel is responsible one for the other" is one of the unique watchwords of our people, as well as a major component of all of our personal and communal endeavors.

Thus, the *Klei Yakar* goes on to explain, our *sedrah* speaks of two different situations: one in which an individual transgresses and one in which a multitude sins. The individual who sins in private will be destroyed; but the multitude that transgresses in public and is not reproved or rebuked involves the entire people in its transgressions and, thus, the entire nation will suffer the punishment of exile from the land, as well as communal punishment.

Our forefathers realized their responsibility, but also the immense blessings which this *arevut* brought us, for, as long we relate ourselves to each other and to our people as a whole, we are always looked upon as meritorious before *HaShem*.

"You are standing firmly today, all of you": You stand firm and victorious in judgment on this day of judgment, as long as you all remain together. This is the blessing we receive this day from *HaShem* Himself, as explained by the Lubavitcher Rebbe, *zt"l*. Let us each resolve truly to fulfill this blessing in our own lives and actions, and thereby receive a *ketivah v'chatimah tovah lanu v'kol Yisrael. Amen.*

❖ CHAPTER 56 ❖

Nitzavim-Vayelech

Rabbi Sholom Steinig

Young Israel of Bayside, New York

The reading of *Parshat Nitzavim* always reminds us of the approach of the Rosh Hashanah and Yom Kippur season. Not only is tonight the beginning of Selichot week, but the very opening words—"You are all standing here this day before *HaShem* your God," call to mind an image of millions of Jews around the world standing in prayer on the *Yomim Noraim*.

Images of *teshuvah* abound in *Parshat Nitzavim*. It may even be said that the entire *parshah* is a metaphor on *teshuvah*, which can be found in virtually every verse. "But it is not with you alone that I am making this covenant" teaches that the covenant of God's granting forgiveness is not extended to those who stand alone but, rather, to those who strive for unity with others so that there shall never be a "you, alone" in Israel.

"Any whose heart strays from *HaShem* our God . . . *HaShem* will not agree to forgive him," is not a threat but literally a plea for awareness. *Teshuvah* is available only for those who first realize that they have transgressed; in order to receive God's forgiveness we must first turn to Him in the knowledge that we have done wrong and are in need of forgiveness; we may then seek it out, regretting our sins of the past year and resolving not to repeat them. "It is something that is very close to you; it is in your mouth and in your heart so that you can do it," tells us how simple the *teshuvah* process can be for every one of us, as long as we just begin to do it. We do not have to start on a high level; *teshuvah* is not only for the spiritually elevated. Even if it starts as only "lip service"—"in your mouth," mere words that, as yet, have no meaning—God guarantees that with a continued effort our attempts to return to Him will eventually be "in your heart"—from the heart, genuine and sincere, thus leading to the ultimate goal of "so that you can do it"—so that we may accomplish it and get it done.

"And *HaShem*, your God, will circumcise your heart and the hearts of your descendants." The Ramban understands "circumcision of the heart" as referring to the removal of any impediments that stand in the way of understanding the truth, any barriers to doing *teshuvah*.

And, finally, we have the outright declaration, "You shall do *teshuvah*, repent, return to *HaShem*, your God . . . ," "And you shall listen to His voice."

The talmudic explanation in *Bava Metzia* (59b) of the verse "It is not in the Heavens," tells one of the best-known of all the stories of our Rabbis, that of how Rabbi Eliezer ben Hyrcanus tried to use a Heavenly voice to convince those who disagreed with him in a halachic dispute to reconsider their decision. This verse can also be seen as a beautiful lesson regarding the *teshuvah* process. Rashi, commenting on this verse, quotes the *Gemara* in *Eruvin* (55a), which explains that "it is not in the heavens" teaches us that even if the Torah were in the heavens, we would have the obligation to go up after it in order to study it. Thankfully, we do not quite have to "climb to the heavens" in order to learn Torah. The *Chidushei Harim* adds that the next verse, "For the matter is very close to you," is a direct outcome of this interpretation. This matter of learning Torah is indeed close to those who are ready to work for it. True, the Torah is not in the Heavens, but if we only show that we are prepared to go up to heaven or cross the sea if that is required to attain the Torah, then indeed God brings it close to us. So, too, is it with *teshuvah*. For the one who is desirous of it, for the one who follows the procedure set down by our Rabbis for doing *teshuvah*, it no longer is a matter that is left to the heavens but indeed comes very close and becomes a part of us. Essentially, it is up to us whether our acceptance for another year shall be in our own hands or if it is to remain beyond our grasp. We must start by wanting it.

After the Torah reading, we return the scroll to the Ark with the verse, "Cause us to return to you, *HaShem*, and we will return; renew our days "*kkedem*" as of old." Rav Avraham Yehoshua Heschel, the Apter Rav understood these words as being a source of encouragement to all who would recite it.

The last word of the verse, *kedem*, is made up of the initials of Kayin, David, and Menasheh, three individuals who were guilty, respectively, of the three most reprehensible sins: murder, immorality, and idol worship. The gates of *teshuvah* were not closed to those three as they sought the chance to return. So, too, the gates of *teshuvah* remain open for all of us who seek to enter. As we begin the process with Selichot this evening, may our efforts be acceptable, and may we all be judged as deserving before God.

❖ CHAPTER 57 ❖

Vayelech

Rabbi Yeshaya Siff

Young Israel of Manhattan, New York

The *parshah* of *Vayelech* is a rather strange *sedrah* to read on *Shabbat Shuvah,* when *Klal Yisrael,* the Jewish people, is immersed in self-preparation for its awesome meeting with *HaShem* on Yom Kippur, the Day of Atonement.

Just imagine the scenario: A dedicated, caring leader who has suffered with his people for forty years is preparing to take leave of them and to deliver his valedictory. We would expect the Almighty to deliver words of encouragement and advice, expressions of hope for the future. At the very least we would expect *HaShem* to comfort *Klal Yisrael.*

But, what do we hear? "And God says to Moshe, behold, you will lie with your ancestors, and these people will arise and go astray after gods of strangers of the land . . . and they will forsake Me and violate the covenant that I have made with them" (Deuteronomy 31:16). This is not even a warning or exhortation, but a prophecy, a statement of fact! And Moshe *Rabbeinu* himself tells the Jewish people "For I know that after I die you will become corrupt and turn away from the path that I have commanded you, and the evil will happen to you . . ." (Deuteronomy 31:29).

It appears that *HaShem* wants Moshe to write the song of *Ha'azinu* (Deuteronomy 32:1–43) and to teach it to the people of Israel—not so much as a *warning* but rather as a *witness* against the people *after* the destruction comes to them. The entire tenor of *HaShem*'s and Moshe *Rabbeinu*'s final words are exceedingly pessimistic and foreboding.

Perhaps the key to understanding why this *parshah* is relevant to *Shabbat Shuvah,* and why *HaShem* and Moshe addressed *Bnei Yisrael* as they did, can be found in an incisive explanation by Sforno (on Deuteronomy 31:29): "I will tell you in that song, and I will testify against you, that I know that you will conduct yourselves in a manner that [will cause] the evil to befall you—

so that you will not ascribe the future to chance, but you will ascribe it to the fact that you have acted corruptly and you will take to heart to return [repent]."

Calamity will surely befall *Klal Yisrael*, the Torah tells us in a manner of prophecy, but it is crucial that we understand *why* and not ascribe calamities to false causes, for, if we are not honest with ourselves and seek to evade the responsibility we bear, then self-correction, or true *teshuvah* (repentance) can never come. If one is unaware of the cause or source of a malady, one can never cure the ailment. Only if we understand that it is our transgressions and our forsaking of God's Torah that brought us the grief of the *galut* will we be able to achieve true *teshuvah*. And *this* is the central lesson of the *sedrah*.

This admonition cries out to us in these days of *teshuvah*. Each individual must be willing to face him/herself honestly and without the myriad of excuses we make for ourselves. We must be willing to recognize where our laxness or even neglect of Torah and *mitzvot* has led us, both personally and collectively as a people. To understand that excuses will simply not do is the true *beginning* of *teshuvah*.

However, there are two types of *teshuvah*—or rather, two stages—contained in our *sedrah* and clarified by the Ramban (Nachmanides on Deuteronomy 31:17–18). In the first stage, the people will have what are called *hirhurei teshuva* ("thoughts of *teshuva*"), feelings that "all is not well because God is not with me." But these feelings are not "a complete confession of sin", explains Nachmonides, but merely a recognition of guilt without the drive to return and correct one's wrongdoings.

The result of this partial *teshuvah* will be a partial easing of the tribulations of the *galut*, but the Jewish nation shall remain still lacking (complete) redemption until such time as the Jewish people fully repent, when they will do a *teshuvah shleimah*, and then the final redemption will come.

Observing the state of our people as we approach the end of this century, we can also observe the beginnings of the final return, after which *Moshiach Tzidkeinu* will arrive to redeem *Klal Yisrael*, as promised by the Torah. We have seen, even in our days, the fulfillment of the warning; we now eagerly look forward to the realization of the redemption, very speedily and in our days.

Rabbi Moshe Teitelbaum

Young Israel of Lawrence/ Cedarhurst, New York

The importance of assuming a consistent venue for davening is implied in the following *pasuk* in *Parshat Yitro*: *Bechol hamakom asher azkir et shemi avo eilecha u-verrachticha*, "In all places where I call out My Name I will come to you and I will bless you" (Exodus 20:21). The *heh* is a definitive "the," which specifies that there should be only one place. Why then does it say *bechol hamakom* ("in *all* places"), which implies that there may be many locations? Furthermore, it should say *tazkir es shmei*, meaning "wherever *you* mention My Name, I will come and bless you." Why does *HaShem* say *azkir et shemi*—"*I* will call out My Name"?

The Prophet, in *Sefer Yeshaiah* (Isaiah 55:6), describes the days between Rosh Hashanah and Yom Kippur as opportune for reaching out to the Almighty: "Beseech *HaShem* when He is present, call Him when He is near." "Said Rabbah Bar Avuha, 'These are the ten days between Rosh Hashanah and *Yom Hakippurim*'" (Talmud *Rosh Hashanah* 18a). On Yom Kippur, the culmination of the Ten Days of Repentance, our most intimate thoughts and prayers are nearer to *HaShem* than at any other time of the year. This closeness is achieved through our observance of the *mitzvot* that He has invested into that specific twenty-four hour period. Its *mitzvot* are unlike those of any other day. It is the only fast day that is *min hatorah* (biblical in origin). It is the only day on which the *avodah* service in the *Beit Hamikdash* is kosher only when performed by the *Kohein Gadol* (High Priest)—but by no one else. It is the only day on which the *Kohein Gadol* entered the *Kodesh Hakedoshim*, the Holy of Holies, to do the *avodah*. From this alone it is clear that *HaShem* is more approachable on Yom Kippur than on any other day of the year.

No moment on Yom Kippur equals the moments of the *avodah*—enacted in the proximity of *HaShem*, achieved through our davening. When the *viduy* (confession service) is read during *musaf* it is the words of the *Kohein Gadol* heard in our midst. When we fall *kori'im* we are transported from our *Beit Hakneset* and are found in the *Azarah* (courtyard) of the *Beit Hamikdash* proclaiming, "Blessed is the Name of His glorious Kingdom for all eternity."

Let us examine this supreme moment of the *Kohein's viduy*. We will raise a few questions along the way. Perhaps through answering these questions we will be able to appreciate the importance of this *avodah*.

"*Kach haya omer*" "And so would he say." The first mention of God's name is *ana HaShem*, "I beg of You, *HaShem*." The second is *ana Bashem*, "I beg of You *with* Your Name," in accordance with the opinion of Rabbi Chagal in Talmud Yerushalmi. Why the change? The Maharil suggested that *Bashem* indicates that the *Kohein Gadol*, at that point, pronounced the name "*Yud Kay Vov Kay*," whereas, when saying *HaShem*, he pronounced it as "*Adnus*." The Taz refutes the Maharil by the strength of a *baraisa* in Tractate *Yoma* (39) that indicates that the name of *HaShem* was pronounced ten times during Yom Kippur; three times each in each of the three *viduyim* and once by the *goral* (lottery) of *se'ir La-HaShem*. Why, then, does the *Kohein Gadol* say, *ana Bashem kapeir na* instead of *ana HaShem*? This is our first question.

Our second question: Why do we bow and say *Baruch Shem* . . . ("Blessed is the Name") upon recitation of the *Shem Hameforash* (Holy Name) during *viduy* and not during the placement of the *goral* on the head of the sin offering, where the *Shem Hameforash* was used as well? Furthermore, the bowing and *Baruch Shem* would accompany only the third enunciation of the Divine Name in each *viduy* but not *ana HaShem* or *ana Bashem*. Why not?

Our third question stems from the next paragraph: "He [the High Priest] too would intend to complete the Name simultaneously with those reciting the blessing. . . ." Why was it so important for the *kohanim* and the people standing in the courtyard to begin *Baruch Shem* as soon as they heard the *Kohein Gadol* begin to say the *Shem* and for the *Kohein Gadol* to conclude the *Shem* at the same moment that they concluded *Baruch Shem*?

Our fourth and final question is the most difficult. The *posuk* reads, *lifnei HaShem titharu*, "Before *HaShem* you will be cleansed." The word *titharu* is the subject of the sentence; it is not meant to be disjoined from *lifnei HaShem*. How, then, does the *Kohein Gadol* enact what seems to be a play on words by saying *titharu*, not as part of the *posuk*, but as a message to the people? As the *Mishnah* and our *Machzor* say, "And he would say to them, "*Titharu*" 'May you become cleansed.'"

The answer to all of our questions lies in the role of *Baruch Shem* . . . "Blessed is the Name of His glorious Kingdom for all eternity" in the *Mikdash*. In the Temple, *brachot* were not answered by *amen*; they were answered by *Baruch Shem*. . . . During *Birkat Kohanim*, each mention of *HaShem*'s Name was answered by *Baruch Shem* . . . but not *amen*. Meanwhile, outside the

Mikdash, *Baruch Shem kavod malchuso l'olam va'ed* was never said out loud except on Yom Kippur.

Baruch Shem . . . is the praise of God heard in heaven above. It was revealed to Moshe on Har Sinai when Moshe ascended to God. It is an accolade that stresses the eternal nature of His Being—transcendent of time and space. The two most important words are, therefore, *l'olam vo'ed* (for eternity). *Baruch Shem . . .* is said only there where the *shechinah* of *HaShem* resides *eternally*. There, the words *l'olam vo'ed* ring true—at least to the *Shechinah*, if not to all mankind.

Mention of the Presence of the *Shechinah* brings us to the next part of our answer. When Moshe was witness to the *Shechinah* as It passed him on *Har Sinai* and *HaShem* uttered the Thirteen Attributes of Mercy, what was Moshe's reaction? He quickly fell to the ground and prostrated himself before the *Shechinah*.

On Yom Kippur, we are told that *HaShem* will be present in the *Mikdash* and in His presence we will be absolved: *Bayom hazeh . . . lifnei HaShem titharu*. The Ari, *z"l*, explained that when the *Kohein Gadol* recited this *posuk* and reached the word *HaShem*, the *Shechinah* continued by speaking through the *Kohain Gadol*'s throat. That is why it says, "they heard the Name 'come forth from his mouth'"; but *he* was not saying it; it was the *Shechinah*, in fulfillment of *lifnei HaShem titharu*. We are given the opportunity to be present as the *Shechinah* awaits our return to *HaShem*.

All four of our question are now answered.

First, why *ana Bashem kaper na*? Because the *beis* means "through the use of" the merciful Name of "*Yud Kay Vov Kay*." The *Kohein Gadol* asks the *Shechinah*, which is present when he says the name of *HaShem* in the context of the *posuk*, to be merciful and forgive—because "*Yud Kay Vov Kay*" is the name of *Midat Harachamim* (the Attribute of Mercy). "By the power," the *Kohein Gadol* asks, "Please forgive".

Our second question was, why we say *Boruch Sheim* and bow only during the recitation of the Name in the context of the *posuk*. The reason is that that is the moment when we are *Lifnei HaShem*, as the *Shechinah* speaks from the mouth of the *Kohein Gadol*. At that moment we bow, as Moshe did when the *Shechinah* passed before him.

Our third question was, why was it was so important for the *Kohein Gadol* to conclude the Name at the same time as the gathered Jews in the *azarah* concluded *Baruch Shem . . .* The answer is that the two most important words are the last two—*L'olam vo'ed*. Those are to be said in the presence of the *Shiechinah* as they are said in *Sh'mayim* above, as Moshe heard the ultimate praise when he went "to God." It is but for a moment, during recitation of the Name, that we can, like angels, offer our tribute to the Almighty with perfection.

Finally, our last question concerning the word *titharu*: Turning to the people to say to them *titharu* is a confirmation of the event of God approached by man and man approached by God. Because of that event, *titharu*: the *Kohein Gadol* confirms that we can indeed become free of *averot*—by cleaving to *HaShem* at that moment.

May we now suggest what the *posuk* in *Parshat Yitro* means when it says, *bechol hamakom asher azkir et Shemi*. The words *azkir et Shemi* refer to the moment when God says His Own Name through the mouth of the *Kohein Gadol*. At that moment, *avo eilecha u-beirachticha*, *HaShem* is with us, to bless us. What is the *brachah*? *Titharu*: we are able to be a pure and good people once again. *Hamakom* refers to the *Beit Hamikdash*. It is the only place on this earth where God's eternal greatness is known. Only there do we say, *Baruch shem* . . . out loud and clearly. But there are many *Beit Hamikdash m'at* such as *Beit Haknesset*, *shuls*, and so on. *Bechol hamakom* means, in every such *Mikdash* built by Jews of Torah faith, *HaShem* will come on Yom Kippur, and in His presence we will receive the *brachah*, the fortunate opportunity of being close and becoming spiritually perfected.

Ki bayom hazeh . . . lifnei HaShem titharu.

Rabbi Moshe S. Gorelik

Young Israel of North Bellmore, New York

There are two levels of *teshuvah*—the private and the communal. The private is an inward corrective experience, self-accounting or *cheshbon hanefesh*. It is also a two-step process.

First of all, we assess our lives. This is illustrated by the anecdote reporting on the dilemma of a disciple on *Kol Nidrei* Eve. While observing his *rebbe*, he noticed that the *rebbe* was not reading the same page as the congregation. Perhaps, he thought, the *rebbe* had dozed off momentarily and, thus, did not realize he was lagging behind. Not wishing to embarrass the *rebbe*, the disciple, appearing perplexed, asked him where he was. The *rebbe* replied that he was at Chanukah.

This message is religiously valuable. Before proceeding to the future, one must reflect on and evaluate the past. How meaningful was our commitment? Was life spiritually inspiring? Was Torah the source of our values?

The second step is preparation for the future. How can one enhance his spiritual content? It requires reflection on life's purpose in order to enrich the daily routine with an added dimension of spirituality. The private *teshuvah* is a psychological and philosophical process. In this spiritual exercise, one's moods shift. There are regret and hope, remorse and encouragement. *Teshuvah* is facing reality while at the same time inspiring new beginnings with renewed optimism and renewed hopes.

The second level of *teshuvah* is communal. This is the awareness of identifying with *Klal Yisrael* and sharing its religious destiny. In his classic code, the *Mishneh Torah* (*Hilchot Teshuvah* 3:11), the Rambam emphatically and unequivocally declared that strict observance of *mitzvot* and adherence to the *halachah* will not guarantee a Jew entrance to *olam haba* unless he shares the pains and distress of Israel and identifies with the national community.

A self-alienated Jew forgoes his religious significance. *HaShem*'s covenant is with *Klal Yisrael*. Detachment from the *Klal* is tantamount to rejection of the covenant. This is reflected by the ritual of reciting the confessions—that is, the *Ashamnu* and *Al Chet*, twice at each *tefillah* on Yom Kippur.

The first recital is affixed to the private *Amidah*. In the quietness of his communication with *HaShem*, the Jew whispers his confession. In the privacy of the moment, the heart is contrite and the soul is humbled. As he stands in the presence of *HaShem*, the spiritual cleansing process begins.

The process is not completed till after the second phase. This phase takes place during the recitation of the public *Amidah*. The words are the same, but the act of confession takes on an additional dimension. The Jew is no longer a private person. He joins his fellow man in *avodat HaShem*. His individual worth is authenticated through his identity with the community. Individuals compose a community, and it is the identity with the community that substantiates his significance.

Identity with the community implies concern and responsibility. The text of the confession is recorded in the plural. The Jew declares, "We have sinned. . . ." My sin is his sin, and his sin is my sin. We apologize for neglecting the needs of others. May a Jew pat himself on the back for adhering to Torah requirements and for the act of *teshuvah*? No, unless he joins with others in a collective experience.

A traditional comment suggests that a common theme links Purim and Yom Kippur. The analogy is suggested by the fact that Yom Kippur can be read as the day that is like Purim. Yom Kippurim Yom—the day, *ki*—that is like Purim. The common theme is a fundamental doctrine, *Kol Yisrael areivim zeh lazeh*, "each Jew is responsible one for the other." The *midrash* (*Shir Hashirim* 8:7) associates this doctrine with the dilemma posed by the Purim event. If the Jews of Shushan were guilty for participating in the festivities sponsored by Ahasuerus, why were the Jews residing in other provinces threatened with annihilation? To resolve this question, the *midrash* declares "*Kol Yisrael. . . .*" All Jews are responsible for one another.

No one may point an accusing finger at another person until he can honestly declare to *HaShem* that he did all that was in his power to contribute to *Tikkun Ha'olam* and for the betterment of a fellow Jew. This is also the message of *Yom HaKipurim*. The plural form of the confession reflects the doctrine of *Kol Yisrael. . . .* We plead for atonement for our personal sins and for the sins of the *Klal*. Why? Because we share the covenant. Our share in the covenant is validated only when we share the communal destiny.

❖ CHAPTER 58 ❖

Ha'Azinu

Rabbi Benjamin Blech

Young Israel of Oceanside, New York

> *"Ki Shem HaShem ekra, havu godel l'Elokeinu"*—"When I will proclaim the name of the Lord, ascribe ye greatness unto our God." (Deuteronomy 32:3)

Does the obligation to recite blessings come from the Torah?

A Jew knows that every important moment requires emphasizing our understanding of its linkage with God. If we eat a piece of food, if we live to celebrate a precious event, for the good times in our lives and even for the bad, we are taught from our youth that there is always an appropriate *brachah* to be recited. But is this requirement to acknowledge the Divine in all things a commandment from the Torah itself, or is it a later addition imposed upon us by the Rabbis?

The correct answer makes a remarkable distinction: most *brachot* are, indeed, *Mi'Drabanan,* from our Sages. It is not God who demanded but we who desired to recite them. There are but two exceptions to this rule. Twice does the Torah text itself make clear that a Jew must verbalize thanks through the text of a blessing. The first appears in the *sedrah* of *Ekev*: "And you shall eat and be satisfied and bless the Lord thy God for the good land which He hath given thee" (Deuteronomy 8:10). This passage, of course, refers to the *Birkat hamazon*—the Grace after meals. When we finish our food, satiety necessitates sanctification.

The second biblical source is the *posuk* in this morning's *sedrah*. From the verse "When I will proclaim the name of Lord; ascribe ye greatness unto our God," we deduce, fascinatingly enough, the *mitzvah* of reciting a blessing before the recitation of words of Torah.

How does one find in this verse an allusion to *birkat Hatorah*? The *Maharsha* in *Berakhot* (21) beautifully explains: The Torah in its totality is the very essence—or, better put, the name—of God Himself. Moshe is telling the people, "When I proclaim the name of the Lord—that is to say, whenever I will read to you portions of the Torah—it is your obligation to ascribe greatness to God by means of a blessing."

THE COMMON DENOMINATOR

The question is obvious. What makes these two laws different? Why should a meal and the study of Torah be the only two situations that warrant a blessing *mi'Doraita* (biblical law)?

A moment's reflection gives us the answer. A human being requires two things in order to survive. The first is food. Without it the body is doomed; death must surely follow. But the Torah has made abundantly clear something that many people take years to realize: "A human being does not live by bread alone." Life is based not only on a "What" but also a "Why." Without a purposeful life, it is not the body but the soul itself that withers and dies. It may be true that "if there is no flour, there can be no Torah." It is equally true, however, that if there is no Torah, the consumption of bread seems utterly meaningless. Lack of physical nourishment causes death; lack of spiritual sustenance breeds a desire for suicide.

The Torah singled out the two most important keys to human existence and imposed the recitation of a *brachah* on both to demonstrate their equality. Bless God for the food you consume and for the Torah you are privileged to study.

BUT WHY THE REVERSE ORDER?

Yet, a striking difficulty still remains. Blessings have two possibilities as to the time when they are uttered. Jewish law teaches us a *bracha l'foneha*—a blessing before [the activity]—blessings that are recited before an act is performed. On the other hand, we also have a *bracha l'achareha*—a blessing after [the activity]—blessings that come in the aftermath of an action.

Note the remarkable way in which the Torah differentiates between the times when we are to give thanks for our spiritual and our physical sources of nourishment. The *birkat hamazon* is, of course, recited after the meal. We have eaten, we are full—and *then* we bless God. With regard to study, however, it is not so. Before we recite even a word of the text, before our souls merge with "the names of the Divine" we must already bless God for the opportunity to have this encounter. How do we explain this disparity?

THE BIBLICAL PRINCIPLE

To understand the answer we must first posit a principle concerning biblical practice. There is a concept developed by Rabbi Samson Raphael Hirsch concerning the "when"—that is to say, the situation—in whose context any Torah law is given. What is the source, for example, of the law of burial? How does the Torah impose upon us the obligation to bury our beloved ones who have passed on? The source is the section in which we find the procedures given for handling the corpses of those put to death by the courts for the most severe transgressions. Individuals who were "stoned" were then to be hanged for a short while. But we were not permitted to allow their bodies to remain there: "His body shall not remain all night upon the tree, but thou shall surely bury him the same day, for he that is hanged is a reproach unto God" (Deuteronomy 21:23).

Every parent, every *tzaddik*, every pious, holy Sage is interred because the Torah said, "thou shalt surely bury him," with regard to a criminal worthy of capital punishment! What is the rationale for such a peculiar placement? Because the Torah tells us that a human being who was created in the image of God may not be allowed to have his corpse strewn about on the face of the earth in a demeaning manner even if he may have committed the worst crimes imaginable. The *mitzvah* of burial is rooted in a human being's kinship to his Creator. And the law of burial is stated in context of a criminal to teach that even in this worst-case scenario burial is still required. How much more so for anyone else?

To summarize the principle: A law is stated in that case or situation where one might least expect it to apply—in order to deduce from there its applicability, as a *kal v'chomer*, in all others.

So, too, the rights of every woman in marriage for food, clothing, and sexual privileges come from the case of the slave girl who is also a second wife. If she can demand her rights as basic to our understanding of obligations imposed upon the husband by marriage, how much more obviously so any other woman!

WHEN IS THE BLESSING OBVIOUS?

Now we may understand why the Torah differentiates between food and Torah with regard to the time of blessing.

The Torah will state the law in that situation where it most needs emphasis. That is why, in the blessing before the meal, when a person is starving and in want, there is no need to make a demand that a human being think of God. "Help me"; "give me"; "O God, if only I could satisfy my cravings, I would be indebted to you forever." So go the promises of people before they have feasted. Once their bellies are full, be it literally or metaphorically, people no longer feel that great need to thank the Almighty. Strange, isn't it, that poor people pray more than rich people—even though rich people have more to be grateful to the Almighty for.

That is why God says eat, be satiated, and then bless. Don't forget blessings even when bellies are full. What the Torah did was address the situation where we might most fear that the law would be forgotten.

Not so, however, with regard to words of Torah. Blessings *after* the study of Torah do not have to be commanded. Observe people who have spent their days absorbing the wisdom and the genius of the words of God. Gratefulness comes from their heart and from their lips as a natural product of having been allowed to share in the essence of *HaShem*. That is not the time when we are afraid there will be lack of blessing. It is, rather, before people have opened the text, *before* they have had an opportunity to grasp the delights and the joys implicit in study of Torah. Make a blessing before you begin to study is the Torah commandment; because the blessing afterward will take care of itself and need not be commanded.

It is the unfortunate reality of life. We are far more aware of our physical hunger than our spiritual starvation. But in retrospect we invariably discover the truth: The finest meal may temporarily fill us—but it is only the study of Torah that leaves us truly fulfilled.

One the eve of the New Year may we learn to put into proper perspective our strivings for the physical and the spiritual so that together we may be insured a year of good health, as well as a year of ultimate blessing.

Rabbi Chaim Wasserman

Young Israel of Passaic-Clifton, New Jersey

HAZIV LECHA

The points at which we stop in the reading of the Torah each *Shabbat* are governed by just a few rules that have become a matter of long-standing tradition. The Vilna Gaon, for example, did not regard the precise stops as unalterably fixed. Rather, we are told, he preferred to invoke the rules as he saw them and to stop at what he believed to be the most appropriate points.

I should like to point out only one such predominant rule as it applies to *Parshat Haazinu*. The universally accepted practice is to avoid beginning and ending with ominous themes. For example, this rule would preclude us from concluding an *aliyah* with a phrase such as *mot yumat* (that is, "he shall surely be put to death") or anything relating to the word *tamei* ("impure"). Similarly, matters of stern rebuke would be avoided with which to start or end an *aliyah*.

Nonetheless, throughout most of *Haazinu* this rule is circumvented. In fact, from as far back as talmudic times, *Haazinu*'s first six *aliyot* were singularly fixed as to where each was to be ended, despite the fact that some of the *pesukim* at the end or beginning of an *aliyah* would not abide by the aforementioned *halachah*. Why so? The entire poem of *Haazinu* (called *Shirat Haazinu*) contains in it ominous predictions of natural consequences of the Jewish future and, Moshe *Rabbeinu* felt that it was essential for the Jews to hear his messages as he prepared to depart from this world. Therefore, the fixing of the *aliyah* stops was to prevent anyone from complaining that for him the *ba'al k'riah* concluded at a "bad" point, perhaps intended to heap a curse upon the head of the one honored with the *aliyah*.

And so, early on, *Chazal* established a mnemonic acronym for the initial letters of the six beginning words of each *aliyah*, commonly known as *HaZiV*

LeCHa, where the *heh* represents the first letter of the opening word, *haazinu*; the *zayin* is the initial letter of *z'chor*, which is the word with which the second *aliyah* begins, and so on for a total of six *aliyot*.

The truth be told, there is universal agreement only as to the starting points of the first two *aliyot*, whereas, for the next four, there are no less than six variations found in the halachic literature, all of which abide by the acronym of *HaZiV LeCHa*.

NETZIV ON ONE *PASUK*

In previous generations, elementary *yeshivot* that followed the philosophy of *ivrit b'ivrit*, learning in Hebrew, would invariably have students commit to memory four or five well-known poetic segments of *TaNaKH*, and Moshe *Rabbeinu*'s song of *Haazinu* was one of them. Accordingly, many youngsters were familiar with all of *Haazinu*. Though times have surely changed in this respect, two or three *pesukim* still remain well known to many because of their use in other contexts.

One such instance, the 4th *pasuk* of the first *aliyah*, is also the opening *pasuk* of *Tzidduk Hadin* recited at the cemetery by mourners and those assembled upon the completion of the burial. There we read: *Hatzur tamim po'olo, ki chol d'rachav mishpat . . . tzaddik v'yashar hu*. "The deeds of the Mighty One (*tzur*) are perfect, for all His ways are just. He is a faithful God, never unfair; . . . righteous (*tzaddik*) and moral (*yashar*) is He."

NeTZiV (Rav Naftoli Zvi Yehudah Berlin, immortal *Rosh Yeshivah* of Volozhin in the last century) invokes this *pasuk* to explain with rare analytical insight the social character of the generation of *tannaim* who sustained the destruction of the second *Beit Hamikdash*. What follows is a partial translation. (This passage is found not in *Haazinu* but in the NeTZiV's preface to his commentary on *Chumash, Ha'amek Davar*, at the beginning of *Bereishit*. In my humble opinion, the complete preface is worthy of translation and annotation so that one day it can take its place alongside other well-known letters of ethical direction such as *Iggeret haGra*, *Iggeret haRaMBaN*, and *Iggeret Mussar* by Rav Yisroel Salanter.)

> *HaTzur tamim po'olo* . . . "The deeds of the Mighty One are perfect, for all His ways are just. He is a faithful God, never unfair; righteous and moral is He." Praising God as *yashar* (moral, straight) is a way of accepting the fairness of the judgment that He meted out with the destruction of the second *Beit Hamikdah*. For that generation was "warped and twisted."
>
> It must be understood that those who lived in that generation were *tzaddikim*, righteous, *hasidim*, they went beyond the call of duty, and

amalei Torah, they worked assiduously at Torah study. However, they were not *yesharim*, morally correct in the manner in which they conducted their worldly affairs. Therefore, because of the senseless hate (*sin'at chinam*) that resided in their hearts toward one another, they would suspect as a heretic anyone whom they saw acting not in accordance with their own particular manner of *yirat HaShem* (awe of God).

As a result of this they committed acts tantamount to murder in the most extreme manner and perpetrated all conceivable evils, which resulted in the *Beit Hamikdash* being destroyed. For this they had to recite *tzidduk hadin* [accepting the judgment that God meted out to them as being just]. For God is *yashar* (moral, straight) and does not suffer the actions of such *tzaddikim* who conduct their affairs in such a twisted manner and not in a morally correct way. For even when their ways are for the sake of Heaven such ways cause devastation to the created world and the destruction of society.

The great praise due our forefathers [Avraham, Yitzchak, and Yaakov] is, above all, that aside from being *tzaddikim*, *hasidim*, and lovers of God in the most extreme manner, they were *yesharim*, morally straight. Witness the fact that they lived in a society dominated by despicable idol-worshipers, and yet they were able to live among them with love, being sensitive to their [human] needs.

This was the case with Avraham when he profusely begged for the welfare of S'dom despite the fact that he so despised them and their king for their wickedness. Nonetheless, [because they were creatures of God] he so desired that they survive. *Midrash Rabbah* notes this when it comments: "God told Avraham, 'You loved righteousness and despised evil. This means you loved to argue for justice on behalf of My creatures and you hated to see them condemned. . . ." Avraham, indeed, was the father to a multitude of nations and acted just as a father would toward a rebellious son, wanting to see that the son is well and good. . . .

Now you will understand why the book of *Bereishit* is known as *Sefer Hayashar*, the Book about those who are moral and straight. . . .

THE ART OF LISTENING

1. The difference between the Hebrew forms of *l'ha'azin* (*haazinu*) and *lishmoa* (*sh'ma*) is that the former always points to a sense of intimacy between the proclaimer and the listener. Moshe *Rabbeinu* was intimate with Heaven. He therefore invokes the verb *haazinu*. Vocal messages can be heard from afar, but Torah messages need an intimate relationship with God in order to be fully perceived.

2. Listening is an act in which we express our being human. Mortimer Adler, educator *extraordinaire*, philosopher and editor of *Encyclopaedia Britannica*, said it so well:

   Of all the things that human beings do, conversing with one another is the most characteristically human. It may be in the long run the only human activity the performance of which will ultimately preserve the radical distinction between human and brutes and between men and machines. . . . Shared thoughts and feelings, understood agreements and disagreements, make humans the only animals that genuinely *commune* with one another. Even though they signal their emotions or impulses to one another, other animals remain shut out from each other. They do not commune with one another when they communicate. The human community would not exist without such communion, which could not exist without human conversation.

3. Active, involved listening by definition is always an exercise in discovery and learning.
4. Consistent practice of the art of listening may be the single most important feature that can guarantee happiness, contentment, and serenity in life amidst all the stress and pressures that abound and that inevitably everyone must face.

Chazak Chazak V'nitchazek!

PART SIX

Festivals

❖ CHAPTER 59 ❖

The Month of Elul

Rabbi Michael Whitman

Young Israel of New Haven, Connecticut

Twice a day (for some of us, three times a day) until the end of Sukkot, we recite *L'Dovid HaShem Ori* (*Tehillim* 27). Yet that psalm contains no *direct* mention of any *yom tov*. Neither does it contain a direct reference to any of the *mitzvot* of the upcoming *yomim tovim—shofar, teshuvah*, fasting, *arba minim*. It is true that we find oblique references to each of the *yomim tovim* such as *ori* = Rosh Hashanah, *yish'l* = Yom Kippur. But aren't these days distinct? Can one paragraph relate meaningfully to the different ways in which we experience each of the upcoming *chaggim*?

As we approach the Days of Judgment, many of us begin to focus on our actions during the past year. We make a *cheshbon hanefesh* as we take stock of ourselves. We begin the process of feeling bad about the mistakes we have made asking *HaShem* for forgiveness, and resolving to be better. This is very important work. But we run the risk of losing sight of what should be our primary goal.

The Rambam states in *Hilchos Teshuvah* (7:6):

> Great is *teshuvah*, for it draws man close to the *shechinah*, as Hoshea states: "Return, O Israel, unto God, your Lord" . . . which means if you will return in *teshuvah*, you will cling to Me. . . . *Teshuvah* brings near those who were far removed. . . . Yesterday he [the sinner] was far from *HaShem*. . . . And today he is beloved and desirable, close and dear. . . .

The goal of *teshuvah* is not just the correction of the *aveirot* we committed so that we will not be punished for them. That is just the tool. The goal is to come closer to *HaShem*, to feel that we are nearer to Him. Thus, the term *teshuvah* does not mean just to turn away from a specific sin but, rather, to *return* to a relationship of intimacy with *HaShem*.

The truth is, there is only one theme to the entire *Yomim Noru'im*, from Elul to *Sukkot*—to come closer to *HaShem*. All of the aspects and *mitzvot* of the *yomim tovim* are different ways of expressing this theme. We wave the *arba minim* in all directions to assert that *HaShem* is all around us. We sit in a *sukkah* to feel enveloped and protected by *HaShem*'s presence.

And that is why one paragraph of *Tehillim* expresses our deepest feelings for the entire season.

> *L'Dovid HaShem Ori: HaShem* is my light and my salvation, whom shall I fear? . . . One thing I asked of *HaShem*, which I shall seek: that I dwell in the House of *HaShem* all the days of my life, to behold the sweetness of *HaShem*. . . . Indeed He will hide me in His shelter. . . . *HaShem* hear my voice when I call. . . . Your presence, *HaShem*, I seek.

Rabbi Samson Raphael Hirsch explains that Dovid *Hamelech* is telling us here that

> This is my goal, to attain God's nearness in every moment and every aspect of my life, ever to keep before my eyes the splendid way in which all earthly affairs are shaped under His guidance, and to seek to increase my understanding of the truths of life by drawing from the wellspring of wisdom set down in the Sanctuary of God's Law.

This paragraph of *Tehillim* gives us a startling example of what *HaShem* is offering us (which we must try to reciprocate and emulate). "Though my father and mother have forsaken me, *HaShem* will gather me in."

I once received a call from a distraught Jewish woman pleading with me to visit her son, who was a patient in a state mental hospital. I visited several times. And this woman kept calling me, begging me to visit again and again. And she pleaded with me to help her son, to get him released. "All he needs," she told me, "is to be home where I can care for him." After a while, I asked a social worker who was familiar with the case, what did this boy do to have caused him to be committed without a chance of release? He had violently attacked his mother and his father, sending them both to the emergency room. Yet his mother was fighting to get him back, to be able to express her love for him. In this paragraph, Dovid *Hamelech* teaches us that the love that *HaShem* has for each of us is even greater.

Chazal have planted this lesson into the beginning of our preparations for the *chaggim* by teaching us that the name of this month, Elul, is the acronym, "*Ani L'dodi V'dodi Li* (I am my Beloved's and my Beloved is mine)." Rabbi Yaakov Weinberg, *shlita*, the *Rosh Hayeshivah* of *Yeshivah* Ner Yisroel, Baltimore, Maryland, explains that the preparation for this season must begin with my knowing that I have a relationship with *HaShem* and that He cares for me.

"*Achat Sho'alti*." There is only one request. May we merit to use every day, every *mitzvah*, every aspect of the upcoming *yomim tovim*, to answer this question, to behold the sweetness of *HaShem*.

❖ CHAPTER 60 ❖

Rosh Hashanah

Rabbi Feivel Wagner

Young Israel of Forest Hills, New York

While the *mitzvas hayom* of Rosh Hashanah is the *shofar* (as ordained by the Torah: "a day of *shofar* sounding it shall be unto you"), it can also be said that the day is identified with *tefillah*, prayer, as well. The time and effort we devote to *tefillah* on these days is indicative of the closeness we feel to *Hakadash baruch Hu*, God, at this time. Prayer is a special gift we received from *HaShem* and, as such, should be treasured and used wisely. Several short comments follow that, it is to be hoped, will contribute to our understanding and appreciation of these *tefillot*.

ZACHREINU L'CHAIM

The addition of four phrases to the *Shemoueh Esrei*—namely, *Zochreinu L'Chaim mi chamocha, u-ch'tov l'chaim tovim*, and *b'sefer chaim*—is a matter of dispute among the *geonim*.

The Baal Halachot Gedolot, among others, says on the basis of Gemara in Berakhot (34) that these phrases should not be said: "A person should not ask for his needs in the first three or last three [*brachot*] of the *Shemoneh Esreh*." The reason is that *Shemoneh Esrei* consists of three components—*shevach, bakashah*, and *hoda'ah* (praise, requests, and thanksgiving). This is the proper way to approach *Hakadosh baruch Hu* and is, according to the Rambam, the required form even for the biblically based commitment of prayer. The first three blessings are of praise, the last three, of thanksgiving, and the middle one(s), of requests. Therefore, it is improper to make a request, even for life, in the middle of the first three or the last three *brachot*. Those who permit the inclusion of these petitions say that there is a distinction between individual requests, which cannot be said there, and public requests, which can be inserted. To explain this differentiation, I refer to Rav Simcha Zissel, the Alter of Kelm (one of the great leaders of the *mussar* movement), who, in his classic volume, *Chochmahu-Musser,* explains the concept of *tefillah* in general as a means for strengthening the *bitachon,* faith, of a person in *Hakadosh baruch Hu,* God.

Man must realize that he is alone—helpless, powerless to deal with the difficulties of life. All his needs—food, shelter, clothing, even his very life—come only from *HaShem.* Man is totally and absolutely dependent on the kindness of *Hakadosh barach Hu* for *everything.* By coming to *HaShem* three times a day, every day, with my list of needs, I express outwardly and strengthen inwardly my belief in this principle. It is for this reason that *shevach,* praise, must come before *bakashah,* request. First I acknowledge His power, majesty, and kindness; then and only then can I discuss my needs.

Requesting public needs, in this case the needs of all humanity and especially life itself, is, therefore, the greatest praise of all. It is a clear and ringing statement that the existence of all creation is dependent on *Hakadosh baruch Hu.* Once I have acknowledged that, I can continue my *bakashot,* my requests.

AVINU MALKEINU

The Talmud in *Taanis* (25b) relates an incident that occurred during the period of the *Mishnah.* During an extremely serious drought, the Rabbis proclaimed a fast day, and the special prayers ordained for such occasions were recited. The great Tanna, Rabbi Eliezer, led the *tefillah,* and yet no rain fell. Rabbi Akiva then stood before the *amud* and began a *tefillah* with the words *Avinu Malkeinu*—Our Father Our King—and was immediately answered. From that time on, *Avinu Malkeinu* took a prominent place in the *tefillah* of *aseret Y'mei teshuvah,* as well as of fast days throughout the year.

Here, too, Rav Simcha Zissel offers a tremendous insight. He defines the power of this tefillah as follows: *Hakadosh baruch Hu* relates to us on two levels—as King and as Father. There is the kingly relationship—one of awe and distance—that we have with the Master of the Universe. There is, however, also the close, loving, warm relationship of a child to a parent that we must feel. It is *our* ability to articulate these relationships through our words, and to feel them through our soul, that cements the specialness of our relationship to *Hakadosh baruch Hu.* This duality is expressed in every *brachah* by the use of both the familiar second person in the word *atah* and the distant third person in the rest of the text of the *brachah.* Yet its clear expression is most evidenced in the words of *Avinu Malkeinu.* This is what *Avinu*

Malkeinu contributed, even beyond the twenty-four *brachot* of the special *Shemoneh Esrei* led by Rabbi Eliezer.

THE *MUSAF SHEMONEH ESREI*

The *Musaf Shemoneh Esrei* of Rosh Hashanah is unique among all other *Shemoneh Esrei* prayers that we recite all year. The weekday *Shemoneh Esrei* contains nineteen *brachot.* The *Shemonch Esreh* for *Shabbat* and *yom tov* contains only seven brachot. In fact, every *musat* contains only seven brachot.

The exception to this is Rosh Hashanah. Our *Chazal* instituted three special *brachot* to express the specialness of the day: *Malchiyot, zichronot,* and *shafarot.* The first *brachah,* that of *Malchiyot,* speaks of the Kingship of *HaShem,* since Rosh Hashanah represents the day of man's creation. The *brachah* of *Zichronot* speaks of the past and *HaShem*'s remembering it. It is connected to the judgment on this day. Finally, *Shofarot,* the last *brachah,* speaks of the various aspects of the blowing of the *shofar.* Its connection to Rosh Hashanah is obvious. These three *brachot* are inserted into the body of the *Musaf Shemoneh Esrei* and thus expand it to nine *brachot.*

Though there is a difference of opinion in the *Mishnah,* in Tractate *Rosh Hashanah,* as to which *brachah* is the one in which *Malchiyot* is inserted, the *halachah* follows the opinion of Rabbi Akiva that *Malchiyot* is included in the *brachah* of *kedushat hayom*—the sanctity of the day. This is the middle *brachah* of every *Shabbat* and *yom tov* Shemoneh Esrei, the *brachah* that discusses the *musaf korban,* the additional sacrifice brought on that day. It contains a prayer for the rebuilding of the *Beit Hamikdash* and the reinstitution of the sacrificial service, and also a plea for the unique sanctity of the particular day. What is the connection between these two themes, *Malchiyot* and *kedushat hayom*? Why was it necessary to include them in one *brachah*?

The answer provides us with one of the basic concepts in Jewish belief. It is not sufficient to believe in *HaShem* only as Creator of the Universe or even as its continuous Master. Torah teaches us that the Creator had a purpose in mind, a purpose revealed to us in the Torah, in its teachings and laws. Some of the Greek philosophers believed in a Creator and proved His existence, but they could not fathom the idea that our small universe or the puny inhabitants of our earth could be of significance to Him. The Torah, on the other hand, categorically denies this philosophy. As Rav Elchonon Wasserman masterfully explains in his *kovetz ma'amarim,* it is incongruous to believe that the brilliant and powerful Creator should create a world for no purpose. There must be a reason, and He must have communicated it to us. That was done through *kabbalat HaTorah.*

We can now understand our *brachah*. Belief in the Kingship of *HaShem* is insufficient; *Malchiyot*, Kingship, needs *Kedushat et hayom*, sanctity of the day. Only through sanctifying our lives by Torah and *mitzvot* can we truly recognize and acknowledge the Kingship of *HaShem* and His role as Creator and Master of the entire universe.

May our prayers be accepted by *HaShem*, and may we all be inscribed for a good and healthy year.

Rabbi Israel Schorr

Young Israel Beth-El of Borough Park, New York

FROM *TASHLICH* TO *AL TASHLICHEINU L'EIT ZIKNAH*

The reply of Rabbi Nechemiah to Rabbi Akiva's question concerning how Rabbi Nechemiah reached old age (as recorded in the Talmud, *Megillah* 28) may be applied to solve the problematical aspect of the two prayers mentioned above. These two prayers—the Rosh Hashanah *Tashlich* service and the *Shema Koleinu* prayer—which are phonetically similar, are also alike in provoking some questions about their aim and name.

It is odd that on these Days of Judgment, when we are cautioned not to utter or pronounce a word that may have a negative connotation we call a prayer by the name *Tashlich* ("to throw, to cast, to discard")—a harsh name, indeed. The name is grim enough in isolation; it is even gloomier in association. It evokes the dreadful prediction "I will cast them into another land as of "*kayom hazeh,*" this day" (Deuteronomy 29:27). Rabbi Akiva comments on the words "*Kayom hazeh*": "As this day will not come back, neither will they [the Ten Tribes] return" (*Sanhedrin* 110:b). It suggests an ominous painting in a drab frame. The name irks, the phrase "what's in a name?" notwithstanding. The aim of the prayer is also perplexing. Of what avail will it be to lower the sins into the bottom of the sea? Will the bulk of water conceal them from the sight of *HaShem*? King David states, ". . . If I dwell in the nether part of the sea, thereto Thy hand will reach me . . ." (*Tehillim* 139:9–10). The prophetic metaphor that *HaShem* will cast the sins into the bottom of the sea, quoted at the *Tashlich* ritual, is meant more as a call for action than as a petition, as we will explain.

When we consider the *Tashlich* petition, the other supplication, *Al tashicheinu* (part of the *Shema Koleinu* prayer) is no less perplexing. We beseech the Almighty, "Do not cast us off when we reach old age; do not forsake us when our strength will end." Would it occur to anyone to think that the Eternal prefers the young and the strong to the old and weak? We read in *Tehillim* (34:19) that "God is nigh to the broken-hearted," meaning the weak and the old—an affirmative assurance to the infirm without their even asking. Then why repeat the petition many times in the holiday prayer?

The answer may be offered that the word "throw" is applied in *TaNaKh* in two different phases. For instance, in Exodus 7:10, "Aaron *threw* the rod before Pharaoh," whereas it is used in a different sense in I Kings 19:19, where Elijah "*cast* his mantle" to Elisha. There are two ways of "throwing"—one from above downward and the other, from one place to another on the same level. The first sense, to "throw down," usually means "to discard; to reject." The other means "to speed up the delivery" from one person or place to another. One way implies recoil; the other, release.

This simple note about the two types of "throwing" may serve to indicate that there are two kinds of sin. The vices that man commits are also of a dual nature. Some are infectious (contagious), able to corrupt the environment. Some are limited to damaging the perpetrator himself but not his surroundings. Some lawbreakers break only themselves; some split the earth, the land, and tear up the roots, whereas others tear out only the twigs. The way to eradicate the evil, in accordance with the formula of Bruriah (the wife of Rabbi Meir) is to erase the sin and save the sinner. We must act in a dual capacity. The sins have to be abolished; however, we must vary the means employed to suit the nature of the different kinds of vices. Those that are contagious, that can corrupt the earth, must be dealt with in a harsh manner; we must cast them, so to speak, into the depths of the sea. That is most likely what the Prophet Michah meant when he proclaimed the Almighty will cast the sins into the ocean (Micah 7:19, opening paragraph of *Tashlich* service). The other type of sins, those that are limited in effect, should be treated with a softer and more lenient approach.

Rosh Hashanah is not only a Day of Judgment for the individual's fate and future; it is also intended to offer a universal lesson for all conditions and ages. Because it is set by the Eternal, it offers a solution to problems in many eras. We, in our present age, are confused and bewildered how to mate crime and punishment. There appears to be a breakdown in the judicial system in our time. The scale of justice is out of balance.

The *Tashlich* ritual offers this lesson: The vices that are infectious, that pollute the atmosphere, should be dealt with harshly; symbolically, they should be cast off the surface of the land and lowered to the bottom of the sea, an area that is not susceptible to contamination by humanity's wrong deeds. The first meaning of the word "throw" should be applied to these sins. The "throwing" should be done in a positive manner because indecisiveness when decision is necessary is liable to produce a morbid state of mind, without hope or peace. The other kind of sin, in which the lawbreaker breaks only himself, has to be dealt with by the second definition, "[Elijah] *threw* the mantle [to Elisha]," which is meant to transfer authority from one prophet to another. This also suggests that the life of man, which is likewise divided with a line of demarcation between old and young, should apply itself to these two alternatives. The young should use the first sense of the term *Tashlich*; the old should use the second sense of the term.

This interpretation may be supported by an inference from the dialogue between Rabbi Nechemiah Hagadol and Rabbi Akiva. Rabbi Akiva asked Rabbi Nechemiah, "By virtue of what merit did you reach such a good old age?" Rabbi Nechemiah replied, "I never accepted presents; I was never exact in my demands to meet my standards; I was generous with my money (*Megillah* 28)." Most likely, what he meant to imply is that to be old graciously is a developing process; one should not "get old," one should "grow old"; one should learn when young how to grow old graciously.

Thus the prayer *Al tashlicheinu l'eit ziknah*. God should not cast us in the frame of the first sense of the word *Tashlich* but should grace us with the interpretation of the second, "and he threw his mantle to him." This presumed interpretation of the dialogue as an aid to solve the dilemma of the two prayers is only an inference. The deeper and more profound meaning of the dialogue is as follows: Rabbi Akiva's question, "Is the antiquity of the Jewish people a drain on their vitality?" as *l'havdil*, the aging of other nations that age causes decay and decline. Does the verse "The one (*echad*) lamb you shall offer in the morning, and the other lamb you shall offer toward evening" (Exodus 28:39) not indicate a difference between the morning sacrifice and the afternoon sacrifice? Rabbi Nechemiah, using himself as a metaphor that the Jewish people should not receive presents, responded that the word *echad* signifies the chosen in the herd which implies that the Jewish people are unique even in that aspect. That age does not decrease their vigor, providing they follow the required virtues—first, that they do not expect "gifts" from alien cultures and habits and, second, that they not demand any restitution for our contributions to them. If we will not take from others, then the *Ribbono shel Olam* will not take from us His Holy Spirit, as it says, "Do not cast us away from Yourself and do not remove Your Holy Spirit from us."

// Rabbi Aaron Parry
Young Israel of Beverly Hills, California

THE POWER OF *TZEDAKAH*

Found in the *chazzan*'s repetition of *musaf* in the Rosh Hashanah *machzor* is the most stirring of the day's *tefillot*—*U'Nesana Tokef.* The story concerning the authorship of this awesome piece of liturgy is, in itself, an incredible episode of Jewish history (see ArtScroll *Machzor,* p. 480). This prayer highlights the essence of the day—*Klal Yisrael* standing in judgment before the Creator with many categories of its existence hanging in balance. "Who will live and who will die . . . , who will be impoverished and who will be enriched, who will be degraded and who will be exalted."

At the conclusion of this *piyut,* the congregation proclaims with confidence; "But *teshuvah,* and *tefillah,* and *tzedakah* can avert an evil decree!" On the surface, notwithstanding the fervent way in which this plea is uttered, it seems more like a statement of fact than a true petition for Divine mercy and amnesty. Furthermore, the tripartite grouping of these components (the three *T*'s), poses a question; we can readily understand the *paytan*'s selection of *teshuvah* and *tefillah* as primary ingredients for annulment of an unfavorable decree, but among all the positive *mitzvot,* why is *tzedakah* singled out as the final attribute of this special formula for arousing *HaShem*'s compassion and pardon?

The centrality of these three elements in Judaism is indicated by their subtle inclusion in the *mitzvah* of *Ahavat HaShem* found in *Kriat Shema;* "And you shall love *HaShem* with all your *heart,* with all your *soul,* and with all your *might*" (Deuteronomy 6:5). *Tefillah* is the paradigm for service of the heart, where one's inner thoughts and feelings are processed, ruminated, and then expressed verbally in words of prayer. Referring to the verse in Deuteronomy (11:13), "To love the Lord your God, and to serve Him with all your heart," *Chazal* concluded that the meaning of the verse under consideration refers to prayer, because this *is* the way a person serves his God—with his *heart*.

Teshuvah, often associated with fasting, self-mortification, and denial, sincere remorse for wrong-doings, and *viduy*, is an *avodah* (religious service) geared for the lofty attainment of purification of one's deeds. This is clearly a function of the *soul*. The deeper one can access his *koach Haneshama*, the greater is he equipped to affect a lasting *shinuy*, or alteration of his thought process and actions.

The final ingredient, *tzedakah*, is a set of all-encompassing actions of Divine service that influences one's entire being, as we will soon discover. In Talmud *Berakot* (61a), we find the words "with all your might" (Deuteronomy 6:5) interpreted to mean, "with all your money." The simple message conveyed is, since there are individuals to whom money is more endearing than their very souls, the Torah needs to empahsize to what extent one must strive in fulfillment of the *mitzvah* of *Ahavat HaShem*. It's an axiom of *Yiddishkeit* that *tzedakah* is a vital occupation, and Torah literature is replete with adulation of its virtue, but just how does charity influence one's entire being? I believe the answer to this question will offer one insight as to why this *mitzvah* is an imperative for invoking Divine mercy and averting an "evil decree."

Shlomo *Hamelech* teaches: "Wealth will not assist a person during a day of His wrath, but charity can save one from death" (*Mishlei* 11:4). The obvious *peshat* in these profound words is that in anticipation of a day of judgment a person can redeem himself with *tzedakah* from the severest of penalties by "bribing" the Judge, literally achieving a new lease on life.

To elaborate more deeply, the Avudraham explains this verse on the basis of the mystical concept that each of the *taryag mitzvot* (613 mitzvot) corresponds to a specific limb, organ, or sinew of the human body. Each time a person performs a Torah precept, or avoids transgressing one, he gives "nourishment" to that correlating part of his anatomy. This "nourishment," as we are taught, can influence a person's physical and spiritual well-being in this world. It is the consummate holistic medicine.

But, as the Avudraham adds, the benefits don't stop in *olam hazeh* (this world). When a person performs a *mitzvah* of the Torah, he is also nurturing that corresponding limb in preparation for the World To Come. Alternatively, if he fails to utilize that specific limb in the fulfillment of a *mitzvah* he effectively has blemished it for *olam habah* (the World to Come). Let's say, for example, one was remiss in the area of *tefillin*. Although the person may be otherwise worthy of being resuscitated at the time of *Techiyat Hameysim*, he will be seen walking around with a missing left arm! An eternal embarrassment indeed!

Enter the power of *tzedakah*. The dynamics of this *mitzvah* are such that when a person gives away a portion of his hard-earned wages, he is essentially sacrificing a part of his being (see also the Sefas Emes on *Parshat Vayikra*; "*Adom ki yakriv mikem korban*. . . ."). Depending on one's occupation, a person either exerts intense mental strain or expends great physical energy. Thus, any act of *tzedakah* is a veritable offering of himself. The magnanimity of one's giving is not lost on the Almighty, of course, and He in His great mercy responds in kind. On each Rosh Hashanah, *HaShem* allows a person's accrued merit of *tzedakah* to "bail him out" of an ugly decree—thus averting any "eternal embarrassment" caused by his laxity in other precepts.

To conclude with a paraphrase of the Chofetz Chaim at the end of his *sefer, Ahavas Chesed*:

> In these times we see with our own eyes how the attribute of strict justice grows stronger in the world from day to day. All kinds of maladies and unnatural deaths abound. There is a lack of Divine influence in the world, so that each day is more cursed than the day before. How much must we increase the prevalence of *tzedakah*. Perhaps in this way we shall overcome the severity of the judgment and the world will become filled with mercy. (Part 2, chapter 3)

❖ CHAPTER 61 ❖

Yom Kippur

Rabbi Naphtali Burnstein

Young Israel of Cleveland, Ohio

One of the highlights of the *Yomim Noraim* is the *Kol Nidrei,* recited at the very onset of Yom Kippur. People all over the world, even many Jews who otherwise do not attend any *minyanim* throughout the year, come to shul on the eve of Yom Kippur to be present for *Kol Nidrei.* What is the connection between *Kol Nidrei* and Yom Kippur, and why is such significance given to this particular part of the *tefillot* of Yom Kippur?

One might suggest that when we enter the holiness of Yom Kippur, a day of *teshuvah* (repentance) and introspection, a closer examination of our speech, and those sins involved with speech, is in order. The *Kol Nidrei* reminds us of one aspect of the power of speech. In particular, it reminds us of the importance of keeping one's word and following through on the commitments, promises, vows, and oaths that have been made in the past.

Whether one interprets the function of *Kol Nidrei* as a nullification of past vows (according to the view of the Rosh) or a declaration to invalidate all future vows (according to the view of *Rabbeinu* Tam), the message is quite clear: Anything a person says or commits himself to is important and must be followed through. With this message in mind, we are then ready to begin Yom Kippur to approach atonement and purity.

Harav Yosef Ber Halevi Soloveitchik, *zt"l,* however, suggests a deeper meaning behind *Kol Nidrei* and its special relationship to Yom Kippur.

As mentioned earlier, some commentaries understand the function of *Kol Nidrei* as a form of *hatorat Nidarim,* retroactively nullifying all vows that have been made during the past year. After concluding this process, one is technically exempt from all vows, oaths, and so on, made in the past that we are permitted to nullify (as dictated to by the *halachot* of *Hatorat Nidarim*).

Other commentaries interpret the *Kol Nidrei* as a proclamation designed to protect the individual from future declarations, vows, oaths, and so on. Through this proclamation one cancels, in advance, any and all validity of those future statements and commitments. A careful analysis of the halachic ramifications of each of these approaches—as well as which approach (if not both) is followed in normative practice, can be found in *sifrei halachah*.

Following the approach of the Rosh, Tur, and others that *Kol Nidrei* is a form of *Hatorat Nidarim*, the following question could be raised. If Yom Kippur (along with *techuvah* of course) allows the individual to achieve atonement for all kinds of sins, why is there a need for *Hatorat Nidarim*? Even if someone violated his/her own commitments, Yom Kippur can atone for that sin without removal of the vow. Why, then, is there a need to remove those past commitments retroactively?

Rabbi Soloveitchik, *zt"l*, says we see, from the necessity of using *Hatorat Nidarim* and not relying on Yom Kippur alone, that it is better to remove a sin totally, and even retroactively, if possible, than to rely on the atonement of *teshuvah* and Yom Kippur.

With all other sins (*Shabbat, kashrut,* sins between man and man, and so on), there is no mechanism to remove those sins as though they never happened. For those sins, our only hope is to achieve complete forgiveness on Yom Kippur.

Sins involving oral commitments such as oaths, vows, and so on, however, allow for the possibility of totally removing the sin or violation as if it were never made at all. If the vow never existed, then obviously it was never really violated. Because of this unique characteristic, found and nullified only through *Hatorat Nidarim*, the individual's sins are retroactively removed—rendering that person pure and innocent.

Rabbi Soloveitchik, *zt"l*, goes a step further. He suggests that if this alternative of totally (even retroactively) erasing a sin exists, and is *not* pursued, even the process of Yom Kippur and its own mechanism of forgiveness will not work. The reasoning behind this is as follows:

There are four components to teshuvah:

1. Regret of the past (*Charatah al ha'avar*)
2. Confession (*viduy*)
3. Leaving the sin (*Azivas hachet*)
4. Acceptance for the future (*Kabbalah al ha'atid*)

The above four categories can also be combined into two basic categories:

1. Regret of the past
2. Acceptance for the future

A major part of regret is *bushah*, a sense of embarrassment. The Rambam, in *Hilchot Teshuvah* (1:1), describes a proper *viduy* (confession) as including the following: "I regret and am *embarrassed* by my actions." The Rambam through his illustration of what a proper *viduy* should include, is teaching us that a person cannot truly regret something from his past without a feeling of *shame* and *embarrassment*. Without a feeling of embarrassment, one cannot be a true *mischaret,* one who has regrets. If *bushah* is a necessary component of *teshuvah,* then it is not sufficient to want forgiveness for a sin committed. There must be an empty feeling and a desire to erase that sin and experience in whatever way possible. An individual who becomes embarrassed by his/her sins and really wants to distance himself from them will look for methods to show *HaShem* that he truly feels this way.

When a person nullifies his vows, he shows a determination to rid himself totally, when possible, of any trace of sin that might remain. Yom Kippur and its built-in *kaparah* will not suffice; therefore, the method of *Hatorat Nidarim* is chosen.

Saying *Kol Nidrei* on the eve of Yom Kippur is the greatest testimony we can have that we are embarrassed about our sins—an embarrassment without which our *teshuvah* would not be complete. What better way do we have to approach Yom Kippur than by proclaiming our sincerest regrets over the past, as reflected in our saying *Kol Nidrei,* thereby showing our commitment to become closer to *HaShem*.

Those who interpret *Kol Nidrei* as a proclamation for the future see in it a statement of commitment toward the future. The Rambam, in explaining what is required in "acceptance for the future", explains that it is not enough physically to remove oneself from past sins. There must be a psychological separation as well. As the Rambam adds (*Hilchot Teshuvah* 2:2), "that *HaShem* should be able to testify that the sin committed will not be repeated." To achieve such a level requires a psychological break and a removal from the past. A mere physical break will not suffice.

Whether we read and interpret the *Kol Nidrei* as referring to the past or the future, its connection to Yom Kippur and *teshuvah* is quite strong, and we should all have its particular significance in mind as we prepare—both as individuals and as a *klal*—for the day we all pray will be a *yom selichah u-mechilah l'kol.*

Rabbi Moshe Faskowitz

Young Israel of Redwood, New York

Life has been described as a parade of marching moments. Life's challenge is to seize the right moment before it marches past. The right moment can provide the inspiration that propels man upward and onward. It can elevate the level of his performance far beyond that which he thought to be the limit of his capabilities.

Ideally, these moments of inspiration and opportunity, of energy and potential, the *she'as hakosher* (opportune time) must be seized before they pass by. Unfortunately, more often than not, they slip from man's grasp to escape and disappear; never to return again.

The prophet Yeshiah (Yeshaiahu 6) expressed this best when he said, "In the year of the death of the King Uziyahu, I saw the spirit of God, sitting upon His throne of glory, surrounded by angels who stood above: and the angels cried out in song unto one another and said, *Kadosh, Kadosh, Kadosh.*" The Prophet then continues and cries out in despair, *oy li ki nidmeiti*, "Woe is to me that I was silent. Woe is to me that I did not join the angels in song." The *Yalkut Shimoni* adds, "for had I joined them in song at that moment, I would have achieved eternal life. I could have been lifted above the human experience and become like one of the angels themselves. If only I had seized the moment; instead I was silent. *Oy li chi nidmeiti.* Woe is me that I let the moment slip by as I stood in silence. A once-in-a-lifetime opportunity never to repeat itself is lost forever."

The Gemara in Tractate *Nedarim* relates the remarkable tale of the wife of Rabbi Akiva. After twelve uninterrupted years of study at the great Academy, Rabbi Akiva finally returned home. He stood at the window poised to enter his home when he heard his father-in-law chastising his wife. "Your husband is worthless," he said. "He is an ignoramus who has abandoned you for twelve years. Forget him!" She responds by saying, "Surely he is studying Torah, and if he could hear me I would tell him to study another twelve years." Rabbi Akiva heeded her words, turned around, and immediately returned to study for twelve more years, after which he returned in splendor and glory, the greatest Sage of his time.

The question that comes to mind is why Rabbi Akiva didn't walk in for one short moment and greet his wife before he returned to the *yeshivah*. Could he not have provided his *Eishet Chayil* with a brief moment of comfort, assurance, and encouragement before he continued his study of Torah? Would a few moments of kindness have impeded him from his ultimate spiritual goals?

Rabbi Akiva, however, perceived at that very moment what the prophet Yeshaiah failed to perceive when his moment came. When graced with inspiration, do not allow the inspiration to fade. Seize the opportunity and act. Had Rabbi Akiva entered his home to speak to his beloved wife even for a few minutes, might he not have wavered? Might his relentless resolve not have been sapped by the emotional longings for the comfort of his wife and family? Rabbi Akiva recognized the moment of truth and grabbed it. He made his decision, never looked back, and ultimately attained a level of holiness and greatness that no other Sage, before or after, was able to achieve.

At the end of *Haftarah Parshat Pinchas*, Eliyahu Hanavi approaches Elisha ben Shefat as he works in the field "and he threw his cloak toward him." A symbolic gesture that said, "Come with me. You have been chosen to be my disciple. You will inherit the exclusive role of *navi LaShem* from me."

Elisha stopped what he was doing, abandoned his cattle, and ran after Eliyahu, thereby indicating his fervent acceptance of Eliyahu's proposal.

"But," he asked, "may I first go and kiss my father and mother goodbye?" "You may go," Eliyahu answered, "for I know you shall return to me!"

What a remarkable exchange. Elisha was about to embark upon a lifelong journey with Eliyahu, perhaps never to see his parents again. Yet he felt compelled to seek permission "to kiss his parents goodbye." Did he believe for a moment that the prophet would deprive him of this simple gesture of love and honor toward his parents? This historic vignette clearly illustrates man's need to seize the moment and not allow it to slip away. Elisha's query to Eliyahu was truly profound, more than the surface words themselves indicate.

"If I go back to kiss my parents, do you think I might change my mind? Am I strong enough to resist the temptations of wealth, comfort, family, and home that I so readily discard now? The intense commitment that I feel at this very moment, can it endure? Will I lose this moment if I don't follow you now? Will love of my parents and family weaken my resolve? Unlike Yeshaiah, I do not want to have to say, *Oy li chi nidmeiti*, why did I let the opportunity fly away!"

In response, Eliyahu said to Elisha, "You may go, for I know you well. You will return to me. You have the strength and commitment firmly imbued in your spirit. You will not fail me or yourself."

It is a sad commentary on human nature that man knows the virtue of seizing the moment yet so frequently lets the moment pass. How often do we hear people lamenting, "If only I had proposed right then! She would certainly have said yes." Or, "If only I had made my pitch right then and there, I would have received the contract." Or, "If only I had said, I am sorry, at yesterday's meeting; that was the perfect moment to apologize." And so on and so forth.

Despite this unhappy assertion, we should recognize that we are not really at fault. These rare moments jump at us so quickly that we are often too confused and overwhelmed either to recognize or to take advantage of them until "later," when it is too late. It almost takes a prophet to anticipate the *she'as Hakosher*, that opportune time those special moments; because we are unprepared, we tend to lose them entirely.

There is, however, one exception to the rule. One *she'as Hakosher*, one moment of intense inspirational potential, that doesn't just jump at us; a moment we can, indeed, anticipate; a moment that can thrust us high and above, a moment that can lift us up and over every challenge of life. That moment is the (*zaman kapparah l'kol toldosom*)—a time of forgiveness atonement for all their offspring—the Holy Day of Yom Kippur, that once-a-year opportunity for *selichah u'mechilah*, for forgiveness and pardon, when the doors of *tshuvah* stand wide open and beckon us all to enter and take advantage of this special day. "It is inscribed on Rosh Hashonah and sealed on Yom Kippur who shall live and who shall die."

At this moment, our very lives are in balance. This is the moment of judgment. How we respond to the opportunity Yom Kippur presents us with is the most critical challenge of our lives. Sincere commitment and resolve to be a better Jew—between man and God and between man and his fellow man—can guarantee the fine future we all long for.

How apropos, then, are the immortal words of Rabbi Yehudah Hanasi: "It is possible for man to attain his whole world in one short moment."

Be prepared to march away with the moment before the moment marches past you.

Rabbi Reuven Drucker

Young Israel of Greenfield, Detroit, Michigan

In my opinion, one of the most beautiful passages in the entire *Tur* (§125) in his description of the spiritual dynamics that operate whenever the Jewish people respond to the *Kedushah* prayer:

> Recount to My children [the Jewish people] what I do when they sanctify Me by reciting, "*Kadosh, Kadosh, Kadosh* . . ." Teach them to raise their eyes heavenward [when they recite these words] . . . for I experience no greater enjoyment in this world than the moment that their eyes are peering into Mine and Mine into theirs [so to speak]. (*Sefer Heichalos*)

Our recitation of *Kedushah* is not merely a declaration of *HaShem*'s holiness, omnipresence, and eternity; it is also an encounter with the Holy One. What, however, is the objective of this meeting?

The *Kehilas Yitzchok* (Vilna) explains with the following *mashal* (parable):

> A man once prepared a regal banquet in honor of his father, who was visiting from a distant land. Upon finishing all the delicacies, the father asked his son to direct the waiter to bring some beer to quench his thirst. The son turned to the waiter and requested that a select bottle of wine be brought from the cellar. Astonished, the other guests reminded the son that his father had ordered beer, not wine. The son responded, "You heard my father's words, but I understood his intent, for I looked into his eyes and saw his true wish was wine. He asked for beer to spare me any embarrassment in case I had no wine."

Eye contact is an intense form of communication between two individuals, for it connects their hearts and reveals their innermost thoughts. When the Jewish people focus upon Heaven during *Kedushah*, *HaShem* takes great delight that they attempt to establish "eye contact" and truly discern His will.

Yom Kippur, more than any other day in the year, provides us with the opportunity to re-establish our "eye contact" with the *Ribono shel Olam*. The pressures of the material world throughout the year sometimes cause us to veer from what *HaShem* truly desires of us. On Yom Kippur, the Jew divests himself of his physical concerns by "resting," as the Rambam explains, from eating, drinking, bathing, and so on (Hilchot *Hil. Shvisas Asar* 1:4). Our *neshamah*, the pure soul, is thus left undistracted to reconnect with *HaShem*'s will. In essence, Yom Kippur is an entire day of *Kedushah*.

It is difficult to look someone in the eye if you know that you have hurt him, but, when we are engaged in the process of seeking forgiveness, such eye contact is a demonstration of sincerity. Gazing upward during *Kedushah* on Yom Kippur necessitates that we review our specific transgressions, our lapses in Torah observance, and sincerely repent by acknowledging our wrongdoing, regretting it, and committing ourselves to avoiding its repetition.

But, from the *Sefer Heichalos*, we learn an additional dimension. After repenting our particular sins so that this eye contact can be re-established, we then enter the second stage of redetermining what our Father in heaven seeks from us in our personal lives. Life's most profound questions need be re-asked: Why was I created? How can I magnify His honor on earth? How well have I performed in serving *HaShem*? Where do I need remediation? How can I restructure my life to enhance my performance?

Our answers to some of these questions will undoubtedly be different, but we are guaranteed one thing. As *Sefer Heichalos* mentioned, *HaShem* also "looks into our eyes." This refers to the *siyata d'Shomaya* that *HaShem* provides—the Heavenly assistance that He gives everyone who seeks Him sincerely—so that we can accomplish our heartfelt plans for spiritual improvement.

Let us all hope that in the merit of our efforts this Yom Kippur, we are *zoche* (merit) to see that time when, "All creatures will bow down before You and form one unit to perform Your will with a perfect heart."

CHINUCH AND YOM KIPPUR

The custom of feeding children who are not required to fast on Yom Kippur is undeniably *halachah l'ma'aseh*, the practical law (see *Mishneh Brurah* 616:9 for details concerning which children are exempted from fasting). Nevertheless, the justification for doing so has given rise to an interesting discussion in the halachic literature. The following is a précis of some of the issues involved.

It should be kept in mind at the outset that an adult who eats on Yom Kippur has violated both a positive and negative commandment (Leviticus 23:27, 29). As we know, parents have the *mitzvah* of *chinuch*—training a child to perform *mitzvot*. Let us review some of the principles of *chinuch*:

1. When a child attains sufficient understanding, we are required to train him to perform the positive commandments (for example, to eat *matzah* on the *Seder* night).
2. When a child attains sufficient understanding, we are required to train him to avoid transgressing the negative commandments (for example, to avoid eating non-kosher meat).
3. If a child who has not attained sufficient understanding decides *on his* own to violate a prohibition (for example, to write on *Shabbat*), the parents are not required to stop him [*Mishneh Brurah* 343:3];
4. However, a parent may not directly engage a child in a prohibited act (for example, put non-kosher food into his mouth), even if he has not attained sufficient understanding.

   Another illustration of this point is the prohibition against bringing a baby *kohein* into a room where there is a corpse, because of the prohibition against defilement. Even though the young child is obviously exempted from performing *mitzvot*, nevertheless, one who carries him into the room causes him to violate what would be a prohibition for an adult *kohein*. Therefore, the person carrying the child has violated Torah law, since he put the child into this circumstance (see *Yevamos* 114a). If however, an infant *kohein* crawls into such a room on his own volition, then there is no requirement to remove him (as number 3 above). [Cf., however, *Mizrachi* to Leviticus 21:1.)

Children who are about 5 years old are required, because of *chinuch*, to eat *matzah* on the *Seder* night (number 1). Why aren't they also required to fast on Yom Kippur?

The Rambam (Hilchot *Hil. Shvisas Asar* 2:11) rules that younger children should not be trained in the *mitzvah* of fasting on Yom Kippur because the lack of nourishment could be detrimental to their health and result in physical danger. Thus, the principle of *pikuach nefesh*, saving a life, overrides the consideration of training a young child to fast. *Minchas Chinuch* (313), however, points out that *pikuach nefesh* allows only the minimum amount of prohibited activity to be performed in order to preserve a life. In this case, we would, therefore, be required to limit the amount of food given to the non-fasting child to the absolute minimum needed to maintain his health. Admittedly, a precise determination of how much food should be provided is not possible, and so no measurements and limitations need be made. However, *Minchas Chinuch* does caution against feeding the child directly (if he is capable of eating on his own), for this would constitute a violation of number 4 above.

In his caveat against directly feeding the non-fasting child, *Minchas Chinuch* echoes the concern of *Mogen Avrohom* (616:2). Both authorities assume that food on Yom Kippur is equivalent to non-kosher food and, thus, cannot be placed in the child's mouth. Chofetz Chaim (*Sha'ar Tzion* 616:9) questions the *Mogen Avrohom*'s assumption. He argues that food on Yom Kippur cannot be considered intrinsically forbidden for a young child as non-kosher food, since it is not forbidden to be eaten by him either by Torah or rabbinic law. As a result, there should be no restriction even about placing food directly in his mouth.

Zichron Yosef (number 6, cited by *Miktra'ei Kodesh*, chap. 43) advances an argument slightly different from that of the Chofetz Chaim. He suggests that food on Yom Kippur is not considered intrinsically forbidden, even for an adult. The prohibition requires only that the individual refrain from eating food, but the food remains a permissible object. Therefore, the restrictions of number four do not apply, and the child may be fed directly. In addition, he opines that younger children who eat on Yom Kippur are actually engaged in the *mitzvah* of *pikuach nefesh* (as per Rambam above). Therefore, a parent who places food in the child's mouth is assisting him and training him in the *mitzvah* of preserving a life. Thus, there should be no distinction made between allowing the child to eat or feeding him directly, as *Minchas Chinuch* suggested.

In section four we discussed directly engaging a child in a prohibited act and gave as an example placing non-kosher food in his mouth. The illustration follows the more restrictive view advanced by *Zichron Yosef*. From *Mogen Avrohom*, however, it would appear that even placing the food down in front of the child would also constitute a direct engagement in a prohibited act. *Mikra'ei Kodesh* (above) cites a statement from Rav Shmuel Salant, *zt"l*, that even according to *Mogen Avrohom*, if the food was not placed directly before the child but, rather, the child needed to maneuver in order to obtain the food, it would not be considered directly engaging the child in a prohibited act and would not be proscribed by number four above.

The weighty responsibility of properly educating our children in the Torah's ways requires our full study of the laws of *chinuch*. It behooves us this Yom Kippur to determine whether we need to improve our performance in any facet of this *mitzvah*.

Rabbi Dovid Plaut

Young Israel of Greater Buffalo, New York

We have heard the statement innumerable times: On Rosh Hashanah, we are judged, and on Yom Kippur the judgment is sealed. What exactly does this mean to us? Once we are judged, why do we need to wait for Yom Kippur? If one would want to argue that everyone is given a last chance, then why can't that chance be before the *Din* (judgment) of Rosh Hashanah? In other words, why can't the *aseret yemai teshuvah* (Ten Days of Repentance) come before Rosh Hashanah, and after that, we could have one final judgment.

Furthermore, we know that Yom Kippur is a day of *kaparah* (forgiveness) and *teshuvah* (repentance). This we know from the *posuk*, "For through this day He will atone for you to cleanse you from all your sins, before *HaShem* you will be cleansed" (Leviticus 16:30). What needs explanation is that the *Gemara* doesn't give a source for the fact that there is a *chatimah* (seal) on Yom Kippur. We know that Rosh Hashanah is a day of *Din*—from the *posuk*, "Blow the *shofar* at the moon's renewal at the appointed time for our festive day because it is a decree for Israel, a judgment day for the God of Jacob" (Psalms 81: 4–5), but where is it derived that Yom Kippur is the day of the *chatimah*?

I think that the most obvious explanation is that *chatimah* is somehow implied in *kaparah*. Since we know that Yom Kippur is a day of *kaparah*, our Rabbis understood that it is also a day of the sealing of the verdict. However, we now have to explain what the relationship is between the two concepts, of *chatimah* and *kaparah*. Another query regarding Rosh Hashanah and Yom Kippur is Rav Yisroel Salanter's famous thought-provoking question, Why does Rosh Hashanah come before Yom Kippur? If *HaShem* will give us atonement anyway, it would seem more logical first to give us the pardon and then to bring us to judgment, not the reverse.

Let us try to define the differences between the basic nature of Rosh Hashanah and Yom Kippur. Rosh Hashanah is the anniversary of Adam's creation. *Hakedosh baruch Hu* (the Almighty) decided to start the world conservatively—that is, with one human being. Although man's destiny was to multiply and inhabit the earth, initially *HaShem* created but one person. Now, there is a big disadvantage with being the only man alive—there is nobody with whom to share the blame if something goes wrong. Also *HaShem* can pay full attention to that one person, which means that Adam was under intense scrutiny. Yet another consequence of being the only human is that there is no one with whom you can be compared. Most of the time we maintain our self-esteem by saying to ourselves, "I'm not as bad as so-and-so."

This enormous source of comfort is one that Adam had to live without in the beginning. Every year, when Rosh Hashanah comes around, we revert to the situation of *Adam Harishon*. Each individual is the only person in the universe, and *HaShem* scrutinizes him or her with total attention. This is the simple understanding of what the *Mishnah* says: "All mankind passes before *HaShem* like members of the flock" (*Rosh Hashonah* 16a). The *Gemara* says that this means that each person will appear in front of *Hakadosh baruch Hu* in a way that will preclude comparison with others.

On Rosh Hashanah it's every man for himself, which also means that each of our deeds is looked at separately. On Rosh Hashanah we cannot comfort ourselves by saying that we are basically good people. Every *tefillah* we pray, every *brachah* we say (or do not say), every word we speak is analyzed and judged. We are stripped of all the alibis; the cloak of collective anonymity is removed. This removal of anonymity is, in fact, the reason for the fear that one experiences when he is brought into court. A person knows that in a court of law the crime that had been committed is considered without taking into consideration anything else about the person, his past or future. This is the *din* on Rosh Hashanah. This adds a new depth of meaning to the statement of *Chazal*, "The Almighty is exacting with the righteous like the shaft of a hair." Generally, the hair on a person's head is looked at as one unit. When it comes to *tzaddikim*, however, *HaShem* divides and dissects their deeds even if those deeds are normally viewed as one whole. This is the comparison between the deeds of a *tzaddik* and God's judgement.

We can now also appreciate the idea of *midat Hadin*, *Hakadosh baruch Hu*'s attribute of strictness. *Midat Hadin* does not have the meaning that sometimes *HaShem* is in the mood to be strict, whereas at other times He is in a mood to be lenient. It does mean that at certain times God looks at the details of a person's life irrespective of other, mitigating factors. That kind of scrutiny is very hard to stand up to.

Midat Hadin is appropriate at the beginning of a creation. Not only is a thing simplest when first made but there is also an initial burst of enthusiasm. Both of these factors give the new creation the energy required to stand up to the exacting standard of *Din*. With the passage of time, things get more complicated, and one's energy wanes. Then the creation is in the second stage, in which everything is looked at as a whole. As events unfold and—this is the case with the creation of man—the world interacts more and more; instead of seeing a series of individual dots, as is done under *Midat Hadin*, we see a whole picture with black and white and shades of gray, all contributing something to the final version.

This is the natural evolution from a Rosh Hashanah perspective to that of Yom Kippur. *Hakadosh Baruch Hu* changes His focus from seeing one person at a time to seeing the whole Jewish nation as one.

"Rabbi Akiva said: Praiseworthy are you Israel. Before whom do you cleanse yourselves? Who cleanses you? Your Father in heaven. . . . Just as a *mikvah* purifies the contaminated, so does the Holy One, Blessed Be He, purify Israel" (Tractate *Yoma*, final *Mishnah*). What Rabbi Akiva stated is that on Yom Kippur *Klal Yisrael* collectively stands before *HaShem* who is *mitahar* them (purifies them). The reason that *Klal Yisrael* gets that *taharah* is only that they stand before God as a nation.

What is a *chatimah* (seal)? The *Gemara* says that the seal of *HaShem* is *emet* (truth). What does that mean? The seal or signature usually comes after a written letter. What is the purpose of it? The body of the letter contains whatever information is to be conveyed, but the signature of the letter authenticates it, says that someone stands behind all that is written. Stating that the seal of *HaShem* is *emet*, tells us that everything in the world—things of all different sizes and colors and shapes—is simply a manifestation of God's truth. In other words, a *chatimah* is a summation, a generalization, or a distillation of something.

Affixing a seal at the end of something is not an arbitrary step but a natural, logical part of a judgment. On Rosh Hashanah everything is looked at in isolated detail, while on Yom Kippur God considers everything together. This concept is supported by the Ritvah (*Rosh Hasanah* 16a starting *K'man*) who asks our question. What is the difference between the verdict of Rosh Hashanah and the seal of Yom Kippur? Seemingly, all that is required of *HaShem* is to say, "so-and-so is guilty or innocent." The Ritva answers that on Rosh Hashanah the judgment is rendered but on Yom Kippur the punishment is assigned.

What is the difference between the verdict and the sentence? In our secular court system we also distinguish between the delivery of a verdict and the sentencing. They are done at different times and are taken as separate phases of justice. Why is this so? Because when we try a case we are interested only in the guilt or innocence of the accused; nothing else matters. However, when it comes to punishment we take the whole situation into consideration. That is why the court is reconvened at a later time. Before sentencing, we take into account the past record of the accused, the various circumstances that may have been operating when the crime was committed, and any other considerations that society may have in this case.

In short, the trial is done with narrow vision, whereas the sentencing is done with a wide view. This is what the Ritva means. Yom Kippur is when the sentencing is done, and "the sealing" as well—because they are really one and the same. Yom Kippur is the day that *HaShem* looks at everything as a whole, and therefore the *din* is sealed and sentence is made. The way the Torah tells this is by saying that Yom Kippur is a Day of Atonement—*Yom Kaparah*. There are many ways to attain *kaparah*, chief among them *korbanot* (sacrifices). Others include learning Torah, performing *gemilut chasadim* (kind deeds), prayer, giving charity, and so on. The common denominator is that *kaparah* is achieved when a person breaks down the barriers between God and *Klal Yisrael*. When a person acts, not out of his own personal goals, but out of a sense of belonging to *HaShem* or *Klal Yisrael*, he achieves *kaparah*. Therefore, it is *kaparah* that underlies the whole essence of Yom Kippur. By fasting, by the *Kohein Gadol* doing the *avodah* for *Klal Yisrael*, we achieve a unity which *HaShem* that, by *HaShem*'s grace, gives us His atonement at the time the sentence or the seal is concluded.

This understanding enhances the words of the S'fas Emes that Yom Kippur stands opposite the *brit* of *milah*. *Milah* stands as an unchangeable sign that we, the Jewish people, are one with God; are essentially righteous people, therefore worthy of *kaparah*. As we say in the blessing after the *brit milah*, "his descendants are sealed with the mark of the holy covenant."

May *HaShem*, in His mercy gives us all a *G'mar Chatimah Tovah*.

The *yom tov* of Yom Kippur is unique in the Jewish calendar in many ways. For example, it is the only *yom tov* on which fasting is required; all the *avodah* in the temple is done only by the *Kohein Gadol*, and only on this day is the *Kohein Gadol* allowed to enter the *Kodesh Hakedoshim*.

However, I think there is one *avodah* (service) that needs more explanation. The main *korbanot* are the *par* (cow) of the *Kohein Gadol*, and the two *sa'irim* (goats) brought by the people. Before offering the cow, the *Kohein Gadol* says the solemn *viduy* (confession) on behalf of his immediate family. Then, after casting the lots on the two goats, he makes the *viduy* on behalf of all the *kohanim*. Then an elaborate, extremely difficult *avodah* takes place that includes bringing in the incense and throwing the blood in the Holy of Holies. Then—almost anticlimatically—the *Kohein Gadol* goes to the final goal and, wihtout any ado, he loads on the unsuspecting goat all of *Klal Yisrael*'s sins. The goat is then escorted by an ordinary Jew to a very unceremonious end at the bottom of a cliff.

How incedible that, despite the elaborate service required to atone for the sins of the *kohanim*, *all* the sins of *Klal Yisrael*—the Jewish people—could be tossed away with such ease! How are we to understand this?

The Ramban says in *Hilchos Teshuvah* (chapter 1), that the power of the *sa'ir hamishtaleach* (the goat that is sent away) is truly remarkable. Without it we need a whole series of steps to attain *kaparah* (atonement). Sometimes we must suffer; sometimes we even must wait for death. However, with the *sa'ir hamisht leach*, that magical goat, *kaparah* was assured. Even now that we do not have a *sa'ir hamishtaleach*, the day of Yom Kippur affects atonement for us. How does that work?

The Maharal of Prague, in the last several pages of his sermon of *Shabbat Teshuvah*, gives an eye-opening explanation of the whole concept of the *Sa'ir Hamishtaleach*. Using the Maharal's basic idea, I would like to explain the atonement of Yom Kippur in the following way. The Talmud in *Kiddushin* says that if a seemingly bad person marries someone on the condition that he is a totally righteous person, we say that the marriage is possibly valid. Even though he may appear to us to be anything but a righteous person, he may have been inspired to repent at the time of his marriage, thereby fulfilling that condition and making the marriage valid. We see from this *Gemara* that, in an instant, a person can transform himself from a wicked person to a righteous one. Righteous means only that he is in control of his decisions and will do the right thing from now on. This in no way exonerates the sins he did up to now; they must be addressed and, in some way, rectified. This is done by the process of *kaparah*. *Teshuvah* changes the person and his future, whereas atonement makes an individual come to grips with the past. The standard *kaparah* is a *korban* (sacrifice). The concept of bringing a *korban* is the thought that we slaughter the animal because we ourselves deserve to be slaughtered for our sins. When the animals blood pours onto the altar, the guilty party must respond as if it were his own blood. That means that the process of *kaparah* is really a process whereby we isolate the exact source of the sins within us. We justify our own continued existence by saying that the sins were not done with our heart and soul. Indeed, they were really done without our consent. A person bringing a *korban* says that the sins can be traced to our body and its cravings. It was a person's animal nature that caused the sin. When we seek *kaparah*, we are acknowledging responsibility, but at the same time we say that the source of the *averah* is our body; however, our soul is still intact and pure. Therefore, we want to sacrifice our body because it alone is responsible for our lapses. The beauty and the paradox of *korbanot* is that we still need our bodies. Try as we may, we cannot separate ourselves from our bodies. As long as we wish to live in this world, our body is not expendable. With all its faults, it is the only one we have. Therefore, we conclude that the need for *korbanot*, or for suffering or, even, death, to achieve *kaparah* arises because the villain lies within ourselves—namely, our *guf* (corporeal self). The difficulty in *kaparah* lies in that we must destroy the sin yet keep the culprit (that is, the body) that allows the sin to occur.

On Yom Kippur we must observe five forms of abstinence. The goal of this is not personal suffering; rather, it is to elevate ourselves to the level where we can shed our body and be like angels. On the holiest of days, Yom Kippur, we do not eat; and although the purpose is not to deny ourselves the food we usually crave, we become a people that no longer needs food. The power of Yom Kippur is to transform the Jewish people into a nation of angels. As the Ramah writes (*Orach Chaim* 610,4), "There are some who wear pure white clothes on Yom Kippur to be like ministering angels." Why the need to be something that we are not? What does it mean that we are like angels for a day? An angel is a creation that has a soul without a body. The angel has a will, and he chooses naturally to follow God's command. An angel does not have to wrestle between body and mind, since, for him, decisions are clear. Once we are like angels, having shed our bodies, we can look back and honestly say that any *averah* (sin) that we have done, was done by a foreign power.

At the time the *averah* was done, the person was commandeered by external forces that caused him to sin. In our Yom Kippur frame of mind, being pure and angelic, we need only to shed our sins by placing them outside the realm of our existence. On Yom Kippur we can honestly say, "I didn't do it." Those sins that we are talking about are someone else's fault. This is exactly what the idea of *sa'ir hamishtaleach* is. This is why we do not need the ordinary forms of *kaparah*; all we need is to recognize that all the sins—every last one of every single Jew—are really external to the essence of our soul. This is done by confessing our sins and sending the goat way out of the city for destruction.

The Maharal cites an interesting *midrash* (*Bereishit Rabbah* 65). Yaakov *Avinu* is called a "smooth person" (*cholok*). Imagine a person with long, bushy hair and a bald person standing next to a threshing floor. In time, the chaff from the threshing settles onto the head of the person with long, bushy hair. However, when the chaff settles on the bald person's head, he is able effortlessly to wipe it off. So Esau the wicked (who is called *sa'ir*—hairy), the whole year, is soiled in sin. How can he possibly clean himself? Yaakov *Avinu* is different; he can attain *kaparah* when Yom Kippur comes around.

This is what the *midrash* means; Yaakov's smoothness allows the sins not to stick to him, thereby making them removable in one quick motion—but only on Yom Kippur. Every moment of Yom Kippur is a priceless opportunity—not only because it comes once a year but because, during that one day, we are on a level that we can only dream about the rest of the year.

❖ CHAPTER 62 ❖

Sukkot

Rabbi Moshe Portnoy

Young Israel of Plainview, New York

THE *SUKKAH*: IS IT TEMPORARY OR PERMANENT?

The two most visible symbols of Sukkot are the *arba minim* and the *sukkah*. The *lulav* and *etrog* are relatively straightforward *mitzvot*. We spend a lot of money to buy a nice set and fulfill the *mitzvah*. The *sukkah*, however, presents some very difficult halachic and philosophical conundrums, even in the way we observe it. Consider the following:

The *Gemara* in *Sukkah* (28b) teaches us that the concept of the *sukkah* is *teishvu k'ein taduru*, that we occupy the *sukkah* in the same fashion that we do our house. In an optimum scenario, we eat our meals, we sleep, we learn, and, generally, spend our time in the *sukkah*. (Our lenient customs in this respect are based on the concept of discomfort, which maintains that if something lessens our joy of *yom tov* substantially, then we are absolved.) Essentially, we must *live* in the *sukkah*. We must make the hut our home for eight (or nine) days.

It goes even further. Even though women are not required to live in the sukkah, in the interest of keeping families together, women should completely partake as their husbands do so that life in the sukkah is as intact as usual. (See *Torah temimah parshat emor*, note 169) This is one side. There is another side, however. The Torah tells us—all seven days—leave your permanent dwelling and sit in a temporary dwelling (sukkah 2a). The Torah wants us to leave our permanent home and move to temporary quarters. The objective is that we live *temporarily* in the *sukkah*. Indeed, anything that might create an enduring living quarter is not permitted—for example, a *sukkah* that is higher than 20 cubits.

In *Pirkei d'Rebbe Eliezer* we find that each of the three Festivals commemorate one of the Patriarchs. Sukkot is in memory of Jacob, who built huts for his cattle on his return to Israel from the house of Laban (Genesis 33:7). The concept is that of impermanence, since Jacob was in transit to Israel and built only temporary shelters.

It is most interesting to note that, even during the temple days in Jerusalem, we erected *sukkot*, even though everyone was in a temporary mode. The *mitzvah aliyah l'regel* of all Jews ascending to Jerusalem on Festivals meant that before we built our *sukkot* we were already living out of suitcases!

The seemingly contradictory concepts lead us to a basic Judaic conclusion. It is the Torah's mandate that we live as if permanently in a temporary milieu, even as we understand that if it ever should achieve real permanence in our minds then we have lost our ulitmate hope of redemption.

As Jacob sent Judah ahead before his coming to Egypt to build a home of Torah (Genesis 46:29) even though his sure knowledge was that Egypt was only a short sojourn, so do we. We create *yeshivot* and *shuls* that we hope will last for a hundred years even while we fervently pray that *Mashiach* will arrive today! Creating Torah eternity in our current situation of flux is a secret that only a Diaspora Jews understands.

Rabbi Daniel Yormark

Young Israel of Eltingville, New York

Is there a connection between the *mitzvot* of Sukkot—the *lulav* and *etrog* and the *sukkah*?

Why do we decorate the *sukkah*?

Why is it that someone who experiences excessive discomfort in the *sukkah* is exempted from the *mitzvah*?

In order to attempt to solve these queries, let us first address a fundamental issue concerning the timing of Sukkot.

The Torah (Leviticus 23:42–43) tells us that the basis for the *mitzvah* of sitting in the *sukkah* is the fact that *HaShem* provided *sukkot* for the Jewish people at the time of the Exodus from Egypt. That being the case, why are we instructed to celebrate Sukkot during the month of Tishrei? Why isn't it observed simultaneously with Pesach?

The Vilna Gaon (*shir Hasirim* 1:4) informs us of the significance of the 15th of Tishrei, the date the Torah tells us to mark the holiday of Sukkot. True, the Clouds of Glory were granted to the *Bnei Yisrael* upon their leaving Egypt. However, following the sin of the golden calf, the Clouds of Glory were removed. On Yom Kippur, the 10th of Tishrei, *HaShem* pardoned His people for that iniquity. On the 11th of Tishrei Moshe issued the command concerning the building of *Mishkan*. During the next two days, the 12th and the 13th of Tishrei, the necessary materials were donated and collected. On the 14th, the *chachmei lev*, those with wisdom of the heart who actually built the *Mishkan*, took the materials from Moshe and, on the 15th of Tishrei, the actual construction began. The Clouds were returned when they started to build the *Mishkan*. For this reason, the Torah tells us to observe Sukkot on the 15th of Tishrei, to mark the return of the Clouds of Glory.

The only difficulty, it would seem, with understanding this explanation is the following: Since the *yom tov* of Sukkot is based upon the Clouds of

Glory that sheltered the Jewish people in the wilderness, why then could we not have a *Chag* (holiday) based upon the *original* granting of the Clouds— when we left Egypt? In other words, why is the *yom tov* of Sukkot, which celebrates the Clouds, "postponed" until the time of their retrieval?

The answer seems to be quite clear. The only difference between the original Clouds and their subsequent return is the manner in which the *Bnei Yisrael* received them. At the time of the Exodus, the Clouds were granted outright to the Jewish people. On the 15th of Tishrei, they were regained through *teshuvah* (repentance). They had been lost and, possibly, would never have returned. Only through the process of *teshuvah* did the *Bnei Yisrael* merit the return of the Clouds. This can be understood by means of the following parable:

A king had many subjects who accorded him the utmost honor and respect. It came to pass that one of the loyal subjects rebelled against the King. Certainly, this caused a deep rift between that subject and His Royal Highness. With time, the rebellious one felt the loss of being distanced from His Majesty. He begged forgiveness and tried to win favor in the eyes of the King. Sensing the sincerity and earnestness of His subject's entreaties, the King acquiesced and welcomed back the former renegade subject. He pardoned him for his iniquity and allowed him to return. It soon became apparent that the close relationship between them was markedly changed following the reunion. There was now a deeper connection, a firmer attachment between the two. Actually, this is the case whenever individuals who are close endure a rift. As long as they are in a state of discord, they feel more distant from each other than strangers who live on opposite ends of the earth. Once they reconcile, however, they are closer than ever.

At the time of the Exodus, the Jewish people were, needless to say, very close with the Almighty. They then strayed and served the golden calf. This resulted in an estrangement, a distancing, a separation between the two. With their subsequent *teshuvah*, the resultant closeness, attachment, and love of *HaShem* for His people was far greater and deeper than it was prior to the deviation. *This* closeness and oneness, this love and endearment, brought about the return of the Clouds, which express an intimacy in which the protective shield of *HaShem* is ever-present and all-encompassing. This closeness results in a permanent annual *mitzvah* of *sukkah*, a yearly opportunity to experience once again and sense the closeness and endearment of that first 15th of Tishrei. Indeed, the return of the Clouds coincided with the building of the *Mishkan*, the vehicle that maintained the close relationship between *HaShem* and His people.

We know that our Holidays are not merely times to reminisce about the "good old days." They are not simply "trips down nostalgia lane." We do not have Pesach merely to remember the events of the Exodus, and Shavuot to remind us of the giving of the Torah. We are taught that, just as there are seasons in nature—that is, spring is a time conducive to planting flowers, and so one—so, too, we have spiritual seasons. Pesach is a time—every year—to harness the spiritual forces of freedom, freedom in a Torah sense. Shavuot is a time—every year—to accept the Torah anew. Sukkot is a time—every year—when we bask in the radiance of the precious *sukkah* and strive to deepen our awareness and recognition that we have a "Shomer Yisrael" Guardian of Israel who "neither sleeps nor slumbers." Since the entire theme of the Clouds is closeness and togetherness, and the intimacy following the *teshuvah* was infinitely greater than the attachment that existed previously, the *yom tov* of Sukkot—which, in essence, is a time to re-experience the Clouds of Glory—is established solely on the occasion of the return of the Clouds through *teshuvah*.

Following *teshuvah*, we are unsullied and untarnished by our wrongdoings. We have been cleansed and emerge pure and pristine. In this state, there is no place for pain. Moreover, there is no place even for undue discomfort. The *sukkah* is a place where, ideally, one should sense the purity of and intimate closeness with *HaShem*. In a sense, one who is unduly uncomfortable is not exempted from the *sukkah*, rather he doesn't belong in the *sukkah*.

Certainly, it follows that a structure designed to express and communicate love and purity would be, accordingly, adorned and decorated to enhance the atmosphere. Hence, we decorate our *sukkot* in a befitting way to help provide the appropriate ambience.

Finally, our Sages tell us that the Four Species—the *lulav, etrog, hadassim*, and *aruvot*—represent four major parts of the body: the spine, heart, eyes, and mouth, respectively. Whereas the soul is pure and perfect, we are accustomed to "blaming" the physical body for our iniquities. Yet, on Sukkot, following *teshuvah*, all has been cleansed, and even the body is *hadar*, elevated and glorified. Indeed, we proudly and triumphantly parade with our *lulav* and *etrog*, which express the grandeur, splendor, and beauty that is the Jew, especially at this auspicious time of year.

In the merit of the *mitzvah* of *sukkah*, may we soon see the fulfillment of the supplication, "Spread over us the *sukkah* of Your peace—upon us and upon all of His people Israel, and upon Jerusalem."

Rabbi Evan Shore

Young Israel Shaarei Torah of Syracuse, New York

> "And you shall take for yourselves on the first day the fruit of a citron tree, branches of palm trees and twigs of a plaited tree and willows of the brook and you shall rejoice before the Lord, your God, seven days." (Levitucs 23:40)

It is this sentence that sets Sukkot apart from all other *yomim tovim*. This is emphasized in the *kiddush* that we recite on Sukkot night when we say, "the holiday of Sukkot, the time of our gladness." Yet the Talmud, in *Taanis* (26b), tells us, "Rabban Shimon ben Gamliel says: There are no greater holidays to the Jewish people than the 15th of Av and Yom Kippur." These two days are specifically mentioned as great happy days; yet the Holiday of Sukkot received the designation of "the time of our happiness." Why?

The Rambam, in *Hilchot Lulav* 8:12, writes, "Even though on all the holidays there is a *mitzvah* to rejoice, during the holiday of Sukkot, in the times of the Holy Temple, there was increased joy, as it says '. . . and you shall rejoice before the Lord your God seven days.'"

The Vilna Gaon attempts to explain the Rambam by pointing out that the Clouds of Glory returned to the Tabernacle on Sukkot after departing as a result of the building of the golden calf. Moreover, the Vilna Gaon points out that it was on the 11th of Tishrei, just days before Sukkot, that the Jewish people began to donate their possessions for the building of the *Mishkean* (Tabernacle). The *Mishkan* symbolized *HaShem*'s desire to dwell once more among the Jewish people

The *Sefer Zman Simchateinu* mentions that *HaShem* saw the *Mishkan* as a sign of God's *chuppah* and *Kiddushin* with the Jewish people. In essence, the happiness that surrounds the holiday of Sukkot is not solely the joy of the Jewish people but includes also the happiness of *HaShem* Himself in His marriage with the *Am Yisrael*, the unique nation of the world.

This happiness is even greater than we can imagine. We learn in Leviticus 23:39, "But on the 15th day of the seventh month when you shall gather in the crop of the land, you shall celebrate *HaShem*'s festival for a seven-day period." The Maharam asks, why does the holiday of Sukkot have the distinction of being called the Holiday of *HaShem*? Why isn't this mentioned in relation to Pesach or Shavuot? *HaShem* is happy and celebrating Sukkot with us because we have been purified from impurity and transgression. However, wasn't this accomplished on the 10th of Tishrei, which is Yom Kippur? By definition, Yom Kippur is a day of forgiveness and atonement; so why celebrate this on Sukkot?

We learn that when an individual is *tamei* (impure), a certain time period must elapse before one goes to the *mikvah* and becomes *tahor* (pure). During the year, we pick up different types of spiritual impurity due to our transgressions. Beginning with Elul, we start the process of purification by preparing ourselves for the Days of Awe. The height of this cleansing process is reached with the onset of Yom Kippur. On *Erev* Yom Kippur we immerse ourselves in the *mikvah*, and during the davening on Yom Kippur we beseech *HaShem* to forgive and purify all of Israel. As the prophet Ezekiel says, "And I will sprinkle pure water upon you, and you shall be cleansed."

However, there is one more immersion that awaits the Jew, and that is found in the *mitzvah* of the *sukkah*. The *sukkah* is the only *mitzvah*, excluding *mikvah*, in which the Jew is totally enveloped. In essence, the *mitzvah* of the sukkah becomes a *mikvah* in which the Jew is totally immersed. *HaShem* looks at His people Israel and takes delight in the elevated spiritual status that we occupy. *HaShem*, if you will, is smiling, joyful, and happy that *Klal Yisrael* is deserving of the closeness and protection afforded by the Clouds of Glory.

The concluding *Mishnah* in *Yoma* teaches us: The *mikvah* of Israel is *HaShem*. Just as a *mikvah* purifies the contaminated, so does the Holy One, Blessed is He, purify Israel. Sukkot, therefore, is truly a time of happiness for both *HaShem* and the Jewish people.

Rabbi Gershon C. Gewirtz

Young Israel of Brookline, Massachusetts

OUR FESTIVAL OF LOVE

Contemporary American culture has a highly developed aversion to anything that is less than a full expression of personal autonomy. "It is my life"; "it is my body"; "it is my choice of lifestyle"; these are refrains that are continuously heard to validate ever-changing variations of personal choice.

With respect to relationships as well, we choose to be in a relationship. "I remain with you because I choose to do so," is the preferred basis for any relationship, whether with a friend, a spouse, or anyone else—even a casual associate.

In light of this, our relationship with God creates significant difficulty. The question each of us may ask is why we maintain our relationship with the Creator. Do we observe *mitzvot* only to receive the many blessings promised in the Torah? Do we refrain from transgressions only to avoid the Torah's curses or to assure our places in the world-to-come? If these are our primary motivations, indeed our sole motivations, of what ultimate value is our observance and what, in fact, is the nature of our relationship with God? Is there opportunity to experience the supreme value of Torah or do we perceive that we merely remain "ensnared" within the realities that the Torah identifies regarding our relationship with a seemingly demanding God?

Thankfully, our quandary is short-lived. Rambam (*Hilchot Tshuvah* 10:1) states that a perception of a relationship with the Almighty as described above is reflective of ignorance and misinformation. One is enjoined from even giving verbal expression to such sentiments. "A person should not say, 'I will fulfill the *mitzvot* of the Torah and study its wisdom in order that I receive its blessings. . . . and I will refrain from sin . . . that I be saved from its curses.'" The most appropriate basis for our relationship with *Hakadosh baruch Hu* is one of love.

In *halachah* 2, Rambam continues: "One who serves [God] from love is involved in Torah and *mitzvot* . . . not because of fear of the evil and not to inherit the good; rather he lives by truth because it is true . . . and this is of the greatest significance."

From our love for truth flows our love for the *Ribono shel Olam*, the Almighty, a very special love indeed. Though the *Orchos Tzadikim* chapter on "*Ahava*" teaches that there are seven expressions of love, each distinct, the love for *Hakadosh baruch Hu* is reflected in only one. It is Rambam, again, who teaches that the pristine love that should fill our souls for the Almighty, should make us "sick with love," not unlike the manifestations of love a man may have for a woman: "And she is always in his thoughts, when he sits, when he stands, at the time he eats and drinks . . ." This is the Torah's goal for each of us.

While, in fact, Rambam acknowledges that such an objective is not easily attainable, nevertheless, it is clearly an ideal of which to be ever mindful.

In truth, this love-relationship is certainly not a one-sided matter. While we have the *mitzvah* of loving the Almighty (Deuteronomy 6:5), we are also very much aware of God's love for us, collectively as *am Yisrael* (the Jewish nation), and individually.

It is commonly understood that we observe the *mitzvah* of *sukkah*, in part, as a commemoration of the Clouds of Glory [Rabbi Eliezer—*Sukkah* 11b] that the Almighty provided to protect the Jewish nation during the period of wandering in the desert. The Mabit [*Rabbeinu* Moshe ben Yosef miTrani; 1499–1579] however, asks why we do not also commemorate the traveling well and the Manna, which were always available to the People. Why do we celebrate only the *sukkah*? His response is most significant.

The God Who gives life is obligated to sustain life; to provide food and water, is expected. The Clouds of Glory, however, were not essential to sustaining life. "The clouds were specifically an expression of God's love for His people." It is, then, God's love for us that we celebrate. Even after thousands of years of persecution, until this very day, *Hakadosh Baruch Hu*'s love for us gives us the strength and determination to survive and flourish.

Sukkot is our Festival of Love. May our celebration of God's love be acceptable to Him; may our love for God grow steadily, and may we be merit that the Redeemer come speedily in our days.

Rabbi Moshe S. Gorelik

Young Israel of North Bellmore, New York

Yom Kippur and Sukkot are thematically interlocked in that the traditional sources underscore the *teshuvah* character of both Holy Days. The intervening four days between Yom Kippur and Sukkot are an integral part of this thematic continuum. They serve as links between the two Holy Days. Perhaps, for this reason, these days adopt a quasi-festive character, as is evidenced by the omission of *tachanun* during the *tefillot*. One must bear in mind, however, though both Holy Days are subsumed under the *teshuvah* rubric, their focus differs.

Yom Kippur primarily is a day of personal *cheshbon hanefesh*—self-evaluation. The limitations on physical comforts and pleasures move the individual to look inward and contemplate life's purpose. A moment of truth confronts the person reviewing the past. In the clear light of this honest evaluation, he or she resolves to embark on a future of moral and religious enhancement. The day is, thus, designated as a *Shabbat Shabbaton*, a time for intense reflection and determined resolution.

Sukkot is a communal *teshuvah* experience. The *halachah* underscores the societal relationship of all the *yomim tovim*. With profound insight, Rav Meir Simcha of Dvinsk, in his remarkable work, the Meshech Chochmah, points out that the lenient rulings with regard to food preparations, including the permissibility of cooking, baking, carrying, and so on, on *yom tov* that otherwise are prohibited on *Shabbat*, encourage the interfacing of people. In this way, communal bonding is deepened and strengthened. Socializing in an atmosphere of spirituality and Torah enriches the national purpose of a people.

The Sukkot observance, however, is distinctive among the *yomim tovim* by the fact that it is a *teshuvah* experience as well. The pervasive theme is the *achdut*—unity—of Israel. This theme is reflected in the *mitzvah* of the *sukkah* and in the symbolisms of the *arba minim*—the four species. In the eighth volume of a brilliant series entitled Eish Dat, the author, the Ozrov Rebbe, Rav Moshe Yechiel Halevi Epstein, underscores the Sukkot theme of unity by drawing upon the massive wealth of talmudic, midrashic, and zoharic sources. The evidence is indisputable. Torah theology as transmitted by the authentic Sages of our *mesorah*, vigorously promotes the *achdut* theme of Sukkot.

Furthermore, the Ozrov Rebbe adds an important dimension to the theme by declaring that the *simchah* of Sukkot is the outgrowth of the *achdut* experience. The *tefillot* define Sukkot as the time of *simchah*, a description not applied to other *yomim tovim*. Genuine *yom tov simchah* is experienced only in the context of a communal fellowship. When *machloket*—dissension—prevails, the warmth of the *yom tov* spirit ebbs. In the absence of *achdut*, the *yom tov* observances—including the rituals of the *sukkah* and the *arba minim*—fail to uplift the *neshamah*. The Talmud spells out the indispensability of *achdut* by referring to the words of the Torah: "all citizens in Israel shall reside in the booths" (Leviticus 23:42). And the Talmud comments, "It [the *pasuk*] teaches that all Israel is suitable to sit in one *sukkah* [the word *sukkah* in the Torah may be rendered in the singular form]" (*Sukkah* 27b). *Achdut* is not a political stratagem, nor is it a sociological necessity. It is the heart and soul of Israel's relationship with *HaShem*, and with it comes the fervor and *simchah* of *Yiddishkeit*.

In a comment on this talmudic passage, Avraham Yitchok Hakohein contributed a brilliant insight on the linkage of the Sukkot theme of *achdut* with the *teshuvah* experience of Yom Kippur. The *achdut* of a people comes about only when the *teshuvah* experience illuminates the minds and rejuvenates the heart with a renewed sense of spirituality. Spirituality is turning to *HaShem*, rejoicing in His presence, and, putting aside our competitiveness, joining with our fellow human beings in beseeching *HaShem* for His atonement. The Jew includes in his *tefillot* concern for others. The plural rendering of the *tefillah* text attests to this idea. When we thrust aside narcissistic attitudes and rekindle our awareness of a common destiny, then, and only then, can we approach *HaShem* for compassion and forgiveness. Thus, *teshuvah* is an act of rejoining destinies. It is a return to the enduring moral and religious values that necessarily include respect for people and a feeling of mutuality with *Klal Yisrael*. Without *achdut*, even the largest *sukkah* is too small. If *achdut* prevails, then *simchah* pervades even a cramped *sukkah*.

❖ CHAPTER 63 ❖

Chol Hamoed Sukkot

Rabbi Aryeh Ralbag

Young Israel of Avenue K
Brooklyn, New York

LULAV AND *SUKKAH* IN THE DESERT?

Did Bnei Yisrael, during their forty years of wandering in the desert, fulfill the *mitzvot* of *arba minim* and *sukkah*? The question might appear esoteric, but it's really more than a mere footnote of history. It's the quest for the Truth—which is *Torah*!

If they did observe the *mitzvah* of *lulav*, then from where did they actually get the palm, citron, myrtle, and willow? Did they grow in the desert? Even the *sukkah*-covering (*schach*) would present a problem, since the Torah mentions "the leftovers from the barn and press" as *schach*. On the other hand, if these *mitzvot* were not preformed in the *Midbar* (desert), why did *HaShem* release them from these obligations? After all, Sukkot is one of the Three Festivals and should be regarded as no less meaningful than the others. *HaShem* should have miraculously provided them the means to observe it.

Most commentaries assume these two *mitzvot* were observed in the *Midbar*. According to the *Tosafos* (*Chullin* 88b, *Eloh*), parts of the desert were fertile in ancient times. The *midrash* (*Shir Hashirim* chapter 4) says that Miriam's well caused vegetation, bushes, and trees to sprout. For this reason, it was only after her passing that *Bnei Yisrael* complained of the *Midbar* "not being a place for vegetation, figs, or grapes." Furthermore, the *Midrash* (*Yalkut Shimoni Novi Chagai*) states explicitly that every tribe dug an irrigation canal from Miriam's well to their camp, where they would plant figs, pomegranates, grapes, apples, and so on. The *araba minim* would surely have grown there. Finally the *Targum* (*Shir Hashirim* 1:15) mentions wine used for the *nesochim* (wine-libations in the *Mishkan*), which came from the "vineyards of Ein Gedi" by the Dead Sea. In ancient times, dates were also grown here, and, for this reason, the city of Ein Gedi was referred to in *TaNaKh* as

Chatsatson Tamar (Rabbi Yehoseph Schwartz, *Tevuoth Ho'oretz*, chap. 7, p. 313). Again, this oasis could have provided the *Bnei Yisrael* with the *arba minim* in the *Midbar*, just as it supplied them with wine.

There is another body of thought that feels that *Bnei Yisrael* never fulfilled the *mitzvah* of *lulav* and *esrog* in the desert. The *pesukim* appear to support this; only in relation to Sukkot does the Torah (Leviticus 13:33–41) separate the command to observe the *yom tov* from the *mitzvot* required to be performed on that *yom tov*. The Torah first commands us to observe Sukkot seven days, with the first and last days being *kodesh*—holy. Only afterwards does the Torah says, "when you gather up the grains of the land," you must take the *lulav, esrog, hadas,* and *aravah*. This implies that the *mitzvah* was given to be observed only *after* the *Bnei Yisrael* entered *Eretz Yisrael* and gathered up the grain of the land.

The Rambam (*Moreh Nevuchim*, part III, chapter 43) posits two of the reasons for the *arba minim*:

> They (*arba minim*) were a *simchah* for them (*Bnei Yisrael*). They departed from the desert, which contained neither vegetation, figs, grapes, pomegranates, nor water to drink and entered a land of trees and rivers. In order to remember this stark difference, they were commanded to take the most beautiful and fragrant of fruit (the *esrog*), the nicest branch (the palm—*lulav*), the most wonderful of bushes, and so on. These were the *most prevalent species* to be found then in Israel and everyone could locate them.

It is obvious that, according to the Rambam, they observed *lulav* and *esrog* only *after* entering *Eretz Yisrael* and finding these four species. This *mitzvah* was a driving force to enable the *Bnei Yisrael* to recall vividly and appreciate the vast difference between the barren desert they had just left and *Eretz Yisrael*—the fertile land of trees and rivers they had just entered.

Both Rabbi Menachem Zerach (*Tsedo LaDerech*, *Maamar* 4, Klal 6, chapter 1) and the *Menoras HaMoar* (*Ner* 3, *Klal* 4, *chelek* 6, chapter 4) paraphrase and quote extensively this Rambam passage and agree with him that the *mitzvah* of *arba minim* was first observed only after *Bnei Yisrael* entered Israel.

Furthermore, Abarbanel (*Vayitkra Emor* 23, 33) buttresses the Rambam. He offers the following reason for the *arovos* (willow branches): "As rivers, streams, and springs of water were not to be found in *Mitzrayim* and surely not in the *Midbar*; therefore *HaShem* commanded them that when they enter *Eretz Yisrael*, the Land of rivers, they were to be joyous in its willows."

With reference to the *mitzvah* of dwelling in the *sukkah*, we find three opinions. According to Rabbi Shlomo HaKohen (*Binyan Shlomo*, introd. 2, *Parshat Re'eh* 12–19), Bnei Yisrael actually built booths during Sukkot and fulfilled the *mitzvah* properly.

In another theory, he posits that the *Bnei Yisrael* fulfilled the *mitzvah* of *sukkah* by remaining during the whole duration of Sukkot under the *Anonei HaKovod* (hovering Clouds of Glory that protected them). These *Anonei HaKovod* could theoretically be considered *schach*. Two requirements for *schach* are that it comes from the ground and not be able to become halachically defiled. For instance, the second requirement excludes metals and all types of vessels because they can become defiled. A cloud, he theorized, comes for the earth, as it says, "and a cloud rose up from the land" (Genesis 2:6). Also, it cannot become halachically defiled.

Thus, according to this line of reasoning, during the year it was optional for *Bnei Yisrael* to remain under the *Anonei HaKovod*—the Clouds of Glory. As a matter of fact, the tribe of *Dan* and the *eruv rav* (false Egyptian converts) were mostly excluded from remaining under these clouds. Because of their sins, they were required to dwell outside these clouds. However, during the week of Sukkot, it became obligatory for *all* of *Bnei Yisrael* to live under the *Anonei HaKovod*; even *Shevet Dan* and the *eruv rav* were permitted to re-enter to fulfill the *mitzvah* of *sukkah*.

A third opinion is cited by the MaBit (*Sefer Beis Elokim, Sha'ar Hayesodos* chapter 37). He states that though Pesach and Shavuot were observed in the *Midbar*, Sukkot was not. He proves his point in two ways. First, there is a halachic problem. If *Bnei Yisrael* had built their own *sukkahs* in the desert, they would then have come up against the situation of "a *sukkah* (an actual booth) under another *sukkah* (the Clouds of Glory, which are also considered a *sukkah*-covering)." The halacha is that a *sukkah* built under another *sukkah* is invalid, unless you sit in the upper one. Secondly, the Torah states that we dwell in a *sukkah* "in order that your future generations know that I caused you to dwell in the *sukkahs*" (Leviticus 23:43). Thus, the *mitzvah* was not obligatory immediately in the desert but, rather, after entering *Eretz Yisrael*—when their generations (that is, children) had to be reminded that their fathers lived previously in *sukkahs*.

It should be obvious by now that there are various differing opinions in regard to the fulfillment of the *mitzvot* of *sukkah* and *arba minim* in the *Midbar*. So, too, every iota of Torah can be analyzed from different angles. Let us make this year, a year of Torah learning so that we may readily merit *Bias Goel Zedek Bimhero BiYomeinu Omen*.

Rabbi Eli Stern

Young Israel of Dayton, Ohio

THE SHELTER OF THE *SUKKAH*

At the beginning of *Parshat Vayera* in *Bereishit* there is a rather enigmatic *Midrash* (*Bereshit Rabbah*) that relates to our *yom tov*. The *Chazal* are explaining how the various acts of *chesed* that Avraham *Avinu* did for the three "Arabs" were all recompensed by *HaShem* to *Klal Yisrael* measure for measure. In fact, in this discussion proof is adduced from *pesukim* in *TaNaKh* for the payback for each *chesed* (water, washing feet, shelter, bread, meat, personal attention) in three stages of our existence (the desert, *Eretz Yisrael*, and the Messianic era).

What is puzzling though is the remuneration for the kindness Avraham showed in giving shelter to the three men from the sweltering heat of the Chevron sun—"and you should recline under the tree" (*Bereishit* 18:4).

In the first and last stages of our existence, the reward is a supernatural shield emanating from *HaShem* and is thus an appropriate analogy to Avraham's shelter. In the desert, we were rewarded with the shelter of the Clouds of Glory that acted, among other things, to shield us from our enemies and the elements: "He spread out a cloud for shelter" (*Tehillim* 105:39). The *midrash*, speaking about the messianic era, quotes a verse in *Yeshaiah* (4:6), "There shall be a *sukkah* for a shadow in the daytime from the heat."

But the reward during the rest of Jewish history, the *midrash* continues, is the *mitzvah* of dwelling in the *sukkah* for a week during Tishrei. "You shall dwell in *sukkot* for seven days" (*Vayikra* 23:42). Living in the *sukkah* may demonstrate our *bitachon*, our inner equanimity that derives from our trust in *HaShem*, but it is manifestly an act of rendering ourselves vulnerable to all our enemies and all of nature's elements. How is this *mitzvah*, then, an appropriate compensation for Avraham's act of providing shelter? There, he protected people from the elements, and here *HaShem* commands us to remove ourselves, ostensibly, from our protection (our homes) and expose ourselves to all the vagaries of nature!

We can explain this *midrash* with some penetrating insights of Rabbi Samson Raphael Hirsch (*Bamidbar* 29:13) that relate to today's *haftarah* from *Yechezkel*. The *navi* speaks about the great apocalyptic wars that will mark the final, wrenching birth pangs heralding the arrival of *Moshiach*. In particular, the forces of Gog and Magog will come against Yisrael and be defeated. Rav Hirsch notes the etymological root of Gog is similar to that of *gag*, "roof." There lies the key to unlocking the struggle of Jewish history.

The Gentile nations of the world (beginning with Nimrod at the Tower of Babel) have tried to fight against *HaShem* through attempts to hermetically seal themselves off from the Divine Providence, *hashgachah*, and punishments of *HaShem*, thus rendering themselves invulnerable to *HaShem*'s system of reward and punishment. Just as they succumbed to the illusion that they had made their borders impregnable with their Maginot lines, they extended their walls heavenward as well. They attempted to create an airtight, metaphorical *gag*—"roof" over their heads in a desperate attempt to eliminate God from the equation of man's actions and their consequences. This spiritual *hubris* will find its ultimate dénouement in the great battles that will proceed *Moshiach*'s arrival, as detailed in the *haftarah*. On Sukkot, the total number of offerings are equal to seventy, corresponding to the seventy archetypical nations of the world. The number of offerings diminishes by the day because the contrast between Yisrael and the nations will diminish until it is distilled into the hard-core opposition of Gog and Magog. And they, too, will be defeated.

The awesome destructive power of heavy rains, floods, and hurricanes should be a clear testament to the futility of trying to "sand-bag" our way through life with yet a higher levee and a bigger roof. But, inevitably, most of the world will fail to draw any lessons from any of this until the epic battle that will defeat Gog and Magog.

The gift of Sukkot is precisely our vulnerability. We remove for seven days the façade that we are sheltered from *HaShem*'s power and His *hashgachah*. We strip the illusion that modern society has foisted upon us that we can cure any disease, conquer any enemy, shield ourselves from temperamental nature, and live the way we want to without interference from *HaShem*. Sitting in our frail booths, exposed to the cold, heat rain, wind, bees, and so on, we recognize the folly of the would-be Gogs and Magogs of our society who would deny *HaShem* any role in our lives—they who think that the answer to all of man's moral ills, which have resulted in numerous catastrophic diseases, is to shore up their hermetically sealed roofs with a stronger vaccine and a safer technique that will finally render them invincible from *HaShem*'s scrutiny.

Ultimately the nations of the world will come, specifically on Sukkot, to render their homage to *HaShem* in the *Beit HaMikdash,* finally admitting that their high-tech roofs were no match for the Jewish ramshackle hut with its thatched roof (*Zechariah* 14:16—*haftarah* of the first day of Sukkot).

THE SECRET OF *CHOL HAMOED*

The Maharal (in his commentary on *Pirkei Avot*) makes some very trenchant observations on the following *Mishnah* (3:11): "Rabbi Elazar Hamodai said: One who desecrates the sacred offerings (sacrifices); who disgraces the Festivals; who shames his fellow man in public; who breaks the covenant of Avraham *Avinu* (*brit milah*); and who brazenly teaches Torah in a way contrary to *halachah*—though he may have Torah and good deeds to his credit—has no share in the World-to-Come."

Although the Maharal never explicitly states so, many commentators say that the mention of the Festivals here refers specifically to Chol Hamoed, the intermediate days of the festivals. What is the common denominator underlying all five of these acts?

The Maharal explains that all five actions represent a denigration of the physical world by an individual who feels he can relate to *ruchaniyut*—spirituality—only through intellectual reflection upon ethereal matters (this sense of dichotomizing the "physical" and "spiritual" worlds is an ancient misconception that classic Christianity still upholds today).

Thus, the meat of the sacrificial offerings is just mundane food; the physical rejoicing that is permitted (indeed, required) during *Chol Hamoed* has no connection to the spiritual; the human being can be embarrassed because he is only flesh and blood; the *brit milah* takes place on the part of the body most prone to lascivious desires and, thus, repulsive; and the Torah is replete with laws dealing with the mundane minutiae of life, and therefore, he has no reverence for it. The punishment entails that the person received the opposite of what he desires. He lives only for the abstract, non-physical world—*olam haba*. He is requited by specifically losing his share in the World-to-Come.

We say that everything in this world can become infused with *kedushah* and become a *keli*, a vessel, a means for *avodat HaShem*. By sanctifying the mundane, by ascribing holiness to physical acts, we allow *HaShem*'s presence to permeate all aspects of our lives. (The concept of *kedushah*—being separated for a purpose—is reflected in the word for sacrifices (*kodshim*) and the word for *yomim tovim* (*mikraei kodesh*).)

On Sukkot, in particular (the only *yom tov* to be called *z'man simchateinu*), the zenith of our joy is reached during the exurberance of the *simchat beit hashoevah* celebrations during *Chol Hamoed,* with music, torches of fire, song, and dance. On *Chol Hamoed,* when some of the restrictions of *melachah* (labor forbidden on *Shabbos* and yom tov) are lifted, we are sorely tempted to view *yom tov* as being temporarily dislodged, following the all-or-nothing dichotomy of our *Mishnah*. It is precisely then—during *Chol Hamoed*—that we must use all the aspects of the mundane that are permitted to us to facilitate an even greater *simchah shel mitzvah*. For instance, on *Chol Hamoed* we might be tempted to dress and eat as on an ordinary weekday. However, our *Chazal* tell us that true joy comes only from enhancing our food and drink, suffusing the mundane with the *kedushah* of *yom tov*.

Rav Hirsch, in the discussion referred to above, says that the real joy of Sukkot is that by our *m'kadesh* sanctifying this world (by observing all the agricultural laws culminating in the harvest and by rejoicing "with cheerful confidence and quietness" that *HaShem* ultimately protects us from all harm) we can attain *olam haba* at the same time.

Rabbi Sholom Gold

Young Israel of Har Nof, Jerusalem, Israel

After the first man ate from the tree of knowledge, God cursed the earth and exclaimed, "thorns and thistles shall come forth from the ground." The *Bnei Yissachar* makes an insightful comment. The word for "thistles" is *dardar* the *mesorah* (tradition) tells us that in a *Sefer Torah* there is the last letter in the *pasuk, Shema Yisrael HaShem Eloheinu HaShem EchaD,* "Listen, Israel God is our Lord, God is one" (Deuteronomy 6:4). The *reish* appears in this morning's Torah reading (also the last letter in the pasuk)—*lo tishtachaveh l'Ei' acheR*—"Do not bow down to another god" (Exodus 34:14). The reason for this, he explains, is that there is only a hairbreadth difference between these two letters. The little appendage on the right-hand side of the top of the *daled* that extends over its vertical leg sets it off from the *reish.* One could easily confuse the two, were they not written in bold, large print. In these *pesukim,* of course, such confusion would be a tragic and blasphemous error.

When Adam did not fulfill the only Divine imperative he had been commanded, he brought confusion to the world; the confusion of *dardar*—spelled daled reish, daled, reish. The *daled,* which represents a clear knowledge of God and the *reish,* which symbolizes a worship and adoration of other forces in the world. In all times, therefore, there would be periods of *daled* and periods of *reish,* times blessed with clarity of vision and times cursed with the clouds of concealment, periods in which man would see God's Hand in history and periods in which man would lose sight of God. Man swings from faith to doubt to disbelief and then, hopefully, back again. Now he sees God as the author of history, and then he blocks God out of his consciousness and sees himself, his wealth, his will, and his resources as the objects of his adoration, to the point of self-worship.

Torah has always insisted that presence of the Divine in history gives life its meaning, purpose, and direction. The ultimate perfection of mankind is envisioned as the reign of God as Ruler of the world. Our celebration of *Shabbat* and *yom tov* is both "a remembrance of creation" and "a memorial for the Exodus from Egypt." God is the Creator and Ruler, both Architect and King, Author and Director, Father and Monarch.

The doctrine of creation carries with it the assumption that there is a moral dimension built into the essential nature of the world expressed through Divine directive. Just as one cannot deny God's role in history, so one dare not ignore or transgress the moral law that governs it. In the end it goes well with the good, while the evil are held accountable.

The need to study Jewish history (as distinct from the history of the Jews) is stated so powerfully by Moshe *Rabbeinu* (Deuteronomy 32:7). "Remember the days of yore, understand the years ("Dor Vador") of generation after generation. Ask your father, and he will relate it to you, and your elders, and they will tell you." Note that the words *dor vador,* are spelled without a *vav* between the *daled* and the *reish*—a reminder of *dardar* at the beginning of the Torah. The study of history requires a distinction between the two, and the ability to perceive the *daled* in all events. All of Torah has, as its purpose, to train the Jew to see Torah as the blueprint of the life of the individual and the community of Israel and the nations.

God tells Moshe in the Torah reading, "You will see My Back but My Face may not be seen" (Exodus 33:23). We are privileged to see and comprehend Him only in retrospect and by hindsight, by reflection and contemplation. When man removes God from the historical equation, he is destined to make errors in judgment that will have far-reaching consequences. To disregard the clear manifestation of God's intervention in history is folly, for His plan will not be frustrated. The *reish* syndrome has appeared during an epoch whose hallmark is clearly *daled*. The underlying theme of the *yomim tovim* as expressed in the Torah and *haftarah* readings is God's overriding presence in history.

As the Prophet Yechezkel says, "Thus I will magnify myself and sanctify myself, and I will make myself known in the eyes of many nations."

Rabbi Aaron Adler

Young Israel Council of Rabbis in Israel

THOUGHTS ABOUT THE WEATHER

Those of us familiar with the annual weather patterns in Israel know all too well that the transition period from summer weather systems of hot and dry air to wintery conditions of cold, wet, windy, and muggy weather can be quite short. The *halachah* gives full expression to this abrupt change of weather patterns through the festival of Sukkot.

We study in the *Mishnah* (*Rosh Hashanah* 1:2), ". . . and on the festival [of Sukkot] we are judged concerning water (that is, appropriate rainfall)." On the festival of Sukkot, the harvest season is celebrated while the immediacy of desired and regulated rainfall during the upcoming months of winter is concurrently recognized. The biblical commandment of the four species, along with the water libation ceremony in Temple days, based upon Oral Tradition, are to be understood as symbolic indications of our utmost dependency upon the Divine for our upcoming water needs (*Taanit* 2b). More direct—and deeply emotional—expression given on Sukkot to the onset of winter is certainly the public announcement declared in our prayers (*musaf* of *Shemini Atzeret*) that it is God alone who "shifts the winds and brings the rain."

A cursory glance at the first chapter of *Tractate Taanit* reveals that the precise date for the rain season in *Eretz Yisrael* is on the third of Cheshvan. It is on that very day that we should include the direct prayer for rain (*Tal U'matar*). On a practical note, Rav Gamliel calls for a four-day delay—until the seventh of Cheshvan (a full fifteen days after the festival of Sukkot)—allowing for those Sukkot pilgrims who resided in the vicinity of the Euphrates River to return home safe and sound (and dry!). And so, the *halachah* was indeed codified in accordance with the opinon of Rav Gamliel

(Maimonides, *Yad, Tefillah* 2:16). The Talmud (*Taanit* 10a) adds that in the Diaspora, the direct prayer for rainfall was not recited on the seventh of Cheshvan but, rather, on the day corresponding to sixty days after the autumnal equinox. In the Julian calendar, the autumnal equinox was observed on October 4. Hence, two months later, on December 4th, the Babylonian Jewish community began praying for rain. Many commentators attribute the change between *Eretz Yisrael* custom (seventh of Cheshvan) and Babylonian custom (December 4th) to the unique topographical and agricultural conditions prevailing in these two different areas. Such an attribution has generated wide halachic discussion concerning the "proper" date for inclusion of the rain prayer in areas other than *Eretz Yisrael* and Babylon. Medieval codifiers were in disagreement whether European countries should follow the December 4 tradition or the seventh of Cheshvan date. As late as the nineteenth century, halachic debate grew in *Eretz Yisrael* and in London, stimulated by the inquiry sent by the budding Australian Jewish community in the Southern Hemisphere.

The critical issue at hand revolves around the all-important question: Does the daily prayer for rain refer to rainfall in *Eretz Yisrael* only, or is it designed for the local rainfall needs? Maimonides' ambiguous comments on the subject (*Yad, Tefillah* 2:16–17, and *Kesef Mishneh* comm.), nevertheless, indicates his apparent opinion that the direct prayer for rain—in the context of the ninth blessing of the daily *Amidah* prayer—is exclusively for rain in *Eretz Yisrael*. Precedent for such a view can be deduced from the Talmud itself (*Megillah* 17b) where explanation is given as to why the ninth blessing (for rain and overall agricultural success) leads into the tenth blessing (ingathering of the exiles)—a view traced to Ezekiel 36:8. This being the case, the obvious question that must be raised is, if local climactic conditions are of no consequence to the ninth blessing, why, therefore, do Diaspora Jews commence with the rain prayer on December 4th, rather than on the seventh of Cheshvan? What relevance do "sixty days after the autumnal equinox" have to do with the agricultural cycle of *Eretz Yisrael*?

A novel response was suggested by our great *Rebbe, Harav* Yosef Dov Ber Soloveitchik, *zt"l* along *halachic* philosophical lines. Our Sages, according to the *Rav, zt"l*, were of the opinion that Diaspora Jewry was to be temporarily placed in a state of reserve for extreme emergency situations. The norm would be carried out by *Eretz Yisrael* Jewry commencing on the seventh of Cheshvan. The first chapter of *Tractate Taanit* delineates the schedule of gradual reactions to drought in *Eretz Yisrael*—a schedule dictated by the increasing of the scope, intensity, and frequency of regimented fast days. This schedule begins with the seventeenth of Cheshvan and brings us generally into the mid-latter half of Kislev (approximately the time of Chanukah). The schedule moves from private fast days for individuals only (that is, scholars), to a communal observance of "private" fast days, to a communal observance of "public" fast days, and to public displays of mourning and desperation. Each stage—more intense than its previous one—reflects the deepening crisis hovering over the community of *Eretz Yisrael*, thereby dictating a stronger—and, hopefully, more effective—response. At the moment of utter despair (middle to end of Kislev), the most effective halachic remedy is called upon. These days correspond roughly with the December 4th date. At this time, world Jewry is drafted into service by joining the prayers of *Eretz Yisrael* Jewry in a unified effort to beg of God to thwart the impending tragedy and disaster. Continues the *Rav, zt"l*: This *halachah*—in microcosmic form—reflects an accurate truth on the macrocosmic level as well. The very role of Diaspora Jewry, in its relationship with *Eretz Yisrael* Jewry, must be understood through its supportive role only! The Jews of *Eretz Yisrael* must take the lead in the redemptive process. However, this process must be augment by a properly sustained support system personified by world Jewry.

As in the case of serious physical drought in *Eretz Yisrael* generating the enlistment of the entire Diaspora Jewish population in joining the prayer efforts and repentance of *Eretz Yisrael* Jewry, so, too, today—in light of the perilous spiritual drought and the dismal cultural climate of modern-day Israel—Diaspora Jewish communities indeed have a role to play.

First and foremost, a unified call for *aliyah* must be issued by the rabbinic and educational leadership. The overwhelming majority of immigrants from Western countries are committed to Torah observance; are committed to the sanctity and covenant binding the Jewish nation and the land; and see the Jews' miraculous return to *Eretz Yisrael*, during the entire twentieth century, as preparatory to the ushering in of the redemptive era. Diaspora Jews can express their solidarity with the spiritual character of Israel by visiting Israel regularly—and, of course, by visiting the right places! It goes without saying that philanthropic activity geared to the growth and support of institutions aimed at protecting Israel's sacred character must be upgraded.

The united efforts of Jews in Israel and throughout the world will ultimately give the nation of Israel the inner strength to weather the upcoming storms in all their manifestations. Let us pray together for a speedy deliverance in our very day.

❖ CHAPTER 64 ❖

Shmini Atzeret/Simchat Torah

Rabbi Simcha Krauss

Young Israel of Hillcrest, New York

The very last *mitzvah* in the Torah, the 613th commandment, is to write a *Sefer Torah*: "And now write for yourselves this song" (Deuteronomy 31:19).

Strangely, the holiday when Jews rejoice with the Torah, Simchat Torah, takes place not on Shavuot, when the giving of Torah, *Matan Torah*, is observed. Neither do we rejoice with the Torah on Yom Kippur, when the second Tablets were given. Rather, at the end of the reading cycle, when the whole Torah has been read, we burst out in the holiday singularly devoted to rejoicing with the Torah, and we celebrate Simchat Torah.

Torah and its meaning, Torah and its issues, are not limited to a particular aspect of our existence. Torah encompasses not only a segment of our life but the totality of life. Torah addresses the Jew not only in a corner of his existence but in the wholeness, fullness, richness, and complexity of his existence. His private life and his public life, the individual and his family, the local community and all of *Klal Yisrael* are addressed by Torah. Hence, only when a Jew passes through a whole year of Torah reading, when the whole of life, its better moments and worse moments, its ups and dows, its joys and tragedies, when under all circumstances we retain loyalty and fidelity to Torah—only then can we truly rejoice with the Torah.

Let us, indeed, look at the context in which this *mitzvah* of *ketivat Sefer Torah*, the writing of a Torah, is commanded.

God tells Moshe that after Moshe's death, the people will go astray and forsake the covenant:

> Then my anger will turn against them . . . and I will forsake them and I will hide my face from them . . . and they shall be devoured, and many evils and troubles shall befall them; so that they will say on that day, 'Are not these evils come upon us, because our God is not amongst us?' And I will surely hide my face on that day . . . *Now therefore write*

> *this song* for yourselves and teach it to the children of Israel. (Deuteronomy 31:17–19)

It is good to observe Torah in all times. Whenever and however a Jew observes the Torah, keeps its commandments and shows devotion to Torah, it is praiseworthy. But when a Jew remains loyal after God has been "silent"; when Jews remain truthful to the covenant in a period when many were "devoured" and "evils and troubles" have befallen them, then indeed that loyalty becomes a model.

It is important to note something else. The Torah does not speak just of retaining loyalties and performing *mitzvot*. The Torah says that exactly after God's "silence" and after all these "evils" befalling *Knesset Yisroel,* the Torah will still be *shirah*—it will be a poem, a song.

The yearly cycle with its ups and downs, the totality of life—not only alone the good but also the not-so-good—nothing deters us from our ongoing "song" to the *Ribono shel Olam—l'maan yezamercha chavod v'lo yidom.*

Rabbi Benjamin Blech

Young Israel of Oceanside, New York

The question begs to be asked: Why now?

The last day of this lengthy holiday period is designated by tradition as Simchat Torah. We rejoice with the word of God; we make *hakafot*; we conclude the reading of all five Books, and we begin again. Yet, by all logic, it would certainly appear that our emphasis is misplaced, our timing ill-chosen. During the course of the year we observe *Shalosh Regelim*. Each of the three pilgrimage festivals has a major historic event as rationale. And Revelation is, of course, the story of Shavuot. We received the Torah on the sixth of Sivan. Indeed, from Pesach to Shavuot we longingly and lovingly count the days marking the passage from freedom to fulfillment, from the rigors of physical slavery to the reason for God's intervention.

The Torah was given on Shavuot. Is not that the *yom tov* on which we should see to it that the annual Torah cycle both concludes and begins anew? Is that not the holiday on which we should express our joy and our gratitude for the greatest gift from God to our people? In short, if Shavuot is described by *Chazal* as *z'man matan Torateinu*, doesn't that automatically confer upon it also the descriptive of *z'man simchateinu* as well?

SHOLASH REGELIM AS A UNIT

The answer, obviously, rests in the fact that Shavuot is only the second in a series of holidays that require completion before true *simchah* is possible. Three times a year the Jews had to go to Yerushalayim to both see and be seen by *HaShem*. Every trip was meant to serve as a step bringing us closer to the Almighty. Every *yom tov* addresses us and makes demands of us. And it is only after we have fully absorbed the complete cycle that we may conclude the entire series with a day known as Simchat Torah.

To grasp the threefold message of *HaShem* as expressed in the *shalosh regalim*, it is necessary to comprehend first the remarkable parallelism of the historic moments of Pesach, Shavuot, and Sukkot with their correspondence in the realm of nature.

Pesach is, of course, sanctified because it is *zeman cheruteinu*. Historically, it commemorates the festival of our freedom. But that is not enough in terms of its halachic identification. It is also the holiday of the spring season. So crucial is this component aspect of the yom tov that the Sanhedrin was commanded to add an extra month, compensating for the difference between the lunar and solar year, in order to insure that Pesach always retains not solely its remembrance of the Exodus but also its identification with a very particular season of the year.

So, too, Shavuot is not only the time of the giving of the Torah but also *chag habikurim*—the time when the first fruits ripened and, in a ceremony carefully described by our Sages, were brought to Yerushalayim, the Holy City. Somehow, the agricultural aspect of the holiday was as integral a part of the observance as the historic commemoration of the moment of revelation.

Finally, Sukkot, the *yom tov* reminding us of our miraculous passage through the desert preserved by Divine intervention with "booths of glory" is also always to be observed as the festival of the harvest.

Why are the specific seasons so relevant to these historic celebrations? In what way does the message of the fields clarify the meaning of the festivals?

NATURE DEFINES HISTORY

The answer allows us a powerful insight into the very meaning and definition of our past. Pesach is to be celebrated because it gave us freedom—but its time on the calendar is to make clear that *freedom from* without any further clarification of *freedom to* may best be compared to the beautiful trees of the field that flower and bloom in the spring. The bloom is the beauty of potential; what it lacks is the fullness of fruit. We are grateful that Pharaoh is no longer our master. But that freedom alone is as transient as buds and as inconsequential as the opening flowers, which please the eye but fail to give us further sustenance.

It is only on Shavuot, when we placed ourselves under the rule of *HaShem*, that God Himself saw the *first fruit* of human progress. At last there was one people that understood life's purpose and meaning. True, God offered the Torah to all people on Mount Sinai, and every other nation rejected what they should have recognized as Divine truth. But even nature itself acknowledges that there are fruits that ripen before others. Shavuot is *chag habikkurim* even as the Jewish people are referred to as *Bni Bichorei Yisrael*—My son,

My *firstborn*, Israel. We are not God's only children; we are, however, God's "firstborn." What in agriculture is known as *bikurim*, amongst the nations of the world is the "firstborn" who hastens to do the will of the Lord. Shavuot must be observed at the time when the first fruits ripen—because historically that is exactly what took place when we became a "kingdom of priests"—a people whose mission would be to serve as priests to the rest of mankind.

And why is Shavuot not yet *z'man simchateinu*? The answer is obvious: How could God and we His people fully rejoice when so many of God's creations still wander blindly in abject ignorance of God's will and His ways? Shavuot is only the second of the three festivals—because nature knows a time of harvest and so, too, will history complement this reality. Indeed, there will come a day of *chag he'asif* when there will be a final and full "harvest"; and only then is the time we can designate as *z'man simchateinu* the time of rejoicing.

What are the readings for the *yom tov* of Sukkot? The *haftarot* all deal with the Messianic Age. The holiday itself speaks of the Jews offering seventy sacrifices—for *all* the nations of the world. We leave the confines of our own homes to sit under the heavens—mindful that God is the God of the entire universe. We shake the *lulav* to all four corners of the earth—because the very God who took us out of the land of Egypt, the House of Bondage, is also the Almighty God who created the heavens and the earth and all that which is within it.

On Shavuot, we remember that we were wise enough to be the first to acknowledge the Creator. Yet every prayer service ends with the hope and prayer that "the Lord will be King over the entire Universe; in that day the Lord will will be one and His name will be one." It is at the conclusion of Sukkot, affirming our belief in a final harvest of mankind to Divine service, that we allow ourselves complete rejoicing. May we do all in our power to hasten that day when the faith of our people becomes the creed of all Creation.

Rabbi Dovid Spetner

Young Israel of Richmond/Congregation Kol Emes, Virginia

"We make a festive meal for the completion of the Torah"
(Midrash *Shir Hashirim Rabbah*).

This *midrash* is quoted as the source for our celebration of Simchat Torah. Although Simchat Torah is one of our most joyous Holidays, we really need to stand back and think about what we mean by "Completion of the Torah." In a sense, how do we ever complete the Torah? Our Torah is that of which "its measure is longer than the earth" (Job 11:9). It is actually infinite in that it is the manifest expression of God's wisdom. Are we not diminishing the Torah and our never-ending responsibility of its study by celebrating its conclusion?

Actually, it is because of these questions that the custom of *chatan Bereishit*—the bridegroom of *Bereishit*—developed. We immediately begin the Torah again from *Bereishit* to illustrate the continuity of our relationship with the Torah.

But still, why celebrate? Let's just keep on going!

The answer, clearly, is that progress has to be incremental. Growth in Torah needs to be like the steps of a staircase, not like a blind elevator shaft where we can not gauge how far we have risen. When we take stock of how far we've come and want to move further, we need to pat ourselves on the back and celebrate.

This cyclical method of completing and recompleting the Torah is not just necessary on a personal level to provide for individual growth. It is an integral part of the Jewish people's relationship with the Torah. On the one hand, the Torah is an ongoing spiritual and intellectual project intertwined with the eternity of the Jewish people. Yet, on the other hand, the authorities who wield it, and the people who study and live it, change with every generation. The Torah of Reb Yehudah Hanasi (author of the *Mishnah*) and the Torah of the *Chatam Soffer* (a nineteenth-century authority) is the same Torah; yet throughout the generations who have studied it, the Torah has expanded (if more so in quantity) through both application and discussion.

This passing of the torch of Torah from one "cycle" of scholars to another has been happening since Moshe first handed the mantle of leadership to Yehoshua. According to the *Klei Chemdah*, this change in Torah authority may be the source for our *minhag* of honoring a Torah scholar to complete the Torah as *chatan Torah*.

The *Gemara* (*Bava Batra* 15) quotes a difference of opinion regarding who wrote down the last eight *pesukim* in the Torah. These last eight *pesukim* begin with, "and Moshe died." The *Gemara* says that one of two assumptions must be made about this *pasuk*. Either Moshe did not write it, or he wrote it even though he was still alive. Rabbi Yehudah concludes that the last eight *pesukim* were written by Yehoshua. Rabbi Shimon maintains that Moshe indeed wrote these words but wrote them *b'dema*, literally, with his tears.

An alternative explanation of Rabbi Shimon's opinion is offered by Rabbi Menachem Azarya, a sixteenth-century Italian kabbalist known as the "Ramah Mipano." He translates the word *b'dema* as having its source in the word *dimua* which means "mixture." As the Vilna Gaon explains, the Torah existed before our world of people, places, and things. It, therefore, must have meaning and interpretation beyond our physical world. The Torah, in its essence, says the Gaon, is a series of particular letters capable of being combined in different ways. It has a hidden, mystical way of being expressed and a practical way, which guides our functioning in the physical world. Moshe wrote the last eight *pesukim* as an undefined string of letters, as yet unbroken into separate words. In this view, even according to Rabbi Shimon, Yehoshua played a role in the last eight *pesukim*; he deciphered the mass of letters that Moshe had written into separate words.

The *Gemara* further quotes a statement in the name of Rav, that these last eight *pesukim* are true *yachid korei otan*—literally "an individual reads them." The *Gemara* goes on to explain that Rav's statement can be agreed upon by both Rabbi Yehudah (Yehoshua wrote them) and by Rabbi Shimon (Moshe wrote them). What, though, does Rav mean by *yachid*, "an individual"?

The Mordechai quotes a view that the word *yachid* is a reference to a *talmid chacham*, Torah scholar. Rav is, therefore, telling us that we should specifically call upon a *talmid chacham* to read the last eight *pesukim* in the Torah. This can be agreed upon by both Rabbi Yehudah and Rabbi Shimon, writes the *Klei Chemdah*, because both agree (as we explained earlier) that Yehoshua played a role in these final eight *pesukim*. That role, however understood, represented the passing of a part of the unique authority of Moshe to the scholars of future generations.

On Simchat Torah, as we complete a cycle of our own study of Torah, we call upon a *talmid chacham* to act as *chatan Torah*, symbolizing another cycle in the Torah's travel through the generations.

Simchat Torah is the last opportunity to fulfill what is often an overlooked *mitzvah*. The *Shulchan Aruch* (*orach chaim* chapter 285) writes that even if a person has heard the Torah read every week on *Shabbat*, he is still obligated to personally review the *sedrah* weekly—twice with *mikra* (reading the words of the *Chumash*) and once with *targum* (explanation). The expression the *Gemara Berakhot* 8 uses to describe this *mitzvah*, is to "complete one's *parshah* [review] with the community." This is best accomplished, according to the *halachah*, by completing your review by the time of the Torah reading on *Shabbat* morning. In a worst-case scenario, one would still be considered to be "completing his *parshah* with the community," if he completes it by *Simchat Torah* when the community completes its review of the entire Torah.

The high educational value of this *mitzvah* must be stressed. Someone who completes the entire *Chumash* annually (preferably with Rashi's commentary), will have a wealth of Torah knowledge under his belt. Yet much of that knowledge is also basic information that every Jew should know. Even if we tell ourselves that we are generally familiar with most of the ideas in the *Chumash*, there is still another issue at work here. That issue is what *Simchat Torah* is all about—*completing* the Torah. *Baruch HaShem*, there is a tremendous resurgence of Torah study today—we have access to *shiurim*, books and audio and video tapes on all topics for all levels. Sometimes, though, we may forget that the Torah was also meant to be *completed*.

Whether an annual review of the *Chumash*, daily *Mishnah* study, *Daf*, or *Amud Yomi*, opportunities abound for completing the Torah. Just as we would not dream of leaving other important projects only half-finished, so it should be with our Torah study. We owe it to ourselves to finish the Torah and enjoy the sense of gratification that comes with it.

The story is told that Rabbi Akiva Eiger, already a prince of Torah in his own time, was called upon to serve as *chatan Torah*. As he approached the Torah, he began to cry, "Here I am, the *chatan* (groom)," he said, "and I still don't know the *kallah* (bride)!" This was not false humility on the part of Rabbi Akiva Eiger; rather it was his powerful grasp of Torah that enabled him to appreciate just how far "the mountain" of Torah really rises.

By our own completion of a cycle of Torah, we open up the vista of new growth in Torah—to the next cycle and the next cycle, as we spiral ever higher.

Rabbi Yehoshua Weber

Young Israel of Canarsie, New York

"The eighth day shall be *Atzeret*, a time you are held back"
(Numbers 29:35).

Names, at least in the Torah's lexicon, are certainly more than ceremonious titles haphazardly appended to designated items. Torah titles define that which they are naming. For example, the Torah calls Pesach, *Chag Hamatzot*, an appellation that highlights the *matzot*, an essential, definitive aspect of the festival. *Chag Hasukkot*, a term the Torah uses for Sukkot, stresses the crux of the *yom tov*, the *sukkah* and its recollection of the clouds and huts of protection that *HaShem* extended to us during our desert sojourn—protection we receive throughout our lives. "Name relevance" must, of course, be true of all our *yomim tovim*. Nothing in our Torah is cursory.

How, then, do we interpret *Shemini Atzeret*? A simplistic translation of the phrase would be *Shemini*: the "eighth" (Shemini Atzeret being an eighth-day addendum to the Sukkot holiday), and *Atzeret*: "held back" (from doing work—according to Ibn Ezra, *Vayikra* 23). Do these two words adequately convey the true essence of Shemini Atzeret? Is Shemini Atzeret merely an eighth-day addendum to the week-long Sukkot *yom tov* with no clearly discernible identity of its own? The word *atzeret* (held back) is also troubling. *Atzeret* seems to lay undue stress on the restrictive, non-productive aspects of the *yom tov*. Should we not rather accentuate the active, productive lessons this *yom tov* most certainly contains? What, really, is the message of Shemini Atzeret?

A glance at two very important numbers should help illuminate this confusing issue. *Sheva*—seven—more than any other number, is the protoplasm, the very building block of Jewish time. The Jewish week is known as *shavua*—"seventhed" and composed of seven days. The Kuzari notes that it did not have to be that way. Society could have structured weeks composed of sequences of eight, ten, or any other number of days. Our twelve-month calendar also heeds the cycle of seven. Rav Shimshon Rafael Hirsch, in his *Collected Writings*, notes that our two festive months, Nisan and Tishrei, are at seven-month intervals from one another. Some other manifestations of this maxim are the seven-year *shemitta*—sabbatical of the land—cycle, the seven-day duration (in Israel) of the Pesach and Sukkot festivals, and the seven-day cycle of ritual purification.

The Vilna Gaon in *Divrei Eliyahu, Parshat Emor* even compiles a list of seven days in which the Torah forbade work: The first and last days of Pesach and Sukkot, Shavuot, Rosh Hashanah, and Yom Kippur. On a somewhat less tangible note, the Rabbenu Bachya, *Parshat Bo* quotes the *midrash* in stating that "whoever has *tefillin* on his head and arm, *tzitzit* on the four corners of his garment, and a *mezuzah* on his door (for a total of seven) is guaranteed not to sin." It is not perchance that the seven aspects of these *mitzvot* combine to form some sort of protecting aura.

Even our lineage is based on the combined accomplishments of seven great people: our three patriarchs and four matriarchs or, alternatively, the seven *Ushpizin*—great leaders of our people—Avrohom, Yitzchok, Yaakov, Yosef, Moshe, Aharon, and Dovid. The *Midrash Rabbah Vayikra* 29 encapsulates this concept by stating that "all sevenths are beloved"; the *midrash* then provides historical proof of this axiom by listing a surprising array of generations and sequences that peaked at the seventh. The seventh of a cycle or sequence is its climax and completion.

The very etymology of *sheva*—"seven"—relays the aforementioned idea. The Maharal, *Ohr Chadash*, page 93, correlates *sheva* to *sova*—satisfaction; after seven we have completed whatever we have set out to do; hence we are satisfied.

Seven is distinct, even from a mathematical standpoint. Of all the basic numbers—one through ten—only seven is both non-divisible (in contrast to six, for example, which can be divided by two or by three) and yet neither can it be multiplied and still remain within the realm of basic numbers (numbers one through ten). Seven cannot be fragmented into equal whole numbers (unlike four, six, eight, nine, or ten) and it is a number so perfect that it need not duplicate itself to achieve greatness—that is, if we multiply seven we leave the realm of basic numbers (unlike one, two, three, four, and five). Seven symbolizes fulfilling our potential; being completely developed; being fully able to stand on our own two feet without any assistance. Our mundane, day-to-day lives are therefore structured in sequences of seven.

Nevertheless, seven is not always the right number. There are moments in our lives that are more ethereal than others; moments that are neither mundane nor day-to-day. These moments do not fit the usual structure of our day-to-day lives. These situations can not be accommodated with the normal cycles of seven; they work within the context of the level beyond seven—eight.

Eight was the definitive number in the Temple, our bastion of most extraordinary spirituality. *Rabbeinu* Bachya (*Vayikra* 9:1) states that "most aspects of the Temple came in multiples of eight; the high priest's eight articles of clothing, the eight spices of the anointing oil and incense, the eight carrying poles (two each for the ark, the table, the golden and the copper altars), and so on." The Maharal, *Ner Mitzva*, makes this concrete by associating *shemini*—"eight"—with *shemen*—excess fat—that is, above and beyond the usual, more than what is necessary.

Circumcision is another *mitzvah* oriented around the number eight; it is performed on the eighth day of a child's life. Eight might figure prominently here because the aim of circumcision is to differentiate us from and raise us above the level of our surroundings. *Tefillin* and *tzitzit* might be other examples. It is entirely possible that the eight strands of *tzitzit* and the eight Torah portions contained in our two *tefillin* allude to the same point. *Tefillin* and *tzitzit* are supposed to be graphic reminders to prevent "straying after our hearts"—reminders to rise above the immorality around us.

Might not Shemini Atzeret belong to the aforementioned "other-worldly" category of *mitzvot—mitzvot* that do not fit into the usual structure of our day-to-day lives? After all, Shemini Atzeret is at the very end of our yearly festival series; it might very well be seen as the year's finale. First we encounter the seven days of Pesach, with the seven Seder *mitzvot*: *Pesach*, *matzah*, and *maror* (for Avrohom, Yitzchok, and Yaakov) and the four cups of wine (for the four matriarchs; see Maharal on the *Haggadah*). Onward we progress through the seven weeks of counting that culminate in Shavuot. On to Rosh Hashanah and Yom Kippur and the seven penitential days between them. Finally, we celebrate the seven days of Sukkot, in which we grip an *etrog*, *lulav*, two *aravot*, and three *hadassim*: the seven parts of the four species. Only after all this are we capable of moving beyond the normal structure of our day-to-day lives and on to Shemini Atzeret; on to the special world of eights. Indeed, Sforno, commenting on *Vayikra* 23:36, notes that Shemini Atzeret "is the *yom tov* in which all *yom tov* festivities are completed."

Shemini Atzeret, a *yom tov* whose name highlights the fact that it is an eighth-day festival, is so much more than an eighth-day addendum. It is a *shemen*—excess (as the Maharal explains)—a holiday of extra and excess potential, one whose capacity goes far beyond that of other holidays. Being called *shemini* (eighth), then, is an attribute rather than a detraction.

Another singular aspect of Shemini Atzeret is its peculiar lack of structure. Pesach and Sukkot have their own particular regimens of positive (*matzah*, *sukkah*, and so on) and negative *mitzvot*. Shemini Atzeret, on the other hand, does not have a legion of distinctive *mitzvot*. The Vilna Gaon (*Divrei Eliyahu*) concludes from the phrase, "and you should only be joyous" (*Devarim* 16), that joy is the only *mitzvah* endemic to Shemini Atzeret: there is nothing else unique about it!

Our earlier idea might help clarify why *Atzeret* "held back" is part of this *yom tov*'s title. Shemini Atzeret does not focus on particular details. We have already absorbed the myriad details of all the previous *yomim tovim*. We are now ready for the unlimited, as-yet-undefined, world beyond that. It is a day to focus simply on being "held back"; as Rashi in *Emor* explains, that *HaShem* tells us, "My sons, please remain with me another day; our parting is difficult." We reveal in the fact that we have another day to spend in Yerushalayim refining the lessons absorbed from all the previous *yom tovim*. Being *Atzeret*, unclear and therefore open to all spiritual possibilities, is part of the greateness of the day.

The ideas espoused flow beautifully with an extraordinary essay by Rabbi Gedaliah Schorr, *zt"l*. He parallels each *yom tov* with one of our founding fathers (see *Tur Orach Chaim* 417)—Pesach with Avraham, Shavuot with Yitzchok, and Sukkot with Yaakov. Shemini Atzeret is unclear; he attempts to correlate it with Yosef. He expounds the connections by exploring the dual meaning of Yosef's name. Upon Yosef's birth, Rochel, who no longer felt unfulfilled as a wife/mother, cried "*HaShem* gathered my shame" (*Bereishit* 30:23) and "*HaShem* should grant me another son" (*Bereishit* 30:24). Rabbi Schorr beautifully connects the two reasons for Yosef's name: Only because Rochel had dealt with and gathered all the outstanding issues of her life ("*HaShem* gathered my shame"), could she move on and ask for yet another son.

The message is relevant for us too. We can and should grow; but first we must fully absorb and understand that which we already have. Only then do we have the right to ask *HaShem* for more. This is Yosef's attribute: Maximizing all that our ancestors gave us so that we can move on and go further. The parallel to Shemini Atzeret is scintillating. Only after we have internalized the message of all the previous seven days of holiday can we expand our horizons and progress to the special world of *shemonah*—eight—Shemini Atzeret. May this Shemini Atzeret truly be a holiday in which we move beyond our mundane, everyday lives on to the extraordinary world of eight.

❖ CHAPTER 65 ❖

Purim

Rabbi Moshe Teitelbaum

Young Israel of Lawrence and Cedarhurst, New York

The *Gemara* in Tractate *Chullin* 139b inquires about a *remez*, an opaque reference to Mordechai in the Torah. *Mordechai min hatorah minayin*? In answer to this question, the *Gemara* quotes the command to Moshe (Exodus 30:23) to procure *mor dror* as the key ingredient of the oil of anointment used to consecrate the *Klei kodesh* (the holy vessels) and Aharon and his Sons. Targum Onkelos translates *mor dror* as *mayro dachyo* which, read quickly together, composes the name Mordechai. Our purpose here is to reveal the message behind this very obscure reference to the hero of the *Megillah*. Our obvious starting point must be an identification of the ingredient *mor* and an understanding of its intended use in the oil of anointment.

Mayro dachyo means "highly refined musk." The Rambam, in *Hilchot Klei Hamikdash* (1:3), explains that this musk was derived from a non-kosher beast. The Ravad asks how can the oil of anointment, used to anoint the holiest instruments of the *Mishkan*, be made of a derivative of an impure nature? The *remez* to the name *Mordechai* is also most unflattering, since *mayro dachyo* is taken from a *davar tameh* (an unclean animal). The intention of *Chazal* in the *Gemara* in Tractate *Chullin* is now more difficult to discern.

In his commentaries on *Parshat Ki Tisa*, Rav Yosef Patzanovsky cites the opinion of *Rabbeinu* Yonah, who permits the consumption of *mor* in our food after it has been processed and refined. Similarly, the oil of anointment was made of ritually pure musk, which sheds its identity and character of impurity once it has been refined. Use of this musk in the oil of anointment was intended to express that, like the musk itself, the mundane—or even the profane—need not remain so forever. The process of consecration effects a radical change and relabeling of both the utensils to be used in the *Mishkan* and the *Kohanim* who will serve *HaShem* there. A mere mortal can become a priest of the Almighty; simple metal objects can become instruments with which to serve Him.

This concept of unleashing latent potential is the basis of the *Gemara*'s comparison of Mordechai to the musk of the oil of anointment. The *midrash* on *Chukat* compared a number of great individuals of very humble ancestry to the waters mixed with the ashes of the red heifer (*parah adumah*) used to bring ritual purity to someone who became defiled through contact with a corpse. Just as the water and ashes cause the *kohein* who handles them to become impure (*tameh*) even though they convey purity (*tahara*) to those upon whom they are sprinkled, so, too, great people can descend from seemingly unworthy forebears. The unworthy ancestors are being compared to the *tumah* brought upon the *kohein* who handles the water of purification, while the worthy descendants are compared to the purity achieved through that very same water. One example of such an individual is none other than Mordechai the *tzaddik*, whose ancestor, Shimi ben Gera, was a wicked enemy of Dovid *Hamelech*. (Other examples mentioned by this *midrash* include Avraham *Avinu*, whose father, Terach, worshiped *avodah zarah*, and the great King Chezkiyah, whose father, Achaz, was a notoriously sinful ruler.)

The message of the *Gemara* in *Chullin*—the hint referring to Mordechai contained in the Targum's words, *mayro dachyo*—is now clear. Just as musk, though derived from a non-kosher beast, is pure and *tahor*, so, too, Mordechai, though descended from impure and wicked ancestry, was a refined and holy *tzaddik* worthy of becoming the savior of all of Israel. When a *tzaddik* is born from parents who are themselves *tzaddikim*, or at least respectably worthy, it is not surprising that the offspring distinguish their family yet again by serving *Hakadosh baruch Hu* with valor. What the *Gemara* in Tractate *Chullin* wishes to prove is that the very same righteousness can emanate from seemingly wicked forebears. The use of musk—derived from unholy sources—to consecrate the *avodah* of the *Mishkan* validates and confirms the intentions that *HaShem* has for us to blossom with greater perfection from one generation to the next.

Mordechai, descendant of Shimi ben Gera, represents our outstanding potential which every Jew carries within himself or herself. We may have modest ancestry, or humble qualifications based on our own past. Yet, within each of us, there is a dormant Mordechai, pure and righteous, waiting to emerge. Our conquest of Amalek is achieved when the nobility within the Jewish people becomes our truest outward identity—when we succeed in shedding the "impurities" of our lives and attain the refinement of the oil of anointment. It is this process of refinement that consecrates us, preparing us to rise, as Mordechai did, to heights of greatness for the honor of *HaShem* and His Torah.

❖ CHAPTER 66 ❖

The Four Parshiot

Rabbi Jeffrey Bienenfeld

Young Israel of St. Louis, Missouri

The opening *Mishnah* in tractate *Shekalim* states, "On the first [day] of Adar, [the obligation to bring] *shekalim* (coins) was publicized." The *Korban Ha'aida* explains that in the *Beit Hamikdash* era, the courts made public declarations in every community reminding the Jews to contribute their *shekalim* to the Temple so that, with the beginning of the following month, the month of Nisan, all sacrifices would be purchased with these newly collected funds.

Subsequent to the *Churban* (the destruction of the Temple), our Sages sought to commemorate this practice by requiring a special Torah portion to be read on what today we call *Shabbat Shekalim*. However, the Talmud in *Megillah* (29b) records a disagreement as to the choice of Torah texts to serve as the appropriate *maftir* portion for this special *Shabbat*. In the view of Rav, the selection was from *Bamidbar* 28:1–8, the obvious preference because it discusses the daily sacrifices, the very purpose for which the *shekalim* were appropriated.

Shmuel disagreed. His choice was from *Shemot* 30:11–26. After all, the Talmud argues, the Shemot selection deals explicitly with the obligation to give *shekalim*, whereas the *Bamidbar* portion contains no mention of the term *shekalim* at all. Shmuel's opinion, however, while accepted as halachically definitive, does have to respond to one significant objection raised in the talmudic debate in *Megillah*. Shmuel's passage from *Shemot* does not discuss the public offerings which, in the view of Rav Tavi, were the primary reason for the *mitzvah* of *shekalim* in the first place.

Shmuel's position is defended by referencing a *baraita* cited by Rav Yosef:

> There are three *terumot*, contributions, mentioned in the Shemot text: of the Altar, for the Altar (*shekalim* for the purchase of the public offerings); of the Bases, for the Bases (*shekalim* for the silver bases used

> to support the Tabernacle); and of the Temple maintenance, for the Temple maintenance (*shekalim* for the repair and upkeep of the Temple complex).

Hence, although not explicitly, the selection chosen by Shmuel does make implicit reference to the public sacrifices as well.

Can there be, however, a deeper understanding of this disagreement between Rav and Shmuel?

The Talmud in *Taanit* (29a) tells us that "When the month of Adar enters, rejoicing is increased."

The reason for this *simchah*, says Rashi, is our anticipation of the holidays of Purim and Pesach and their powerful motif of *geulah*—redemption. How then is this joyful mood enhanced by requiring the recitation of *Parshat Shekalim*? Rav apparently was of the view that the message of the *korbanot* was of primary significance in facilitating this rejoicing. Rashi in *Shemot* (30:15) explains that the daily sacrifices served to atone for the sins of Israel. True *simchah* is inconceivable until every Jew, through his donation of a *machtzit hashekel* (half-shekel), commits to a collective responsibility for the transgressions of the entire community. Only when the daily offerings effected such an atonement could the cleansed Jew feel worthy to merit redemption and thus genuinely rejoice.

Now, Shmuel, while certainly accepting this insight, felt that the message of the *shekalim* was not to be restricted to this lesson alone. Atonement is not the only prerequisite for *simchah*. There must be, in addition, a positive affirmation of the worth of each individual Jew as well. According to Shmuel, the *maftir* selection contained just such an affirmation.

The *baraita* of Rav Yosef was fairly explicit, for, apart from the public offerings, *shekalim* were also donated for the bases of the Tabernacle and for the upkeep of the Temple. And yet, without a foundation, no House of God could stand, and without daily maintenance, the most magnificent Temple could not preserve its beauty. Every Jew, through his *machtzit hashekel* donation, had thus a share in both the foundation and the splendor of the Temple.

Shabbat Shekalim, then, was a time to give visible and public recognition for such ostensibly commonplace activities as well. Each and every Jew was thus complimented and his contribution communally acknowledged by virtue of its very public solicitation on Rosh Chodesh Adar. How much better to feel appreciated and worthwhile than to have one's small, modest deeds given such proud applause! What better way to generate a mood of *simchah*!

If indeed it was this lesson that Shmuel sought to teach, then the *haftarah* choice clearly supported this message. The Prophetic selection for *Shabbat Shekalim* (II *Melachim* 12) discusses how Yehoash appealed for funds to repair the Temple. Imagine, not for the sacrifices, not for the other lofty purposes, but simply to restore and renovate a place of holiness. It was this task alone that merited the attention of the Navi! (See Radak on II *Melachim* 12:14 and Talmud *Ketuvot* 106b.)

It has been reported in the name of HaRav Yosef Dov Halevi Soloveitchik, *zt"t* that should one forget to recite the designated *haftarah* for *Shabbat Shekalim*, one is required to say it at *mincha* with the attendant blessing. Why? Perhaps the reason is simply to stress that without the *haftarah* reading one might not properly grasp the essential message of the *maftir*, and that is that every Jew has a contribution to make toward the ultimate redemption of our people. For some, that *machtzit hashekel* might take the popular distinctive form of Torah study; for others, it might involve the quiet routine sweeping of the study hall. In both cases, the Jew is recognized for his effort. It is valued and appreciated; it is necessary and vital. And . . . it releases bountiful *simchah*!

The *Sefat Emet* makes a remarkable observation in comparing the months of Elul and Adar. Both precede two of the four New Years discussed in the Talmud. In Tishrei, the individual is judged; in Nisan, the collective is judged. Tishrei requires the preceding month of *Elul* to be set aside for *teshuvah*; so, too, Nisan requires Adar for the same purpose. But the *teshuvah* for each month is different. For Elul, it is a repentance born of fear and trembling; for Adar, it is a repentance inspired by joy and happiness. Convinced that my life is worthwhile and meaningful, confident that my relatively anonymous efforts are noticed and gratefully acknowledged, I yearn to improve and enhance my religious life and honestly feel I can, with God's help, be successful in that attempt. With such a buoyant mood of *simchah*, the prospects of a complete redemption become a more optimistic reality.

Adar enters and heralds a spirit of rejoicing filled with optimism and hope. The Jew is beckoned to participate, and he hesitates. Perhaps he is not worthy: a blemished past, a tiresome routine, an uneventful life with little to recommend itself. Comes along *Shabbat Shekalim* with its powerful *maftir* and ignites the spark of simchah for everyone. It declares: If you are committed to the *klal* (the community of Israel), then no sin is beyond forgiveness and no task is too insignificant. The *machtzit hashekel*, three times over, reinvigorates the Jewish soul and arouses renewed faith that redemption can be ours if we, as a community, can inspire individuals to attain and appreciate their true greatness.

Rabbi Chaim Wakslak

Young Israel of Long Beach, New York

Parshat Parah is the third of the four special Shabbat readings that are read in the weeks that precede the *yom tov* of Pesach. These four are: *Parshat Shekalim, Parshat Zachor, Parshat Parah,* and *Parshat Hachodesh*. Each of these special *parshiyot* commemorates a specific event, but, taken as a group, they also form a lesson for the preparation for each year's *yom tov* of Pesach. On a more global level, these *parshiyot* illustrate the principles necessary for the ultimate redemption of *Klal Yisrael*.

Parshat Shekalim discusses the *machtzit hashekel* (one-half coin), a donation that was required of every Jew in the time of the *Beit Hamikdash* and that allowed each member of *Klal Yisrael* to have a portion in the *korbanei tzibbur* (community sacrifices) that were sacrificed throughout the year. The concept of *machtzit hashekel* evolved to symbolize other charitable deeds and contributions and is often used as a metaphor for *gemilat chesed* in our day. In more recent times, it stood for proactive acts of kindness designed to combat the *shekalim* that were given by Haman to destroy the Jewish nation.

Parshat Zachor calls upon us to remember the actions of the nation of Amalek and destroy their memory. How are we to combat Amalek? Our only weapon is the study of Torah. And our enemies know this: Haman, a member of Amalek, was overjoyed when his lottery determined that his evil plan would occur in the month of Adar, the month of Moshe *Rabbeinu*'s *Petirah* (passing). Why would this add to Haman's glee? If he simply saw it as a positive omen for his plot, then, surely, there would be some righteous Jewish leaders who had died during any particular month. But, of course, Moshe *Rabbeinu* is not simply a leader; he is the very essence of Torah, and our Torah is called *Torat Moshe*. These two forces exist in the world: When Torah is diminished, God forbid, Amalek flourishes, but when Torah is strong, Amalek cannot survive.

Parshat Parah teaches us that the ashes of the *parah adumah* were the exclusive mechanism by which a person who was a *tomei meit* (impure through contact with a dead body) could achieve a status of *taharah* and be eligible to sacrifice the *korban Pesach*. The *parah adumah*'s purpose in purifying the *B'nei Yisrael* so that they might be able to sacrifice the *korbanot*, as well as the entire procedure of preparing the ashes of the *parah adumah*, are concepts of service to *HaShem* (*avodah*). These three *parshiyot* together illustrate that, in the words of *Pirkei Avot* (1:2), "The world depends on three things—on Torah, on the service of God, and on kind deeds."

It is interesting that all these concepts are also reflected in our celebration of the *yom tov* of Purim. The four *mitzvot* of the day—reading the *Megillah* (*Torah*), *mishloach manot* and *matanot l'evyonim* (*gemilut chasadim*), and *seudat Purim* (*avodah*, as the table of a person is likened to a present *mizbeach*, an altar)—present to us in an even more concentrated manner these basic principles.

There is one additional *Shabbat* reading; *Parshat Hachodesh*, which commemorates the *mitzvah* of *kiddush hachodesh* (sanctifying the new moon) that was given to *Bnei Yisrael* for the first time when Moshe, Aaron, and *Hakadosh baruch Hu* sanctified the month of Nisan while the Jews were still in Egypt. In addition, *Parshat Hachodesh* reflects a concept of renewal and recommitment, teaching us that it is not enough that we acknowledge the principles of *Torah*, *avodah*, and *gemilut chasadim* but that, before the *yom tov* of Pesach, we are called upon to make a rededication to these principles so that we can appropriately celebrate the *yom tov* of Pesach—the *Chag Hageulah*. As our Rabbis teach us: Our ancestors were redeemed in the month of Nisan and the future redemption will also take place during the month of Nisan.

This concept of preparation for the *yom tov* of Pesach seems to make a great deal of sense. We are cognizant that preparation for the month of Tishrei, the other New Year, takes the entire month of Elul (four weeks); so, too, the New Year that begins in the month of Nisan requires preparation.

The ashes of *parah adumah* are the exclusive mechanism by which an individual can purify him or herself from *tumat hameit* (defilement from contact with a corpse). Had *Bnei Yisrael* accepted the Torah without committing the sin of the golden calf (*eigel hazahav*), they would have been free of the *malach hamavet* (the angel of death). As the *Gemara* states in Tractate *Eruvin* (42) (Shmot 32:16): The tablets were God's handiwork and the script was the script of God, *charut*—engraved on the tablets. "Read it as *cherut* (free), not *charut* (engraved)." One who accepts the Torah is free, free from the *yetzer hara* and the *Malach Hamavet*. Therefore it is the responsibility of the mother (*parah adumah*) to clean up the excrement of the child (*eigel hazahav*).

The commandment of the *parah adumah* is referred to as a *chok*—a concept that exceeds the comprehension of man. Why is it that the Torah stresses the *chok* aspect of this *mitzvah*?

The tragedy of death in this world was a consequence of the transgression of eating from the *Etz Hadat* (Tree of Knowledge).

Our Rabbis indicate that the underlying motivation of Adam and Chava was their arrogance in demanding knowledge and insight and not being satisfied with a total dependency on *HaShem*. It is for this very reason that the *parah adumah*, which acts as an antidote to *tumat hameit*, should be a concept that totally defies man's intellect.

Rabbi Asher Schechter

Young Israel of Merrick, New York

This week we read the special reading of *Parshat Hachodesh*. The Jewish calendar is described and laid out to Moshe with the words, *Hachodesh hazeh lachem rosh chadashim, rishon hu lachem lichodshei Hashanah* (Exodus 12:2). Loosely translated, this month is the first month in the Jewish year. Many *halachot* of the Jewish Lunar-Solar Calendar are derived from this one *posuk*.

Rashi points out that *Niskashe Moshe al molad halevanah*—Moshe had difficulty fully understanding the phenomenon of the *molad*, the New Moon. He was not sure how much of the moon has to be visible for us to be able to be *Mekadesh Hachodesh*, declare the new month. *HaShem* had to point to the actual new moon in the sky and explain *Kazeh reeh vikadesh*—this is how the new moon should look when you are *Mekadesh Hachodesh*.

Rashi continues with a question. The moon is generally visible only at night. A new moon is especially hard to see and would be discernible only in the darkness of night. However, the Torah teaches us that *HaShem* spoke to Moshe only during the daylight hours (see Exodus 7, Leviticus 7, and Numbers 15). If that is the case, how did *HaShem* communicate with Moshe and point to the new moon, since it would be visible only at night and *HaShem* did not communicate to Moshe at night? Rashi answers as follows: *HaShem* spoke to Moshe just before *shekiyas hachamah*, sunset, and taught him the rules of the Jewish calendar. When Moshe asked *HaShem* more details about the *molad*, *HaShem* said to him, "Wait here a few minutes until it gets dark, and you will see what the *molad* looks like." Therefore, we see that the communication took place during the day, and the vision took place at night.

The above interpretation by Rashi raises some interesting questions. First, what is so difficult about the *molad halevanah* that Moshe had difficulty understanding? Most of us know what a new moon looks like and even a *mahshehu*, a tiny speck, of the new moon is considered a *molad*. What was

Moshe's quandary? This issue is raised by many *meforshim* (see *Mizrachi, Sifsei Chachomim*, and others).

Second, there are two other places in the Torah in which Moshe had similar questions and *HaShem* had to show Moshe a vision to explain the subject to him. In both instances, *HaShem* used a firery image to display the subject for Moshe. One item was the *machatzis hashekel*, the half-shekel, that every male Jew over the age of twenty had to donate to the Mishkan. Moshe had difficulty understanding the nature of this coin; so *HaShem* then displayed a firery coin before him (see Exodus 30:13 and Rashi, ibid.). Also, when the commandments about the *menorah* for the *Mishkan* were given, Moshe had difficulty envisioning the Menorah. *HaShem* then displayed a firery *Menorah* for Moshe to fully explain the intricacies of its design. Why did *HaShem* wait until close to *shekiyas hachamah* to show Moshe the real *molad*? Why did He not use a firery *molad* to display the rules of the new moon, as He did with the other two subjects?

Although *Ein hamikra yotzeh midei pshuto*—the *pasuk* must have a simple straightforward meaning—and surely there are ways to explain the above commentary by Rashi in its simple form—I would like to offer a homiletical perception into the discussion between Moshe and *HaShem Yisborach*. *Am Yisrael* is often analogized to the moon, and the *umos ha'olam*—the nations of the world—to the sun. The Jewish calendar is basically defined by the moon (although there are some aspects that are related to the sun). The main *yomim tovim* of Pesach and Sukkot fall during the full moon, and Rosh Hashanah falls on a new moon. Every month *Klal Yisrael* prays special *Kiddush Levanah* prayers hoping the rebirth of the moon will coincide with a rebirth of the Jewish Nation and spirit. Almost all the *umos ha'olam* follow the solar year and are often associated with the sun in aggadic discourses.

Moshe had difficulty understanding why the Jewish people would have to live the existence of the moon throughout history. The moon waxes and wanes, and so would *Klal Yisrael*. There would be good times of peace and prosperity, and there would be times of persecution and hatred. There would be times of religious zeal and fervor, and there would be times of apathy and religious disobedience. As *HaShem* was telling Moshe that the Jew must follow the moon for his calendar and holiday schedule, Moshe wondered why *HaShem* did not give us the more powerful and imposing sun to guide our *mazal*. Why would the Jew be subjected to the power, shine, and glory of the *umos ha'olam* while the Jewish moon was waning?

HaShem answered Moshe at the time of *shekiyas hachamah* with the following message: It is true that the moon waxes and wanes. The moon stays but a short time in its full state before it begins to wane. However, even when it seems that the moon is about to disappear and be removed from sight, it immediately reappears and that begins the *molad* once again. Thus, there will be difficult and hard times for *Klal Yisrael,* but *HaShem* promises that even at the hardest of times there will be a renewal and a *Kiddush Halevanah.* However, if we look at the *umos ha'olam,* we see that their existence is compared to the sun. Although many empires have had their day in the sun, when their sun sets there is only darkness. Their days of glory are over forever without any renewal of hope and promise.

Thus *HaShem* gave Moshe a lesson that history has proven time and time again. As much as the Jew is persecuted and as much as the *umos ha'olam* attempt to destroy us, we will wax and wane but always be there to continue the mission of *HaShem* and His Torah. We look back at history with pride as we see all those who were so powerful in their prime but today are mere museum relics and artifacts of an era long forgotten. *Ki ani lo shanishi v'atem bnei Ya'akov lo chlisem* (Malachi 3:b)—For I, *HaShem,* have not changed and You the sons of Jacob, have not perished.

Rabbi Shmuel Greenberg

Young Israel of White Plains, New York

The commemoration of *Shabbat Hagadol* is discussed in the *Shulchan Aruch* (*Orach Chaim*, chapter 430). It says the following: "The *Shabbat* before Pesach is called *Shabbat Hagadol* [the Great *Shabbat*] because of the miracle that occurred on that day." The *Mishnah Berurah* comments that the miracle was that the *Bnei Yisrael* took a lamb, which the Egyptians considered sacred, and used it for a *korban Pesach* (Paschal sacrifice). Despite their anger, the Egyptians did not react adversely or retaliate. This event took place on *Shabbat*, the tenth day of Nisan.

An obvious question that must be asked is, why do we commemorate this miracle on the *Shabbat* before Pesach instead of the tenth day of Nisan? After all, our holidays, without exception, are celebrated on the date of the occurrence and not the day of the week.

There is a well-known custom of reciting the *Haggadah* (Ramah, *Orach Chaim, Siman* 430) on *Shabbat Hagadol*—the *Shabbat* before Pesach. This raises another question as to why there is no comparable custom before Sukkot? We obviously do not sit in the *sukkah* or take a *lulav* on the *Shabbat* before Sukkot, so why do we recite the *Haggadah* during the *Shabbat* before *Pesach*?

When the *Haggadah* is recited on *Shabbat Hagadol*, the above custom is to recite up to "*HaShem* built the *Beit Hamikdash* for us." Obvsiously, we must also attempt to understand why we conclude the reading of the *Haggadah* at that point.

Another point of interest is raised by the Rambam in *Hilchot chametz u'matzah*, chapter 7, where he writes the following: "Remember this day that you went out of Egypt, just as it says, remember the day of *Shabbat*." What is the connection between *Shabbat* and Pesach?

The most significant question I would like to raise is in regard to the very name of the holiday, Pesach—Passover. This name is derived from Exodus

12:13, in which *HaShem* says, "I will see the blood, and I will pass over you." When *HaShem* was engaged in killing the firstborn of Egypt, he spared the homes of *Bnei Yisrael* by passing over them. Ostensibly, there were many other great miracles performed in Egypt for which the holiday could have been commemorated; the name could have reflected the Exodus from Egypt itself.

In *Parshat Vayakel,* dealing with a construction of the *Mishkan* (Exodus 35:1), we learn the prohibition of the thirty-nine categories of work on *Shabbat* (Tractate *Shabbat* 97a). These thirty-nine activities correspond to the thirty-nine activities necessary for the construction of the *Mishkan* (Sabbath 49b). Why do we learn the activities of *Shabbat* from the *Mishkan*? What relationship do these *mitzvot* have with each other?

First we must focus on the essence of *Shabbat*. *Shabbat* can be perceived as a day when *HaShem* enters into the Jewish home. We live in a mundane world in which God's Being is not always readily apparent. However, when the Holy *Shabbat* arrives, we prepare our homes for the entrance of the Divine Presence. *Shabbat* derives its meaning from the word *shevet* (to dwell) as it says in the *pasuk* "How wonderful it is when brothers dwell together." (Psalms 133:1) By observing *Shabbat,* we allow God to dwell, so to speak, in His own world. Now we can see that *Shabbat* and the *Mishkan* share a common goal. Both *Shabbat* and a *Mishkan/Beit Hamikdash* provide a dwelling for the Divine Presence.

"The customs of the Jewish people are sacred." In all homes on Friday evening we sing *Shalom Aleichem,* a song based on the talmudic passage *Shabbat* 119b. We welcome the angels who accompany us to our homes: *Boachem leshalom*. Then we proceed to ask these angels to bless us: *Barchuni leshalom*. In the very next and last stanza we say, *tseitchem l'eshalom, malachei hashalom*—"leave in peace, angels of peace." This request is rather perplexing. It does not seem very respectful to ask the angels for a blessing and then, immediately afterward, ask for their departure.

On the basis of the previous insights into *Shabbat,* however, we can understand the sequence of the song Shalom Aleichem is most appropriate. The role of these angels would be analogous to the mission of secret service agents of a king. It is their duty to check a premises in anticipation of the arrival of the king. After an affirmative determination of safety has been reached, the agents leave, allowing the king to enter; so it is with these Angels of Peace who are engaged in the service of God and enter our homes to see if it is acceptable for God's presence. When they have made that determination, they immediately leave, and we herald the royal entrance of "the King of all kings, The Holy One, blessed be He."

This great achievement of being in God's presence began on Pesach. The *pasuk* says, "I will see the blood of the sacrifice, and I will pass over you."

On the surface, this is an act of omission by *HaShem*. Simply understood, *HaShem* promised the *Bnei Yisrael* that they will be spared from any harm. However, when we analyze the *pasuk*, we realize that it does not merely say, "I will turn aside from your homes or pass by in a manner to avoid them." Rather, it is telling us of a positive action on the part of God; the *pasuk* states, "I will intentionally pass over your homes."

The Divine Presence swept over each and every Jewish home. This was indeed a momentous occasion and the highlight of the Exodus. We ascended to the greatest heights and attained a great level of holiness, from God Himself, "not represented by an angel" but the very holiness of the *shechinah*, descended upon our homes.

This idea can be traced to the *Mechilta*. Commenting on the *pasuk* "And they shall take of the blood" (Exodus 12:7), the *Mechilta* states that the receiving of the blood of the *korban Pesach* had to conform with all the laws of sacrifices. If the *korban Pesach* was modeled after the basic principles of sacrifices, where was the *Beit HaMikdash*, and where was the *mizbeach* (altar) that are needed for a sacrifice? It would seem self-evident that the *bayit*—the home of each Israelite—was a *mizbeach* and a *makom hamikdash*.

It is now understood why the *Shabbat* before Pesach is called *Shabbat Hagadol*. The greatness that *Am Yisrael* demonstrated on Passover night by having a rendezvous with God emanated from *Shabbat*. In fact, the date of 10 Nisan is not significant; rather the focus was on *Shabbat*. It necessitated that the preparations of the *korban* that would facilitate *HaShem*'s coming to the *batei Bnei Yisrael* originate on *Shabbat*.

Now we can place the entire concept and being of *Shabbat Hagadol* in perspective. We recite the *Haggadah* on *Shabbat Hagadol* to connect the highlight of *Pesach*, "I will [intentionally] pass over your homes," with its source, *Shabbat*; however, we read the *Haggadah only* to the statement *uvana lanu et beit habechirah*—"and built for us the House of His choosing (The Temple)." By so doing, we have a threefold strength of *Shabbat*, Pesach, and *Beit Habechira*, the common denominator being the dwelling of the Divine Presence among *Bnei Yisrael*.

It is of interest to note that we do not say *tachanun* throughout the month of Nisan, since most of the month is considered to be a *chag* (festival). One could ask concerning this whether Nisan is merely a collection of days on which we do not say *tachanun*, whether there is a theme.

The first twelve days of Nisan are considered festive, and *tachanun* is not recited, since it was on those days that we celebrated the *Chanukat Hamishkan*, the inauguration of the tabernacle that accompanied the Jews in the desert. That particular celebration was the completion of the Pesach phenomenon. We have now come full circle. The *Mikdash* is the result and culmination of the joy of Pesach. Now *Bnei Yisrael* had the dwelling of the Divine Presence in a permanent residence.

This Pesach we must try to achieve, the level of "I will pass over you" so that God's Presence will once again sanctify our homes; thus, the objective of Pesach—"Pass Over"—will once again be accomplished.

Rabbi Yoel Schonfeld

Young Israel of Kew Gardens Hills, New York

WOMEN AND ROSH CHODESH

The Tur (O.C. 417) states that many women have the custom of not doing work on Rosh Chodesh, as this monthly occasion has special significance for them. Citing a *midrash*, the Tur explains that as a reward for their nonparticipation in the sin of the golden calf, women were given Rosh Chodesh as a day of special observance. Although many women did adopt Rosh Chodesh as a nonworking holiday, the *Ramah* in *Shulchan Aruch* indicates that many communities did not develop this custom in full. Today, most women do work on Rosh Chodesh, although some refrain from certain domestic type of work such as sewing and knitting. We note that some women are particular about attending the synagogue for *Birkat Hachodesh* the *Shabbat* prior to Rosh Chodesh.

What the Tur does not explain, however, is the relationship between the sin of the golden calf and Rosh Chodesh. Why was the *mitzvah* of Rosh Chodesh chosen above all others to be the payback for the women's resisting that particular temptation?

In *Shemot* (32:1) the Torah states, "And the people saw that Moshe was delayed in returning from the mount." Rashi, commenting on this verse, explains that this delay in time is what drove the people into a panic, and that this panic led to the creation of the golden calf. Convinced that because their leader, Moshe, was tardy, he would not return at all, they thought they were all headed for disaster. In their frenzy, they plotted to substitute a statue of a golden calf for Moshe. In other words, their actions were controlled by time. Proper timing, according to their thinking, would have had Moshe descend at a particular day and at a particular hour. His lateness sent them spinning to the point that their reasoning power was impaired. Time had gotten the best of them.

Let us now go a bit further. As we know, the *mitzvah* of Rosh Chodesh—which is that the Jewish people, via a *Beit Din*, declares a New Moon—was the first *mitzvah* given to the Jewish people as a nation. "This month will be unto you the first of the months of the year" (Exodus 12:1), is how the Torah introduces this *mitzvah*. Sforno, in his commentary on this *pasuk*, explains that this *mitzvah* is what separates a slave mentality from a freed mind. When the Jews were enslaved, they were dominated by time, for their time was not theirs to control. Now that they were liberated, time was theirs to control. Thus, from the very outset, the Jews were to be entrusted with the duty of proclaiming the New Moon, upon which rests the remainder of the Jewish calendar.

By not panicking during the episode of the golden calf, by staying aloof from the sin that was committed, women showed that they were not held in the clutches of time. Rather they remained poised, even though the timing might have meant that their leader would not return. In return for this noble display of their ability to think and behave as a freed people, they were given the gift of Rosh Chodesh.

The *Gemara* in *Shabbat* (147b) relates a remarkable incident. Rabbi Elazar ben Arach, whom we are told in *Pirkei Avot* (2:12) was the most outstanding young scholar of his time, traveled to a far-off island that was devoid of Torah. After remaining on this island for some time (Exodus 12:1) and becoming attracted to their worldly delights, Rabbi Elazar returned home to his colleagues, who welcomed him by calling him to read from the Torah portion of that week. When he came to the words, *Hachodesh hazeh lachem*—"This month is unto you" (Exodus 12:1)—Rabbi Elazar could not read the words properly. Instead, he read, *Hocheresh haya Leibam*—"Their hearts were silent."

The particular words that Rabbi Elazar mispronounced are of great significance. It was precisely the *mitzvah* of Rosh Chodesh, which is the great indicator of renewal and rejuvenation (see Hirsch's commentary) and which proclaims man's ability to use time to his own best interests on that island in a state of mental stagnation. Therefore, the words from his mouth spoke of deafened hearts. He had lost the precious gift of controlling time, the gift understood so well by our Jewish women.

In the *zechut* of *nashim tzidkaniut* (righteous women) we were delivered from Egypt. In their *zechut* may we see the ultimate redemption in our time.

❖ CHAPTER 67 ❖

First Days of Pesach

Rabbi Daniel Yormark

Young Israel of Eltingville, New York

> Why is it that on all other nights we eat *chometz* and *matzah*, but on this night of Pesach we eat only *matzah*?
>
> Said Rabban Gamliel: "Anyone who does not recite the following has not fulfilled his obligation: 'This *matzah* is eaten because the dough did not have time to rise before the time for the redemption arrived.'"

The answer to the first of the four questions is plain and clear: There simply was not enough time for the dough to rise. Consequently, the *Bnei Yisrael* had no choice but to eat *matzah*.

However, we have a principle: "Matters of great import do not come about by happenstance." The Almighty had performed the Ten Plagues, the greatest miracles from the time of creation. He was yet going to Split the Sea. Surely, if He willed it, the Jews could have waited for the dough to rise. Or, they could have eaten other food altogether. What then, was the need for *matzah*?

With the Exodus, a special nation came into existence—a nation that is like no other, a nation which is not bound by the ephemeral. A nation unique in that it is eternal, destined to endure hardships and travail and still continue to survive. How is it possible that nations with mightier armies, more land, better economies, and more powerful alliances eventually fall by the wayside, but *Klal Yisrael*, even through a difficult two-thousand-year exile, is still here?

As we read in the *haggadah*: "In every generation they rise up against us to destroy us, and the Holy One, Blessed is He, rescues us from their hands." Only the relationship, connection, and attachment with *HaShem* affords the *Bnei Yisrael* this eternity.

Simply stated, God is eternal. By virtue of being the People of God, the nation also takes on the quality of eternity. Every Jew is instilled with a soul that is a part, as it were, of God Himself. Just as God is eternal, every Jew, as well as the nation as a whole, is eternal.

The human being is created with a need for food. A regular supply of nutrition is needed for survival. What kind of food does God designate to be man's source of sustenance?

Following Adam's downfall when he ate from the Tree of Knowledge, we find that God told him (*Bereishit* 3:18) "Thorns and thistles will it [the land] grow for you, and you will eat the grass of the field." Upon hearing this, Adam began to cry. "Shall I and my donkey eat from one trough?" To which *HaShem* replied, "By the seat of your brow, you will eat bread" (Talmud *Pesachim* 118a).

What upset Adam so, and how did God appease him?

When Adam was banished from *Gan Eden* (the Garden of Eden), he dreaded entering the outside world. He viewed it as a place where he could readily and quickly forget his unique Divine nature, resulting in a weakening of his connection with his Creator. Adam feared that, if he subsisted on the same food as the animal world, the splendor and majesty of being created *B'tzelem Elohim*, in the mirror image of God, would soon be lost.

God assured him that he would retain his uniqueness. Unlike all other creatures, which ingest only raw, unprocessed food, the human being cannot do so. Much of that which he eats, primarily anything from the animal world, as well as grains, will require some sort of cultivating and refining before being consumed. Animals not only do not know how to process raw food; they have no need to do so. An animal is a physical being. What you see is what it is, and it has no problem consuming its food in its raw, original state. In addition to having physical qualities similar to those of animals, man is endowed with a pure and holy *neshemah* (soul), which so permeates his physical body that he cannot digest his food in its raw state.

The processing and refining of food in order to make it fit for human consumption is achieved by means of employing the intellect, *neshamah*. For bread, the wheat kernel must be harvested, ground into flour, sifted, kneaded with water to make dough and, finally, baked. The Divine aspect of man becomes an essential ingredient in his sustenance, thereby ensuring that he will retain his Divine quality even while living in the material world (see Rabbi Samson Raphael Hirsch, and Maharsha in *Pesachim*).

On Pesach night, the nation of Israel came into being. Is there any more appropriate sustenance for an eternal nation, a people who are to elevate themselves and represent the ultimate human being than a food that includes *neshamah* and intellect in the recipe? Surely *matzah* is a most accurate prescription for one created in the image of God!

One difficulty remains. Why the emphasis on the bread being unleavened? Why wouldn't leavened bread suffice?

Eternity is a difficult concept to grasp. However, by definition we know that it is infinite; it is not bound by time. The quickness with which *matzah* is prepared expresses this concept. *Matzah* is a food not bound by time. It is prepared with a minimal lapse of time, as opposed to bread, which requires a passage of time in its preparation.

At the Seder, we eat *matzah*. We know that is comprised of flour and water. There is so much more, however. The intellect and eternity of the *neshamah* are infused into the *matzah*. When we ingest *matzah*, we are elevating ourselves above the animal world. We are doing nothing less than nourishing ourselves with eternity.

With the arrival of Pesach, once again we begin the cycle of the *Shalosh Regalim*: Pesach, Shavuot, and Sukkot. Each *Regel* is an opportunity for growth in a particular area of *avodat HaShem*.

Pesach is the festival of freedom. It is vital to note that our definition of freedom differs greatly from that of contemporary western society. Whereas the world around us defines freedom as the right to do whatever one pleases, we explain it quite differently. "The only one who is truly free is one who is occupied with Torah."

Beginning on Pesach with the eating of *matzah*, we begin to count the *omer*, anticipating the receiving of the Torah, our ultimate key to eternity. Next year in Yerushalayim!

Rabbi Pesach Lerner

Executive Vice President, National Council of Young Israel

FOUR CUPS OF WINE

The Talmud (Tractate *Sanhedrin* 91b) relates that when Alexander the Great conquered the Land of Israel, the Egyptians came to Alexander and lodged a long-standing complaint against the Jews. "It is written in the Torah," they declared, "that when the Israelites left Egypt they borrowed gold and silver vessels from our ancestors; so far these items have not been returned. We now demand that this debt be repaid."

One of the Sages of Israel, Gabiha ben Pessissa, undertook the defense of his countrymen before Alexander the Great. "It is true," he said, "that this debt is still outstanding, but we have a counterclaim. The Torah says 'and the sojourn of the Jewish people in Egypt lasted 430 years (Exodus 12:40–41).' Six hundred thousand Jews worked for the Egyptians for 430 years and received no wages. Settle this account," said Gabiha ben Pessissa, "and we will return the gold and silver our ancestors borrowed." The enormous sum demanded by the Jews deterred the Egyptians from pressing their claim (in fact, the Talmud explains that, because of the counterclaim, the Egyptians fled their homes and left their full fields and vineyards to their Jewish neighbors).

In connection with this episode discussed in the Talmud, Rabbi Shmuel Ideles (often referred to as the *Maharsha*) poses a difficult question. How could Gabiha ben Pessissa suggest that the Jewish People were entitled to the wages of six hundred thousand workers for a period of 430 years? In truth, the Jews did not remain in Egypt for more than 210 years, and the actual period of slave labor was only for 86 years. Was Gabiha ben Pessissa not concerned that he would be challenged and have his counterclaim dismissed?

Rabbi Dr. Marcus Lehmann of Mainz, Germany (circa 1850) answers the *Maharsha*'s question as follows: The Torah tells us (Exodus 13:18), "and the

Children of Israel went up *chamushim*—armed—out of the land of Egypt." The great commentator, Rashi, provides another explanation to the word *chamushim*—a fifth. Only a fifth, 20 percent of the Jewish people left Egypt, whereas four-fifths of them died and were buried, in Egypt, during the three days of darkness. Therefore, since the number of Jewish people that left Egypt included 600,000 working males, there must have been five times that amount—3 million—during the years of Egyptian bondage. Thus 3 million Jewish male workers served the Egyptian nation for the 86 years of actual servitude. It all equals out; whether 600,000 worked for 430 years or 3 million worked for 86 years, Gabiha ben Pessissa had no reason to fear a challenge by the Egyptians. Had they countered his claim by contending that the Jews had labored for only 86 years, his reply would have been obvious.

Rabbi Dr. Lehmann adds a beautiful addition to his answer of the *Maharsha*'s question. The custom, at the Pesach Seder, is to drink four cups of wine in commemoration of the four expressions of freedom and deliverance the Jewish nation experienced, "and I will bring you out . . . and I will deliver you . . . and I will redeem you . . . and I will take you to Me as a people . . ." (Exodus 6:6–7). Another reason for four cups of wine, explains Rabbi Dr. Lehmann, is as follows: The servitude of the Jewish people was originally intended to last 430 years, five times the actual 86 years. There were four periods of 86 years that we did not work. We raise our cups of wine once for each one of those periods of 86 years. We praise the Almighty for His deliverance of four sets of 86 years each time with a *kos*, a cup of wine. The *gematria*, the numerical value, of the word *kos* is 86. With our *kos* of 86, we thank *HaShem* for His deliverance of an 86–year period.

NOT JUST HOW, BUT WHEN

> The Wise Son—what does he say? "When your son asks you on the morrow, saying, what are the testimonies, statues and ordinances that *HaShem* our God, has commanded you, . . ." (Deuteronomy 6:20).
>
> The Wicked Son—what does he say? "What is this service for you?" (Exodus 12:26).

What is the difference between the Wise Son and the Wicked Son? Both address the question, "what are the testimonies," "what is this service"—using the second-person pronoun, "you," seemingly excluding themselves.

The answer commonly given is that the difference is not indicated by the second person pronoun but by the fact that the Wise Son said "*HaShem*, our God." The Wise Son clearly accepts that *HaShem* is his God. The Wicked Son, on the other hand, leaves God out of his discussion. Another interpretation, perhaps, lies not only in how the question is asked but also when the question is asked.

It is the Wise Son who inquires into the nature of the various commandments. The Wise Son participates in the Pesach Seder. He has joined in the eating of *matzah* and *maror*. He was part of the discussion of the *Haggadah* and the miracles that occurred to the Jewish People. His inquiry into the reasons for the Commandments *follows* his involvement—"when your son asks you on the *morrow* . . ."—please explain to me that which we have already performed. The Wise Son believes in the Torah and our traditions. The Wise Son's lack of understanding does not prevent him from his performance of the *mitzvot*. The Wicked Son, on the other hand, poses his challenge to "this service" before the Pesach Seder has even begun. To the Wicked Son, our traditions are foreign unless he fully understands and agrees with their importance and relevance to his lifestyle. For the Wicked Son, there is no acceptance or trust; to him the Torah responds, "had he been in Egypt he would not have been redeemed."

In Judaism, we are taught to question and challenge—but only once we have accepted the premise. We say at the end of davening every *Shabbat* and *yom tov, Ein Keloheinu, ein Kadoneinu*—"there is none like our God, there is none like our Master." It would be more logical to first ask, "*Mi Keloheinu, mi Kadoneimi*—who is like our God? Who is like our Master?"—and then respond. However, in Judaism, we must first accept God's sovereignty as our foundation and them, as the Wise Son did, ask all our questions.

Rabbi Asher Bush

Young Israel of Stamford, Connecticut

HA LACHMA ANYA, A DIFFERENT KIND OF INVITATION

As the Seder opens, an invitation is issued as we recite the words *Ha Lachma Anya*—"This is the bread of affliction. . . . All who are hungry should come and eat, all who are in need should come and celebrate." These words are, indeed, very gracious and sensitive; they are also completely out of place. The time to issue this invitation was a week or two ago or, in a pinch, a few days ago. It certainly should not be now, as the meal is about to begin. To recite these words as we sit down to eat seems to serve little purpose, as there is nobody in need of a meal who will hear them.

These words, however, are not uttered to bring in new guests; they are for the benefit of any guests already at the table. A guest sitting at a table surrounded by somebody else's family, may very well feel ill at ease—even embarrassed. We, therefore, recite these words of invitation as a way of telling our guests that they should not feel uncomfortable, that tonight is the night to have guests. In fact, we can hardly have a proper Seder without them.

Rav Nisan Alpert, *z"l*, pointed out that in saying *Ha Lachma Anya*, we are not just being kind to our guests; we are also speaking to ourselves. This reminder is said at the beginning of the Seder, a time when we spend our night praising and thanking God for having brought us out of the land of Egypt. Before we can do that, however, we must step back and remind ourselves that, as bad as those years in Egypt were, as much as we suffered there, our sojourn in Egypt was not in vain because there was a Divine purpose and plan behind it all. The ultimate purpose in these four hundred years of exile and servitude was to give us moral and spiritual perfection. We were there to learn the importance of being concerned with the problems and sufferings of others—a kindness we never received from our hosts, the Egyptians. We were there to learn that the fate of each individual Jew is bound up with that of every other Jew and that, as one extended family, we should have the capacity to demonstrate the concern that loving members of a family have for each other ("You shall love your neighbor as yourself"). This is a fact that Yosef himself testified to as he told his brothers, "For God has sent me down here to provide bread before you" (*Bereishit* 45:5). Despite the many hardships and indignities that he suffered, Yosef understood that he was in Egypt for a purpose, and because of that he could no longer be concerned only with himself but with the burdens of others as well. It is for this reason, Rav Alpert explained, that we start off with *Halachma Anya*—to remind us that, as grateful as we should be for the Exodus from Egypt, there are many valuable lessons we needed to learn there. There are no random events in the world, only learning opportunities.

This same idea is expressed by the Malbim in his commentary on the *Brit bein Habesarim* (The Covenant between the Pieces). It was at this time that God told Avraham, "You should know that your children will be sojourners in a land that is not theirs, and they will subjugate them and afflict them for four hundred years. And also the nation that they serve, I will judge, and afterwards they will go out with great wealth" (*Bereishit* 15:13, 14). Many of the commentators ask what offense Avraham committed that this punishment should be decreed.

To this most vexing question, the Malbim answered that, indeed, Avraham had done nothing to be punished; the decree of four hundred years of exile was not a punishment at all. God had just promised him that he and his children would, indeed, inherit the Land of Israel (at this point Avraham was not yet sure that he was going to have children at all). Avraham thought that God was giving this to him as an act of *tzedakah* (translated here as an unearned charitable gift). To this God responded that neither the Land of Israel nor having children were an act of *tzedakah*—Avraham had earned these two things with the great *mesirat nefesh* (risking his life for the sake of God) he had demonstrated in Ur. Upon hearing this, Avraham worried: "Perhaps I have earned the right to possess and dwell in Israel, but what about my children?" To this question God answered, "Your children, too, will be able to merit the Land of Israel throughout the generations through the *Zechus Hakorbanos* (Merit of the Sacrifices)."

On this last point, the Malbim explained that each of the offerings that Avraham brought at this time were not just animals; they were symbols for different human traits. The calf is a symbol for the refusal to accept the authority of one's master, as an ox will accept a yoke, whereas a young calf will not. The goat is a symbol for greed, as even after it has been domesticated it will continue to wander about looking for more and more food. The ram is a symbol for indulgence and lust, as an animal of great strength and power. Avraham divided each of these animals in the middle, symbolizing the fact that he had already mastered each of these potentially destructive traits. Through his life experiences, Avraham had reached the high spiritual level where bringing these offerings was nothing more than an expression of his inner self. But the question remained, how were his children to reach that level? To this, God answered that they would need to go into the long, bitter exile and slavery of Egypt. Through those four hundred years of suffering, the Jewish people would become worthy of standing at Mount Sinai to receive the Torah. It was an experience that we would perhaps rather have done without, but the results made it all worthwhile.

When we start the Seder with *Ha Lachma Anya* it is not just because our hindsight shows that some good can be found in the Egyptian experience; it is far more. As the Malbim has explained, from the very beginning it was God's plan that we would profit from our experiences there. Only from the poverty and degradation of our Egyptian slavery could we learn how to serve our true Master without being led astray by the pursuit of profit, power, or pleasure. It was only from the pain and suffering of our Egyptian slavery that we could learn to bear the burdens of our fellow Jew in need: *Ha Lachma Anya*, all who are hungry should come and eat, all who are in need should come and celebrate.

Despite its deep symbolism, *Ha Lachma Anya* remains in its simplest form a warm offer of hospitality. Not only are these words an open invitation to the stranger and the needy; Pesach itself serves as the very symbol of *hachnasas orchim*. This is pointed out by Rashi in a most unexpected context. Lot had left behind the righteous house of his uncle Avraham for the wealth and prosperity of S'dom, despite its reputation for evil. Subsequently, God decreed destruction for this wicked region. Following the unsuccessful attempt by Avraham to intercede, two angels, in the appearance of men, come to visit Lot. Lot invites them to spend the night. They refuse, but he persists until they finally relent. He prepared a festive meal and baked *matzah* for them. At first glance, it might seem natural to suggest that he made *matzah* because it could be made quickly, not needing to rise. However, Rashi does not give this explanation, stating instead that Lot fed them *matzah* because it was Pesach. Aside from the obvious question about the chronology of this event in relation to the Exodus, the very idea seems to make no sense. After all, wasn't this the same Lot who had (as we said already) left his uncle's righteous household to indulge in the decadence of S'dom? Wasn't this the Lot who was about to do what no decent man would do, as he offered his two daughters to a mob of men in order to save two strangers? How could it be that he was observing Pesach; did he really care about such matters? Through the use of the word *matzah* and its obvious connection to Pesach, the Torah is telling us that, even at this moment, as Lot sunk to the depths of depravity as he offered his daughters to the mob, there was still some good left in him. He may have become enamored with the riches of S'dom, and he may have forgotten about the meaning of virtue, but Lot still understood what *hachnasas orchim* meant—even when it was not a very popular activity. Not only did Lot insist that they stay with him, not only did he make sure that they had the best, but he literally risked his life for the sake of his guests. This is the ultimate in *hachnasas orchim,* and this is what Rashi meant when he said that Lot was observing Pesach.

The holiday of Pesach was not yet created in Lot's time, but, since the very beginning, it has served as the symbol of a home that wants nothing more than to say the words, "All who are hungry should come and eat, all who are in need should come and celebrate."

Rabbi Moshe Teitelbaum

Young Israel of Lawrence/ Cedarhurst, New York

In the *kiddush* for *Shabbat* that we recite every Friday night, we declare that the *Shabbat* day is a remembrance of our Exodus from Egypt. How does the sanctity of the Seventh Day of Creation serve to commemorate *HaShem*'s taking us out of Eypt?

We turn to the *mitzvah* of *Sippur Yetziat Mitzrayim,* which we fulfill by reciting the *Haggadah* on Pesach night. The section of the Seder called *Maggid* is introduced by the *Ha Lachma Anya,* which describes the *matzot* at the table as the staple food of our enslaved ancestors in Egypt. The words *Lachma Anya* are taken to mean "poor man's bread" or "bread of affliction." From this introduction, it would seem that the *matzot* of Pesach serve to remind us of the servitude and oppression we endured while in Egypt.

Later, in the words of *Maggid* itself the *matzot* are defined as a very different reminder altogether. Rabban Gamliel is quoted as saying that we must verbally describe the presence of *matzot* at the Seder table. The *Haggadah* goes on to explain that *matzot* are eaten to remind us of haste and to relive that haste in which we left Egypt. Our ancestors had no time to let their dough rise, so speedily did *HaShem* cause them to pack their belongings and leave *Mitzrayim* in just one night.

This explanation contradicts the reason for *matzah* mentioned in the *Ha Lachma Anya*. The *Ha Lachma Anya* describes *matzah* as the poor man's bread eaten while we were in Egypt, whereas in *Maggid* it is a remembrance of the haste with which we left Egypt.

The process of the *Haggadah* is *Matchil B'gnut U'mesayem B'shevach*. We begin with talking about the evils to which we were subjected and follow with the virtues and benefits that were attained with the help of *HaShem*. In the spirit of *Matchil B'gnut,* the *matzah* is first described as the bread eaten during the years of our affliction. Later, when we are

Mesayem B'shevach, it is the bread that reminds us of the lightning speed with which *HaShem* freed us.

This thematic process does not, however, integrate the two very different identities of *matzah*. The *pasuk*, in *Devarim* 16:3, cites both identities and concludes with the *mitzvah* of remembering the Exodus from Egypt every day of our lives: "You shall not eat leavened bread with it, seven days you shall eat unleavened bread with it, the bread of afflictions; for in haste did you come forth out of the land of Egypt; that you may remember the day when you came forth out of the land of Egypt all the days of your life."

From the words "for in haste" and "bread of afflication" in the same *pasuk*, it is clear that these two identities co-exist in the *matzot* of *mitzvah* with some common origin or ingredient in both.

A slave laborer bakes his dough without letting it rise because his time isn't his own. He is obligated to his master and must rush to his every beck and call. "The bread of afflication" reminds us of our minute-to-minute responsibilities to our task masters.

"For in haste" reminds us of this same pressing obligation—but to *HaShem*: the Ari, *z"l*, taught that if we had remained in Egypt any longer we would not ever have escaped. The fiftieth gate of *Tumah* was awaiting us—we would have remained Egyptians forever. The speed with which we left Egypt was necessary for the beginning of our service of *HaShem*. The haste is a characteristic of our new commitment to be His People, not Egypt's. Where we used to devote our every moment and rush from task to task for the sake of a slave-master, we were from that night on committed to do the very same in service of *HaShem*. That is why the *Haggadah* here refers to *HaShem as* the highest master and ruler—the King, King of Kings, the Holy One, blessed is He.

Accordingly, "bread of affliction" and "for in haste" both describe our haste to serve—our service, first, to the Egyptians, then to *HaShem* alone. The change from servitude to Egypt to the service that is *avodat HaShem* is reflected in the movement of themes from *Ha Lachma Anya*—poor man's bread to the *matzah* that was made in haste, that did not have time to become leaven.

Just as an aside, it is interesting to note that the *matzot* described in the quote from *Parshat Bo* were actually baked in the morning after the *Bnei Yisrael* had left the city of Ramses, not before. The dough had been prepared many hours earlier but had (miraculously, according to some commentators) never risen. This was a way of expressing the urgency of our moving quickly to become followers of *HaShem*, even though a whole night should have been enough time for the dough to rise.

We now return to our original question—the relationship of the Exodus from Egypt and *Shabbat*. *Shabbat* focuses all of our week's efforts toward *avodat HaShem*. It reminds us that all of our six days of achievements are for His sake. As we have seen the Exodus from Egypt and the haste of our exit were intended to highlight the very same message: all our work, every effort, all of our rushing should be for His sake.

Our times see man and woman rushed and harried as never before. The preciousness of time is so keenly felt in a society so severely pressed for a little more of it. *Shabbat* and the Exodus from Egypt both remind us whose time it is after all. They ask us, "Who are we rushing for?" For yet another undeserving "master" that has undue control over our lives? Or, we hope, for the greater purposes of the only worthwhile *Adon* man has ever known—the King, King of Kings, the Holy One, Blessed is He.

❖ CHAPTER 68 ❖

Chol Hamoed Pesach

Rabbi Yoel Schonfeld

Young Israel of
Kew Gardens Hills, New York

The term *Chol Hamoed* is a difficult one. *Chol*, by definition, means weekday—that which is secular. *Moed*, literally an appointed time, means holiday—that which is sanctified. These are two contradictory terms that seem to coexist in a happy union as the intermediary days in the middle of the Pesach and Sukkot holidays.

The term *Shabbat Chol Hamoed* compounds our difficulties. Not only do we have fusion of *Chol* and *Moed*, but we now add a new dimension of the ultimate sanctity, that of *Shabbat Kodesh*. Here, we cannot reconcile *Chol* with *Moed*. Here, we cannot interpret the *Chol* as being sublimated to a higher level of *kedushah* through the *Moed*, as we can say of *Chol Hamoed* falling on a weekday. If the day is *Shabbat*, then it cannot tolerate *Chol*; if it is *Chol*, then it cannot sustain *Shabbat*.

Of course, we can simply explain this as a vernacular, the simplest and most convenient way of referring to the occasion. It is the time when the intermediary days of *yom tov* coincide with *Shabbat*. However, if we look at the Talmud (*Betza* 17) and the Rambam (*Hilchot Tefilla* 2) we find a striking reference to this period. Here the occasion is referred to as *Shabbat Shechol B'chol Hamoed*, "*Shabbat* that occurs on *Chol Hamoed*." *Shabbat* does not "occur" on any time other than its own fixed time of the seventh day of the week. The phraseology of *Shabbat Shechol B'chol Hamoed* suggests something extraordinary about this whole idea of *Shabbat* and *Chol Hamoed* coinciding—or is it colliding?

Apparently, when *Shabbat* is given the opportunity to meet with *Chol Hamoed*, the entire day is sublimated. The *Shabbat* is a different *Shabbat*, and the *Chol Hamoed* is a different *Chol Hamoed*. Although we do not normally see this in the *tefillah* of *Shabbat Chol Hamoed*, there is one place where this idea is distinguished. At the end of *Kedushah* for *musaf* on *Shabbat Chol*

Hamoed, there are those who recite *Adir Adirenu*. This in spite of the fact that *Adir Adirenu* is said neither on *Shabbat* nor during *Chol Hamoed*. When *Shabbat* and *Chol Hamoed* coincide, there is apparently a call to elevate the *tefillah* at some point.

The message we should take from this is clear: the mundane, the secular, the materialistic in life take on an altogether new existence when coupled with *kedushah*, with the spiritual. We may say that in this instance the whole is greater than its parts.

For this reason, we read the *Shir Hashirim* on *Shabbat Chol Hamoed*. As Rabbi Akiva said in the *Mishnah* (*Yadaim* 3:5), if all the songs are holy, then the song of *Shir Hashirim* is the holiest of holiest. What could be taken as erotic poetry, becomes the ultimate expression of affiliation with God when infused with an understanding of *kedushah*. The *Sefas Emes* adds that during this festive time of celebration the Jew must channel his earthly drives to the service of God. That is the reason we read the *Shir Hashirim* at this juncture.

The *haftarah* for *Shabbat Chol Hamoed* relates Yechezkel's famous vision of the Dry Bones. Here the Prophet vividly depicts a scene in which bones of those long since deceased spring to life and develop anew as functioning bodies. It is the ultimate inspiring call for the Jewish people to keep their faith in the future despite a dreadful past. The Talmud (*Sanhedrin* 92b) debates whether this vision of the resurrected bones is to be taken literally or allegorically. Rabbi Yehudah ben Besera, the *Gemara* relates, stood up and declared, "I am a descendant of those people and here are the *tefillin* of my grandfather, who was one of them." The fact that the *tefillin* were displayed is significant. It is only by showing that he remained true to his grandfather's traditions that we can consider those bones as coming to life. If a Jew cannot transmit his spiritual legacy to the next generation, then, indeed, he tragically becomes relegated to nothing more than a heap of bones following his passing. Here too, as in *Shir Hashirim*, the message is that it is only through spiritual elevation that the physical has any meaning.

Much is done to commemorate the memory of the six million *kadoshim* of the Holocaust who fell victim some fifty years ago. Lecture series, literature, and Yom Hashoah commemorations are the most popular way of memorializing the martyrs. However, without a spiritual meaning, without a religious ritual associated with their memorials, the memory of the six million will simply fade with the coming generations. Religious Jews still feel the pain of the fall of Jerusalem two thousand years ago because of the Tisha b'Av fast and its *Kinot*. We recall the victims of the Crusades with *Av Harachamim* recited every *Shabbat* before *musaf*. The memory of these Jews has not been lost to time. The youngest of Orthodox Jews identify with these age-old victims.

The Holocaust account is being seriously challenged today by anti-Semitic revisionists. We must realize that what may appear today to be a radical hypothesis will tomorrow become accepted doctrine. The next generation will simply not believe the "exaggerated" account provided by the Jews clamoring for world sympathy.

The only way we can perpetuate the memory of the victims of this most awesome tragedy is to give their memory religious significance. *Kinot* and *Tehillim* must be a part of the commemoration if it is to assume any meaning at all.

Without the spiritual we will be left with *Chol*: but no *Shabbat*.

❖ CHAPTER 69 ❖

Yom Sh'viei VeAcharon Shel Pesach

Rabbi Hershy Worch

Young Israel of Pawtucket, Rhode Island

"And the Children of Israel came through the sea on dry land" (Exodus 14:22).

Were they in the sea or were they on dry land? Asks the *midrash*, continuing, "From here we learn that each individual had to throw himself into the sea before it parted."

Nachshon ben Aminadav, prince of the tribe of Judah, was first to jump into the sea. It reached his nostrils before splitting for him. Did Nachshon know what would happen, or was he committing suicide? Did all those who followed, the six hundred thousand, did they know the sea would split, or did they expect to drown? Were they expecting some sort of miracle to occur?

Another question that begs to be asked, concerns the "Great Wealth," promised to our Father Abraham, that was brought out of Egypt.

It is well known that when the Jewish people left Egypt, they emptied it of treasure, leaving it like an ocean without fish. There was nothing left for them to borrow or take. Yet we are told that seven days later, Moshe had to drive them away from the scene of the Splitting of the Red Sea, that they were so busy plundering the booty, stripping the corpses of the Egyptian dead, that they would not move on. Furthermore, we are told: the value of the spoil picked at the seashore was hundreds of times greater than the loot hauled out of Egypt. The *Midrash* makes a ratio comparison as that of dots of silver to lines of gold. How empty could Egypt have been, if there yet remained the vast treasure carried by the pursuing army that later drowned in the sea?

The answer is, of course, that there is treasure, and then, there is treasure!

What was so precious that we brought out of Egypt with us on the first night of Pesach? What could possibly have been worth those hundreds of tormented years, the slavery, the pain or the degradation?

First of all, we realized that we could not manage our own lives. Intelligent and well-meaning though we were, children of the Holy Patriarchs and Matriarchs, twelve tribes of God, alone we were not enough. Nothing we ourselves were capable of was going to stop our descent to the lowest depths of defilement.

This may seem at first glance like a very unpretentious truth until you realize that many a civilization has gone from evolution to extinction with no inkling of its implication.

Secondly, while we were in Egypt, we came to believe that only a power infinitely greater than ourselves was capable of managing and governing our life's affairs and maintaining a sane balance in them. Throughout the year that revealed the Ten Plagues, we became imbued with the profound awareness that the God of our Fathers is the Creator of the World, and no one else—that we had failed in all our attempts to control our Egyptianization, that, while it is true we had not intermarried, we had maintained our identity as the Children of Israel, we spoke Hebrew and dressed as Jews, it was not enough. If there are fifty gates of impurity, we had passed through forty-nine of them. We could not and cannot do it on our own; we are powerless. In order to be delivered out of Egypt, we would need the Almighty to act as midwife. To have our Jewish gold separated from the dross that was Egypt, we would need an omnipotent, caring, and loving God. What priceless knowledge this is!

Now to return to the question we asked at the outset, what happened at the sea?

Knowing intellectually that something is true is only the first step. Being able to act on that knowledge is a much more difficult matter. What happens when our fears meet our challenges? There we were at the Red Sea, the Egyptian cavalry and army bearing down on us; there was nowhere to run.

Moshe said, "*HaShem* has said 'be quiet'; he will do the fighting for you. Why are you crying at me? Tell the children of Israel to begin moving."

This was the first real moment in history when our fears met a challenge. It was a triumphant moment because we made the decision to turn our will and life over to the care of *HaShem*. To answer the question; did Nachshon know the sea was going to split for him? He didn't stop to ask. Turning life over to the care of God, precludes such meaningless speculation. When I know I'm being taken care of, what does it matter whether I'm being told to walk or stand still? To jump into the sea or into the flames?

When it was all over, when we began realizing what had happened to us, the jump we had made, the quantum leap, the purest act of faith, we couldn't get over it. We sat together on the seashore going over it, again and again. This was wealth beyond anything we had dreamed. That we could give up managing our own lives and turn it over to the care of a kind, caring, loving God? It was totally unprecedented. It was revolutionary. It was even greater wealth than we had brought out of Egypt with us. Moshe had to get us moving, urging us away from there. He knew it was not the end of our spiritual journey; there was more to come.

It is said that the riches we brought out of Egypt were given to us in the merit of the Jewish women, whereas the riches we acquired at the Sea were in the merit of the Jewish men. The hidden meaning to this is the realization that we were out of control, that only *HaShem* could straighten us out, was achieved passively. We did no more than watch the plagues befall the Egyptians. It took no participation on our part. Passivity is often symbolized in Jewish stories by "woman." The realization we could make leaps of faith required action on our part. We ourselves had to do the jumping—intellectualizing about faith in God would not save us. Action is denoted in this story by the symbol "man."

Rabbi Reuven Stein

Young Israel of Patchogue, New York

> *Yalkut Tehillim*: "The sea saw and it fled." What did it see? The coffin of Yosef. *HaShem* says to let the sea flee in honor of Yosef, about whom is said that when his master's wife was trying to seduce him, he fled and ran outside.

The commentators ask, "Why didn't *HaShem* directly command the sea to split? Why was it necessary to have the sea first view the coffin of Yosef?" *HaShem* wanted the *Bnei Yisrael* to learn an important lesson. The *Bnei Yisrael* were used to being slaves and had just been freed. The freedom that they now had gave them much opportunity. Would they take charge of their lives and use their Divine intellect to grow and become the *Am Segulah*, or would they let things just happen? The sea did not want to split because that would involve going against its natural flow. Normally, the Will of *HaShem* is for nature to go on its natural course. The sea then saw Yosef, who represented the greatness of man inherent in the Jewish people. Yosef could have gone along with his nature—that of a young man attracted to a beautiful woman—but he used his strength of character to show that a Jew can rise above his nature. The sea then realized that *Bnei Yisrael* was greater than itself and it would be required to split. *HaShem* wanted the *Bnei Yisrael* to visualize this important lesson of their inherent greatness. That is why He didn't command the sea to split directly.

This thought was similarly expressed by Rabbi Mordechai Gifter, *shlita,* the *Rosh Hayeshivah* of the Telshe Yeshivah, in Cleveland, Ohio. Why was the first commandment to the Jews the *mitzvah* of *Hachodesh Hazeh Lechem*—the New Moon? *HaShem* wanted the *Bnei Yisrael* to realize that time belonged to them, "this month is yours." You are to become free masters of your own destiny. You must not be a slave to time. A Jew has the ability to use time to reach great heights.

With this thought, we can also answer the question that many of the commentaries ask: "Why did the *Bnei Yisrael* wait till the seventh day to sing *shirah* for the miracle that *HaShem* did?" They could have sung *Shirah* on the first day. We must first understand the concept of *Shirah*. *The Shiurei Daas* explains that *Shirah* is not just a plain song that anyone can sing. *Shirah* is an outpouring of the soul. When a person has tremendous feelings of devotion and elation, his soul must then express itself through *Shirah*. True, the *Bnei Yisrael* had witnessed miracles in Egypt, but the sense of tremendous elevation and opportunity only took place at the splitting of the sea when they became witness to the fact that man's greatness could transcend nature. This helps us to understand Rashi's comment (15:2), "Even a maidservant at the sea could envision what the prophets could not." Even the lowest of people now understood that they can control and rise above their destiny. This is also why we count the *omer* after Pesach—to show that we can take command by taking these steps of improving each day to lead ourselves to *Kabalas Hatorah*.

The Chanukas Hatorah answers why the *Bnei Yisrael* waited until the seventh day by using a halachic approach. The *Gemara* says in *Kiddushin* 16 that a slave who must work for six years and who leaves before the six years must recompoense his master by finishing his work at a later time unless his master passed away. The Jews had left Egypt after 210 years instead of 400 years and worried that they would have to return and finish their time. It was only on the seventh day, when they witnessed the death of their masters, that they could feel at ease and sing *Shira* with heartfelt joy.

Reb Moshe Shwab, *zt"l*, the former *Mashgiach* in Gateshead Yeshivah in England, asks the following question: Why does the Torah hint at the rebellion of some of the Jews toward *HaShem* at the splitting of the sea? (Talmud *Yerushalmi Tanis* 5:5 and *Pesachim* 11) In *Devarim*, Rashi explains that the sin of *Mul Suf* included one group of Jews who rebelled at that time and wished to return to Egypt. Rav Shwab explained that not always will a person be perfect and reach the highest levels. *HaShem* performs miracles and demonstrates His love for us despite our shortcomings. This is part of the great love that *HaShem* has for the Jewish people. This also motivates us to sing *Shirah*, in recognition of this love.

STORY FOR LAST DAYS OF PESACH

Two brothers had been business partners for many years. They always quarreled. Once, they got into a fight and one of the two brothers, in a fit of rage, swore that he would never come to see his brother again. His brother passed away, and he wanted to know if he would be allowed to visit his brother's grave or if that would violate his oath. Great rabbis pondered this question, trying to bring proofs from many sources. Twelve-year-old Yechezkel Landau, who would later become the world famous Noda BeYehuda, found a proof from the Torah that it would be permitted for the brother to visit the grave. Moshe *Rabbeinu* told the Jews that they would never see the Egyptians again. We find just a few verses later that, "Israel saw the Egyptians dead on the shores of the sea." Seeing someone after death is not the same as seeing them alive. Therefore, the living brother could visit his dead brother's grave.

The *Gemara Pesachim* 118 quotes Rav Elazaer ben Azaria saying, "The difficulties of *Mezones shel Adom*—of making a living—are compared to the difficulties of splitting the sea. The Chidishe Harim explains that, just as the *Bnei Yisrael* were in trouble from all sides and the salvation came from an unexpected avenue, so we have the same experience in earning a livelihood. Sometimes it comes from unexpected sources. *The Baal Aserah LeMeah* explains that splitting the sea was not automatic but required prayer and effort. The quest for a livelihood also requires prayer and effort and does not come automatically.

Rabbi Bernard Weinberger

Young Israel of Brooklyn, New York

LIBERTY OR FREEDOM

There are two separate and distinct miracles: *Yetziat Mitzrayim* (the Exodus from Egypt) and *Kriat Yam Suf* (the Splitting of the Red Sea). As a matter of fact, it is questionable whether, if one were to recite only the *Shirat Hayam* (Praise of the Sea), would he be satisfying the requirement of *Zechirat Yetziat Mitrayim* (remembering the Exodus from Egypt). These are, actually, two episodes celebrated on two distinct days; the first days of Pesach relating to *Yetziat Mitzrayim* and the latter days of Pesach relating to *Kriat Yam Suf*.

The question, therefore, that emerges is, why was *Kriat Yam Suf* necessary at all? The Jews went out of *Mitzrayim* with a healthy head start. Why couldn't *HaShem* lead them in such a way that the Egyptians could not catch them? Why did *HaShem* take the Jewish nation back towards *Mitzrayim* so that the Jews would be perceived as being lost and then have the Egyptians catch them, which necessitated the suspension of the rules of nature inherent in *Kriat Yam Suf*?

The *midrash* tell us that the angel of the Red Sea argued against *HaShem*'s splitting the Sea, saying "Both these and these are idol-worshipers. Why split the Sea for one and not for the other?" The difficulty that is inherent in this *midrash* is why this question was not raised at *Yetziat Mitzrayim* but only now at *Kriat Yam Suf*. Most commentators suggest that at *Yetziat Mitzrayim, Klal Yisrael* enjoyed cohesion and *achdus*, and when they are united as one nobody will complain against them. However, at the *Yam* we are told that they split into four different opinions (see commentaries on Exodus 14:13–14), and when Jews are split among themselves they are vulnerable.

I want to suggest a deeper and more penetrating response. There is the famous and troublesome question asked on the Gemara (*Megillah* 10) that says that the angels in Heaven wanted to recite *Shirah* (praise) at the splitting of the Red Sea and the Almighty rebuked them with the admonition, "My handiwork is drowning in the Sea, and you want to recite *Shirah*." And, obviously, the question is why the Jews were allowed to say *Shirah* when God's handiwork was drowning in the Sea.

The Exodus, if it was to be meaningful, had to have two parts, liberty and freedom. Liberty is to remove the bondage, to escape the enslavement, and to be liberated from the burdens of the master. *But*, and a crucial *but* it is, the master remains and the threat hovers overhwelmingly that the slave may be returned to his erstwhile captivity. Freedom entails more than that. Freedom means that the threat has been removed, and there is no longer the danger of being put in that position again. Alas, we have been witness, in our generation, to people who have been liberated from the most horrible experience humans have ever been witness to; yet not all these people have been freed. Too many still have nightmares and worries, even if unfounded, that it could happen again. The main ingredient of freedom is absent, even though they are totally liberated and even enjoying successful lives. *Yetziat Mitzrayim* and *Kriat Yam Suf* are two sides of the same coin of the Exodus. The Jews were liberated from *Mitzrayim* but they did not become free men until after *Kriat Yam Suf* (this could also explain the two terms of *yeshuah* and *geulah*).

A fascinating *midrash* tells us that when the passage says, "And the Jews saw *Mitzrayim* die on the banks of the *Yam*" (Exodus 15:30), *Mitzrayim* is used in the singular, not the plural of Egyptians. The *midrash* derives from this that each Jew saw the death of the very same *Mitzri* who punished and enslaved him. In other words, it was his taskmaster whom he saw perish; and that meant he was now experiencing freedom, not just liberation. Little wonder, then, that the Rabbis said only that the angels were not allowed to sing the *Shirah* at the death of the Egyptians. The Jews did recite *Shirah*—not for the death of the Egyptians but for the removal of the *Mitzri* from his heart and mind. In short, the Jews were celebrating the experience of freedom from within and not the death from without.

We know that Passover is referred to in the Torah as the "The Morrow of Sabbath" (*Vayikra* 23:15) in the *mitzvah* of *Sefirat Ha'omer*. Why is Pesach called *Shabbat*? Because *Shabbat* represents a God-given gift unrelated to human endeavor, and therefore Pesach is called *Shabbat* because, as the name indicates, *HaShem* had to pass over the unreadiness of the Jew to be redeemed. As the *midrash* indicates on the passage in Song of Songs (2:9), "My beloved, behold he cometh leaping upon the mountains skipping from the hills," indicating that *HaShem* skipped over the fact that the Jews were not yet suited for liberation. The difference between *Shabbat* and *yom tov* (suffice it to say, within the purview of this message) is that *Shabbat* is a gift, whereas *yom tov* is something we need to earn by ourselves.

A gift needs no explanation. I give a gift out of love, no explanations necessary. *Yetziat Mitzrayim* was a gift—therefore the angels couldn't protest as to why *HaShem* did what He did for the Jews. But *Kriat Yam Suf* was something that the Jews had to earn by themselves and so needed the selflessness of Nachshon ben Aminadov to save them.

Note that the *midrash* uses the expression, "they had to earn their resolve." Hence, we received our liberty as a gift from God but, when it came to the freedom at *Yam Suf*, we had to earn it. Note, if you will, that at *Yetziat Mitzrayim* the killing of the Egyptians took place at night, but the Exodus did not occur until morning. At *Kriat Yam Suf*, however, it was the reverse; the crossing of the Sea was by night and the drowning of the Egyptians was by day. Night is *Din*—judgement. Day is *Chesed*—kindness. The Jews deserved *Kriat Yam Suf Al Pi Din*; therefore, it could be at night.

It was *Kriat Yam Suf* that we earned and that rendered Pesach a *yom tov*, redeeming the first days, which were originally *Shabbat*.

Rabbi Dovid Plaut

Young Israel of Greater Buffalo, New York

The character of the first two days of Pesach is tied to *Yetziat Mitzrayim* (the Exodus from Egypt), whereas the final days of Pesach derive their character from *Kriat Yam Suf* (Splitting of the Red Sea). There are several notable differences between the events of *Yetziat Mitzrayim* and *Kriat Yam Suf.* First of all, by *Kriat Yam Suf* we see for the first time serious divisions occurring in *Klal Yisrael. Chazal* tell us that when the Jewish people found themselves caught between *Mitzrayim* and the *Yam Suf,* four different groups developed with different approaches on how to handle the situation. One group said that we should all jump into the sea. A second group recommended that *Klal Yisrael* should return peacefully to Egypt. A third group felt that they should fight the attacking Egyptians, and the fourth group put forth the rather novel idea of making loud, frightening noises to scare the army away. (I believe that these groups are sequenced in order of the increasing amount of *emunah* they had in *HaShem*. The first had no *emunah* and chose suicide. The second had a little *emunah* and chose re-enslavement. The third had even more and elected the military option, and the fourth had the most *emunah* and wanted to do only a minimal effort—*hishtadlut*—letting *HaShem* do the rest.)

Another instance of this newly discovered division is that during the crossing of the Red Sea, *Chazal* tell us, each Tribe had its own wall of water surrounding them. Finally, we have the famous statement of Rav Yossie Hagelili, who compared the ten plagues in Egypt to one finger, and the plagues at *Kriat Yam Suf* to a hand. He concludes that there were five times as many plagues that took place at *Kriat Yam Suf.* This, too, is a sign of increased diversity at *Kriat Yam Suf.*

Another difference between the events of *Yetziat Mitzrayim* and *Kriat Yam Suf* is pointed out by the *Avnei Nazer* as quoted in the *Sheim Mishmuel*. He asks why is it that the *Klal Yisrael* had to do *mitzvot* to merit their Exodus from Egypt. We know that *HaShem* asked them to do *milah* and *korban Pesach* (The Pascal Sacrifice). But to experience miracles five times as great at *Kriat Yam Suf*, we don't find any requirement for *Klal Yisrael* to do any *mitzvot*. On the contrary, when *Klal Yisrael* wanted to pray, *HaShem* said that now is not the time for prayer, move ahead. We see that *HaShem* was actually discouraging *Klal* Yisrael from doing good deeds; why?

The Avnei Nazer answers that if the Jews were to have *mitzvot*, the Egyptians would not have entered the Red Sea. By this time, the Egyptians realized that the Jews were protected by *HaShem* and if they had seen *Klal Yisrael* doing *mitzvot*, they would have immediately realized that *HaShem* would protect them from the Egyptians, and the Egyptians would have retreated. However, by not allowing them to do *mitzvot*, the Egyptians were lulled into thinking that *HaShem* would not protect them. What does the *Avnei Nazer* mean? How does he know that doing *mitzvot* would have made such a crucial difference in the eyes of the Egyptians? What is really the difference between *Yetziat Mitzrayim* and *Kriat Yam Suf*?

The Avnei Nazer says that at *Yetziat Mitzrayim* there were *mitzvot* and *HaShem* saved and rewarded *Klal Yisrael* for doing those *mitzvot*. In other words, *Yetziat Mitzrayim* was a consequence of what they did and what they did not do. *Klal Yisrael* maintained their language, their clothing, and so on, and they made a *korban Pesach*. *Klal Yisrael* probably viewed themselves as a people who were superior in their deeds; and that was *Klal Yisrael*'s ticket to leave *Mitzrayim*. But, the Egyptians felt, take *Klal Yisrael*'s *mitzvot*, their good deeds, away from them, and they'll be just like us. This was the Egyptian's fatal miscalculation. So *HaShem* said, do not do any *mitzvot*, do not pray, just walk and see what will happen. The angels were also lulled into the same frame of mind. They, too, said that the Jews were identical to the Egyptians. "*Halolu Ovday Avodah Zorah, V'Halollu Ovday Avodah Zorah.*" Take away their *mitzvot*, and they are just like the rest of them.

Another consequence of the lack of *mitzvot* at *Kriat Yam Suf* was that the Jewish people began to split. Nothing binds *Klal Yisrael* together like everybody doing the same *mitzvah*. At *Kriat Yam Suf*, *HaShem* gave no instructions; there was nothing to keep *Klal Yisrael* in line and, so, people naturally had different opinions and dissension grew. The difference between one tribe and another became important even at a time when such differences had no special significance, all because *Klal Yisrael* did not have any *mitzvot* to do. God wanted to teach the world a lesson they would never foget. The uniqueness of *Klal Yisrael* is not in their deeds alone.

Mitzvot are not the bottom line distinction between Jew and non-Jew. *HaShem* revealed that He chose *Klal Yisrael* because of who they are, not merely because of what they do. The Egyptians never dreamed that *Klal*

Yisrael could be elevated so high so fast. Why did *HaShem* choose *Klal Yisrael*? Rashi in *Beshalach* Exodus 14:15 says, ". . . because of their exalted forefathers and because of their pure faith in Me they will be saved from the Egyptians." *Emunah*, pure simple faith in God, is the only explanation for such a closeness of God to His chosen nation.

We can now understand much better why *Klal Yisrael* sang a *shirah* after *Kriat Yam Suf* and not after the ten plagues of Egypt. The feeling of closeness that *Klal Yisrael* felt, could only give rise to the highest form of praise, which is *shirah*. Can you imagine what an exhilarating experience it is to be singled out like that? Even the lowest member of *Klal Yisrael* could experience that feeling of being wanted and loved by *HaShem*. No wonder that even a maidservant achieved the level of prophecy of Yechezkel!

I believe that this helps explain something else as well: Why the Egyptian army (and Pharaoh also, according to some explanations) were killed. Surely chasing after *Klal Yisrael* in a menacing way is not worse than what they had done to them for the years in slavery. If they deserved to be spared after the ten plagues, why did they deserve to be killed now? The answer is that at *Kriat Yam Suf*, *HaShem* conclusively and decisively chose *Klal Yisrael* as His nation. The angels in Heaven said, "What is the difference between this nation and the other (Egypt)?" If the angels couldn't see a difference, then no one else in the world could see it. Moreover, after the Red Sea split for *Klal Yisrael*, the Egyptians went right to the very same place where *Klal Yisrael* had just been.

From the *pesukim* it seems that the punishment of the Egyptians occurred *B'soch Hayom*, within the sea. What the Egyptians were doing by entering the dry sea bed was making it clear that they were the same as *Klal Yisrael*; at a deep-down fundamental level, there is no difference between the two. The sea split for *Klal Yisrael*, and it split for the Egyptians too. True, the Egyptians were not being wicked toward the Jews; however, what they were doing was much worse. They were implicitly questioning *Klal Yisrael*'s true Jewish identity. That left *HaShem* with no choice but to destroy the impostors and declare for all time who *Klal Yisrael* truly is.

❖ CHAPTER 70 ❖

Yom Yerushalayim

Rabbi Aaron Cohen

Young Israel of Fith Avenue, New York

Yerushalayim has always held a very special place in the hearts and minds of the Jewish people. A golden city, filled with *kedushah*, symbolic of peace and kindness, evoking memories of a glorious past and a yet more promising future, somehow above the constraints of time, wear, and tear; such are the associations with Yerushalayim. Other nations of the world are also enraptured by the aura and enigma of Yerushalayim and wish to share in its treasures. What is the "status" of Yerushalayim?

We must delve into two topics to answer this question: The etymology of the name "Yerushalayim" according to *Chazal* and the first appearances of Yerushalayim in the Torah.

The *midrash* (*Bereishit Rabbah* 56:10) tells us that "Yerushalayim" is, in fact, composed of two parts. The first—*Yeru*—derives from the name that Avraham assigned to *Har Hamoriah* (Yerushalayim; Rashi, Genesis 22:2) subsequent to *akedas Yitzchak*: "And Avraham called the name of that place *HaShem Yireh*, God shall see." (Genesis 22:14) The second half of the name—*shalayim*—originates from the designation of Shem, son of Noah, who called it *Shalem* (Genesis 14:18).

What is the significance of these two components that constitute the name "Yerushalayim"? The *Meshech Chochmah* (Genesis 22:14) elaborates upon this *midrash*. Shem, a survivor of a generation that was steeped in corruption and moral depravity, focused on the universal ethical and moral values he saw reflected in this unique place and, therefore, called it *Shalem*—a place of peace and justice. Avraham, however, who independently discovered God and then devoted his life to teaching others God's Providence and the need to follow His laws, revealed another aspect of Yerushalayim—a place where God will reveal Himself as the Master of and Provider for the world. Both these aspects—the universal-ethical and the spiritual-religious—are to be found in Yerushalayim and, therefore, they join to form its name.

Moreover, Rabbi Mordechai Breuer perceives the manifestations of these two facets in the initial references to Yerushalayim in the Torah. The first instance occurs following Avraham's triumph over the kings who had taken Lot captive. Malki-Tzedek, king of Shalem (Yerushalayim), "a priest to the most high God" (Genesis 14:18), blesses Avraham, and Avraham, in turn, gives him a tenth of the spoils of the battle. A second, very different exchange then takes place between Avraham and the king of S'dom. The king offers the booty to Avraham in exchange for the prisoners of war that Avraham redeemed. This time, Avraham adamantly turns down the offer and swears that he will not take "from a thread even to a shoelace" (Genesis 14:23) from the spoils. Avraham chooses *Shalem*—Yerushalayim, which manifests peace and justice, high ethical and moral standards—while firmly rejecting S'dom, which stands for the injustice and immorality associated with its locality.

As mentioned earlier, Avraham experiences yet another encounter with Yerushalayim when God sends him there for *akedas Yitzchak*. This time, however, Avraham does not view Yerushalayim as a city of universal values but as a place that represents God's special relationship to the Jewish people. Realizing this, he subsequently calls the place *HaShem Yireh* (Genesis 22:14)—meaning that God will choose this as the dwelling place for His presence.

We learn an important lesson from Avraham's encounters with Yerushalayim. True, Yerushalayim is *Shalem*, a city of peace, of wholesomeness, of proper ethics and morals, a city with universal appeal. In addition, however, it represents the message of *HaShem Yireh*, a facet that only the Jewish people can appreciate and bring to realization. Strikingly, as Avraham and Yitzchak approached their destination, Avraham turned to the accompanying servants: "You stay here with the donkey and I and [Yitzchak] will go to there" (Genesis 22:5). Avraham sensed that this meeting with Yerushalayim would be different; the Yerushalayim that served as home to the *shechinah* in the *Beis Hamikdash* is the exclusive inheritance and heritage of the Jewish people.

A dispute exists regarding the *kedushah* of Yerushalayim today. The Rambam holds that Shlomo *Hamelech*'s sanctification of Yerushalayim and the *Beis Hamikdash* endowed them with their special *kedushah* for all time, whereas the Ravad argues that, with the destruction of each *Beis Hamikdash*, the *kedushah* of Yerushalayim and the *Beis Hamikdash* dissolved as well (*Hil. Beis Habechira*, 6:14–15).

The Chasam Sofer (*Teshuvos Chasam Sofer, Yoreh Deah* no. 233, 234) was asked: According to the Ravad, doesn't it appear as if Yerushalayim and the *Beis Hamikdash* have *lost* their unique *kedushah*? The Chasam Sofer replied, most adamantly, that the special *kedushah* of Yerushalayim remains unaltered and can never be removed; the dispute of the Rambam and Ravad is relevant only to specific *halachos*, such as the prohibition of an impure person entering certain locations in the *Beis Hamikdash*. The *kedushah* of the *Beis Hamikdash*, Yerushalayim, and *all* of *Eretz Yisrael*, however, is intrinsic; it has always existed and will never be annulled. The unique character of these chosen places is not dependent on any person's sanctification; long before Yehoshua, Shlomo, or Ezra lived, Adam and Noach brought *korbanos* there; Avraham offered Yitzchak there, and Yaakov dreamt there of a ladder ascending to heaven. That "Gateway to Heaven" that Yaakov envisioned is part of the essence of the *Beis Hamikdash* and Yerushalayim, the Chasam Sofer explained, and the presence of the *shechinah* has never and will never be diminished.

Strikingly, the Avnei Nezer (*yoreh deah* Teshuvah #454, sec. 33) follows precisely the same reasoning in concluding that it is preferable to live in Yerushalayim. Even according to the opinion that the specific laws relevant to Yerushalayim were annulled with the destruction of the *Beis Hamikdash*, the inherent *kedushah* of Yerushalayim exists from the very creation of the world, and one who dwells in Yerushalayim lives in the shadow of *HaShem*'s presence. Who could deny the significance of this opportunity?

The special journey of Avraham to Yerushalayim for *akedas Yitzchak*, which designated Yerushalayim for all time as the capital of the Jewish people, the city in which their special relationship with *HaShem* would become most manifest, parallels yet another journey that Avraham undertook—his trek to *Eretz Yisrael*. Then, Avraham is commanded suddenly, *Lech lecha—Go!*—and is asked to begin his travels without a clear destination in sight: *el ha'aretz asher areka*—To the land which I will show you (Genesis 12:1). The Ramban there provides an explanation of the implicit demand made on Avraham; he writes that Avraham was uprooted from his land, birthplace, and father's house, "and he wandered and traveled from nation to nation and from kingdom to yet another people, until he reached the land of Canaan."

Strikingly, when *HaShem* requests of Avraham that he offer Yitzchak as a sacrifice, He says once again "*Ve-lech lecha*"—the same double verb emphasizing the power and authority inherent in the request. And, once again, *HaShem* conceals the destination: *Veha'aleyhu sham le'olah al echod heharim asher omar eylecha*—And offer him up on one of the mountains that I *will* designate to you (Genesis 22:1). Only on the third day of wandering, uncertain of where he would stop, did Avraham see the mountain that *HaShem* had chosen. Why did *HaShem* make these difficult and agonizing demands on Avraham when sending him on these two journeys?

The following truism sheds some light: a goal or objective becomes all the more precious and treasured if it is not taken for granted. In order for

Avraham to appreciate fully the gifts of *Eretz Yisrael* and Yerushalayim, in order for him to feel the full value of their unique *kedushah*, he first had to wander, looking forward with anticipation to his final destination. In this context, Avraham's concluding statement becomes much more meaningful and poignant: "*Vayikra shem hamakom Hashem Yireh*—And Avraham called the place 'God shall see.'" As Rashi and others explain, this means, "This is the place that God shall choose." At this point, Avraham appreciated fully the significance of the selection of Yerushalayim as *HaShem*'s chosen city.

We, too, have wandered for many centuries, always looking forward with longing and yearning to the day that we would return to *Eretz Yisrael* and Yerushalayim and merit to see them restored to their full glory. Now that we have been granted our wish of seeing these holy, chosen places back in our care, we must take heed to offer thanks and gratitude for the return of these treasures and look forward to the day when our dreams will be fully realized, when we will merit seeing the *kohanim* and *leviim* serving in the third *Beis Hamikdash, bimheira beyamainu. Amen.*

Rabbi Benjamin Blech

Young Israel of Oceanside, New York

What is the one crime for which we most deserve to be punished as a people? According to the Rambam, the sin is implicit in the statement repeated over and over again in the section of the *Tochechah: v'halachtem imi bekeri*—"if you walk with Me with casualness" (Leviticus 26:27). The word *bekeri*, for Maimonides, is to be identified with the same root as the word *mikreh*—by happenstance or coincidence. The crime to which God refers that will draw forth His continued wrath is the Jewish people's failing to recognize that everything that occurs in the world is due to Divine Providence; the sin of sins is to proclaim coincidence and meaningless accidents as supreme rulers of human destiny. The antidote to this crime is to be sensitive to "the finger of God" in the events of our history. For our generation in particular, survivors of the Holocaust who have been privileged to witness the beginning of messianic redemption through the birth of Israel, there is a very special obligation to perceive the miraculous intervention of *HaShem* in our return after millennia to *Eretz Yisrael*, as well as to Yerushalayim. Let us not fail to take note of the remarkable messages of this day as they identify clearly the author of our newly established day of rejoicing. Permit me to share with you four remarkable insights:

1. Yom Yerushalayim is the twenty-eighth day of the month of Iyar. In letters, 28 is a *kof* and a *chet*—two letters that make the word *koach*—"strength" or "power."

Elie Wiesel, the scribe of the Holocaust, movingly described the uniqueness of our generation: "We are the most cursed of all generations, and we are the most blessed of all generations. We are the generation of Job, but we are also the generation of Jerusalem."

The final solution as envisioned by our enemies was genocide. The final solution as predicted by our prophets was Jerusalem.

The Holocaust represented the vulnerability of the Jew. Returning to our homeland gave us dignity. That is the meaning of Yom Haatzmaut, marking the re-establishment of the State of Israel. The liberation of Jerusalem, spiritual center of the land of our fathers, returned to us the ultimate strength of our people.

Kol HaShem bakoach—"The voice of the Lord came in strength" (Psalm 29:4).

On the twenty-eighth day of Iyar, the day of *koach*, we acknowledge God's strength in fulfilling His prophecies, even as we recognize the gift of the return of the spiritual strength of our people through Jerusalem.

2. There is one sin so common among the sons of man that the prophets constantly inveighed against it. Moses was concerned with it in his last speech to the people before his passing. In his final oration, recorded in the Book of Deuteronomy, the Jewish leader warns lest "your heart be lifted up and you forget the Lord, your God, who brought you out of the land of Egypt, out of the house of bondage . . . and you say in your heart, 'My power and the might of my hand have gotten me this wealth'" (Deuteronomy 8:14–17). Mankind should never confuse blessings from the Almighty with personal achievement. "But you shall remember the Lord, your God, for it is He that gives you power to get wealth" (*ki Hu hanotein lecha koach*)—it is He and He alone who gives unto you *koach*, strength (Deuteronomy 8:18).

Koach comes from God alone. Could Jerusalem have been liberated on any day other than the twenty-eighth of Iyar, the day of *koach*? It is the date itself that proclaims beyond question that "This is the day that the Lord has made; we will rejoice and be glad on it" (Psalm 118:24).

3. The ultimate purpose of Jerusalem is powerfully portrayed by King David in the Book of Psalms: *Yerushalayim habenuyeh ke'ir shechubrah lah yachdav*—"Jerusalem that is rebuilt is like a city that attaches to it together" (Psalm 122:3). Its function is to create unity among all Jews. Its goal is the word *yachdav* ("together")—the kind of togetherness manifested at Mount Sinai when "all the people answered together and said, 'All that the Lord has spoken, we will do'" (Exodus 19:8).

Yachdav in *gematriah* (numeric value) is 28 (*yud*=10, *chet*=8, *dalet*=4, *vav*=6; total 28). Jerusalem, the city of unity, "was liberated on the twenty-eighth day of Iyar of *koach*. After all, is not *yachdav*, Jews being as one, the ultimate *koach* (28), power, of our people?

4. Before the miraculous events of the Six Day War, Jews were forbidden by the occupiers of Jerusalem to pray at their holiest site.

The Temple of old was built on Mount Moriah. That spot had previously been sanctified by the first Jew, Abraham, as he brought Isaac up as an offering on that very mountain to express his unqualified commitment to the commandments of God. That very spot, too, is where Adam had brought the first sacrifice ever offered by a human being to his Creator.

Tradition has it that the very mountain that served as the location for the first two Temples will have built upon it the Third and final Temple as well. It is called *Har Habayit*—the Mount of the House. In *gematriah*, "to the mountain of the house," *Lehar Habayit*, is 652 (*lamed*=30, *heh*=5, *resh*=200, *heh*=5, *bet*=2, *yud*=10, *tet*=400; total, 652). We returned *Lehar Habayit* (652) to the temple mount in modern times on Yom Yerushalayim. Can it be mere coincidence that the *gematriah* of Yom Yerushalayim, as well, is 652 (*yud*=10, *vav*=6, *mem*=40, *yud*=10, *resh*=200, *vav*=6, *shin*=300, *lamed*=30, *yud*=10, *mem*=40)?

Rabbi Nachman Kahana

Young Israel of the Old City, Jerusalm, Israel

VIEWS ON *ALIYAH* (AFTER 25 YEARS IN ISRAEL)

Twenty-five hundred years ago, the prophet Yeshaiah summarized what would be the religious and social condition of the Jewish nation in messianic times with the statement *V'tihi haemet ne'ederet*—"and the truth shall be concealed." The *Gemara* in *Sanhedrin* 97a explains the prophet's intention: "the truth shall be divided into many herds (*ne'ederet—adarim*)." With this as an indication, one may justifiably conclude that the Messiah is not far off, for today even rudimentary issues of Jewish life are inundated with dissent and partisanism.

Within this kaleidoscope of divergence and diversity, there is no issue so basic to our physical existence and so fraught with implications for our spiritual survival as the centrality of *Eretz Yisrael,* and its corollary—*aliyah*. It is on this very issue that our halachic authorities are extremely divided in their opinions. On one side, there is the authoritative voice of Ramban stating that it is a *Torah chiyuv* to go up to the Land and a transgression to permit the Gentile to remain its possessor, whereas, on the other side, diametrically opposed to Ramban, we hear some contemporary opinions that it is a transgression to establish an independent national entity in *Eretz Yisrael* prior to the Messiah and, therefore, preferable to leave the Gentile in possession of the land.

An Orthodox Jew, by definition, uncategorically accepts *halachah* as the medium through which God conveys His will to the chosen people and, as such, as the corner-stone of our faith. *Halachah* is based on the Written Torah—*Mishnah, Gemara, Rishonim,* and *Acharonim*. However, at times of profound halachic ambiguity precipitated by dramatic social upheaval and historic transition (as today), an extra-halachic system, paralleling the formal codifications of *Shulchan Aruch* and, at times, surpassing them in authority, comes to the fore—*Daat Torah*. This sublime methodology of Jewish thought is a formidable instrument, emanating from an intuitiveness acquired through long years of commitment to Torah study and total submission to a life of *kedushah*. It is the merger of intellect and emotion, the meeting of soul and body in that undefined grey area dividing conscious thought and prophecy.

In addition to the classic methods of determining halachic conclusions utilized by each side in defense of its position, *Daat Torah* has been used most extensively in attempts to define how one must discharge his obligations with regard to *aliyah*. This has resulted in total confusion for those seeking guidance in what is demanded of one committed to a Torah way of life.

Now, though it is beyond the authority and ability of this writer even to voice an opinion in those areas concerning which Torah leaders are in controversy and, most certainly, in the area of *Daat Torah*, it is the aim of this article to point out three realities of life in *Eretz Yisrael* about which there can be no disagreement. These three arise out of our experiences of more than two decades in *Eretz Yisrael* and should be weighed very seriously by those in *galut* when considering the path one must take.

1. CONTINUATION OF THE *TANAKH*

The most fundamental theme of the 24 books of *TaNaKh*, second only to the belief in One God and the revelation at Sinai, is God's dialogue with His chosen people in the chosen Land. Even those books whose events occurred in *galut*, such as *Megillat Esther*, are based on the background of *Eretz Yisrael* and our redemption from *galut*.

Were there a prophet among us today and were it permitted to add chapters to the *TaNaKh* detailing God's miracle to His people, how much could be written! There is probably no one who lived through the Six Day War and witnessed the unification of Yerushalayim who did not feel an irrepressible urge to sing praise, *Ashirah LaShem ki Gaoh Gaah* (Exodus 15:1). Who did not feel part of the victorious army of King David upon entering in 1967 the cities of Shechem, Yericho, Bet Lechem, and Chevron? And did we not become one with the soldiers of Gideon or Barak upon learning that our air force had destroyed 450 enemy aircraft in the first hours of the war!

To live in *Eretz Yisrael* today, regardless of the negative elements present in certain areas of our lives, is to become emotionally and spiritually united with the characters and dramas of the *TaNaKh*. No abstract theorization or dialectic can in any way diminish this very real fact of life, which when translated into practical terms, results in profound feelings of *Yirat Shamayim* that cannot be felt in the *galut* experience.

2. THE JEWISH PERSONALITY

Historically, there has been a weeding-out process regarding who may enter and remain in *Eretz Yisrael*—a process of "survival of the spiritual fittest," commencing with the masses who succumbed in the plague of darkness for not wishing to leave Egypt and continuing with the *dor hamidbar* and up to our own times, where we witness the great number of Jews who leave *Eretz Yisrael* in voluntary *galut*. It would appear that *Eretz Yisrael* can retain only a very unique type of individual.

What are the character traits which constitute the classic Jewish personality? According to what image should our educators mold the coming generations? Is the "ideal" Jew that one who is molded in the image of the *mussar movement*, or the young man from the Hesder *Yeshivah*, as familiar with a *Gemara* as he is with a tank? These questions are not being posed for their anthropological or sociological ramifications but for their great spiritual importance.

Through "natural" selection, a very unique type of religious individual is being formed, albeit slowly, today in Israel—one who is very conscious of his chosen role in history; who no longer retains the unending patience of the Jew in *galut* but wishes to implement the dreams of generations as liberated freemen on the soil where kings and prophets once stood. As parents of children born in *Eretz Yisrael*, we can testify to the great pride they have in all things Jewish and their readiness to protect this land at all costs.

Safra v'seifa, the book and the sword: this is the unique personality of the classic Jew. This fact of life cannot be ignored, and its development cannot be emulated in any Jewish community outside of *Eretz Yisrael*.

3. THE BEIT HAMIKDASH

A Torah individual living in *Eretz Yisrael* is continuously made aware of a fact that rarely crosses the mind of his *galut* counterpart—that the most essential element in our national existence, the Holy Temple, is lacking. The almost total indifference and ignorance regarding the present state of affairs on the Temple Mount relegates the *Beit Hamikdash* to the realm of mythology in the minds of religious Jews *chutz la'aretz*. Lip service is paid at the end of the *Amidah* prayer "that the *Beit Hamikdash* be rebuilt, speedily in our days," but no impression is left on the heart.

The *midrash* on *Tehillim* (Psalm 17:4) records that though King David's army was comprised of the most erudite Torah scholars of his time, nevertheless many fell in battle, the reason being "that they did not demand the building of the *beit hamikdash*." And the *midrash* concludes with the following *kal v'chomer*—that if the soldiers of David, in whose time the *Mikdash* was not yet a factor in their religious experience, were punished for not demanding its construction, then we who knew the *Mikdash* in our past must certainly long for its restoration.

Now, even if it were politically feasible to build the Temple, we would not be permitted to do so in view of the many halachic problems yet to be resolved. Nevertheless, I claim that it is vital to one's wholeness as a Torah Jew to include the consciousness of the *Mikdash* on one's list of spiritual priorities. A test of this consciousness is the feeling one experiences at the *Kotel*. If one feels an urge to dance and rejoice, then his spiritual sensitivities have been dulled, for the *Kotel* is a mere retaining wall of the Temple Mount, which today houses two of the most significant mosques in the Islamic world. How can one rejoice at the sight of a hundred thousand Muslim worshipers occupying, every Friday, the area that God hallowed for His Temple, while we stand at the foot of the Mount and consider that to be a great *zechut*?

To live in *Eretz Yisrael* is to develop a clearer insight into our spiritual needs, an insight unattainable by one not living in *Eretz Yisrael*.

Summary: Regardless of the halachic positions maintained by rabbinic authorities today, the responsibility of religious Jews to live in *Eretz Yisrael* arises out of three undeniable realities:

1. To be part of God's dialogue with His people through miraculous events in *Eretz Yisrael*
2. To be part of the process of regaining the classic Jewish personality, as a means of better understanding the essence of the Torah
3. To be cognizant of the absence of the *Beit Hamikdash* and to long for its restoration.

❖ CHAPTER 71 ❖

Shavuot

Rabbi Moshe Teitelbaum

Young Israel of Lawrence/Cedarhurst, New York

A woman once came to Rebbe Yisrael of Kozhnitz complaining that her husband wanted to leave her because he no longer found her attractive. The Kozhnitzer Magid said to her, "Maybe you really aren't attractive to him anymore?" Upon hearing the Rebbe's response, the woman cried out, "He chose me as his bride and stood with me under the *chupah*, and I was beautiful in his eyes. Together we endured years of hardship, always at each other's sides, through thick and thin. It's true that I'm now a little older, a little tired, and my face is a little wrinkled. But how dare he now claim that I am not attractive!"

The Magid understood that the woman was right. He rose to his feet, turned his eyes toward Heaven, and said: "*Ribono shel Olam*, this is the argument of *Klal Yisrael*. When Your children stood at the foot of Mount Sinai and said, *Na'ase Venishma*, they were to You like a bride—You chose them from among all of the nations. So how can You now say *chas veshalom*, that because of the sins and mistakes that we've made over the years, in a troubled and challenging world, that now we are ugly in Your eyes?"

We seem to be very far from the noble and virtuous Jews who accepted the Torah from *HaShem* at Mount Sinai. At times we have disobeyed and disregarded the Torah, sullying our own image to the point where we are arguably no longer the unique and exclusive People chosen by *HaShem* the way a groom chooses and cherishes his bride. At times it appears as if we are no longer worthy of being an *Am Segulah* and shouldn't hope for any better treatment from *HaShem* than we already receive.

This, the Kozhnitzer Magid said, is a mistake. We are forever, unconditionally, the Chosen People. But where at *Ma'amad Har Sinai* was this promise made to us? And why?

Before *Matan Torah*, *HaShem Yisborach* introduced the idea of our becoming a chosen people endowed with majesty and priestliness (Exodus 19:6): "and you shall be to Me a kingdom of priests and a Holy Nation; and these are the words that you shall speak to the children of Israel." On the words, "and these are the words," Rashi comments: "Say these words, no less and no more." Throughout the Torah, there are hundreds of messages spoken by *HaShem* and delivered by Moshe, but only in this instance does *HaShem* say not to add to, or omit from, that which He has said. Why here, specifically, does *HaShem* say: These are the words, no less and no more?

Rabbi Menachem Mendel of Kotzk offered the following explanation: The Rambam (in *Hilchot zechiyah umatana* chapter 3) rules that if someone gives a gift on a certain condition, then the condition must be a double condition in which the stipulation is stated in both positive and negative terms. For example, one would have to say "If you fulfill A, B, and C, then this gift is yours. And if you don't fulfill A, B, and C, then this gift is not to be yours." Otherwise, if the condition isn't double, the gift belongs to the recipient even if the stipulation is never fulfilled.

In these *pesukim, HaShem* said to the *Bnei Yisrael* (Exodus 19:5), "and now if you will listen well to Me and observe My covenant you shall be to Me a treasure from among the nations because to Me is the world." But *HaShem* never expressed it as a double condition. He didn't say, "and if you don't do the Torah you're not a chosen people." Moshe, concerned only with our fulfillment of Torah life and its observance, might have done one of two things. He could have omitted the promise of our becoming an *Am Segulah*, a beloved nation or he could have added the negative half of the condition, stipulating that if we don't fulfill the Torah we won't remain the *Am Segulah*. Therefore, *HaShem* said "Don't say less—do promise that they will be a Chosen People. And don't say more—don't make it a double condition. Because the Will of God is that even if, *Chalilah*, we won't fulfill the stipulation of "If you will listen well . . . ," we are to receive the gift of being His Chosen People nevertheless. Why would *HaShem* do so? Why did He promise to cherish us—no matter what we may be lacking spiritually—for better and even for worse? He must have seen the inner core that comprises the soul of our nation that remains pure and holy. In this core there is a compassionate nature that is reflected in our relationships to one another, and there is a striving for closeness to the Almighty through our observance of *mitzvot bein adam Lemakom*. Mitzvot between man and God. These are the traits of greatness characteristic of the Jew. *HaShem* saw within us the promise of our remaining forever deserving in His eyes.

As the Magid of Kozhnitz prayed to *HaShem*, we too *daven* that *HaShem* should once again see us a certain way: "If not our outer beauty, then see our inner devotion. If not our fulfillment of every *mitzvah* today, remember our sacrifices of yesterday. And we on our part will endeavor to live up the name and title of a unique and exceptional people—a kingdom of priests and a holy nation."

Rabbi Pesach Lerner

Executive Vice President
National Council of Young Israel

> Rabbi Elazar said, "All agree, with regard to the *yom tov* of Shavuot that it is mandated to be also for *you*" (that one attend to his personal needs of eating and drinking). What is the reason? It is the day on which the Torah was given to Israel
> (Tractate *Pesachim* 68b).

There is a discussion in the Talmud on the subject of how one should occupy oneself on *yom tov* (Jewish Holiday). Should an individual be festive and eat and drink, or should one use the day only in the service of God, praying and studying Torah? Rabbi Eliezer says that one may *either* eat and drink or pray and study Torah. Rabbi Yehoshua says, divide the day so that half of the day should be used in the service of God and the other half should be used in festive eating and drinking (see Talmud *Beitzah* 15b).

However, all agree that on the holiday of Shavuot one must enjoy the festival with food and drink. Although Rabbi Eliezer is of the opinion that a *yom tov* may be observed *either* by devoting it exclusively to God or exclusively to oneself, he agrees that the *yom tov* of Shavuot must be celebrated with eating and drinking. What is the reason? Because it was on Shavuot that the Torah was given to the people of Israel.

A question must be asked: It would seem that, especially on the day of *Matan Torah*, the giving of the Torah, we should be busy with spiritual activities. This is the day that should be set aside specifically and exclusively for God. Why is this the day—of all days—when one must celebrate with food and drink?

The Talmud (Tractate *Shabbat* 88b) relates that when Moses ascended to the Heavens to receive the Torah, the angels asked of the Almighty, "What is man born of woman doing in our midst?" God responded that he came to accept the Torah. The angels challenged, saying that this secret treasure that has been hidden for nine hundred and seventy-four generations before the creation of the world—You wish to give it to flesh and blood?

God requested that Moses answer them. Moses responded, "Master of the World, this Torah that You are giving to me, what is written in it?" "I am your God that took you out of Egypt." Moses asked the angels, "Did you go down to Egypt, were you enslaved by Pharaoh? Why should the Torah be yours? . . . What else is written in it?" "You should have no gods before Me. Remember the *Shabbat* to keep it Holy. Do not swear falsely. Honor thy Father and thy Mother." "None of these commandments apply to the angels," said Moses; "the Torah was made for the human being."

Moses was able to defeat the angels only because he proved that the Torah was ordained to be given to flesh and blood. Only mankind is capable of using the Torah to perfect itself into spiritual physical beings. Through the observance of the *mitzvot* of the Torah, only man—to the exclusion of the angels—can elevate his physical being into a true spiritual force.

It is precisely on Shavuot, the day of *Matan Torah*, that we celebrate the holiday through physical pleasures—human activities that we can and must use in the service of God. When we rejoice through eating and drinking, we show that we truly deserve receiving the Torah because we use the *mitzvot* to elevate and sanctify our human existence.

The Talmud (*Avodah Zarah* 11a) relates that Antoninus and the Prince, Rabbi Yehudah, were among the wealthiest men in the world and that they could afford for their dining tables summer foods even during the winter and winter foods even during the summer. The commentary of *Tosafot* ask that it appears from the story in the Talmud that Rabbi Yehudah benefited and enjoyed the physical pleasures of this world. Yet, in Tractate *Ketubot* 101a, we are told that, at the end of Rabbi Yehudah's life he pointed his ten fingers upward and exclaimed to the Heavens, "I have not benefited from this world even one small finger's worth." The *Tosafot* explain that, although Rabbi Yehudah was so wealthy that he offered his guests the finest foods available, he himself never partook and so he did not benefit.

The *Vilna Gaon* has another answer to the dilemma of *Tosafot*. Rabbi Yehudah the Prince did eat and partake of the foods found on his dinner table. However, everything that he ate and every physical activity he performed was not for his personal pleasure. His every action was for the sake of Heaven to enable him to better serve his Creator.

Rabbi Yehudah was able to say that he had not benefited from this world; the message of physical celebration on Shavuot, the elevating and sanctifying one's human existence, was the daily challenge and success of Rabbi Yehudah, the Prince and the mission of the Jewish nation.

Rabbi Reuven Fink

Young Israel of New Rochelle, New York

In Jewish tradition, Shavuot commemorates the day that the Torah was given at Sinai. Every year we acknowledge and mark this historical event. The question is: How does the notion of accepting the validity and authority of the Torah impress us? How do we react to the binding nature of the affirmation of *Na'aseh V'nishma* that we celebrate on Shavuot?

Interestingly, the Talmud records two altogether different reactions or responses to the revelation at Sinai and its impact on subsequent generations. The more famous of the two is featured in Tractate *Shabbat* (89a) in the chapter that deals at length with the event of the acceptance of the Torah by the Jewish people.

> A Jew baiter saw Rava learning Torah. . . . He said to Rava, "You are a rash and impetuous nation who place your mouths before your ears. . . . First you should have ascertained the degree of difficulty of the Torah, and only then have decided to accept it!"

A second reaction to *Kabbolat HaTorah* is found in *Pesachim* 68b.

> Rav Yosef celebrated and rejoiced on the holiday of Shavuot. He said, "If not for that day (Shavuot)—there are many Yosefs in the marketplace."

Here we have two models, two possible insights into the giving of the Torah and the Jewish people's acceptance of the *mitzvot*—the duties and responsibilities that define the essence of the Jewish experience. One approach is that the Torah is very difficult. It impinges on living the good life in a very profound way. The sum total of obligations and restrictions that are entailed in *Sh'mirat Hatorah* is a significant burden that we would sometimes rather do without. To be sure, there are aspects of Judaism—even difficult ones—that we might embrace, but the all-overwhelming and all-encompassing nature of the Torah—that is too much to bear. But bear it we must because that is our responsibility and our heritage. Difficult though it might be, we must adhere to the full range of rituals and customs and pass them on to our children. If only our ancestors had not acted so impulsively! If they had first experimented with the Torah, they would have acknowledged, *ess is shver tzu zein ah yid* (it's difficult to be a Jew) and, perhaps, they would not have been so rash and impulsive. This is one assessment of the day of Shavuot.

There is, however, another approach. The life of Torah for all of its complexities and detailed observances, contains within it an ennobling quality. Torah has the ability to refine the human personality. It has the *imprimatur* of the Divine. It allows man to be a part of eternity. It has the ability to tap into the spiritual dimension of man and bring out the inner person and to integrate the physical and the spiritual components into one being. The Torah invests the Jew with a vision of the future and teaches him what priorities he should have in life. That is what Rav Yosef means when he says, "If not for the day of *Matan Torah*, there are many Yosefs in the marketplace." In the marketplace of ideas and ideals there exist many approaches to the good life which most of the world embraces. It is the life of Torah, however, that makes the Jewish people unique and special. It is a privilege that Rav Yosef humbly acknowledged. All the other "Yosefs" of his time died in obscurity, and nobody remembers their names or their lives. They were all *Ploni Almoni* (John Does). Rav Yosef teaches us that if want to have the *Shem Tov* (good name and reputation) it will be the dedication to and the love of Torah that will give us that good in life, and a share in Jewish destiny. When our ancestors said *Na'aseh V'nishmah* they were not acting rashly. They had the insight to choose eternity and goodness for themselves and for all the generations after them.

Rabbi Fabian Schonfeld

Young Israel of Kew Gardens Hills, New York

> "Hew thee two Tablets of stone *like* unto the first and I will write upon the Tablets *the* words that were on the first Tablets which thou didst break" (Exodus 34:1).

After the great spiritual experience on *Har Sinai* and the revelation that produced it, there followed the great act of betrayal on the part of the Jewish people, the national treachery of the golden calf. Subsequently, after the plea of Moshe for forgiveness, *HaShem* instructed him to attempt again to present another set, *Aseret Hadibrot,* to the people, as described in the verse quoted above.

A careful reading of the text shows that the second set of tablets are described as *karishonim*—"*like* the first"—whereas the words to be engraved on them are described as *the* words.

Should not the wording be the same for both—namely: *like* the words, not *the* words? This distinction caused the Sochatchover Rebbe, in his seminal work *Shem Mishmuel,* to explain as follows, in a manner that has great implication for our so-called modern age.

Said the *Shem Mishmuel*: The Tablets were, after all, only *chomer*—material such as stone and rock, which were plentiful on *Har Sinai.* Once a material substance breaks, it cannot be mended or repaired. The *contents*—the words—can, however, be exactly the same. Matter and form are apt to change as time goes on, but meaning and ideas remain the same—are indeed, eternal. Thus, the tablets can only be *karishonim*—*like* the first, whereas the words are *hadevarim*—exactly the same.

For Orthodox Jews living in the modern world, this has very important implications.

The outer forms of Torah observance are often subject to change. We do not necessarily wear the same outer garments, we do not necessarily have the same appearance but we do have the same *tallit*, the same *tzitzit*, and the same *tefillin*.

The modern *mikvah* may have a beauty-parlor appearance, but the *dinim* and *halachot* are the same as they were in the days since they were promulgated by Moshe *Rabbeinu*.

The modern kitchen may be technologically centuries apart from the one used in ancient days, but the laws of *kashrut* have not changed. The computer-age electronic devices give us all kinds of advantages on *Shabbat*, but the *hilchot Shabbat* have not changed.

Finally, the educational opportunities for our young people are unprecedented, but the *hashkafah*, which keeps our young people loyal and faithful to our sacred Torah traditions, has not changed.

The tablets, the outer forms, are subject to change, not the *devarim*. Thus, the tablets are *karishonim*, but the words are *hadevarim*—the same eternal words spoken on *Har Sinai* thousands of years ago.

Chazek Chazek V'nitchazek!

About the National Council of Young Israel

The National Council of Young Israel (NCYI), founded in 1912, serves as the coordinating agency for nearly 150 Orthodox congregations comprised of 25,000 member families throughout the United States and Canada. NCYI also serves as a resource to its sister organization in Israel, "*Yisrael Hatzair*—the Young Israel Movement in Israel."

As the premier Orthodox synagogue network, the goal of National Council of Young Israel is to broaden the appeal of the traditional community synagogue as the central address for Jewish communal life by providing religious, educational, social, and communal programming. This is accomplished by rendering services through our various departments:

Synagogue Support Services
Youth and Young Adult Activities
Young Israel Council of Rabbis
Kosher Certification and Education
Yisrael Hatzair—Young Israel in Israel
Lay Leadership Education and Development
Outreach Programs and Resources
National Speakers Bureau
Rabbinic Training and Placement
Sisterhood Services
Synagogue Endowment Fund
ACHVA Summer Programs
Political Action
Women's League

Senior League and Health Facilities
University Campus Religious Programming
Publications (*Viewpoint* Magazine, Weekly Divrei Torah Bulletins, Professional Rabbinic and Lay Leadership Newsletters)

National Council of Young Israel is a grass roots organization which takes its direction from its national lay leadership, delegates from each branch synagogue, and branch rabbis and presidents. Join NCYI and become part of this great motivating force in North American and Israeli Jewish life. For more information, contact: National Council of Young Israel, 3 West 16th Street, New York, NY 10011 Tel: 212-929-1525 or 800-617-NCYI / Fax: 212-727-9526 / e-mail: ncyi@youngisrael.org or http://www.youngisrael.org